AFRICA IN CONTEMPORARY PERSPECTIVE

A Textbook for Undergraduate Students

Edited by

Takyiwaa Manuh

and

Esi Sutherland-Addy

First published in Ghana in 2013 by
Sub Saharan Publishers
P.O. Box 358
Legon-Accra
Ghana.
email: saharanp@africaonline.com.gh
www.sub-saharan.com.

© IAS and Contributors 2013

ISBN 9978-9988-647-37-7

Cover design: Patrick Awuah Antwi

Contents

ACKNOWLEDGMENTS

As editors, the fact that this volume has taken far longer to appear in print than we would have wished has not diminished our initial conviction about the book's importance and relevance. During that long period of gestation, we benefitted from the generosity of several persons and we wish to place on record the enormous debts that we have accrued.

We wish to acknowledge most sincerely the initial assistance from the University of Ghana through the World Bank-funded Teaching and Learning Innovation Fund (TALIF) grant to the Institute of African Studies that helped us pay some of the costs of commissioning the chapters and publication. We are grateful to the staff at the Accounting Section of the Institute for their assistance in administering the grant.

We thank all the contributors for sharing in our conviction about the importance of the volume and for their patience and forbearance. We can only hope that the ready uptake and use of the volume by readers in Ghana, and around Africa and elsewhere will more than make up for the delay that they have endured. We remember especially our late colleague, Reverend Dr. Abraham Akrong, who passed on a few months ago.

The following staff members, students and associates of the Institute assisted us as we prepared the volume for publication- Emmanuel Ekow Arthur-Entsiwah, George Bob-Millar, Korklu Laryea, Patrick Awuah Antwi, and Eyram Fiagbedzi- and we remain grateful for their assistance. Mr. and Mrs. Hans and Kwadua Roth welcomed us to their airy home on the hills at Kitase, near Aburi, and permitted us to spend some time in their guest quarters for a writing retreat, and we remember them with great affection. The Botchweys at The Place, also near Aburi, were also hospitable to us, and we thank them.

In the period since we embarked on this project, there have been rapid developments on the continent and many commemorative moments which call for an immediate sequel to this foundational volume. We believe that the issues, omissions and disagreements arising from this volume should spur responses from the growing pool of scholars working to produce knowledge and epistemologies for a renascent Africa, and we look forward to their appearance.

PREFACE

THE AFRICAN GENIUS

Speech by Dr. Kwame Nkrumah, President of Ghana, on the occasion of the opening of The Institute of African Studies at the University of Ghana , Legon, 25th October, 1963.

Ladies and Gentlemen:

I am very happy to be with you on this occasion and to welcome you to this official opening of the Institute of African Studies.

I regard this occasion as historically important. When we were planning this University, I knew that a many-sided Institute of African Studies which should fertilise the University, and through the University, the National, was a vital part of it.

This Institute has now been in existence for some time, and has already begun to make its contribution to the study of African history, culture and institutions, languages and arts. It has already begun to attract to itself scholars and students from Ghana, from other African countries and from the rest of the world.

The beginning of this present academic year marks, in a certain sense, a new development of this Institute. Already, the Institute has a team of seventeen research fellows and some forty post-graduate students — of whom about one- third come from Ghana and the remainder from countries as diverse as Poland and the United States of America, Nigeria and Japan. We hope soon to have students and fellows from China and the Soviet Union.

This Institute is no longer an infant, but a growing child. It has begun to develop a definite character of its own; it is beginning to make itself known in the world. This, therefore, is a moment for taking stock and to think afresh about the functions of the Institute, and of the University within which it is set.

What sort of Institute of African Studies does Ghana want and need to have? In what way can Ghana make its own specific contribution to the advancement of knowledge about the peoples and cultures of Africa through past history and through contemporary problems?

For what kind of service are we preparing students of this Institute and of our Universities? Are we sure that we have established here the best possible relationship between teachers and students? To what extent are our universities identified with the aspirations of Ghana and Africa?

You who are working in this Institute— as research workers and assistants; teachers and students — have a special responsibility for helping to answer these questions. I do, however, wish to take this opportunity to put to you some of the guiding principles which an Institute of African Studies situated here in Ghana at this period of our history must constantly bear in mind.

First and foremost, I would emphasise the need for a re-interpretation and a new assessment of the factors which make up our past. We have to recognise frankly that African Studies, in the form in which they have been developed in the universities and centres of learning in the West, have been largely influenced by the concepts of old style "colonial studies", and still to some extent remain under the shadow of colonial ideologies and mentality.

Until recently the study of African history was regarded as a minor and marginal theme within the framework of imperial history. The study of African social institutions and cultures was subordinated in varying degrees to the effort to maintain the apparatus of colonial power. In British institutes of higher learning, for example, there was a tendency to look to social anthropologists to provide the kind of knowledge that would help to support the particular brand of colonial policy known as indirect rule.

The study of African languages was closely related to the practical objectives of the European missionary and the administrator. African music, dancing and sculpture were labelled "primitive art". They were studied in such a way as to reinforce the picture of African society as something grotesque, as a curious, mysterious human backwater, which helped to retard social progress in Africa and to prolong colonial domination over its peoples.

African economic problems, organisation, labour, immigration, agriculture, communications, industrial development — were generally viewed from the standpoint of the European interest in the exploitation of African resources, just as African politics were studied in the context of the European interest in the management or manipulation of African affairs.

When I speak of a new interpretation and new assessment, I refer particularly to our Professors and Lecturers. The non-Ghanaian non-African Professors and Lecturers are of course, welcome to work here with us. Intellectually there is no barrier between them and us. We appreciate, however, that their mental make-up has been largely influenced by their system of education and the facts of their society and environment. For this reason, they must endeavour to adjust and re-orientate their attitudes and thought to our African conditions and aspirations. They must not try simply to reproduce here their own diverse patterns of education and culture. They must embrace and develop those aspirations and responsibilities, which are clearly essential for maintaining a progressive and dynamic African society.

One essential function of this Institute must surely be to study the history, culture and institutions, languages and arts of Ghana and of Africa in new African centred ways — in entire freedom from the propositions and pre-suppositions of the colonial epoch, and from the distortions of those Professors and Lecturers who continue to make European studies of Africa the basis of this new assessment. By the work of this Institute, we must re-assess and assert the glories and achievements of our African past and inspire our generation, and succeeding generations, with a vision of a better future.

But you should not stop here. Your work must also include a study of the origins and culture of peoples of African descent in the Americas and the Caribbean, and you should seek to maintain close relations with their scholars so that there may be cross fertilisation between Africa and those who have their roots in the African past.

The second guiding principles, which I would emphasise, is the urgent need to search for, edit, publish and make available sources of all kinds. Ghanaian scholars who at an early period were actively concerned with the study of Ghana's history and institutions and helped to prepare the way for the creation of this Institute — such as Carl Reindorf, John Mensa Sarbah,

Casely-Hayford, Attoh-Ahuma, Attobah Coguano. Anthony William Amu — understood how much the development of African Studies depended on the recovery of vital source material. Indeed, the search, publication and our interpretation of sources are obviously processes that must go hand in hand.

Among non-African students of Ghana's history and institutions, one of the most distinguished was undoubtedly Captain Rattray. By his intellectual honesty and diligence, he was able to appreciate and present to the world the values inherent in a culture, which was, after all, foreign to him. It is impossible to respect an intellectual unless he shows this kind of honesty. After all, Academic Freedom must serve all legitimate ends, and not a particular end. And here the term "Academic Freedom" should not be used to cover up academic deficiencies and indiscipline.

I would therefore like to see this Institute, in co-operation with Institutes and Centres of African Studies in other African States, planning to produce what I would describe as an extensive and diversified Library of African Classics. Such a library would include editions, with translations and commentaries or works — whether in African, Asian or European languages— which are of special value for the student of African history, philosophy, literature and law. I can think of no more solid or enduring contribution which the Institute could make to the development of African Studies on sound lines during the second half of the Twentieth Century, or to the training of future generations of Africanists.

Here in this Institute of African Studies you have already made a useful beginning with the collection of a substantial body of Arabic and Hausa documents. This collection has revealed a tradition of scholarship in Ghana about which little was previously known, and I hope that it will throw a new light on our history as part of the history of Africa.

I also regard as important the work which you are doing in the collection of stool histories and other forms of oral tradition— of poetry and African literature in all its forms— of which one admirable expression is Professor Nketia's recently published book entitled "Folk Songs of Ghana", and Kofi Antubam's latest book on African culture. Other Ghanaians have done equally admirable work in this field. I may mention here Ephraim Amu, whose work has created and established a Ghanaian style of music and revived an appreciation for it. Our old friend, J. B. Danquah, has also produced studies of Akan culture and institutions.

Much more should be done in this direction. There exist in our Universities, Faculties and Departments, such as Law, Economics, Politics, History, Geography, Philosophy and Sociology, the teaching in which should be substantially based as soon as possible on African material.

Let us take an example. Our students in the Faculty of Law must be taught to appreciate the very intimate link that exists between law and social values. It is therefore important that the Law Faculty should be staffed by Africans. There is no dearth of men and women among us qualified to teach in the Law Faculty. This applies equally to other Faculties. Only in this way can the Institute of African Studies fertilise the Universities and the Nation.

The magnitude of the changes taking place in Africa to-day is a positive index of the scale and pace necessary for our social reconstruction. Our Universities should provide us with the force and impetus needed to maintain this reconstruction.

After years of bitter political struggle for our freedom and independence, our Continent is emerging systematically from colonialism and from the yoke of imperialism. The personality of the African, which was stunted in this process, can only be retrieved from these ruins if we make a conscious effort to restore Africa's ancient glory. It is only in conditions of total freedom and independence from foreign rule and interferences that the aspiration of our people will see real fulfilment and the African genius find its best expression.

When I speak of the African genius, I mean something different from Negritude, something not apologetic, but dynamic. Negritude consists in a mere literary affectation and style, which piles up word upon word and image upon image with occasional reference to Africa and things African. I do not mean a vague brotherhood based on a criterion of colour, or on the idea that Africans have no reasoning but only sensitivity. By the African genius I mean something positive, our socialist conception of society, the efficiency and validity of our traditional statecraft, our highly developed code of morals, our hospitality and our purposeful energy.

This Institute must help to foster in our University and other educational institutions the kind of education which will produce, devoted men and women with imagination and ideas, who, by their life and actions, can inspire our people to look forward to a great future. Our aim must be to create a society that is not static but dynamic, a society in which equal opportunities are assured for all. Let us remember that as the aims and needs of our society change, so our educational institutions must be adjusted and adapted to reflect this change.

We must regard education as the "gateway to the enchanted cities of the mind" and not only as a means to personal economic security and social privilege. Indeed, education consists not only in the sum of what a man knows, or the skill with which he can put this to his own advantage. In my view, a man's education must also be measured in terms of the soundness of his judgment of people and things, and in his power to understand and appreciate the needs of his fellow men, and to be of service to them. The educated man should be so sensitive to the conditions around him that he makes it his chief endeavour to improve those conditions for the good of all.

As you know, we have been doing a great deal to make education available to all. It is equally important that education should seek the welfare of the people and recognise our attempts to solve our economic, cultural, technological and scientific problems. In this connection, it will be desirable for your master's degree courses to be designed with such problems in mind. It is therefore important and necessary that our Universities and the Academy of Sciences should maintain the closest possible liaison in all fields. This will result not only in the efficient planning and execution of research, but also in economy in the use of funds and resources. Let me emphasise here that we look to the Universities to set an example by their efficiency and their sense of responsibility in the use of public funds. They must also set an example in loyalty to the Government and the people, in good citizenship, public morality and behaviour.

In order that the students may obtain the maximum benefit from their education in our Universities, it is imperative that the relationship between them and their teachers should be as free and easy as possible. Without this close interaction between mind and mind and the common fellowship of a University, it will be impossible to produce the type of student who understands the larger issues of the world around him.

Are we really sure that our students are in touch with the life of the nation? The time has come for the gown to come to town. In this connection, I can see no reason why courses should not continue to be organised at the Law School in Accra for Lay Magistrates, Local Government staff and other officers both in Government and industry, who wish to acquire a knowledge of the law to assist them in their work. The staff of the Law Faculty in this University should be able to organise such courses for the benefit of the people in the categories I have mentioned.

It should also be possible for individual Lecturers and Professors on their own initiative to give lectures on subjects of their own choosing, to which the whole University and others outside it are invited. This would make possible the greatest freedom in discussion and the widest contacts between our Universities and the general public. I would like to see this become an established practice in our Universities.

Furthermore, I would stress the need for the Institute to be outward looking. There may be some tension between the need to acquire new knowledge and the need to diffuse it — between the demands of research and the demands of teaching. But the two demands are essentially interdependent. And in Ghana the fact that we are committed to the construction of a socialist society makes it especially necessary that this Institute of African Studies should work closely with the people— and should be constantly improving upon its methods for serving the needs of the people— of Ghana, of Africa and of the world. Teachers and students in our Universities should clearly understand this.

What in practice does this mean? In part this objective — of serving the needs of the people — can be achieved by training this new generation of Africanists — equipping them, through our Master of Arts and Diploma courses, with a sounder basis of knowledge in the various fields of African Studies than former generations have had. It is because of the great importance that I attach to the training of well-qualified Africanists who can feed back this new learning into our educational system that — in spite of the serious shortage of secondary school teachers — I have agreed that teachers who are selected for these post-graduate courses should be released for two years to take them.

An Institute of African Studies that is situated in Africa must pay particular attention to the arts of Africa, for the study of these can enhance our understanding of African institutions and values, and the cultural bonds that unite us. A comparative study of musical systems, for example, or the study of musical instruments, drum language, or the oral traditions that link music with social events, may illuminate historical problems or provide data for the study of our ethical and philosophical ideas.

In studying the arts, however, you must not be content with the accumulation of knowledge about the arts. Your researches must stimulate creative activity; they must contribute to the development of the arts in Ghana and in other parts of Africa. They must stimulate the birth of a specifically African literature, which, exploring African themes and the depth of the African soul, will become an integral portion of a general world literature. It would be wrong to make this a mere appendage of world culture.

I hope that the School of Music and Drama, which works in close association with the Institute of African Studies, will provide this Institute with an outlet for creative work, and for the dissemination of knowledge of the arts through its extension and vacation courses, as well as through regular full-time courses. I hope also that this Institute, in association with the School of Music and Drama, will link the University of Ghana closely with the National Theatre movement in Ghana. In this way the Institute can serve the needs of the people by helping to develop new forms of dance and drama, of music and creative writing, that are at the same time closely related to our Ghanaian traditions and express the ideas and aspirations of our people at this critical stage in our history. This should lead to new strides in our cultural development.

There are other fields in which a great deal remains to be done. In addition to publishing the results of its research in a form in which it will be available to scholars, the Institute must be concerned with its diffusion in a more popular form among a much wider public. While there are many channels through which this new learning can be spread — including radio and, in the very near future, television — I am particularly anxious that the Institute should assist the Government in the planning and production of new textbooks for use in our secondary schools, training colleges, workers' colleges and educational institutions generally.

I have attempted to indicate briefly some of the principles, which should guide the institute in its work. It is for you to develop, amplify and apply these in relation to the actual possibilities that present themselves to you. Of one thing I am sure, that Ghana offers a rich and exciting field of work and a friendly and sympathetic environment for scholars and students from any part of the world who wish seriously to devote themselves to a study of Africa and African civilisation.

Hence it will, I hope, be possible to say of this Institute — and, indeed, of our Universities — as the historian Mahmut Kati said of another famous centre of learning — 16th Century Timbuktu — I quote "... In those days Timbuktu did not have its equal ... from the province of Mali to the extreme limits of the region of the Maghrib, for the solidity of its institutions, its political liberties, the purity of its morals, the security of persons, its consideration and compassion towards the poor and towards foreigners, its courtesy towards students and men of learning and the financial assistance which it provided for the latter. The scholars of this period were the most respected among the Believers for their generosity, their force of character, and their discretion..."

Finally, I would hope that this Institute would always conceive its function as being to study Africa, in the widest possible sense — Africa in all its complexity and diversity, and its underlying unity.

Let us consider some of the implications of the concept of African unity for the study of African peoples and cultures, and for the work of your Institute.

It should mean, in the first place, that in your research and your teaching you are not limited by conventional territorial or regional boundaries. This is essentially an Institute of African Studies, not of Ghana Studies, nor of West African Studies. Of course, you are bound to take a special interest in exploring the history, institutions, languages and arts of the people of Ghana, and in establishing these studies on a sound basis — as indeed you are already doing.

But these investigations must inevitably lead outwards — to the exploration of the connections between the musical forms, the dances, the literature, the plastic arts, the philosophical and religious beliefs, the systems of government, the patterns of trade and economic organisation that have been developed here in Ghana, and the cultures of other African peoples and other regions of Africa. Ghana, that is to say, can only be understood in the total African context.

Let me illustrate this point.

As you know, Ghana has always been one of the great gold-producing areas of the world. Much of the gold from our mines was exported by our people, who conducted this trade as an exclusive state enterprise, to Jenne on the Niger, whence it was transported by canoe down the Niger to

Timbuktu — the great entrepot and meeting place of river-borne and desert-borne traffic. At Timbuktu the gold was transferred to the camel caravans, which carried it across the Sahara to the commercial centres of the Western Maghrib — whence part would be re-exported to Western Europe.

It was normal for African trading firms to have their agents in Jenne and Timbuktu, in Marrakesh and Fez, with trade connections stretching southwards to modern Ghana and northwards as far as England. Thus, in the early nineteenth century we find in Timbuktu, the home of the University of Sankore, merchants visiting their business colleagues in Liverpool, while merchants from North Africa took part in trade missions to Kumasi.

Another distinct commercial network had grown up around the Kola trade, linking Ghana and its neighbours with the Hausa States and Bornu, and thus — by the central Saharan trade routes — with Tripoli and Tunis. These commercial contacts were naturally reflected at the level of culture. The languages, literature, music, architecture and domestic arts of Ghana have made their impact, in a great variety of ways, through these ancient links on the wider African world, and beyond.

Very few of you may know, for example, that Baden Powell based the idea of the Boy Scout Movement, including the left-hand shake, on the concept of Ashanti military strategy and youth organisation.

Consider a Ghanaian writer like Al-Hajj 'Umoru, who lived from about 1850 to 1934, whose Arabic works, in poetry and prose, have so far been collected by the Institute of African Studies. Al-Hajj 'Umoru belonged to a family of Hausa traders and scholars — his great-grandfather had taken part in 'Uthman dan Fodio's revolution. Born and educated in Kano, he travelled along the kola route to Salaga where he settled as a young man and built up a school of Arabic and Koranic studies; at the time of the Salaga wars, he migrated to Kete-Krachi; well-read in classical Arabic Literature, he collected around him students from various parts of West Africa, and described in some of his poems the disintegration of African society consequent upon the coming of the British.

Similarly, we cannot hope to understand adequately the mediaeval civilisations of West Africa — ancient Ghana, Mali, Songhay, Kanem, Bornu, Oyo — without taking full account of the civilisations which emerged in Eastern, Central and Southern Africa — Meroe, Aksum, Adal, Kilwa, Monomotapa, Mogadishu, Malindi, Mombasa, Zanzibar, Pemba, Chang' Amir — exploring the problems of their inter-connections, their points of resemblance and difference. In North Africa, too, powerful enlightened civilisations had grown up in Egypt, Libya, Tunisia, Algeria and Morocco. These cities, states and empires developed their own political institutions and organisations, based on their own conceptions of the nature and ideals of society. These institutions and organisations were so efficient, and their underlying ideas so valid, that it is surely our duty to give them their place in our studies here.

Nor must the concept of African unity be thought of in a restrictive sense. Just as, in the study of West African civilisations, we have to examine their relationships, by way of the Sahara, with North Africa and the Mediterranean world, so, in studying the civilisations of Eastern and Southern Africa, we have to recognise the importance of their relationships, by way of the Indian Ocean, with Arabia, India, Indonesia and China.

The 11th Century Arab geographer, Al-Bakri, who gave the first full account of the ancient Empire of Ghana, also gave the first description of the Czech city of Prague. -

When we turn to the study of modern Africa we are again confronted with the necessity of thinking in continental terms. The liberation movements, which have emerged in Africa have clearly all, have been aspects of a single African revolution. They have to be understood from the standpoint of their common characteristics and objectives, as well as from the standpoint of the special kinds of colonial situation within which they have had to operate and the special problems, which they have had to face.

So, while of course no single institution can possibly attempt to cover the whole range of African Studies in all their multiplicity and complexity, I hope to see growing up here in this Institute, a body of scholars with interests as many-sided and diversified as our resources can allow. We should in time be able to provide for our students here opportunities for the study of the history, the major languages and literatures, the music and arts, the economic, social and political institutions, of the entire African continent — so that, though individual students will necessarily have to specialise in particular fields, there will be no major sector of African Studies that will be unrepresented here.

This is not, I think, too ambitious an aim. And I am glad to know that the Institute is already taking steps to develop research and teaching both in North African and in East African History — with their prerequisites, Arabic and Swahili.

At the same time, we must try to ensure that there is the same kind of diversity among the student body. While we are glad to welcome students from Asia, Europe and the Americas, we have naturally a special interest in developing this Institute as a centre where students from all parts of Africa can meet together and acquire this new learning — and thus take their places among the new generation of Africanists which Africa so urgently needs; where the artificial divisions between so-called "English-speaking", "French-speaking", "Portuguese speaking" Africans will have no meaning.

The Encyclopaedia Africana, sponsored by the Ghana Academy of Sciences, should provide a forum for African scholars working together and setting forth the results of their research and scholarship.

Scholars, students and friends; the work on which you are engaged here can be of great value for the future of Ghana, of Africa and of the world.

Here let me pay tribute to your Director, Thomas Hodgkin, for the energy and thought with which he has carried out his work. It is to his credit that such a firm foundation has been laid at this Institute.

Ladies and Gentlemen: I now have great pleasure in declaring the Institute of African Studies formally and officially open.

LIST OF TABLES

LIST OF MAPS

LIST OF FIGURES

NOTES ON CONTRIBUTORS

Marian Ewurama Addy retired as Professor of Bio-Chemistry at the University of Ghana and is currently Principal, Anglican University College, Ghana

Olive Akpebu Adjah is Senior Assistant Librarian, Institute of African Studies, University of Ghana.

Akosua Adomako Ampofo is Professor and Director, Institute of African Studies, University of Ghana.

Alexander Agordoh retired as a Senior Research Fellow, Institute of African Studies, University of Ghana.

Kojo Opoku Aidoo is Senior Research Fellow and Coordinator, History and Politics Section, Institute of African Studies, University of Ghana.

Abraham Akrong was Senior Research Fellow at the Institute of African Studies, until his untimely demise in 2011.

Osman Alhassan is Senior Research Fellow, Institute of African Studies, University of Ghana.

Kojo Amanor is Associate Professor at the Institute of African Studies, University of Ghana.

Kwame Amoah Labi is Senior Research Fellow and Deputy Director, Institute of African Studies, University of Ghana.

Richard Asante is Research Fellow, Institute of African Studies, University of Ghana.

Alexander Asiedu is Associate Professor, Department of Geography and Resource Development, University of Ghana.

Albert Awedoba is Professor, Institute of African Studies, University of Ghana.

Joseph R.A. Ayee retired as Professor of Political Science at the University of Ghana and is currently Deputy Vice-Chancellor at the University of Kwa-Zulu Natal, South Africa.

Ebenezer Ayesu is a Research Fellow at the Institute of African Studies, University of Ghana.

Delali Badasu is Senior Research Fellow, Regional Institute of Population Studies, University of Ghana.

John Collins is Professor of Music at the Department of Music, School of Performing Arts, University of Ghana.

Mary Esther Kropp Dakubu is Professor Emerita, Institute of African Studies, University of Ghana.

Ebenezer Laing is Professor Emeritus, Botany Department, University of Ghana.

Takyiwaa Manuh is a retired Professor of African Studies, University of Ghana .

Lord C. Mawuko-Yevugah is a lecturer in International Relations at the University of the Witwatersrand, Johannesburg, South Africa.

Dan Obeng-Ofori is Associate Professor, College of Agriculture and Consumer Sciences, University of Ghana.

Francis Nii-Yartey is Associate Professor of Dance at the Dance Department, School of Performing Arts, University of Ghana.

Brigid Sackey retired as Professor of African Studies and is currently Professor at the Centre for Social Policy Studies, University of Ghana.

Kodzo Senah is Associate Professor, Department of Sociology, University of Ghana.

Esi Sutherland-Addy is Associate Professor and Coordinator of the Language, Literature and Drama Section, Institute of African Studies, University of Ghana.

INTRODUCTION
Takyiwaa Manuh and Esi Sutherland-Addy

Institutional Foundations

The Institute of African Studies (IAS) was established in 1961 at the University of Ghana and charged with ensuring African-centred perspectives in all aspects of the production and dissemination of knowledge.[1] In addition to its foremost task of research, it was also to design and coordinate an introductory, multidisciplinary course on Africa which all students of the University of Ghana would be required to take. This course was designed to ensure a sound basis for further inquiry and enlightened self knowledge about Africa and its people among students who were likely to take up leadership roles on the continent. The African Studies programme has thus been part of the offerings at the University for almost 50 years. Under the over arching theme of "Society, Culture and Development in Africa," the curriculum for the course has evolved over time to reflect salient issues such as environmental change in Africa, gender in African societies, technology and development in Africa, and health and disease in Africa, including new epidemics such as HIV and AIDS. The course incorporates research findings of Fellows of the Institute as well as the changing pedagogical and academic focus of the University. Thus from the 2011/2012 academic year, the new General Studies programme of the University necessitated further changes in the structure of the course. A course in African Studies is also a requirement at all other public universities in Ghana, with the University of Cape Coast establishing a full undergraduate course in African Studies, while some private universities have also adopted the requirement.

Given the significance of the African Studies programme in Ghanaian tertiary education both historically and currently, as well as its necessary multi-disciplinary nature, the lack of textbooks or readers that bring together a body of knowledge on the themes, issues and debates that have informed and animated research and teaching in African Studies in Ghana over the past half-century is a matter of deep concern for teachers and students alike. This becomes even more important when we consider the need for knowledge on Africa that is not Eurocentric or sensationalised, but driven from internal understandings of life and prospects in Africa. Dominant representations and perceptions of Africa usually depict a continent in crisis threatened by conflict, disease, famine, technological backwardness, 'failed' and neo-patrimonial states and a lack of integration into the global economy. Many of these same representations are also disseminated around Africa and absorbed, willy-nilly, by many Africans, including intellectuals and students. There is also deep contestation over whether and how to teach about Africa to African youth and students, who often end up buying into self-destructive myths about African inferiority and lack of achievement, perpetuated through 'standard' textbooks and the dominant interpretative frames of the disciplines. Indeed our readers will find that this volume is not entirely exempt from the effect of these representations. Students of African politics on the continent are therefore as likely as students in Europe and the USA to be fed on a diet of the 'neo-patrimonial' African state and sensationalist accounts of its workings- 'the politics of the belly' (Bayart 1993) or 'Africa works- disorder as political instrument' (Chabal and Dalotz 1999), as further demonstration of African irrationality and immaturity, although this is rather more reflective of the subservience of many African intellectuals to western intellectual ideologies and epistemologies.

Knowledge Production for Africa

In contrast to such accounts, what are needed are representations and accounts that seek to understand and appreciate African societies and their politics, rationalities and challenges on their own terms, as well as perspectives that bring out Africa's rich and deep history and cultures, and African knowledge production and knowledge systems over a diverse range of fields and subjects. Knowledge production from such perspectives counteracts the distortions, simplifications and binaries that have been used to present and 'explain' Africa, while decentring the power and authority claimed by other, more 'knowing' interpreters, who have been in the habit of informing Africans about themselves.

As a consequence of increased access to education and to higher education in particular, over the past five decades in several parts of Africa and the sheer size of African populations, there are now many more African scholars both on the continent and elsewhere, who study different aspects of the economies, histories, religions, languages, arts, cultures, and science and technology in Africa.[2] For many such scholars, the study of Africa cannot be a passing fad, or in fulfilment of an academic requirement, because their very lives, presents and futures are bound up with the fortunes of the continent. They are also close to the reality that they study. Increasingly therefore, it is such scholars who generate the richly textured and detailed studies that are serving to animate intellectual life and debates within and across disciplines throughout Africa, even if the terms and forms of such engagements are not framed after academic fashions elsewhere, particularly in the West, or recognised and cited in their indexes and texts. However the concern cannot be merely about presence, but in how such scholars contribute to re-create the social and natural sciences in Africa as unified bodies of knowledge that are relevant for addressing social, cultural and technological realities in the continent.

In the midst of rampant global economic crises, unsustainable consumption and production systems, environmental and ecological degradation and failed development, especially in several parts of Africa, it is increasingly recognised that development visions and perspectives that are rooted in Africa's own histories and experiences, including its relations with others, and the knowledge that communities have developed, both in the past and contemporaneously, to deal with others and to survive, may hold the key to the continent's future development and prospects, and to restoring dignity and hope to the nearly one billion African population. The different bodies of national African Indigenous Knowledge Systems (IKS), the so-called 'traditional' knowledges and systems, for example, are known to be richly endowed, and they have been utilised by the majority of African populations in both rural and urban locations to deal with several medical and health conditions, and to provide food, nutrition, and environmental protection, among other interventions and survival strategies. While this is known and accepted, systematic efforts have not been made, especially by intellectuals, to study, restructure, coordinate, manage and exploit such knowledge systems in innovative ways, in order to help produce sustainable and culturally acceptable solutions to several of Africa's developmental challenges particularly in the areas of health, agriculture, natural resource management and conservation, nutrition and food security. Rather than attempting to play 'catch-up' in the face of dwindling funds and infrastructure for research after a Western mode, African researchers and scholars who embrace IKS are more likely to produce robust and new knowledges and technologies rooted in their own contexts and realities, that can foster local solutions for socio-economic development and growth, the creation of local economic enterprises and systems and their articulation with the so-called formal sectors, as well as exploring the potential of IKS for innovation and commercialisation (Neba et al. 2012). It is in such ways that Africa's competitive edge across several domains of knowledge production, and not only in raw material production and exploitation, may be realized, to allow for real diversification of economies and the elimination of poverty and under-development. For these to occur however, the compartmentalisation of knowledge into discrete disciplines will need to evolve into more interdisciplinary modes of knowledge production, while science education needs to better integrate IKS and to develop interfaces and synergies to develop the necessary innovations. Current modes of research and of knowledge production in which the researcher, as *knower*, relates to local populations as merely 'informants' and 'respondents,' will also need to change, to embrace them fully as *knowers* and partners, and co-producers of knowledge, in new meaningful, participatory and sustainable relationships. This will also entail better thought out collaborations between African higher education institutions and the various indigenous knowledge communities to engender trust and cooperation for mutually beneficial results. These mutually reinforcing activities should in turn reshape the teaching and learning in schools and communities and affect pedagogy and instructional systems. An example of how this can be done is provided by Botswana's Centre for Scientific Research, Indigenous Knowledge and Innovation (CesrIKi) which has worked actively with traditional medicine practitioners from rural and peri-urban villages using a recently developed "Screens-to Nature" technology, a field deployable method for testing and documenting biological activities of medicinal plants. This has provided a 'novel platform for generating potentially useful knowledge from IKS with a significant potential for wide scale application in other African IKS settings' (Andrae-Marobela et al., 2012).

Such an approach resonates with the question posed by Nigerian political theorist, Claude Ake, concerning how the knowledge developed and appropriated by Africans on the basis of their historical experiences could be valorized in the pursuit of democracy and development (Ake 1996). These same questions are pursued by Nabudere (2006) who terms it as *self -understanding* to organise ourselves to *'move forward in history'*, in which Africans position ourselves as authentic human beings who have made a contribution to human civilisation, given Africa's position as the cradle of humankind that has contributed the building blocks of the human heritage, which we share with others.

It is on the basis of such self-confident and resurgent epistemologies that Africa can hope to end its erasure from the global counts of knowledge production or other measures of global and national and regional progress (see Mouton 2008). For Ake and several others including Mafeje (2000), Adesina (2008) and Nabudere (op cit.), African social sciences in particular, but also the natural sciences, must take their local intellectual, political and existential contexts seriously at the same time as they also seek to be globally reputable. As noted by Mafeje, "If what we say and do has relevance for our humanity, its international relevance is guaranteed" (Mafeje 2000:67, quoted in Adesina, 2006). In this way, the practice of much of the scholarship in Africa will advance beyond its current status as translation or data-gathering for 'others' in the global division of intellectual labour, to be recognized as capable of generating theories and ideas that are relevant for African people and their lives. This also requires that scholarship should critically appraise its links with African policy-making and assess what it can contribute to formulating policies that support and help regenerate African peoples and societies while safeguarding its autonomous space. It is with such ambitions that the textbook has been designed and written.

Africa in Contemporary Perspective- Themes and Approaches

The textbook, *Africa in Contemporary Perspective* presents and analyzes broad information on Africa's physical features, demography and languages; social, political and cultural institutions and practices; economic life, production systems, livelihoods and human security; health, the environment, the state of science and technology on the continent; and artistic expression and performance, as a basis for engaging with representation and discourses about Africa. Several contributors are primarily concerned with the practical implications of the themes which they discuss for improving the livelihoods of the peoples of the continent, while others concentrate on demonstrating how alternative epistemologies could yield different perspectives on Africa today. The 22 chapters of the book are each viable as stand-alone pieces. However, they have been incorporated into five broad thematic sections and a final section on resources for studying Africa.

Overview- Geography, Language and Population

The overview chapters on the geography, population and languages of Africa in Section One set the scene for a lively discussion of the multilayered facets of the continent that are captured by other chapters in the volume. Beyond providing a mental image of the land mass, climatic features and vegetation of Africa by region, the opening chapters expand on the notion of Africa as a vast lived space of great antiquity. While the natural, human and cultural attributes of the continent are presented as resources, contributors also emphasize the challenges inherent in managing these apparent abundant resources, and the need therefore for carefully calibrated strategies to manage the tensions and the dynamic relationship between human activity, including population and environmental pressures, and resources (Chapter One). Africa is a continent of enormous natural resources including forests, rivers and lakes, minerals, and oil reserves, and the chapter presents their salient features for each of the five regions of Africa- North, West, Central, East and Southern Africa. However these geographies are also accompanied by challenges in soils and weather conditions and production processes that have not allowed optimal exploitation and benefits for the population.

As is well known and highlighted in the literature, the basic right of Africans to assert their own definitions of their humanity and way of life has been subject to several distortions. One of these concerns language use. Kropp Dakubu (Chapter Two) notes that one of the greatest attributes of human beings is our ability to create and use language to express our innermost feelings, through personal conversation and also through poetry, song and story, and in literature both oral and written. These artistic expressions of feelings and ideas are considered to be among the supreme creations of the human spirit. This assertion permits a discussion of the legendary linguistic diversity of the continent in historical perspective, before adding on the layer of issues raised by the encounter with European languages which have become a major vector of political and economic hegemony in Africa. In similar manner to linguistic diversity, the population of Africa is often posed as a problem in dominant discourses and policy, and Chapter Three on population introduces readers to basic demographic tools for understanding the dynamics of Africa's population. Africa's population is also a huge resource for the continent, but its youthful nature, combined with continuing high fertility and mortality rates, and the disproportionate burden of disease and poor management and policy choices have not allowed full development and optimisation of this crucial asset.

Setting the tone for the volume, the chapters in Section One are not restricted to a static view of Africa's past. While explaining conceptual frames of reference developed by African societies as regards the natural, social and cultural environment, contributors to this section also signal the frontiers of change that are relevant to dealing with current predicaments and challenges. Whether it is a question of natural resources, population or the fundamental human attribute of language, contributors present facts in both historical and contemporary perspective, sometimes in response to epistemological distortions or to policy implications. Themes which get a preliminary airing in the overview section are subsequently examined from various angles. The ideological and ontological underpinnings of African cultures and societies as a whole raise a vital cluster of issues which impact on the study of contemporary Africa. Indeed no aspect of the processes of change and the elusive modernisation in Africa can be said to offer more of a challenge than that of coming to terms with inherited ways of knowing and belief systems within the context of an invasive colonial experience. Tied into this is how African people might critically embrace their history and culture in the face of globalisation and other pressures.

Cultural, Social and Political Institutions

In Section Two, contributors present some basic cultural, social and political ideas and practices underlying African social life, belief and governance systems, the advent of monotheistic religions into the continent and the interplay between these and indigenous African religious and political systems. In Chapter Four, readers are made aware of the highly nuanced notions of gender in several African societies which allow persons who are male by sex to be socially accepted as female and vice versa, at the same time as gender-based discrimination against women are pervasive in those same societies. The chapter also discusses gender as an analytical tool for assessing the social, cultural, political and economic conditions of African societies with particular reference to two major areas, namely (1) family, work and livelihoods, and (2) leadership, politics and citizenship. Chapter Five examines the historical processes that led to the emergence of African diasporas with a particular focus on the main trajectories by which Africans ended up outside of the continent, the features of slave lives and the survival strategies of those communities. Of particular interest are African retentions in the Diaspora and political and ideological movements created by African descended peoples, particularly Negritude and Pan-Africanism, which have had extremely important resonances with the continent.

Notions of culture in dialectic with the notion of development are among the most misconceived and misapplied, particularly when connected to Africa. For a variety of reasons some of which are related to the processes and economic systems which led from slavery to colonialism, there is often a tendency to simplify and essentialise African ways of life. In addition, they are set within a paradigm which places these ways of life at the lowest rungs of the 'development' ladder. The section encourages an exploration of the various perspectives from which these notions can be viewed, completely debunking the static perspective and emphasizing their dynamism (Chapter Six). Particular emphasis is placed on concepts which often appear in scholarship on African peoples such as "world view." In this section there is an attempt to examine worldviews as they were developed and lived among different African societies prior to encounters with other cultures and how they continue to change and affect the lives of contemporary Africans (Chapters Six and Seven). Differences notwithstanding, there are profound similarities running through the worldviews that have produced a general pattern of belief systems and practice in African societies. Indigenous world views are brought into the realm of contemporary African life, demonstrating the contradictions raised by factors such as the generation gap and the adoption of Abrahamic faiths and religions.

The issue of Abrahamic faiths in Africa is discussed in this section from the perspective that scholarship in the study of Islam and Christianity in Africa is coming to grips with the dynamic transformative roles of indigenous African religions and cultures in the spread of Islam and the process of Christian evangelization (Chapter Eight). Whether it is about the millennium-long relationship between Africa and Islam, or in the stuttering start of Christianity in the fifteenth century in most of the continent and its relationships with the political and economic conquest of the continent especially in the 19th and 20th century, what is clear is that there is an African perspective to put forth – an African story to tell. The story includes the construction of conflicts between 'Western' interests and those of major Islamic powers in terms of a clash between Judeo Christian and Islamic forces since the turn of the century which has affected the African continent in a number of ways. There are also proxy wars over natural resources such as occurred in the Sudan and South Sudan, and sectarian violence in Nigeria. It is evident that the emergence of Pan-Islamic and Christian fundamentalism has begun to turn Africa into a theatre of struggle for ideological dominance.

Traditional leaders in Africa have been regarded as important custodians of world views in both historical and contemporary times. Here again lies a vexed and complex confluence of systems, interests and ways of life. In Chapter Nine, traditional leadership is set alongside modern leadership, and the challenges posed by their coexistence are highlighted, with solutions being proposed to these challenges. Concerning leadership generally, an argument is developed about a causal relationship between the persistent development crisis of a resource–rich continent and poor leadership. Proposals are made for a new political paradigm of transformational leadership, which emphasises not only strategic vision and strong ideological convictions of a leader, but also the personal resolution and political will to put them into practice.

Development, The Economy, Livelihoods and Human Security

Culture is frequently evoked in the same breath as development as has been noted above, while the notion of "development crisis" occurs frequently in discussing leadership in Africa. There is therefore the need in this volume for a robust and extended discussion of development, especially as it relates to livelihoods and the economy, which is a matter of concern in several chapters

6

(e.g. Chapters 1, 4, 6, 11, 13 and 15). Section Three is dedicated to this important topic from the perspectives of development theory, agricultural development, the economy and human security. The section opens with Chapter 10 which presents the historical underpinnings of development theory and interrogates development within the framework of political economy. Here, the account of the evolution of the dominant political economy at the global level slots discourses around development into a complicit ideological relationship. It becomes evident that any attempt to abstract development as a set of prescriptive technical solutions or scientific theories, betrays an over-simplification and a distortion of the socio-political implications of the phenomenon. This inevitably leads to a questioning of any attempt to conflate development with modernisation, such that the Global North becomes the paragon of progress to which the Global South must aspire. The chapter uses the example of agriculture to illustrate how productive activities in African societies were transformed into a cheap source of primary materials for the Global North, and it also demonstrates how at the household and community level, gender inequalities and inequities can be exacerbated by 'development' policy.

Agriculture remains central to Africa's social and economic survival, as shown in statistics on its contribution to gross domestic product (GDP), and the proportion of the population involved in agriculture on the continent (Chapter 11). Without a reinvigorated agriculture sector based on higher productivity and yields, Africa cannot hope to achieve food security and robust poverty reduction. Such growth would however be dependent on a number of conditions including the modernisation of agriculture and farm inputs, crop improvement and animal husbandry, conservation techniques, empowerment of women, and the establishment of incentive systems to attract the participation of the youth and more educated persons into the sector. Governments would also need to take on multiple policy roles aimed at ensuring sustainable agricultural practices and more secure livelihoods for farmers.

A discussion of agriculture and livelihoods begins to reveal the ways in which African communities, families and individuals have become vulnerable to deepening insecurities. Human security has become an important field of inquiry within which sundry phenomena which threaten the daily lives and dignity of human beings are assessed, and readers are introduced to this in Chapter 12. The bulk of the chapter focuses on the post colonial African state, with brief references to some factors affecting security in pre-colonial Africa. Chief among these factors were the principles which guided governance, in particular the pact between the rulers and the ruled, by which those in power were also responsible for ensuring the security of the community. The chapter tracks the policy choices made by the majority of post independent African states as well as the external pressures exerted on their economies such as the Structural Adjustment Programmes which have directly resulted in threats to the survival of individuals and communities. Isolating the areas of public health and conflict, the authors discuss among other effects, the direct consequences of the HIV and AIDS pandemic and civil strife on women and children, and acknowledge the effectiveness of women's participation in the resolution of conflict. The poignancy of this point is buttressed in the global acknowledgement of the role that Liberian women played in restoring peace to the country after the civil wars (1989-2003), and the joint award of the Nobel Peace prize to President Ellen Johnson Sirleaf and Ms. Leymah Gborwee both of Liberia, and Ms. Tawakkol Karman of Yemen in 2011.

Examining the state of human security prepares the ground for a broad examination and critique of the performance of African economies in Chapter 13. The chapter provides a broad and critical overview of development policy-making and policy outcomes in postcolonial Africa, and uses the 'development crisis' as a point of departure to tease out key challenges and debates which have shaped and influenced development policy choices and outcomes in the postcolonial era. The evolution, implementation and outcomes of the structural adjustment policies since the early 1980s are also analyzed, together with the new poverty reduction architecture which replaced the SAPs in the late 1990s. Africa's economic outlook and development prospects at the beginning of the new millennium are also explored within the implications of key changes within the global economy including the emergence of new global powers for Africa's development prospects. Finally, the chapter takes stock of Africa's performance on key indicators such as job creation, gender equality and democratic governance and argues for an African-led development trajectory that relies more on mobilization of internal resources and less on aid and externally-guided development policies.

Health, Environment, Science and Technology

In Section Four, two areas of intense challenge for the continent- health and the environment- are combined with an innovative approach to the promotion of science and technology in teaching, learning and community life, as critical ingredients in setting Africa firmly on the path of sustainable and problem-solving development and emergence from poverty. As we know, health is situated at the fulcrum of development from a human development perspective. Chapter 14 demonstrates that health is not the absence of illness, but a metaphor for individual and communal harmony, and the author makes an important contribution in helping us understand the social reproduction of health and well being in the African context, and the health seeking behaviour of the majority of African people. Reading the chapter requires a willingness to abandon the empiricist stance and to accept that perception is reality, as the author asserts. The proposition is that health care delivery and systems would be more efficient if the training of health personnel, particularly those in the 'allopathic' facilities, incorporated an understanding of the African sense of health and well-being. According to this perspective therefore, Western healthcare systems in Africa must undergo a necessary process of indigenization in order to provide a wide-ranging continuum of medical services, instead of generating a clash of incompatible systems.

The discussion on the environment in Chapter 15 reinforces the position taken by the authors of several chapters of this volume (Chapters 1, 2, 4, 11 and 12) about critical indicators of human development in Africa which require significant improvement for Africans to experience the well-being promised by the continent's resources. The debate around the relationship and articulation between human beings and their environment is thus intensified. Once again this is a node around which critical questions of development play out. The natural resources described in Chapter 1 of this volume for instance, are shown to be rapidly degrading, drawing attention to the question of the exploitation of natural resources and whose interests need to be placed at the centre of such activities. The list of environmental issues is alarming, ranging from deforestation and biodiversity loss to various forms of pollution affecting the very basis of life such as water and air. Issues brought to the fore include the apparent clash between the resource requirements for higher and better standards of living and the need for safeguarding and ensuring the interests of future generations. In particular, water is isolated here (as it was earlier in the discussion of human security) as a predictable cause of conflict on the continent. In the circumstances, contributors call for a review of the model of political economy and technological choices that might be made by African states. The section on health, science, environment and technology seeks to advocate the adoption of home-grown solutions as the crux of the strategy to stem the tide of environmental degradation, poor health and technological inadequacy and redirect it towards sustainable growth. But the section contains within it a paradox of perspectives, one which is cautionary and lacking in optimism, and the other which is visionary.

The authors set up a lively and provocative discussion which brings science and technology into the discourse on social and economic policy, social mobilisation and education as well as development strategies. Authors also invite readers to look at conceptual issues which should form the basis of strategic thinking and action and they discuss invention and innovation, insisting that 'bringing something completely new into existence' as well as re-engineering existing phenomena to adapt them to changing requirements are both necessary processes. They advocate the facilitation, institutionalisation and management of invention and innovation as central to an emergent continent. For the contributors to this section, the major paradigm shift required for science and technology to play its pivotal role in the development of Africa lies in advocacy to enable policy makers, the research community and other community members to understand its essential value and commit to developing a multi-faceted enterprise. The approach advocated by Addy and Laing (Chapter 16), and shared by Senah (Chapter 14) and Alhassan (Chapter 15) involves the exploration of indigenous processes and knowledge which they have termed "the Sankofa Idiom" in a process involving scientific rigour and vigilance in safeguarding African intellectual property in a globalised knowledge economy. It is pertinent to note that this section also contains several recommendations based on recurring epistemological questions as well as agenda setting themes throughout the volume which seek to align the science and technology enterprise with the emergence of an alternative path towards African development.

Artistic Expression and Performance

The final section of the volume, Section Five, is dedicated to artistic expression in Africa. This constitutes a vibrant and dynamic aspect of the lives of Africans which continues to be integrated into the daily and ceremonial life of peoples of the continent. Rituals and festivals for example, offer a rich platform for the performance of a communal aesthetic and ethos. Chapters in the section are on the literary arts (Chapter 17), visual arts (Chapter 18), as well as on dance (Chapter 19), musical traditions (Chapter 20), and popular entertainment (Chapter 21). The authors seek to both lay out the features of a range of art forms and to demonstrate the contexts of their use and performance, while also emphasising their importance in expressing the universe of ideas and beliefs developed by Africans. The arts are shown as assisting in understanding African societies better while some art forms also play the role of social commentary and intervention. The authors bring to the fore the ways in which the arts have evolved over the years, guiding the reader in the appreciation of contemporary manifestations of African arts. Perhaps, what is most exciting is the variety of ways in which these facets of the arts are constantly in dialogue with each other, creating synergies; or the ways in which the arts can act as a vehicle for challenging societal norms such as the suppression of females and jural minors.

Section Five also takes up the quest to resist the presentation of African cultural manifestations in a linear hierarchy which excludes the indigenous from contemporary manifestations. For example, in an attempt to avoid the tendency to place oral literature in a static time warp, the discussion covers both oral and written forms contemporaneously. Contributors are also keen to demonstrate the fact that the creativity, aesthetic satisfaction and affective intensity have been integrated into the entire spectrum of African life ways. Thus the contexts in which art works are made and used are carefully accounted for. In this process the reader is exposed to regional cultural affinities which are not stressed often enough. Many African societies became dependent on art works literally as historical documents and as tools for communication, while the symbolic value of the arts up to the present tends to facilitate their incorporation into acts of worship and ritual both within particular ethnic and multi-ethnic contexts.

Inevitably, contributors tackle the vexed question plaguing the dominant scholarship as to whether the aesthetic value of the arts exists in inverse proportion to the functionality of the art form. The issue of the vectors of change is also picked up in this section. There is a discussion of internal and external sources of change in form and function of the arts. However, artists are credited with agency in selecting new themes and technologies to produce new art forms or variations on a traditional theme. Transnational (ethnic) manifestations of the arts are also given significant attention in the section, and the survival of African arts in the Diaspora as well what Africa has made of its exposure to the arts of other continents is also explored. This is particularly prominent in the discussion of the visual arts, dance and popular entertainment.

Resources for studying Africa

The volume has argued forcefully for interdisciplinary modes of knowledge production and the integration of African indigenous knowledge systems in knowledge production in Africa. Current modes of research and of knowledge production in which the researcher, as knower, relates to local populations as merely 'informants' and 'respondents,' will also need to change, to embrace them fully as knowers and partners, and co-producers of knowledge, in meaningful, participatory and sustainable relationships. This aspiration does not however take a simplistic or essentialist view that epistemologies and bodies of work which have evolved in the area of African Studies are invalidated. The different chapters of the volume are indeed a resource for studying Africa from disciplinary and thematic perspectives and reflect major findings and theoretical arguments in the area of African Studies and cognate fields of study. But there are often complaints about a dearth of reference materials and sources in African Studies, leading to students and researchers selecting other fields in which to work. The final section of the volume (Ch.22) specifically addresses this particular issue and provides a quick guide to a range of sources to serve the needs of students and researchers interested in African Studies. In addition to providing guidelines for citing references, it examines materials that provide a general overview of African Studies, reference sources available in the subject area, and other information resources including major libraries, museums and on-line sites and platforms. Also included among sources are references to communities of scholars conducting researchin African Studies such as subject associations.

Conclusion

We have argued for renewed knowledge production about and for Africa, to undergird growth and renewal on the continent. Rather than buying into external representations of Africa, with its 'lacks' and aspirations for Western modernities, we insist that African scholars in particular should be in the forefront of promoting understanding of the pluri-lingual, overlapping, and dense reality of life and developments on the continent, to produce relevant and useable knowledge. The continuing and renewed interest in Africa's resources, including the land mass, economy, minerals, visual arts and performance cultures, as well as bio-medical knowledge and products, by old and new geopolitical players, obliges African scholars to transcend disciplinary boundaries and to work with each other to advance knowledge and uses of those resources in the interests of Africa's people. In order to do this successfully, we must abandon the pretence of omniscience as well as disdain of Indigenous Knowledge Systems, which continue to provide sustenance and solutions to the everyday existential problems of the majority of Africans. We must work actively with practitioners and communities to study, restructure and exploit such knowledge systems in innovative ways to produce sustainable and culturally acceptable solutions to existing challenges in the areas of health, agriculture, natural resource management and food security, as well as new and emerging issues.

But to attempt a comprehensive overview of these emerging issues which ought to be tracked in the African context would be like trying to catch a torrent of rain in a calabash. Some emergent issues, such as the powerful thrust of China into the continent, hold no surprises as they are in effect iterations of established patterns and relations between Africa and others. On the other hand, the notion of an emergent Africa is a shift in the dominant discourse that reflects the influence of factors like the proactive response by Africans to new information and communication technologies.

In addition to these, environmental change in general, and climate change in particular, have gained global attention as phenomena around which the world and societies as we know them are likely to be subject to fundamental transformations. Adaptation and mitigation strategies are being proposed to manage their impacts, but specific African responses are also needed which combine strategic thinking with proactive knowledge production and management to ensure sustainable human-centred development of the continent.

Africa in Contemporary Perspective is dedicated to recording and recovering Africa's culture and memory. The editors recognise that the sheer breadth and density of Africa as subject, and expect that this volume will serve as a stimulating introduction. There are many resources for producing textbooks in each of the thematic areas highlighted in the book, as indeed exist for each of the chapters. A textbook on popular performance, or on development discourses in Africa, can be produced with the rich material from the teaching resources that have been accumulated over the years within the African Studies Programme at the University of Ghana. The current volume which is long overdue, can only be a prelude of many that we hope will be produced by fellow scholars working on the continent. We eagerly await their appearance in the very near future, obstacles to publication notwithstanding.

References

Adesina, J. 2008. "Archie Mafeje and the Pursuit of Endogeny: Against Alterity and Extroversion" *Africa Development*, Vol. XXXIII, No. 4, 2008, pp. 133–152

Ake, C. 1996. *Democracy and Development in Africa*. Washington: The Brookings Institution Press.

Andrae-Marobela, K. , A.N. Ntumy, M. Mokobela, M. Dube, A. Sosome, M. Muzila, B. Sethebe, K.N. Monyatsi, and B. N. Ngwenya. (2012) 'Now I heal with pride: The application of Screens-to-Nature Technology to Indigenous Medical Knowledge in: Chibale, K., Masirimembwa, C., Davies-Coleman, M. (eds.) *Drug Discovery in Africa*, Springer Verlag, Germany.

Bayart, J-F. 1993. *The State in Africa: The Politics of the Belly*. London: Longman

Chabal, P. and J-P.Dalotz 1999. *Africa Works- Disorder as Political Instrument*. London and Bloomington: The International African Institute and Indiana University Press.

Lauer, H., and K.Anyidoho (Eds.) 2012 . *Reclaiming The Human Sciences and Humanities Through African Perspectives*. Accra: Sub Saharan Publishers

Mafeje, A. 2000. "Africanity: A Combative Ontology", *CODESRIA Bulletin*, (1):66-71.

Mkandawire, T., 1997, 'The Social Sciences in Africa: Breaking Local Barriers and Negotiating International Presence', The Bashorun M.K.O. Abiola Distinguished Lecture presented to the 1996 African Studies Association Annual Meeting, *African Studies Review*,Vol. 40, no. 2, pp.15-36.

Nabudere, D. W. 2006. 'Towards An Africology of Knowledge Production and Regeneration.' *International Journal of African Renaissance Studies*. Vol.1 (1): 7-32.

Neba, A., K. Andrae-Marobela et al. 2012. 'Higher Education Institutions-Industry Stakeholder Relationships: A Case Study of the University of Botswana's Centre for Scientific Research, Indigenous Knowledge and Innovation's (CesrIKi's) Partnership with the Indigenous Knowledge Systems (IKS) Community in Botswana.' Unpublished report prepared for The Association of African Universities

Odotei I and A. Awedoba 2006. (Eds) *Chieftaincy in Ghana: Culture, Governance and Development* Accra : Sub-Saharan Publishers.

Olaniyan, T and A. Quayson 2004. (Eds) *An Anthology of Theory and Criticism*. Oxford: Blackwell Publishers .

Endnotes

1. See Preface above.
2. See for example the publications and activities undertaken under the umbrella of CODESRIA, the Council for the Development of Social Science Research in Africa, based in Dakar, Senegal. <www.codesria.org>.

SECTION 1: AFRICA–GEOGRAPHY, POPULATION & LANGUAGE

CHAPTER I

GEOGRAPHY OF AFRICA
Alex B. Asiedu

Introduction

Africa is a continent bestowed with resources, yet only negative images dominate its portrayal in both academic scholarship and popular media. Africa is the second largest continent after Asia, and has a total area of about 19 million km², covering 23 percent of the world's total land area. It stretches across the equator with its southern tip at Cape Agulhas near the Cape of Good Hope, at 35° S and the northern coast between the straits of Gibraltar and Tunisia at about 35°-37° N. Africa stretches roughly 8000 km from north (Egypt) to south (South Africa), and its widest point is 7000 km from east to west. Africa has 54 states including island republics off its coasts in the Indian and in the Atlantic Oceans. The largest and the most important of these islands is Madagascar.

The relief of the continent is varied. Although Africa is mainly composed of plateaux, in some places there are depressions which are below sea level, while elsewhere there are mountains rising to over 5000 m. Lake Assai, for instance, lies many hundreds of meters below sea level, whereas such long-extinct volcanoes as Mt. Kilimanjaro (5895m) and Mt. Kenya (5194m) rise thousands of feet higher. Many of Africa's plateaux and highlands provide sustenance, and in some cases, refuge for some of the continent's densest and most productive populations. For instance the Ethiopian, Drakensberg (in South Africa), Cameroon and Atlas Mountains (a mountain range across a northern stretch of Africa through Morocco, Algeria, and Tunisia) include peaks between 3000m and 5000m and support dense populations living in various eco-zones between 1000m and 2500m above sea level.

Africa has several of the world's great rivers, of particular importance being River Congo (4,700 km long), River Nile (6,650km) and River Niger (4,180km). The continent is also well noted for its lakes including Lake Victoria, Lake Tanganyika and Lake Malawi, which support dense and productive populations. The longest river on earth, the Nile, originates from Lake Victoria-Nyanza and derives two-thirds of its waters from the Ethiopian Highlands before emptying into the rich Nile Delta. In modern times, the lower Nile has become an important source of hydroelectric power, as well as vital irrigation water to Egypt and Sudan which benefit from the electric power generated from the Aswan Dam.

Although a large part of the continent lies within the tropics, considerable variations in climate occur. Of particular importance are differences in rainfall. A few parts of the continent experience heavy rainfall, while there are other areas that receive extremely low and unreliable rainfall. Temperatures are high everywhere in Africa except at high altitudes and during winter in the extreme north and south. The Sahara and the rest of continent to the south are generally hotter than any other part of the world of comparable size. The only major exception to this is the south-eastern part of the continent, which is considerably cooler on account of its greater altitude. Variations in climate are largely responsible for the great differences in natural vegetation which occur in Africa. In the wettest parts of the continent, notably in the D.R. Congo Basin, dense forest occurs, but in the driest areas plant life is very scanty. The patterns of plant cover and the animal life of the continent basically depend on the availability of water in the soil. The amount of rainfall, its seasonal distribution, the relief of the ground surface, the nature of the underlying rocks and soils also influence soil water availability. Increasingly, the activities of people as cultivators, woodcutters and charcoal-makers among others, have been modifying the natural pattern of the vegetation.

As at 2010, 911 million people—or about 13 percent of the world's population—lived in Africa. The most populous countries are Nigeria (158.2 million, UN 2010), Egypt (84.5 million, UN 2010), Ethiopia (84.9 million, UN 2010), and the Democratic Republic of Congo (DRC) (67 million, UN 2010). Distribution of the population is highly uneven, and some parts of the continent, particularly the vast Sahara, have few permanent residents. Others rank among the world's most densely populated areas, notably the Nile Valley of Egypt; the Atlantic coastal stretch from Côte d'Ivoire to Cameroon; Rwanda; Burundi; and South Africa's province of KwaZulu-Natal. The extensive areas of the continent which remain sparsely settled include the deserts of the north and south-west, swampy plains in south-east Angola, Zambia and Central DRC. Overall, Africa's population density was 31 persons per sq km (79 persons per sq mi) in 2006. This compares to 461 in Europe, 530 in Asia, 80 in North America, and 168 in South America.

The continent-wide population growth rate peaked at 3.43 percent in 1979 and remained relatively high through the 1980s, averaging 2.69 percent. Rates have lowered since. In 2005, Africa's growth rate was 2.08 percent, which is still high compared to other continents. When one considers the continent's population growth rate, the vast arid and semi-arid regions, and the diminishing availability of arable land, there are serious grounds for concern about Africa's future capacity to feed its own people. As on other continents, pockets of population density in Africa have emerged in various rural areas because of favourable local climates, fresh water supplies, cultivable land, or useful minerals.

One of the characteristic features of Africa, which has an important bearing on economic and political affairs, not only on the continent as a whole, but also in individual countries, is its variety of races, languages and religions, as discussed in chapters 2 and 7 of this volume. Some of the peoples of Africa have been on the continent for thousands of years, whereas others, such as the Europeans, settled later.

The economic life of most African countries is still to a large extent dominated by agriculture, although in some parts of the continent, mining, forestry and fishing are also of considerable importance. In the recent past many African countries have developed modern manufacturing

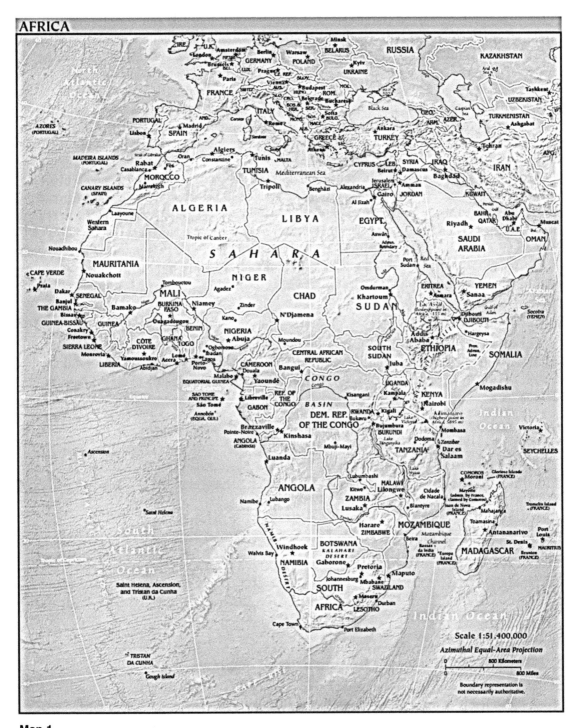

Map 1

Source: *Courtesy of the University of Texas Libraries, The University of Texas, Austin*

industry. The export trade, to a large extent, is made up of primary products such as agricultural products, minerals and timber. The import trade is made up mainly of a wide range of manufactured goods. A great deal of the trade of most African countries is with the highly developed countries of Western Europe and North America.

The political geography of Africa consists of some 54 modern nations, including island republics, off its coasts. With the current exception of Western Sahara (which is under domination of Morocco), these African countries are independent states with their own political institutions, leaders, and identities. All these countries belong to a continental forum called the African Union.

Considering the vastness of this continent and the diversity of its physical and human features, a discussion of the regional geography of Africa will be better done on sub-regional basis, starting with the Southern Africa sub-region, followed by the Eastern Africa sub-region, the Central Africa sub-region, the West Africa sub-region and the Northern Africa sub-region. Geographic features or themes that are explored include relief and geology, drainage, climate, vegetation and soils, population, agriculture, manufacturing and mining. In some instances, tourism and regional economic integration have been added.

Southern Africa

Southern Africa comprises ten countries: Angola, Botswana, Lesotho, Malawi, Mozambique, Namibia, South Africa, Swaziland, Zambia, and Zimbabwe. The region covers a total surface area of 2,310,776 sq. miles, with South Africa representing about 24% of this landmass (see Table 1).

Table 1 – Area, Population and Population Density of Southern Africa Nations

Country	Area(square miles)	Population(Mid 2006) (Millions)	Density (Per square mile)
South Africa	471,444	47.3	100
Mozambique	309,494	19.9	64
Angola	481,351	15.8	33
Zimbabwe	150,873	13.1	87
Malawi	45,745	12.8	279
Zambia	290,583	11.9	41
Lesotho	11,718	1.8	154
Namibia	318,259	2.1	6
Botswana	224,606	1.8	8
Swaziland	6,703	1.1	169
Total	2,310,776	127.6	941

Source: *World Population Data Sheet, Population Reference Bureau, 2006*

Relief and Geology

The sub-region's landscape and resources vary from country to country on account of contrasts in relief and geology. The greater part of the sub-region consists of plateau land, whose rim tends to be high, with the ground sloping gently towards the interior like a saucer. The rim, which is often called the Great Escarpment, is most marked in the east where it is known as the Drakensberg Mountains. The peak of the Drakensberg is called the Thabana Nttlenyama (3,483m), and is found in Lesotho.

From the crest of the Drakensberg Mountains the land dips away to the region known as the Veld. The High Veld is over 1200m high, and is either flat or gently rolling. To the north of River Vaal there is an extension of the High Veld called the Witwatersrand. From the High Veld the land dips gently westwards towards the Middle Veld and to the Kalahari. The lowest part of the Kalahari (Lower Veld) is a broad depression occupied by the Okavango Swamp and the Makari-kari Salt Pan (Senior and Okunrotifa, 1983).

In Zimbabwe, the high plateau extends in a belt across the country from south-west of Bulawayo to the north-east of Harare. Here, it is known as the High Veld, and is everywhere above 1,200m. From Harare, the highland curves eastwards to the Mozambican border, where it is known as the Eastern Border Highlands. In certain places, the Eastern Border Highlands rise to over 2,400m.

The relief of Malawi is characterized by great differences in height which occur within a short distance. A very important relief feature is the Great Rift Valley which is a continuation of the East African Rift Valley System. The Great Rift Valley is occupied in the north by Lake Malawi and in the south by River Shire which drains the lake into River Zambezi. To the east of River Shire are the Shire Highlands which rise to 2,100m in Mt. Zomba and 3,350m in Mt. Mulanje. In the north of Malawi, there are large areas of high plateau, such as the Nyika and Vipya plateaux.

In most parts of Zambia, there is a level or gently rolling plateau surface of between 900-1500m. In some places the plateau surface is cut into by the faulted flat-floored valleys of rivers such as the Zambezi and the Luangwa. In Angola, the coastal plain is almost narrow everywhere. From this plain, the land rises gently in the north, and more steeply in the central and southern sections, to the plateau surface which occupies a large part of the country. Much of the Bie plateau in the centre of the country is 1500-1800m high. In Mozambique, the coastal plain is wider than in Angola and a large part of the country lies below 400m. The plain is narrowest in the north, becoming much wider in the centre and south. In the north, bordering Lake Malawi, there are mountains rising to over 2,400m.

The explanation for the patterns of relief in this sub-region and in Africa as a whole lies in the succession of events in Africa's geological history. This history can be divided into two ages, the pre-Cambrian and the Cambrian (Grove, 1998). The pre-Cambrian began with the origin of the earth, about 4.5 billion years ago and rocks found in southern Africa which are about half this age, occupy much of Zaire-Angola and the Zimbabwe-Transvaal Orange Free State region. Bordering them are the regions where folding has taken place within the last 200 million years.

Drainage and Water Bodies

The Southern Africa sub-region has a number of important rivers. Some of these, such as the Zambezi and Limpopo, flow into the Indian Ocean, whereas the Vaal joins the Orange which empties into the Atlantic Ocean. The flow of some rivers varies quite remarkably for several years. The discharge of the Zambezi, for instance, was 40 per cent greater on average in the 24 years after 1946 than it had been in the last 20 years preceding that date. These variations can be attributed to increased use and environmental degradation in their catchment areas. The two most important lakes in the Southern Africa sub-region are Lake Malawi and Lake Victoria.

These water bodies are of immense economic importance to the sub-region. The Zambezi for instance, was dammed in the 1950s at Kariba and provides about half the energy needs of Zimbabwe. The Kariba is also on the tourist circuit from Harare to Victoria Falls and the Chobe and Wankie game reserves. Since the 1970s, Zambia has also been supplied with electricity from a plant at Victoria Falls. Downstream Kariba, below Tete in Mozambique, is the Cabora Bassa Dam which was completed in 1976 and generates 680MW of electricity per year. The Vaal, a tributary of the Orange, flows through the industrial heartland of the Southern Transvaal, about 65 km south of Johannesburg. The Vaal has been carefully controlled for irrigation as well as to supply industries of the Witwatersrand and Vereeniging in South Africa. Its flow has been supplemented by water from the eastward flowing headwaters of the Tugela River. The Orange River itself is deeply entrenched and offers few opportunities for irrigation.

The headwaters of the Limpopo River cut through the quartzite ridges of the Witwatersrand and the Bankeveld to flow across a remarkably level plain called the Bushveld Basin. This plain coincides with the surface of an enormous mass of granitic and norite rocks around the rim of which, at the base of the igneous complex, are a number of strongly mineralized zones. Other rivers which drain the sub-region include Cuanza, Cunene, Okavango, Chambeshi, and Luangwa.

There are also several important lakes and swampy areas in Southern Africa. Both Lake Tangayika (only the southern tip of which is within the sub-region) and Lake Malawi occupy the floor of the rift valley, and are very steep. Lake Kariba is man-made and resulted from the construction of the Kariba Dam across River Zambezi. Lake Meru was formed partly by faulting and partly by warping. Bangweulu, Lukanga and Okavango are some of the major swampy areas in the region.

Climate and Vegetation

(i) Climate

Because of greater distance from the equator, Southern Africa generally has lower mean annual temperature than for example, West Africa. In most coastal areas, mean annual temperatures are about 20° C–25° C. Places on the west coast, however, tend to be rather cooler than places on the east coast due to the influence of the cool Benguela current, which flows northwards along the west coast. The east coast, on the other hand, is influenced by the warm waters of the southwards flowing Mozambique current and its continuation, the Agulhas current. In some parts of the sub-region, particularly in Lesotho, the temperature is greatly reduced because of the height. Temperature drops at an average rate of about 0.6°C for every 100m gain in height. The annual range of temperature is small everywhere but tends to become rather larger with increasing distance from the equator.

The rainfall of Southern Africa is very unevenly distributed. Rainfall is generally heaviest in the east of the sub-region, and becomes progressively lighter towards the west. The eastern coastal area receives rainfall from the easterly winds. These winds blow from the Indian Ocean and bring warm, moist air. When the winds meet the Drakensberg Mountains, the air is forced to rise and is cooled. Much of its moisture is deposited as rainfall in the eastern coastal area.

Rainfall is highly seasonal. Most of the rainfall occurs during the southern summer, from about November to April when the Inter-Tropical Convergence Zone lies well to the south of the equator and a low pressure system develops over the sub-region. Winds are drawn from the sea into the low pressure belt. On the eastern side they are drawn across the warm Mozambique current, and pick up substantial amount of moisture which they deposit as rain on reaching the land. On the western side, however, the winds are drawn across the cool Benguela current, and bring much less rain.

During the southern winter (May-October) there is little rainfall, and the sub-region comes under the influence of high pressure and the winds from the sea are much weaker. However, the extreme south-western part of Southern Africa (the Cape region), receives most of its rainfall during this time. Much of Southern Africa is affected by unreliable rainfall, with great variations in amount from one year to another. This creates problems for agricultural development in the region.

(ii) Vegetation

The pattern of natural vegetation in Southern Africa is closely related to the amount and seasonal distribution of rainfall. In the wetter eastern coastal areas, there is sub-tropical forest, with evergreen trees, palms, tree ferns and lianas. Away from the coast, large areas in the north of the region are covered by tropical grassland (savanna). Further south in the eastern interior there is temperate grassland. The grasses here are generally shorter than in the savanna, and there are very few trees. In the drier areas further west, grassland is replaced by various kinds of semi-desert and desert vegetation. In the southwest of Cape Province, the climate is similar to that experienced around the shores of the Mediterranean Sea. Here the type of vegetation is known locally as Machia, which consists of low shrubs. These are evergreen and are adapted to survive the summer drought by having hard, leathery leaves which reduce transpiration. In a small area, midway along the south coast of the Republic of South Africa, rainfall is moderate and is fairly evenly spread over the year. Here temperate forests are to be found, with evergreen trees.

Population

The Southern African sub-region on the whole tends to be sparsely populated, but there are great differences in population density (See Table 1). The factors influencing population density in the sub-region include relief, rainfall, soils, the distribution of tsetse fly, the distribution of mineral deposits and accessibility.

By far, the most densely populated of the countries is Malawi. In the past, the population of Malawi increased as a result of immigration, particularly of people from Mozambique in search of work on the country's tea plantations. This trend, however, has changed within the past four decades. Instead, large numbers of migrant workers leave Malawi to work for long periods in other countries, especially in South Africa. Within Malawi, the population is very unevenly distributed. The highest concentration is in the south of the country, particularly in the areas around Blantyre, Zomba and Lilongwe. The southern part of the country is the most accessible and was the first to be economically developed by Europeans, and so job opportunities there are greater than in the north. The population generally becomes less dense as one moves northwards. This is because the north is less accessible and is less well developed. Also, there are large areas of high plateaux such as the Vipya and the Nyika plateaux, where the climate tends to be less pleasant and the soils stony and shallow.

Although very mountainous and poor in minerals and agricultural potential, Lesotho is the second most densely populated of the Southern African countries (See Table 1). The pressure of population on the land has led to the cultivation of very steep slopes, and to overgrazing. As a result soil erosion has become a serious problem. Because of the difficulty of making a living in the crowded and over-crowded homeland, large numbers of men migrate to work, particularly in South Africa. About two-thirds of the population of Lesotho live in the extreme west of the country, in the so-called "lowlands". The extreme east of the country is 2300m high and population there is much less dense, as the slopes are particularly steep and the soils are thin.

Swaziland, the third most densely populated country in the sub-region, can be divided into four regions running north to south across the country. They are the High Veld, Middle Veld, Low Veld and the Lubombo Mountains. The High Veld is hilly, with steep slopes and heavy rainfall. Much of the High Veld is now occupied by forest plantations. The Middle Veld, with its rolling and adequate rainfall for crop growing, is the most densely populated part of Swaziland. The Low Veld, on the other hand, is rather thinly populated. Although a number of important irrigation schemes have been developed, rainfall totals are low to promote any appreciable cultivation. The Lubombo Mountain area is also generally thinly populated because of the rugged relief.

The three most thinly populated countries of Southern Africa are Namibia, Botswana and Angola. Namibia is thinly populated because it suffers from extreme dryness. Large parts of the country are almost uninhabited, including the Namib Desert along the coast. The only settlements in the Namib are in the mining centres. The greater part of Botswana is occupied by the Kalahari Desert.

The civil war that engulfed Angola for over two decades has contributed to the low population. It is remarkably light along the southern coastal area, which suffers from dryness but is dense on the plateau, particularly on the Bie plateau.

In Zambia there are several belts of fairly dense population, particularly along the railway extending from Livingstone to the Copper Belt, the eastern plateau, the mid-Zambezi floodplain, and the lower Luapula basin. Thinly populated areas include the area between the mid-Zambezi valley and the line of rail, and the Luangwa valley. Much of these areas are infested with tsetse fly and are not suitable for cattle rearing.

In Mozambique, the most densely populated areas tend to be in the north of the country, particularly along the coast. Also fairly densely populated is the coastal area in the south.

In Zimbabwe, population tends to be densest on the High Veld, particularly along the main railway, where temperatures are pleasantly cooler than elsewhere and the rainfall is more abundant. Transport facilities are also good, thus favouring commercial agriculture.

There are great variations in population density in South Africa. The densest population occurs along the east coast, where the rainfall is moderately heavy and fairly reliable, and where

Natural Vegetation in Africa

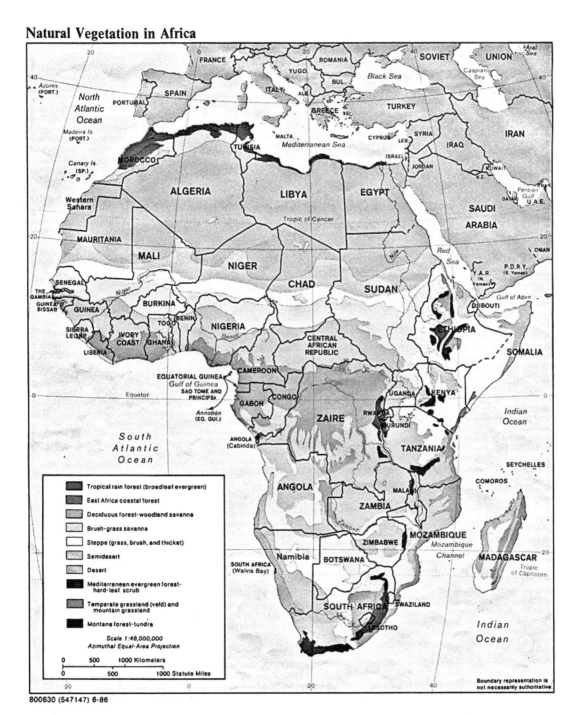

800630 (547147) 6-86

MAP 2

Source:_Courtesy of the University of Texas Libraries, The University of Texas, Austin_

conditions are favourable for growing a wide variety of crops. Also fairly densely populated is the south-western corner of Cape Province, where water for irrigation is available and where conditions are favourable for growing wheat and fruits. Another concentration of population occurs in the area known as the Rand, around the metropolis of Johannesburg, where mining and manufacturing provide good job opportunities. A vast area in the western part of the Republic is thinly populated. This area is extremely dry and is only suitable for animal rearing.

The Economy

The region has the largest economic sector on the continent, with South Africa being the hub of most activities. Economic patterns at the beginning of the 1960s were partly the result of two factors: the known physical resource base and the countries' colonial economic history. These factors are still very relevant in facilitating growth and are also interconnected, since the location of mineral reserves was an important determinant of the pattern of white settlement, which was in turn, a decisive factor influencing the economic and political policies which shaped the different countries' economic geography.

Two fundamental aspects of economic patterns in South Africa, Zimbabwe, and Namibia were shaped by policies designed to create and maintain racial inequality. First, land was divided between whites and blacks in an unequal manner, and white areas received the bulk of transport and other infrastructural investment. Furthermore, land ownership in both rural and urban areas was almost entirely a white preserve, and rural land designated for African occupation was mainly held under conditions of traditional, communal tenure. Second, a plethora of restrictions and impediments was implemented to limit the occurrence of permanent African urbanization, which also encouraged the circular migration of men without their families.

Agriculture

In all the countries of the sub-region, with the notable exception of South Africa and Zambia, agricultural products form a very important part of the export trade, in spite of the fact that large parts of Southern Africa suffer from low and unreliable rainfall. Widely different agricultural systems are found in the sub-region, operated by both indigenous African and former settler farmers.

Most of the sub-region's farmers produce mainly for subsistence and farms are generally small and methods used are simple. Subsistence farmers practise some form of bush fallowing called the *Chitimene* system which is particularly important in parts of northern and central Zambia. Much use is made of hand tools such as the hoe, and in some cases cattle-drawn ploughs are used, although there are countries where mechanization is also practised. The traditional patterns of farming are however, changing and more farmers are producing an increasing proportion of the region's cash crops.

In South Africa however, the bulk of the commercial crop and livestock production comes from European-owned farms and ranches. The main grain crops are maize and wheat. The most important area noted for maize growing is the so-called Maize Triangle, which extends roughly between the towns of Mafikeng, Middelburg and Bloemfontein. Wheat is particularly important in the winter rain area to the north of Cape Town.

Fruit growing is very well developed in South Africa. The fruits are supplied to local and international markets. A very important area for fruit growing is the south-western part of Cape Province. Grape vines are of particular importance inland from Cape Town. Citrus fruits such as oranges, grapefruits and lemons are important in some of the areas where temperatures do not fall below freezing point. The most important growing areas are in the valleys of rivers which drain into the Limpopo.

Sugar cane is a very important crop in the coastal belt of Natal and some of it is exported. Tobacco is an important crop to the north and west of Pretoria, particularly around Rustenberg. Cotton is grown mainly in the Transvaal.

Livestock rearing is important in South Africa. Cattle are mainly concentrated in the eastern part of the country where rainfall is heavier and more reliable. Both beef cattle and dairy cattle are reared. Dairy farming is particularly important in areas close to towns as they provide the main market for fresh milk. Beef cattle are mainly kept on mixed farms on the High Veld. Sheep farming, mainly for the production of wool, is very important in the drier areas of South Africa, especially in the Great Karroo and eastern Cape Province. Large numbers of goats are also kept, mainly for the production of mohair.

Mozambique is an important producer and exporter of cashew nuts. The cashew tree grows wild on sandy soils along the coastal belt of the country where it forms the continuation of the cashew growing area of southern Tanzania. Planted cashew trees now also occupy a vast area of land. Most of the cashew nut crop is exported to India.

Coconuts are also important, especially in the coastal areas of Mozambique, particularly around Quelimane. Coconuts are grown both by African and white farmers on large plantations. The exports include copra, coconut oil and coconut cake. African farmers, particularly in the north of the country, also grow cotton. Groundnuts, sisal, sugar cane, tea and tobacco are the other important cash crops grown in Mozambique.

Angola is the only country in Southern Africa which is an important producer of coffee, although small quantities are produced in several other countries. Most of Angola's coffee is of the *robusta* variety and much of it is exported to the United States of America for making instant coffee. Cotton, sisal and sugar are the other important crops grown in Angola.

Large-scale mixed farming is of particular importance in Zimbabwe where until the 1970s about two-fifths of the total land area was set aside for the sole use of white farmers. The bulk of what is produced on these farms is intended for sale. Considerable use is made of modern machinery and methods. Maize is very widely grown in the mixed farming areas. Tobacco growing is mainly concentrated in Mashonaland and part of the adjoining Manicaland Province. Wheat is grown particularly in the Low Veld. Cotton is fairly widely grown while sugar is grown on large plantations in the south-eastern Low Veld, particularly on the Triangle and Hippo Valley estates.

Cotton, groundnuts, sugar cane, tea and tobacco are the important cash crops grown in Malawi. The main cotton growing area is the Shire valley. Part of the region's cotton crop is used by the local textile industry. The bulk of the country's groundnut production comes from small-holdings in the Lilongwe and Kazungu districts. Both nuts and groundnut oil are exported. The Lower Shire valley in Malawi is also an important area for growing sugar cane. Tea plantations are found on the lower slopes of the Shire Highlands where rainfall is fairly heavy. Farmers also grow tea around Nkhata Bay near Lake Malawi. Most of the country's tobacco production comes from small farms. Sugar cane and tobacco are important cash crops in Zambia. Sugar cane is grown in the Kafue Flats region near Mazabuka, while in Lesotho only about one-eighth of the country is suitable for cultivation. The rest is too mountainous and is only suitable for livestock rearing.

The low and unreliable rainfall limits agriculture in Namibia. In the areas which were reserved for Africans during colonial rule, the people are subsistence farmers who grow crops such as millet, and rear cattle and sheep. White farmers control most of Namibia's commercial agricultural production. This consists largely of livestock rearing. Cattle and sheep are reared in large ranches, many of which depend on deep wells for their water. In addition, there are some irrigation schemes on the tributaries of River Orange.

Like Namibia, agriculture in Botswana is hampered by low and unreliable rainfall. In good years the eastern part of the country receives as much as 700mm of rain, but the rest of the country gets much less. Most of the cultivated land is in the extreme east of the country. In that area Africans grow maize, sorghum and beans for subsistence. Some white farmers also cultivate maize and cotton.

Because of the low rainfall, livestock rearing is much more important in Botswana than crop growing. Most Batswana keep large numbers of cattle, sheep and goats. There are also some white-owned cattle ranches in the eastern part of the country, and around Ghanzi in the west. Meat and hides are important export items, and there is also a considerable trade in live animals.

In relation to its size, Swaziland has a greater agricultural potential than any of the other countries of Southern Africa. The main agricultural area is the Middle Veld, where large parts are used by farmers for growing subsistence crops and for grazing. Also some cash crops such as citrus fruits, cotton, tobacco, and pineapple are grown. In the Low Veld there are white-owned ranches and crops such as sugar cane, citrus fruits, and cotton are grown.

Fishing

Fishing is of great importance to South Africa and Namibia, and to some extent, Angola, Malawi and Zambia. It is of only minor importance in Mozambique, Zimbabwe, Botswana, Lesotho and Swaziland. In South Africa, fishing is particularly important over the Agulhas Bank, which is off the south coast of the Republic. The water here is shallow and helps make fishing easy. Important species of fish caught include cape hake (stockfish), South African pilchard and cape anchovy. Large quantities of fish are canned, and there is also considerable production of fish meal and fish oil. South Africa's important fishing ports include Cape Town, Port Nolloth, Durban, Saldanha Bay and Port Elizabeth.

In Namibia, the cool waters of the Benguela currents, which are rich in fish food, wash the coast of Namibia. Some of the important species of fish caught include South African pilchard, cape anchovy, and rock lobster which is a shellfish and is mainly exported. Important fishing ports in Namibia are Walvis Bay and Luderitz.

The fairly large area of continental shelf off the coast of Angola, and the cool and plankton-rich waters of the Benguela current, which support a large fish population make fishing very important along the coast of Angola. Some of the important species of fish caught include the horse mackerel, sardines and anchovies.

Even though Malawi is a land-locked country, fishing is important. The rivers and lakes of Malawi abound in fish. Lakes Malawi, Chilwa and Malombe, Khota-kota and Nkhata Bay and the lower part of River Shire are all important fishing areas. Tilapia and catfish are some of the important types of fish caught. A small amount of frozen and dried fish is exported.

Fish forms an important part of the diet of many of Zambia's people. This is because many of the lakes, swamps and rivers of the country are fairly rich in fish. Lakes Tanganyika, Bangweulu, Meru, Kariba, and Rivers Luapula and Kafue, and the Lukanga swamps are important fishing grounds for Zambia. There is considerable trade in fresh, dried, and smoked fish within Zambia, and the main market for fish are in the towns of the Copper belt.

Mining

Southern Africa as a whole is very rich in minerals. Almost all the countries have significant mining industries. South Africa is exceptionally rich in minerals. Over a number of years, it has ranked first in the world in the production of gold, chromium ore, platinum and vanadium; second in manganese ore; third in antimony, asbestos, diamonds and uranium; fourth in phosphate rocks. The country also produces about seven-tenths of the gold used in Western Europe. The oldest gold mining area is around Johannesburg on the central plateau of the Rand. Other gold mining areas are around Klerksdorp and Welkom. Many of the gold mines are deep.

South Africa is a major producer of coal. Some coal is mined in the Newcastle and Vryheid areas of Natal. Most of the country's coal, however, now comes from the Transvaal and Orange Free State coalfields. Much of the coal is burnt in thermal power stations to generate electricity. Other consumers of coal are industry and the railways. Some is also exported.

Diamond mining is also very important in South Africa. Almost half the diamonds produced in South Africa are gem quality. Important diamond mining areas include Kimberly and the areas around Pretoria and Postmasburg. Other important minerals produced in South Africa include copper, platinum, uranium and chromium ore. Uranium is a by-product of the gold mining industry.

The economy of Zambia depends very heavily on mining, particularly copper, which is mined in a belt about 130km long and 30km wide, called the Copperbelt. The Zambian Copperbelt is an extension of the copper producing area of the Shaba province of Zaire (now Democratic Republic of Congo (DRC)). An important by-product of the copper mining industry is cobalt which is useful in the making of magnets, turbines and cutting tools. Lead and zinc are mined at Kabwe, as well as coal, which is found at Maamba in the Zambezi valley.

Zimbabwe has a wide variety of minerals, including gold, asbestos and coal. Most of the important mineral deposits are located near the Great Dyke, which is an area of granite rock running for some 560km across the country.

Angola is rich in minerals. It is also an important producer of petroleum, iron ore and diamonds, although during the mid-1970s there was a drop in production because of the effects of the civil war. Angola's important petroleum production area is the oilfields in the shallow waters off the coast of the Cabinda Enclave. Also near Luanda, petroleum has been produced since 1953. The most important iron ore mining centre is near Cassinga with most of the iron ore mined here exported to Europe and Japan. Diamonds are mined near Dundo and areas bordering the diamond mining area of the Kasai region of the Democratic Republic of Congo. Other minerals such as copper and manganese ore have been mined in Angola at various times. Angola has a number of hydro-electric power stations, particularly on the Cuanza and Catumbela Rivers.

The mining industry makes an important contribution to the economy of Namibia, with minerals accounting for a greater proportion of the country's export trade. Of particular importance are diamonds, which occur in the coastal strip of the Namib desert to the north of the mouth of the River Orange. Diamond mining takes place mainly between the mouth of Rivers Orange and Luderitz. Copper, lead and zinc ores are mined around Tsumeb, to the north of Windhoek. Uranium deposits can be found near Rossing.

In Botswana, diamonds which are a very important export commodity, are produced at Orapa and Jwanang in the south of the country. Copper and nickel ores are mined at Selibe-Phikwe. There is some coal produced near Morupule.

Minerals are of little importance to the economies of Mozambique and Malawi, although several important mineral deposits like coal iron and oil are known to exist.

Manufacturing

The share of manufacturing in GDP varies widely between countries in the sub-region. The share of manufacturing has increased in the past 30 years, but there have been no fundamental shifts in the nature of the economies which still essentially rely on trading primary products for manufactured goods. In Malawi, Mozambique, and Swaziland the export sectors are dominated by agricultural products. In Zambia, Namibia, Angola, and Botswana minerals dominate exports, and manufacturing industry has remained fairly insignificant in the Lesotho economy. Zimbabwe's industrial sector is by far the most sophisticated and successful in the sub-region, apart from South Africa.

South Africa is the most industrialized country in Africa. Manufacturing contributes more to her economy than do mining and agriculture combined. The main manufacturing centres include the Rand, the areas around the ports of Cape Town, Durban and Port Elizabeth. A wide variety of manufacturing establishments are found in South Africa. One group of industries is those associated with agriculture, and to a lesser extent with forestry and fishing. Another very important group of industries comprises those associated with minerals. Chemical industries are also of considerable importance as well as those associated with the manufacturing of textiles, clothing, footwear and arms.

The manufacturing industry is also well developed in Zimbabwe which exports large quantities of manufactured goods to neighbouring African countries. Like the other countries of the sub-region, many of its industries are concerned with the processing of local agricultural products, minerals, timber and fish both for the local market and for export. Factories which process agricultural products are mainly located in the producing areas, in order to reduce transport costs.

In Botswana, there is the extraction of diamonds at Orapa and the smelting of copper and nickel ores at Selebi-Phikwe. In Swaziland there are saw mills and a large pulp mill, together with cotton ginneries, sugar factories, and canneries for citrus fruits. In Namibia copper ore is smelted, and there are factories for canning meat and fish, as well as the production of fish meal and fish oil.

Fish processing plants are important in Angola, where in the coastal towns there are fish canneries and factories for making fish oil. There are also saw mills in a number of the countries producing planks, railway sleepers, plywood and veneer. There are also a number of mills for the manufacture of wood pulp and paper at Norton and Umtali in Zimbabwe, at Alto Catumbela in Angola, and at Chinteche in Malawi.

In recent times a number of industries have grown up in all of the countries of the sub-region, which produce for the local markets goods which in the past had to be imported. These import-substitution industries are mainly located in towns, near to their main markets.

Tourism

Southern Africa is an important tourism destination and tourism constitutes a major source of foreign exchange earnings in countries such as South Africa, Zimbabwe, Namibia and Mozambique. There are many wildlife reserves, including the famous Kruger National Park in South Africa. Most of the tourists originate from within the sub region itself. However, visitors from Europe, North America and Asia have grown rapidly in recent years.

Other important attractions of the sub region are coastal beaches, the lake shore beaches of Malawi, wildlife reserves, and some spectacular scenery such as the Victoria Falls.

Sub-Regional Integration

In 1980 the Southern African Development Coordination Conference (SADCC) was formed as a regional grouping. It included all the states of Southern Africa (excluding South Africa) and Tanzania to press for black majority rule in South Africa and Namibia. In 1995, with black majority governments in power throughout Southern Africa, SADCC was renamed the Southern African Development Community (SADC) with a broader agenda to enhance socio-economic and political development.

Eastern Africa

The spatial extent of Eastern Africa has always been difficult to establish. This is due to certain historical, cultural and environmental reasons. The region consisted of two major regions in the past. 'East Africa' originally referred to Tanzania, Kenya and Uganda which shared the same colonial history and various common services such as railways and postal services. "The Horn of Africa" in turn referred to countries bordering the Red Sea and its immediate environs. Ethiopia, Somalia, Eritrea and Djibouti fall into this category. This discussion merges these two sub-regions into the Eastern Africa region.

Relief and Drainage

East Africa is mainly a plateau region. Parts of the plateau are very old in origin while parts have been affected by faulting or warping or volcanic activity.

Faulting has produced the great depressions called the Rift Valley system, which is characterized by high mountains that tower above the plateau surfaces and a number of lakes. Volcanic activities have been responsible for the formation of characteristic landforms of the area. Volcanic cones and widespread lava flows are some examples of these land forms. Mountains Kilimanjaro, Elgon, Kenya and Meru represent some of the notable volcanic cones that were created on lines of weakness extending from the main rift valley. Lake Victoria, which is Africa's largest lake, is found here. Furthermore, River Nile, which is also the continent's longest river, takes it source from this part of the continent.

Climate, Vegetation and Soils

All parts of the region are within 12°C from the Equator and because of this fact, places at sea level have high temperatures throughout the year. These temperatures, however, vary greatly from place to place due to altitudinal differences. The tops of Mounts Kilimanjaro and Kenya are permanently snow covered, while lowland coastal areas such as Mombassa and Dar es Salaam have mean annual temperatures of about 27°C.

There are also large spatial variations in rainfall received. Large parts of the region, however, suffer from extreme dryness. More than half of the region as a whole has a mean annual rainfall of less than 800mm. Two main types of rainfall are experienced. Areas close to the Equator are affected by the Equatorial type which is characterised by double maxima rainfall. Areas bordering the Indian Ocean, the highland areas of the interior and those surrounding Lake Victoria and other major water bodies experience this type of rainfall. Further away from the Equator, the tropical type of rainfall occurs. It is characterised by a single rainfall maximum that affects the area from about November to April. Much of Central and Southern Tanzania, the extreme north of Kenya and Uganda, most parts of Ethiopia, Eritrea, Somalia and Djibouti experience this type of rainfall. Another significant characteristic of rainfall here is its unreliability in terms of the amount received within the year and also variations in the rainy seasons from year to year.

Because of the dryness prevailing in the region, tropical rainfall forest vegetation is largely confined to the wettest areas, particularly in Western Uganda and along the coast. There is, however, considerable diversity in the spread of this vegetation. In the relatively wetter areas, there is savanna woodland which consists of grasses interspersed with trees, particularly deciduous trees. In the drier areas, there is savanna grassland which usually consists of grasses with scattered trees, especially the baobab tree. In the extremely dry areas, semi-desert scrub, with drought resistant thorny bushes, dominate. On higher grounds, montane vegetation consisting of a succession of different vegetation zones is commonly found.

The main soil types found here are the *oxisols, ultisols* and *vertisols*. *Oxisols*, which are highly leached soils with low base nutrients for plant growth, are found largely in the humid areas of the region, especially along the coast while *ultisols* are widespread in the moist to sub-humid parts of Kenya and Uganda. *Ultisols* are relatively less weathered than the *oxisols* and support some of the densest agricultural populations in areas where tea, rubber and banana crops are grown. *Vertisols* are confined to the sub humid to arid areas of Western Ethiopia and other surrounding regions. These soils respond well to agricultural activities when cultivation is supplemented with irrigation agriculture. In Ethiopia, *vertisols* support extensive cultivation of cotton, corn, sorghum and millet.

Population

Because most of the people in the sub-region are involved in agriculture, population concentration is determined largely by the amount and reliability of rainfall received. Areas with highest densities occur in places with mean annual rainfall of at least 750mm, as it is in such areas that intensive crop cultivation is possible. Uganda which receives appreciable rainfall has the highest population density of 297 persons per square mile. Other factors that influence population densities here include the incidence of tse-tse fly, the nature of the soil and the reduction of temperature with altitude.

Generally there are four (4) main areas of high population density, all related to availability of rainfall (see Table 2):

 i.   Lands bordering Lake Victoria, particularly southern Uganda, where plentiful rainfall is available for farming activities;

 ii. The lower slopes of highland areas of Mounts Kilimanjaro and Kenya where plentiful rainfall is available for agriculture. The Kikuyu of Kenya originate from and farm these areas;

 iii. The coastal areas and islands of Zanzibar and Pemba are important agricultural areas because of the heavy rainfall received there;

 iv. Central Ethiopia, which is a highland region west of the Rift Valley belt, has well watered agricultural lands that support high densities of population and cattle.

Table 2 – Area, Population and Population Density within Eastern Africa

Country	Area(square miles)	Population (mid 2006) (millions)	Population Density per sq. miles
Ethiopia	426,371	74.8	175
Tanzania	364,900	37.9	104
Kenya	224,081	34.7	155
Uganda	93,066	27.7	297
Somalia	246,201	8.9	36
Eritrea	45,405	4.6	100
Djibouti	8,958	0.8	90

Source: *World Population Data Sheet, Population Reference Bureau, 2006*

Some salient characteristics of population growth and distribution in the area are as follows: large population increases experienced in the last forty or so years seem to represent the most fundamental change in the region's geography. Population increased from about 50 million in 1965 to around 150m in 1997 and then to 189.4m in mid 2006. However, it has become clear in recent years that the region is at the onset of a demographic transition which suggests that falling birth rates should be quickly following the falling death rates.

Variations in birth and death rates within countries are often the result of migration. In national terms this involves massive refugee movements across frontiers due to supposedly "failed" nation states, especially of Sudan, Ethiopia, Uganda, Eritrea and Djibouti. Kenya has become the major destination of these refugees.

While urbanisation is proceeding at a very fast rate and accounts for about 6-9% of the increase of population in urban areas, it is important to note that over three-fourth of the population in East Africa are still rural dwellers.

Another significant population growth characteristic is the effect that the AIDS menace has had on population numbers. There is a grim possibility that HIV infections may rise steeply enough to reduce growth rates in countries like Uganda, Kenya and Tanzania.

The Economy

Agriculture

The economy of the region is also dominated by agriculture which, employs close to three-quarters of the working population. Despite this high level of participation, the region's agriculture continues to suffer from widespread famine which has turned catastrophic at certain times. For example during the 1983-85 period, close to half a million people died in Ethiopia mainly due to famine. A further half a million crossed the border into Sudan due mainly to famine and civil war. Famine in the region has been attributed to a plethora of factors which include drought and rapidly increasing population eking out a living from the land in areas experiencing environmental degradation and civil wars.

Various agricultural systems are prevalent here. They include the following: peasant farming which is the commonest type and which is usually small scale in size, with acreages cultivated not exceeding 5 hectares per head. Under this system, crops are grown mainly for subsistence and a system of fallow is applied to allow the soil to regain its fertility after years of cultivation; in some highland areas, particularly in Kenya, there are large-scale mixed farms. These are farms that usually occupy several hundreds of hectares and specialise in the cultivation of cash crops as well as fodder that is used to feed farm animals. Cash crops produced here include wheat and barley. Plantation agriculture is also very important here, especially in Kenya and Tanzania where expatriate farmers and multinational companies dominate the sub-sector.

In areas where rainfall is low and unreliable, livestock farming is dominant. It is very important among certain ethnic groups like the Masai, Boran, Turkana and Karamojong. Cattle is the most valuable animal among these ethnic groups but goats and sheep are also reared. Commercial ranching is also practised mainly by residents of European extraction who specialise in the rearing of beef cattle for sale.

Coffee is the region's most important export crop. Both arabica and robusta varieties are grown throughout the entire region. Cotton is the second most important export crop, especially in Uganda, Tanzania and Ethiopia, followed by others such as sisal, cashew, cloves, sugar cane and pyrethrum.

Fishing is also a very important economic activity. Most of the catch comes from lakes and rivers. Lake Victoria serves as the largest fishing ground in the region. Fish species caught in the lake include *tilapia, haplochromis and bagrus.* Only about ten percent of fish caught in the region come from the sea.

Mining

Minerals have limited economic importance in the region. Many mineral deposits exist but most of them are either not rich or large enough to provide a major source of income. In fact mineral exports continue to account for just about one-tenth of the region's total export. Another reason for the smallness of the industry is that some of the deposits occur in remote and inaccessible areas and so high transport costs make it financially unattractive to develop them.

Gold mining has however assumed greater importance in recent years. Tanzania and Ethiopia, for example, have attracted a lot of attention from major multinational companies involved in the exploration of gold and some discoveries have been made. In the Geita province in Tanzania, for example, substantial gold deposits have been discovered and mining is ongoing. Tanzania also produces diamonds (at Mwadui where open cast methods are employed), salt, limestone and phosphates. Uganda also produces copper, limestone and phosphate while Kenya has soda ash, limestone and fluospar mines. Kenya's limestone is used to manufacture cement near Mombassa and the Athi River, while the fluospar is used in the production of hydrochloric acids, which is an essential flux in the steel industry.

Manufacturing

Generally industries are not as fully developed here as compared to Southern Africa. Most of the existing ones specialise in the processing of local raw materials. They include factories that process local agricultural products. These industries are widely distributed and are located mainly in the producing areas in order to reduce transport costs. Examples include coffee pulperies, tea factories, sugar factories, sisal factories, cotton ginneries, cashew nut shelling plants, vegetable oil mills, fruit and vegetable canneries, meat canneries, flour mills and creameries for producing dried milk, butter and cheese.

A small number of industries process forestry and fishing products. They include saw mills, plywood factories and pulp and paper mills. Other industries also process locally produced minerals. They include the concentration and smelting of copper ore at Kasese and Jinja in Uganda, drying of soda ash at Lake Magadi in Kenya, extraction of diamonds at Mwadui in Tanzania and the manufacture of cement and fertilizer in Kenya, Tanzania, Uganda and Ethiopia.

In addition to the processing of local raw materials, a number of industries have been established with the intention of reducing the region's dependence on imported manufactured goods. These import substitution industries manufacture a wide range of products including textiles, clothing, footwear, chemicals, electronics, metal and petroleum-related products mainly for local markets.

Tourism

International tourism has developed into a very significant economic sector over the past decades. Perennial sunshine and warmth, an attractive coast, the world's greatest concentration of wildlife, magnificent scenery composed of snow capped mountains and major water bodies are some of the major attractions. The culture and way of life of the people, especially the Masai of Kenya and Tanzania, have attracted tourists in increasing numbers from all the major regions of the world. Kenya and Tanzania are the major tourist destinations but Uganda is gradually making some strides. It is widely acknowledged that the Serengeti Plain in Tanzania and the

Somalia-Masai region in East Africa possess some of the largest concentrations of wildlife in the world. The industry has generated substantial foreign exchange, employment opportunities and encouraged the establishment of affiliate industries like handicraft and souvenirs in the respective countries.

Sub-regional Integration

The East African Community (EAC) is the regional intergovernmental organization of the Republics of Burundi, Kenya, Rwanda, Uganda and the United Republic of Tanzania with its headquarters in Arusha, Tanzania. The Treaty for Establishment of the East African Community was signed on 30th November 1999 and entered into force on 7th July 2000 following its ratification by the original three partner states, Kenya, Uganda and Tanzania. The Republic of Rwanda and the Republic of Burundi acceded to the EAC Treaty on 18th June 2007 and became full members of the Community with effect from 1st July 2007.

Central Africa

This sub-region, which is constituted by the following nine countries –Cameroon, Central Africa Republic (CAR), Chad, Gabon, Congo, Democratic Republic of Congo (DRC, formerly Zaire), Equatorial Guinea, Rwanda and Burundi- has a combined land area of about 5.4 million km². Despite their continued socio-economic ties with East Africa, Rwanda and Burundi have been included here for certain past and contemporary political and other socio-economic development reasons even though they continue to use port facilities in East Africa since they are landlocked.

Relief and Drainage

With heights averaging 300–500m above sea level, the sub-region forms part of Lowland Africa which is clearly distinguished from the contiguous Highland Africa regions of Southern and Eastern Africa where highlands tower over 1250m above sea level. The only exception here however is Mt. Cameroon which rises to about 1300m high.

The region is drained by one of the major river systems in the world, the Zaire (Congo) River. Flowing from Lake Bangweulu in Central Africa and draining the entire Congo rain forest region into the Atlantic Ocean, River Congo is the tenth largest river in the world. It carries the second largest volume of water in the world after River Amazon in South America. It has enormous potential for hydro-electricity and to date several hydro power generating plants dot its river-scape, providing electricity to nearby modernising cities. Another important drainage system here is the Lake Chad basin. This basin, which is a very important water resource, is centred on an impoundment of Lake Chad as a final recipient of surface water available from rivers that originate from wetter southern regions of Nigeria, Cameroon (Chari and Logone Rivers) and the Central African Republic (CAR), and from seasonal streams in the north. The effects of sustained droughts, high evapo-transpiration rates and human actions have reduced its water levels considerably.

Climate, Vegetation and Soils

Climatically, the sub-region falls within the humid equatorial belt which affects the northern sections of Congo, Gabon and the narrow coastal strip of Cameroon. Mean monthly temperatures here hardly fall below 64.4°F (18°C). Rainfall is consistent all year round with monthly averages exceeding 2.4 in (6cm). In interior regions, rainfall decreases with the approach of the dry season and also have two periods of concentrated rainfall interspersed with two dry seasons. Parts of Gabon, CAR, Southern Congo, DRC, Rwanda and Burundi are some of the areas that experience these sub-humid conditions.

The sub-region is dominated by the tropical rain forest. This vegetation which is commonly referred to as either Central African or Congolian rain forest, is found predominantly in Cameroon, Gabon and Equatorial Guinea, and occupies an area of about 918,680 square miles or 2.3m square km. Characterized by uniformly high temperatures and rainfall, this forest belt is dominated by broad–leaved evergreen trees, with high diversity of species which are structured into 3 layers – high, middle and lower layers. The belt represents the most extensive evergreen vegetation in all true rainfall forest zones on the continent (Osei and Aryeetey-Attoh, 1997) and produces substantial amounts of hardwood that is exported overseas.

Two major soil types are found here. Within the humid region are *oxols* which are heavily weathered. In parts of Cameroon where they are found, they support large plantation crops of rubber and oil palm. Another significant soil type is *ultisols*. Developed largely in most semi-humid climatic areas, *ultisols* are less weathered than *oxisols*. Found mainly in Rwanda and Burundi, they support the cultivation of rubber, coffee, tea and banana.

Population

National population growth rates have generally assumed high levels over the past four or so decades in the region. Table 3 shows these population dynamics. Growth rates exceeding 2.8%, which could lead to the doubling of population within a time period of twenty five years and, a population quadrupling within fifty years has been realized in the Democratic Republic of Congo (DRC). Indeed, rates exceeding 8.4% per year have been achieved in DRC over the 1960-1997 period. Generally, however, even after recent decades of rapid growth, population totals in the area remain small in absolute terms. Wide variations in population density also exist in the sub-region. Remarkably the sub-region is the most urbanized on the continent with rates exceeding 40% of the population. DRC, Congo and Gabon have urbanization levels rivaling those of some Latin American countries and an overwhelming primacy exists in the two capital cities situated along the banks of the Lower Congo River- DRC's Kinshasa and Congo's Brazzaville (Atsimadja, 1992). A combination of the above factors, that is low population totals and high urbanization levels mean that settlement density, particularly of the rural population, is very thin. This may help explain why much of the sub-region's tropical forest and savanna still remain in good, if not pristine condition. The limited market potential and the small base for large-scale infrastructural development that are associated with the sub-region however have often been blamed on the low population densities.

Significant recent happenings that are likely to impact on future trends in population growth within the sub-region include the AIDS menace and the genocides that occurred in Rwanda and Burundi in the late 1990s. Grim forecasts on AIDS infections, as in other parts of sub Saharan Africa, depict a very worrying outlook.

Table 3 – Area, Population and Population Densities of Central African Countries

Country	Area (square miles)	Population (in millions) 2006	Population Density per sq. mile (2006)
Democratic Republic of Congo (DRC)	905,351	62.7	69
Cameroon	183,568	17.3	94
Rwanda	10,170	9.1	890
Chad	495,753	10.0	20
Burundi	10,745	7.8	729
Central African Republic(CAR)	240,533	4.3	18
Congo	132,046	3.7	28
Gabon	103,347	1.4	14
Equatorial Guinea	10,830	0.5	47

Source: *World Population Data Sheet, Population Reference Bureau, 2006*

The Economy

Agriculture

Even though agriculture is the largest sector and the dominant employer in the sub-region, production is inadequate to feed the population. Food imports, therefore, supplement local production.

A number of factors account for the low agricultural productivity. First, the high temperatures and heavy rainfall that are experienced promote extensive leaching of nutrients from the soils and this leads to low organic content, poor and easily degraded soils. Second, the use of slash and burn methods of cultivation and the repeat cultivation of drier margins of forestlands have the tendency to degrade extensive areas if the increasing population numbers result in growing rural densities. Third, the culture of food collection from the forests is widespread. For example, certain indigenous societies in the Democratic Republic Congo (DRC) still operate a traditional gathering economy of collecting nuts, snails, wild fruits and small animals from the forest. Finally, government policies in general have also negatively influenced the sector. For example, past currency overvaluations have rewarded food importers at the expense of local producers and exporters.

Agricultural products from the region include the following: cotton from the semi-forest regions of Chad, cocoa, rubber and oil palm from the forested areas of Cameroon, Gabon, DRC and Congo, tea and coffee from parts of Cameroon, Burundi and Rwanda. Most of these products are exported. In semi-arid parts of the region where conditions are too dry for cropping, and water and grassland are available, livestock farming is practiced. However, the presence of tse-tse fly tends to limit the southern extent of this agricultural activity. The numerous major rivers and their tributaries, together with Lake Chad, represent important inland fishing basins in the region. Maritime fishing is also of great importance.

Mining and Industry

The sub-region abounds in substantial mineral wealth and is reckoned as one of the most richly endowed on the continent. The Shaba province in DRC, for example, is second only to the Witwatersrand in South Africa in terms of known mineral wealth in Africa. Variations, however, exist in the extent of endowments within the respective countries in the sub-region. Minerals obtained here include copper and zinc at Kipushi in the Shaba Province. The concentrated ores obtained are railed to Lubumbashi for smelting and conversion to blister copper. About half of the world's output of cobalt is produced at Kolwezi which is located in this province. Other minerals available from Shaba include manganese, zinc, cadmium, silver, diamond and practically all the world's supplies of radium. Gabon, Cameroon, and recently Chad and Equatorial Guinea also exploit oil in commercial quantities. The region is gradually becoming a major oil producing region in the world and major multinational companies are engaged either in oil prospecting or production. CAR has a wealth of diamonds and other valuable minerals. Rwanda and Burundi are, however, poorly endowed with mineral resources. Manufacturing industry is very small and poorly developed in the region. With the particular exception of Cameroon, all the others have smaller manufacturing sectors.

West Africa

Generally, West Africa has been defined as the region lying between the Gulf of Guinea in the south and the southern boundary of the Sahara Desert, even though there are three West African countries that extend into the Sahara. The sub region is bounded on the west by the Atlantic Ocean, while the eastern boundary follows the crest of the Mandara-Adamawa-Cameroon Highlands.

Relief and Drainage

Most rivers in West Africa flow into the Atlantic Ocean or southwards into the Gulf of Guinea. For instance, the Senegal and Gambia empty into the Atlantic Ocean, while the Niger, Volta and Sassandra empty into the Gulf of Guinea. The River Niger, the longest in the sub region (4,200km long), has its source in the Fouta Djallon Highlands, and flows in a northeast direction then bends in a southeast direction before turning south towards the coast at the Niger Delta in Nigeria. The seasonal fluctuations of the water volume in these rivers limit them considerably for navigation. Also several of the rivers are interrupted in places by rapids, and sand bars at the estuaries. On the other hand, most of the rivers have the potential for hydroelectric power.

The coastline of West Africa is varied. A considerable part of the Gulf of Guinea coast is smooth and exposed to winds. There are few good natural harbours, but there are extensive lagoons.

Climate and Vegetation

All parts of West Africa, except for very high locations, are hot throughout the year. It is only in a few places that the mean temperature of the coolest month falls below 20° C. The annual range of temperature is generally small; along the Gulf of Guinea coast it is usually less that 5° C, rising to about 10° C-15° C inland from the Gulf of Guinea.

The daily range of temperature is usually much higher than the annual range, being lowest during the rainy seasons when there is most cloud, and highest during the dry season when there is little cloud.

The coastal area from Sierra Leone to south-eastern Nigeria (except for a small area around Accra) receives heavy rainfall. Going inland from the Gulf of Guinea the rainfall decreases in amount, as the rain-bearing winds gradually lose their moisture carrying capacity. Along the Gulf of Guinea coast, the rainfall is generally spread out over the whole year but there tends to be double maxima (two periods of particularly heavy rainfall, separated by two rather drier periods).

The position of the Inter-Tropical-Convergence-Zone (ITCZ) explains why there are big variations in the amount and seasonal distribution of rainfall. The ITCZ is the zone where the south-westerlies and the northeast trade winds meet. These two seasonal winds dominate the climate of the region. In July the ITCZ is situated at about 17°N–20°N, and most parts of West Africa come under the influence of the moist south-westerlies and so receive rainfall. In January, the ITCZ is situated not far to the north of the Gulf of Guinea. At this time of the year only the Gulf of Guinea coastlands come under the influence of the south-westerlies and so have some rain. The rest of West Africa comes under the drying influence of the north-east trade winds (Harmattan), and receive little rain.

In West Africa there is a close relationship between the plant life of a given location, and the amount and seasonal distribution of its rainfall. In areas of heavy rainfall there is usually tropical rainforest. This occurs along much of the Gulf of Guinea coast but there is a gap in the forest around Accra, because of the unusually low rainfall in that area. Along parts of the coast there are mangrove swamps, and they are particularly extensive in the Niger Delta.

To the north of the forest lies the savanna zone, where the nature of the vegetation varies according to the amount of rainfall received and the length and severity of the dry season. Near the forest edge, the rainfall is moderate and the dry season is not too severe. Here, there is Guinea savanna consisting of a mixture of trees and tall grasses. The trees generally shed their leaves during the dry season, and the grasses wither and die. Many of the trees have thick bark, which helps to protect them from the frequent bush fires. North of the Guinea savanna is the Sudan savanna zone where grasses are shorter and there are fewer trees as compared to the Guinea savanna belt. The Sahel savanna is the most northerly of the savanna zone. Here the grasses are very short and widely spaced and thorny bushes are also common.

Within the desert proper, plant life is scanty and plants are especially adapted to withstand rather dry conditions. Plants in this area usually have small leaves to reduce water loss by transpiration and long roots to reach down to water deep below the surface.

Population, Migration and Urbanization

In West Africa there are great variations in population density. It ranges from 29 persons per square mile in Niger to about 377 persons per square mile in Nigeria (see Table 4). Much of the West African coast, between the Senegal and Congo Rivers, is densely populated, especially near the rich alluvial sands of the Niger River Delta and the mouths of other West African rivers.

Broadly speaking, it is possible to distinguish two main east-west zones of high population density. The most densely populated zone extends along the coast from Sierra Leone to South-eastern Nigeria and corresponds roughly with the zone of high forest. The largest concentrations of population are found within the Ibo, Ibibio and Yoruba traditional areas of Nigeria, southern Benin, Togo, and southern Ghana. In most parts of this zone, rainfall is heavy and fairly well distributed over the year, and so it is possible to grow high-yielding root crops such as yams. Conditions are also suitable for such important tree crops as cocoa, coffee, oil palm and rubber. In parts of this zone there exist valuable mineral deposits, providing opportunity for employment in mining.

Table 4 – Area, Population and Population Density of West Africa

Country	Area (square miles)	Population (mid 2006) (millions)	DensityPer square Miles
Benin	43,483	8.7	200
Burkina Faso	105,792	13.6	129
Cape Verde	1,556	0.5	312
Gambia	4,363	1.5	338
Ghana	92,100	22.6	245
Guinea	94,927	9.8	103
Guinea Bissau	13,946	1.4	97
Cote d'Ivoire	124,502	19.7	158
Liberia	43,000	3.4	78
Mali	478,838	13.9	29
Niger	489,189	14.4	29
Nigeria	356,668	134.5	377
Senegal	75,954	11.9	157
Sierra Leone	27,699	5.7	205
Togo	21,927	6.3	288

Source: *World Population Data Sheet, Population Reference Bureau, 2006*

The other densely populated zone extends across the Sudan savanna, from the coastlands of Senegal and Gambia to northern Nigeria. Particularly high densities occur in the groundnut growing areas of Senegal and Gambia; around Ouagadougou in Burkina Faso; in north eastern Ghana and in parts of northern Nigeria. In this zone, although the rainy season is fairly short, the rainfall is sufficient for growing such crops as millet, guinea corn, cotton and groundnuts. Cattle rearing is possible in this zone thus making manure available for the land.

There are two thinly populated areas. Population is most sparse in the extreme north of the sub region, and also in the so-called middle belt. Unreliable rainfall, the presence of the tse-tse fly and also slave raiding in the past have contributed to the sparse population in these zones.

Urbanization

Urban expansion is the most notable change in the geography of West Africa over the last 25 years. Only 7 per cent of West Africa's population was urbanized in 1965, but by 1985 the figure had reached 31 per cent. Currently, Lagos, one of the world's largest metropolitan areas and its surrounding suburbs are home to close to 17 million people. By 2015 the population of the Lagos metropolitan area is expected to be more than 23 million. Other major cities such as Accra are rapidly becoming major urban centres in the sub region with population growth rates of 8 to 10 percent per year.

The word "urbanization" as being used, reflects the movement from rural areas to urban areas (Aryeetey-Attoh, 1997). People move to urban areas for a variety of reasons most of which are usually bound up with expectations of a better quality of life. Higher incomes, combined with a less poverty-ridden existence than in the rural areas, access to better health facilities, better schooling, the sheer desire to escape from family pressure in the village, and to experience the "bright-lights" of the city are common reasons for these movements.

Rapid growth of cities has overtaken planning and prevented the implementation of quality standards. Development has been piecemeal and school and health facilities which in theory are more readily accessible than in the villages are nevertheless far from sufficient to meet the demands of rapidly growing populations. Water supply is poor everywhere; provision for refuse collection is inadequate in most cities, and disposal of waste more difficult.

The Economy

Agriculture

Agriculture in West Africa is as important now as it was at independence. However, it has declined relative to the service sector in recent times even though it is still of crucial importance in absolute terms, involving over 70 per cent of the population of most countries. Drought, population growth and therefore environmental pressures, and major changes in government policy towards agriculture are some of the factors explaining the state of agriculture in the sub region (see Chapter 11).

Most of the sub region's agricultural production is in the hands of peasant farmers and pastoralists. Mixed farming is not common and most West African cultivators have very little if any animal manure to put on their land to keep the soil fertile. To overcome this problem, in many areas, a system known as bush fallowing is practised. This involves cultivating a plot of land for a year or two and letting it lie idle for several years to allow the soil to regain its fertility.

In the forest zone important food crops grown include root crops such as yams, cocoyam and cassava; cereal crops such as maize and rice; vegetables such as tomatoes, okras and pepper; and tree crops such as plantains, bananas and oil palm. In the savanna region important food crops include millet, guinea corn, groundnuts, and various kinds of beans. In the past, crops were grown entirely for subsistence purposes. Although in many areas farming still contains a large subsistence element, West Africa is an important producer of crops for export. Cocoa is very important in Ghana, Cote d'Ivoire, and to some extent Togo, Nigeria and Sierra Leone. Rubber is important in Liberia and Nigeria, with smaller amounts coming from Cote d'Ivoire. However civil war of more than a decade affected rubber production levels in Liberia. Unlike cocoa and rubber, the oil palm is native to West Africa. It grows widely throughout the forest zone in a belt of varying width from Guinea Bissau to South-eastern Nigeria. Groundnuts are grown for subsistence in many parts of West Africa, and in some parts of the savanna zone they are an important export crop. Important producers are Nigeria, Senegal and Gambia.

Livestock rearing is also important in this sub region. In the south, only dwarf, humpless breeds of cattle such as the Ndama are kept. These breeds are more resistant to the trypanosomiasis disease, which is spread by the tsetse fly, than are the larger humped Zebu cattle. In the north, Zebu is mainly reared by the Fulani, who make seasonal movements with their livestock. Other animals kept in the more northernly parts of West Africa include sheep, goats and donkeys.

Fishing

Fish forms an important part of the diet of many West Africans. In some areas, rivers and lakes are important sources of fish. A few countries such as Senegal, Ghana, Cote d'Ivoire and Mali have a small surplus of fish for export, but most of the others do not even produce enough fish for their own needs, and have to import large quantities.

Most of the sub region's catch comes from the sea and various fishing methods are used. In the shallow waters of the coastal lagoons, cast-nets and various kinds of fish traps are used. Beach seine nets are operated from sandy beaches along the coast. Much of the fishing in the open sea is done from large dugout canoes fitted with outboard motors. Small motorized vessels also operate from a few centres such as Takoradi, Tema, and Elmina in Ghana.

Deep sea fishing fleets also exist in some of the countries. The boats have refrigerated holds in which the catch can be kept in good condition. Many rivers are important source of fish, as are several of the lakes such as Chad and Volta.

Part of the West African catch is eaten fresh, but a large part is preserved by such methods as smoking, salting and sun-drying. Modern fish processing plants exist in a few places. There are canneries for sardines and tuna in Dakar, Abidjan and Accra.

Mining

The development of mining in the region has considerably changed the economies of most countries. Liberia is rich in iron ore, and since the 1960s this has replaced rubber as the country's main export. The ore is mined by open-cast method. The only other mineral mined to some extent in Liberia is diamond, which is mined by small operators.

Nigeria is very rich in minerals and is one of the world's leading producers of petroleum, tin, and columbite. It is also a minor producer of coal. Nigeria's oil comes from the Niger Delta region where it is produced both on land and from off-shore wells. Most of the oil is exported in its crude form. Large quantities of natural gas occur with the petroleum in Nigeria. Local market for the gas is largely undeveloped and so much of it is flared. There is an on-going project to utilise this flared gas for productive purposes within Ghana, Togo, Benin and Nigeria.

The important minerals produced in Ghana are gold, diamonds, manganese ore and bauxite. Gold is mainly mined by deep-pit and open-cast methods and modern machines are also used to explore diamonds. However a number of small-scale miners using rudimentary methods operate alongside these well-established mining concerns. Most of Ghana's diamonds are industrial stones, with only a small proportion being gem stones. Manganese ore is mined by open-cast method near Tarkwa, and is exported for use in steel making. Bauxite occurs in several deposits in Awaso, Nyinahin and Kibi. Diamond mining is also of considerable importance to Sierra Leone and Liberia while bauxite is exploited in Guinea.

Manufacturing

Generally, manufacturing is an underdeveloped activity in the West African region. Countries with much more developed manufacturing sector include Cote d'Ivoire, Nigeria and Ghana. Much of the modern industrial activities in these countries involve the processing of raw materials. Processed foods are largely consumed by the sub region's expanding urban populations, while raw materials such as minerals, petroleum, and timber are processed almost entirely for export.

The bulk of the rest of West Africa's manufacturing output consists of consumer goods such as textiles, footwear, beverages and detergents. The technology used in manufacturing ranges from rudimentary tools used in small-scale cottage industries to large-scale factories. Although its impact on the national economy is frequently underestimated, the cottage industry sector of the economy produces significant amounts of goods both for local consumption and for the tourist trade. Textile and footwear plants, on the other hand, can be sizable, often requiring modern machinery.

Manufacturing in the sub region grew in the 1960s and 1970s in countries like Nigeria and Ghana but declined in the 1980s and 1990s for several reasons. For instance Nigeria relied too heavily on extracting and exporting petroleum and neglected its manufacturing sector. Secondly, war and political unrest disrupted development efforts and caused the role of manufacturing to decline.

The development of manufacturing industry has also been hindered by a general lack of investment capital, as well as by misguided economic strategies and corruption. In addition, multinational corporations have tended to discourage local manufacturing, seeking instead to trade their manufactured goods for raw materials.

Tourism

Tourism's contribution to the development of some of the economies of West African countries appears to be expanding. Countries such as Senegal, Gambia, La Cote D'Ivoire and Ghana offer a variety of tourism experiences to visitors and tourist arrivals and receipts have been on sustained increase in recent years. According Hoff and Overgaad (1974), Ghana has a comparative advantage over her rivals in the West African sub region in the development of beach-centered resorts and national parks. However,the unstable political and social conditions in the sub region have led to inadequate investment in the industry.

Sub-regional Integration

The Economic Community of West African States (ECOWAS) is the main sub regional integration organization formed to encourage economic, social, and cultural development in West Africa. Founded in 1975 by the Treaty of Lagos, ECOWAS began operation in 1977. Its 15 member states are Benin, Burkina Faso, Cape Verde, Côte d'Ivoire, The Gambia, Ghana, Guinea, Guinea-Bissau, Liberia, Mali, Niger, Nigeria, Senegal, Sierra Leone, and Togo. ECOWAS is administered through a secretariat, which is based in Abuja, Nigeria. Since its inception, ECOWAS has moved to liberalize trade by gradually reducing restrictions on the movement of goods, services, and people between member states. It has also improved communications and transport within the region. Some member governments, however, have been slow to implement agreed-upon policies at a national level and to pay their contribution to community funds.

North Africa

North Africa is made up of the following countries- Egypt, Sudan, Libya, Morocco, Algeria and Mauritania. Historically these countries fell under two main groupings – Egypt and Sudan belonged to the Nile Valley region while the rest constituted the Maghreb region. The entire region is quite unique within the continent of Africa. It is the only sub-region that falls outside the Sub-Saharan Africa block and this can be attributed to a number of factors. Geographically, the Sahara desert has constituted a great impediment to physical communication and smooth interaction of this area and the rest of the continent. In addition, North Africa is more closely linked to the Middle East in terms of religion, history, commerce and accessibility. Moreover, due to its close proximity with Southern Europe, being separated by the strait of Gibraltar which is only about 15 kilometres wide, North Africa has also had strong cultural, historical and economic ties with Europe. It is, therefore, natural that these countries interact more with Europe and the Middle East than with the rest of Africa even though it is part of the African mainland.

Relief and Drainage

Much of the region lies below 1000 metres high but as in other parts of the continent, some high grounds tower above the general plateau surface. The Atlas, Tibesti and the Ahaggar (hoggar) mountains are good examples of such elevated surfaces in the region. These highlands rise to heights exceeding 3000 feet above sea level. One major geographical feature in the region is the Quattara depression which is found within the Sahara desert and whose formation continues to attract different and varied hypotheses.

The River Nile is the main drainage system in the region. The River receives water from three main tributaries– the White Nile, the Blue Nile and the Atbara River. Egypt and Sudan have built a number of dams to regulate the River's flow which has been characterized by serious seasonal fluctuations. There have also been several attempts to regulate the use of the Nile's water by countries through which it flows. Between Khartoum and Aswan, there are a series of cataracts in the River's valley and these impede navigation. Below Cairo is the Nile delta where it splits into different tributaries before entering the Mediterranean Sea.

Climate, Vegetation and Soils

Two major climatic types are experienced here. These are (a) the dominant arid and semi-arid climatic type and (b) the Mediterranean type which is limited to coastal areas. With increasing distance from the Equator than most parts of the continent, the annual range of temperature is large. Northern Egypt, for example, has temperatures of about 23°C during the northern summer but there is a much cooler period during the northern winter when mean monthly temperatures are usually below 15 degrees Celsius. The annual range of temperature here is generally more than 15 degrees Celsius. The daily range is usually very large. Cairo, for instance, has a daily range of 18°C and this has been attributed to low cloud cover at night-time, leading to a drop in temperatures. In the Mediterranean region the summers are hot but winters are warm.

Rainfall decreases as one moves from the south to the north of the Nile region. Parts of Southern Sudan have an annual rainfall of more than 1400mm but this reduces to about 200m around Khartoum. Further north into Egypt, rainfall is less than 100mm and it is also irregular, apart from the narrow strip along the Mediterranean coast. Within the Mediterranean belt, most of the rainfall is experienced during the northern winter, and the summers are generally very dry.

The vegetation pattern is closely related to the amount and seasonal distribution of rainfall. In relatively wetter areas of Southern Sudan, savanna woodland vegetation thrives. Going northwards, as the rainfall decreases in quantity and the dry season becomes longer and more severe, the savanna vegetation becomes poorer. Parts of Sudan and most parts of Egypt, Algeria, Libya, Morocco and Mauritania have desert vegetation except along the coastal belts to the north where the Mediterranean climatic zone has Mediterranean vegetation. This vegetation has 2 belts– (a) the highland or wetter belt with evergreen forest and (b) the drier or lowland belt, which has low evergreen shrub vegetation, called *maquis*. These shrubs have tough leathery, waxy or spring leaves which help to reduce transpiration. It must be indicated here that as a result of past crop cultivation and pastoral activities, especially in the higher region, the vegetation has degraded substantially. The over-exploitation of the area by the ancient Romans, pastoral activities of nomadic Arabs, sharp increases in population growth and the cutting and burning down of large tracts of natural woodland during the long years of liberation wars in the period 1954-62 have often been cited as explicit examples of factors contributing to the deterioration of the region's vegetation (Grove, 1998).

Three main soil types are present in the region. The most famous is perhaps the alluvial soils that are found in the Lower and Upper Nile valleys. The major soil type here is the *vertisols*. These soils are very productive under irrigation. In the White Nile basin of southern Sudan, the *vertisols* have a characteristic dark clay content and do very well when cultivation is supplemented with irrigation agriculture. Within the Sahara desert, a soil type called *entisols* is present. They are deficient in soil organic layers and this restricts their potential for agricultural production. The soils of North Western Africa, including those of the Mediterranean region and northern Sahara, commonly include an alluvial horizon rich in carbonates. In the heavier rainfall areas, near the coast, they are often reddish in colour. Because of high relief, soils around the Atlas Mountain region vary greatly over shorter distances and rates of erosion are high with reservoirs silting rapidly. Desertification and soil erosion are very serious ecological problems here. Cultivation of marginal lands, burning of charcoal and increasing population numbers have been cited by Joffe (1992) as aggravating the situation.

Population

The region supports densely settled agricultural populations, especially in the Maghreb (north of the Atlas Mountains in Morocco, Algeria and Tunisia) and the Nile River delta area. Egypt, Morocco and Tunisia have population densities that are significantly higher than those of the other countries (see Table 5). The well-watered and temperate conditions available through the Mediterranean climate have supported the production of a rich variety of foods, fruits and wines in the Maghreb region. This long standing tradition led to the description of the area as "the breakfast" of Rome's ancient Mediterranean empire (Khapoya, 1998).

Similarly, by turning the desert of the Sahara into productive agricultural farmlands through irrigation along the Nile, most people living within ancient and modern Egypt and Sudan have been able to raise nutritional standards through the cultivation of fruits, grains and the raising of animals. Population concentration along the Nile valley, Nile delta and the Maghreb coast represents probably the highest on the continent and continues to increase rapidly. The Nile valley in particular, together with the Southern Transvaal industrial and mining region of South Africa, constitute the most densely populated regions on the continent. Ninety percent of Egypt's population is concentrated in the Nile valley and delta and the density of population here is over 1000 persons per km^2, making it one of the densest areas of the world.

Table 5 – Population, Areal Extent and Population Density for North African Countries

Country	Area (square mile)	Population Mid 2006 (in millions)	Population Density per sq. miles
Algeria	919,591	33.5	36
Libya	679,359	5.9	9
Mauritania	395,954	3.2	8
Morocco	172,413	31.7	184
Tunisia	63,170	10.1	160
Egypt	386,660	75.4	195
Sudan	967,494	41.2	43

Source: *World Population Data Sheet, Population Reference Bureau, 2006*

In addition to these population distribution characteristics, growth rates averaging 2.3% to 3.1% were experienced during the period 1960-90. In addition, the region has also witnessed substantial population movements. The neglect of agriculture in favour of investments in industry, mining, beach tourism and infrastructure has aggravated the problem in recent years. Rural-urban drift seems to have abated and instead labour migration abroad has increased sharply and has become a popular and growing phenomenon. Migration to Europe and oil rich Middle Eastern countries has provided alternative destination for migrants to earn a living. Remittances from these overseas-based workers have contributed enormously towards economic development within these originating countries.

The Economy

Agriculture

As indicated in the preceding section, the massive population concentrations in the region can be partly attributed to the intense pursuit of agricultural activities. With the particular exception of Libya and Mauritania, all the countries are endowed with sizeable arable and pastoral land. Even in Libya, past and recent attempts to irrigate the Jefara plain, the Jabal al Akhadar region and the Sirte area of the Sahara and the use of the Senegal River in Southern Mauritania for similar purposes seem to lessen cultivable land availability problems in these countries.

Generally, agriculture is practiced under a dual system in the Maghreb region. These are intensively farmed modern agricultural practices that are often dependent on an irrigation system and primarily designed to serve the European and Middle Eastern markets. Export crops like citrus and olive oil are cultivated and individual landholdings usually exceed 50ha. These exports generate up to 80% of agricultural exports. Morocco, Algeria and Tunisia are well noted for this type of agriculture (Joffe, 1992). Within the Nile region, a number of factors account for the high productivity. These include the availability of extremely rich alluvial soils formed by materials deposited in the past by the Nile flood; availability of water for irrigation purposes; and the existing large internal and external markets that exist. A combination of these factors makes it possible for farmers here to undertake multiple cropping. They cultivate two or three crops a year over the same piece of land. Major crops cultivated include wheat, barley, vegetables, cotton, oranges, maize, rice and sugar cane.

Livestock, especially cattle and sheep, are kept under a mixed farm system. In Southern Sudan, some form of subsistence agriculture, using bush fallowing methods is employed to grow crops such as banana, beans, maize and millet, without irrigation. In the north of the country, the Gezira irrigation scheme and other minor ones have been developed for the large scale cultivation of cotton and other crops. Apart from Morocco and Mauritania, fishing is of less importance here. In spite of these developments in the sector however, the region remains a net food importer.

Mining

The region is well endowed with mineral resources. Almost all of the countries produce hydrocarbons which contribute significantly to export earnings. Libya and Algeria are major producers while Morocco, Tunisia, Egypt and lately Sudan, also produce oil for export. Hydrocarbons contribute close to 99% of Libya's export earnings and constitute the major export commodity in Algeria and Tunisia. Morocco is the largest phosphate exporter and the largest producer in the world, while Tunisia is a moderate exporter. Egypt produces some phosphates and iron ore while Algeria has iron ore and Sudan some salt.

Industry

Algeria and Egypt are the most industrialized countries in the region. About one-fifth of the Egyptian workforce is employed in industry compared with about half who are employed in agriculture. Industries in Egypt are primarily concerned with the processing and manufacturing of locally produced raw materials like cotton, sugar cane, fruits, vegetables, tobacco, crude oil, natural gas and iron ore and they are mainly located in Cairo, Alexandria and towns in the Nile valley and delta. The most widespread ones are those involved in cotton spinning and weaving and related activities.

In Algeria, industries have very strong linkages with the oil industry. Large investments have been concentrated in the refineries and plants which liquefy and utilize natural gas. Refined oil and natural gas are major export commodities. Ammonium nitrate and other forms of fertilizers are also manufactured alongside plastics. Iron and steel, cement and paper are the other major products. Industry accounts for about half of her national output while farming represents only 10%.

To a greater extent, industries in Libya, Morocco and Tunisia mimic those in Algeria. In Libya in particular, a number of oil based industries are either in operation or have been planned while Morocco and Tunisia have relatively more diversified manufacturing bases than pertains in Libya. In Sudan and Mauritania however, manufacturing is less developed and consists of the processing of some local agricultural products and the manufacturing of simpler kinds of import substitution consumer goods.

Tourism

The region is a very important world-class tourism destination. In Egypt, Tunisia and Morocco, tourism receipts contribute substantially to foreign exchange earnings. Historical, cultural and beach tourism are major attractions and with increasing visitations to the Sahara desert, the region is gradually becoming a major player in the international tourism industry. Egypt's Sphinx at Giza near Cairo, the temples at Luxor and deluxe cruising along the Suez Canal and on the Mediterranean Sea, are major attractions that help to bring over three million visitors into the country annually. This rakes in over 3.5 billion dollars to the national exchequer annually. Tunisia and Morocco have also developed a well functioning tourism industry that is based on beach tourism, heritage site visitations, and tours to the interior of the desert. Libya, Mauritania and Sudan are relatively less endowed and have less developed tourism industries, while Algeria's tourism industry is now on a sound development course after years of stagnation under near state monopoly. Its potential for the future is quite immense.

Regional Integration

The Arab Maghreb Union is a Pan-Arab trade agreement aiming for economic and political unity in North Africa. The idea for an economic union of the Maghreb began with the independence of Tunisia and Morocco in 1956. It was not until thirty years later that five Maghreb states – Algeria, Libya, Mauritania, Morocco and Tunisia – met for the first Maghreb summit. The following year in 1989, the agreement was formally signed by all member nations. There is a rotating chairmanship which is held in turn by each nation. However, traditional rivalries between Morocco and Algeria, and the unsolved question of Western Sahara's sovereignty have blocked union meetings since the early nineties, despite several attempts to re-launch the political process.

Conclusion

This chapter has provided insights on the geography of resource endowment and utilisation in the various sub-regions on the continent. Also highlighted are some of the impediments constraining the smooth harnessing of these resources for development. It is very clear from the text that the continent abounds in numerous natural and cultural resources which if effectively and judiciously utilised, could hasten the current slow pace of development.

Tackling critical and nagging development problems such as unsustainable use of resources, high and sometimes uncontrollable population growth rates, rapid urbanization, rural depopulation, the AIDS epidemic, political and ethnic strife and economic mismanagement is critical in achieving development goals and should therefore attract priority attention. The development agenda of the continent should also facilitate the promotion of the integration of regional and continental economies in order to enhance better use of resources, expanded markets and better governance.

Review Questions

1. With reference to any of the major geographical regions in Africa;

    i.   Outline the major characteristic features of vegetation zones and assess the role climate plays in the spatial distribution of these vegetation zones.

    ii. Describe the distribution of soils and relate this to the distribution of agricultural productivity.

2. On what grounds would you consider the geography of either the northern or southern African region to be unique in Africa?

3. In what ways has the location of the Sahara desert hampered the development of the adjoining countries ?

4. Examine the bases and prospects for manufacturing industries in either western or eastern Africa.

5. Describe and account for the distribution of either mineral resources or population in Central Africa.

References

Aryeetey-Attoh, S. 1997. "Urban Geography of Sub-Saharan Africa," in Aryeetey-Attoh, S.: *Geography of Sub-Saharan Africa*, Prentice Hall: New Jersey. pp 182-186.

Atsimadja, F. A. 1992. "The Changing Geography of Central Africa" In G. Chapman and K. Baker (eds), *The Changing Geography of Africa and the Middle East*. London and New York: Routledge. pp 80-113.

Chapman, G. and K. Baker. 1992. "Introduction- Independence: Promise at the new Dawning" In G. Chapman and K. Baker (Eds.), *The Changing Geography of Africa and the Middle East*. London and New York: Routledge. pp 1-111.

Cohen, S. 2005 (Ed.) "Africa" In *The Columbia Gazetteer of the World Online*. New York: Colombia University Press.

Hoff and Overgaad Planning Consultants, 1974. *Tourism in Ghana-Development Guide* 1975-1990, Danish International Development Agency (DANIDA), Copenhagen, Denmark.

Grove, A.T. 1998 *The Changing Geography of Africa*. Oxford: Oxford University Press. 2nd Edition.

Joffé, G. 1992 "The Changing Geography of North Africa". In G. Chapman and K. Baker (eds), *The Changing Geography of Africa and the Middle East*. London and New York: Routledge. pp 139-164.

Khapoya, V.B. 1998 *The African Experience: An Introduction*. Upper Saddle River, New Jersey: Prentice Hall 2nd Edition

Konadu-Agyemang, K. and K. Panford (Eds.), 2006 Africa's Development in the 21st Century: Pertinent Issues, Opportunities and Challenges. Aldershot, Hampshire, UK: Ashgate International.

O'Connor, A. 1992 "The Changing Geography of Eastern Africa" In G. Chapman and K. Baker (eds), *The Changing Geography of Africa and the Middle East*. London and New York: Routledge. pp 114-138.

Osei, W.Y. and S. Aryeetey-Attoh. 1992 "The Physical Environment" in S. Aryeetey-Attoh (ed) *Geography of Sub-Saharan Africa*. Upper Saddle River, New Jersey: Prentice Hall pp 1-34.

Rakodi, C. 1997. *The Urban Challenge in Africa: Growth and Management of Its Large Cities*. Tokyo and New York: United Nations University.

Senior, M. and P.O. Okunrotifa. 1991. *A Regional Geography of Africa*. London: Longman.

Stock, R. 2004. *Africa South of the Sahara – A Geographical Interpretation*, 2nd Edition. New York: Guildford Press.

———<www.prb.org/pdf06/06WorldDataSheet.pdf>

CHAPTER 2

THE POPULATION OF SUB-SAHARAN AFRICA
Delali M. Badasu

Introduction

In the past, the African community ethos was built on the numerical strength of people (wealth in persons). Among families, childlessness was stigmatised while a large progeny was considered prestigious. The larger the number of people, the greater the wealth created by production of goods and services and trading. Labour requirements in the predominantly agrarian or pastoralist communities encouraged adherence to pro-natalist values that encourage preference for large family sizes and the need for children to provide labour for farming activities and household chores. Family labour was important for all aspects of agricultural production and families depended greatly on their children for both subsistence and commercial production, and children were also seen as providing security in old age for parents. In addition, in the centralised political systems the power of a king or chief was also reckoned by the number of his subjects, since as a king, he needed a large army to fight battles and to protect his territory, while an expansion of kingdoms meant that more tribute would be paid by subjects.

But in contemporary Africa and Sub-Saharan Africa (SSA) in particular, a high rate of population growth is now considered a liability as far as economic progress is concerned. Recently, other demographic concerns have emerged as areas of equal importance, especially those of . infant, child and maternal mortality, reproductive health and the Human Immuno-Deficiency Virus/Acquired Immune Deficiency Syndrome (HIV and AIDS), rapid urbanisation and population-related environmental degradation. Indeed, Sub-Saharan Africa's population is distinct from that of other major regions of the world in many respects, including continuing high fertility and mortality rates. In general, population issues evoke emotions and contentious debates. A proper understanding of population issues is a prerequisite for developing informed attitudes and appropriate behavioural change towards them. This chapter discusses both the longstanding issues in Africa's population as well as the more recent concerns with the aim of helping undergraduate students to understand population issues and to seek to address them in whatever capacity they find themselves in now or in the future.

Some basic demographic concepts that are relevant for easier understanding of the population issues discussed in the present chapter can be found in Appendix A. The reader should also refer to the other chapters in the volume that discuss the physical environment, political economy and socio-cultural contexts of Sub-Saharan Africa (Ch. 1,10, 13,4,6,7,14). These will enhance understanding of the interrelationship between the concepts and population patterns, trends and processes.

Population Patterns and Dynamics

The features of the population of Sub-Saharan Africa are distinct from those of other major world regions in several ways. The main characteristic is its fast rate of growth. However, as in other areas of the world, another feature is the concentration of the population in some countries and geographical areas that are rich in natural resources, or have better economic opportunities.

Patterns of Population Growth and Distribution

The rate of natural increase or the difference between birth and death rates, accounts to a large extent, for the fast growth of population in Sub-Saharan Africa. The average rate of natural increase was 2.6 % in 2011, or almost twice that of other less developed countries (1.7%); almost twice that of the whole world's (1.2%), and twenty-five times that of the industrialised countries (0.2%) [See Table 6].

Table 6 – Population Patterns and Components of Population Growth of Sub-Saharan Africa, 2011

REGION/COUNTRY	Population Mid-2011 (Millions)	Net Migration Rate per 1,000	Births per 1,000 Population	Deaths per 1,000 Population	Rate of Natural Increase (%)	Total Fertility Rate	Percentage of Population of age <15	65+
WORLD	6,987		20	8	1.2	2.5	27	8
MORE DEVELOPED	1,242	2	11	10	0.2	1.7	16	16
LESS DEVELOPED	5,745	-1	22	8	1.4	2.6	29	6
SUB-SAHARAN AFRICA	883	-1	38	13	2.6	5.2	43	3
WESTERN AFRICA	313	-1	40	14	2.6	5.5	43	3
Benin	9.1	0	40	11	2.9	5.4	44	3
Burkina Faso	17.0	-1	43	12	3.1	5.8	45	2
Cape Verde	0.5	-5	22	5	1.7	2.5	32	6
Cote d'Ivoire	22.6	-1	37	13	2.3	4.9	41	4
Gambia	1.8	-1	39	9	3.0	5.0	44	2
Ghana	25.0	-0	31	8	2.3	4.1	38	4
Guinea	10.2	-1	39	13	2.7	5.3	43	3
Guinea Bissau	1.6	-1	39	16	2.3	5.1	41	3
Liberia	4.1	-1	43	12	3.1	5.8	43	3
Mali	15.4	-5	45	15	3.1	6.4	48	3
Mauritania	3.5	-1	33	9	2.4	4.4	40	3
Niger	16.1	-0	48	12	3.6	7.0	49	2
Nigeria	162.3	-0	41	16	2.5	5.7	43	3
Senegal	12.8	-2	36	9	2.8	4.7	44	2
Sierra Leone	5.4	-0	37	15	2.2	5.0	42	4
Togo	5.8	0	36	8	2.8	4.7	42	4
EASTERN AFRICA	336	-1	39	11	2.8	5.3	44	3
Burundi	10.2	5	42	10	3.2	6.4	46	3

REGION/COUNTRY	Population Mid-2011 (Millions)	Net Migration Rate per 1,000	Births per 1,000 Popu-lation	Deaths per 1,000 Popula-tion	Rate of Natural In-crease (%)	Total Fertil-ity Rate	Percentage of Population of age <15	65+
Comoros	0.8	-3	36	8	2.8	4.8	43	3
Djibouti	0.9	0	29	10	1.9	3.7	35	3
Eritrea	5.9	0	34	8	2.6	4.7	43	4
Ethiopia	87.1	-1	37	10	2.7	2.0	44	3
Kenya	41.6	-0	37	10	2.7	4.7	42	3
Madagascar	21.3	-0	35	6	2.8	4.6	43	3
Malawi	15.9	-0	42	15	2.7	5.7	45	3
Mauritius	1.3	-0	12	7	0.5	1.5	22	7
Mayotte	0.2	-0	33	3	3.0	4.2	46	2
Mozambique	23.1	-4	41	14	2.8	5.6	45	3
Reunion	0.9	0	17	6	1.1	2.3	25	8
Rwanda	10.9	0	33	12	2.1	4.6	42	3
Seychelles	0.1	0	18	8	0.1	2.4	23	8
Somalia	9.9	-12	43	15	2.8	6.4	45	2
Tanzania	46.2	-1	40	11	2.9	5.4	45	3
Uganda	34.5	-1	46	12	3.4	6.4	48	3
Zambia	13.5	-1	46	15	3.1	6.3	46	3
Zimbabwe	12.1	0	34	15	1.9	4.1	44	4
MIDDLE AFRICA	131	-0	43	16	2.7	5.7	45	3
Angola	19.6	1	43	15	2.8	5.7	47	3
Cameroon	20.1	-0	37	15	2.2	4.8	41	4
Central African Rep.	5.0	0	37	15	2.1	4.7	41	4
Chad	11.5	-2	45	16	2.9	6.0	45	3
Congo	4.1	-1	36	11	2.5	4.7	40	4
Congo, Democratic Repub-lic of	67.8	-0	45	17	2.8	6.1	46	3
Equatorial Guinea	0.7	5	37	15	2.3	5.3	39	3
Gabon	1.5	1	27	9	1.8	3.4	35	4
Sao Tome and Principe	0.2	-9	34	7	2.7	4.6	44	3
SOUTHERN AFRICA	58	-0	22	14	0.7	2.5	31	5
Botswana	2.0	2	26	14	1.2	3.1	32	4
Lesotho	2.2	-2	27	15	1.2	3.1	37	4
Namibia	2.3	-0	26	8	1.7	3.3	36	4
South Africa	50.5	-0	21	14	0.6	2.4	30	5
Swaziland	1.2	-1	30	14	1.5	3.5	38	3

Source: *Population Reference Bureau (2011).*

As Table 6 shows, the population of Sub-Saharan Africa is unevenly distributed. Nigeria is Sub-Saharan Africa's most populous nation, with almost a fifth of the continent's population; in 2011, Nigeria had 162.3 million inhabitants, or 18.4% of the total SSA population of 883 million. There were six other countries with populations of over 30 million: Ethiopia (87.1 million); Democratic Republic of Congo (67.8 million); South Africa (50.5 million); Tanzania (46.2 million); Kenya (41.6 million) and Uganda (34.5 million). The populations of another four countries were above 20 million- Ghana (25.0 million); Cote D'Ivoire (22.6 million); Madagascar (21.3 million) and Mozambique (23.1 million). The populations of the remaining thirty-eight countries were below 20 million; they ranged from 0.1 million in the small island country of Seychelles, to 13.5 million in Zambia.

The average population density for the sub-continent was 78 persons per square mile in 2011, compared to the average of 123 for the rest of the world, and 162 for the Less Developed Countries. Thus population density is relatively low in Sub-Saharan Africa, although there are wide variations among countries. As can be seen from Table 6, the most densely populated countries in Sub-Saharan Africa are the islands of Mauritius and Mayotte, which have more than a thousand persons per square mile. Among the continental countries, Rwanda is the most densely populated, with a density of 829 persons per square mile, compared with only 6, 7, and 8 persons per square mile respectively in Namibia, Botswana and Mauritania. Western and Eastern Africa have the highest population densities, not only because of more habitable environments, but also due to the huge population concentrations in the most populous nations which are all found in these two sub-regions. The low population densities in Middle and Southern Africa are due to the excessive humid climate in the former and the arid environment in most parts of the latter. With the exception of Nigeria (385 persons per square mile), and Ethiopia (170 persons per square mile), the population densities of the most populous countries, Democratic Republic of Congo (64 persons), Tanzania (99 persons), and Kenya (145 persons), are not far above the average for the whole region.

Population densities also vary greatly within various countries and sub-regions. In the Western, Central Africa and Southern Africa sub-regions, population is concentrated along the coasts and in the capital cities. In Ghana, for example, almost a tenth of the population enumerated in the population census of 2000 lived in the capital city of Accra alone. Population estimates for the mid-1990s show that nine-tenths of Kenya's population lived on the well-watered lands along the shores of Lake Victoria and nearby highlands around Nairobi. Most of Tanzania's population is concentrated in the fertile eastern shores of Lake Malawi and around Lake Victoria in the highlands. Most Ugandans live on the relatively small fertile crescent of land around Lake Victoria or in Kampala, the capital, which is on the shores of the lake. In Burundi and Rwanda, population density is extremely high between Lake Victoria and the smaller lakes along the western branch of the Rift Valley. (See also Ch. 1)

Components of Population Change

As noted, the rapid rate of population growth in Sub-Saharan Africa region has been due to the rate of natural increase. Both the Crude Birth Rate (CBR) and the Crude Death Rate (CDR) were high, between 40 and 50 per one thousand live births and deaths respectively, until the last quarter of the 20th century. Since then, death rates have declined over the past three or so decades. Although they are still high by world standards, mortality rates, particularly infant and child mortality rates, have dropped significantly, and are even reversing in some countries.

Death Rates

The Infant Mortality Rate (IMR) exceeded 100 deaths per one thousand live births in many African countries up till the 1980s. The highest rates were recorded in Malawi (165), Gambia (193), and Sierra Leone (200), and the rates ranged between 100 and 149 in thirty other countries. According to the Population Reference Bureau's 2011 World Population Data Sheet, current Infant Mortality Rates are around 100 per one thousand live births and below, in 30 out of the 49 SSA countries. In the Southern African sub-region, the average is 49 (See Table 6).

The main factors that have contributed most to improved survival rate of infants and children has been improved health technology and associated public health and medical advances, including expanded immunisation programmes. Subsequently, the incidence of childhood killer diseases has reduced and some are even near eradication.

Treatment and some level of control of malaria, yellow fever and some other major causes of death have also contributed to reduction in mortality rates among all age groups. Better living conditions following provision of better ventilated housing and improved environmental sanitation and provision of sanitation facilities, access to safe drinking water and wider availability of flush toilets in urban communities also contributed to decline in mortality.

Formal female education has also been one single factor that has contributed to the higher survival rate of infants and children. Better personal hygiene, better understanding and acceptance of children's health and nutritional needs associated with formal education, have helped mothers to care for their children better. Consequently, children have better survival chances with increase in female education.

Compared however with the average Infant Mortality Rates of the higher industrialised countries (5), and that of the world (44), current Infant Mortality Rates in Sub-Saharan Africa are still high. The rates in other developing regions are also significantly lower than those in SSA. The average rate for South Central Asia, for example, stood at 53 deaths per thousand live births in 2011. The Maldives, which belongs to this region, has made a lot of progress in child survival efforts, and recorded the lowest rate of 11 in 2011. Worst of all is the stagnation of the decline in mortality and for that matter life expectancy at birth in Sub-Saharan Africa. In Southern Africa, for example, there has been a loss of 15 years so that current life expectancy is the same as it was in 1955 (Tabutin and Schoumaker, 2004: 487). The main factors responsible for this situation include worsening economic and living conditions, social and cultural practices that negatively affect health behaviour and the effect of the spread of HIV and AIDS.

Birth Rates

The levels of birth have remained high in Sub-Saharan Africa despite the fall in infant and child mortality rates. The average number of children that Sub-Saharan African women bear during their reproductive ages was between 6 and 8 until the 1980s, when a few countries recorded declines in their CBR and Total Fertility Rate (TFR).

The Crude Birth Rate which was between 40 and 50 live births per one thousand population up to the 1970s is still high. It is between 30 and 20 in most countries in the 2011 Population

Reference Bureau. The average TFR for SSA in 2011 is 2.4 (See Table 6). The lowest rates were in the countries where fertility decline began in the 1980s. In the whole of the Southern African sub-region it now ranges from as low as 2.4 in South Africa, to 3.5 in Swaziland. Niger has the highest TFR of 7.0. Generally, the poorest countries have the highest fertility rates. Since fertility decline has been recorded in the countries that have higher levels of socioeconomic development, it may be inferred that improvements in living conditions can also bring about a fall in the fertility rate in the other countries.

Improved survival chances of infants and children have not resulted in significant drops in birth rates in Sub-Saharan Africa as a whole, except in a few countries. This is because production systems have not altered significantly and family labour is still important for all aspects of production in low technological agricultural and pastoral production systems. Lack of pensions and social security in many countries also mean that families continue to depend greatly on children in their old age.

Fertility rates are also high, compared with prevailing rates in other regions of the world. The average for the world is 2.5, while that of the industrialised countries is 1.7, and 3.0 for the developing countries. As a result of the high fertility rate and high proportion of children and adolescents in the population, Sub-Saharan Africa has the world's youngest population. The high proportion of children and youth accounts for high age dependency and the potential of the population to grow into the future even when replacement fertility is attained. This population momentum accounts for the relatively reduced impact of the HIV and AIDS on the growth of the population in the sub-continent.

Though fertility levels are still high in Sub-Saharan Africa and remain the highest in the world, when we consider fertility levels in the sub-continent over a longer period of time from the middle of the 20th century to present times, we can observe that TFRs have dropped from between 6 and 8, to between 4 and 6, and even more in a few countries, as noted earlier.

Family Planning Programmes

Persistent high fertility, declining death rates, and resultant rapid population growth, necessitated the adoption of family planning programmes by Sub-Saharan African countries as a means of controlling births through the use of modern contraceptives. The motivation of Sub-Saharan African countries and other developing countries to adopt family planning programmes came from the United Nations' General Assembly's resolution on "Population Growth and Economic Development" at the 1962-63 session. The resolution called attention to the consequences of rapid population growth for the economies of developing countries. It also proposed the active involvement of the UN in seeking solutions to the problems of rapid population growth in the developing world. Since then, international population conferences every decade since 1974 have addressed the consequences of rapid population growth for economic development.

Until 1994 when a new paradigm "reproductive health" was adopted at the International Conference on Population Development (ICPD), held in Cairo, Egypt, the programmes had a narrow perspective and objectives, setting demographic targets that aimed at reducing fertility levels within set periods. The programmes also focused on women and were implemented under maternal and child health programmes in the health sector. Under the new paradigm, the scope of reproductive health programmes has been implemented within a wider context that recognizes the social and cultural contexts of reproduction. Consequently, women's education, employment, human rights and related issues, male involvement in family planning, and a multi-sectoral approach, have been characteristic of reproductive health programmes, not only in Sub-Saharan Africa, but elsewhere in the developing world.

Kenya was the first Sub-Saharan African country to launch an official family planning programme in 1967. Ghana followed suit in 1970, a year after adopting a national population policy. Since then, many other countries in the region have launched national population policies and/ or family planning programmes, with a main objective of controlling rapid population growth.

Most family planning programmes implemented in Sub-Saharan Africa have achieved modest success. Knowledge about modern contraception has been high, reaching as high as 90% in some populations, but attitudes to family planning have not been positive and practice has been low. This is exemplified by the Knowledge-Attitude-Practice (KAP) gap in contraceptive use. Presently Contraceptive Prevalence Rate (CPR) or the percentage of married women aged 15-49 years using modern contraceptives in 2011 is 29%, which is relatively low, compared to the average rates of 59 % in Less Developed Countries and 72% in industrialising or industrialised countries. The lowest CPR in the sub-continent in 2011 was recorded in Chad (3%), and the rate was not much higher in many others. The highest rate was in Mauritius (76%). There were a few others whose rates are also high- Reunion (67%), Zimbabwe (59%), Cape Verde (61%), Namibia (55%), Botswana (44%), Kenya (46%), Lesotho (47%) and Swaziland (49%).

Where CPR is high, fertility decline has been experienced. Kenya's record TFR of 8 in the 1980 reduced to 4.7 in 2011. TFR was below 5.0 in all the others countries where contraceptive usage rates are relatively high (See Table 6). It was only in Ghana that fertility has declined significantly from 6.4 in 1988 to 4.1 in 2011 though CPR had remained low, and was only 24% in 2011. The decline has been attributed to high rates of abortion by some demographers, while others call for further investigation into the process.

Many factors account for the limited success of family planning/reproductive health programmes in the sub-continent. They include implementation shortcomings such as the focus on women (it is only recently that male involvement has been considered), urban-biased approaches to the provision of the services, and logistic problems, among others. Cultural and religious practices that put a high premium on large family size also affect acceptance of modern contraception. The objections to adoption of family planning methods in Sub-Saharan Africa have also been attributed to suspicions about the long-term objective of the programmes which are claimed to be neo-colonialist or imperialist strategies to keep the African population low, so that it does not far exceed the white population. Such arguments are however debatable, considering that anthropological studies on several African societies indicate that traditionally they used some methods of birth control, including abortion and infanticide, to manage population. The fertility trends and levels in the region are explained further by the demographic transition theory and the cultural context.

The Demographic Transition Theory and the Cultural Context of Fertility

A demographic theory known as the Demographic Transition Theory explains the long-term pattern of change in the fertility, mortality and the associated population growth rates that are viewed as consequences of socioeconomic progress. The theory identifies four stages of the process (See Annex).

In the first stage, both birth and death rates are high and population growth is negligible. This stage is typical of traditional or agrarian societies and populations that depend on hunting and gathering. In the second stage, the death rate begins to fall as socio-economic conditions improve. The birth rate however remains high because socio-cultural institutions that encourage large family size change more slowly than the conditions that result in declines in death rate. The population increases fast as a result of the widening gap between birth and death rates. The third stage follows when the birth rate begins to drop sharply as the processes of modernisation and associated urbanisation, particularly female participation in formal education and paid employment, discourage large family size. The death rate still falls, but at a slower pace and the population growth rate now decreases. The fourth stage is reached when both death and birth rate are at their lowest and are about the same. The rate of natural increase approaches zero. This condition is referred to as **zero population growth** (ZPG) because the difference between the death and birth rate yields on slight increases in population.

Basically, all the industrialized countries have entered the fourth stage. Some of those countries have even reached what is now considered the fifth stage, where the death rate exceeds the birth rate, resulting in declining national population (see Figure 1).

The low levels of development in Sub-Saharan Africa explain the high levels of fertility and the associated rapid population growth. Death rates have been declining as some level of socio-economic progress has been achieved. But the proportion of females who receive formal education and are employed in paid jobs is still low in the region and the cultural practices that encourage large family sizes have not yet been eroded.

Culturally, as in other areas, Africa is not homogenous. More than 800 languages with numerous dialects are spoken in the region (See Chapter 3). Traditional African societies share some common beliefs, cultural values, customs or traditions especially regarding fertility behaviour and related areas. Religious beliefs in a Supreme Being and several lesser gods or deities and practices including ancestral worship are the most characteristic (see Chapter 7). Associated with this religious system are beliefs about reproduction and pro-natalist practices. The general concept about life is that there is life after death and the dead are in touch with the living and bless them with offspring. Infertility is a curse and a sign of the displeasure of the ancestors, while children are a blessing from God/the gods. The value of children is high and derives from the economic value of children as family labour and as valuable security against old age. Until recently, it has been considered prestigious to have many wives and children, with the wealth of a man measured in terms of his family size, while a woman was honoured when she bore many children, but was stigmatized if she could not bear children. There are many African proverbs that buttress the importance of children and large family size. Some of the proverbs cited by Korem and Abissath (2004) are as follows:

Even ghosts want to increase in number (Akan, Ghana)
It is better to have a rebellious child than to remain childless (Ewe, Ghana)
A woman whose sons have died is richer than a barren woman (Kikuyu, Kenya)
A child is greater than money (Ibo, Nigeria)
Children are the reward of life (Congo)
There is no wealth where there are no children (Liberia)

Despite the high value placed on childbearing and large family size, African traditional family values generally scorn prolific childbearing, premarital childbearing, premarital sex and extramarital sexual relations that result in childbearing. Marriage establishes the line of descent in patrilineal societies and provides security for the child. Post-partum abstinence and prolonged breastfeeding practices ranging from two to three years and other abstinence practices are observed to ensure the survival of the child and the good reproductive health of the mother. Some anthropological studies show that abortion and infanticide were practiced in some communities to regulate birth, family size, "undesirable" births (sometimes twins) and to prevent the birth of a child whose paternity could not be established. Rites of passage such as puberty rites for girls ushered them into adulthood, ensured virginity at marriage, and supervised entry into sexually active adulthood and marriage in some societies (Nukunya, 1969: 89; Sarpong, 1974: 73-74).

Descent is also an important concept about life and a feature of the traditional African society that affects fertility behaviour. The individual's existence is linked with his/her relationship with the ancestors through the living elders of the clan or kin group who are in direct touch with the ancestors either in a patrilineal or matrilineal descent group. This is the vertical relationship in the lineage based on age. The horizontal is defined as that with the members of the descent group who are peers or generation group who are members of the lineage and in the wider society. The individual is defined as a member of a society, a descent group or lineage. Individualism had little value and expression compared with communalism, except of course in areas of life where individual responsibility is required. Polygyny, early marriage of women, widow inheritance, fostering, extended family and kinship systems and the associated rights and obligations are practices that ensure the continuity and increase of the lineage and the survival of society. Such communal concepts underlie the belief among the Akan of Ghana that the land belongs to the dead, the living and those yet unborn. It also explains the corporate practices in land ownership and settlement patterns among lineages of the Ewe of Ghana and the belief among the Kikuyu of Kenya that the land could not be sold as it belonged to the ancestors. Members of a lineage therefore ensured that the lineage was not only sustained but increased in population size.

Gender roles are also important in African systems of kinship and marriage (see Chapter 4, this volume). Patriarchy, defined as a "system of social structures and practices in which men [fathers, uncles, brothers or elder males] dominate, oppress and exploit women" (Walby, 1990: 214) or a "sexual system of power in which the male possesses superior power and economic privilege" (Eisenstein, 1979: 17) in Eurocentric and Western feminist discourse, has been applied to African societies to explain the low socioeconomic status of women, their limited access to means of production (particularly land) and greater involvement in reproductive activities. However, the notion of patriarchy as an institution where male dominance operates in a system that emphasizes kinship ties above all others, including the conjugal, has been challenged in a number of ethno-historical works. They assert that more egalitarian, symmetrical and complementary male-female relationships in production and reproduction exist in traditional African societies, such as pre-colonial Igbo societies, than has been portrayed in colonial and other sociological and ethnographic works. But, today, gender inequalities in many areas, especially education, paid employment and access to critical resources for livelihood affect development. Low levels of female educational attainment account for high rates of early childbearing.

Christianity and Islam, the two predominant religions, Western education and lifestyles, and the general process of modernization have transformed some aspects of African traditional values, systems of belief and institutions such as marriage since Africa's contact with the Middle East and Europe. In spite of these transformations, practices pertaining to childbearing have not been altered significantly.

Population Growth

In terms of absolute numbers, the population of Sub-Saharan Africa has grown over the past two thousand years. It increased steadily between 4000 B.C. up to the beginning of the 20th century (See Table 7). SSA's share of the world's population has been significant, fluctuating between 4.6% and approximately 17% before 1900, and it has doubled since 1900, from 5.8% to 12.7% in 2011.

The rate of increase of Sub-Sahara's population was very dramatic during the second half of the 20th century (See Table 7). The population change was a little over 75% during the first fifty years when it increased from 95 million in 1900 to 167 million in 1950. A dramatic, almost fourfold, increase was recorded between 1950 (167 million) and the year 2000 (661 million), while over 15% of the population in the year 2000 had been added by 2011.

Table 7– Proportion of the World's Population in Sub-Saharan Africa (SSA), 4000B.C. to 2011 A.D.

Year	Population (in Millions)		Percentage (%) of World Population in Sub-Saharan Africa
	Sub-Saharan Africa	World	
-400	7	153	4.6
0	12	252	4.8
500	20	207	9.7
1000	30	253	11.9
1500	78	461	16.9
1750	94	771	12.2
1850	90	1,241	7.3
1900	95	1,634	5.8
1950	167	2,530	6.6
2000	661	6,081	10.9
2011	883	6,987	12.6

Source: *Weeks (2002: 24) and Population Reference Bureau (2011)*

Considered among the world's twenty most populous countries, two Sub-Saharan African countries, Nigeria and Ethiopia, took the 14th and 19th positions in 1950, but moved to the 10th and 18th positions by the year 2000 (See Table 8). Nigeria's population increased approximately fourfold from 32 million in 1950 to 123 million by the year 2000. Estimates show that by the year 2050, Nigeria will move up higher to become the world's sixth most populous country with a population of 307 million and Ethiopia will be the tenth, with 173 million people.

Table 8 – The Twenty most Populous Countries in the World: 1950, 2000, 2050

Rank	1950		2000		2050	
	Country	Population (in millions)	Country	Population (in Millions)	Country	Population (in millions)
1	China	563	China	1,262	India	1,628
2	India	370	India	1,014	China	1,394
3	Soviet Union	180	United States	275	United States	422
4	United States	152	Indonesia	225	Pakistan	349
5	Japan	84	Brazil	173	Indonesia	316
6	Indonesia	83	Russia	146	Nigeria	307
7	Germany	68	Pakistan	142	Bangladesh	255
8	Brazil	53	Bangladesh	129	Brazil	221
9	United Kingdom	50	Japan	127	Congo (Dem. Rep. of)	181
10	Italy	47	Nigeria	123	Ethiopia	173
11	Bangladesh	46	Mexico	100	Mexico	153
12	France	42	Germany	83	Philippines	133
13	Pakistan	39	Philippines	81	Egypt	127
14	Nigeria	32	Vietnam	79	Russia	119
15	Mexico	28	Egypt	68	Vietnam	117
16	Spain	28	Iran	66	Japan	101
17	Vietnam	26	Turkey	66	Turkey	98
18	Poland	25	Ethiopia	64	Iran	96
19	Ethiopia	22	Thailand	61	Sudan	84
20	Egypt	21	United Kingdom	60	Uganda	82

Source: *Weeks (2002: 20), Population Reference Bureau (2004)*

It is estimated that by 2050, the Democratic Republic of Congo and Uganda will also be among the world's twenty most populous countries. The former will have 183 million people, a higher population than Ethiopia's, thus taking the ninth position, while the latter will be in the twentieth position with a population of 83 million (See Table 8).

Urbanization

As populations grow, the tendency for human beings to congregate in large numbers to take advantage of resources is very high. The phenomenon of urbanization has been observed to be evolving rapidly. This section examines urbanization from the point of view of its demographic implications for Africa.

Worldwide, countries differ in the ways in which they classify their population as "urban" or "rural." Typically, a community or settlement with a population of 2,000 or more is considered urban, but the cut-off point may be high. In Ghana, for example, settlements with populations of 5,000 and over are classified as urban. Some countries consider availability of some services and facilities in their classification. (See the United Nations *Demographic Yearbook* listing of country definitions which is published annually.)

Sub-Saharan Africa is the least urbanised region of the world. In 2011, the rate of urbanisation which is the percentage of a country's population living in urban areas or towns was 37% in Sub-Saharan Africa, compared with an average of 44% for all Less Developed Countries and 75% in the More Developed Countries (Population Reference Bureau, 2011). The most urbanized parts of the sub-continent are on the coast of West Africa. West African coastal towns and others such as Dar es Salaam in East Africa and Cape Town and Durban in South Africa, began to develop when Arab merchants and European traders established links with Africans at the ports of these towns for trading purposes. Later, when colonial governments established plantations and extractive industries in the interior, particularly in Eastern and Southern Africa, railroads were built to connect the towns in the interior with the coastal towns and their ports. This was done to facilitate the transportation of agricultural raw materials, minerals and other export commodities to the ports for shipping to Europe. After independence, Sub-Saharan African countries continued to rely on export production and maintained the coastal towns as capital cities, making the port cities still important.

Other towns in the interior are at railway junctions along major rivers or near sources of valuable minerals (mining towns such as Johannesburg in South Africa; and Tarkwa, Konongo and Obuasi in Ghana, which are near gold mines). Some Sub-Saharan African towns that were relatively small grew as trading activities became important, following contact with European and other traders, for example, Lagos (Nigeria) and Salaga (Ghana) which were slave trading posts.

Trade and commercial activities continue to play a dominant role in economic activity in Sub-Saharan cities and towns. Industrial production has not been an important economic activity in them, and though attempts have been made to industrialize economies, they have not been strong enough to support large cities. Even where the rate of urbanization increases fast and is high as in the case of Benin (43% in 2011), rural-urban drift rather than economic progress in the urban sector is responsible. The largest city in the sub-continent is Lagos, whose population has exceeded 9 million. The others are capital cities in which populations of one million or more people reside: Dakar (Senegal), Abidjan (Cote d'Ivoire), Accra (Ghana), Ibadan and Kaduna (also in Nigeria), Kinshasa (Democratic Republic of Congo), Luanda (Angola), Addis Ababa (Ethiopia), Dar es Salaam (Tanzania), Kampala (Uganda), Nairobi (Kenya), Harare (Zimbabwe), and Maputo (Mozambique). South Africa, which has a more vibrant economy than most others in the region, has five cities with a million or more people – Pretoria and Johannesburg in the interior and Durban, Port Elizabeth and Cape Town on the coast.

In spite of the fact that Sub-Saharan Africa is the least urbanized region of the world, its rate of urbanization is the fastest growing worldwide. Only 35 million lived in urban areas in Sub-Saharan Africa in 1950 (Boehm, 1995: 435). In 2011, some 357 million Sub-Saharan Africans resided in urban areas, more than seven times the number about 50 years ago.

Vast differences in the rate of urbanization exist among and within the various sub-regions of Sub-Saharan Africa as well as among the countries. While half the population in Southern Africa live in towns and a little over a third in West Africa (45%) and Central Africa (44%), only a fifth (22%) do so in East Africa. In Southern Africa, the rate of urbanization exceeds 60%. It is 62% in South Africa, 62% in Botswana and the least urbanized country, Lesotho, has an urbanization rate of 23% (Population Reference Bureau, 2011: 11). The rate for Burundi in East Africa, the least urbanized in SSA, is only 11%. On the other hand, the average rate is as low as 22% in

Eastern Africa, but Djibouti's is as high as 76%. In Middle Africa also, the rate of urbanization ranges from 28% in Chad to 86% in Gabon. The disparities are not as high in West Africa as in the other sub-regions. With the exception of Guinea (28%), Burkina Faso (24 %), and Niger (17 %) all the others have between 30% (Guinea-Bissau) and 62% (Cape Verde) rate of urbanization.

Three factors account for the rapid population increase of the urban population of Sub-Saharan Africa: rural-urban migration, natural population increase or natural increase, and reclassification of previous rural communities as urban as they experience population increase and change their character.

Urbanization and Rural-Urban Migration

The pace of urbanization in Sub-Saharan Africa was fastest during the 1960s and early 1970s when the economies of most countries in the region were booming as agricultural and mineral exports attracted favourable prices. The average rate of urban population growth in the region was more than 4.64% between 1965 and 1970 (United Nations Economic Commission for Africa, 1995: 17).

A migration theory known as the "Push-Pull" Hypothesis explains the movement into urban areas. The theory suggests that circumstances at the place of origin (such as poverty and unemployment) repel or push people out of that place to other places that exert a positive attraction or pull (such as a high standard of living or job opportunities).

Prior to the mid-1970s, rural-urban drift contributed most to rapid urbanisation in the region as the emerging independent states invested in building their capital cities/towns and other regional centres and also implemented urban-biased economic development policies. Employment opportunities in the public sector expanded during that period. These developments resulted in a number of pull factors that attracted migrants into urban areas. Salaried employment attracted many rural residents who moved to urban areas. Some were also attracted by better educational opportunities, social amenities and facilities (water, health care, sanitation etc.) and infrastructure being provided in the urban areas and general higher living standards. The attraction of modern lifestyles in towns drew still more people from rural and economically deprived communities. The main factors that tend to push rural residents out of rural areas into towns include deteriorating agricultural lands due to population pressures on farmland and droughts in some countries (particularly in the Sahel), poor market facilities, transport networks and lack of banking credit systems for small-scale farmers and a general lack of interest in the agricultural sector among young graduates from secondary school. Most new migrants moving to urban areas today in Sub-Saharan Africa work in the informal sector as self-employed service providers or employees working for small and medium businesses.

Since the mid-1970s, as most countries in the sub-continent have experienced a downward trend in socioeconomic development, natural increase has begun to account for population increase in urban areas. As the economic crisis continues to prevail in the region, the gap between urban and rural economies has been narrowing. Consequently, there has been a slow down of the rural-urban drift (ECA, 1995: 17). Some urban residents even returned to their hometowns in the face of hardships in the urban community. Other urban residents also emigrated to Europe and North America. But urban population increased at 4.38% in the 1990s compared to 3.68% in Asia where economic growth was faster.

Problems Facing Urban Communities

Urban populations in Sub-Saharan Africa have grown far faster than resources have been available to keep up with the demand for public services, utilities and facilities. Remarkable population growth is expected in Sub-Saharan African urban centres as result of the high rate of natural increase. Meanwhile, as the national economies continue to face crisis of development so do the economies of the urban sector. As observed, the urban bias in development has seen the benefits of development more concentrated in urban areas. But cities and towns have not been centres of industrialization and manufacturing, and depend on the exports of agricultural and other raw materials. Therefore the interdependence of urban and rural production which can be derived from urban sectors that thrive on industrial production has been non-existent (Songsore, 2003). So, both urban and rural economies have grown weaker over the past two to three decades and this has resulted in several challenges. Many urban areas in Sub-Saharan Africa, like others in the developing world are "at the crux of the struggle to achieve better living standards" as they face rapid population increase, rising poverty levels, and inadequate public services and facilities (Hinrichsen et al. 2002: 1, 7).

In the face of all these, urban migration has not declined to the same degree that opportunities of employment and investment in public utilities and services decreased. Cities and towns which have been islands of development in a generally economically poor sub-continent continue to attract new migrants who look for non-existent jobs. Crime rates have increased among unemployed urban residents. Increasing commercial sex work has also been associated with worsening economic conditions. Other problems that have been associated with rapid urbanization in Sub-Saharan Africa include inadequate housing and increasing urban poverty. Some Sub-Saharan African cities such as Nairobi and Dar es Salaam have had large proportions of their populations, between 34 and 60%, living in deprived slums or shanty or squatter towns. Inadequate provision of sanitation facilities and services with associated poor environmental sanitation have plagued many urban communities leading to persistent high rates of mortality from environmentally related diseases among urban residents (See also Chapter 15 on the environment and development).

Meanwhile, many SSA governments have implemented economic policies, such as Structural Adjustment Programmes (SAPs) that included the laying off of labour in the public sector and payments for social amenities and services, especially in the health and educational sectors. Privatisation of public corporations has also been part of structural adjustment policies. This has led to higher charges and fees for services and products of the hitherto subsidized services. As employment opportunities continue to reduce, general living conditions have become worse over time; many urban residents live in deprived areas where access to basic facilities and amenities is limited. As is well known, SAPs have had particularly adverse effects on women.

Health

A number of health indicators show that the health status of the population of Sub-Saharan Africa has been poor, compared to the health condition in the world's major regions. They include Infant Mortality Rate, Child Mortality or under-five mortality and Maternal Mortality Rate. The survival rate of children and the rate at which mothers die as a result of child-birth and related causes are the most striking indicators. Children in SSA have the lowest survival rates worldwide. Maternal deaths are also high, exceeding 1,000 per 100,000 live births in some countries. It is only the Southern African region, where the standard of living is relatively higher, that average mortality rates are lower than the averages for the entire region. The average of 870 deaths per 100,000 live births for SSA in the year 2000 is very high, compared to the averages of other regions- Southern Asia (260), South America (170), North Africa (130), and East Asia (60). Life expectancy rates have been affected by stagnant decline in mortality due to the effect of HIV and AIDS and other economic factors.

The mortality rates are reflections of the standard of living and some socio-cultural factors also that determine health behaviour. Large proportions in both urban and rural areas do not have access to safe-drinking water, sanitation facilities and also suffer from malnutrition and therefore have poor health outcomes. Increasing poor environmental sanitation in urban areas also affects the health of many residents.

Reproductive Health

Reproductive health is defined as the state of complete physical, mental, and social well-being and not merely the absence of disease or infirmity, in all matters relating to the reproductive system and to its functions and processes. The cultural factors that determine access to contraceptives, particularly in the case of adolescents or the youth, for example, has been examined in the provision of reproductive health services.

Reproductive Health of the Youth

The proportion of Sub-Saharan Africa's population that is aged between 10-19 years is large, comprising 25% of the population of the region. The health needs of this segment of the population are therefore important as a result of this demographic reason.(See figure 1) Furthermore, the development or prosperity of the region will largely depend on the condition of the youth in all aspects of their life. Their reproductive health and well-being is perhaps the most crucial.

Figure 1– Africa's Diverse and Youthful Population

Source: *Courtesy Gifty Afia Oware-Aboagye,2010 MILEAD Fellow*

A number of components of the reproductive health of the youth have been identified as important for the transition of the youth to adulthood. They include continued school attendance leading to delayed sexual initiation, marriage and childbearing. Adolescence, the period of transition to adulthood, is the time when young people develop physically, emotionally and intellectually. But many factors, particularly adherence to traditional norms, account for the absence of the achievement of high levels of education and consequent delayed sexual initiation and childbearing.

Many youth, especially girls, either do not go to school or drop out and marry early. Many others do not marry early but are sexually active. They do not use modern, Western contraceptive methods as traditional culture frowns on these among young unmarried people. They therefore engage in high risk sexual practices that expose them to Sexually Transmitted Diseases (STDs) and HIV infection and the hazards of induced abortion which they sometimes seek from unauthorized sources such as quack doctors or peers. The youth have therefore been the targets of HIV in-school and out-of school programmes.

The reproductive health of women in Sub-Saharan Africa has also been affected by several cultural practices such as food taboos (especially during pregnancy and childbirth) and gender relations that limit their reproductive health rights or make them dependent on the spouses' decision or control thus increasing their vulnerability to STDs and HIV and AIDS. These, in addition to limited access to health care and the effect of poor nutrition, have been addressed in reproductive health/ family planning programmes.

The Human Immunodeficiency Virus and Acquired Immune Deficiency Syndrome (HIV and AIDS)

Since 1999, the year many experts thought that the epidemic peaked, the number of new infections globally has fallen by 19% (UNAIDS Global Report, 2010). Nonetheless, Sub-Saharan Africa continues to bear an inordinate share of the global HIV burden: 23 million people living with HIV and AIDS (Ibid). The outbreak of the HIV and AIDS has brought with it new challenges to the reproductive health dimension of health the world over. By the late 1970s and early 1980s HIV and AIDS was identified as a major health problem (Sai, 1999). The Population Reference Bureau (2011: 10) estimates show that at the end of 2009, 0.8% of the world's population aged 15 to 49 years was infected with HIV and AIDS. According to the Population Reference Bureau (2011), the global figure for persons aged 15-49 infected with HIV and AIDS remained unchanged (8%).

The proportion in Africa however declined from 4.8% in 2001 to 4.3% in 2009. But the rate of infection in Sub-Saharan Africa remains the highest and the most challenging considering that the region generally has higher rates of poverty and mortality than any other region of the world. The impact of the HIV/AIDS on various aspects of life has therefore been most severe in Sub-Saharan Africa. At the end of 2009, Sub-Saharan Africa recorded 67% as persons living with HIV and AIDS even though only 11.5 % of the total world population reside in the region.

HIV and AIDS Prevalence Rates in Sub-Saharan Africa

The average rate of infection for the Sub-Saharan African region greatly masks the wide variation among the countries. The rate of infection among those aged 15 to 49 years in 2009 ranges from 0.7% in Mauritania to 25.9% in Swaziland. Generally, the rates of infection are highest in Eastern and Southern Africa. The eastern African countries that have the highest rates currently are Zimbabwe (14.3 %), Zambia (13.5%), Malawi (11.0%) and Mozambique (11.5%). In southern Africa where the infection rates are highest, three countries have prevalence rates that exceed 20%, with Swaziland recording the highest rate of 25.9%; Namibia recorded the lowest figure of 13.1% at the end of 2009. In terms of the absolute numbers with HIV and AIDS, South Africa has the largest number, about 20 million people (Population Reference Bureau, 2011). Eastern and southern African countries and La Cote d'Ivoire in West Africa have the highest HIV and AIDS prevalence rates in the region. They ranked among the top 15 HIV and AIDS prevalence countries in Africa and the Caribbean (See Table 9).

The Mode of Spread of HIV and AIDS in Sub-Saharan Africa

After sub-Saharan Africa, the Caribbean has a higher HIV prevalence than any other area of the world, with 1 percent of the adult population infected (UNAIDS, 2010). The major route by which HIV and AIDS is spread in Africa is heterosexual intercourse. Women are particularly vulnerable to HIV infection; more than half of people living with HIV are women. It has been estimated that 93% of all adult cases are contracted through heterosexual intercourse. Transmission from mother to infant during pregnancy, delivery or breastfeeding is another major mode of spread of the virus in the region. Some people are also infected by the virus through blood transfusion and the use of blood products. As drug use is increasing among young people who are also often sexually active it is expected that shared needles may also become important route of infection in Sub-Saharan Africa in the course of time.

Table 9 – HIV and AIDS Prevalence Countries

Africa			Outside Africa		
Rank	Country	Percent of Population	Rank	Country	Percent of Population
1	Swaziland	26.1	1	Bahamas	3.1
2	Botswana	23.9	2	Belize	2.3
3	Lesotho	23.2	3	Haiti	1.9
4	South Africa	18.1	4	Jamaica	1.7
5	Namibia	15.3	5	Trinidad and Tobago	1.5
6	Zimbabwe	15.3	6	Barbados	1.4
7	Zambia	15.2	7	Dominican Republic	0.9
8	Mozambique	12.5	8	Brazil	0.6
9	Malawi	11.9	9	Puerto Rico	-
10	Central African Rep.	6.3	10	Suriname	1.0
11	Tanzania	6.2	11	Peru	0.4
12	Gabon	5.9	12	Honduras	0.8
13	Uganda	5.4	13	Martinique	-
14	Cameroon	5.1	14	Grenada	-
15	Cote d' Ivoire	3.9	15	Dominica	-

Source: *PRB, 2010; UNAIDS, 2008*

Control and Prevention of the Spread of HIV Infections

Researchers and other experts who have studied the spread of HIV have concluded that the control of the virus in Sub-Saharan Africa and elsewhere will be achieved by three means: development of a vaccine against the virus, a decimation of the disease itself or control of the spread of the virus by means of behavioural change. Since the first two have not been a possibility, behavioural change has been considered the most probable solution to the spread of the virus (Anarfi, 2001).

The control of the spread of HIV as well as its prevention, like any other disease, has depended on the understanding of the nature of the virus and how it is transmitted from one person to another. Identifying the population that is at risk of contracting the disease has also been an important prerequisite for successful education of people about the virus and how they could protect themselves against the disease.

Early studies focused mainly on the biological and individual or group risk behaviour that put people in danger of getting infected with the virus. Commercial sex workers, long distance drivers, homosexuals and intravenous drug users were targeted for education (Awusabo-Asare and Anarfi, 1999). People who have multiple sexual partners or who are not in marital or stable relationships, for example, unmarried but sexually active young people, added to the list of the population at risk.

Following the limited success of strategies adopted to control the spread of the virus that have been based on the epidemiological understanding of the virus and its spread, recent researches have considered the socio-cultural contexts within which people's behaviour expose them to the virus. The social, cultural, political, economic and environmental factors that have also hindered or increased the rate of spread of the virus have been examined.

Regarding the socio-cultural dimensions of the risk of contracting the virus, gender inequality has been singled out as a crucial factor that has determined the differences in the vulnerability of men and women to contracting HIV and AIDS (Sai, 1999; Wodi, 2004). In many African societies, a double standard has been adhered to with respect to sexual or reproductive health behaviour and the rights of men and women. While in many societies women are expected to marry as virgins or keep to one partner, their husbands or male partners are allowed multiple partners before and within marriage. Married women may therefore be at a greater risk of contracting the virus than others when their husbands engage in extra-marital sexual relations or have a record of previous promiscuous sexual behaviour. Some other factors including the tendency for women to marry at an early age, their financial dependence on partners or husbands, as well as the expectation that they will bear children, make them more vulnerable to contracting the virus. The biological make-up of women also makes them more susceptible to contracting the HIV. On the other hand, lack of male circumcision explains greater female-male transmission in some African societies (Simonsen et al. 1988 and Bongaarts et al. 1989 cited by Orubuloye et al.1999: 1).

Puberty rites have been emphasized recently in the fight against HIV and AIDS. As discussed earlier, rites of passage served many purposes in traditional African societies. Puberty rites were means by which adolescents were ushered into sexually active adult life. As such traditional educational processes have been abandoned, premarital sex has been condoned and become a main factor responsible for increased risk among young people. Some people have suggested that these rites be repackaged for contemporary African society to control sexual promiscuity among young people (see Chapter 7).

HIV infection is not curable but it is preventable, and efforts have been made to control its spread. Educational campaigns aimed at creating awareness about the virus, the modes of its transmission and its prevention have been embarked upon. The media, health workers, educational institutions, NGOs, and more recently, religious organizations, have been in the forefront of such campaigns. There has however been little or moderate achievement of the goals of campaigns at all levels of society.

The main achievement of the educational campaigns has been the creation of a high rate of awareness in the population about the virus. Despite the high rate of awareness about HIV and AIDS, behavioural change needed to prevent further spread of the virus has not been forthcoming. A number of factors have been responsible for this situation.

Some people deny the existence of the virus. Among some young sexually active students in Ghana, for example, the acronym AIDS has been distorted to become "American Idea to Discourage Sex." Such an attitude may not encourage young people to examine their sexual behaviour in the light of the spread of the virus.

Some people have also held the view that the virus is a punishment from God or supernatural forces for those who commit adultery or engage in sexual immorality. There is also the perception that a person can contract HIV and AIDS when someone attacks him through the occult or *juju*. These are some of the reasons why some HIV and AIDS patients seek healing from traditional healers or through prayer. Some go to the extent of believing that male patients can be cured by sleeping with virgins.

The findings of some studies have also identified people who hold fatalistic opinions about contracting the disease. Hence the expression "all die be die"- literally translated to imply that as one is going to die in any case then it does not matter how s/he dies (Awusabo-Asare, 1999). Research, especially qualitative research, is also needed for a better understanding of the spread of HIV and how social and cultural factors such as gender and stigmatisation of victims affect its spread.

Population, Environment and Development

The majority of the population in SSA derive their livelihoods directly from the environment by means of agricultural production, mining, and other primary economic activities. The conditions of the environment and the impacts of human activities are important factors that affect the people especially as the population has been increasing rapidly. Indeed the concern about the relationship between environment and population is one of the most important on the agenda for human development worldwide (See also Chapters 1, 12 and 15).

Population and Development Theories

Several perspectives exist on the inter-relationships among population, environment and development. We examine some that are pertinent to the situation of the sub-continent. The main issue that has been addressed by the various viewpoints on population and development is the ability of human beings to provide subsistence for increasing numbers using a finite resource base. The concern about population and development has therefore centred on the question of survival; simply, population change and its consequences for the well-being of society. The philosophical dimensions of the answers to the question of survival are twofold. The first one is about production and the role of technology has been the main focus of concern. The second dimension is on distribution of the resources. The arguments about distribution have addressed egalitarian and inegalitarian systems and which of the two should be the goal of society (Wiman, 1984).

The Malthusian Population Thesis

A theory on population expounded by an English clergyman and economist, Thomas Robert Malthus, (1766-1834) is one of the most influential works ever written on population and development. He published his work in a series of articles that first appeared in 1792. Malthus propounded his population theory in the 1798 article titled *An Essay on the Principle of Population*, based on the population of England at the time. His main argument was that population, when unchecked, increases in a geometrical ratio (1, 2, 4, 8, …) while subsistence only increases in arithmetical ratio (1, 2, 3, 4, …). In the short run, Malthus argues, improvements in technology and productivity can lead to better living standards but these also encourage additional population growth. Increase in population tends to exceed the means of subsistence in the long run and the main societal consequence is starvation and poverty. Eventually, there will be decline in the standard of living since more people have to share the same finite resource base. Malthus recommends that births must be controlled through late marriage or celibacy or moral restraint or it will be checked by natural population restrictions such as famine, disease and war; and the consequences will be poverty (Shelley and Clarke, 1995: 83- 84).

The Malthusian population theory has been criticised on a number of accounts. The main criticism against the theory was that Malthus was skeptical about long-term impacts of advanced technology that can increase efficiency of resource use. 20th century adherents of the Malthusian population theory, the **Neo-Malthusians**, however argue that even when production methods improve as a result of advances in technology, rapid population growth leads to diversion of resources to indirectly productive sectors (health and education) to meet such immediate needs of children rather than investment in directly productive sectors such as agriculture and industry. Consequently, there will be constrains on the development process. The Neo-Malthusians however advocate the use of modern contraceptive methods for birth control instead of the moral restraint that Malthus recommended.

The Neo-Malthusian argument about population pressures on resources has been the basis for the implementation of family planning and other population programmes in SSA.

The Marxian Perspective on Population and Development

The most articulated reaction to the Malthusian population theory came from the founder of modern communism, Karl Marx (1818-1883), a German political philosopher and economist resident in England from 1949, and his contemporary and co-founder of modern communism, Friedrich Engels (1820-1895), also a German socialist and political philosopher resident chiefly in England from 1842.

The main Marxist thought on population states that poverty is not a consequence of unchecked population growth, as argued by Malthus, but a consequence of inequalities in capitalist systems of distribution of resources which are characterized by exploitation of the working class and unfair economic structures. The Marxist perspective also rejects the Malthusian population law, arguing that there are no universal population laws, rather each population's developmental experience can be explained largely by its historical processes. The Marxist viewpoint attributes the underdevelopment of Africa, for example, to the colonisation process and other inequalities in world trade and other partnership systems.

The main Marxist argument is that population growth encourages increases in production. Such a viewpoint which states that population growth increases the resource base as additional populations contribute rather than take away from the resource base is known as the **cornucopian thesis.** It basically advocates that population growth is desirable rather than detrimental. The cornucopian position was adopted by the Chinese communist leader Mao Zedong (1890-1976) who rejected population control and said that "Every stomach is attached to two hands." It was after his death that China began to implement its controversial one-child birth control policy (Shelley and Clarke, 1995: 84). In fact, the cornucopian thesis has been held by some African leaders too, especially in the past. They extend their argument by stating that Africa has more than enough resources needed for its people, in particular land, and need not control its population growth. But since the 1970s, more and more governments have acknowledged that rapid population increase, even if it is not the cause of underdevelopment, contributes to the problems of development in their economies. Subsequently, family planning programmes have been implemented in many countries, though with limited success.

Other Population and Development Hypotheses

Some perspectives on population and development argue that population pressures on resources can lead to economic development. Some of the proponents of such theories argue that population increase provides a chance for economic progress. Two 20th century proponents of this viewpoint are Ester Boserup and Julian Simon. Ester Boserup (1965) postulates that in pre-industrial societies, increase in production occurred in response to population growth. Making observations on empirical data from such societies, she concludes that rather than bringing about poverty, population increase creates the necessity for agrarian societies to develop better production techniques such as intensive cultivation that soon facilitates division of labour. According to her, the overall effect of the technological innovation that is stimulated by population growth is growth in the agricultural sector as productivity increases. Food supply also becomes more stable. The benefits are invested in other sectors. The division of labour resulting from the process also promotes efficiency in production that engenders economic progress. She therefore proposes that population pressures in the developing world can bring about progress in their economies if agricultural technology is improved.

Julian Simon (1981) also argues that population pressures bring humans the opportunity to develop advanced technology to meet the needs of an increasing population. Simon argues that human resourcefulness and enterprise can forever respond to the problems of an increased need for resources through advancement in technology and the results will be better living standards. Therefore, knowledge is the ultimate resource. Simon's perspective has shaped the notion held by some population experts and policy-makers that development rather than birth control is a better approach to population management in the developing world. This argument has been supported by empirical evidence from developed countries where economic and technological advancement has not been without reduction in fertility levels.

A critical examination of the conditions of population and development in Sub-Saharan Africa shows that technological advancement in agricultural production and other sectors of the economy may offset the present bottlenecks in the developmental process of the region. Many resources in the region are yet to be fully developed as the level of technological advancement is still very low.

The Concept of Sustainable Development

More recent concerns about the population-development interrelationship have focused on environmental issues, specifically since the 1992 International Conference on Population and Environment in Rio de Janeiro (see also Chapters 10 and 15, this volume). With the paradigm shift, the main concern has been about the implications of unrestricted exploitation of resources for the ability of the environment to continue to support the human race into the future. The concept, **sustainable development**, has been the guiding principle in the policies and developmental frameworks that consider this new paradigm. Simply defined, sustainable development is development that satisfies the needs of the present generation without compromising the ability of future generations to satisfy their needs. Such an approach to development requires that resources, both renewable and non-renewable, are not exploited for present needs only but preserved for future generations too. It also requires the adoption of environmentally-friendly practices in production and consumption such as the use of biodegradable substances.

The main objectives of sustainable development are broad, encompassing a number of inter-related issues such as improving human well-being, particularly alleviating poverty, increasing gender equity, improving health, human resources and stewardship of the natural environment.

Poverty alleviation has been the framework of development in many developing countries, including those in Sub-Saharan Africa. Health and gender issues have also become important components of contemporary development efforts in many developing countries. With respect to gender equity, efficiency and increased growth in production in the agricultural and other sectors that women dominate are some objectives for the adoption of policies that seek to improve women's access to critical resources such as land and credit. Stewardship of the environment underscores government policies worldwide that address environmental degradation and pollution in all aspects of production. Stewardship of the environment may be equated to sustainable development. The sustainable development approach indeed provides a wider scope within which population, environment and development interrelationships can be examined though the implications of the other viewpoints must not be neglected.

Population and the Political Economy of Development in Sub-Saharan Africa

Prevailing economic conditions in SSA and associated population and development processes can be attributed to a variety of factors, including the political and economic processes that began from the era of colonialism and have been exacerbated by contemporary external political and economic sources. These, in addition to limited investment in the agricultural and manufacturing sectors, overdependence on cash-cropping for exports since the colonial era and the lack of advanced technology have been some of the major setbacks to economic development in Sub-Saharan Africa, quite apart from some aspects of the population processes of the region.

The period of colonialism has been generally considered as a catastrophic set-back for African civilization because of the loss of human and natural resources and the consequent interruption of pre-colonial conditions in the region. The redrawing of political boundaries by colonial states cut across ethnic lines, dividing kin groups and their neighbours, while grouping diverse ethnic groups under one state. This has been one of the causes of ethnic polarisations and clashes in the post-independence era. Political instability, civil wars and other types of conflicts have been experienced in most countries in the region, some of which can be linked to the political structures and institutions established under colonialism.

Widespread civil wars, political turmoil, ethnic conflicts and religious clashes in Sub-Saharan Africa from the 1970s have also been human factors that contribute to famine in the region. For example, in the Horn of Africa- Eritrea, Sudan, Ethiopia and Somalia- long and intermittent civil and other forms of conflicts have also been causes of famine. Starvation and bloodshed resulting from conflicts have created millions of refugees in Sub-Saharan Africa. The loss of human life and opportunities for development that have been associated with the various forms of conflicts are also a challenge to the economic progress of the region. Furthermore, various aspects of bad governance manifested mainly in corrupt practices and expenditure on ammunition also drain national coffers and create increasing inequalities among citizens. (See also Ch.12)

Sub-Saharan Africa has remained the poorest of the world's major regions by technological and living standards. Standards of living, however, vary greatly within the region. The per capita Gross National Income Purchasing Power Parity (GNI PPP), for example, ranged from US$280 in Malawi to US$7,240 in Mauritius in 2009 (World Bank, 2009). The low levels of economic development contrast strikingly with the vast natural resources that the region is endowed with.

The Millennium Development Goals and Development in Sub-Saharan Africa

At the turn of the new millennium, the international community has emphasized "human or people-centred development" as an alternative to the economic growth and development, and associated modernisation paradigms. This new paradigm focuses on human well-being and views people as the most important catalysts or agents of development and its ultimate beneficiaries. For this reason, new and alternative measures of development and progress such as the **Human Development Index (HDI)** and the **Human Poverty Index (HPI)** have been adopted to replace gross Gross Domestic Product (GDP) and other commodity indicators of development (Onimode, 2004). The HDI is a composite measure of economic, health and social indicators while the HPI is not only about income but also access to basic human needs such as food, water, housing and sanitation.

The September 2000 United Nations Millennium Summit identified a number of problems that are considered impediments to development: poverty, hunger, disease, illiteracy, environmental degradation and gender inequalities. The summit set eight time-bound goals, popularly known as the "Millennium Development Goals (MDGs)" that are to be achieved by the year 2015:

1. Eradicate extreme poverty and hunger;
2. Achieve universal primary education;
3. Promote gender equality and empower women;
4. Reduce child mortality;
5. Improve maternal health;
6. Combat HIV and AIDS, malaria and other diseases;
7. Ensure environmental sustainability;
8. Develop a global partnership for development.

Despite the efforts made so far to achieve the MDGs, evidence suggests that Sub-Saharan Africa and many other developing countries cannot achieve them by the set date of 2015. The percentage of people living under $1 a day exceeds 80% in Uganda and Guinea Bissau, and it is between 50 and 75% in several other countries including Tanzania, Gambia, and the Central African Republic (Africa Development Bank, 2007). High rates of morbidity and mortality are some of the consequences of malnutrition. Sub-Saharan Africa therefore has the highest Infant Mortality Rate (IMR) of 96 per 1,000 live births, almost twice the rate of Asia (54) and many times those of Europe (7) and North America (7). The IMR is above 100 in 16 Sub-Saharan African countries and between 75 and 100 in 14 others. High rates of maternal mortality, high rates of morbidity from HIV and AIDS and malaria, and poor governance resulting in political conflicts are characteristic of the Sub-Saharan African population (PRB 2006, 2007a).

It has been emphasized that the MDGs cannot be achieved without addressing population questions (UNFPA, 2002). It has also been asserted that though decades of research have not concluded on how demographic change affects economic development and vice versa, there are some associations between the two and they influence each other both directly and indirectly through other factors (PRB, 2007). One such association has been identified as the **demographic dividend or bonus**. The demographic dividend is the benefit that accrues to a country when its fertility drops and the age structure of the population changes such that as the youthful population reaches the working age and have fewer children than previous generations, a very large working-age population can result relative to the dependent (children under 15 years and the elderly) that have to be supported. Certain conditions must be met, though. Investment must be done in health and education and appropriate economic and labour policies adopted. Furthermore, stable and effective governments are required for implementation of effective economic, social and political policies. Some countries in East Asia, particularly China and South Korea, are reaping the demographic dividend following their demographic transition and drop in fertility between 1965 and 1990. But a demographic transition does not guarantee economic growth. Examples of this are found in Bangladesh where economic growth has lagged behind demographic change and in Iran where job shortages have encouraged brain drain (Ashford, 2007).

The population and economic conditions of Sub-Saharan Africa indicate that the human development approach to development and the pursuit of the MDGs may yield the demographic dividend. Strategies to achieve the goals are needed so that the future population of Africa is a bonus rather than a bane.

Conclusion

The population of Sub-Saharan Africa has features that distinguish it from those of other major regions of the world. Rapid population growth and its implications for development of the sub-continent has been a long-standing issue of concern and debate. Many other issues concerning the population such as health, environment and poverty have been receiving equal attention.

Population processes in Sub-Saharan Africa are intricately linked with many political, socio-cultural and environmental variables. Socio-cultural transformations beginning from the colonial era in particular, such as migration and ethnic conflicts have had implications for population processes that affect development in the region. In the post independence era, economic policies and governance have also contributed to population patterns and trends. The conditions of the population, especially the health and the resource bases- land and other natural resources- have been deteriorating fast. These and other areas of concern need urgent attention so that a steady improvement in health and development can be achieved. When this happens, population, which was considered as an asset in the past, will no longer be or perceived as a liability in the region. Human resource development will then be an integral part of socioeconomic development that will lead the sub-region to yield a demographic dividend.

It must be noted again that issues such as health and stewardship of the environment were important in traditional notions of population management. Pro-natalist practices have paid attention to the health of children and mothers, for example in the practice of prolonged breast-feeding and postpartum abstinence. The concept of the human being, extended family system, fostering and other practices provided social security and a safety net for people in traditional society. It is the transformation of some of these institutions that resulted in many social problems such as child neglect and street living. Indigenous concepts of population, environment and development must not be neglected when adopting policies that promote sustainable development in the region. Indeed, for the Sub-Saharan African region, protection of some traditional practices and valuable cultural practices must be part of sustainable development objectives.

Review Questions

1. What are the main features of Africa's age structure?
2. Explain the following concepts:
   a. A young population;
   b. Infant Mortality Rate (IMR);
   c. Total Fertility Rate (TFR);
   d. Reproductive health.
3. Distinguish between the following terms

    a.   Fertility and fecundity;

    b.   Morbidity and mortality.

4. Discuss four factors that promote and sustain high birth rates in Africa.

5. How would you account for the limited success of family planning programmes in Africa.

6. A migration theory known as "Push-Pull" hypothesis explains the movement into urban areas. Explain and state the major problems of cities.

7. Why is the HIV and AIDS pandemic no more considered solely as a medical issue in Africa? With this in mind, if you were the Minister of Health in an African country with the HIV and AIDS pandemic, what measures would you put in place to address the issue? Answer with reference to a specific country.

References

Aase, A. and S, Agyei-Mensah 2005. "HIV and AIDS Epidemic in Sub-Saharan Africa: Geographical Perspectives". *Norwegian Journal of Geography* 59(1): 1-5.

Africa Development Bank 2007. *Africa: Progress Towards Attaining the Millennium Development Goals*. Tunis: Africa Development Bank.

Agnew, C.T. (1995). "Desertification, Drought and Development in the Sahel". in T. Binns, *People and Environment in Africa*. Chichester: John Wiley & Sons, pp137-149.

Aryeetey-Attoh, S. 2003. *Geography of Sub-Saharan Africa*. 2nd ed. Upper Saddle River: J. Pearson Education Inc.

Ashford, L. S. 2007. *Africa's Population: Risk or Opportunity*. Washington D.C.: Population Reference Bureau.

English, P. L.1997. *Geography: People and Places in a Changing World*. 2nd ed. Eagen: West Publishing Company.

Fellman, J., A. Getis and J. Getis 1996. *Human Geography: Landscapes of Human Geography*. 5th ed. Dubuque: Brown & Benchmark.

Government of Ghana 1994. *National Population Policy*. Rev. ed.. Accra: National Population Council.

Haupt, A. and T. T. Kane 1998. *Population Handbook*. 4th International ed. Washington D.C.: Population Reference Bureau.

International Institute for Applied Systems Analysis 2002. "Population in Sustainable Development". *Population Network Newsletter (POPNET)*, 34 (Spring).

Korem, A. and M. K. Abissath 2004. *Traditional Wisdom in African Proverbs: 1,915 Proverbs from 40 African Countries*. Accra: Publishing Trends Ltd.

McFalls, J. Jr. 2003. "Population: A Lively Introduction". 4th ed. *Population Bulletin* 58(4). Washington D.C.: Population Reference Bureau.

Population Reference Bureau (PRB) 2005, 1990, 1999, 1985, *World Population Data Sheet*. Washington D.C.: PRB.

_____. 2007 *Population & Economic Development Linkages 2007 Data Sheet*. Washington D.C.: PRB.

Sai, T. 1999. *Why is Africa Losing the Battle Against AIDS?* Accra: Ghana Academy of Arts and Sciences.

Shelley, F.M. and A. Clarke 1994. *Human and Cultural Geography: A Global Perspective*. Dubuque: Wm. C. Brown Publishers.

Simon, J. 1981. *The Ultimate Resource*. Princeton: Princeton University Press.

United Nations Economic Commission for Africa (UNECA) 1995. *Population and Sustainable Development with Particular Reference to Linkages Among Environment, Urbanization and Migration in ECA Member States.* E/ECA/POP/TP/95/3(b)/3. Addis Ababa: UNECA.

Weeks, J. R. 2002. *Population: An Introduction to Concepts and Issues.* 8th ed.. Belmont: Wadsworth/Thompson Learning.

World Bank 2004. *African Development Indicators.* Washington D.C.: World Bank.

WHO/UNAIDS/UNICEF 2010. 'Towards Universal Access: scaling up priority HIV and AIDS interventions in the health sector'

UNAIDS Report on the Global Aids Epidemic, 2010.

Population Reference Bureau 2011. 2011 World Population Data Sheet, available at www. prb. org (accessed 08-08-2011).

Appendix

Basic Demographic Concepts

Demography is the scientific study of human populations, their sizes, compositions, distributions, densities, growth, fertility, mortality migration and other causes and consequences of changes in these factors. The discipline has developed the methods and principles by which population is studied and presents them under major themes (Haupt and Kane 1998:57, Shryock et al.1976:1). We consider only those that are relevant for the purposes of the present chapter.

Age and Sex Composition

Age and sex composition are the most basic characteristics of a population and are essential for the analysis of many other characteristics of a population. Age "0" refers to children who are under one year or have not yet celebrated their first birthday; they are called **infants,** while those aged 1 to 4 years are technically called **children.** All children who have not yet celebrated their fifth birthday are called **under-fives. Adolescence** refers to the transition period between childhood and adulthood. The years 15 to 45 or 49 years are **childbearing** or **reproductive years** for women. For economic analysis of population, all persons under 15 years are referred to as **children** and **young dependants**, while the age bracket 15 to 64 years is called the **economically productive** and those aged 65 years and over are **old dependants.** The ratio of those in the dependent ages to those in economically productive ages is referred to as the **age dependent ratio.** It is often used as an indicator of the economic burden of the economically productive. It is expressed mathematically as follows:

$$\frac{\text{Population under 15 years} + \text{Population aged 65 years and over}}{\text{Population aged 15 – 64 years}} \times K, \text{ where } K = 100.$$

Many developing countries have high birth rates, with between 40 and 50 per cent of their populations below 15 years, resulting in high age dependency ratios. The use of the age dependency ratio in measuring economic dependency has to be taken with some caution though, as there may be many in the economically productive ages who may not be productive, while some children under 15 years (especially in poor economies) participate in paid employment. Some adults aged 65 and over may also be still economically active.

When the proportion of children and young adults in the population is high, the population is referred to as a **young population** and has potential for growth. An o**ld population** has a relatively high proportion of middle-aged and elderly people. In general, the populations of developing countries are young while those of developed countries are old.

The **sex ratio** is the most commonly used measure in analysIs of the sex composition of a population. It is the ratio of males to females in a given population and it is usually the number of males for every 100 females. It is expressed as:

$$\frac{Pm}{Pf} \times K,$$

where Pm represents the number of males, Pf is the number of females and K= 100.

A sex ratio of 100 is a balance of the sexes in the population. When the sex ratio is above 100, it means there are more males in the population than females. There are more females than males when it is below 100. Sometimes, the concepts gender and sex are used synonymously. This is erroneous. **Sex** is the classification of the human population on the basis of biological characteristics into males and females or boys and girls or men and women, while **gender** refers to the culturally defined roles, rights, responsibilities, obligations and associated privileges for men and women. Gender is as dynamic as culture itself is and varies from one society to another (see also Chapter 4)

A commonly used technique that graphically depicts the age-sex structure composition of a population is called a **population pyramid.** The proportion of population in each age group (usually five-year age groups) is represented as a bar chart horizontally in ascending order from the lowest age group to the highest.. The shape of the pyramid depicts the cumulative result of past trends in fertility, mortality, migration processes and immigration policy and also foretells future trends of population growth. There are three general shapes with associated age structure and trends of future population growth: 1) broad-based depicting high fertility rapid population growth or high growth potential, 2) cylindrical, showing slow growth, and 3) narrowing base, typical of declining population.

A concept associated with the broad-based pyramid is **population momentum.** It is the tendency of the population to continue to grow even after replacement-level fertility has been achieved. This is due to a current high proportion of children and young persons in the population who will enter their reproductive ages in future so that even when fertility levels fall they will, by virtue of the large number, continue to add large numbers of children to the population.

Fertility

The concept of **fertility** is sometimes confused with **fecundity**. Fertility is the actual birth performance while fecundity is the physiological capacity of individuals or couples to reproduce or have children. Three most commonly used measurements of fertility that are relevant for our analysis are now considered.

The **Crude Birth Rate (CBR),** also known as the birth rate, indicates the rate of birth in a population per 1,000 population in a given year. It is represented mathematically as follows:

$$\frac{\text{Number of births}}{\text{Total population}} \times K, \text{ where } K= 1000$$

In 2004, crude birth rates in developing countries where fertility levels are generally high, ranged between 35 and 50 live births per 1,000 population, compared with 10 in many industrialized countries.

The **Total Fertility Rate (TFR) is t**he average number of children that would be born to a woman by the time she comes to the end of her reproductive years if she conforms to the age-specific fertility rates (the fertility rate of specific age groups in the population), in a given year. The TFR is currently between 5 and 7 in most Sub-Saharan African countries while it is below **replacement-level fertility** in some industrialised countries such as Italy and Spain. The replacement-level fertility is the level of fertility at which a couple has only sufficient number of children to replace themselves, considered to be a TFR of 2.1, or about two children per couple in the industrialised countries. A higher rate is required in developing countries because of higher mortality rates that require more than two children to replace their parents.

Morbidity and Mortality

The frequency of disease, illness, injuries, and disabilities in a population is referred to as morbidity, while mortality is about deaths that occur in a population. Both are indicators of the health status of a population and more often than not, a reflection of the standard of living of a population. In Africa, the rate of morbidity is high because of poor environmental sanitation and high prevalence rates of malaria, upper respiratory infections, diarrhoea and other diseases.

The **prevalence rate** is a commonly used measure of morbidity. It is the number of persons in a population who have a disease at a given point in time per 1,000 population. The rate includes all cases that have not resulted in death or cure. The prevalence rate of HIV and AIDS is a good example. It is measured for ages 15- 49 years as shown below:

Number of persons aged
<u>15- 49 with HIV and AIDS</u> x K, where K= 100
Total Population aged
15- 49 years

A simple measure of mortality that is often used is the **Crude Death Rate (CDR),** sometimes referred to as the death rate. It is the number of deaths in the population per 1,000 population in a given year. It is represented mathematically as follows:

<u>Number of deaths</u> x K, where K= 1000
Total population

The mortality rates of those who are most vulnerable to disease and death- infants, underfives and women in their reproductive years- are the most commonly computed mortality rates.

The **Infant Mortality Rate (IMR), i**s the number of deaths of infants (children under age 1) per 1,000 live births in a given year. It is expressed mathematically as:

Number of deaths of infants
<u>under age 1 in a given year</u> x K, where K= 1000.
Total live births in that year

The number of women who die as a result of complications of pregnancy or childbearing in a given year per 100,000 live births in that year is referred to as the **Maternal Mortality Rate or Ratio (MMR)**. It is computed as follows:

<u>Number of maternal deaths</u> x K, where K= 100,000
Total live births

In 2004, the average IMR for the Sub-Saharan African region was 96 compared with 7 for industrialised countries. Current MMR exceeds 1,000 deaths per 100,000 live births in some Sub-Saharan African countries, while it is below ten in many industrialised countries.

A concept used to describe the average number of additional years that a child at birth is expected to live is **Life Expectancy at birth**, often referred to as life expectancy. Life expectancy can be calculated for any other age and is determined principally by the level of development and associated living standard, including access to health service. According to the Population Reference Bureau's estimates for 2004, the average life expectancy at birth was 76 years for the industrialised countries, 65 years for developing countries and as low as 49 years for Sub-Saharan Africa, the world's poorest region..

Population Change

Three processes or events account for changes in any population: births, deaths and migration. **Natural Increase (or Decrease)** is the difference between births and deaths in a population in a given time period, usually a year. It is expressed as:

NI= B-D, where NI is natural increase during the time period, B is births and D is death during the time period

The NI can be expressed as a rate, **Rate of Natural Increase** which is the change in the population size within the given period that is explained by difference in births and deaths as a percentage of the base or initial population. The **Growth Rate** on the other hand is the rate of change, (increasing or decreasing), that takes into account the natural increase and net migration of the population.

A concept of population change referred to as the **Doubling Time,** estimates the length of time it takes a population to double itself if it grows constantly at the current growth rate. It gives a more vivid picture about population change than the natural increase and the growth rate. It is estimated approximately as 70, divided by the growth rate (percent), at which the population is growing constantly and expressed as:

$$\frac{70}{\text{Growth Rate (\%)}}$$

For example, a population that is growing constantly at 2% will double itself in 35 years (70÷2). The populations of most Sub-Saharan African countries have been growing at between 2% and 4% over the past three to four decades. Their populations therefore double between 17 and 35 years, contrasting with the declining populations of Italy and Spain and those of other industrialised countries.

Population projection is the computation of future changes in population numbers by making certain assumptions about future trends in the rates of fertility, mortality, and migration based on different sets of assumptions.

CHAPTER 3

LANGUAGE AND AFRICA
Mary Esther Kropp Dakubu

Language pervades human life. More than anything else, articulate spoken language distinguishes human beings from animals. It is our most useful tool, our most spectacular cultural creation, and at the same time an inherent endowment of our species as well as an inescapable force that gives form to our lives. Human society without the means of communication provided by spoken language is hardly imaginable, and the position of people who for one reason or another cannot speak, for example those born deaf, is very difficult. Such people have to develop language through another medium, usually signed or written language, and those who do not succeed in doing this live barely human lives. In many places in this world, people have regarded those who speak languages different from their own as inferior, uncivilized, perhaps not even quite human. Yet from the earliest known times people who could speak more than one language have played an important role in society and history, although this fact has rarely been acknowledged. Governments pass laws about what language people should use, especially in public and government agencies, and hostility over language issues is unfortunately quite common. All of these things are as true in Africa as anywhere else. Plainly, to understand African cultures and societies in the contemporary context we need to know something about how the language phenomenon is played out on the continent.

In this chapter, we will first think about why language is important in society generally and in Africa in particular, and about the relationship between languages and their speakers. After briefly reviewing the distribution of languages in Africa, we will look at some of the problems related to language, particularly problems related to education and acquiring the culture of literacy.

Language, Society, and Language in African Society

Large numbers of languages are spoken on the continent of Africa. We will look at this more closely later, but anyone living in Africa knows by personal experience that most African countries, especially African countries south of the Sahara, have large numbers of languages. In the face of this diversity of languages, many questions arise. What are the implications of the language situation for education or for national and regional political and economic integration? Is it possible for so many languages to survive and thrive in the modern world? Is it even a good thing that they should? More generally, how do Africans manage to communicate with each other within the same country and how can they communicate regionally? Everything we do as societies and groups of individuals depends on communicating with each other through language. Therefore, the fact that people speak many different languages seems bound to have an effect on their relations with each other.

There is another question that goes even deeper. Language is a very important part of our psychological make-up. We learn our first language as very small children, by interacting with

There is another question that goes even deeper. Language is a very important part of our psychological make-up. We learn our first language as very small children, by interacting with the people closest to us. Because it is part of our earliest personal beginnings, our own or first language, our "mother tongue", tends to symbolize for us what is most precious in our lives. We use this language to express our innermost feelings, through personal conversation and also through poetry, song and story, in literature both oral and written. These artistic expressions of feelings and ideas are considered to be among the supreme creations of the human spirit. What hope is there for understanding each other, if we hide our real feelings and our best creations from each other in languages we do not all understand?

We must realize that these are questions about world society, not just African society. It is no accident that the story of the Tower of Babel is one of the best known stories in the Bible, for it rationalizes linguistic diversity in terms of divine punishment for human hubris or pride. While it is a story of God's punishment for human over-reaching, it is based on an explicit ac-knowledgement of the importance of language for humanity and the power it gives to human beings. It must be one of the earliest arguments ever recorded for the value of a single universal language, although it also condemns the idea. If everyone had a language in common, human beings could rival their Creator! Another way of interpreting the story is that diversity of lan-guages and therefore lack of communication is a metaphor for disunity, and the converse of the principle that there is strength in unity.

On the other hand, if many languages were to disappear because many communities adopted another language that let them communicate with more people, what would the people have lost in terms of culture, social identity, and their individual psychological identities? Do we re-ally want a world, or a country, in which there is only one way of saying things? In fact, there are known cases where languages have indeed disappeared. In the late nineteenth century at least two languages were recorded in the Volta Region of eastern Ghana that by then were only partially remembered by a few elderly people, and have since disappeared completely. It seems their communities were wiped out and scattered by Ashanti invasions. Other cases of "language death" are known from South Africa.

Apart from such drastic events, sections of the speakers of a language quite often shift their language to one spoken by another group of people. Sometimes this is a result of war and domi-nation, sometimes a result of peaceful migration into another language area. It is noticeable that when this happens, the adopted language as used by the new speakers tends to take on new fea-tures, usually brought in from the language the people have given up. Thus in northern Ghana the Nankansi and the Gurensi speak different dialects of Farefare that came into existence partly because the Nankansi once used to speak Kasem and carried over some features of it when they gave it up in favour of Farefare. Even without this kind of influence from another language, a language tends to break up as the community that speaks it grows, diversifies and spreads out. Different parts of the community invariably introduce new features that become characteristic of their way of speaking the language. Thus in south eastern Ghana the Krobo and the Ada speak the Dangme language, but there are definite differences of pronunciation and even of vocabulary. We refer to these kinds of differences, between Nankani and Gurene or between Krobo and Ada, as differences in dialect. They seem to indicate that just as in other areas of culture there is a strong human tendency to introduce changes into languages, reflecting the changing conditions of life and also whether or not different groups communicate with each other often. Consequently, even if a country or a region has a single language, it is rarely uniform. A living language is never static.

It is a sign of how deeply people (not only African people) feel about language that it is often treated as though it had a power of its own. This attitude to language is shown in many attitudes and practices that we take for granted and hardly think about. For instance, nobody likes to be insulted. But what is an insult? There are different ways of insulting someone, but the usual and most powerful way is by saying something, uttering words, that you know will make the other person feel very badly, demeaned and humiliated. It is an extraordinary fact that mere words can do this, even if no one else is around to hear them. That is, language has the power to hurt, quite apart from any other accompanying action. This is even more true of oaths and curses; the very fact of having uttered certain words creates a situation that has to be dealt with. Exactly which words of course will vary from place to place and language to language. When people marry in a Christian ceremony, they become husband and wife by virtue of the fact that a religious authority has uttered the words "I now pronounce you man and wife." Words therefore do more than allow us to communicate with each other; we treat them as if they actually do things, and our ideas about language and the behaviour connected with it are organised in such a way as to make sure that it is true, that in fact they do.

Our feeling for the importance and the power of language is also expressed in many religious practices. In every religion the act of uttering words of prayer is believed to have power. Sometimes the words of prayer and invocation of the deity are disguised by "talking in tongues", which no one can understand except God – the Pentecostal churches adopt this practice. Or the prayer and invocations may be disguised in a secret language that only God and priests or others who have been initiated into its use can understand. Many African religions and cults, including the Yeve cult of the Ewe-speaking people, practise this. Both kinds of disguised language are believed by those who use them to have special powers. The very fact that they feel the need to disguise it is evidence of the power that the believers find inherent in the words being uttered.

In our social interactions, much depends on whether the people we speak with think we are being polite, and whether we in turn think they are responding politely. To a very large extent, it is the words we use that determine whether we are being polite or not. Most languages have words equivalent to "please", "thank you", "excuse me", and it makes a big difference to the nature of our personal relationships that we use them on the proper occasions. If we have to disturb someone at their work we can do so politely and get a positive reaction or rudely and get a negative one, depending on the words we use to do it. The tone of voice we use, our gestures, and other aspects of behaviour that accompany our speech also make a difference to how what we say is received. Every child learning to become part of a society learns that in that society there are certain words you cannot use in speaking to an elder, and other words that you should always use. How we use our language makes a big difference to what people think of us, and our success in life generally.

In many African cultures, terms of address and the use of names are very important, and not always straightforward. Whether or not you are regarded as a sensible, intelligent and responsible person is likely to depend on whether you know how to address people properly. Chiefs are usually addressed in a different way from other people. Wives may be expected to use particular terms when addressing their husbands and members of their husband's family, and to avoid others. The necessity of avoiding certain names is sometimes carried to extreme lengths. Among the Zulu of South Africa, traditionally wives not only have to be careful how they address members of their husband's family, and avoid pronouncing their names, they are not allowed to use ordinary words in ordinary conversation that even sound like names of the husband's close relatives. The women have therefore developed an elaborate parallel vocabulary to make it possible to avoid these words. This practice is known as *hlonipha* (see Finlayson 1978, also Alexandre 1972: 105.)

The South African case is an extreme one, but there are many other instances where people try to avoid certain words, particularly names. Among the Ga of Ghana, children are named after their elders in their grandfather's generation, and to some extent are spiritually identified with the elder whose name they bear. Most people avoid calling these names out loud, since it would be rude to call an elder like that. For this reason a small child may be called "Nii" (grandfather) or "Naa" (grandmother). Many if not most other languages of the area have comparable customs.

It seems that in many places, a person's name is not merely a word. It is thought to have some kind of spiritual power. In some cultures, a person's "real" name is kept secret, because knowledge of it gives the knower power over the owner. (Many folktales refer to this belief. A character finds out the name of another character by trickery and this knowledge gives him power over the other, or enables him to do some difficult task.) Among the Igbo of Nigeria, and in several other societies, men undergo ceremonies to mark specific stages of their lives, and take a new name each time. Even when the belief in the power of names is less strong people may still avoid using a person's "real" name, because frequent use of it might cause suspicions of bad intentions or simply because it is considered rude. For reasons like these, in most of Ghana, adults are commonly known and referred to as "So-and-so's mother" or "So-and-so's father", or some other nickname, rather than their actual name. In many places one can get to know another person very well without learning his or her "real" name.

Another common practice that indicates how seriously people take language and its power is the widespread practice of making sure that the chief's speech is not heard directly by ordinary people. An Akan chief always has a "linguist", a spokesman who officially relays the chief's words to the assembled people. There are many explanations for this practice, ranging from the practical problems that might arise if the chief made a mistake to the spiritual danger to others of his utterance, but generally related to the preservation of power. For similar reasons, Yoruba Obas wear a bead veil that covers the face, so that ordinary people cannot see them speak.

There is actually a great deal of variation in Africa in the way in which people regard the relationship between political power, especially the power of chiefs and kings, and the art of speaking. In Burundi, the Tutsi aristocrats prided themselves on their oratorical ability, which they made an effort to develop, while the Hutu commoners did not learn these skills (Albert, 1964). Among the Mande and the Wolof of Senegal and Mali, on the other hand, skill in oratory and artistic linguistic performance is considered to be unseemly for people of noble birth, who practise dignified reticence. The language arts are left to the griots, who in the past served noble families – their patrons. Today, many griots practice language arts professionally, for money. The attitudes of the Tutsi and the Wolof are quite the opposite of each other, yet both imply that language is a very important aspect of political power, both for what is said and for the way it is said. Although a Mande prince never speaks at length in public, he cannot maintain his political and social position without his griot who does it for him, just as an Akan chief without a linguist is unthinkable.

Not everything to do with language is so serious. People also love playing with language. Jokes and riddles are often about language; they play with the fact that words and expressions in the language have particular intonation patterns, similar sounds but different meanings, or different sounds but similar meanings. Poetry, proverbs, prayers and songs also make use of patterns of sound and meaning that people have noticed in their language, for more serious purposes or just for enjoyment. Depending on the subject matter and what the particular words are associated with, these patterns within the language can be very funny, or they can be very beautiful. They are also very difficult if not impossible to translate. The beauties of the oral art of a particular language are very hard to communicate to those who do not speak it, and the first things to be lost when a language is no longer spoken. Everywhere in Africa people, admire a good orator. S/He does not necessarily express different ideas from other people, indeed most often s/he does not. What people admire is how the orator says it, the way s/he uses the language.(See further Ch. 17)

The Many Languages of Africa

We began with a number of questions related to the facts that a) language is important, and b) Africa is very well supplied, some would say oversupplied, with different languages. People sometimes talk as though multilingualism were a terrible handicap, and that these questions imply that Africa has insoluble communication problems, which are interpreted to mean insoluble development problems. Of course it is true that there are problems, but they are not necessarily insoluble, nor is multilingualism necessarily a major factor in them. As we examine some of the issues involving language and communication we shall not solve the problems, or even suggest solutions, but if we understand the problems better we may find that they need not be problems at all.

Let us take the question of how Africans communicate with each other, given that they speak so many different languages. One way is to use a European language that has been learned in school, but that is not the only solution or even the most widespread one, especially if we look beyond official policies to what happens on the ground. Not only do African countries tend to have a lot of languages, to be multilingual, but their citizens themselves tend to be multilingual. That is, large numbers of people, although of course not all, speak more than one African language. This is especially common in urban areas all over Africa. In southern Ghanaian towns and cities, for example, most people who are not Akans speak a little Akan or Hausa (or both) in addition to their own language. People who travel for trade or work over wide areas often learn a particular language that is spoken by large numbers of people – these are the "languages of wider communication" and include Hausa in the eastern part of West Africa, Dioula in western West Africa, and Swahili in East Africa. Akan in Ghana could also be classified as such, since it is spoken by many people who have different mother tongues. Each of these languages is spoken by millions. Thus people quite often are able to speak a language that is not indigenous to their own country. When a language is spoken among people from different groups and it is not the first language of any of them, it is called a "lingua franca". Many people in Ghana and Togo speak Hausa as a lingua franca, and many people in Tanzania, Uganda and Kenya speak Swahili as such. The kind of spoken Arabic that is learned in schools in the Arabic-speaking countries serves as a lingua franca, although with regional variations, among the educated classes of those countries. So, while it is true that there are indeed problems of communication among the different communities within countries and between countries, it is also certainly true that communication over very wide areas does take place, and was taking place long before European languages appeared on the scene.

Many people fear that, since language plays such a large part in our personal and public lives, multilingualism, especially official multilingualism, will give rise to misunderstandings that can even result in violence. This is mainly because languages are usually associated with particular ethnic groups, who may be perceived as significantly more (or less) powerful than others, or parts of a country that may also be perceived as richer than other areas. When groups or sections within a country are not getting along well, their languages often come to symbolize the differences between them; they become symbols or "indexes" of the opposing groups. When India became independent in the 1950s there were serious riots in major cities over the choice of the official languages, and there were serious demonstrations in South Africa when a previous government made Bantu languages and Afrikaans, rather than English, the languages of all schools for black Africans. Although a few of them (such as Ghana) have sometimes discussed it, West African countries have refrained from making one of their languages the official language for fear of arousing resentments like these, that could lead to serious unrest or even violence. However, to say that multilingualism causes hostility is putting the cart before the horse. The politics of language choice can be quite complicated, but it normally has to do with the ambitions of the social groups associated with the particular languages and not with the nature of the languages themselves, or the mere fact that the languages are many. It would probably be an aid to national integration if there were one single language that everyone could speak, or at least read, for then it would be relatively easy to get a message across to everyone in the country. This does not mean, unfortunately, that the existence of such a language is a guarantee of peace and good will within a country. The very worst inter-communal violence in African countries has occurred in Rwanda, Burundi, and Somalia, countries where everyone speaks the same language. In Somalia there is even a standard written version of the Somali language, yet this does not seem to be a strong force for national unity in that extremely disunited country. Language differences sometimes come to symbolize differences among groups of people, but they are rarely the actual cause.

The Languages of Africa: an Overview

Before we discuss language-related social problems further, since we are specifically interested in Africa it will be useful to have an overview of what languages are spoken on the continent, the relationships among them, and convenient ways of referring to them. A very large percentage of the languages now spoken in the world are spoken in Africa. Most of these are spoken only in Africa, but at least one (Arabic) is spoken on another continent (Asia, in the Near East) as well. Many of Africa's languages are closely related or similar to one another, especially when they are spoken by people who have lived near each other for a long time, Ahanta and Nzema of south western Ghana for example. Others, such as Hausa (in Nigeria and Niger, and spoken as a second language in other countries) and !Kung (in South Africa), are as extremely different as it is possible for languages to be. Some, like Swahili in East Africa and Yoruba in Nigeria, are spoken by millions of people, while others, such as Ebang (Sudan) and Animere (Ghana) are spoken by only a thousand people or less. Whether it is spoken by many millions or a few hundreds, every language is a flexible and dynamic creation of the human mind, that makes communication among people possible about every conceivable topic and on every aspect of its speakers' lives.

One of the first things people ask about African languages is, how many languages are there? One respected contemporary scholar has mentioned the figure of 1,900 (Bendor-Samuel 1989: vi). The truth is, however, that we do not really know. This is partly because the people who write about such things are still discovering that there are people speaking languages the scholars had never heard about. It is also because counting languages is not so easy as we might think. Do the Fante and the Asante speak the same language, or different languages? What about the people who speak Bambara and those who speak Dioula? Or the people of Burundi and the people of Rwanda? It all depends on the criteria you use for separating one language from another. One criterion is whether or not a way of speaking is written. On this criterion, Fante and Asante are different languages because they have different writing systems, and so are Kirundi and Kinyarwanda. Hausa is written very differently in Nigeria and in Niger, which would mean that there are two different Hausa languages. By the same criterion, there is just one language called Arabic.

Another criterion ignores the written form, if any, and says that if people can talk to and understand each other without much difficulty, and without one of them having to spend time to learn the other's language, then they speak the same language, even though there may be obvious dialect differences. If they cannot converse in this way, then they have different languages. By this criterion (known technically as "mutual intelligibility"), Fante and Asante are one and the same language, as are Bambara and Dioula, Kirundi and Kinyarwanda. On the other hand, by this criterion Arabic is really a whole group of languages, because people from different parts of the Arabic-speaking world, say Egypt and Morocco, have considerable difficulty understanding each other if they have not also learned a lingua franca version of the language. (We have met this concept in the foregoing discussion.) People tend to refer to the local ways of speaking Arabic as "local dialects", but they are not at all as similar as, say, the Fante and Akuapem dialects of Akan. People thus have different attitudes to variation within their own language. These differences in attitude, rather than the language differences themselves, may be politically important.

Academic linguists usually employ the second criterion, focusing on the spoken language, because they are interested in finding out the details of all languages, whether written or not, and because large areas of Africa traditionally did not use writing. The estimate of 1,900 African languages is based on this criterion. This does not mean of course that written language is not important. The problem of which written language to use, and how to develop a written language, is a matter of great practical concern for many reasons, as will be discussed below.

With such a large number of languages to deal with and discuss, it is useful to be able to sort them in some way, preferably a way that is based on similarities and differences among them.

Map 3 – Language Families in Africa

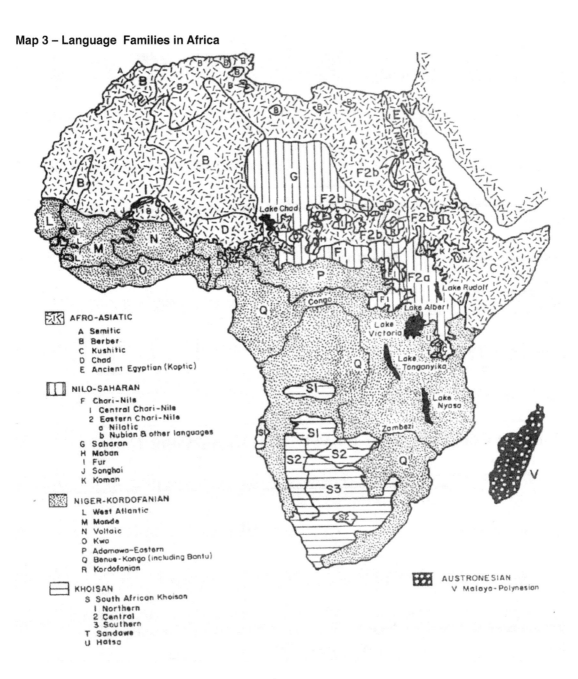

AFRO-ASIATIC
A Semitic
B Berber
C Kushitic
D Chad
E Ancient Egyptian (Koptic)

NILO-SAHARAN
F Chari-Nile
1 Central Chari-Nile
2 Eastern Chari-Nile
a Nilotic
b Nubian & other languages
G Saharan
H Maban
I Fur
J Songhai
K Koman

NIGER-KORDOFANIAN
L West Atlantic
M Mande
N Voltaic
O Kwa
P Adamawa-Eastern
Q Benue-Kongo (including Bantu)
R Kordofanian

KHOISAN
S South African Khoisan
1 Northern
2 Central
3 Southern
T Sandawe
U Hatsa

AUSTRONESIAN
V Malayo-Polynesian

Courtesy Awedoba, A.K., 2005 *Culture & Development in Africa with Special Reference to Ghana page* 62; Institute of African Studies, University of Ghana, Legon

The indigenous languages of Africa have been classified into four huge groups, known as families or "phyla": Niger-Congo, Khoisan, Nilo-Saharan, and Afro-Asiatic. Not everyone accepts this grouping, but it is more widely accepted than any other and is convenient to use. It means that as far as we can tell, all the languages of Africa trace their descent back to one of just four languages, which must have been spoken many thousands of years ago. On the ground they are arranged, more or less, with Afro-Asiatic languages in the far north, Khoisan languages in the far south, Niger-Congo languages in the west but spreading southeastwards into the southern half of the continent, and Nilo-Saharan languages in the east and central regions.

Only the Afro-Asiatic family is native to more than one continent; the Niger-Congo, Khoisan and Nilo-Saharan languages are spoken only in Africa (apart of course from languages carried by recent migrants from Africa to other parts of the world). Most branches of Afro-Asiatic in fact are strictly African – including Ancient Egyptian, Berber languages, the Cushitic languages of Somalia and Ethiopia, and the Chadic branch that includes Hausa. However the Semitic branch, that includes Hebrew and Arabic, first developed in the Near East. A sub-branch migrated back to Africa and became the modern Ethiopian Semitic languages which include Amharic and Tigre. Today of course there are large Arabic speaking communities in Africa, especially North Africa, that have been there for a thousand years or more.

Map 4 – The Niger-Congo Language Family

Courtesy Awedoba, A.K., 2005 *Culture & Development in Africa with Special Reference to Ghana page 62*; Institute of African Studies, University of Ghana, Legon.

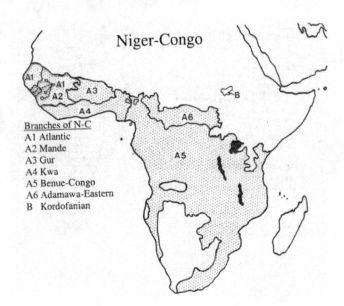

Niger-Congo

Branches of N-C
A1 Atlantic
A2 Mande
A3 Gur
A4 Kwa
A5 Benue-Congo
A6 Adamawa-Eastern
B Kordofanian

The largest family of African languages by far is the one called Niger-Congo, with more than a thousand languages, stretching without interruption from Senegal to South Africa. It has even been claimed (Heine and Nurse 2000: 11) that it is the largest family of languages in the world, with 1,436 languages included in it. If this is true, then the figure mentioned above, of 1,900 languages for all of Africa, is certainly too small! The Niger-Congo family of languages includes all the languages indigenous to Sierra Leone, Guinea, Liberia, Cote d'Ivoire, Ghana, Togo and most of the Republic of Benin, the languages of southern and most of central Nigeria, and the huge group of languages known as Bantu that spreads throughout the southern half of the continent.

The smallest family is the Khoisan. These languages, numbering about 30, are spoken far to the south, mainly in South Africa, Botswana and Namibia, by small numbers of people. Before historical times there undoubtedly were more of these languages, spoken by more people. Today the largest is Nama, spoken by about 100,000 people. The Nilo-Saharan languages spoken in central and east Africa range from Kanuri, the language of Maiduguri in north-eastern Nigeria, to the language of the Maasai in northern Tanzania. The Songhai language (known in Ghana as Zabrama) of the north-eastern part of the Niger valley in West Africa has also been grouped with these languages, although some scholars disagree.

As far as sound features are concerned, African languages generally (but not every individual language) are noted for the sounds kp and gb and for the important role played by differences in the tone or pitch of syllables in making distinctions among words and grammatical forms. The Khoisan languages are famous for their unique "click" sounds, a type of consonant that occurs nowhere else in the world and that was made famous by South African singer Miriam Makeba, with her "Click Song". Because of this they have sometimes been called the Click languages. There is a large specialist literature on these matters (for further information see the bibliography, especially Sebeok [Ed.] 1971; Bendor-Samuel [Ed.] 1989; Heine and Nurse [Eds.] 2000).

African Multilingualism

An important aspect of the distribution of languages in Africa is that most countries are "multilingual" – that is, several languages are spoken in a country, not just by foreigners and immigrants but by the indigenous inhabitants. Some African countries are more multilingual than others. Most of North Africa is Arabic speaking, but Morocco, Mauritania, Algeria, Libya, all have minorities that speak indigenous Berber languages, and southern Egypt has Nubian (Nilo-Saharan) languages. In Sub-Saharan Africa we can mention as relatively "monolingual" (that is, having only one indigenous language) Botswana (mainly Setswana but also Khoisan languages), Lesotho (which was deliberately set up to include one ethnic group with one language), Somalia, Rwanda and Burundi. However, most countries have anything from half a dozen indigenous languages to several hundred. Nigeria is the most diverse of all, with more than 500 languages, including several from each of the main groups except Khoisan. Perhaps this is not surprising, since Nigeria also has the largest population of any African country. Yet Egypt, with the next largest population, is one of the countries where only one language is spoken by the vast majority. Tanzania, while not an especially large country in terms of population, is unique in that it has at least one language from all four great families, although most of the people speak Bantu (Niger-Congo) languages.

African multilingualism becomes even more impressive when we recognize that while the continent has almost 2,000 indigenous languages, spoken by anywhere from a few hundred to several million people each, these are by no means the whole story. Numerous languages of European origin, mainly French, English and Portuguese and to a lesser extent Spanish play an important role in communication within African countries, between African countries, and between Africa and the rest of the world. In many countries one of them is the "official" language, spoken and written for all governmental and educational purposes. According to the language used these countries are called anglophone, francophone, lusophone or hispanophone, even though in most cases only a small fraction of the population is fluent or even literate in the language. In some areas such languages have been "indigenized", and are the mother tongues of African communities. The Krio of Freetown, a development from English, is one of these. Another is the Portuguese of the Azores. We must also mention Afrikaans, a development from Dutch. It is the language not only of the descendants of European settlers in South Africa known as the Boers, but of many other people, especially in the hinterland of Cape Town. However, for most Africans, European languages are still foreign, learned in school, and since many Africans still do not go to school this means that many do not learn any. At the same time, we have to admit that many African cities have "street" versions of the official European language, for instance Pidgin English in Nigeria, and the popular French of Abidjan and Dakar. The fact that these unofficial versions of official languages have appeared and seem to be growing indicates just how practically important they are for ordinary people. In a city like Accra, English is part of the popular repertoire, so that most people speak at least one of Akan, Hausa, and English, and not a few speak all three – one language of Ghanaian origin, one of Nigerian origin, and one imported from Europe, not to mention Ga, the indigenous language of Accra, and/or their mother tongue.

The proper language to be used in formal education under these conditions has been the subject of debate for more than a century. Obviously the choice is important. Language is the single most important tool available to teachers and learners; it is simply not possible to teach someone who has no language, but a child who knows a language can certainly be taught. There have been historic cases of teachers who succeeded in teaching a child who had been deaf and dumb from early childhood and never acquired a language (the American Anne Mansfield Sullivan, the teacher of Helen Keller, is a famous example) – but what made these teachers especially outstanding was that they found ways to teach the child a language. Knowledge of a language is the basis of all further learning. Every normal African child learns a language, and therefore can be taught, or what is more important, can learn. So what is the problem?

If there is a problem, it seems to be related to the fact that there are so many languages to use – an embarrassment of riches, so to speak. Providing teachers and reading materials for the children of every language community in a country such as Ghana or Nigeria, or any of their neighbours, is logistically and financially a daunting prospect. We may therefore wonder whether the presence of a European language, usually inherited from a former colonial power, has been an advantage or a disadvantage, since it adds another to the plethora already existing. On the positive side, we recognize that exactly because of their recent colonial past the European languages used in Africa are the big ones, spoken world wide and not only in their home countries and Africa. English in particular is still spreading as a language of science, learning, diplomacy, technology and international business. Even speakers of very large languages with old, well established literatures, such as French, Arabic and even Chinese, are busy learning English for these very practical purposes. To many it seems obvious, therefore, that it is advantageous to the citizens of any African country that English should be the language of education. French is not growing as an international lingua franca in the way that English is, but it is still spoken and written by many millions more than most African languages, so the same argument holds for francophone countries as for anglophone.

Another advantage, perhaps, is that it is easier and more economically efficient, and also more equitable, to produce books and teaching materials in just one language for everyone. If different parts of the country are using books in different languages it is more difficult to ensure that all the books intended for Class 4, for example, are at the same level and of the same quality. And it is obviously cheaper to publish a book once in one language instead of in twenty languages.

Another common argument is that using a single external language means that no group has an advantage over any other, as you would if your language but not someone else's were the language used in school and Parliament. If the language is foreign to everybody, all are equally at a disadvantage, according to this argument.

On the other hand, there are counter arguments to all of these. Probably no one would argue against introducing one of the major European languages at some stage of the educational process, since that seems to be the trend world-wide, and it is important that some (at least) of a country's citizens should be able to communicate with the rest of the world. The disagreements are likely to be about what language should be used in the early years of schooling. One problem is that the easy availability of materials in English or French sometimes results in failure to create learning materials in any language whether local or foreign that are relevant and meaningful to young children in the local context. Where such materials have eventually become available it has often taken a very long time, decades after independence, for education authorities to see the need for them. It is too easy to take over what someone else has already done, even if it is nearly meaningless to the children and teachers who use it.

We may also argue that it is not really true that having a foreign language as the language of education puts everyone at an equal disadvantage. However, instead of the advantage going to those whose mother tongue is the official one, or one of the local languages used in school, it goes to those whose parents have the money to pay for private schools that give their children a head start in the language, or even to take them abroad. The inequality is then based on economic class, rather than region or ethnic group.

Since teachers and pupils alike depend on language to communicate with each other, it is natural to expect that children will learn best when they understand the language they are being taught in. Indeed, the educational psychologists who study these things are unanimous that children learn everything much better when they at least begin their schooling in their own language. Children learn new languages fast, and there are many countries where they get their schooling quite successfully in a second language. Nevertheless, even children in rich countries with relatively well funded school systems learn to read best in the school language when they have first learned to read in their own. Learning to read and learning a new language are not the same thing, and children who have to do both at once have a very difficult task. It is not really surprising that so many find it beyond them and drop out of school. It can be argued that since learning to read for the first time in the mother tongue is much more efficient, and results in a much lower school drop-out rate and better performance in all subjects, it is actually more cost-efficient to teach the early grades in the children's own language, not English, despite the higher initial cost. If a child cannot even write his/her name after being taught in English for five years, as happens in many Ghanaian schools, then those five years have been a complete waste of money.

It is sometimes argued that African languages don't have the vocabulary for use in modern educational and other public contexts. The implication seems to be that unlike other languages that have adapted to modern needs, African languages are not so flexible. Or is it their speakers that are thought to be inflexible? At any rate it is quite unfounded. Languages change to fulfill the needs of their speakers, and as the culture develops, so does the language. If it is thought necessary, the speakers can deliberately intervene to develop new ways of speaking their language.

The case of Swahili provides an interesting example of deliberate modernization and a contrast to what pertains in most West African countries. It is the only case of an African language being adopted as an official general language in a highly multilingual country. Swahili was not at first a major language in Tanzania, at least not in the sense of being the mother tongue of a dominant community. It is the native language of a very small group on the coast of Tanzania and on Zanzibar, but that small group is and was very active in trade, and in pre-colonial times it became widely known as a trade language, a lingua franca among the people the Swahilis traded with and especially those who worked for them. In colonial times, first the Germans and then the British found it very useful, and encouraged its use in the colonial administration, partly because Tanzania is very fragmented linguistically, with no language spoken by more than about a tenth of the population (Polomé and Hill 1980). Under the British, an East African Swahili Committee was founded to develop new vocabulary and determine the proper spelling of the language. This eventually became the Institute of Swahili Research in the University of Dar es Salaam. Newspapers were published, and the language became the language of primary schooling everywhere in the country. English was maintained as the language of higher education, but there is no doubt that the general adoption of Swahili has been a major factor in making literacy nearly universal in Tanzania. Another advantage, according to those who support this approach, is that there is less danger that a serious linguistic divide will develop between the educated elite and the rest of the people, since although Swahili is not so much used at post-secondary levels it is nevertheless a language of both oral and written communication used at all levels of society throughout the country. In Uganda and Kenya, with much larger competing indigenous communities, no such development took place, even though in those countries too Swahili is very widely spoken as a lingua franca.

Language, Writing and Education

It is noticeable that the debate over what language should be used for what purpose is really not about what languages should be spoken, except at the very earliest levels of education, but about what languages should be adopted for reading and writing. It is therefore worth reflecting on the relationship between spoken and written language. It can be viewed in different ways. We can look at a language as an abstract system of signs and the rules for using them. This system can then be expressed in a variety of media – usually, the medium of oral audible speech, or the medium of material visible writing. Computer languages are expressed in invisible, inaudible electronic signals and can also be expressed in a special form of writing. In historical fact, however, the written languages that we know have been derived from spoken languages.

That is, a spoken language existed before a way was devised of expressing it in a visible form that could be read and understood even when the original writer, substituting for a speaker, was not around. There is no doubt that spoken language is our primary mode of communication. No human culture has existed without a spoken language, but most have existed without ever writing it down.

Spoken language goes back to the earliest beginnings of humanity, but written language goes back only about 5,000 years. Many cultures use pictures and abstract signs to represent ideas. These visible images can serve as reminders of ideas, provided those who see them know what they mean. They can be painted, carved, woven, or represented in any other available visual medium. For example, the Akan adinkra symbols are stamped onto cloths, carved as emblems on linguists' staffs or even cast as cement blocks, to represent proverbs and sayings. However although they may be said to "mean" a particular proverb, they do not represent it as language; one cannot use them to represent a specific series of words that have never been depicted before. This is exactly what spoken language can do, and what writing can also do, by matching visible graphic signs to audible spoken ones, word by word. As I write these words I can imagine myself saying them out loud, and as you read them you could repeat them out loud and sound almost exactly the same as I would, and understand it, I hope, as well as if I were there with you. Probably, writing in this sense, as a direct representation of spoken language that can easily be converted back to speech, has been invented only once, in ancient Sumer in the area of what is now southern Iraq around 3,000 BC. All other forms of writing that we know of, including Ancient Egyptian hieroglyphics and the oldest forms of Chinese writing, seem to have been acquired, adapted and developed from this original invention, directly or more often indirectly. This includes the alphabetic writing that most of us use today, and the Latin method of writing from which it has been developed over the past 2,000 years (Gelb 1962).

Most African languages, especially the languages of Sub-Saharan Africa, were not written before modern times. Most of those that have writing systems acquired them only after contact with either the Arabic or the European literacy-based trading cultures. We might wonder why this is so. Today, the fact that a language is written has acquired a certain prestige. Many people think that if a language is written as well as spoken it must be somehow more advanced than one that is not, and that its speakers must therefore also be somehow more advanced. The written form thus becomes a symbol of the prestige of a language, and therefore of its speakers. However if we think about the main uses of writing, and what the ancient cultures that had writing used it for, we can perhaps see why traditional cultures were not inspired to invent it. Most of the written records that we have from ancient Sumer (not written with pen and ink but scratched into clay tablets, which were then baked to preserve them) are bureaucratic records, of things like taxes and inventories. The Ancient Egyptian writings are also of this kind or they are religious, not so much theology as incantations, spells and prayers, which were considered powerful in written as well as in spoken form, and instructions about how to perform rituals properly. Bureaucratic records and religious formulae account for the bulk of what the ancients used writing for. Letters to absent friends, newspapers and story books came much later, and were never the original reason for adopting writing. Even in today's modern states many people use reading and writing mainly for business purposes, especially if they get their news and entertainment mainly from television. In the absence of a bureaucratic state, therefore, and in the absence of an elaborately codified state religion, our forebears did not feel any need for writing. Nowadays of course things are quite different; no state and no society that hopes for material prosperity can do without writing.

It is not true of course that no ancient Africans had writing, for Ancient Egyptian writing is junior only to that of Sumer. Other indigenous writing systems include the script used by Ethiopian languages like Amharic, which is a development of the ancient writing system of south Arabia (not Arabic), and the North African Berber writing system, not much practiced today, which is also ancient. The original purposes of the Ethiopian writing system were religious. Several Sub-Saharan languages, including Swahili and Hausa, began to be written in Arabic-style script a few hundred years ago, after its speakers came into contact with Arabs, their religion, their trading culture and their writing. However most African languages have acquired writing within the past century and a half, either through the efforts of Christian missionaries or encouraged by them, and therefore using the Latin-derived writing systems of those missionaries' own languages. These writing systems have been spread by teaching them in schools whose original aim was to create a literate class of Christian clerks. Here too, the original purpose of introducing writing was bureaucracy, business and religion.

Whether we read and write mainly in our own language or in another that we have to learn for the purpose, becoming literate is always a complex process, and some people have more talent for it than others. Learning those peculiar signs and how to put them together seems simple once we have done it, but it is not. One problem is that although the written language is based on the spoken language and reflects it, there is never an exact match between what is spoken and what is written. This is partly because many of the subtleties of spoken language, inflections and emphases of the voice, not to mention syllable tones, are difficult if not impossible to write with our present system. This is why we speak of a language being "reduced" to writing, at the same time that we consider this "reduction" a form of "development!" More generally, the difficulty comes from the inherent nature of language. A major reason for writing is the desire that the language product should endure over time. We want to read something written five or fifty years ago and still understand it. Therefore a system of spelling and writing must be conservative. If we want people distant in time or space to understand what we write, we must stick to some common form of the language that should not change too quickly. Yet, we have seen that change is part of the dynamic of a living language. To come back to the language of education, this means that as in every other aspect of our lives, there can never be a final perfect solution. Even English speaking children have to learn a "correct" way to write their language, because nobody anywhere speaks exactly like the written standard, although some people's spoken language is much more like the written language than other people's. Still, it is undeniably less of a strain to learn with a language that you hear around you every day than with one you never hear, or hear spoken only by people who do not speak it very well. The character of the African societies of the future will depend very much on how these problems are recognized and dealt with today.

Review Questions

1. How do you address older people in your own language? Do you address them all in the same way? What would be the consequences of behaving differently?

2. What is the significance of the fact that drumming in Africa is often based on spoken language?

3. What languages, besides the local language, do most people in your town speak, and why? Do you know how to write your own language, or would you like to? If not, why not?

4. Which African countries use an African language in the national government? for local government? for university teaching? Which countries use a foreign language?

References and Suggested Further Reading

Albert, E. M., 1964. "Rhetoric", "Logic" and "Poetics" in Burundi; cultural patterning of speech behaviour. American Anthropologist 66.6,2: 35-54.

Alexandre, P. 1972. *An Introduction to Language and Languages in Africa*. Translated by F.A. Leary. London, Ibadan and Nairobi: Heinemann.

Amonoo, R. F., 1989. *Language and Nationhood: Reflections on Language Situations with Particular Reference to Ghana*. Accra: Ghana Academy of Arts and Sciences.

Bamgbose, A. (Ed.), 2000. *International Journal of the Sociology of Language 141: Sociolinguistics in West Africa*. Berlin: Mouton de Gruyter.

Bendor-Samuel, J. (Ed.), 1989. *The Niger-Congo Languages*. London and Lanham, Md.: University Press of America, Inc.

Boadi, L.K.A., 1994. *Linguistic Barriers to Communication in the Modern World*. Accra: Ghana Academy of Arts and Sciences.

Dakubu, M.E. Kropp, (Ed.). 1988. *The Languages of Ghana*. London: Kegan Paul International.

Finlayson, R. 1978. "A preliminary survey of hlonipa among the Xhosa." *Taalfasette* 24.2: 48-63.

Gelb, I.J., 1963. *A Study of Writing*. 2nd edition. Chicago and London: University of Chicago Press.

Heine, B. and D. Nurse, (Eds.). 2000. *African Languages, an Introduction*. Cambridge: Cambridge University Press.

Polomé, E. C. and C.P. Hill, (Eds.), 1980. *Language in Tanzania*. Oxford University Press.

Sebeok, T. A., (Ed.). 1971. *Current Trends in Linguistics Vol.6: Linguistics in South West Asia and North Africa. Vol.7: Linguistics in Sub-Saharan Africa*. The Hague and Paris: Mouton.

Yankah, K. 1995. *Speaking For the Chief, Okyeame and the Politics of Akan Royal Oratory*. Bloomington and Indianapolis: Indiana University Press.

SECTION 2: CULTURAL, SOCIAL & POLITICAL INSTITUTIONS

CHAPTER 4

GENDER AND SOCIETY IN AFRICA- AN INTRODUCTION
Akosua Adomako Ampofo

A woman gave birth to a king. – Akan proverb

Introduction

In African societies proverbs contain and reflect the wisdom, philosophies, religion, customs, traditions and practices of the people. The proverb referred to above demonstrates that African people recognise the inherent complementarity of the sexes and view women and men as mutually interdependent. Thus, while the ultimate authority figure among Akan states in Ghana is a male ruler, women, and not even necessarily biological mothers, are seen as necessary to bear, nurture, raise and train men to the point where they can become fitting kings. Recognition of the importance of a "mother" in producing the king also helps us to understand the rationale for having a *queen mother* in the Akan system to select the king and counterbalance his powers, evidence of the appreciation of different gender roles for females and males. In this chapter, attention is drawn to the multiple ways in which African societies are gendered, and the specific ways in which the relations between women and men impact on societies and the lives of individuals, with particular reference to the Ghanaian context. The chapter also introduces students to the concept of gender and its usefulness as an analytical tool for assessing the social, cultural, political and economic conditions of African societies. The discussion focuses on women and men's relative positions in two major areas, namely (1) family, work and livelihoods, and (2) leadership, politics and citizenship. Specific changes that may have occurred over time in gender roles and practices from the "pre-colonial", through the "colonial" to the "post-colonial"/contemporary time are also examined.

In examining the relative situations of women and men in African societies a few factors need to be borne in mind. The first is that Africa is a vast continent with diverse peoples, cultures, languages and historical experiences (see also Chapters 1, 3, 6). Thus, while the Chapter makes some general observations, it urges sensitivity to unique local differences. For example, while "female genital mutilation" has been widely discussed as a violation of women's rights in Africa, it can be noted that the operation is actually practised in a minority of African societies,

94

and that there are different forms with varying physical and psychological effects.[1] Secondly, while this chapter uses gender as the lens through which peoples' lives and relationships are examined, it is important to stress that there are several other factors such as class or economic status, ethnicity, and age that also affect the position and situation of women and men in Africa; thus girls born into middle-class, affluent homes are more likely to complete university and end up in decision-making positions than sons of peasant farmers. The third point concerns the use of the terms "pre-colonial," "colonial" and " post-colonial," to delineate social, political events, processes and outcomes and to suggest historical and political changes, as if these were discrete and completely cut-off periods.[2]

What is Gender?

The term *gender* has become popular not only in academic and development discourse but also in everyday parlance. For many it is simply a synonym for "women", as if men also do not have a gender. For others it serves as a code to point to inequalities between the sexes, although as noted earlier, there are many other dimensions of inequality. Thus while it can be argued that gender was not the most significant stratifying principle in "traditional" African societies, even among African societies that exhibited several complementarities between men and women, still men as a group generally had more rights and privileges than women. Many of women's rights and their enjoyment of certain privileges were tied to their relationships to men (as their fathers, husbands or brothers) or, as in some societies, to women becoming "men" in a social sense. In the contemporary period, Western ideas about gender have been introduced through academic scholarship, the media, multinational corporations, development agencies and national governments. Together they affect gender relations and the relative position of women and men in Africa today both positively and negatively.

While almost everyone is born with a particular sex and we are either female or male, we are not *born* with a gender, but *grow into* one, or are given one. We can say therefore that females and males are born, but women and men are made. Thus gender is useful as a social construct which is defined by the beliefs, norms and practices of particular societies. For example, we generally determine that someone is a girl or woman if she behaves in a manner the society considers to be feminine. Likewise someone is defined as a boy or man if he fits generally accepted constructions of being masculine. It is these social and local understandings of gender that determine what it means to be feminine or masculine and what the appropriate behaviours for women and men, girls and boys are, or should be. It should thus be clear that these understandings will not be the same across the world or even among different societies in Africa. Nor are they fixed in time, but rather they can change over the life course. Thus, it is possible to be a biological female, but belong to the male gender and vice versa. We will use two examples to illustrate that gender is not necessarily equal to sex.

The Concept of Gender: 'Female Husbands' and Men who become Women

Among some African societies, biological females were allowed to do "men's work", to inherit property and titles and marry other women, thus becoming *de jure* men. This institution of social marriage between two women was practised among the Igbo of south western Nigeria, some communities in East Africa such as the Agikuyu, Akamba and Nandi of Kenya, the Nuer of Sudan and the Lovedu of South Africa. These "woman-woman" marriages have been documented in more than 30 societies throughout Africa (Duley and Edwards, 1986). The female husbands were not expected to dress or behave like men in order for the rights and responsibilities of husbands and fathers to be bestowed on them. Rather, the practice centred around procreation, and particular females became "men" by marrying wives and raising children for their patrilineages. Essentially the female husband married another woman by paying the bridewealth for her, and then selected a suitable male genitor to father children for her with this wife. Among the Nuer, if the wife had sexual relations with a man the female husband had not approved, the latter could demand damages from the offending man. The wife's children by the male genitor belonged to the female husband. She had full control over them, and the children would address the female husband as "father". In the East African groups where woman-to-woman marriage was practised, women who were legally married to men but who were unable to have children themselves, or who had only given birth to daughters could "marry" women to have sons for them. Among the Igbos and Lovedu, a man without an heir could choose a daughter to be his "son". These "female sons" then became the heads of their families and were expected to marry other women to raise heirs for the family or lineage. While the practise was essentially intended to ensure the continuation of the lineage, wealthy women married to men could also marry wives thus strengthening their social status and the economic importance of their households. While some have tried to suggest that the practice of woman-to-woman marriage is proof of same-sex sexual relations between women, there is no evidence that there were sexual relations between the female husband and her female wife.

Although gender concepts seem to privilege maleness, and thus females who took on male characteristics or roles also enjoyed the privileges normally accorded men, social gender roles were not neatly assigned to biological sex or to the male status (see Figure 2 below). The second example taken from among the nomadic Gabra of Kenya (Wood, 1999) helps us understand the ways in which sex and gender are not necessarily synonymous. Among the Gabra, when boys became men they moved outside the main camp, while women lived inside, in the main camp. When the men became elders, they became *d'abella* and moved from the outside where the other men were, to the main camp inside to be with the women, where by definition and ritually they became female. We can thus consider them to be "male women".

Inside the camp they become custodians of, and responsible for, the reproduction of tradition. They took charge of ceremonies and prayers and on formal and ceremonial occasions they were referred to with the feminine pronoun. As with the female husbands, the Gabra men who moved into the female space would not begin to behave like women per se, even though several elements of their behaviour, practices assigned to them and even their dress can be said to "belong" to the "side of women" (Wood, 1999:66). For example, they would squat to urinate, rather than stand up and hold their penises.

D'abella also shared restrictions and prohibitions which applied to women: they were no longer allowed to eat meat from animals killed by natural causes; they could not, like other men, wear sacrificial blood on their foreheads nor use the red ceremonial paint used by men. Among the Gabra the left is associated with female, and while *d'abella* do not dress like women, they tie their cloth on the left side of their body and wear the seams of their turbans on the left.

Figure 2 – WoDaabe Fullani Youth at the Geerewal (Beauty Contest)

Credit: *Carol Beckwith and Angela Fisher- http://www.africanceremonies.com/*

They also receive tobacco with their left hand rather than the right. *D'abella*, like women, are expected to smell good, and it is interesting that smelling good is associated with health, cleanliness and purity, which are considered as female characteristics among the Gabra. There are several other notions that liken *d'abella* to women, but we can conclude by examining their roles as mothers and reproducers. Children are not expected to be afraid of *d'abella*, just as they are not supposed to fear women. In this sense *d'abella* are like mothers and belong to the class of individuals whom children do not fear because just as places where mothers are serve as locations of safety and comfort for their children, so would spaces inhabited by *d'abella* and indeed *d'abella* themselves, serve as sanctuaries for the wider Gabra society. Thus, if a man was pursued by an enemy he only had to touch the hem of a *d'abella's* cloth or grab a pole within his tent to find protection. Further, just as mothers were secluded after childbirth, when Gabra men became *d'abella*, they too would be secluded, and they shared with women the same term used for the seclusion, *ulma*.

We noted earlier that female husbands do not engage in same-sex sexual intercourse; in the same way *d'abella* are not homosexuals. They continue to have sexual intercourse with their wives and lovers with whom they may have children and they remain heads of their households. It should therefore be clear from these two examples that gender is not necessarily equal to sex. Male does not necessarily = "man" and female does not necessarily = "woman" in the strict biological sense. In fact, contrary to some arguments that have been made against the usefulness of gender as a significant concept in Africa, the fact that biological sex does not seem to separate people into neat, discrete, distinct, or separable categories for all time, would be an argument for the value of gender as an analytical category in Africa. Both the female husbands and the *d'abella* remain biologically female and male respectively, but assume a gender that typically belongs to the opposite sex. *D'abella* do not become *female* nor do female husbands become *male* (sex); however *d'abella* do become social *women* while female husbands become social *men* (gender). Thus *d'abella*, male women, are distinct from female husbands. Further, Gabra men only become *d'abella* late in life as do female husbands, who attain this status as a result of particular circumstances such as infertility or the absence of a male heir. This option to "change" gender was especially true in times of crisis such as inability to bear children, or the absence of men to take up particular roles.

Historicising the Gender Paradigm

Since the series of United Nations international conferences on women first initiated in the mid 1970s, there has been a growing interest in understanding the relative position of women and men within social institutions, political structures, and family relationships, especially in developing countries. Within these contexts, the interest has also been with women's and men's relative access to economic, social and political resources. Most of the studies undertaken to examine these issues reveal that women are not equal beneficiaries with men of Africa's resources. They also reveal that today women lag behind men on most of the indicators of well-being such as access to education, health care, credit, and land; enjoyment of human rights, and so forth. Further, women's positions and contributions in the course of history have been subsumed or hidden, within larger social themes that have tended to reveal men's lives and experiences as the experiences of all human beings. For example, while it is generally well known that many men went to prison during Africa's struggles for independence, the fact that women also joined actively in these struggles and some also ended up in prison is less well known.[3] Hence, recent scholarship on gender in Africa reflects a fundamental interest in uncovering the attitudes and practices that support inequalities in women and men's lives. Essentially gender studies in Africa seek to do two things: (1) To shed light on women's contributions to African societies by reclaiming their histories (often referred to as *herstories;* and (2) To show how women and men have experienced, and continue to experience social, political and economic conditions and changes differently.[4]

In order to understand *gender* it is useful to understand the concepts of feminism and patriarchy, from which it was born, since these are parent and grandparent as it were of the concept of gender. There are several brands and strands of feminism but at a minimum they share the following components: 1) A recognition that women as a group generally suffer from greater inequalities in the world we live in than men, not because of some inherent deficiencies, as some had previously thought, but because societies are structured in ways that privilege men relative to women. This male privilege is referred to as patriarchy, which comes from the literal meaning, "the rule of the fathers". 2) A commitment to bringing about greater equality between women and men. This goal is to be achieved via two routes. One of these is through the work of activists and practitioners to make laws, policies, and even influence public thinking to be non-discriminatory and more female friendly. The second route is through the study of women and men's relative positions in order to understand *how* these inequalities manifest and are created, transmitted and reproduced. For example this recognition and commitment to bringing about greater equality between women and men led to the establishment of the Association of African Women for Research and Development (AAWORD) in Dakar, Senegal in 1977, which envisioned an agenda for African feminism through scholarship and activism.

Initially efforts to "improve" the lot of African women, especially among Western scholars and development organisations, were directed at extending the benefits of development to include women, hence the Women in Development (WID) paradigm. Several activities were initiated at local, national, regional and international levels to "integrate women into development". Usually this was done by providing women with services and resources that they had lacked such as health care, credit, and so forth, so that they could participate *in* development. Subsequently it was argued through the Women and Development (WAD) paradigm that women *were*, or had in fact always been actively involved in development through their many activities such as farming and trading, and even care of children and families, but that it was the development process itself that was problematic and needed to be envisioned. Eventually there was a shift to the Gender and Development (GAD) perspective that stressed the nature of relations between women and men which, in turn, was predicated on notions of masculinity, femininity and appropriate behaviours and spaces for females and males. This shift was intended to provoke analysis of the social and structural factors that underpin women's and men's unequal positions, including the differential impact of policies and programmes on them.

The academic study of gender in Africa generally grew out of African feminists' concerns with the need to develop debates and theories grounded in the continent's unique contexts rather than relying mainly on Western sociological and feminist theorising. Thus, an African gender analysis is grounded in an understanding and appreciation of our historical experiences, including imperialism and racism, as well as how our "traditional" societies were configured

Women and Men in Africa

Family, Work and Livelihoods

The constructions of gender among so-called pre-colonial African people often meant that women had available to them a number of different roles that were complementary to those of men and played important social roles as mothers, sisters, wives, chiefs, queens and priestesses. Scholars of Akan society, for example, note several characteristics of gender relations that suggest marked jural equality, a lack of basic sex discrimination in the roots of the kinship terminology and similar social commitments and responsibilities. Studies of coastal Ga and Fante women traders of Ghana note their financial autonomy and household decision-making clout. However, if we apply the criteria usually employed in analyses of status – power, wealth, and social position – women as a whole enjoyed fewer of these than men. Colonial rule, when it came, allowed a few women to have access to modern education, which provided them with new opportunities for autonomy. However, in other respects colonial rule removed certain traditional structures which had allowed considerable autonomy, such as independent access to resources and economic ventures, and the mutual dependence of the sexes based on an efficient division of labour. In their place, the colonial rulers introduced new forms of subordination through differential access to the resources in the "modern" economy. While the above summary is an over simplification since there exists no "generic" pre-modern period, it is also true that certain structural impositions of the colonial and modern states have had implications for the relative positions of men and women. Thus, it is necessary to read accounts by "outsiders" with caution as they sometimes present distortions that arise out of using a different cultural lens. For example, several European accounts about African marriage contend that these were devoid of romantic love because of the practice of so-called arranged marriages. This was because Europeans interpreted the practice as being similar to that found in Europe between royal households to cement an empire. Certainly the kings and rulers of African kingdoms and states also sought to cement political alliances by arranging marriages between their daughters and sons. However, by and large marriage in Africa remains a relationship between two families, often from related lineages, who both have a vested interest in the survival of the marriage and the well-being of the couple. Since the families of both the bride and the groom are interested that heirs may be produced, labour power provided, and familial and social ties cemented, they would rarely foist an entirely unwilling spouse on their children. Families spent considerable time and diplomacy in learning about the prospective spouse and determining the opinions of their own daughters and sons.

Much of the late 19th and early 20th century studies of Africa by Western anthropologists and historians describe men and women's lives and experiences in binary, opposite, and hierarchical terms. So, for example, women were described as being located "in the home" or the "private sphere," while men were described as being present in the "public space", thereby implying that men's lives as hunters and warriors were more highly valued than women's work as subsistence food providers or reproducers of the family. More recent scholarship argues that men's and women's relationships then were probably a lot more complementary and supportive of each other than they are today, even as they operated in different spheres of social, economic, and political life. This does not mean that there were no hierarchical relationships. Quite the contrary, hierarchy and respect for seniors and elders were very important. However, individuals might be hierarchically related to each other in some, but not in other areas and relationships, rather than a generally global view that all men were superior to all women. Women and men each had their responsibilities and obligations – to their lineages, to their clans, to marriage partners and affines, as well as to their children.

To understand the organisation of work and livelihoods we should understand that female and male marriage partners, and even sometimes siblings, may belong to different kinship, descent and residence groups. First, everyone is held to belong to a lineage that is either of unilineal descent (matrilineal and patrilineal), dual descent, or cognatic descent. Unilineal descent means that members of the lineage trace their ancestry from a common ancestress (matrilineal) or ancestor (patrilineal). In dual or double descent systems, individuals trace their lineages through both their mother and father's lines. Most lineage systems in Africa are unilineal.[5] Members of the lineage typically live together in extended families made up of conjugally-based family units. The system of descent largely determines residence, inheritance of property, organisation of work and control over resources, rights of parents over their children, and succession to office, to name a few.

Residence patterns are generally influenced by the type of lineage system. Thus, residence of a nuclear unit, consisting of a husband, his wife or wives, and children, among matrilineal groups is usually duolocal, where each spouse lives with her/his own matrikin, while among patrilineal groups residence is generally virilocal, and women move to live with their husbands' lineages. In the latter system an adult male, upon marriage, leaves his father's household and sets up his own nuclear home sometimes within the same larger compound in which his father also lives with his wives and their children. A woman moves to live with her husband after marriage and is given a separate hut for herself and her children (especially if the marriage is polygynous) or she shares a common residence with her husband. Traditionally, the matrilineal Akan practice a duolocal residence system where spouses continue to live with their matrikin after marriage, and since children belong to the matrilineage, they usually live with their mother and her family.

There are often variations from the norm, as for example, among the Ewe of Ghana and Togo. Where residence is virilocal, many women remain in their parental homes after marriage, at least for a season. Their children, who are members of their father's lineage rather than their own, typically stay with their mothers during this period. In some cases the children remain with their mother's patrikin even after a wife moves to live with her husband. The Ga of Ghana are another exception to the general residence pattern found among patrilineal groups. They practice a bi-local residence pattern; individuals live in the compound of the parent of the same sex; that is, girls live with mothers and boys with fathers. Sometimes older men, especially widowers, or men whose wives have effectively "retired" from marriage, (that is women who remain formally married but who perform few of the typical functions of a wife) may return to live in their matri-compounds with their female kin. Such men are sometimes regarded as 'hopeless' men because they are dependent on the very people they are supposed to support. Further, even among the matrilineal, duo-local groups, women may sometimes choose to move in with their husbands during the course of their marriage. Often the decision to live with husbands is a conscious strategy and may change over the course of the marriage. It is more common among women in their twenties and thirties who may have several young children and require the extra resources of their husband to take care for them. This arrangement also makes cooking and sexual relations between spouses easier to negotiate and arrange.

Certain specific practices can be said to have implicitly subordinated women to men in "traditional" societies. Practices such as early marriage, wife inheritance, polygyny, wife seclusion, widowhood rites and female genital cutting have the effect of privileging a perceived corporate or community balance, or men's needs or rights, over those of the woman. In early marriage or child betrothal, young girls are given in marriage to older men who usually already have wives, and who have the option to choose the young girl and pay her bride wealth. She on the other hand, has little choice in the matter since the decision is taken by her parents, father, or maternal or paternal kin. Usually the marriage is not consummated sexually until the girl attains physical maturity; however, in some societies the young bride is actually expected to engage in sexual intercourse and, with young immature female bodies carrying pregnancies and going through labour, a condition known as vaginal or obstetric fistula, normally caused by obstructed labour, can result.[6] Arrowsmith, Briggs and Lassey (2002) note that, "it seems there is ... a road to obstetric fistula that begins when girls grow up in nutritionally marginal circumstances, are married around the age of menarche, become pregnant while still adolescents ..." They go on to write that practices such as the forcible enlargement of the vaginal tracts of child brides so that sexual relations can commence may further complicate the situation. In northern Nigeria a practice known as *gishiri* is responsible for some cases of fistulas (Ampofo, Otu and Uchebu, 1990).[7] This condition, although once common in Western Europe and the United States, is almost unknown in these regions today, and its incidence has also fallen in Latin America and Asia (Wall *et al*, 2002). Arrowsmith et al. also associate the disease with poor maternal health care services, a fact that is also associated with continuing high rates of maternal mortality in Africa.[8]

Both the practice of polygyny as well as wife inheritance are centred around ensuring male access to the bodies and labour of females. Both are constructed as being for the greater good of the community, and indeed co-wives often enjoy cordial relations and benefit from sharing domestic work and care of children. Polygyny ensured men's access to the labour of wives and children and further ensured that virtually all women in the community were married, had a male provider/protector, and had a legal union in which to bear children. As has been indicated above, most wives of farmers had the obligation together with their children, to provide labour on their husbands' farms while the fruits of this labour were largely controlled by the men who determined its distribution. Nonetheless polygyny was closely associated with social status and commoners and ordinary men rarely had more than one wife.[9] Even so, up until today women rarely have a say in whether their husbands will take a co-wife, or whom they will marry; women often experience polygyny as extremely painful, as shown in the lives of the two female protagonists of Mariama Bâ's (1980) novel, *So Long a Letter*.

Some of the practices around polygny suggest that it was acknowledged not to be the ideal situation. Among the Fante, when a man wanted to marry an additional wife he was expected to pay his wife a pacification fee, literally known as *ebien dze*, "it belongs to two", because it was anticipated that whatever resources a husband had to contribute to the household would now have to be shared among two wives (and their children). A co-wife is referred to as a *kora*, rival, and the issue of *ebien dze*, frequently precipitates divorce, which was not considered ideal. Nonetheless there are indications that polygyny was highly valued among some groups.

Among the Dagomba for example, the value of polygyny is institutionalised by the idea that a hundred children by one wife are considered as one child, whereas two by two different wives are considered as many. A man is expected to beget a male regent and a female regent from different women. Another interesting finding is that while among many societies women and men enjoyed the same rights to divorce, proven adultery of a wife was almost universally an instant ground for a man to divorce her, while women did not typically have the same rights since a man's female partner could frequently be seen as a prospective wife.[10]

Among the patrilineal and patrilocal Luo of Kenya, a widow and her children, as well as the family property, belong to the husband, and when he dies, to his family. Thus widows are "inherited" so that their families and they themselves can continue to enjoy community cohesion. According to Agot (2005: 364), in widowhood inheritance the brother or a cousin "takes over" his widow even though the relationship does not constitute a formal marriage, nor are sexual relations necessarily an integral part. The notion is that "being taken over" by her late husband's brother will discourage a widow from abandoning her marital home. It is also expected to restrain a widow from seeking sexual liaisons outside her husband's clan, and to give childless widows an opportunity to bear children, especially sons, (through the deceased's brothers) who would continue the lineage of the deceased. All of these then entitle the widow to social and economic support from the inheritor and enable her to participate in specific social events during farming seasons and during ceremonies associated with rites of passage of close family members. Agot notes that women say that they agree to be "inherited" so they can ensure the well- being of their children.

While widow inheritance as understood among the Luo and several societies across Africa is meant to ensure community harmony, it is interesting that no corollary practices for community edification are found for widowers. Further, these practices frequently involve physical and emotional trauma to women.[11] Finally, women's gender roles and the constructions of femininity and masculinity—such as behaviour that sanctions polygyny, extramarital relations, and multiple partners for men, as well as the enormous work burdens that many women confront—make women particularly vulnerable to HIV infection and result in poor care when they become infected. Perceptions about men's and women's sexual rights are associated with behaviour that sanctions male infidelity and men's right to multiple sexual partners while women are expected to be monogamous and faithful. At the same time condom use is not popular among men in Africa and in a context where women feel unable to refuse sex to non-monogamous partners, this increases their vulnerability to HIV-infection. (See Ch.2) The matrilineal kinship system has been said to provide a safety net for women against the risks of divorce, widowhood, illness, and bankruptcy since, upon marriage, wives retain their use-rights to property (typically land to farm) within their own lineage and frequently continue to live with, or very near to, members of their lineages. The emphasis on maternal kin as a residential unit among matrilineal societies, or even patrilineal ones such as the Ga, serves to destabilise eurocentric images of the family and household as male-centred. Under colonialism, European preconceived notions about the form of the nuclear family, and how its members should organise their lives together, meant that African women were not always positioned in favourable ways in their relationships to African men. Colonial assumptions about husband-wife-children relationships determined women's new positions within colonial states as men were expected to be "bread winners", i.e. income earners, while women became 'home makers'. Thus women were increasingly socialised to depend on men for their own support and that of their children when traditionally no "self-respecting African woman" failed to be an "autonomous economic contributor" (Mikell, 1997: 9). Indeed, this economic contribution can be seen not only through women's provision of labour power by giving birth to several children, but also by their direct production of food for their families, and later, surpluses for sale. Both men and women conceive of their roles in society as determined by their membership in corporate groups– families and lineages– towards whom they have responsibilities and through whom they receive benefits such as access to resources.

Another aspect of African marriage not understood by Europeans was the practice of duo-local residence. European family values of the 18th and 19th centuries, and even today, were that a husband, wife and their children should live in a single space set apart from other family members. This separate space was expected to foster emotional bonding and shared goals among spouses and their children. However, duo-local residential systems permit individuation and provide both spouses the freedom to live and organize their lives with their lineage members. Thus men and women could carry out activities with siblings, who, after all, would always be their relatives while spouses could be separated by divorce, abandonment or death. On the other hand the co-residence of spouses in the more typical European nuclear format affords both spouses greater access to each other's time and resources than when they live separately. However, this sharing of a common pot is not always seen as a positive outcome among individuals previously used to maintaining separation of incomes and resources. In discussing conjugal arrangements among contemporary Ghanaian migrants in Canada, Manuh (1999) shows how nuclear conjugal arrangements, particularly the maintenance of a "joint account", can lead to mistrust and conflict. She describes resentments that arise over perceived unequal disbursements of these common funds to the lineage members of wives and husbands, eventually leading many couples to decide to practice a system more in line with what pertains in Ghana, where each spouse is responsible for different aspects of family welfare, with women typically being responsible for food and children's clothing and men, who usually earn more, are typically responsible for rent and utilities.

Traditionally within the lineage, members are entitled to several rights and privileges. Individuals usually received a plot of land to cultivate, a place to live, and assurance of care and support from the lineage in times of difficulty. Women's rights are generally tied to their relationships to men who may be their fathers, uncles, brothers and husbands. Often a father's or uncle's rights over, and responsibilities to, his daughter are transferred to her husband upon marriage. Individuals also have ties of affiliation and responsibilities, to parents, siblings, aunts/uncles, cousins, and affines. Indeed, the importance of the family can be seen in the absence of a word for 'cousin', 'aunt', grand-aunt/uncle among many groups across Africa. Among many societies, cousins are referred to either as brother/sister, or the "sons/daughters of my mother/father's sisters/brothers". Generally, the behaviour considered appropriate between parents and children is extended to the siblings of both parents. An individual's relationship with her or his father's siblings is one of deference and respect, and often the greatest respect is reserved for a father's female kin. For example among the Dagomba of Ghana, a father's sister commands even greater respect than a father's brother. Indeed among the Anlo Ewe, the relationship is formalised in specific terms with "deep mystical overtones" (Nukunya, 1966: 41). This makes the fostering of children very important, so much so that the practice is institutionalised among the Dagomba. In this case a man's sister has rights over her brother's daughters, and his first daughter is usually given to her to raise as her own.

Traditional resource allocations in marriage dictated that men would provide particular products: fishermen would give fish and hunters game, while farmers provided major crops such as yams. Women, on the other hand, were expected to contribute the vegetable ingredients to go with the meal. Farming systems were generally arranged along gender lines. There were men's farms, and often men's crops, and women's farms, with their own crops. Among the Igbo of Nigeria for example, yam was considered a male crop. However, even on "men's farms" wives and children provided labour. Men performed the "heavier" work of clearing the farms, and both men and/or women were involved in planting depending on the crop, while women predominantly, ensured that the farms were kept weeded and also harvested the crops. Although women worked on their husbands' farms, they also had smaller ("subsistence") plots on which they grew food for the family's meals. With the introduction of a cash economy wives also began to sell some of the crops from their husbands' as well as from their own plots, and to accumulate surpluses which they could use to purchase other goods. Indeed, across most of Africa women were expected to engage in independent productive activities, and young girls often received their own capital upon reaching maturity. Among the Nnobi of Nigeria, a girl's father would arrange cocoyam and yam seedlings on sticks and give these to his daughter as farming capital upon marriage. If she was a first or favourite daughter, she also received a palm tree. Her mother gave her a female goat, livestock, spices and vegetable seeds, seasoning ingredients for cooking, ladles, pots and pans. The she-goat would bear kids which could be sold for cash (Amadiume, 1990). The idea of a woman being merely a "housewife" is still frowned upon, and among the Akan, a woman who is not engaged in any economic activity is labelled *Obaa kwadwofo*, a lazy woman. One husband, in a study of traders in Kumasi, commented that he would feel ashamed as a father "to satisfy his vanity and convenience by keeping a wife at home to wait on him at the expense of his children's higher education or food supply" (Clark, 1994).

Following the establishment of colonial administrations in West Africa, retail trade in fish, vegetables, and "imported items" came to be conducted by women. Economic autonomy was also important for women because, as indicated earlier, inheritance systems did not necessarily assure women economic assets through marriage either in the matrilineal or the patrilineal system (though in the latter case a woman could more readily expect life-time support from her sons, if not from her husband's lineage). This made it necessary for a woman to have economic assets of her own. While men had access to the labour of wives and children, women did not command the labour of others, and thus, with colonialism's culture of domesticity women were not only excluded from formal sector work but also disadvantaged in cash-crop farming.

Nonetheless work and production in so-called traditional societies revealed a high level of complementarity. An example from coastal fishing communities such as the Ga and Fante may suffice to illustrate this. When fishermen returned from sea their wives would collect the husbands' share of the fish at the beach and either sell it directly or smoke it before they sold it. At the end of the fishing season a wife would render accounts to her husband, from which she deducted her sales commission. With her share of the profit the woman was expected to trade, although much of the trading capital built up in this way could be claimed back by the husband during the lean season to be spent on repairs and maintenance as well as on food. However, Hagan (1983) and Robertson (1976) argued that the sale of fish makes the female population the ones who control "the husbands' purse strings" and also control the circulation of money in the society. Under colonialism, and the development of the modern post colonial state, men began to move into formal white and blue collar work. The accelerated development of private property, as opposed to property vested jointly in the lineage, and a cash-based exchange economy, led women and men to increasingly develop unitary relations, sometimes in opposition to each other. Spouses had less information about each others' work and resources and tensions over contributions to the common nuclear pot have emerged (Adomako Ampofo, 2000).

Leadership, Politics and Citizenship

Around Africa, indigenous political roles and relationships, like familial ones, are generally corporate in nature. Traditional African political systems were generally configured with God and the various deities at the apex, followed by leaders some of who were viewed as divinely ordained even when they were typically selected from a pool of eligible candidates. If the population became unhappy with its leaders there were ways of withdrawing support and sanctioning the leader and there were individuals, both female and male, who had the authority to initiate such proceedings.

Although some descriptions seem to suggest that African women were virtually legal minors under the male guardianship of fathers or uncles which passed upon marriage to husbands, others suggest that women and men were both autonomous beings with separate but complementary responsibilities. While family, lineage and community heads tended to be men, women had both formal and informal roles as important political players and decision makers. Indeed it has been noted that on no other continent do women play as many different and important political roles as in Africa. Oral history teaches us that both women and men played important roles as leaders and political actors in pre-colonial Africa – as kings and queens, chiefs, priests and priestesses, warriors, leaders of clans, lineages and clans and that women were important actors in the making of states (Figure 3). Several military groups had female wings who actually led war companies and women were celebrated in poetry and performances. For example, women are celebrated in the poetry of the *Ifa*, the major Yoruba divinity (see Chapter 17).

Among some groups a kind of "duality" of power was built into the political system as for example among the Swazi and Sotho of Southern Africa, and the Asante, Baule, Hausa and Wolof of West Africa. This duality reflects the cosmological balance of male and female. Among the Swazi, the queen is responsible for ritual assignments that ensure the well being of the state. Among the Asante, the *Asantehemma,* the occupant of the female stool of the state, served as a counterpoint to the king, and was a member of the general assembly of Asante rulers and participated in the legislative and judicial processes such as the making and unmaking of war, and distribution of land, which was, and remains, a basic resource (Arhin, 1983). Often referred to in the literature as "queen mother" the *Ohemma* is not necessarily the king's mother, and she does not draw her authority and status from her relationship to him although the two come from the same matrilineage. Both the king and queen ruled through a council of elders and held separate courts. The existence of the queen at the highest level of state organisation is seen as a further example of the perceived complementarity of male and female, and in this case male and female power. The *Ohemma* was charged with the responsibility of consulting with members of the council to select the *Asantehene,* from among eligible male successors. Only she could begin destoolment (impeachment) proceedings against a king. Additionally, she could herself occupy a male stool, performing all the duties of her male counterparts, including the performance of rites normally barred to women on account of menstrual taboos. There are several accounts of women who took up prominent leadership positions,[12] and Aidoo (1985) describes the role played by several important Asante women leaders. She notes that Nana Dwaben Ama Seewaa whom she describes as a "female chief" ruled Dwaben chiefdom from 1841-1850. After having lost a major civil war with Asantehene in 1831 the people of Dwaben were forced into exile in south eastern Ghana, but it was Nana Ama Seewaa who, after successful negotiations with the then Asantehene Kwaku Dua I, led her people back to Asante in 1841, and, with the help of her daughter and successor, Afrakuma Panin, is said to have rebuilt their ruined capital. There were other women who resisted foreign interventions such as the Berber prophetess Kachina who held back the Arab invasion (ca. AD. 575-702) and the prophetess Nehanda of Zimbabwe who led the resistance against the imperialist Cecil Rhodes from 1863-1898.

However, in most accounts of powerful and influential women it is noteworthy that women experienced restrictions based on menstrual flow. Among most African people the concept of blood ties is central to the transmission of lineage membership. Among matrilineal groups like the Asante, this blood is transmitted by the mother during pregnancy and childbirth. Akyeampong and Obeng (2005) refer to Thomas Bowdich's statement of the origins of this system, "if the wives of the sons are faithless, the blood of the family is entirely lost in the offspring, but should the daughters deceive their husbands, it is preserved." However, Asante thoughts on matriliny are about more than marital infidelity. It was also about the valuable role of women as biological reproducers of the state by transmitting their blood to the next generation, epitomised in the notion that an Asante village was established by "a core of women . . . who have children there, and whose daughters there give birth to other daughters who will constitute the matrilineage" (McLeod in Akyeampong and Obeng, 2005). Indeed the family or lineage could survive only as long as there was a female member; "If the female sex became extinct ... no matter how many men there were, the abusua (family) would last only the span of these men's lives" (Aidoo, 1985: 18). A woman's power as a reproductive force was thus directly linked to her childbearing years. Thus, women past their childbearing years, were viewed as "ritual men". Biologically they were still women, but spiritually they were men. This was not merely symbolic, as such women also assumed several external or physical male manifestations – they earned the right to cut their hair short in the manner known as *dansikran*, they wore their cloths in the male fashion over one shoulder rather than wrapped around across their chest, and could drink liquor in public and pour libation (Akyeampong and Obeng, 2005).

Figure 3 – Modjadji- The Rainqueen

Modjadji- The Rainqueen- *http://rainqueensofafrica.com/tag/lovedu/*

This is another example of the fact that gender roles are often more social than biological, even if, in this case, they are tied to biology through the cessation of childbearing.

Nonetheless, Mikell (1997) notes that male dominance existed at many levels, including within the household and at the level of popular culture. Generally, while African men could speak up to express their opinions, women, especially when they spoke in public, tended to speak as representatives of a group. The Aba women's demonstrations of 1929 in Nigeria is an example of women leading and organising, but on behalf of women's specific interests, which while also beneficial to the larger community, did not threaten men's dominance and privilege. In this case women traders responded to the British government's imposition of taxes on their trading activities by mobilising their female-controlled kinship networks to resist the colonial government by refusing to pay the taxes.

Over the last few hundred years both women and men have experienced transformations in their identities. Colonial rule, contact with new religions, access to Western education, a modern cash economy and formal wage sector have all played important roles in these transformations. Consolidating colonial rule required that the British "contain men and women on terms unfamiliar to them, imposing Western notions of household organization and gender on local conceptualizations, and to instil new ...notions of housewifery..." (Hansen, 1991: 5). To a large extent therefore, modernisation also brought exclusion. Women were not recognised in the colonial chiefs list, for example, nor as members of the native councils and courts (Arhin, 1983). Among the Swazi, Mikell notes that attempts to modernise the traditional state resulted in the retention of power in the position of the *ngwenyama* (king) and the *liquoquo* (male royal council), but in the subversion of the power formerly held by the *indlovukati* (queen). The change from traditional to "modern" farming systems enhanced men's prestige at the expense of women's by widening the gap in their levels of knowledge, and by introducing changes in production patterns which often reduced women's roles to those of mere labourers while men earned cash directly from large, often state-owned, marketing companies for the sale of the produce. Essentially, sex discrimination, which was inherent in missionary education as well as the colonial administrative systems, was reinforced. The colonial emphasis was on male education, specifically to prepare men for entry into the civil service. Female education, when girls went to school at all, was geared towards domestic training (for example subjects such as "home management" and "cookery"). The colonial officials, by superimposing the Victorian and 19th century European aristocracy's notions of appropriate gender roles and relations, introduced relations in which men were perceived as, and trained to be "breadwinners", while women were expected to "support" men.[13] This bias set the tone for certain inequities that remain until this day. The indissolubility of Christian marriages in the 19th century created a desperate situation for many couples, especially women, who, having sought escape from a poylgynous husband, now found themselves inescapably yoked to a partner they had no use for. New income opportunities for men opened in the formal sector, mainly as white and blue-collar workers in the civil service and European enterprises. Naturally there were only few women in these sectors, and even when they gained entry, restrictions applied. In many of the British colonies, once a woman got married she had to resign from the Civil Service. Thus, marriage under the colonial order brought new levels of dependency for wives as they were expected to become "housewives" and homemakers for men employed in the formal sector. As Christianisation in many countries encouraged monogamous church-based marriages, women began to take on the title and role of being a "Mrs", especially where they could thus distinguish themselves as the "legitimate" wife from other wives and girlfriends a man might have. Among an emerging middle class elite, this distinction then allowed women to be identified as married or single. The idea of a male "breadwinner" and a female "housewife" was reinforced, creating the myth that some women merely sat at home and did no work while the husbands went out to earn an income. By assuming non-equality and comparativeness of men and women's roles, western ideology led to the situation where roles were assigned a more hierarchical position with the result that women's progress assumed a stronger association with their relationship with men than would seem to have hitherto been the case. This was the case even where colonial interventions appeared to relieve women of traditions that subordinated them within domestic spheres. Mikell (1997) argues that this was done by categorizing women as wives, thus separating them from kinship structures and creating vulnerabilities that continue to exist. An example one might look at is the resistance, across Africa, to see marital rape as a crime. Under many customary marriages, women and men continue to be members of their lineages even after marriage, and thus a woman's physical body "belonged" to her lineage and not her husband's (as evidenced by the fact that lineage members and not spouses bury the dead). Contemporary arguments often make references to the unmitigated sexual access of a man to his wife's body, often justified on the basis of the payment of so-called "bride wealth" or "bride price"; and yet any payments made by a groom to his bride or her family upon marriage did not entitle him to abuse her.

Gender Issues in Contemporary Africa

In this concluding section we will briefly examine some of the differences in women's and men's positions and the implications of gender in Africa today. Institutions and processes, while they may not overtly discriminate against women, are not therefore gender neutral in their outcomes. Whether one looks at agricultural systems, the modern industrial sector, state and market institutions, or the effects of economic reforms, it is clear that specific prescriptions, policies and practices affect women and men differently. This calls for a critical examination of institutions as gendered mediators of development policies and practices.

Relative to men, women continue to be under-represented and under-acknowledged in the "modern" economy and public sector. Women are to be found mainly in the agricultural labour force where they produce mostly subsistence crops, while men are farm managers or owners of plantations. Women also market about 60 percent of food crops in Africa and constitute most of the labour force in retail trading generally, especially in West and East Africa. The formal labour market in the "modern" economy is also greatly segregated by sex, and men's jobs are generally better than women's in terms of remuneration and career opportunities. They are also generally more varied than those available to women. Women are clustered at the bottom of most establishments in semi-skilled, poorly paid jobs that reflect historical barriers, in terms of educational qualifications, colonial reinforcement of a culture of domesticity for women, and cultural prejudices, to women's entry into a number of occupations. In the private sector women are to be found mainly in clerical and service positions while men are disproportionately to be found in the administrative and managerial class. Women's heavy reproductive work burdens as well as their lack of education and training limit their opportunities within formal sector work.

Indeed, in the area of education today disparities can be found not only in terms of male and female access, but also in terms of completion rates, attainment levels, and stereotypes in the curriculum content. This was not always the case; early post-independence governments, particularly in former British colonies, were keen to open up access to social goods to their societies and large numbers of women attended primary and secondary school in the 1960s. Former French colonies were slower to admit women, and in Muslim areas such as the Muslim north of Nigeria, women experienced greater restrictions. However, as competition for privileged positions in government and state bureaucracies generally favoured men, women were increasingly domesticated, and relegated to the role of "supporting men" as "housewives." More boys secondary schools were built and tertiary institutions often had only one residence hall for women thereby restricting access. Although since the 1990s sex-based gaps are closing at the primary school level in many countries, huge gaps remain at secondary, and particularly the tertiary levels. Also, more women are functionally illiterate than men. Specific factors exacerbate educational problems for girls, including early marriage, teenage pregnancy, domestic and agricultural responsibilities, and discriminatory punitive practices (and sometimes even policies) such as the expulsion or transfer of pregnant schoolgirls while the men or boys who father their children are not held accountable. Sexual harassment is an issue that receives insufficient attention even where it is acknowledged to exist, which it frequently is not. And yet harassment of girls by teachers, persons in authority in educational institutions and also boys, is an important contributor to gender disparities in education. Indeed, harassment is experienced even by women faculty and staff.

In the area of work, both women and men continue to be active contributors to African economies. A gendered division of labour remains and women continue to be responsible for domestic work, which is typically not paid for and thus remains invisible. Today almost all African countries have implemented one version or another of structural economic reforms. In the 1980s they were referred to as Structural Adjustment Programmes (SAPs). In the 1990s, and by the twenty first century, they have been implemented mainly under the rubric of Poverty Reduction Strategies (PRSPs). However well meaning, these reforms cannot be viewed in isolation from the global economic restructuring that has occurred, for this process in itself has social, economic and political implications not only at the global or international level, but also nationally, and at the local and household levels. For example, Zimbabwe and South Africa are among the most highly industrialized nations on the continent and have provided more opportunities for formal-sector employment for their populations than any other sub-Saharan African economies; however, due to South Africa's agreement with the World Trade Organization requiring lower tariffs on clothing and textiles, thousands of women in these sectors have recently lost their jobs due to competion with lower priced imports. Several writers agree that these structural reforms may have severely worsened the economic situation for women, who are then thrown into new levels of dependence on men. In addition, as the state withdrew from the provision of social services, as the provision of these services was made cost-effective, it fell to women to pitch in to provide care and support for families thereby further increasing their already over-burdened domestic and reproductive roles.

However, these effects were not uniform across the continent and in some contexts women benefited from reforms. In Ghana, trade liberalisation advantaged women by streamlining access to imported goods such as clothing while in Kenya and Uganda, trade liberalisation increased women's access to employment in non-traditional, export oriented goods, such as flowers and fruit. However, these advantages may be limited to the low-wage sector of the labour market. In other cases it was men who suffered the brunt of economic reforms as industries became highly feminised to exploit cheap female labour. This has thrown some men into new levels of dependence on women and is associated with increasing levels of domestic violence as masculine identities are threatened. As in other parts of the world domestic and gender-based violence remains an under-reported crime because of the stigma associated with it as well as fear of reprisals. Unlike many industrialised countries, however, most African countries do not have adequate customary or statutory laws to deal with gender-based violence although there are laws against assault and some forms of rape (Adomako Ampofo et al. 2004). Violence against women is becoming an area of concern for many individuals and civil society organisations. Some have explained violence in the postcolonial African state as a structural development from colonial rule in Africa. For example, Mama (1997) explains how colonialism was itself both a violent and a gendered process that exploited pre-existing social divisions within African cultures. The coercive control of women that was endemic to colonialism—e.g., rape as a form of military conquest and the domestication of women—has continued in the post independence period and been sanctioned by repressive political, particularly military regimes. This has been most sharply manifest, perhaps, in the attacks on women under military rule in Ghana and Nigeria in the 1980s when women traders were blamed for the ills of the economy and publicly whipped and molested. Wife battering, which is associated with cultural understandings of men's right to control and physically discipline women and girls, remains the most prevalent form of gender-based violence. Sexual assault of women, girls, and boys is one of the most hidden forms of violence, largely because the perpetrators are typically known to the victim, and are often the trusted family members or close relatives who would have been expected to provide protection. The rape of young boys by older male relations or friends is doubly traumatising because not only is trust broken but gender roles are destabilised. In African societies where homosexuality is largely stigmatised and rarely discussed, boys who are sexually assaulted by older men have fewer gender frameworks to help them understand or address their experiences.

All across the continent, women's groups, including church groups, were active in the struggle for independence as well as for specific women's rights. Russell (1989) notes that even in South Africa where African women were physically and sexually assaulted for their participation in political struggles by male security forces, black revolutionary politics was prioritised over feminist political demands. Nonetheless, although women were important players in the independence struggles of African nations, post colonial states have seen men more visibly present in the nation building project, while specific women's concerns have often been trivialised. In Ghana, Kwame Nkrumah's post-independence government is credited with creating space for women, even unschooled women (such as market women) and commoner young men within the ruling party, and giving them responsibility for organising at the grassroots (Manuh, 1991; Obeng, 2003). After independence women were appointed to ministerial positions alongside men. However, this was not generally the case across Africa and, political patron-client relations tended to favour men, particularly elite men, for political office. Men are over represented in both elected and appointed political positions and today, after 50 years of independence, only 10.9 percent of Ghana's legislature is female, compared to 10 percent in 1960.

Most governments do not prioritize women's needs as equal citizens. This is clearly reflected in attitudes to legislation around domestic violence, sexual harassment, rape and maternal mortality (despite a disproportionate interest in women's "reproductive health"). So-called reproductive health services have paid a lot of attention to family planning, but in Nigeria, for example, it has been estimated that between 800,000 and 1,000,000 fistulas remain unrepaired (Arrowsmith et al. 2002) while pregnancy-related deaths remain high around Africa, partly as a result of poor health services or lack of access to those that exist.[14] What the failure of attention to women's specific concerns – such as domestic violence, maternal mortality, and political representation – has led to, in many instances, are tensions between women and men, particularly in a context of economic crises and hardship.

However, all across the continent women, women's groups, separately or in alliance and coalitions with men, are seeking new ways to respond to situations of economic reforms, poverty, gendered human rights abuses, lack of social infrastructure and political alienation. Women (and some men) are calling men into discourse with them to discuss gender issues. Civil society and women's groups are also calling governments to account and pressurising them to address gender concerns. Hopefully such advocacy will help individuals, groups, institutions, as well as governments, to become more sensitive and open to addressing issues of gender in African societies.

Review Questions

1. Discuss two examples of social and cultural practices that affect the relative positions of women and men in Africa, and their relations with each other.

2. Select any institution (an example could be a school, government or non-government body, or a religious organisation) and examine how gender is factored (or not factored) into the organisation's philosophies, planning, choice of activities and how these activities are carried out.

3. Conduct research on major sectors of the social and political economy, comparing women and men's representations by sex. Discuss possible explanations for these differences, the impacts they might have and how the gaps might be reduced.

4. Keep a journal in which you note your observations about gender roles and relations in everyday life – from the media, among your family and friends, through a novel etc. Ensure diversity in your observations and concentrate on a variety of issues that also reflect ideologies and representations. In your journal also speculate on why a particular phenomenon exists, how it came to be, its relevance, and what challenges, if any, it poses for women's well being in Africa. Feel free to express your opinions about what you observe, but make sure that you justify and qualify your feelings and observations.

References

Abu, K. 1983. "The Separateness of Spouses: Conjugal Resources in an   Ashanti Town." in C. Oppong (Ed.) *Female and Male in West Africa*, London: George Allen & Unwin. pp. 156-168.

Abou-Zahr, C. and E. Royston. 1991. *Maternal Mortality: A Global Factbook*. Geneva: World Health Organisation.

Adomako Ampofo, A. 2000. "Resource Contributions, Gender Orientation, and Reproductive Decision Making in Ghana; the case of Urban Couples." *Research Review NS* 15(2): pp 93-125.

Ampofo, K., T. Otu and G. Uchebo 1990. "Epidemiology of vesico-vaginal fistulae in Northern Nigeria." *West African Journal of Medicine* 9: pp98-102.

Agot, K.. 2005 "HIV and AIDS Interventions and the Politics of the African Woman's Body." (In) L. Nelson and J. Seager (eds.). *A Companion to Feminist Geography*. Malden, Massachusetts: Blackwell Publishers. pp. 363-379.

Aidoo, A.A. 1985. "Women in the History and Culture of Ghana." *Research Review*, NS., 1 .

Akyeampong, E. and P. Obeng. 2005. "Spirituality, Gender and Power in Asante History". In

O. Oyewumi (Ed.) *African Gender Studies: a Reader*. New York: Palgrave Macmillan. pp 23-48.

Amadiume, I. 1990. *Male Daughters, Female Husbands*. London: Zed.

Arhin, K. 1983. "The Political and Military Roles of Akan Women." In C. Oppong (Ed.) *Female and Male in West Africa*, London: George Allen & Unwin: pp 91-98.

Bâ, M. 1980. *So Long a Letter*. Oxford: Heinemann.

Hansen, K. T. 1991. "Introduction; Domesticity in Africa." In, K. T. Hansen (Ed.) *African Encounters with Domesticity*. New Brunswick: Rutgers University Press. pp.1-33

Hagan, G. P. 1983. "Marriage, Divorce and Polygyny in Winneba." In C. Oppong (Ed.) *Female and Male in West Africa*. London: George Allen & Unwin. Pp. 192- 203

Mama, A. 1997. "Postscript: Moving from analysis to practice?" In, A. Imam, A. Mama and F. Sow (Eds.) *Engendering African Social Sciences*. Dakar: CODESRIA.

Manuh, T. 1991. "Women and their Organizations during the Period of CPP Rule in Ghana, 1951-1966" In K. Arhin (Editor), *The Life and Work of Kwame Nkrumah*. Trenton and Accra: African World Press/SEDCO Publications.

Manuh, T. 1999. "'This place is not Ghana': Gender and Rights Discourse among Ghanaian men and women in Toronto." *Ghana Studies* (2): pp 77-95.

Mikell, G. 1997. (Ed.) *African Feminisms- The Politics of Survival in Sub-Saharan Africa*. Philadelphia: University of Pennsylvania Press.

Nukunya, G. K. 1966. *Kinship and Marriage among the Anlo Ewe*. London: The Athlone Press.

Obeng, P. 2003. "Gendered Nationalism: Forms of Masculinity in Modern Asante of Ghana." In L. Lindsay and S. Miescher (eds.) *Men and Masculinities in Modern Africa*. Portsmouth, NH: Heinemann.

Robertson, C. 1986. "Women's Education and Class formation in Africa, 1950-1980." In, C. Robertson and I. Berger (Eds.) *Women and Class in Africa*. London: Africana. pp. 92-113.

Russell, D. 1989. *Lives of Courage: Women for a New South Africa*. New York: Basic Books.

Vellenga, D. D. 1983. "Who is a Wife? Legal Expressions of Heterosexual Conflicts in Ghana." In C. Oppong (Ed.) *Female and Male in West Africa*. London: George Allen & Unwin. Pp. 144-155

Wall, L. L., S. D Arrowsmith, N. D. Briggs and A. Lassey. 2002. "Urinary incontinence in the Developing World: The Obstetric Fistula." In P. Abrams, L. Cardozo, S. Khoury and A. Wein (Eds.) *Incontinence*. Plymouth: Health Publication Ltd. Pp. 893-935.

Wood, J. 1999. *When Men are Women: Manhood among Gabra Nomads of East Africa*. Madison: University of Wisconsin Press.

Suggested Reading:

1. Adomako Ampofo, A., J. Beoku-Betts, M. Osirim and W. Njambi. "Women's and Gender Studies in English Speaking Sub-Saharan Africa: A Review of Research in the Social Sciences." *Gender and Society*. Vol 18(6): 685-714

2. Cole, C., T. Manuh and S. Miescher. 2007. (Eds.) *Africa After Gender?* Bloomington: Indiana University Press.

3. Shefer, T., K. Ratele, A. Strebel, N. Shabalala & R. Buikema (Eds.) *From boys to men*. Cape Town: UCT Press.

Useful Internet Reference Sites:

Agenda: is a feminist media project journal dealing with issues and themes that effect women in Southern Africa; http://www.agenda.za

Bridge: Institute for Development Studies journal on gender and development;

http://www.ids.ac.uk/bridge/reports.html

Feminist Africa: Continental focus journal on gendered implications of African concerns; http://www.feminsitafrica.org

Jenda: A journal of culture and gender in Africa; www.jendajournal.com/jenda

Kubatana: An archive on women; http://www.kubatana.net/html/archive women/021216iewad.asp?sector

Endnotes

1. The literature discussed in this chapter is selective and illustrative and not exhaustive, thus students are strongly urged to search further. For this purpose a list of recommended readings and useful websites is provided at the end of the chapter.

2. The term pre-colonial conjures up images of a vast continent, which is static or unchanging for centuries, with a menu of shared "traditional" practices and customs that were only interrupted by the advent of colonial forays into Africa. In reality, African societies were extremely dynamic and went through immense changes long before the advent of the European merchants, missionaries, slavers and colonialists. Where the term "post-colonial" is used, it is simply to denote that the colonial enterprise in Africa brought in a short period of between 100-200 years, changes so drastic and frequently severe, that the periods before and after deserve some differentiation.

3. For example Manuh (1991, op. cit.) notes that women like Akua Asabea and Leticia Quaye, both active with Kwame Nkrumah on a political newspaper *The Evening News*, and who took part in the resistance to British rule dubbed the "Positive Action Campaign", were convicted and imprisoned by the British.

4. Men's studies or discourses on Masculinities are gaining ground in African Studies; however, the focus of this corpus of work still tends to be more on men's specific experiences than on gender relations per se.

5. Also see Chapter 4 of this volume.

6. According to Wikepedia, the online free encyclopedia, vaginal fistula "is an abnormal fistulous tract extending between the bladder and the vagina that allows the continuous involuntary discharge of urine into the vaginal vault. It is often caused by childbirth (in which case it is known as an obstetric fistula), when a prolonged labor presses the unborn child tightly against the pelvis, cutting off blood flow to the vesicovaginal wall." [Source: http://en.wikipedia.org/wiki/Vesicovaginal_fistula]

7. *Gisiri* is the Hausa word for salt and is often used to refer to the encrustations of salt on the outside of water jars. The belief is that an imbalance of salty or sweet foods can cause this film to grow over the woman's vagina. Random cuts are then made in the vagina by a local midwife with a razor, knife, or piece of broken glass to "open the way" for the baby. The insertion of caustic substances into the vagina and the practice of female genital cutting can also lead to fistulas developing.

8. The commonly accepted definition of a maternal death is "the death of a woman while pregnant or within 42 days of termination of a pregnancy irrespective of the duration and site of the pregnancy, from any cause related to or aggravated by the pregnancy or its management, but not from accidental or incidental causes" (AbouZahr and Royston 1991, op. cit.). While maternal mortality ratios are 430 per 100,000 live births for the world, 27 per 100,000 in the industrialised world, they are a staggering 870 for Africa as a whole and 1020 for West and 1060 for East Africa respectively.

9. Bowditch (181: 289-90) reported that "the higher orders" of Asante men practised polygyny "to an excess" but that most men of the "lower orders" had only one wife, if any.. Similarly, Fortes (1949:124) noted that the plurality of wives among the Tallensi, for example, was mainly the privilege of older men and that "three quarters of married men under 45 have only one wife each (1949:124).

10. Aidoo (1985, op. cit.) states that an Asante woman had as many grounds as her husband for terminating an unsatisfactory marriage, including the husband's adultery, impotence, neglect of maintenance and sorcery.

11. In some societies the practice required widows to drink water used to bathe the deceased's corpse; to be isolated for periods ranging from a few days to several months; or to be deprived of certain foods and sleep. Today the contneud practice brings with it the risk of HIV-infection. In the case of the Luo, this is the ethnic group with the highest prevalence of HIV infections in Kenya.

12. Mikell (1997) also lists great-wife Mmanthatisi of Sotho as another great leader.

13. Aidoo (1985) notes that these Western ideals of womanhood that were imposed on African women only applied to a small minority of Europe's aristocracy and that the majority of European women of that time experienced "drudgery and exclusion" (p.16).

14. Ghararo and Abedi (1999) observe that any pregnant patient could develop fistulas as a result of substand-ard care.

CHAPTER 5

AFRICA AND ITS DIASPORAS
Ebenezer Ayesu

This chapter examines the historical processes that led to the emergence of the African diaspora with a particular focus on the main ways by which Africans ended up outside of the continent in historical times. Africans are on record as having visited and having dealings with other peoples in antiquity. And since the second half of the 20ᵗʰ century, the community of Africans living outside the continent has grown and is developing into an increasingly complex post colonial phenomenon. But the focus of this chapter is not on the encounter between Africans and other peoples in antiquity or the evolving contemporary movements of continental-born Africans. Rather, the chapter focuses on the historic African Diaspora that emerged from the Indian Ocean Slave Trade, the Arab Slave Trade and the Trans-Atlantic Slave Trade, since these were the main conduits by which the largest number of Africans found themselves outside of Africa. It details the features and conditions of slave life and also discusses slave survival strategies and resistance. In the final section, the chapter examines the ideological offshoots of the historical experiences of Africans and African-descended peoples, such as Pan-Africanism and Negritude.

The African Diaspora

In its broadest sense, the African diaspora refers to all the communities and societies of Africans that are found outside of the continent of Africa. These communities and societies constitute a 'diaspora' of Africa because of their historical links to the continent.[1]

The word 'diaspora' is of Greek origin and means "dispersion or scattering", an allusion to the scattering of Israelites from Palestine following the Babylonian captivity. Diaspora was thus originally used to refer to all Jews and Jewish-descended peoples who found themselves domiciled in territories outside of the land of Palestine or Israel which is considered their homeland or original home. (Members of the Jewish diaspora were, in a manner of speaking, dispersed from their home). The notion of a diaspora implies two things: firstly, the existence of a 'homeland' from which a people moved, and secondly, the existence of a new community or communities outside of the homeland in which the dispersed people have settled. For members of the African diaspora, Africa is the homeland and the new communities in which they live form the diaspora of the homeland.

The emergence of an African diaspora is a product of history- the long and complex history of the African continent and its contact with peoples from other parts of the world. That history by far predates European contact with Africa in the 15ᵗʰ century.[2] As a diaspora, these African-descended communities, in spite of their complex diversities, reflect certain characteristics, which are not unrelated to the particular historical circumstances that gave rise to them. Firstly, people of the diaspora often portray a sense of longing for the homeland from which their forebears came. This sense of longing produces an elevation of Africa in the minds and perception of many diasporic Africans. Africa is fondly conjured up as that distant land of glory from which they came and to which they may return some day. Some African-Americans speak of "Africa, the land of kings and queens, princes and princesses". The Rastafarians often refer to Africa as their "Zion, flowing with milk and honey". There have been also calls for diasporic Africans to repatriate back to Africa as championed by leading black nationalists like Marcus Garvey.

Such reclamations and affirmations are occasioned by the underclass status and the deprivations that these African-descended peoples have historically suffered. By reclaiming the African past, sometimes to the point of romanticism, diasporic Africans give themselves a sense of self-worth and dignity. This psychological boost is important for survival in the harsh social and economic conditions in which diasporic Africans have lived.

For proponents of the Back-to-Africa movement, repatriation was seen as a way out of the deprivations of the African diaspora. Marcus Garvey, leader of this movement in the 1920s, held the view that Africans in the diaspora could never attain any respectable degree of equality and freedom until they separated themselves from the white-dominated societies of the Americas and the Caribbean. He also saw repatriation as key to the economic revival and dominance of the entire African race. Ironically, Garvey was never to set foot on the continent of Africa. On the other hand, W.E.B. Dubois was of the conviction that the talented one-tenth of the African American community should be nurtured to become world class leaders not only in their community, but in the American society as a whole because they had contributed significantly to building it. Du Bois was to be hunted out of the United States for his communist leanings and to spend his last days in Ghana.

The sense of longing for Africa is often reinforced by another characteristic of displaced persons, which could be traced to the marginalisation and alienation that they tend to suffer in their new or adopted societies. Diasporic Africans have largely been on the periphery of the societies they live in and they have suffered and continue to suffer many deprivations. It began with their status as slaves in the new societies in which they found themselves. After emancipation, they continued to face racism and social, economic and political exclusion.[3] These deprivations are reflected in their lack of access to resources, the poverty of their communities, the difficulties in formation and maintenance of families, and high rates of violence and crime. Even in countries where people of African descent form the majority population, the social structure and economic arrangements tend to place persons of darker hue at the bottom of the social ladder, and countries such as Haiti and Jamaica have been cited as exhibiting these traits.

Another feature of the African diaspora is the cultural continuities or retentions it has with the continent of Africa. Studies of African-descended communities reveal many cultural practices that also occur on the continent. These continuities are sometimes maintained as found on the continent or have been altered to some degree. They may indeed be retained in a form which is fixed and therefore predates the way it is currently practised on the African continent. These continuities are seen in the religious, linguistic, socio-economic and political lives of diasporic Africans. Arising from the social, political and economic differences between the homeland and the new societies of settlement, Africans in the diaspora have had to create or construct new ways of adapting to their environment. For instance, the *Santeria*, *Candomble* and *Vodoo* religions combine strong elements of African religion and influences of Catholicism.[4]

But it should be noted that while there are cultural similarities between continental Africans and diasporic Africans, there are also differences. These differences are conditioned by location,

117

environment, and their particular experiences. For instance, research shows that the plantation systems in the Americas differed from one place to the other. Plantations in the south of the United States were somewhat different from those in the Caribbean and other parts of South America. Also, the different European groups that were the dominant class in most of these societies interacted differently with their black slaves and freed persons. In the process, different sensitivities and attitudes were developed to race-related issues. It has been established, for instance, that conceptions of race in Brazilian society are different from those in the United States; whereas in the latter society the 'one drop' rule made anyone with African blood irredeemably black, in Brazil, the issue of gradations was more complex and crossed colour lines. Therefore the lumping together of the different nationalities of the African diaspora- African-Americans, Afro-Brazilians, Afro-Caribbeans and Afro-Europeans—conceal real socio-cultural diversities, but together they constitute the diaspora of Africa.

The Emergence of the African Diaspora
The emergence of African-descended communities in the modern world outside of Africa has been largely the result of three main movements:
   a. The Indian Ocean Slave Trade;
   b. The Arab Slave Trade, and;
   c. The Atlantic Slave Trade.

The Indian Ocean Slave Trade
The slave trade in the Indian Ocean started well before the 15th century and ended only in the 20th century. It is difficult to define the exact limits of the Indian Ocean, but for our purposes we shall confine ourselves to the movement of slaves from the east and southern African coast to the Far East across the Indian Ocean.

Most of the slaves were taken from the Horn of Africa, or present-day Somalia, and from along the East African coast. Indeed slave dealing from this region is believed to have begun from as early as the 1st century AD. Additional factors which aided the trade were the settlements that were created along the East African coast by Arabs. The East African coast was appropriately close to the Arab world and supplied items of trade which the Arabs required. These included kola nuts, ivory, slaves, spices and leather.

Arab traders and Arabs fleeing the many wars in the Arab world contributed tremendously to the founding of major trading posts and towns along the East African coast. Clear examples are Mogadishu, Brava and Kilwa, which were founded in the 10th century. The island of Mafia, the Comoro Islands and Madagascar were founded in the same manner in about the 10th century as well.[5] As a result, several millions of Bantu-speaking peoples were taken to Mesopotamia to work on large sugar cane farms and to construct dams in Southern Iraq. H. Deschamps described the African involvement in the dam construction as "the first model of a great tropical construction project involving the labour of hundreds of Negro slaves."[6] However Deschamps' views discount the labour of African people involved in the construction of the pyramids in Egypt.

The slave trade in the Indian Ocean was governed by the monsoon winds. The Greeks in Hippalos first observed these winds. Four months in a year (during the winter months in the Northern Hemisphere) North East winds blew ships coming from Arabia and North-west India towards the east coast of Africa. For about six months in the summer, winds blowing from the South West provided for a return journey across the Indian Ocean to the Indian sub-continent or to Asia. If we consider that the beginning of winter in Europe and North America marks the beginning of summer in Asia and the beginning of summer in Europe marks the beginning of winter in Asia, then it is easy to imagine that African slaves arrived in Asia completely unprepared for the climatic conditions in which they found themselves.

As items from the Far East, especially pottery came in from China and Persia, the demand for slaves increased and these were obtained from the area between Mogadishu and Pemba. Other valuable items obtained from the East African coast were ivory and iron. So lucrative and rewarding was the trade along the East African coast that when the foremost African historian Ibn Battuta visited Mogadishu and Kilwa in the 14th century, he could not help but notice the prosperity in which Arabs created a mercantile society and mixed liberally with indigenes of the East African coast and hinterland and thus creating the Swahili culture, civilisation and language.[7]

The settlement of Arabs along the East African coast and the conversion of Africans to the Islamic religion only temporarily obstructed the slave trade. This is because Islam as a religion frowned upon the taking of Muslims as slaves. Slave dealers therefore had to go further into the interior, to non-Muslim societies, in order to have access to slaves. The slaves bought by the Arabs found their way to the Near East principally through Yemen and the Persian Gulf.

Map 5 – Map showing the dispersion of Africans from the continent

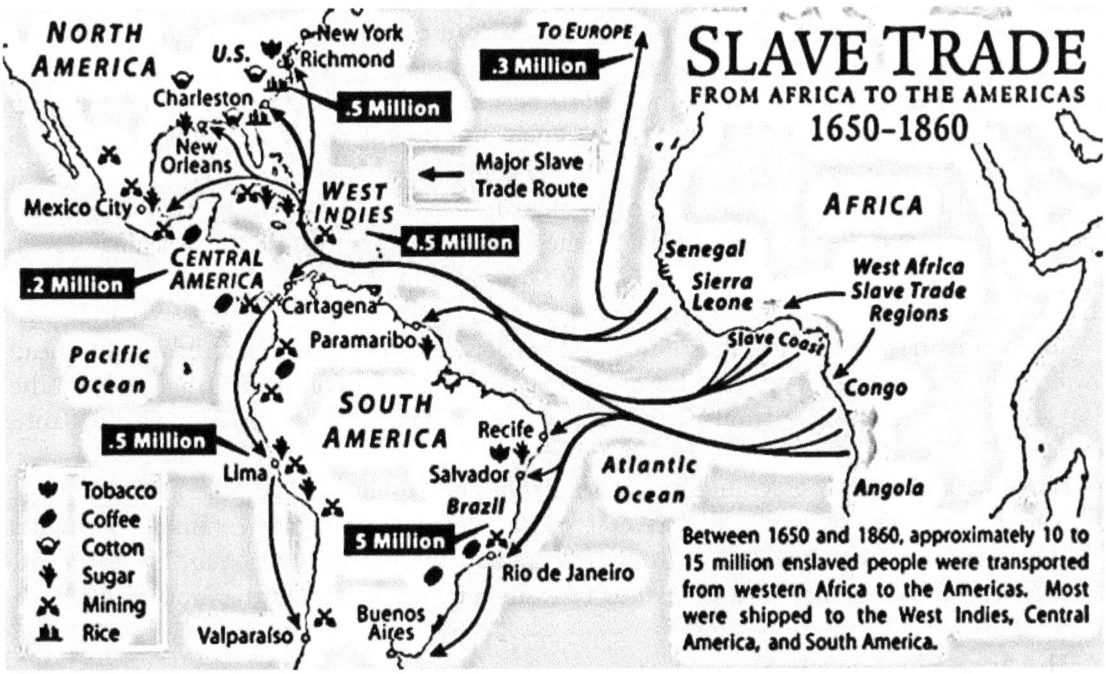

Source: Neil A. Frankel (2007, 2008), Slavery in America, Slave Trade
From Africa to the Americas 1650-1860, http://www.slaverysite.com/
Body/maps.htm or Slave Trade From Africa to the Americas (17)
http://www.slaverysite.com/slave%20trade.htm/

The scale and extent of the trade

African slaves were taken to as far as China. For instance, during the 12th century, the inhabitants of Canton used African slave labour. There was the exportation of Africans to India as well, and this was on an even bigger scale. In the 11th and 12th centuries Muslims conquered and ruled the Ganges region of India, and introduced into the area African slaves from the East African coast. This was later extended to Ceylon (present-day Sri Lanka), and in this area slaves from Ethiopia who were called *habshis* or *siddis* were much sought after.[8]

The African slaves served as soldiers and sailors and some even rose to high positions in the different chiefdoms and kingdoms. For example, the sovereign of Bengal owned 8,000 slaves in the latter part of the 15th century, some of whom were so influential that he himself became deeply suspicious of them and even tried to eliminate them. Consequently, King Fath Shah tried to rid his kingdom of some of these influential African slaves. In return, some of the African slaves conspired and killed him and two African slave soldiers ruled over Bengal from 1486-1493. This of course occasioned severe reprisals as the Asians who succeeded them had the Africans persecuted to the point that they had to seek refuge in Deccan.[9]

In the closing decade of the 16th century, the Dutch worked their way to Indonesia and began creating settlements along the way. In the process, Madagascar became an important slave-dealing centre. When subsequently settlements were created in Mauritius and the Cape of South Africa, involvement in the slave trade across the Indian Ocean increased in dimension. By the middle of the 17th century, the English and the French and other European nations had joined not only in the movement along the East African coast, and therefore in the creation of settlements, but also in the trade across the Indian Ocean. As a clear illustration of the widespread nature of involvement in the trade, one scholar noted slave brokers in 1726 buying Malagasy Islanders and re-selling them to the English of Bristol, the Dutch of Batavia and the French of Martinique as well as the Arabs of Boina and Majunga.[10]

As a result of the massive scale of involvement in the trade, slaves from the East African coast sold somewhat cheaper than the slaves who were sent across the Atlantic. A scholar noted: "a slave in Barbados costs from £750 to £1,250 whereas in Madagascar with some £12 of merchandise one can buy all one wants. We can get a fine chap there for an old suit."[11]

The interesting point about the trade across the East African coast is that it did not only head towards the Indian Ocean, but also towards the Atlantic Ocean. For example slaves from the East African coast, especially from Madagascar and Mozambique, populated in the main, Santo Domingo.

Notwithstanding the foregoing, the African continent could best be described as a huge human reservoir where especially, the east coast offered slave traders of four continents great human cargoes in the 19th century. The Indian Ocean area, even more than the Atlantic side, fell increasingly into the hands of dealers in black flesh as the century wore on.

The Arab Slave Trade

The Arab Slave Trade is closely related to the advent of Islam in Africa. It is important therefore for us to begin looking at Islamic attitudes to slavery. Islam recognises the existence of two worlds. These are:

a. The Abode of Islam, which comprised the community of adherents of the Islamic religion/faith, and

b. The Abode of War, made up of the community of unbelievers, any person considered in Islam as an infidel and non-believer.[6]

It is believed that the first duty imposed on believers by Allah is to extend a peaceful invitation to all persons in the abode of war to join the Islamic religion. Where the invitation is accepted, the person naturally becomes a Muslim and therefore is not affected by the consequence of refusal. But where the invitation is rejected, it is the duty of Muslims to wage war (holy war or *Jihad*) on such persons and upon conquest, they are taken into slavery. It is only after a long period in slavery after a sincere acceptance of the Islamic religion, that a person is subsequently admitted into the abode of believers. One sheds his "cloth" of slavery and becomes a free person. However, the master of the Muslim has to be persuaded that one has been converted. Thus it was not automatic that one became a Muslim upon conquest.

One of the first areas that Islam spread as part of evangelisation was North Africa, where anybody it came into contact with was considered an infidel to be conquered. Islamic incursion into the Western Sudan in particular occurred around the 9th Century A.D. Soon thereafter the great Empires of Ghana, Mali and Songhai developed in that order, utilising the resources of Islam, including its intellectuals, and trade to develop (See also Chapter 8, this volume). The wars waged by Islamic adherents for the purpose of acquiring slaves led partly to the collapse of these empires.

The first wave of slaves in large numbers to be taken away was after the Battle of Tondibi in 1591 when Muslims advanced on Songhai. This led to the defeat of Songhai and over 1200 prisoners of war were taken, in addition to several camel loads of gold dust. The success of that enterprise intensified the process of the Arab slave trade. Thereafter, the capture of Africans-whether of the forest region or from the Sudan or North Africa, became a regular feature of the business, which was conducted by Muslims who came from the Middle East. All of this was justified under the ideology of Jihad.

As the trade developed, three main routes came to be established:

i. The East-West route, which started from West to East. It ended up on the Nile where the slaves were taken towards the Red Sea to the East.

ii. The route running from Tripoli through Central Sudan.

iii. From the Nile Valley to the Northern borders of Egypt.

These sets of routes moved from North Africa to South Europe and the Middle East (the coastal route).

Major cities including Timbuktu, Tezzan, Ghatt, Kano, Tunis and Daffur emerged as a result of the trading activities. Slaves were obtained mainly from the Sudanic Belt and the area directly below it. Those obtained from modern day Burkina Faso, Ghana, and Liberia invariably had to travel for over 3,000 km east to the shipping points.

Many of the slaves, particularly those from the savannah and the forest region, would have been sold for the fifth or sixth time, by the time they got to the point of export. The whole enterprise was a chain which allowed traders to break off at centres where they could sell their 'goods' and return to their respective homes.

Travel Conditions

Those Muslims who were actually involved in the slave trade were called *Gehlabis*. They treated their slaves in a most inhumane manner, worse than they treated their camels. The camels carried the *Gehlabis*, the cargoes of water and food items and also other items of trade such as elephant tusks, gum, gold and any other thing the owner might have purchased, while the slaves walked the entire journey. Sometimes, slaves less than 12 years of age were carried by camel. Those who lagged behind out of sheer exhaustion were whipped along. There was a special whip, *Kubash*, which was used for this purpose.

Caravans usually set off at dawn and did not halt until evening. The journey was an interminable one through endless arid sands. The few oases appeared to offer little solace from the punishment of the heat and lack of water. Water was rationed and due to its scarcity, slaves did not have more than one drink a day. One could therefore imagine the number of slaves who died of thirst and not of physical illness. Caravan owners of the time would have thought nothing of sacrificing exhausted, parched slaves to preserve provisions for the journey.

From the North African coast, the slaves were shipped off and sold to Arabia and the Persian Gulf. The journey across the sea to Arabia was a nightmare because the slaves were carried in very small boats called "dhows" which were very hazardous and could not sometimes survive the ravages of the sea. Upon arrival in Arabia, the slave if male, would be circumcised (if not already circumcised), and given a bizarre name that no man would like to bear. Before the slaves were sold to south Europe, the Persian Gulf or Arabia, they were carefully assessed in the following manner:

1. Opening of mouth (for inspection of teeth)
2. Questions were asked about their appetite.

Those who had good appetite were deemed to be healthy and therefore desirable, while those who did not have a good appetite were sold for very little.

Each slave was accompanied with details of his service record (the number of times sold before), price paid at each sale, and what his previous owners thought about him. Sales were organised publicly, three times a week.

After a sale was completed, an official of state issued a deed of sale which sealed the sale that "X" has been sold to "Y". Raymond Muluy, writing about the number of Africans taken from Africa into Arabia, the Persian Gulf and Southern Europe, stated that in about 7th century A.D. about 100,000 slaves were taken. According to him that number increased to about 200,000 in the 8th century, and to 500,000 between the 10th and 13th centuries. From the 14th century onwards, the figure soared to over 1,000,000, reaching a peak of 2,000,000 from the 15th century to the 19th century.

The Trans-Atlantic Slave Trade

The Transatlantic Slave Trade, by far the largest forcible transportation of human beings from one part of the earth to the other, can best be understood as part of the process of European expansionism starting from the early 1400s. The trade lasted from about 1440 to 1880, but was at its peak in the 18th and 19th centuries.

European exploration and exploitation of the Americas created the need for labour to work on the large plantations and mines that were established. These plantations produced sugarcane, coffee, cocoa, rice, indigo, tobacco and cotton, to feed industrial production in Europe. However the indigenous Amerindian populations proved unequal to the task of working these plantations. Many of them died from exhaustion and the new diseases- mumps, measles and small pox– that were introduced by the Europeans. Also, because of their knowledge of the terrain, the Europeans found it difficult to control their escape from the plantations. European indentured labour was also an unsatisfactory answer to the labour needs created in these plantations. Unused to the tropical and sub-tropical conditions of the Americas, the European indentured servants fell victim to tropical diseases like malaria and yellow fever. Upon escape, these European indentured labourers could also easily blend into the colonies' white ruling class. In any case, the racism that inhered in European expansionism made this category of workers unsuitable for the menial work that needed to be performed. African slave labour, which was not unknown in Europe,[7] was deemed the best possible solution to the labour question in the Americas. Donald Wright aptly captures the perceived suitability of African slaves for the American plantations:

> They came from an environment where those who survived into adolescence acquired some immunity to such ...diseases as smallpox, mumps and measles, as well as to such tropical maladies as malaria and yellow fever. This meant they lived three to five times longer than white labourers under difficulties on plantations, and longer still than Native Americans.

And then he adds:
> Also, when Africans ran away they could neither go home nor be mistaken for members of the planters' society...
> They were thus the best economic solution for plantation owners seeking inexpensive labor.[8]

African slaves were thus exported in droves to work the plantations of the Americas for the benefit of Europeans and Europe. In the process, a triangular trade developed between Africa, Europe and the Americas. In the first leg of the triangular trade, European merchants purchased African slaves on the African coast with European manufactures. The slaves were transported to the Americas where they were sold. The merchants then purchased products from the Americas like sugar cane, cotton and tobacco, and transported them to Europe where they were sold, manufactures procured, and then they headed back to Africa to buy slaves with the goods, thus completing the cycle of the triangular trade. This triangular trade integrated Africa into the international economic order of the modern world, and provided the historical basis of the strictures within which Africa has had to operate in the international economy.[9]

Beginnings of the Trade

The Atlantic Slave Trade started in a trickle and grew slowly through the 17th century. Indeed the initial trade between the Europeans, particularly the Portuguese, and the peoples of West Africa had items other than slaves as the mainstay. Initially spices, ivory, pepper, wax and gold were the main items in the trade. The trade in gold was particularly profitable,[10] while slaves were a minor item of trade at this stage. However, as more plantations were established and mines opened up in the Americas, the demand for slaves increased.

Sources of the slaves

The slaves exported were mainly from the coast and interior of west and west-central Africa between the mouth of the Senegal River in the north and Angola in the south. This coastline thus came to be known as the Slave Coast. A few of the slaves also came from Mozambique and the island of Madagascar.

Adu Boahen identifies four main ways by which Africans became slaves. First, criminals could be punished by being sold into slavery. Also, free Africans could become slaves through raids organised by other Africans with the support of a few Europeans. Domestic slaves could also be resold, as well as prisoners of war.[11] Pawns and debtors were also sometimes sold into slavery. It should be stressed that the high demand for slaves by Europeans on the coast heightened the tendency to sell people into slavery on the least pretext.

Most of the exported slaves were adult males and only one in ten slaves traded to a European was under the age of ten.[12] The number of women slaves was estimated at about half of the number of men. This was unlike what pertained in African domestic slavery where women were preferred over men because they served both productive and reproductive functions. As is well known, some of the female slaves who found themselves in the Americas were compelled to provide sexual services for their white masters and to reproduce to replenish the slave stock.[13] In this respect, the slavery experience for women differed from that of men.

The Conduct of the Slave Trade

Initial attempts by some European traders and pirates to seize Africans on the coast did not prove successful as they faced resistance from them.[14] Soon the realisation dawned that the best way to proceed was to bring goods that were needed by Africans in exchange for slaves. The European traders thus established outposts on coastal ports and neighbouring islands where the slave transactions between them and African merchants and rulers occurred.

The Europeans rarely went inland to procure slaves, but mainly served as shippers. African rulers and merchants devised ways of supplying slaves and moving them to the coast. Some of the slaves were brought down in caravans while to the east of the Niger Delta, commercial associations (known as trading houses) were created to see to the procurement and delivery of slaves.[15] Once the slaves were brought to the coast, they were carefully examined by the Europeans, who subsequently went into negotiations with the African merchants over the price. Once the price had been agreed to by all sides, the transaction was then concluded. African slave traders exchanged slaves for manufactured European goods of various kinds: guns, gunpowder, calico, rum, beads, iron and copper bars, and the cost of slaves rose steadily through the years.

The slaves thus procured were then packed on the slave ships for onward transportation to the Americas. The Middle Passage was a gruelling experience for the slaves as the terrible conditions on the ships did not allow for any comforts. Though the European merchants took care to have as many of the slaves as possible landed alive at the end of the journey in order to increase their profits, the sanitary conditions on the ships were anything but satisfactory. The trip across the ocean lasted between 25 to 60 days depending on the origin, destination, and wind.[16]

Numbers involved

As noted above, the slave trade started on a small scale in the 1400s and 1500s, and then peaked in the 18th and 19th centuries. Though we may never know the exact number of people involved, historians have generated estimates that help to give us an idea of the number of slaves forcibly transported to the Americas and those who died on the high seas. According to Adu Boahen (op cit.), an average of 13,000 slaves a year were exported between 1530 and 1600. The number rose to about 27,000 a year in the 17th century, 70,000 in the 18th century, and a whopping 135,000 a year by the 1830s. Of these, quite a number died in the Middle Passage, or the voyage from the African coast to the Americas.

Conservative estimates peg the entire number of the men, women and children exported as slaves to the Americas at about 11 million. Others suggest that the numbers involved were many more. To some historians a more accurate figure would be anything between 15 and 22 million.[17] Of these, about 16 percent are estimated to have died in the Middle Passage.[18] The disputes over the numbers however do not obscure the monumental tragedy that the trade constituted for Africa.

Effects of the Trade

Some historians have claimed that the Transatlantic Slave Trade brought some economic advantages to Africa. A careful study of the nature of the trade and its duration however, cannot lend any credence to such claims. As one historian puts it the "trade did not confer benefits of any kind on...Africa."[19] Another says that it was "an unmitigated misery– a crime unredeemed by one extenuating circumstance."[20]

The slave trade had many enduring effects on African society. One of these effects was an increase in the incidence of warfare and raiding. While Africans had fought among themselves before the advent of the slave trade, its inception helped to increase the rate at which states and communities engaged in warfare against each other. Other violent acts like raiding also increased as they became the source of obtaining slaves for onward sale to the Europeans on the coast. The introduction of more sophisticated weaponry by Europeans during this period made warfare more brutal and destructive. In the process, anxieties and apprehensions about personal and collective security were also heightened.

The trade also resulted in the loss of population, particularly of the most economically active, in the affected parts of the continent. Many people died due to the violent methods of slave acquisition and the horrible conditions in which those who were captured were kept. The traders' interest in young and active males and females also meant that the most virile segment of the population were prone to enslavement and export. Instructions from the Directors of the

African Company in London to their agents on the coast is revealing on this point. The directors asked the agents to procure 600 slaves who should

> all be good merchantable Negroes, viz. two-thirds males, one third females, six-sevenths of each cargo to be about 16 and 30 years of age and upon no account to exceed 30, one-seventh boys and girls of which none should be under 10 years of age.[21]

Furthermore, the trade led to the decline of many indigenous industries such as bead-making, pottery, cloth weaving, gold and bronze casting. As the slave trade increased in importance, knowledge and skills were also affected and these industries went into decline.

The Transatlantic Slave Trade also marked the integration of Africa into the modern world economy on terms that were not fair and this has been greatly detrimental to Africa's development. This unfairness has characterised Africa's economic relations with the rest of the world since then and Africa has been the poorer for it.

The slave trade also had some psychosocial effects which have been long lasting and more difficult to deal with. The prejudice and suspicions that exist among ethnic groups around Africa up to today can partly be traced to the slave trade. Suspicions against Asante and Dahomey, for instance, are partly rooted in the roles they played in slave-acquisition during the Transatlantic Slave Trade. Sometimes, these suspicions also surface in the relations between continental and diasporic Africans; thus some diasporic Africans view continental Africans as the descendants of those who sold their ancestors into slavery, and therefore the cause of their plight.

The Transatlantic Slave Trade has also contributed to the racism and mindless prejudice that Africans and African-descended peoples face in the world today. The ideological justifications for the trade that emanated from Europe and America portrayed the African as an inferior being who occupied the lowest order in the evolutionary scheme of things. The period of slavery in which the most menial of labourers was more likely to be African-descended did not help matters and deepened the image and perception of inferiority. As a result all kinds of complexes have developed among the descendants of both the slavers and the enslaved. These psychosocial problems may well be the fundamental challenges to surmount to allow the African world, both continental and diasporan, to come into its own. It is to address these issues that various intellectual and cultural movements, foremost of which are Pan-Africanism and Negritude, emerged.

The Pan-African Movement

Though there is no single definition for it, Pan-Africanism can be said to be a philosophy or ideology based on "the belief that African people share common bonds and objectives, and advocates unity to achieve these objectives."[22] As a historical movement, it encapsulates motley ideas of unity centred on African and African descended peoples. The ideology has sometimes been applied to all black African people, at other times to black people of African descent, and also to all peoples in Africa including Arab North Africans or to all countries in Africa.[23]

Pan-Africanism has produced many prominent persons as its exponents, advocates, thinkers and practitioners. On this roll of honour one may find names like Edward Wilmot Blyden,

Sylvester Williams, W.E.B DuBois and George Padmore, among others. The movement has been marked by the holding of periodic congresses starting in the post-1945 phase of the Pan-African movement. Kwame Nkrumah occupies pride of place as one of its lead exponents and practitioners. The movement, at its congresses, considered developments on the African continent and the plight of Africans in the diaspora. It strongly condemned racism, colonization of the continent, and all forms of discrimination against Africans. It developed strategies and a powerful ideological framework aimed at ridding the world of racial discrimination particularly manifested against Africans and establishing self government for African states and peoples.

Certain key features of Ghana's stance as an independent nation manifested a Pan-Africanist and in some cases, a Garveyite orientation. These include iconography such as the Black Star in the middle of the national flag, and support to independence struggles around the continent. Ghana today is privileged to house the remains of many Pan Africanists, some of whom are not fully acknowledged. It is significant that the mortal remains of four of the best known are all to be found in Accra, namely those of Kwame Nkrumah, W.E.B. Du Bois, Shirley Graham Dubois and George Padmore.

Negritude

The term 'Negritude' or 'the awareness, the defence, and development of African cultural values,'[24] was first used by Aimé Cesaire in his poem, *'Cahier d'un retour au pays natal'*. It refers to a collective identity of Africans globally, born of a common historico-cultural experience of oppression. The movement originated as an act of intellectual and artistic defiance by African and Afro Caribbean students living in Paris in the 1930s, led by Leopold Sedar Senghor of Senegal, Leon Damas of Guadeloupe and Aime Cesaire of Martinique. In asserting the 'Negro identity', these writers turned to the various cultural expressions such as those developed in the French Caribbean which were deeply rooted in the African continent and mirrored in the experience of the Middle Passage and slavery. The concept represents a historic development in the formulation of African diasporic identity. It is the affirmation by diasporic Africans of the overwhelming pride in black heritage and culture.

Internally, the French colonial policy of assimilation, which propagated French civilisation in Africa at the expense of African culture, propelled exponents of Negritude to press hard the agenda of propagating African cultural heritage in the face of the French onslaught. In addition, Africans from the French colonies in Africa had to contend with discrimination from the French educational establishment in France.

Through journals and publications, exponents of the concept sought to uphold black aesthetics and intellectual capabilities.[30] They also condemned the overt colonial identification with French culture, which had led to a 'collective boveryism' and the denigration of African culture. In addition, they called for strong collaboration between black intellectuals and workers to uplift the image of the black race.

Conclusion

The concept of the African diaspora has historically been understood as referring to the unity of black existence as a phenomenon arising out of the events of the Trans Atlantic slave trade and the new world economic order. Arising out of the struggles to abolish the slave trade and end slavery, several movements developed to help realise the aspirations of people of African descent to assert their rights as equal citizens as well as their rights to a homeland and to human dignity. Later encounters and engagement between Africans born on the continent and in the diaspora led to the creation of intellectual and cultural movements which facilitated the pace of decolonisation in Africa and the attainment of civil rights in the Americas. Pan-Africanism and Negritude were key expressions of this impetus and continue to varying degrees in animating public thought and discourse on the conditions of Africans and African-descended persons around the world. In the contemporary period, the concept of the African diaspora must be expanded to include emerging communities of continental-born Africans around the world. These communities are made up of emigrants who have left the Continent for a variety of reasons including flight from economic decline and conflict, and the quest for a better life for themselves and their children riding on the promises of globalization. Unlike the historic African diaspora however, members of these communities are able to maintain linkages with their countries of origin, with many sustaining a transnational existence. Of interest for scholars working on Africa will be the connections and relationships that may develop between the old and the new African diasporas on the one hand, and the on the other hand, the new forms of engagement that may emerge between Africa and its diasporas.

Review Questions

1. What were the similarities and differences between the trade in Africans directed towards the Indian Ocean and that across the Atlantic?

2. It has been contended by some that the Atlantic Slave Trade was beneficial to Africa. Do you agree? Give reasons for your stand.

3. What is your understanding of the notion of Diaspora especially in relation to Africa? In your opinion what should be the relations between Africa and its diaspora in the contemporary period?

4. Attempt a concise account of the evolution of Pan-Africanism.

Suggested Readings

Berlin, I. 1998. *Many Thousands Gone: The First Two Centuries of Slavery in North America.*Cambridge: Harvard University Press.

Berlin, I. 2003. *Generations of Captivity.* Cambridge: Harvard University Press.

C. Eric Lincoln and L. H. Mamiya. 1990. *The Black Church in the African American Experience.* Durham: Duke University Press.

Herbstein, M. 2001. *Ama: A Story of the Atlantic Slave Trade* (Novel) New York, E-reads Publication.

Thornton, J. 1998. *Africa and Africans in the Making of the Atlantic World, 1400-1800.* Cambridge: Cambridge University Press.

Endnotes

1. *The World Book Dictionary,* Vol. 1 A-K, World Book Inc., 1960, p.580.

2.. W.T.W. Morgan 1969. *East Africa: Its peoples and resources.* London: Oxford University Press.

3. R. Nettleford, 1979, *Caribbean Cultural Identity: The Case of Jamaica.* UCLA Latin American Centre Publications: University of California. Pp. 212-213.

4. R. Nettleford, op. cit., p.1. As in the North American spirituals in W.E.B. Du Bois' *The Souls of Black Folk',* a variety of arts and practices provided refuge for Afro-Caribbean pride and African Culture. These were commonly portrayed in the calenda, bamboula and laghia dances; the kric-krac folktales and the Creole arts. The forced migration of great numbers of Africans to various parts of the Americas brought in its wake the grounds for the continuation of African traditions in this 'new world.' For more details on Africans contribution to music, dance and folktales to the New World. See Bruno Nettle, *Folk and Traditional Music of the Western Continents.* New Jersey: Prentice-Hall Inc. 1973.

5. W.T.W. Morgan, op.cit., p. 25

6. Nieuwenhuis Tom 2001 'Politics and Society in Early Modern Iraq: Mamluk Pashas Tribal Shayks and Local Rule between 1802-1831.'*World Archaeology* Volume 33 Number 1: pp. 30-31.

7. *Global Studies* (9)- Africa's Early History. <www.historyteacher.net/Globalised Africa

8. L.H. Ofosu Appiah, 1969, *Slavery: A brief History*, Waterville House, Accra.

9. Deccan is a vast plateau in India encompassing most of central and southern India. The name Deccan is anglicised form of the "prakrit dakkim". See Wikipedia- The Free Encyclopedia. See also, The Slave Dynasty of Bengal. www.webindia123.com/history/medievalslaverydynasty

10. Gwyn Campbell 1981 'Madagascar and the Slave Trade 1810-1895.' *The Journal of African History*, Volume 22 Number 2, p. 208.

11. For more on the trade on the east African coast, see, Campbell, "Madagascar and the Slave Trade. 1810-1895. *The Journal of African History,* Vol. 22, No. 2, 1981, pp. 203-227.

12. Gunasekara Victor 1999 'Slavery and the Infidel in Islam: Essays on Islamic Theory and Practice.' *Queensland Humanist* Volume 33, Number 1.

13. Earlier slave trades like the Trans-Saharan Trade, which developed from the 10th to the 14th century, brought some African slaves to especially the southern European states of Spain and Portugal, the Mediterranean region and Arabia. See A. Adu Boahen, 1966, *Topics in West African History* ,London: Longman.

14. Wright, op cit.

15. On this topic, see Walter Rodney, *How Europe Underdeveloped Africa* (Washington, D.C.: Howard University Press, 1982); and Eric Williams, *Capitalism and Slavery* (Chapel Hill: University of North Carolina Press, 1944.

16. Adu Boahen, 1966, *Topics in West African History,* London: Longman.

17. Boahen, op. cit.

18. Wright, op cit.

19. See M. A. McLaurin, *Celia, A Slave* (New York: Avon Books, 1991, and S. Block, "Lines of Color, Sex, and Service: Sexual Coercion in the Early Republic." In Linda Kerber and Jane De Hart (eds.), *Women's America,* 5th Edition New York: Oxford University Press, 2000. The former is a classic work that tells of the harrowing experience of a young female slave in the US. It clearly bears out the peculiar conditions of female slaves in the Americas.

20. Particular reference can be made to the activities of the pirate Hawkins who seized some Africans in the Senegal region. For more on the development, see, Basil Davidson, (1996), *The African Slave Trade,* Oxford: James Currey.

21. Wright op. cit.

22. Wright, op cit

23. See P. D. Curtin, 1969, *Atlantic Slave Trade: A Census*, Madison: University of Wisconsin Press; Per Hernaes, 1995, *Slave, Danes, and African Coast Society: the Danish Slave Trade from West Africa and Afro-Danish relations on the Eighteenth Century Gold Coast*, Trondheim: Department of History, Norwegian University of Science and Technology; Inikori, J. E., (Ed.), *The Atlantic Slave Trade: Effects on Economies, Societies, and Peoples in Africa, the Americas, and Europe*, Durham: Duke University Press.

24. Wright, op cit.

25. Boahen, op. Cit, p. 112.

26. Ibid.

27. Cited in Boahen, op. cit, p. 112.

28. Ronald Walters, "Pan-Africanism," Microsoft Encarta Reference Library, 2004.

29. Ronald Walters, ibid.

30. Senghor, L.S. 'The Struggle for Negritude' in, J. Reed & C. Wake, ed., *Senghor: Prose and Poetry*, London: Oxford University Press, 1965, p. 97.

CHAPTER 6

THE CULTURAL FRAMEWORK OF DEVELOPMENT
A. K. Awedoba

Introduction

It is important to have some understanding of the concept of culture given the abuses of the concept in public and private discourses. For some, it is nothing more than past forms of behaviours and attitudes, what are best labelled as 'traditional'. Modernists who accept this view see no place for culture in modern societies and would seek to expunge any relics of it (the so called outmoded customs) from society. On the other hand, traditionalists bemoan the passing of an age – the loss of culture and the 'good old ways'. They therefore hanker after a reassertion of culture. From one perspective, culture can be said to be the past, the present and the future.

'Culture' is one of those terms or concepts that we encounter often in every day life and in academic discourse. It nevertheless defies definition. Numerous definitions have been attempted in the past, but few, if any, have gained universal acceptance or have escaped damaging criticism. It is not so much that the various definitions are wrong; rather the problem lies in the polysemous nature of the concept which has more than one meaning and in fact means different things to different people. The World Conference on Cultural Policies' (MONDIACULT, 1998) definition of the concept states as follows:

> Culture is that whole complex of distinctive spiritual, material, intellectual and emotional features that characterize a society or social groups. It includes not only arts and letters, but also modes of life, the fundamental rights of the human being, value systems, traditions and beliefs

It is noteworthy that UNESCO takes the position that:

1. Each culture has its dignity and value, which must be respected and valued.
2. The diversity of national cultures, their uniqueness and originality are an essential basis for human progress and development of world cultures.

The term 'culture' has an undeniable Indo-European etymology (derivation) and also reflects a specific set of experiences. If we survey African languages, we shall no doubt come across terms that can translate the basic import of the concept 'culture'.

In the English language it is possible to describe a person as 'cultured' or 'uncultured'. A city may sometimes be described as rich in culture, which would seem to imply that some cities may be poor or less rich in culture. These two usages or images of culture conjure a certain meaning of the term which suggests the pursuit of certain socially or culturally desirable activities or elitist pursuits pertaining to leisure classes such as those to do with the exhibition and appreciation of finer arts including classical and related music and the theatre arts, literature, etc. This is akin to T.S. Eliot's notion of culture as personal accomplishment in manner, morals, learning, sensitivity to artistic forms of expression, etc.[1] For Eliot very few individuals, if any, can boast of the totality of personal accomplishments necessary for attainment of the status of 'cultured person'. This type of definition is not wrong although not every scholar would necessarily agree with this somewhat narrow view of culture. It would simply imply that the working classes and the rural peoples whose way of life does not allow much time for their leisurely activities lack culture. Certainly such people too have their culture and idea of culture no matter how different from that of their upper class counterparts.

Going back to the time of Tylor, culture has been often defined as "the totality of a people's way of life" and as "that complex whole which includes knowledge, morals, religion, customs and habits or any other capabilities acquired by man as a member of society"[2]. Clyde Kluckholn describes culture as 'a way of thinking, feeling; believing...' and observes that it is the main factor permitting people to live together as a Society[3]. For him, culture embodies pattern or norms; it is acquired; and it includes material and non-material or in other words, tangible and non-tangible aspects of life. To quote his words:

> . . . [culture] consists of patterns, explicit and implicit, of and for behaviour acquired and transmitted by symbols, constituting the distinctive achievement of human groups, including their embodiments in artefacts. . .

We may attach the term 'culture' to a variety of human activities such as 'tissue culture', but it is possible to attach the term to the following as well: 'political culture', 'business culture', 'culinary culture' etc. From the point of view of sociologists and anthropologists, as Ember and Ember (1981) remark, it can be '...a set of learned beliefs, values and behaviours generally shared by the members of a society or population'[4]. While tissue culture is based on procedures that specialists have learnt and are able to carry out, this type of culture must be distinguished from others. Culture in the sociological sense, takes its reference from society– human society to be exact, a body of persons who regularly hang out together and see themselves as such. They need not live together and in these days of internet connectivity, they need not even know each other. Culture is seen to pertain to the group or the society collectively. Thus, what is peculiar to the individual and has no implications for the rest of society or community or group of which that individual is a member is to be regarded as idiosyncratic. This is not to deny that sometimes it is from the individualistic that we trace the genesis of cultural norms. Culture is, from the perspectives of some writers, patterned behaviour, and these patterns imply regularities, even if people may not be overtly conscious of these regularities. Predictability could even be implied in such understandings of culture.

From our perspective as students interested in human development, it is essential to appreciate that culture and the norms and patterns that it embodies are associated with sanctions, both negative and positive. The negative sanctions may have embodied in them a penal element, while the positive can be seen as rewards and positive inducements. The sanctions may furthermore be physical or non-physical, and verbal criticism, rebukes, and insults exemplify the latter. The sanctions may also be ritual or non-ritual ones, negative or positive. Members of the community are compelled, even coerced, into complying with certain of the approved norms. It may be that there is the fear of the ancestors punishing the offenders, or that the rest of society would not take kindly to anyone violating their norms. Even negative gossip may have an effect on compliance. Also the fact that my neighbours will say and think of me as a good person may be powerful enough to make me wish to comply with the norms of the group.

However, culture does not always imply absolute compliance with established norms. Contrary to what is sometimes supposed, individuals are not slaves of culture, nor does the culture deny individuals the opportunity to exercise their creative impulses and imaginations. There are always those grey areas where society has not taken a stand and does not prescribe what should or should not be done. Culture could, but does not, necessarily stifle creativity. Culture does not insist on uniformity in everything people do. Because of the existence of variation, it is not unusual to have intra-cultural variations that are manifested in what may be described as sub-cultures. Youth for example, may espouse ways that are different from those of their seniors and elders, just as women may do things that men do not normally do, or know how to do, as is the case in societies where gender differences are enshrined and entrenched. Given the division of labour along gender lines that obtains in some African cultures, women are socialised to know more about culinary arts than men. While boys may be adept at throwing stones, girls may exhibit clumsiness handling a stone as a weapon. Similarly fisher folk may have better understanding of the sea and aquatic culture than farmers or pastoralists, and courtiers may understand the norms of court etiquette better than ordinary people. Bankers know more about the business of managing money matters than ordinary people, and the writer would be at a loss about how to proceed at the stock exchange where shares are dealt with. There is hardly any group of people who do not appreciate these differences in knowledge and expertise and in ways of perceiving and doing things.

An attempt at cataloguing the constituents of culture easily generates a long list which should include among others- language and literature, general knowledge, technology and science, law and jural issues, religious beliefs, food ways and preferences, music and artistic performance, work habits, taboos, etc. In some sense, culture becomes holistic and all encompassing, with synergies between the above components. Societies can differ however as to the extent of this holistic character of culture. Contrary to some view points, the economy, the political realm, science and technology, religion are all aspects of the culture, although the emphasis on domains can differ from context to context and society to society. Culture brings under its scope the tangible and the intangible. In some societies there is a close synergy of the different aspects and domains, in the so called rural communities more than the urban ones. The social, the economic, the political, the religious, the technological and the philosophical etc., can be so intricately interwoven as to make it impossible to fully understand and appreciate some institutions in isolation and without their interfaces. We can illustrate this as follows:

The school curriculum and timetables in Ghana have for long emphasised what has been labelled as 'drumming and dancing'. During culture studies periods, pupils are expected to learn and appreciate Ghanaian traditional drumming and dancing. This has been criticised as inadequate, and as equating culture with drumming and dancing. While there is some justification in the criticism, it cannot nevertheless be doubted that culture can be taught through drumming and dancing. A full understanding of Ghanaian drumming and dancing culture will need to consider a number of issues which are social and economic, religious and technological. Linguistics, history and philosophy are all involved. Arguably, knowledge of botany and physics cannot be dispensed with in the manufacture of Ghanaian drums and musical instruments. All this illustrates the point about the inter-connectedness of domains in culture.

In any appreciation of culture, context and environment are necessary. The physical environment and the world around us influence our societies, outlooks and cultures, even if we cannot assert any determinism in all cases. Changes in the human and physical environments can indeed result in palpable changes in a people's way of life. This writer has demonstrated this elsewhere (Awedoba, 2002)[5]. The effect is not uni-directional, since human activities (cultures) may also change the physical environment for better or for worse, wittingly or unwittingly. Environmental degradation is not a new idea in Africa, where human activity has led to the transformation of ecosystems even within our lifetime. In parts of Northern Ghana, the substitution of traditional millet cultivars unable to guarantee reasonable yields due to weather changes, with corn and new early maturing varieties of sorghum, seem to have changed local lifestyles considerably. A traditional dry season (socially defined) that should begin in November after the harvests and the cessation of the rains comes earlier, because the harvests are gathered in, in early October, with the harvesting of the sorghum crop in September. Dry season activities must therefore begin earlier than in the past.

But just as the immediate environments can play critical roles in our ways of life, so also can the cultures of neighbours. The theory of cultural diffusion may have since ceased to be a serious explanation for similarities in cultures; nevertheless societies have been known to borrow from each other and this continues, even at a more rapid pace, as it becomes easier to view on the television, events taking place in other cultures, and to read on the internet about what is happening in the world outside our homes, and watch in videos films and documentaries portrayals of life in other places. It may be that it is not every new thing that we see that is adopted, or if adopted, is retained. Sometimes the borrowed idea or artefact may, with time, become so internalised that it loses its 'otherness' and becomes accepted as authentic and even 'traditional'. The processes of cultural diffusion and inter-cultural exchange continue unabated in today's world, as globalisation gains ground and ushers us into the culture of the 'global village'.

Culture as an Artefact

Whatever is said about culture, it is important to observe that it is an artefact, and humanly-made. This enables us to distinguish between things that are natural or have resulted from non-human causes, and things that originate in human society and culture. This writer's favourite illustration has been to compare the birthmark and the so-called 'tribal mark' or scarification. The distinctions are not however watertight. As the term implies, people with birthmarks are born with them, and most people would agree with this. The 'tribal mark' however can have cultural meanings in some societies. Culture arguably continues to invade nature as it were, and will make greater inroads with advances in technology.

Culture, Society and the Individual

The definitions of culture often situate it in a society, as we have remarked above. Maquet (1972: 9) defines society as a group of men and women (one may include children, to avoid any doubts), living and working together, who by their complementary activities, provide at the same time for the survival of the group and the satisfaction of the material and psychological needs of an individual[6]. One may doubt that members of a society always have to live together or work together, and we know types of societies where people may live together, but do not work together or may work together, but do not live together. This definition of society may not be comprehensive enough and may not easily embrace the school debating society or several other kinds of societies, like the Ghanaian society, but at least it contributes to an understanding of the concept. In any case, it does not limit us to elite society, as other usages would suggest. Maquet maintains that a culture is '. . . the totality of ways of living, working and thinking and the totality of what results from these activities. . . as constituted in a given society'.

The society-culture dynamic should account for the idea of a wider culture, a national culture, an ethnic culture, a village culture etc. It does not imply a contradiction to talk therefore of 'African culture', despite the diversities that Africa as a continent contains. Likewise it is not a mistake to talk of 'Ghanaian culture'; Ghana's National Commission on Culture may seem ambivalent as a name, but there are good grounds for isolating a 'Ghanaian culture', as I have argued in Awedoba (forthcoming: 46-48)[7]. In Ghana's case, P.N.D.C. Law 238, passed in August 1990, setting up the 'National Commission on Culture,' does not exhibit any such ambivalence as it stipulates that the National Commission on Culture should seek, among other things, to '. . . promote the evolution of an integrated National Culture thus creating a distinct Ghanaian personality to be reflected in African and world affairs. . .' The Law recognises that a national culture is not a given and that it has to evolve or be brought about consciously. The Commission confirms this in its brief profile[8].

Culture is seen to pertain to the group or the society collectively. The point has been made above that what is peculiar to the individual is usually to be regarded as idiosyncratic. Nevertheless it is individuals who bond together to form a group and the society. In any society or group however, it is not always all members who adhere to the norms or the tenets of the collective ideology.

Individuals may from time to time exhibit behaviours that go counter to the norms of society. The group or the society itself may, on certain occasions, set aside its own norms; this is known to happen in quite a few societies on days specifically designated for this. A classic example is the **Apoô** festival of the Brong of Techiman. The bounds of propriety are relaxed during these festivities such that behaviour that would under other circumstances be forbidden can be condoned. It is almost as if on these occasions, status differences are nullified or suspended just as some of the norms are put in abeyance. One student of the Ndembu society of Tanzania, the anthropologist Victor Turner (1969)[9], and Needham (1980) in their studies of 'rites of transition' and 'symbolic reversals' affirmed the existence of what one may call 'organised deviations' from the cultural norms. Unorganised deviations also occur, involving individuals motivated perhaps by self-interest or compelled by personal needs. The notion of culture does not therefore deny deviance, and some might even argue that it is deviance that proves the rule. Brongs consider **Apoô** behaviours to be necessary for the sanity and orderliness of their society. It is seen as a cleansing exercise by means of which the debris or detritus resulting from social life may be aired and cleared away. Thus, on **Apoô** occasions, an ordinary person may tell people in authority unpalatable truths and get away with it. As Asihene (1980: 15)[10] explained, the name of the festival derives from the word **po** i.e. "reject' 'the resentment, grudge, or nuisance the soul has harboured for the year...".

It is not just the occasional setting aside of the norms of society that culture is presented with; culture does not and should not have to imply absolute compliance. Contrary to what is sometimes supposed, individuals are not slaves of culture, nor does the culture deny individuals the exercise of their creative impulses. Some of the changes that occur in cultures may in fact stem from individuals, particularly those imbued with charismatic qualities and attributes, like statesmen and women, pop musicians, sportsmen and women etc. whose idiosyncratic behaviours, speech styles, and other mannerisms may have become popular and widely emulated by their fans. Thus, not only can the idiosyncratic be subsumed under culture, it could be the template based on which aspects of a people's culture may be derived or modelled.

There is circularity apparent in the argument at this point; the idiosyncrasies may in fact be the product of an individual's synthesising patterns already in existence, but they could equally stem from the individual's makeup or constitution. A person who lisps may do so basically because of a speech defect and the same may apply to those whose speech has a nasal timbre. This is to be distinguished from the case of the individual who has a tendency to pronounce 'ship' and 'sharp' as 'sip' and 'sap', or 'thin' as 'tin'. This behaviour would be cultural in the sense that the absence of certain sounds in his/her language such as /•/ and />/ explains the mispronunciation. He or she is substituting (though unconsciously) for unfamiliar English sounds, those sounds of his/her first language or mother tongue that he/she considers closest to these peculiar English sounds or 'phonemes', as the linguists like to call them. Indeed, it might be that other individuals who share this person's mother tongue have an identical problem. These types of idiosyncrasies are in fact not idiosyncrasies at all, but cultural manifestations. On the other hand, a person may walk in a peculiar way because of a physical defect, and this can be regarded as idiosyncratic, however, others may choose to learn to walk in the same way because they have decided to pattern their behaviour on their 'hero's' gait. When this becomes common within a society or group, what began as a peculiarity of some individual ceases to be merely an idiosyncrasy.

The peculiar physiological features referred to of the individual may or may not of themselves be due directly to culture; at least, they cannot be directly attributable to one's activity as a member of a society. To take an earlier example: the birthmark that some people may have somewhere on their bodies is not human-made, as it could not have been inflicted deliberately. However, some features of the individual such as the facial marks or other body marks inflicted at infancy or in the course of initiation rites can be situated in culture and bear meanings in the context of the person's society. It may be that the marks identify the individual's ascribed status, his or her membership of an ethnic group, clan or lineage, an association or even his or her birth order, as when a baby whose immediate elder sibling did not survive infancy is given a body mark. They may also be for therapeutic reasons, as when children are inoculated, or for religious reasons, as in the case of circumcision in those cultures where this is practised. Aesthetic reasons, as the story of Akiga among the Tiv of Nigeria shows, can also account for body scarification[11]. These kinds of explanations could not be advanced for the birthmark that a child comes into this world with. This is not to deny that given superior scientific knowledge, it would not be possible some day to predict the birthmark or account for it in terms of cultural activities. In fact in some cultures, birthmarks have been accounted for within the context of the religious belief system. A spear wound or scar may have a cultural explanation too, even if it was not a premeditated act. All this goes to explain the fact that it is in order to dichotomise between idiosyncratic and the collective event, so long as we do not erect water-tight boundaries between the two categories.

Culture as a Legacy

Culture has also been described as a 'Social Legacy'. In this respect some people seem to equate culture and tradition. Many aspects of our cultures can indeed be traced to the past. Human society is built on past knowledges and discoveries. It is common knowledge that progress cannot be achieved from a continual process of re-invention. There is no need to re-invent the wheel. Society endeavours therefore to improve upon what already exists or is known in order to chart the way forward. Culture therefore implies the utilisation of tradition or the management of what has been handed down from group to group.

There is however the need to distinguish between culture and tradition. There is currently much confusion in people's minds about these two concepts with the result that the two are equated. This need not be the case, especially when in some understandings of tradition, the modern is excluded. Modernity and tradition are often opposed or contrasted in such a way that what is traditional cannot be modern, and what is modern cannot be traditional. Given such a dichotomy, it is easy to see why some people, the 'traditionalists,' hanker after culture and are wary of contemporary ways, while the 'modernists' hate culture and consider it incompatible with the present life of a society.

Culture, Tradition and Modernity

Along side the dichotomy is the perception that tradition is associated with backwardness, the simplistic way of life, small scale communities, the rustic, the non-scientific, the non-literate, the irrational and the illogical, and with custom-bound communities, with the additional implication of outmodedness, to mention a few presumed attributes of tradition. However, tradition or what is traditional does not have to imply all of this or even any of it. What is more, tradition is sometimes no more than an invention put up to serve a purpose, be it a negative one or a positive purpose. Sometimes it is no more than just a label and description. In the same way, modernity too can be an invention. If the difference between the modern and the traditional were premised purely on what is current- here and now, there would really be no difference at all. In fact, the traditional is modern too, especially if modern means current. The modern and the traditional can also be seen as relativities. What we might call 'traditional' was once modern and what is now labelled as modern, will one day become traditional or 'colo' (or colonial). For there to be a difference, the modern must be seen as novelty or innovation. However, this is not how modernity ought to be seen, i.e. as lacking a past or rootedness. It would seem from some perceptions that the rootedness of modernity is external- located elsewhere, more often than not, in western European norms and practices. This way of thinking equated modernisation

137

with westernisation. Again, those who hold on to such perceptions and hanker for the modern way reject culture, while those who see it as loaning from Western norms tend to have lukewarm attitudes to modernisation which they see as betrayal of self worth. However, apart from the cases where it is attributable to borrowing, modernity too can be said to have its traditions, as it is often a rehash of ideas that are not really new. All this should throw into doubt several dichotomies that some people assume to obtain, such as the dichotomy between the modern and the traditional, the opposition of culture and modernisation, the contrasting of culture and westernisation or the equation of culture and tradition on the one hand, and modernisation and westernisation on the other.

Legacies that imply continuities are however important in the kinds of cultures that we have been associated with in Africa. These continuities are made possible by the processes of cultural transmission. It is important to understand that the social legacies in question could be negative or positive, or even ambivalent in the current condition. However, it is not only legacies that constitute culture. A culture can be said to receive its stock through both vertical and horizontal transmission, contrary to some perceptions. Vertical transmission is inter-generational. Older generations transmit their ways and norms to succeeding ones. A horizontal transmission applies to the learning of the ways of the group by new peers that come in. Transmission in this respect is not necessarily wholesale in the sense that if A (a1, a2, a3) is being transmitted, what is captured may be A (a2, a3) + x. Modification and customisations are not excluded in the cultural process.

The transmission of cultures is made possible by the willingness of people to learn. Culture is learnt. It is acquired and not inherited. People are not born with their culture. This means that a Chinese child born into an Ewe cultural background can learn to behave, to see things and to do things like any average Ewe person in the community, even if his/her racial features are different. The variety of sanctions deployed in the community compels and facilitates the acquisition of the cultural norms and standards of our communities. We may learn by participant observation, but there are also situations where we are taught overly to feel, think and do things in the approved ways. There may even be a prize for getting it right or wrong.

Culture is Dynamic

A misunderstanding of the meaning of culture sometimes results in the perception that culture is bad for development, as it sets society back by attempting to replicate past conditions in contemporary societies that have undergone substantial change. Some people tend to see culture as static and fossilised in perspective. There is no doubt that linkages can be traced between the ways of life of our predecessors and our ways. However, culture is also dynamic. It allows for change, an ongoing process that is not always immediately perceptible or palpable, except in rare circumstances where change amounts to revolution. While certain sectors of society may for good reason hanker for change, there are also sectors that also for good reason, express nostalgia about the 'glorious past'. The concept of a golden age has been with human beings perhaps ever since the dawn of civilisation. There may even be a social as well as environmental aspect to this craving for a return to older times that we find in some people in some of our so called more traditional societies. The forests were once more luxuriant and richer and men and women did not have to labour to gain the means of a livelihood, nor did they entertain anxieties although they lacked the sophisticated technologies of contemporary times. As resources were in abundance, there was less need for human competition and conflict. That was 'paradise' and it makes sense to long for a return to those days, even if there is also a realisation that this is a forlorn hope. It could be argued, rightly or wrongly, that environmentalists and demographers with their concerns for environmental pollution and the destruction of eco-systems, rapid population growth, destruction of the ozone layer and their general comments about the state of the contemporary world, place them squarely in the camp of the *nostalgists*. Yet it makes sense also to look forward to the future and to the new technologies and discoveries in the pipeline which, it is hoped, would improve knowledge and the quality of life. There has always been room in society for both the progressivists and the nostalgists. Indeed a person could be a nostalgist in one domain and a progressivist in another. This takes us to the subject of development.

Development and Culture

Development, as a concept, has been defined differently over the years, but simply put, development is progress and the betterment of the human condition. Progress is change and development, like culture, is dynamic. In fact, culture is development, or put another way, development is the dynamic interface of culture. Some scholars suggest that the way to bring development about is to create opportunities for exercising freedoms and the provision of options that allow for informed choices. Development is, above all, people-oriented and people-centred. It needs to be emphasised here that although in the past, countries were ranked as 'developed', 'developing', 'undeveloped' or 'under-developed' (which echoes ego-centric Victorian evolutionist ideas of social progress with Europe at the pinnacle of human social evolution), development is not the monopoly of any country, since no country in the world today can say it has solved all its problems or has attained utopia. Even in the opulent countries of the world, not all citizens are happy with life; for some, life has lost its meaning, the suicide rate is high and artificial stimulation (use of narcotic drugs) seems required, to enable individuals to keep living at all and not commit suicide.

Development, as currently conceptualised, aims at addressing all forms of vulnerability and deprivation and this is an aim that culture also shares, even if there may not be a readily available operational concept in Ghanaian languages for 'development'; the Akan concept of *mpontuo*, has been suggested. The ideas that cohere in the meaning of development are not new to African peoples; in fact, the rethinking on development as a concept and shift from an economy-centred perspective patterned on westernisation, owes much to the fact that the earlier emphases had failed to incorporate the perspectives of communities, as if these did not matter, and those of the individuals whom development should aim at benefiting also. It is instructive that Ghanaian definitions of wealth and poverty, as reflected in wise sayings and behaviour patterns, stress more the quality of life that people ought to live than mere quantification of value, and show that wealth and poverty are regarded as holistic and transcend the material components. This emphasis on the holistic, which is not new to African systems of thought, is crucial. Development is concerned with the holistic dimensions of wealth and health, and with poverty reduction and generally with opportunity and well-being.

When it comes to the nuances, societies and cultures may differ in the specificities of development and their priorities, and of course on their modes and modalities for operationalising development. In the past, it seemed that development meant westernisation– making the so called under-developed states adopt Western ways and approaches. Development was seen as a condition that a developed country had attained, which could be measured in per capita income statistics, based on dollar or sterling currency values. Paradoxically, the development of Japan did not derive from a wholesale adoption of Western European ways, yet for a long time it was felt that to develop, countries in Africa and elsewhere should westernise. Premised on this thinking, many well-meaning development projects in African countries ended up as abysmal failures, because they had failed to take into account simple questions like whether the people really wanted what was being presented to them, whether their priorities did not lie somewhere else, whether the strategies being adopted were the appropriate ones that could work, or even whether the imposed project did not cause dislocations in the society and environment thereby engendering worse problems. It has since been realised that development needs to be tailored to the needs of specific communities and should take into account the specific environment.

Rather than being overly concerned with the state, the needs of communities and individuals have been scripted into the concept of development. The Millennium Development Goals (MDGs) may be cited in illustration. They target issues like eradication of extreme poverty and hunger, universal primary education by 2015, gender equity and empowerment of women in all aspects of life, as well as ensuring that children do not die needlessly, mothers enjoy good health, and killer diseases like HIV and AIDS, malaria and others that tend to be endemic in the deprived sectors of the society are checked and eradicated. The MDGs also include the development of global partnerships for development. It is stipulated that the principles of sustainable development be integrated into the policies and programmes of countries and should aim at reversing the loss of environmental resources. Arguably, the perspectives of the individual, the community and the nation are included, even if it would appear that the specific goals are determined from outside Africa.

Current concepts of development, such as those projected by multilateral agencies such as the United Nations Development Programme (UNDP) and some international NGOs, support and prioritise individual rights; for example the UNDP states its concept of *Human Development* as follows:

> The process of widening people's choices and the level of well-being they achieve are at the core of the notion of human development. Such choices are neither finite nor static. But regardless of the level of development, the three essential choices for people are to lead a long and healthy life, to acquire knowledge and to have access to the resources needed for a decent standard of living (UNDP 1997:13-14)[12].

A concept of development which emphasises individual rights and empowerment may seem at first sight to be at odds with a cultural concept that prioritises community rights. Yet deep down, there cannot be conflict since the concept of culture and its manifestation in particular African societies does not really deny the individual his/her rights, unless these seem to be antithetical and grossly subversive of community viability.

In spite of societal differences, the culture of a people or community is important to any development that is people-centred. Culture and development need not be antithetical, as is sometimes assumed; culture can in fact be an enabler, setting the parameters for development, facilitating the developmental process, and even providing the means for attaining developmental goals. For example, the United Nations Population Fund (UNFPA) has since decided as a matter of policy to reflect cultural sensitivity in its programming. It seeks information on the cultural context to be able to ascertain the ways in which programme objectives can be made relevant to the grassroots and to ensure also that programmes exploit cultural synergies.

One lesson that the student of development or the developer, if there is anyone like that, might have to learn, is that a people's culture is crucial to their existence and sense of self respect and self worth. Therefore it cannot be toyed with. It cannot be set aside in favour of another society's culture without their consent and participation, not even in the name of development. However negotiation is possible when interventions are planned.

The Encompassing Character of Development

If it is true that development implies empowerment, the exercise of choices and the betterment of the conditions of the communities, individuals and nation states, then it is not just one domain of life that is the issue, but in fact all facets of life. While in the past, development was perceived as economic, it is now widely accepted that it is multi-dimensional and holistic. It shares this feature with culture. Development is certainly economic, as economic growth impacts on the well-being of the aggregate as well as on the individual. Every day, communities around Africa cry for good roads, electricity, potable water, food to eat etc. When the economy is buoyant, these amenities will be available and the quality of life may be enhanced. Culture necessarily affects the economy in positive or negative ways, since economic activity is not carried out in a vacuum.

Culture, Development and Leadership

Equally important are the political dimensions that underpin development; issues of law and order, the existence of peace or its opposite, the mechanisms for resolving conflicts, or the opportunities for the exercise of what are seen to be civil liberties and rights. Again there is a cultural input to all this. Many African countries attempt to superimpose Westminster models of government and politics. What aspects to borrow or not to borrow, what traditional institutions they should or should not replace, and how they should blend or even how to customise borrowed political institutions, are all issues that impinge on the cultures of African peoples. There are also questions of cultural legitimacy here.

Questions such as who holds or should hold power and exercise authority and on what terms; how power and authority ought to be and are exercised are crucial too. These are issues of cultural concern and various traditional systems have had to grapple with these and devise various solutions to such questions. While nobody is suggesting a return to traditional modes of accessing and using power and authority, nevertheless modern systems may draw useful lessons of governance from some traditional political institutions such as chieftaincy and the earth-priestships (the *tendaana* of Northern Ghana). Even when leaders were not directly elected through adult suffrage, they enjoyed popular acceptance and a variety of ritual and non-ritual mechanisms ensured that they remained accountable to their people. This is not to imply that all is necessarily well with these institutions. Chieftaincy for example has had its share of bashing in recent times in Ghana and rightly so, but so have modern politicians.

It may be argued that leaders of the likes of Bokassa in the Central African Republic (who crowned himself emperor), Mobutu (Sese Seko) of Zaire (now the Democratic Republic of the Congo), and Idi Amin (Dada) of Uganda, failed their people because they tried to cast themselves in the mould of African kings of old (see Kirk-Green, 1991 on the African Head of State), i.e. trying to return to traditional cultures.[13] There is a difference however; the post-colonial dictators did not have the legitimate bases to carry on in this fashion, especially as they themselves had chased and hounded the remaining monarchs out of office. Whatever legitimacy they may have had as elected heads of state, they soon lost it. African traditional rulers on the other hand had legitimacy and were not unregulated, given the institutional checks and balances on the African monarch's exercise of power, including the resort to ritual suicide. The era of traditional dictatorships of the types found in Old Dahomey, or in Chaka's Zululand, ended with European colonisation. Unfortunately, the few African monarchs who were lucky to have survived, such as the Swazi kings, do not sometimes seem to realise that cultural change necessitating changes in the approach to governance has come to pass. While in the past, absolute power went hand in hand with absolute responsibility, as one researcher remarked[14], now an absolute monarch such as the Swazi king can reign irresponsibly and treat his kingdom as a personal estate.(See also Ch.14)

Many parts of Africa have experimented with borrowed political institutions and political cultures without having achieved meaningful tangible results. The experimentations continue, sometimes at the instance of international donors. Innovations in governance, whether in the form of military or civilian dictatorships, have however set back development. They entrench an oligarchy whose narrow interests government policies are often aimed at promoting, to the detriment of the public. Consequently, economic and socio-cultural growth has not taken place, and the majority remain disempowered and live in poverty and despondence. This has not contributed to peace and stability, a situation that in turn could not enhance development. Conflicts, it has been argued, are driven not so much by ethnic diversities, as is sometimes suggested, but rather by poverty and the competition for scarce resources; it has therefore been argued that improving governance prevents conflicts, enhances conflict resolution and lays down the most basic requirements for rapid development in all directions. Perhaps it is time to customise political institutions that underpin African cultures. In Ghana's case, there has been a call for the institutionalisation of an Upper House of Parliament where chiefs and other community leaders would have roles to play in the management of the nation.

It is important to remind the reader that local leadership institutions are now being brought into the picture more fully than before, as they have been proven to be the means for effecting dialogue with and within local communities and getting them to adopt partnership roles in development schemes. In Ghana, there are a variety of such institutions that include chiefs, queen mothers, religious personalities, elders, youth and women's leaders, associational leaders and so on. They act as the spokespersons of their communities and for their constituents. They voice local concerns and interests, and this is important since true development should involve and empower the grassroots and prioritise their concerns. Unfortunately, it is widely accepted that the progress and betterment of many communities are being checked by the interminable disputes that rage on as a result of competition for power and authority in some local communities. Many Ghanaian communities have chieftaincy and succession disputes, some of which seem intractable. It may be pointed out that although disputes are not new and can be said to be scripted into some African social organisations, as anthropological studies show, one wonders whether the magnitude and the devastating nature of such conflicts are not due to globalisation. In the past, competing princes might fight with magical weapons and the damage was very negligible. If there were skirmishes they involved close kin, often maternal relatives of the princes. Today, competitors fight with machine guns and dominant political parties are involved. The arena of war soon becomes the whole nation which becomes polarised, rather than the small scale unit of the traditional state.

Culture, Development and Religious Beliefs

The religious issue is a cultural one and has implications also for development. It would not be an exaggeration to describe religion as the foundation of African belief systems (see Ch.7). In many African communities, the person who cannot reconcile himself or herself to his/her gods (the ancestors included) and to kin (they might bewitch him/her, given a cause), lives in fear of the present and the hereafter and lacks the peace of mind to go about his/her business. Though we may not all agree with this statement, it remains a valid characterisation of many Africans—educated and uneducated, urbanite and rural. For many, the traditional gods, divinities and ancestral spirits are alive. Associated with some of these are taboos and regulations about how life should be lived. In addition, many Africans today believe in new gods and espouse faiths not usually regarded as originally African[15].

Religion is an emotive issue which has in the past triggered wars, but religious conflicts are by no means a thing of the past. Despite this background, the inclination to engineer religious homogeneity still persists. Many crimes have indeed been committed in the name of religion. Also religion is being used to exploit people and set back development. It is important however that the religious beliefs of communities, groups and individuals be respected. Neither the state nor its agencies should be seen to interfere or to toy with people's religious beliefs without good justification. To do so is to sow the seeds of insecurity and undermine development directly or indirectly. The current problems of Northern Nigeria for example, are a pointer to the instability and insecurity that can result if religious freedoms and rights, which are cultural rights, are denied or are not respected.

In some African societies, religious beliefs have been demonstrated to have played a crucial role in community development. One cannot imagine what the crime rate would become if people lost faith in God, the gods or the ancestors, and their capacity to sanction wrong doing. Some religious beliefs have in the past protected the sanctity of life, property, interpersonal relationships and even the environment, functions that some of these beliefs continue to perform. However, the concept of outmoded religious beliefs and practices has come to stay. Though the 'outmodedness' of some of these beliefs requires proof, some have been demonstrated to impact negatively on development and on the well-being of individuals and communities. We only have to recall negative practices like *trokosi* (a form of female servitude akin to slavery) in Ghana, and ritual murders of several kinds which have a religious base. Female genital mutilations that seriously undermine health and degrade women have a religious dimension in some African societies, even if this is not the only one.

Culture, Development and Health

Related to religion is the health issue, which again is as much a developmental concern as it is cultural. There are cultural beliefs to the effect that spirit beings control the health and well-being of people. They bring about ill-health and death, but can be the source of healing too. 'Traditional' medicine thus becomes an alternate and alternative help-seeking system in many communities, taking a broader perspective on health. Some of the recipes of 'traditional' healers and medical experts have been proven to be efficacious, but some too have ended up endangering life. Some of the healers' approaches, which are non-alienating, but take account of the cultural environment, have provided lessons that some biomedical practitioners have found worthy of emulation (see also Senah, Chapter 14, this volume).

In the domain of health, culture and development coincide. If a people are not healthy in mind and body, they do not enjoy a good quality of life and it is meaningless to talk about development to such people. They cannot be expected to thrive, whether economically or politically, or in any other domain. This brings to mind the role of pandemics like HIV and AIDS, diseases like malaria, acute respiratory infections, onchocerciasis, as well as urban and rural health and sanitation, availability of clean and safe drinking water, and many more, in the development of African peoples. HIV and AIDS can be described as sapping the spirit and strength of individuals and communities in Africa today. The affected, usually people in their productive ages, can no longer sustain themselves and their families; caring for the sick entails high costs for relatives and ultimately for the nations; and when the sick die, surviving relations are saddled with funeral expenses, not to mention the uncertainties that result from social disruption. In some highly affected areas, the feeling of insecurity is rife, together with that of blame and shame. Many are those who have been orphaned by the pandemic, and for such children, their development is put on hold. The effect of such pandemics is severe on culture. It is for these reasons that sound reproductive health has become an issue of critical importance for all stakeholders.

Health impacts on the society and culture, as it can influence and be influenced by cultural norms and practices. In fact, what is, or is not, an illness, has a cultural definition. Similarly, the modes of intervention, treatment and help-seeking can be influenced by cultural beliefs. The cultural background influences decisions as to whether people should seek treatment for a disease or not, and where to find it. It is not coincidental that social scientists now are required to team up with biomedical specialists in public health research, and in the search for cultural meanings to health issues and the strategies for prevention and containment of pandemics like AIDS.

Culture, Development and Performance Arts

Cultural forms like the fine arts- music and dance, theatre, illustration and painting, poetry, sculpture and the whole gamut of artistic expression- have a place in development, despite the equation between development and the economy. There is a tendency to see the finer arts as falling within the purview of culture and devoid of any developmental connection. It cannot be doubted that giving some people a good song will see them through their day. In the same way, for some people a good story can make or unmake their day, and the stanzas of a poem can ring in the ears for days. The effect of music on work, creating and sustaining psychological moods or alleviating stress and pain, cannot be gainsaid; it can be magical. Artistic expression is a right that individuals and their communities should enjoy and has implications for well-being.

Artistic performance also serves as an effective channel for communicating development messages to individuals and communities and imparting to them knowledge and information. The concept of a theatre for development has gained currency in recent decades (see also Sutherland-Addy, Chapter 17, this volume). The humour and the graphic dramatic illustrations that theatrical performances contain can have deep-seated effects on audiences, even surpassing the ability of words. The fight against HIV-AIDS does employ theatre, dance and music to critical effect in Ghana. Perhaps one could wish that the performances themselves incorporated more African cultural elements than appear to have been the case.

Culture, Development and Education

Culture, as has been pointed out previously, is learnt. Formal and informal learning processes are involved in the acquisition of cultural knowledge and expertise. Education and information are also crucial for meaningful development as people and communities need information and education if they are to enhance the quality of their lives and be able to make informed decisions and choices. The UNDP, UNICEF and UNESCO like any other development agencies, consider education as one of the three most crucial requirements for human development. Here we are not talking exclusively of formal education; informal and non-formal education are also very necessary. One of the worries of development agencies and specialists today is the fact that formal education has not progressed far enough in African communities. As at 2000, the illiteracy rate was nearly half of Ghana's population (45.9%); 54.3% of adult female Ghanaians were considered as illiterate in 2000, while in the Northern Regions illiteracy was rated at over 70% (Ghana Statistical Service, 2002)[16]. If it is considered that 18.6% of Ghana's population have no more than primary schooling, then those with effective literacy skills remain but a small percentage. Through access to secondary and tertiary education, the quality of human resources improves as the necessary skills are acquired for development. Unfortunately, with a rapid rate of social change, the traditional processes of education have largely fallen into disuse.

Education and communication are the means for effecting behaviour change to ensure development. If good decisions and policies cannot be disseminated or explained in such a way that people understand what the issues are, and what choices and options exist, and to be able to make inputs, then they cannot be expected to adopt behaviours that would promote the good of society or make beneficent choices. Given the importance of education, governments have been called upon to adopt free compulsory universal basic education policies.

Making education free should make it affordable for all and sundry, it is hoped, but some would also argue that in addition to making it affordable, the hidden obstacles, often cultural in nature, such as attitudes to formal education for boys and girls, distance from school to the home, the opportunity costs of schooling to parents and children, and school quality and the extent to which the school environment is alienating, among others, would also have to be identified and addressed if the set objectives are to be achieved. For education to succeed, it must be appropriate and culturally meaningful.

The media for communication in Ghana today include radio, television and the newsprint. There is still the need to emphasise the use of local languages in view of the low literacy rates and the inadequate command of the English language among many citizens. However, English remains the official language of the country and almost all written communication is in English. It has been argued that effective education should take account of the local environment, but this is not easily accomplished when the medium of instruction and communication in basic level schools is different from the child's mother tongue. School textbooks project foreign images and issues, while not much effort is made to incorporate local materials and draw examples from the localities. In this respect, the educational systems in place in African communities have been faulted for being out of tune with the local cultural environment.

Culture, Development and Environments

The physical and natural environments also are important and need to be properly managed to ensure sustainability and expedite development processes. There has to be an awareness of the constraints placed on the environment and the consequences of its ruthless exploitation. Mining ventures, in their use of dangerous chemicals for example, have ruined irreparably the sources of livelihood for many communities in mining areas. Water supplies are unsafe and even the soils are rendered unproductive for farming and other uses. Countries that are late to start on the path to technological and scientific advancement, such as those of sub-Saharan Africa, tend also to be rich in biodiversities and would need to protect these resources from loss. The role of science and technology (particularly non-African technology and science) in development has usually been stressed, perhaps over-stressed to the detriment of other important components. The argument is not that Africans should reinvent the wheel so to speak, or that they jettison it because someone else was first to invent it. The problem lies more in uncritical adoption of technologies that are not appropriate without any thought for customisation (see also Addy and Laing, Chapter 16, this volume). Development could be enhanced and improvements achieved in group and individual well-being by the introduction of appropriate technologies. The introduction of high-yielding crops and labour-saving devices certainly enabled more to be produced to meet human needs and for labour to be saved with the possibility that time and energy could be reallocated to other competing needs, including leisure. Unfortunately, this has a telling effect on the fragile environments and eco-systems, the destruction of which jeopardises societies and ways of life.

However, while the demands made by western industries and markets for developing world raw products and the sophisticated technologies imported to make extraction more efficient and thorough, are blameable for environmental degradation, some African cultural practices that have persisted, such as setting bush fires cannot be ignored when it comes to a roll call of culprits.

Though development, as has been argued, is holistic, with different dimensions or components, it is important nevertheless to note that the different domains do not work in isolation, but in synergy to achieve beneficial results. For example, the achievement of economic growth is enhanced by a healthy population that is empowered and educated to understand the issues, and is equipped with the skills to function. Such comprehensive empowerment would strengthen the commitment of the people to achieving the objectives of development, given the assurance that the wealth created in the process would be shared equitably, since empowerment ensures equity. On the other hand, empowerment cannot be genuine if the share out of the cake is not acceptable, people lack a voice to express their concerns and to obtain redress, and if people cannot themselves do anything to improve their lot, but have to be dependent on others. There would then be no peace and stability. There is no need for a reminder of the saying that it is idle hands that respond readily to the call to arms and to mischief making. This is illustrated by the fact that while in the past there was employment for all and most people were gainfully employed, today, the same cannot be said. Many of the youth are idle and they are beginning to be the source of instability. One only has to open the newspapers to see the extent to which youth unemployment is undermining development. Globalisation cannot be excused as the culprit.

The Outmoded

This chapter cannot be concluded without further remarks on 'outmoded customs', a pet phrase in Ghana, and indeed around Africa, today. There are people for whom any artefact, belief, feeling or practice that is distinctively African or non-Western is deemed to be misplaced and outmoded. For such people, African marriage practices, family norms (especially the extended family), systems of reciprocity such as gift-giving, foods and culinary practices, dress codes, exhibition of courtesy, African religious practices, African languages, chieftaincy and leadership institutions, etc. have no place in the contemporary society; they are outmoded. There are even those who are ashamed of their dark skins and seek to change their appearance by bleaching; their skins too are outmoded. The same might dye their hair or perm it into a long flowing mane that resembles Caucasian hair. For some of these people, African Studies has no place on the University curriculum or timetable. As such attitudes are not based on any rational considerations, we can only label them as exhibitions of prejudice and loss of faith in oneself.

It would be myopic not to realise that aspects of a people's culture can be ambivalent and, depending on perspective, can be said to be positive or negative. The important thing is to assess and identify the negative sides of issues and deal with them, while exploiting the beneficial aspects of any cultural institution.

There is no doubting the fact that certain aspects of culture, whether African or non-African, can pose problems for modern development, especially when there is retention of certain practices, norms and beliefs that have lost their utility value for the majority of the present generations of society. In many African societies today, there is talk of 'outmoded' customs and practices. These may be aspects of culture that have lost their positive values as society itself has changed considerably to obliterate the logic of such practices. Nevertheless, a conservative core still continues to uphold such aspects of a by-gone culture, despite the disaffection of the majority of society. 'Outmodedness' as a concept cannot however be anything new since when viewed against the backdrop of a changing dynamic, outmodedness must have always existed. Change must involve conflict and negotiation, since change itself often is gradual rather than a sudden transformation of life. Nonetheless there is need to be careful about the rampant labelling of any practice or norm which is associated with traditional ways as outmoded.

The glib denigration of culture is unfortunate, especially as nothing is usually being suggested as replacement. Bashing sometimes leads to the call for legislation to outlaw some norms. Often, those who call for such measures do so on the basis of rumour; as they themselves may not have much acquaintance with the offending norm and certainly cannot claim any understanding of its logic and its pervasiveness within a nation state. Take the case of widowhood rites. There is evidence that in some ethnic groups in Ghana, the rites are vicious and endanger the life of the widow. Where such rites require sexual intercourse with a stranger in order to shed the pollution of a spouse's death, the risk of contracting or passing on HIV and AIDS cannot be ruled out. From such reports, it becomes only too easy for a 'knowledgeable' person who mounts the podium to call for laws to criminalise the performance of widowhood rites. Once you have such laws in a country, all nationals are obliged to conform. However, the person who has called for the law may not even know what constitutes widowhood rites, what diversities exist in the country where these rites are concerned, and whether in all cases widowhood rites are negative. Such uninformed denigration of culture is dangerous and cannot be the way to development.

Development enshrines the right to be consulted and to be listened to; the bashers of culture are not in the mood for any of this. In the pursuit of development, communities and individuals are entitled to a voice when it comes to affairs that pertain to, or concern their lives. This is where it has to be realised that dialogue and persuasion are far superior to legislation and compulsion in regulating life on issues that are deemed to affect societal development, especially when the community happens not to share 'Big Brother's' concerns on what is best for the generality. Indeed we create legal problems when we have a series of laws that cannot be enforced and do not have any merit in the eyes of the ordinary person. A situation where many people cannot sympathise with some 'bad' laws and therefore violate them, can degenerate into situations where even good laws cannot be enforced.

Conclusion

The importance of culture to development is suggested by the recent growing interest in culture as it manifests itself in various communities. It is multi-dimensional, some will say, all encompassing. It may in the long run be nothing more or less than an abstraction, but it does not exist in a vacuum. Whatever it is, it is learnt and is transmitted. It is subject to change and for that reason, has been described as dynamic and interactive. It need not be seen as sacrosanct, and we can negotiate about what to retain or drop. Negotiation is on-going, although it may not take an organised format. It can be assumed that every society wants what is good for it and therefore shapes its culture according to its needs. The fact that something was done in the past does not make it cultural.

As the meaning of development shifts from concerns with economic indicators such as per capita incomes and the quantification of gadgetry, to concerns about well-being, aspirations and freedoms for not only national states, but even more importantly for communities and individuals, for men and women, adults and children, handicapped people and non-handicapped people, the realisation has dawned that development in the third world cannot be simply the imposition of westernisation. All countries are developing, although some appear to be doing better than others. In this respect, culture and development can be seen as bedfellows, rather than as enemies. Though outmoded beliefs and norms can stand in the way of progress, this should not be seen to mean that it is culture which is opposed to progress, since outmoded norms are themselves often in the process of re-negotiation as their logic changes in the face of new knowledge. It could in fact be argued that rather than attempt to import foreign ideas and experiences and even technologies wholesale and implant them in another culture, effort should be made to customise the import so that it meets the needs of the beneficiary. In this respect it can be argued that development rather should conform to community and individual aspirations and take into account local environments– both physical and social. The articulation between culture and development is a dynamic one.

Review Questions

1. What do you understand by culture and development as concepts? Show in what ways the two exhibit similarities and/or differences.

2. To what extent does an analysis of the UNO's Millennium Development Goals illustrate the concept of development?

3. What would you consider as the diacritical marks of culture?

4. For some, culture is about drumming and dancing. How would you explain how we could study a people's culture through drumming and dancing?

5. What in your view are 'outmoded customs'? Outline some of the approaches and interventions that you would consider appropriate for the eradication of undesirable practices in our communities.

6. Consider the importance of 'cultural sensitivity' to programme implementation in Ghana.

Suggested Readings

Benedict, R. 1935. *Patterns of Culture*. London: Routledge and Kegan Paul.

Bentsi-Enchill, K. 1971. *Institutional Challenges of Our Time*. 4th J. B. Danquah Memorial Lecture. Accra: Ghana Academy of Arts and Sciences.

Crewe, E and E. Harrison 1998. *Whose Development*? London: Zed Books.

Eade D. (Ed.) 2002. *Development and Culture*. Oxford: Oxfam GB. (The volume contains several chapters on different aspects of culture and development such as Cultures, spirituality and development; culture, liberation and development; faith and economics in development; women's resistance and development etc.)

Eliot, T. S. 1948. *Notes Towards the Definition of Culture*. London: Faber.

Fortes, M. 1971. 'The Family: Bane or Blessing?' University of Ghana Open Lecture, Accra: Universities of Ghana Press.

Fugelsang, A. 1984. 'The Myth of a People's Ignorance". *Development Dialogue* 1-2, pp42-62.

Sherageldin, I and J. Martin-Brown (eds.) 1999. *Culture in Sustainable Development: Investing in Cultural and Natural Endowments*. Washington D. C. World Bank.

Endnotes

1. T. S. Eliot 1948. *Notes Towards the Definition of Culture*. London: Faber

2. E. B Tylor 1873. *Primitive Culture* London: Murray

3. C. Kluckhohn and Henry A. Murray (eds.). 1948. *Personality in Nature Society and Culture* . New York: Alfred A Knopf.

4. M. Ember and C. R. Ember 1981. *Cultural Anthropology*. Engelwood Cliffs: Prentice-Hall.

5. A. K. Awedoba 2002. *Culture and Development in Africa*. Legon: Institute of African Studies.

6. See J. Maquet 1972a. *Civilizations of Black Africa*. New York: OUP and 1972b *Africanity, the Cultural Unity of Africa*. London: OUP.

7. Revised and enlarged issue of Awedoba 2002.

8. See the Commission's website - http://www.ghanaculture.gov.gh/default.asp?

9. V. Turner 1969. *The Ritual Process*. London: Routledge and Kegan Paul.

10. E. V Asihene 1980. *Apoo Festival* Tema: Ghana Publishing Corporation.

11. Akiga 1939. *Akiga's Story* (The Tiv Tribe as seen by one of its members) Translated by Rupert East. London: IAI/OUP. Reprinted 1965.

12. UNDP 1997. *Human Development Report 1997*. Oxford: Oxford University Press

13. A. H. M. Kirk-Green 1991. "His Eternity, His Eccentricity, or His Exemplarity: A Further Contribution to the Study of H. E. the African Head of State". *African Affairs* 90(), pp163-187

14. M. W. Young 1966. "The Divine Kingship of the Jukun: A Re-evaluation of some Theories". *Africa* 36(2), pp135-153.

15. There are those who would disagree with any suggestion that Islam or Christianity is non-African or foreign to the Africa continent, but this is not the place to debate the issue.

CHAPTER 7

AFRICAN WORLDVIEWS
Brigid M. Sackey

Introduction

The notion of 'worldview' refers to the way a particular people or society understands or perceives the world in which it finds itself. It embodies ideas and beliefs which human beings have about the origins of the universe, their relations with and obligations to other human beings, as well as the natural elements or ecology and cosmological phenomena. As the concept of worldview is rather comprehensive, this chapter will focus on only certain fundamental aspects of it. It will emphasise the worldviews as they were developed and lived among different African societies prior to encounters with other cultures and how they continue to change and affect African peoples contemporaneously. These views include beliefs and/or practices that tend to confront the young inquiring, yet bewildered mind which often has difficulty in appreciating what may be called 'authentically' or 'traditionally' African. This is especially true of most African Christians and contemporary young people who have adopted and internalised foreign cultures in preference to their local worldviews.

If a worldview refers to the ideas and beliefs people have about the world, then there are as many worldviews as there are different peoples and cultures. Since Africa has a diversity of ethnic groups and cultures that differ considerably in many aspects from others, each ethnic group may have its own particular views about the world that have been shaped by specific beliefs, practices and traditions, and which are as such restricted to the people through which they have evolved. As stated earlier, a worldview is closely related to the ecology and climate. For example, people who depend on farming for their subsistence will formulate ideas about their world around those elements that play a crucial part in sowing and harvesting, while people engaged in marine fishery will pay attention to the sea and the weather and know when it is feasible to go to sea and when it is not. It is therefore not possible to take one worldview as perceived by one group of people and regard it as typical of all others. Yet, various differences notwithstanding, and given the fact that not one or a standard African worldview exists, there are profound underlying similarities running through the worldviews that have produced a general pattern of belief systems and practice in African societies.

Significance of Worldviews

Worldviews are significant because they help human beings make sense of the world in which they live; they help explain inexplicable phenomena and occurrences in human society and give people a way of understanding their world. But the fact that the worldview supplies people with answers to the questions which arise in the human world does not imply that the answers are scientific or objective verities. They are answers which a people have found to be most practicable and meaningful to them. By giving people a way of interpreting and understanding their own existence, worldviews equip them emotionally, intellectually and culturally to face the hazards and challenges of life. Without a worldview, the existence of human life would be meaningless. Worldviews therefore serve as guidelines to people as they go through changes in their lives and reflect upon them. Worldviews thus are not stagnant but dynamic; they may be changed to suit modernising influences or repackaged to counter them. The following two examples may give some clarification on the topic.

The first example concerns the practice of traditional puberty rites that were banned by European missionaries and colonisers as indecent, pagan and uncivilised. Puberty rites are one of the most important rites of passage for females and males in many societies. The term 'rite of passage' was first used by the French social anthropologist, Arnold van Gennep in 1908 to describe the ceremonies which accompany changes at the different stages in the life of an individual. It is believed that every human being passes through these stages: birth, puberty, marriage and death, and certain rites are performed at each of these stages to allow the smooth transition from one stage to the other. Puberty signified the attainment of adulthood or maturity and sought to preserve cultural values or worldviews pertaining to virginity (especially of young girls, while at the same time cautioning them against moral laxity); among boys, initiation rites were meant to instil courage and responsibility. The rites also tended to defer the onset of sexual activity in young people at least until they had gone through the ceremonies which were usually not performed until after the onset of menarche (menstruation) in girls and biological maturity in boys (breaking of the vocal cords, appearance of pubic hair etc.). With the current alarming incidence of HIV and AIDS and teenage pregnancy around Africa, there have been calls from various individuals, organisations and sectors of the public to resuscitate and repackage aspects of the rites that aim at chastity or abstinence that the HIV and AIDS campaigns also emphasise (Sackey, 2001). Some rites involve the shedding of blood, such as the performance of female circumcision or female genital mutilation, facial and other bodily scarifications. As global consensus has been reached on human rights and values (a 'global worldview' as it were), these practices have come under scrutiny and have not only been deemed cruel and inhuman, but have been also recognised as providing avenues for the spread of HIV and other communicable diseases.

The second example seems quite apposite in the contemporary university setting in Africa. The Ghanaian slang term, *apuskelele,* refers to a young female dress fashion that many in society regard as immoral because "it exposes your shape, your breast, your belly, and your back. And when the men see that, they ridicule you. It can also be a very short skirt, mini skirt or tight trousers."[1] Yet this same fashion in America and Europe is generally acceptable and does not breach any moral code or value, and supports the view that different peoples have different worldviews, with what is abhorred in one society being condoned or even appreciated in another. From the foregoing two examples, it becomes obvious that a worldview does not comprise only so-called archaic rituals, but may include new views on self-expression and representation of the body.

The academic study of worldviews extends into the realm of other disciplines such as philosophy, anthropology and religion. Philosophers generally identify and relegate worldviews into a sub-division of philosophy called 'natural philosophy' or 'metaphysics' as this was "conceived as the effort to grasp the fundamental explanatory principles of nature" (Manicas, 1987: 9). Anthropologists sometimes maintain the term *worldview* itself or may speak of 'belief systems,' while scholars of religion may speak of 'doctrinal systems' or 'theological beliefs.' However, in the case of African worldviews, Western authors of religion hardly refer to them as 'theological' because they do not count the indigenous, ethnic-based African religions or what is widely known as *African Traditional Religions* (ATRs) among the so-called 'world religions,' comprising Judaism, Buddhism, Hinduism, Christianity and Islam.

A major reason often given for placing ATRs in a category of its own is that most African societies did not possess the knowledge of, nor did they develop their own writing systems so as to enable them to codify, compile or document their belief systems or worldviews as others have done in the form of scriptures, for example the Bible (Christianity), the Koran (Islam), or the Torah (Judaism). But the question can be asked how Africans who did not develop and keep their worldviews in written form have been able to sustain their culture over the years and indeed to withstand the test of time and the onslaught of powerful foreign influences? Especially in the contemporary period, much attention is being given to esoteric systems of codification such as the hieroglyphics of Ancient Egypt and the complex marking of the *Ifa* divination system of the Yoruba (Abimbola, 1997). These studies demonstrate that the situation in Africa, as far as systems of codification are concerned, is far more complex than has been made out to be. Another answer to this question may be found in proverbs and other forms of African cultural heritage. For example, an Akan proverb says: *nipa wu a, ne tekyerema nporo*, to wit, even though human beings die, their tongues (words) do not rot. In other words, the wisdom, knowledge and philosophy embodied in peoples' words or speeches live on when these are transmitted to younger generations as verbal knowledge gets imprinted on the psyche much more firmly. It can be further argued that although Islam has a scriptural basis, Muslims' main mode of transmitting Islamic religion and culture is by memorising the verses of the Koran, also a verbal action, rather than through writing. (See also Ch.3)

Another claim used in denying African worldviews the acknowledgement that they deserve is the misrepresentation that Africans do not have a history, and that Africa's history began with colonisation by Europeans who also wrote Africa's history. On the contrary, Plavoet (1996: 46-104) contends that even though literacy is important in the history of a society, it is not the beginning of its history. Human beings as well as their societies, cultures and religions are, by the mere fact that they exist, or existed for a specific period in a specific place, time- and space-bound. Regardless of script or writing, it is important to note that Africans have, by means of oral culture, been able to deal with philosophical ideas about the ultimate quest or reason for human existence, as other peoples have done with script. The ideas or beliefs of the people have evolved with time and though they were not written down or codified as coherent belief systems, they do not exist in chaos. They are shrouded in philosophical complexities that are systematically embodied in the form of myths or stories, proverbs, symbols, gestures, art, etiquette, music, dance, drum language etc. and have been transmitted through teaching and imitation, to the younger generation who observe the actions of older generation, or undergo periods of formal training (see also Chapters 3, 17, 19 and 20, this volume). According to Mbiti (1975: 31), African peoples observed the world around them and reflected upon it. They looked at and pondered over the cosmic elements, namely the sky, sun, moon, and clouds above; the rain, rainbow, animals, insects, plants, rivers, lakes, rocks and mountains. They deliberated on the earth below and formed ideas about how things look the way they do and where they are located. From this premise we discuss below African ideas about God, divinities, ancestors and the moral order.

Religious worldviews

African worldviews generally reflect two distinct worlds, namely a material, visible world, and a spiritual and invisible world that are interdependent and constantly interacting. The invisible world is made of spiritual beings that include a Supreme God, a multitude of spiritual beings known variedly as deities, divinities or gods; spirits of ancestors or shadows of human beings that have died, and both benevolent and malevolent spirits (especially witch spirits). The visible world harbours human beings and other tangible creatures, including the sky elements, trees, rivers, rocks.

God is at the centre of African beliefs, and dominates and penetrates all other spheres. Belief in God is taken for granted, but exactly how this belief in God originated is highly debatable. According to Mbiti (1975: 40-41), it is a very ancient belief in African religious life, and he gives three possible explanations. First, the belief in God might have arisen through reflecting on the universe, how it came into being and who caused it to evolve. People realised at a very early date that the universe must have had an origin and, using their imaginations, they acknowledged that a spirit being, God, must have been the creator. Second, the idea of God must have probably arisen because of the limitations of human capacity. Human beings ostensibly realised their own limitations and weakness in power and knowledge. This was particularly the case in the face of death, calamity, and natural phenomena such as thunderstorms, earthquakes, epidemics, and diseases that human beings could not control or understand. Such situations might have led people to speculate that there must be someone greater than themselves and greater than the world, who had full control over it. This idea of a creator made it logical and necessary for human beings to depend on the one who was more powerful than human beings. Third, the belief in God may have been suggested by the forces of nature, particularly the powers of the weather, storms, thunder and lightning, rain, and the phenomena of day and night, together with the expanse of the sky with its sun, moon and stars. Human beings tended to name where these mighty forces emanate as the abode of this God (called heaven by Christians) with God as its controller, and the human abode – earth, where human beings are at its centre.

In Africa, each ethnic group has a principal name for God, which is unique as it is not shared by any other spiritual being, and neither does the name for God exist in the plural form. For example, there is generally a belief in one God named variously in Ghana as *Onyame*[2], (Akan), *Nawuni* (Mamprusi), *Nayiwum* (Talensi), *Ataa-Naa-Nyonmo* (Ga), *Mawu-Lisa* (Fon), and *Mawu* (Ewe, Ga-Dangbe). In Nigeria, God is known as *Chuku* (Igbo), *Oludumare* (Yoruba), and *Oghene* (Urhorbo). God is called *Ngewo* among the Mende of Sierra Leone, *Akposso* by the Uwolowu (Togo) and *N'gai* among the Masai people (Kenya and Tanzania). The Zulu (South Africa) call him *Unkulunkulu*, while the Baryanwanda in Burundi refer to God as *Imana*. That God is the creator of all things is fundamental in African worldviews. According to some societies, creation is still in process, new things are still being made and will continue to be created in time (Opoku,

1978: 19). For this reason there are many names which describe God as creator. Even though Africans do not have writing, this idea can be inferred from tales often called "creation myths" or "origins stories." It is very important to clarify these terms since myths for example have different meanings.

Viewing creation through myths

At the popular level, the term 'myth' is generally understood as the equivalent of "fairy tale" or "fantasy." Others consider myths as 'primitive' philosophy of metaphysical thought. Still others view myths as a post-scientific mode of thought. However, a myth should be seen as a rationale not only for religious practices, but as stories that give meaning to certain events, ceremonies and behaviour which, though might have happened in the remote past, still have a bearing on present day existence. There is a myth behind everything Africans do and believe in. Each society has its own myths, which tell of how the world was created, how it will end, and the relationship of human beings to spiritual entities. Some of the popular myths that explain why the sky is up high and not easily accessible are as follows: Oral traditions in many African societies say that sky/ heaven (and by implication God) used to be very close to the earth and human beings could communicate with God without any restrictions. The myths blame women for the separation between God and human beings. A Yoruba myth, for example, attributes this state of affairs to a greedy woman who took a large quantity of food from heaven and could not finish it and as a result, heaven was removed from the reach of humankind. In another Yoruba myth, a woman with dirty hands touched and infected the sky, causing it to be removed from its former location. Among the Akan of Ghana, an old woman is supposed to have caused sky/God to move up higher to its present location. The myth says that God, *Onyame*, and human beings used to live close together until an old woman invented and began to pound *fufu* (the staple food) regularly, using a mortar and a pestle. The pestle hit God each time the woman raised it high. *Onyame* complained several times, but since the woman would not heed his complaints, he moved up farther and farther into the sky. Seeing what had happened, the old woman persuaded the community to re-establish a closer relationship with God by asking the whole community to bring out their mortars which were piled on one another to make a ladder. However, they discovered that they needed only one more mortar to get to the sky and the same old woman suggested that they remove the bottom-most mortar and place it top-most. When they did this, the whole pile of mortars crumbled down. Thus, the sky stayed up high, leaving the earth below.

Regarding creation, the Christian Bible has adopted Jewish creation myths to explain how the world, its inhabitants and contents came into being. But since Christianity is counted among the world religions as indicated earlier, its myths also tend to be regarded differently, not as 'myths,' since myths are supposed to be for the 'superstitious' minded, scriptless cultures. As Sutherland-Addy (1997: 20) argues, "what is considered in Judaeo-Christian dogma has in fact been the ideology that has often cushioned the Bible from being recognised as a great compendium of mythical narratives along with many others in the world."

The following examples of African myths tend to have a similar perception that the world was created just as in Judeo-Christian beliefs. But although there are parallels in these myths, it can be argued that ideas or cultures can develop independently of each other, though when cultures clash it becomes difficult to determine the claim to authenticity or ownership of a particular idea. Thus the Yoruba believe that the earth was originally a watery and marshy waste, and *Oludumare*, the Almighty, lived in the heavens with the divinities. The divinities used to visit the earth and play and hunt by walking on spider's webs, which served as bridges. *Oludumare* decided to turn the watery and marshy waste into solid earth. Therefore he summoned the chief of the divinities, *Orisha-nla* and entrusted him with the assignment and gave him loose earth in a snail's shell and a hen and a pigeon, which were to spread and scatter the loose earth. On earth *Orisha-nla* emptied the snail's shell and at once, the hen and the pigeon began to scatter it, covering a significantly wide area of the marshy waste. When *Orisha-nla* had completed the assignment, *Oludumare* sent his messenger, the chameleon, which walks with circumspection, to inspect the work. He reported that the world was both wide and dry. According to the Yoruba, the place where creation began was called *Ife*, which means wide. This was how the holy city of the Yoruba got its name. It was after the creation of the earth that human beings were formed in heaven by *Orisha-nla* and *Oludumare* breathed into the bodies. *Orisha-nla* is believed today to be carrying on forming human bodies.

Among the Akan, *Onyame* first created the sky, then the earth, rivers and plants. Finally he created human beings and animals. God created the spirits of the waters, rivers and plants. In another Akan creation story, *Onyame* simply dropped a ladder from heaven and allowed human beings, male and female together, to descend and populate the earth. Interestingly, the Akan believe that it is this same ladder that shows up at death for human beings to walk up back to *Onyame*. Thus the saying, *owu atwer baako mmfrow*, i.e., each individual will climb the ladder of death.

In the above myths, God either performed the creation himself or delegated it to his subordinates under careful supervision. In most Akan creation narratives, even when the creator is a male principle, both man and woman are made to appear, to descend, or are moulded together, thus stressing complementarity. Above all, there are a number of female creator gods, and among the Uzo (Ezon or Ijaw) of southern Nigeria, *Temearu* or *Wongyi (Wonyengi)* is the creator. In some parts of the Republic of Benin and neighbouring Togo, *Nana Buku [Buruku]* a female, is the chief creating deity (See Sackey, 1996). An Akan folktale alludes to a female principle called *Antwiwaa (Ankywaa) Nyame* as the creator God. According to the tale, *Antwiwaa Nyame* was the owner of the Akan stool on which she sat when creating the world. Holding a big bow and arrow in her hands, she would shoot the arrow to particular places where she wanted her creation to be located.[3] The attribute, Onyame *baatan pa* (the good nurturing Nyame), supports the femaleness of God as the word *obaatan* refers to the caring qualities of women.[4] While some societies depict God as solely male and others as female as we have seen, other Africans believe God to be a dual principle manifesting as both male and female or symbolising complementarity. For example, the Fon of Benin perceive God as female and male as shown in the duality of *Mawu-Lisa*, *Mawu* being the female, and *Lisa*, the male parts respectively. The Ga people of Ghana call God *Ataa-Naa-Nyomo*, which translates as grandfather/grandmother God, depicting God as balanced gender. It is important to note that gender complementarities have existed in African religions and other realms long before the currents of women's liberation and empowerment in the West. (See also Ch. 4)

In 1887, A.B. Ellis wrote a book in which he doubted the knowledge of God among the Akan or the *Tschii Speaking Peoples of the Gold Coast*. He claimed that even if they did, then they borrowed it from European Christian missionaries on the coast. Later, he recanted on this idea when he wrote his book, *The Ewe Speaking Peoples of the Gold Coast* (1889). This misconception was partly due to the apparent absence of temples for the worship of God. According to Erivwo (1983: 358), in the whole of tropical Africa, only the Asante and the Gikuyu (Kikuyu) of Kenya seem to have a structured worship of God at a particular location with priests through whom offerings were made to him. The Urhobo erected altars for *Oghene* for regular worship, though they do not have temples and priests. Otherwise God can be worshipped in sacred groves, special shrines or anywhere. The people of the Gold Coast, for example, knew they had a strong conception of God whom they generally did not build temples for or approach through mediums (priests/priestesses) because God is accessible to all as depicted in the proverb, *wo pe asem aka akyere Nyame a, ka kyere Mframa,* or "if you want to speak to God, speak to the wind". It is said that the Asantehene, king of the Asante (of Ghana) every morning as he wakes up touches an *adinkra* symbol that hangs at the head of his bed and says: *Onyame biribi wo sor, ma no mmeka me,* meaning "God, release your mighty power above to touch me." This is an acknowledgement of God's presence, might and easy accessibility. Similarly among the Urhobo of Nigeria, *Oghene,* God, can be approached by everybody. The daily worship may take the following form: a man wakes up in the morning, takes a chewing stick and brushes his teeth with it. After this he looks up to heaven holding up the stick as he addresses this prayer:

> *Oghene, Ubi Ukpabke, Obe Ode Oteakpovworhurhu,*
> "I know neither what is in front nor what is behind, I have taken no-one's
> property; if anyone is after me or after my property, O God, you know him."

Having prayed thus, he uses the chewing stick to describe a circle round his head, and casts it on the altar of *Oghene* (Erivwo 1983: 360). This performance indicates the protective power of God, his justness and knowledge on which human beings depend. (See Figure 4- Osun worshippers).

Figure 4 – Osun Worshippers, Nigeria

The Divinities

In the Judeo-Christian Bible, angels were present during the creation myth recorded in Genesis. Similarly, from the Yoruba creation myth narrated earlier, it is evident that *Oludumare* did not live alone. The *orisha* whose chief is the *Orisha-nla*, were already in existence and acted as his messengers. These messengers in ATR have been given the name divinities, deities or gods, though each society has its own name for them such as *orisha* (Yoruba), *abosom* (Akan), *won* (Ga), *trowo* (Ewe), *vodu* (Fon). The divinities are spirit beings localized in some forms of natural phenomena such as trees, rocks, stones, hills, rivers, the sea and some animals. They may be male or female and are approached through the medium of a priest or priestess (*okomfo*, Akan; *olorisa*, Yoruba; *wontse*, Ga). Others are represented by anthropomorphic (or resembling a human being) imagery. Akan deities generally are spirits, as opposed to the Yoruba where the concept of apotheosis or deification (making a god of a human being) of human heroes is prevalent. Deification of human beings raises the status of the dead person to that of a deity or god. This resembles the practice by Roman Catholics whereby human beings because of their good deeds are beatified (blessed) or canonised as saints. In the secular world, such persons are honoured often in their life time and sometimes posthumously as honorary members of certain groups in the society, or they are accorded titles such as Dr., Sir, or *Nana*.

As has been discussed above, certain ethnic groups including the Akan, believe that God, signified by the sky, used to be so close to human beings who could even touch it. According to mythology, when God detached himself from human beings, he sent the divinities (*abosom*, plural; *obosom*, singular) which are spirit beings to attend to the immediate needs of human beings. Their very origin and the functions for which they were created, place them in a special relationship with the Creator, but they are never put on a par with God. Unlike *Onyame*, these spirits are approached through a medium.[5] *Onyame* does not compete with the deities; neither do the Akan *abosom* compete with each other as existed in the ancient Greek religious pantheon. They simply recognise each other's jurisdiction and may even collaborate.[6] Though the deities are subordinate to God, they nevertheless possess some autonomy in reacting to human conduct. It is believed that, like the ancestors, the *abosom* reward good human conduct with abundant rain, food, children and general prosperity, while they punish adverse conduct with drought, famine, diseases, infertility and even death. These 'checks and balances' on human conduct by the deities are means of exercising their function as custodians of morality. The *abosom* are also generally concerned with medicine and healing, but in addition they have their specific functions and limitations. Every deity has its own jurisdiction. Some are concerned with fertility, others with curing small pox and other epidemics, or with harvests, war and peace, while yet others reveal secrets, apprehend witches, and settle disputes etc.

From the foregoing, it seems the divinities have positive and responsible functions, yet it is also believed that they can be used for evil purposes by individuals and invariably it is the negative aspects that are embellished. In fact, the concept of deities is the greatest aspect of African worldviews that has posed a great challenge in the relationship between Christianity and ATR. While Christians regard the existence of many deities as polytheism (the worship of many gods), ATR practitioners think otherwise. They believe the deities form an integral part of their religious cultures and Christian efforts to have them relinquish this theology will render ATRs incomplete. They also believe that the deities are spirit beings who represent God on earth as God moved farther up with the sky. Also, what is called deities may sometimes not be *abosom* in the view of the adherents. For example, among the Akan, the lower spirit world is believed to be hierarchically structured with the *abosom* at the apex of this hierarchy, while other powerful sources called *asuman* occupy the lowest rank. Even though both are equally powerful and their cults are similar, the *asuman* are spirits that inhabit small man-made objects that can be carried or hung in the house such as charms. The *asuman* perhaps represent what can be termed 'fetishes' in the proper sense of the word, namely handmade objects by human beings in which mystical power resides. Such objects can be bought, sold, or reproduced by their owners, while an *obosom* which dwells in a river, tree or mountain cannot be bought. While human beings acknowledge both the protective and destructive powers of the *asuman*, they are generally believed to be destructive and are therefore responsible for evil. On the other hand the saying, *Onyame ma wo yare a, oma wo adur n so*, meaning "when God gives you sickness, he also gives you medicine" seems to indicate that misfortune can also come from God and that in the Akan worldview, God has a balanced nature. He is good, yet he can punish people for wrongdoing. In effect the sickness is a temporal measure or lesson for the wayward to come back home, or for the evil one to reconcile with what is good. Good and evil co-exist to make the moral order functional, and to remind human beings of the power of God. The *abosom* therefore are sources of morality and good conduct for Africans and Ghanaians generally and the Akan specifically.

Ancestral Veneration

In African worldviews, human life is generally perceived as a cycle. Thus, a person is born, grows into adulthood, marries, produces offspring, dies and is reincarnated. Death therefore is not finality, but a means to new life. Those good family members who have died are referred to as ancestors and it is these that the living family members venerate through communication in forms such as libation. The ancestors are believed to live the same life as they lived on earth in a certain location called *asamando* by the Akan, as they wait in turns to be reborn. The abode of the dead lacks the concepts of heaven and hell. There is simply one place where all the dead go and that place is not described in terms of punishment or reward, though the dead have the power to reward the living for good conduct and punish them for adverse behaviour. They also act as intermediaries between the living family members and the spirit world. Here the view that the dead climbs a ladder back to God, as stated earlier, seems to be contested if there is no idea of heaven. Do the dead perhaps climb up to *Onyame* to give account of their life on earth before they descend to *asamando*? This is possible, since according to another tendency in the Akan worldview, the abode of the dead is believed to be here on earth. This discussion is a pointer to the fact that there are no standard worldviews as they vary even within the same ethnic group.

In African worldviews, death is one of the phases that a human being passes through. As a rite of passage, the correct performance of certain ceremonies is meant to help usher the dead smoothly into the spiritual world or to give him/her a 'fitting burial', as it is termed in Ghana. A fitting burial is of utmost importance both for the dead and the living because of the potential for the power of the dead to inflict good or bad luck on the living. In a sense, the dead are dependent on the living properly performing the rituals so as to put them to rest, while the living are dependent on the dead to link the family with the spiritual power which the ancestors com-

1">

1">

mand. However, in the contemporary period, a 'fitting burial' has been misconstrued to mean expensive burial ceremonies, rather than strict conformity to laid down procedures to prepare the dead for the spiritual world. This is manifested in elaborate expenditures with regard to luxurious and costly coffins, shrouds or suits and expensive make-up of the corpse, and elaborate feasting in the form of excessive drinking, eating and dancing that sometimes may be mistaken for a joyful party which often ends up in debts to the family after the burial. The incurrence of debt after a funeral can give rise to family quarrels and disintegration. In view of this fact, some traditional authorities in some regions of Ghana including Ashanti and Brong Ahafo, as well as Christian churches, have advised communities and individual members of society to desist from expensive funerals which tend to make meaningless the traditional understanding of a fitting burial. The effectiveness of this advice remains to be measured.

Moral Values

We started off by saying that Africans do not generally have scripts and therefore do not have written documentation on their worldviews. This reality, as we also established, does not indicate that absence of writing means chaos, as other alternatives to sacred writing exist, among which is the moral order. The moral code of a society deals with ideas of what is right and good and what is wrong and bad. These ideas of right and wrong are generally referred to as moral/cultural values. According to Gyekye (1996: 55), moral values are those forms or patterns of conduct that are considered most worthwhile and thus cherished by a society. They are not only principles of behaviour, but also goals of social and individual action. Examples of moral values are kindness, generosity, hospitality, politeness, respect, truthfulness, honesty, reliability, and hard work. On the other hand, conduct that is deemed morally wrong includes murder, robbery, rape, lying, greed, envy, disrespect, backbiting and laziness. However in modern times, human beings seem to have compromised the ideas of wrong and right. Armed robbery, rape and even murder have increased greatly and indiscipline in traffic has soared in the capital cities and towns especially in Accra, Kumasi, Takoradi, Cape Coast (Ghana). The situation in Nigeria has been described as 'brutal' and 'chaotic' and 'inhuman' by both nationals and travellers to Nigeria. Law enforcement seems to have relapsed in most African countries and there appears to be the need for greater police reinforcement. This contrasts with what Williamson (1954) wrote in his book, *Akan Religion and the Christian Faith* that in the olden days, there were no policemen because the gods were the policemen for the people. According to him, "The customs and traditional ways of life sanctioned by the spirit-ancestors and the gods provided the framework of the Akan ethical code" (Williamson, 1954: 108-9). The question that comes to mind is what happened to this moral code? It may be surmised that encounters with other cultures, particularly Western, have influenced people to do away with the respect for the moral order. Another consequence of the encounter between Western and African culture was the denigration of everything African: "Their worst fault lay in the condemnation of African culture. African art, dancing, music, marriage and even names were condemned as pagan, barbaric or evil" (Boahen, 1975: 87).

Do African cultures qualify as pagan, barbaric, fetish, and evil? Perhaps we may be able to find answers to these when we know what the terms mean. The term *pagan* comes from the Latin word *paganus* and was used to describe village dwellers in contrast with town or city dwellers.

160

It was a sociological mark of distinction between the rustic, unpolished and unsophisticated on the one hand, and the enlightened, civilised and sophisticated on the other. In the early times of religious intolerance, the word pagan was used to describe a person who was not a Jew, Christian or Muslim. Later, the word acquired a derogatory application especially with regard to Africans as they were thought to have no religion. As we have seen, Africans do have religion and although it differs in some way from Western religions, it also has its own moral code, the breach of which merits sanctions. Again, African religions have been described as pagan because they do not claim to hold the 'absolute truth' as do Christianity, Judaism and Islam. Christianity unquestionably believes that there is one absolute truth which is found in Jesus Christ as the truth, the way and the life. Similarly, Islam views the absolute truth as emanating through Mohammed whom it regards as the last of the prophets. African religions cannot be traced to one human founder. Moreover, Africans believe that the truth is not the monopoly of any one individual or group as is illustrated by the Ewe saying: "the truth is like a baobab tree, no one individual can embrace it," as the baobab tree is huge, with a circumference that one person's hands cannot encircle. To Africans, the truth of religion is that it must be functional, namely to be able to provide human beings with their existential needs be it food, health, shelter, or money.

Another word that is associated with ATRs is *fetish* or *fetishism* which came up earlier on. The word *fetish* comes from the Portuguese word *fetico*, which means man-made. It was used to describe any work of art or religious objects made by hand, including the amulets, talismans and mascots that Portuguese visitors to Africa encountered. Since these objects were considered as gods by the Portuguese, they referred to them as *fetish*. During a research trip to the famous *Akonnedi* shrine in the town of Larteh in Eastern Ghana and a shrine at Enyan Abaasa in the Central Region, I inquired to be shown the deity. But the answer I received was that the god was not localised as it was a spirit that hovered around and manifested through possession. Dissatisfied with the answer, I pointed to wooden carvings I saw in the *abosom dan mu* or shrine at Enyaan Abaasa (see Figure 5 below). In response, *Okomfo Aba Tum*, the priestess in charge, told me that those dolls were not the gods; rather they were playthings for the gods who sometimes during their visits liked to play with them. In other words, spiritual beings take on certain human conduct during their interactions with human beings to deflate their spiritualness so as to be at par with them. Although there seems to be an aspect of fetishism with regard to the amulets, talismans and the wooden dolls, ATRs as a whole cannot be described as such since the gods are spirits and not man-made, and can change their habitation at will.

African worldviews and particularly African practices have been described as barbaric and evil. Perhaps, the former practice of human sacrifice, female circumcision or female genital mutilation, scarification and fighting animals during certain puberty and initiation rites are some of the practices that led to this labelling. Whatever good reasons might have been given for these practices, what is important now is that they are no longer practiced by many African peoples. It is hoped that with intense education, those who still practice female genital mutilation will come to terms with its harmfulness and abolish it and retain aspects of puberty rites that are progressive for individual and community development. Thus moral values as worldviews are processual and are always changing; they shape society and they in turn are modified by society.

Conclusion

As we have tried to demonstrate in this chapter, it is important to examine African worldviews in order to achieve a better understanding and appreciation of African cultural heritages. In turn this will help to relieve us as Africans from "mental and spiritual bondage" as a result of Christianisation and European domination, which "make[s] [African] people despise their own culture....for it makes them lose their self-respect and, with it, faith in themselves" (Busia, 1962:7). Contrary to assertions that African religious beliefs and practices do not amount to a worldview because of the absence of writing or that African worldviews do not deserve acknowledgement because Africans do not have a history, the chapter has demonstrated that Africans possess esoteric systems of codification such as the hieroglyphics of Ancient Egypt and the complex marking of the Ifa Divination system of the Yoruba.

Figure 5 – Shrine Ghana

Source: *Photo credit: Brigid Sackey*

By means of their oral and material cultures, Africans have also been able to deal with philosophical ideas about the ultimate quest or reason for human existence, as other peoples have done with script. Further, the chapter notes that African worldviews generally reflect two distinct worlds, namely a material, visible world, and a spiritual and invisible world that are interdependent and constantly interacting, and that God is at the centre of African beliefs, dominating and penetrating all other spheres.

Review Questions

1. What is the relationship between The Supreme God, the deities and human beings?

2. 'The development of African countries lies in the conscious return to their religious worldviews'. Discuss

3. Write critical short notes on the following concepts that have been used to describe African religious worldviews:

   - Fetishism

   - Paganism

   - Polytheism

Suggested Reading

Abimbola, W. 1997. *Ifá: an exposition of Ifá literary corpus*. Brooklyn: Athelia Henrietta Press.

Adu Boahen. 1975. *Ghana. Evolution and Change in the 19th and 20th Centuries*. London: Longman.

Amponsah, K. 1975. 'Topics on West African Religion'. *Religious Studies*, Vol. 2. Cape Coast: Mfanstiman Press Ltd.

Arens, W. and I. Karp (Eds.) 1989. *The Creativity of Power*. Washington, D.C: Smithsonian Institution Press.

Busia, K. A. 1962. *The Challenge of Africa*. New York: F. Praeger.

Erivwo, S.. 1983. "The Worship of Oghene", in E.A.A. Adegbola (ed.).*Traditional Religion in West Africa*. Accra: Asempa Publishers.

Forde, D.. 1954. *African Worldviews*. Oxford: Oxford University Press.

Gilbert, M. 1989. 'Sources of Power in Akuropon-Akuapem: Ambiguity in Classification,' In W. Arens and I. Karp (eds.), *The Creativity of Power*. Washington, D.C: Smithsonian Institution Press. Pp. 54-90.

Gill, J. H. 2002. *Native American Worldviews. An Introduction*. New York: Humanity Books

Gyekye, K. 1996. *African Cultural Values: An Introduction*. Philadelphia Pa / Accra: Sankofa Publishing Company

Manicas, P. 1987. *A History & Philosophy of the Social Sciences*. New York: Basil Blackwell.

Mbiti, J. S. 1975. *Introduction to African Religion*. London: Heineman

Opoku, K. A. 1978. *West African Traditional Religion*. Singapore: FEP International Private Limited.

Platvoet, J. 1996. "The Religions of Africa in their Historic Order", in J. Platvoet and J. Olupona (Eds.) *The Study of Religions in Africa. Past, Present and Prospects*. Cambridge: Roots and Branches.

Sackey, B. M. 2001. "Cultural Responses to the Management of HIV and AIDS: Repackaging Puberty Rites." *Research Review*, N.S. Institute of African Studies, University of Ghana, Legon. 17 (2): 63-82.2003.

Sackey,B.M. "*Apuskeleke*: Youth Fashion Craze, Immorality or Female Harassment?" *Etnofoor*, XVI (2): 57-69.

Sarpong, P. K. 1974. *Ghana in Retrospect*. Accra- Tema: Ghana Publishing Corporation.

Sutherland-Addy, E. 1999. *Perspectives on Mythology*", Accra: Goethe-Institut.

Williamson, S. G. 1954. *Akan Religion and the Christian Faith*. Accra: Ghana Universities Press.

Endnotes

1. See Sackey (2003: 58) for varied opinions on this fashion code.

2. Even though in the Twi Bible, Christian missionaries used the word *anyame* as the plural form of deities, which are correctly called Abosom and never anyame since the latter are not at par with *Onyame*. See discussion on *Abosom*.

3. This story was narrated by my most senior grandmother, Nana Adwoa Amissah, when she was already 92 years old. Ampom Darkwa, formerly of the Institute of African Studies gives two oral traditional sources about Ankyewaa Nyame. The first refers to her as the ancestress of the *Oyoko* clan whose origination myth says that she descended from heaven with her retinue and landed at Asiakwa in Asante. The other Ankyewaa Nyame is named as the ancestress of the Aduana clan, the autochthonous people, who existed before Odomankoma, the creator, emerged from the ground. Whether these three are the same is not evident (See K. Ampom-Darkwa, "The Akan Cosmogony.").

4. The word *baatan/obaatan* refers to a woman who has had a child. The childbirth pains that she suffers create a special mother-child love or bond between them. This emotion causes a mother to be sensitive and caring for her child.

5. Although Rattray's *Ashanti* (1927) and Busia's "The Ashanti",in *African Worlds* edited by Daryll Forde(1955) report of priestesses for God, *Onyame*, among the Asante. There has not been evidence of this practice or knowledge of it among the wider Akan group

6. In 1987 I witnessed this unique solidarity of the *abosom* in my matrilineage home. The family *obosom*, the area *obosom* and the great *obosom* of the sea all worked together to detect the whereabouts of a missing family member. In fact the services of a different *okomfo*, rather than the lineage's own were used to avoid accusation of prior knowledge from sceptical Christian members of the family.

7. Ghana Statistical Service (2002). *2000 Population and Housing Census*. Accra: Ghana Statistical Services.

CHAPTER 8

ISLAM AND CHRISTIANITY IN AFRICA
Abraham A. Akrong

Introduction

The usual focus in the study of both Islam and Christianity in Africa has often been on the impact of Islam and Christianity on African societies. However recent scholarship in the study of Islam and Christianity in Africa is coming to grips with the dynamic transformative roles of traditional African religion and culture in the spread of Islam and the process of Christian evangelization. Any meaningful assessment of the impact of Islam or Christianity on African societies therefore, cannot be done without due consideration of the contribution of African religions and cultures to the planting, growth and nurture of Christianity and Islam in Africa. This requires a methodology that gives due recognition to the role and place of traditional religions and cultures in that process[1].

As we shall observe later, the process of Africanisation of both Islam and Christianity, which is often criticised by the orthodox establishment of both religions, was the very instrument that aided their spread and growth. Thus the story of Christianity and Islam in Africa is essentially the story of African spirituality coming to terms with Christianity and Islam through a dialectical process of tension and accommodation. It is within this context of dialogue, protest and accommodation that African Christianity and Islam have grown and made progress. The approach to this study of Islam and Christianity in Africa will focus on the history of both religions on the continent from the perspective of how they have been fashioned as products of Africa spirituality. This will help us to analyse the various forms of Islamic and Christian expression as *religio*-cultural responses to the religious needs and concerns of adherents.

The dynamic of African people's interaction with traditional religions and cultures and these foreign religions has produced unique African forms of both Christianity and Islam. The essential African elements in their growth and spread are what have inspired the now popular description of religion in Africa as a triple heritage of African traditional religion, Islam and Christianity. The concept of *triple heritage* that runs through the thought of Wilmot Blyden, Kwame Nkrumah and lately, Ali Mazrui, is a recognition of the transformative power of traditional religions and cultures that has Africanized both religions and endowed them with elements of African religion and spirituality. This has also made it possible for Christianity and Islam to affect each other through the mediation of traditional spirituality. Sulayman Nyang, the Gambian scholar, writes:

"In my view the African encounter with the Abrahamic tradition has been very inspiring and elevating. The message of Abraham as echoed by the Old Testament prophets, Christ and Mohammed, is still vibrating in the African spiritual firmament. The ringing of the church bells and the booming voices of latter–day Bilals summoning fellow believers to prayers makes it crystal clear to observers that Africa has finally joined the growing commonwealth of believers in the Abrahamic tradition".[2]

Both Christianity and Islam come from a common root that has been described as the Abrahamic tradition, made up of Judaism, Christianity and Islam. These religious traditions share common traits because of their common origin in the Semitic culture and also their historical connections through their acclaimed common ancestry to the patriarch Abraham. Significantly this common Semitic cultural base has a lot of commonalities with Africa traditional culture in many respects and has formed the basis of the easy identification with this tradition. As we shall note later on, most African indigenous churches feel very close to the Old Testament. The Semitic cultural context which is akin to the African world-view becomes a point of contact for most Africans in the appropriation and understanding of the revelation of God in the Abrahamic tradition. In the same way, Islam and Christianity have found a home in African traditional culture, which account for their impact on African societies.

History and Origins of Islam

We start with Islam in Africa not because Islam is older than Christianity, but because Islam was the first world religion that came into contact with African societies, although Christianity existed in Ethiopia even before the emergence of Islam as a religion.

The foundation of Islamic religion is the affirmation that God has spoken to human beings in the *Qur'an*. According to Islamic theology, this divine communication is the final stage of a chain through the prophets of Judaism and Christianity. These prophets are: Adam, Abraham, Moses, the great Prophets of Israel, Jesus Christ, and lastly, the Prophet Mohammed, the chosen Prophet of God through whom God sends his eternal message in its definitive form.[3]

The Prophet Mohammed in Islamic theology is the seal of all the prophets and the Qur'an, the revelation of all revelations.[4] Initially the message of the Prophet Mohammed was addressed to the people of Mecca, who were his own people. But the Meccans rejected his message and their subsequent hostility led to the Prophet's migration to Medina in 622 BCE. This event, which is a landmark in Islamic history, is known as the *Hijira* (the Flight). It was in Medina that the Prophet Mohammed developed the theology, social and political organization of the nascent Islamic community *(Umma)*. The new community recited the *Shahada* – the confession of the divine unity and the prophethood of Mohammed: *"There is no God but Allah and Mohammed is his prophet.* The Islamic community observes the *Salat:* the five daily prayers. They also practise *Sawn* -fasting in the month of Ramadan; the act of alms giving, *Zakat,* and make an annual pilgrimage to Mecca–*Haji*. In addition to these religious observations, which have come to be known as the five pillars of Islam, they were engaged in *Jihad*, which means "striving in the path of Allah". This was expressed in the following forms: *Jihad* of the heart- the purification of the soul from evil thoughts and desires; *Jihad* of the tongue - instructing people on the path of righteousness; *Jihad* of the head – the administration of Islamic discipline; *Jihad* of the sword - the defense of Islam to convert unbelievers and enemies. The Islamic community was ruled by the *Sharia*, the sacred law of Islam revealed to the prophet by Allah. The sacred law or *Sharia* was elaborated upon and codified by successive Islamic legal experts.

Under the successors of the prophet Mohammed, the Islamic community he founded was transformed into a vast empire.[5] This transformation was achieved through the peaceful preaching and teaching of Muslim missionaries, and by the Jihad of the sword. The first Caliph and Successor of the prophet Mohammed brought the Arabic peninsula under Islamic rule and pushed forward into Palestine. The Caliph Umar advanced the Islamic religion as far as Damascus, Syria. This break-through opened the way for Islamic advancement to Mesopotamia and Asia.

Islam in West Africa

The penetration of Islam into West Africa started in about the seventh century through trade contact between the Islamic communities in North Africa and West Africa. This contact became intense in the early part of the eighth century with trade in slaves, gold, salt and horses. The Islam that came to West Africa during this period was from merchant missionaries mostly from unorthodox sects, who later became the object of Jihad and reform of West African Islam, beginning with the Almoravid Jihad in the eleventh century, in what might be described as the second wave of Islam in West Africa.

The trans-Saharan trade produced merchant missionaries in the market place who were the main agents for the initial spread of Islam in West Africa. The trade attracted many North African traders to settle in commercial towns along the terminals of the trade routes. The commercial centres of the trans-Saharan trade that sprang up were Tahert, Wargla and Awdaghost. Later, Muslim quarters were established in the capitals of the West African states of Gao, Ancient Ghana and Takrur.[6]

The majority of the early merchant missionaries who spread Islam were from the heretic sects of the Kharijites.[7] The Almoravid movement which played a great role in the islamisation of West Africa launched a jihad movement in Western Sahara in the eleventh century, ostensibly to spread Islam and also to rid the religion as practised of its heretic teachings. This jihad was done through conquest and subsumed the reform agenda under the expansionism of the Almoravids.

The Almoravid jihad movement had little success in 'purifying' Islam and setting up an ideal Islamic society. A few unorthodox practices were stamped out, but the significant achievements of the Almoravid movement lay in the fields of learning and missionary activities by Islamic communities, which kept alive a tradition of reform in West African Islam. This reform impetus runs through the traditions of reformed spirituality of Abdullah-al-Maghili of the sixteenth century, to Osman Dan Fodio in the nineteenth century.

In West Africa from about 1000-1600, the majority of the people who converted to Islam came from the ranks of the ruling elite merchant class and from among the inhabitants of towns. For this reason Islam made little impact on the way of life and beliefs of farmers, fishermen and people in the rural areas in general.[8] The principal agents of spread of Islam in this period were Muslim merchants who performed the role of Muslim missionaries, scholars and religious specialists, acting as religious, political, and moral guides, judges, doctors and diviners.

The initial spread of Islam through the work of these merchant missionaries and sustained by the various Muslim communities created by the Almoravid reform movement was followed by the spread of Islam through West African kingdoms whose rulers became the instrument for the spread of Islam.

Figure 6 – Larabanga Mosque, Ghana

Source: *photo credit: Institute of African Studies, University of Ghana, Legon*

The various West African kingdoms had different relationships with Islam. Most of them converted to Islam, but failed to create Islamic states. There were of course rulers like Sunni Ali of the Songhai empire, who ridiculed Islam and ignored it, and the rulers of the Mossi kingdom who were openly hostile to Islam. Elsewhere in the Volta Basin some of the rulers simply tolerated Islam, others were sympathetic to it and used Muslims as advisers, allowing Muslims to become part of the political and social system.   Few rulers in the Volta basin converted to Islam and Muslims in this area generally tended[10] to live apart from the society and as a result preserved more of their Islamic identity while having relatively little impact on the people as a whole. There were however other rulers in West Africa who became converted to Islam and became champions of the Islamic cause. Rulers like Mansa Musa and Askia Mohammed were celebrated Muslim rulers who were able to link West African Islam to mainstream Islam in North Africa and Arabia. But even these great champions of Islam were not able to introduce Islamic laws into their kingdoms.

The generality of people did not see Islam as a religion that necessarily excluded traditional religion, but rather as a useful companion. Islam in the various Muslim kingdoms was seen merely as an adjunct to traditional religion rather than an alternative. The Muslim kings saw themselves as rulers over both Muslims and traditionalists because their subjects were both. For this reason, Islam in West Africa for all its impact remained a religion of the rulers, the official classes, the merchants and townspeople, but it was not the religion of the people.[11] After about eight hundred and fifty years of Islamic presence in West Africa therefore, its main strength was among the privileged classes, and the various Islamic communities preserved and sustained Islamic scholarship and reformed spirituality, while the mass of the people generally combined Islam and traditional religion. What could therefore be called the pure practice of Islam was confined to the privileged classes: rulers, administrators, scholars and merchants living in isolated Muslim communities in a sea of traditional religion and culture.

Even among those kings, administrators and scholars, who went on pilgrimage and waged the Jihad of the sword, the profession of Islam did not imply a fervent adherence to the legal, moral, doctrinal and ritual demands.[12] Apart from Takur, which could be described as a Muslim state, there was resistance when attempts were made to administer the state on Muslim principles. This led to various forms of compromises and accommodations. While the rulers used and appointed Muslims to important positions in their administrations as interpreters and secretaries, they also made room for non-Muslims. They used Muslims mainly because of their literacy skills within social and political systems based on beliefs in traditional religion.

Prior to colonialism Islam was the dominant foreign religion in West Africa, which many Africans had embraced mainly through trade contacts. However, the expansion of Islam in West Africa was not a mere by-product of trade. Islam was seen by Africans as a prestigious and transforming religion that could bring social changes into traditional society and provide rulers with administrators as well as legal and religious experts for the expansion and development of the state and empire.[13].

At the personal level, Islam provided a new vision of life, the world, human existence and destiny. As a new religion of change, it provided skills and techniques that helped the socio-political transformation and growth of traditional society. In spite of all the advantages that Islam brought however, adherence to Islam brought into focus points of conflict between Islam and traditional religion as well as points of convergence that facilitated the Africanization of Islam and its easy assimilation by African Muslims. This process of Africanization was the genius of the two dominant brotherhoods in West Africa, the *Tijanniyya* and the *Qadiriyya*.

The Sufi mystical tradition out of which these communities emerged created an accommodative religious framework that allowed for the re-interpretation of Islam in idioms of African spirituality and made it possible for people to see a continuity between Islam and traditional religion. This perceived continuity between Islam and traditional religion on the popular level allowed for what might be called the Africanisation of Islam or the interpretation of Islam on the patterns of traditional religion. This process allowed for the assimilation of aspects of Islamic practices into traditional culture which also led to the transformation of aspects of traditional culture in conformity with the Islamic ethos. It is this dialectic of conflict, accommodation and transformation which created the conditions for the spread and growth of Islam as a religion that could address the needs and concerns of Africans. In this way Islam became a popular religion seen as linking the believer to a universal faith and relevant to the immediate needs of Africans.

However the dominance and prestige of Islam as a universal and transforming religion was challenged by the imposition of colonial rule. Colonialism introduced a new socio-political order backed by the Christian religion. Although it halted the spread of Islam through the mainly nineteenth century Fulani Jihad movements, its imposition facilitated the peaceful spread of Islam on the strength that Islam was a universal religion with special appeal to Africans.

Colonialism was received by the Muslim communities in West Africa with great apprehension and suspicion. Many African Muslims saw the colonial project as a tacit agenda to replace Islam with Christianity. There were many different responses to colonial rule. Some Muslim communities saw colonialism as a form of evil, which had to be avoided at all costs. Those who saw colonialism as evil refused to have anything to do with it. They withdrew socially, psychologically, mentally and culturally from any contact with colonialism and its attendant European culture. There were militant radical groups like the Bomidele, Sabbanu and Muridiyya, which believed[14] that it must be overthrown through an international Muslim Jihad to rid the world of its evil influence. There were still other Muslim communities which believed that Islam could accommodate colonialism and work through its structures. Their strategy was to work with colonialism but reject its more baneful influence. This accommodationist approach created a helpful point of contact for Muslims in dealing and operating within the structures of colonialism until the demise of colonial rule. It is important to note that despite the many misgivings about colonialism, the peaceful atmosphere it created through the halting of the Jihad expansionism of Muslim states with their hegemonic empire building ambitions allowed Islam to spread in a peaceful way. But this peaceful spread of Islam met with resistance from the revival of traditional religion.[15]

The demise of colonialism gave impetus to West African Islam like Islam elsewhere, to revive its communities and strengthen its links with world-wide Islam to assert its presence in the modern world. In Africa this revival of Islam meant its increased visibility that was championed by a new breed of West African Muslim scholars trained from Muslim centres world-wide. This new breed of Muslims are struggling to change the image of Islam in West African societies as a religion which is compatible with the intellectual demands of the modern world. More importantly, the links with world-wide Islam have attracted a lot of interest from different world centres of Islam. Indeed we may be witnessing what can be described as a new modern wave of Islamic presence in West Africa aimed at changing the image of the religion as a way of reclaiming West Africa for Islam.

Islam in West Africa today displays a great continuity with the past. However there are significant developments that are influencing its direction. The resurgence of Islam in the modern world finds expression in the various attempts to unify it against the dominance of secularism often associated with Christian modernity. This is a movement of pan-Islamic recovery of the Muslim *Sharia* as the basis of a new civilisation both as an alternative to, and bulwark against, secularism. The spirit of this world-wide recovery is often described as Islamic fundamentalism, which is often perceived as aligned to international terrorism. The crusade to revive the *Sharia* as a bulwark against secularism is what has energized Muslim communities world-wide to establish Muslim states on the pattern of the idyllic nascent state which was headed by the prophet Mohammad in Medina. The establishment of the *Sharia* in a number of Nigerian states is an aspect of this revival of the *Sharia* in the modern world.

The variety of responses to modern secularism comes from the conviction that Islamic civilization or the *Sharia*, cannot be marginalized in the reshaping of the modern world. Muslims in West Africa, whether one labels them as conservatives, modernists or fundamentalists, may not necessarily advocate the establishment of an Islamic state, but are generally convinced that certain Islamic ideas and principles are relevant to the social, intellectual and cultural well being of West Africa.[16]

Islam in East and Central Africa

The Sudan belt or northern Sudan (between 10° and 60° N) that stretches across Africa has been identified as the location where Islam has made its deepest impact and gained most adherents in Africa. This belt is divided into three areas: West, Central and Eastern or Nilotic Sudan.

The history[17] of Islam in East Africa falls into three periods. The first period was the early settlement of Muslims mainly of Arab descent on the Coast, while the second period was the *Shirazi* culture which produced a number of Islamic communities along the Coast. These two phases of the spread of Islam was disrupted by the Portuguese, whose presence affected trade and the life on the Coast. The third stage which followed the decline of Portuguese power led to the formation of the state of Zanzibar and the revival and transformation of *Shirazi* culture, which created the context for Islamisation and the later development of a local Bantu Islamic culture that helped in the spread of Islam in East and Central Africa.

The people of the East African coast were brought into contact with Islam through trading contacts with Southern Arabia, Persia, Indonesia and China. It was through this maritime trade that Islam was introduced by Muslim traders to the East African coast. The Muslim traders traded in slaves, gold and ivory and founded settlements along the coast, which later became centres of Islam. This contact promoted intermarriage between Arab and Persian traders and Bantu women which produced the Bantu–Islamic civilisation (the Swahili culture), a combination of Arab-Persian Islamic culture and Bantu culture.[18]The development of this Bantu Islamic civilization was however disrupted by the Portuguese in the fifteenth century, leading to the impoverishment of *Shirazi* culture on the whole east coast. Zanzibar emerged as a main trading centre that facilitated the spread of Islam into inland regions, mainly in the nineteenth century. The revival of trade contact led to the development of Islamic villages and towns and the conversion of many Bantus to Islam. There were however kingdoms like the Baganda kingdom that resisted the spread of Islam, although Muslim traders were able to exert a limited influence on the Baganda court.

The fortunes of Islam in East and Central Africa improved with the establishment of European rule later in the nineteenth century. Colonial rule and the suppression of the slave trade opened up the region, facilitating trade and allowing for the peaceful spread of Islam. The rapid spread of Islam mainly in the second half of the nineteenth century coincided with colonial rule and the work of Christian missions, which affected its fortunes. The association of Arab traders with the trade in slaves negatively affected the appeal of Islam to many Bantus. Some ethnic groups like the Yao were however converted, but Islam on the whole could not penetrate into many Bantu groups in East and Central Africa. In Kenya, hostile Maasai and Galle groups did not facilitate the spread of Islam in many parts of the country.

On the whole, the spread of Islam in East and Central Africa was through the Swahili culture. But while many people spoke the Swahili language and were affected by the culture, they remained largely unaffected by Islam.[19] The Swahili culture that spread from Somalia to Zanzibar was developed by the following communities: the Shirazi, a mixture of Asiatic and Bantu cultures; the Afro-Arabs, Arab descendants of those who became part of the Shirazi civilization; and assimilated groups of Bantu people composed of mostly household and liberated slaves. Inland Bantus acquired features of Swahili culture but retained much of Bantu culture. Those on the Comoro Archipelago can be classified as coastal Swahili. Their culture is basically Bantu, but they devoted themselves to Islam and founded communities which dedicated themselves to the study of the *Sharia* and served as Qur'an teachers, and helped to strengthen Islam on the coast. Thus, there were two modes of the spread of Islam in East Africa: the formation on the East coast and off-lying islands of new African Islamic societies and its spread into the interior, especially between 1880 and 1939.[20]

The contact between Arab-Islamic civilization and Bantu culture produced an African Islamic regional culture whose roots and outlook on life remained non-African. The societies that were formed as the result of contact with Islam did not expand outwardly to create communities and kingdoms as instruments for the propagation of the religion, but rather Islam spread through absorption of individuals. On the whole, the impact of Islam on the Bantu culture resulted in the spread of Swahili civilisation, which did not create Muslim communities as beacons of Islamic teaching and spirituality, but rather the conversion of isolated individuals. For this reason, Islam in East Africa bears the marks of a foreign religion unlike in West Africa. Most ordinary Bantus resisted the spread of Islam because of its association with slavery and the stratification of Swahili society. Conversion remained largely an individual affair which was made possible through de-ethnicisation and assimilation into a Swahili civilization itself deeply stratified into classes. However, the attraction of Islam to the Bantus lay in its universal culture, which for many people became a mark of distinction; the dress code, eating habits, unique rituals and the association with the literate religion of 'the Book'. Invariably on the popular level, Islam was added to traditional religion, but as a universal religion with a world-wide reach.

Islam in East and Central Africa could be viewed from the prism of three inter-related phases: germination, crisis, and gradual orientation. The germination phase is the assimilation process that produces shock and crisis based on Islamic demands on traditional culture. The consequence however was new attitudes that modified social and individual behaviour. The shocks that assimilation brought did not lead to the perception that Islam and traditional culture were incompatible, but rather parallel systems that could co-exist with each other and therefore did not require total rejection of traditional religion in the name of Islam. For example the *Salat*, which is the Muslim ritual prayers, is performed together with many aspects of traditional cultural practices. The gradual orientation comes from the accommodation of traditional religion to Islam, which allows for a smooth transition from traditional religion to Islam; the more rigorous demands of Islam are accommodated within the logic of the idea that Islam and traditional culture are parallel religions that can co-exist in the life of the individual who belongs to both traditional culture and Islam.

In spite of the many inroads that Islam made into Bantu traditional culture through their accommodationist strategy, Islam remained weak in East and Central Africa because it did not produce clergy, scholars, and missionary communities like in West Africa, which could sustain the spread of Islam. The spread of Islam in the nineteenth century through the conversion of individuals, rather than communities, exposed Islam to competition from Christian missions which became associated with modernity.

One of the greatest challenges facing contemporary Islam in East and Central Africa is from Western secular civilisation, which is challenging the very principle on which Islamic civilization is based. The effect of secularization means that it is the secular state and not the Islamic *Sharia* that will decide on issues of law, education, economic and social matters that affect the life of the individual. The clash is essentially between the medieval outlook of Islam and modern Western secular civilisation. In the face of these challenges, it seems that Islam is retreating from visibility in the society, a process which conservationists are fighting very hard to resist, but which is rather leading more to the marginalisation of Islam in modern public life. The younger generation is attracted to Christianity as the religion that can equip one to function well in the modern society while Islam is associated with the urban poor and backwardness. The modernization process which is determining the tempo of modern life is making Islam lose its appeal as a civilization compatible with the rhythm of social change and modernity in Africa. The real effect of secularisation on Islam is that it is narrowing the domain of Islam by restricting its sphere to the molding of the lives of individuals.

The recent resurgence and Islam's claims to visibility in the public arena is part of the attempt by Islam to burst out of its self–imposed isolation and present itself as a viable alternative to Western modernity to roll back the tide of secularization to which it attributes much of the problems that the world faces today. African Muslim communities have not been left out of this world-wide attempt to redefine Islam as a world civilization that can be considered as an alternative to Western modernity. One of the important phases of Islam in Africa is the world–wide revivalist movement in Islam to regain its proper place as a world civilization has been expressed differently by various Muslim communities in Africa. For most of the communities especially in West Africa where Muslims are in the minority like Ghana, this resurgence means breaking the barriers that have kept Muslims from active participation in the modern society for fear of being contaminated by Christianity through the structures of modernity. In these communities, the recovery of the image and prestige of Islam means that Muslim youth should avail themselves of educational opportunities and encouraging them that one could be Muslim, educated and socially mobile in a modern society. In countries where Muslims are in the majority with significant political leverage and long history of Islamic rule as for example in the Gambia and Northern Nigeria, the revival of Islam takes the form of the introduction of the *Sharia* as the law that must regulate the life of Muslims in the modern state.

Christianity in Africa

The first contact between Africans and European Christianity came as a result of the ambition of Henry the Great to find an alternative route to India that would go around the Muslims of North Africa. He sent ten expeditions between 1421 and 1451 for this purpose and in 1498 they succeeded in finding an alternative route to India that would by-pass the Muslim world. In addition to the goal of securing an alternative route to India, Prince Henry also wanted to explore the possibility of a Christian kingdom in Africa. It was also his intention to carry the message of Christ to the Africans along the coast where the Portuguese set up trading centers. For this reason he included Catholic missionaries in his trade expeditions. It was Portuguese Catholic missionaries who made the first contact between Western European Christianity and Africans. The fist contact was with the *Bakongo* people through their chief *Manikonyo* in 1491. Another Portuguese contact with Africans was in the kingdom of *Monomatapa*. And although the King of *Monomatapa* was baptized in 1652, the mission work there died. The Portuguese missionaries were neither successful in penetrating the inland of the coast of East Africa to convert the people, nor successful in converting the East Coast towns. The Portuguese Catholic missionaries then turned their attention to Ethiopia. There they believed they would find the Christian kingdom of Prester John, only to be disappointed by the way the Ethiopian Coptic Church practiced Christianity.

Figure 7 – Ethiopian Coptic Church

Photo credit: *Uri Eshkar*

The missionary aspect of the ambition of Prince Henry to find an alternative route to India did not succeed because all the contacts that the Catholic missionaries made in this period did not bear fruit but nevertheless brought up Africans as a potential missionary field to the notice of Western Christendom.

There were also Protestant missionary attempts in the eighteenth century that was able to make contact with Africans but these did not bear immediate fruits just like the Portuguese Catholic experiment. Dutch and British merchants in West Africa like the Portuguese also had chaplains who made attempts at converting the African community around the forts and castles, but these contacts were not lasting. The Protestant missionary effort in South Africa was too weak to make any impact. Like the other Protestants, the mission of the Moravians to the San in South Africa was obstructed by the Boers. Although these early attempts were not successful in terms of converts like the Catholic effort, it also brought Africa to the attention of Christians in Europe as a potential mission field with great possibilities for spreading the Gospel.

The eighteenth and nineteenth century religious revivals in Europe led to a renewed interest in missions and Africa was one of the main targets of this renewed mission interest. The mission agenda for Africa was to rid the continent of the slave trade and replace it with education, honest work and the Gospel. [21] After many efforts in West Africa, most missionary bodies felt that Sierra Leone as a colony of freed slaves was the perfect place to launch missionary work. The Church Missionary Society (CMS) started work among the freed slaves in Sierra Leone, followed by the Wesleyan Methodist Mission. Thus by 1815, there were indigenous churches of African settlers as a result of the work of the CMS and the Methodist Mission. In 1792, the Moravians mission started work in South Africa. They were followed by the London Missionary Society and other mission bodies followed suit. By 1815 several mission bodies were firmly established in two areas in Africa namely, Sierra Leone and the Cape Province in South Africa.[22]

The work of the CMS progressed in Sierra Leone. They established villages for liberated African slaves, set up schools and trained the new converts in such vocations as masonry, carpentry, tailoring and other trade skills. In 1827 the CMS established Fourah Bay College to give further training to converts who had completed the mission schools. The Wesleyan Mission also recorded great success in terms of converts and the establishment of schools.[23] The success of these missionary efforts in Sierra Leone among the freed slaves led to intense missionary work in neighbouring Liberia where the Methodist Episcopal Church established a strong missionary presence. Another area of missionary activity in West Africa in the period 1815–1840 was in the Gold Coast now Ghana, where the Basel Mission sent their first mission in 1828. In spite of initial set-backs as a result of missionary casualties, the work continued and from 1840 onwards, when the European missionaries were replaced by African Moravian freed slave missionaries from Jamaica, the Basel Mission was able to expand its work into the inland of the Gold Coast. In 1834 the Wesleyan Methodist Missionary sent a missionary to Cape Coast to start work on the coast, which later expanded inland.

By 1840, Christian missions were well established in South Africa. On the West Coast, there was a strong Christian foundation in Sierra Leone, the Gambia, Liberia and the coast of the Gold Coast. The mission in this period laid the foundation for the later great success of mission work in Africa. There was explosion in the success of mission work in Africa from about 1840 onwards. This was due to the intensive contact between Africa and Europe and improved information about Africa, especially through explorers, attracted the curiosity of many Europeans. More important, through colonialism much of the hinterland of Africa was opened up through improvements in transportation and roads, the suppression of slavery and intra ethnic wars. These conditions enhanced the work of missionaries and put missionary work in this period on a new aggressive and progressive thrust to win the African continent for Christ.

The rapid growth of Christianity in West Africa in this period was through the pioneering and energetic work of Samuel Ajai Crowther, who used Sierra Leone as the launching pad for the spread of the Gospel in other parts of West Africa like Nigeria. Crowther was a Yoruba-born slave who was rescued from a slave ship and sent to Sierra Leone, where he was educated. He was entrusted with the Niger Expedition planned by the CMS to sail from the Guinea Coast to the inland parts of West Africa up to Nigeria. The great ambition of the expedition was to stop the slave trade inland and open up Nigeria for the spread of the Gospel. The expedition was not able to stop the slave trade, but was able to open up Nigeria for evangelization. Samuel Crowther was later consecrated bishop in charge of the CMS Mission in Africa and has been justifiably given the title 'The Apostle of the Niger' for the work he did in opening up the hinterland of West Africa for the spread of the Gospel. The Wesleyan Mission followed up on the CMS work in Nigeria, then the Baptists, and the Church of Scotland in Eastern Nigeria in 1847. By 1878, the Gospel was firmly established in Nigeria.

In the 1840s, the Gospel made great progress in South Africa but there were still areas that it had not reached. It was the path-breaking work of the Scotsman, David Livingstone, that helped the spread of the Gospel in Southern Africa. David Livingstone was sent in 1840 by the London Missionary Society to South Africa as a missionary. Livingstone was able to explore the inland of Southern and Eastern Africa, which helped the later spread of the Gospel in this region by other mission bodies like the Church of Scotland in Malawi in 1876.

Up to about 1878, mission work in Africa was confined to mainly coastal towns. For this reason from 1878 to 1914 there was a great determination on the part of the mission bodies to penetrate the inland of the Africa coastal regions. In Senegal, the French encouraged the Catholic Church to work among the people in the inland region. And in this same period, between 1878 and 1914, there was effective mission presence in Senegal, Gambia, Sierra Leone, Liberia, Gold Coast, Togo, Benin and Nigeria. There was similar expansion of mission work in Central Africa, Cameroons, Gabon, Belgium, Congo and Angola. In South and Eastern Africa, progress was made in mission work in South Africa, Basutoland (Botswana), Rhodesia (Zimbabwe), Northern Rhodesia (Zambia), Nyasaland (Malawi), Kenya, Uganda and Tangayika (Tanzania).

The trajectory of the history of the planting of Christianity in Africa from 1815 to 1914 was checkered. The sowing of the seed from 1815 to 1840 met with many obstacles, hostility from slave traders, opposition from various ethnic groups, and the inhospitable climate which took its toll on the missionaries. In spite of these difficulties, modest gains were made in the period 1840–1878 which sustained the momentum for the next stage in 1878-1914, the golden age of mission work. In this period, colonial rule opened up countries, stamped out slavery, and contained ethnic conflicts so that missionaries could carry out the work of evangelism with relative ease, not to mention the finding of cures for malaria, which helped to preserve the life of many missionaries.

From 1914 to 1960, the churches established by the mission bodies entered a period of local church autonomy based on the ideals of self-supporting, self-governing and self-propagating local African churches. The various local churches established local Christian Councils, which were later to play important roles in the socio-political transformation of post independent African societies.

The Encounter between Christianity and Traditional Culture

The spread of Christianity in Africa through mainly the nineteenth century movement brought missionary Christianity face to face with African traditional religion and cultural institutions. It is important to note that Christianity was presented as part of the Western European civilizing mission in Africa together with commerce and colonialism. For this reason, in addition to the spiritual values that Africa might have appropriated in the conversion process, Christianity was also presented as a modernising movement, which could be appropriated through Western culture. The presentation of Christianity as a function of Western civilisation made the Christian Gospel excessively Western as if one needed to be Western in cultural orientation before one could be a Christian. The identification of Christianity with Western culture made the Christian message unnecessarily foreign to Africa culture.[24] Furthermore, the identification of Christianity with Western culture placed Western culture and African culture at the opposite ends of an evolutionary scheme of a supposed progression of human cultural development from its primitive beginnings to its advanced forms. The polarisation of Western and African culture created the perception that African culture, which was defined as primitive, is a culture that must be rejected before one could become Western and Christian. And African culture was also presented as not only primitive, but also demonic, and therefore incompatible with Christianity.

The missionaries set up a rigid system of rules for the new converts to prevent them from falling back into African culture or paganism, defined as all that is ungodly, immoral, indecent and inhuman (see Ch. 7). For this reason the converts were expected to have nothing to do with their traditional culture which was defined as pagan and ungodly. The views of the missionaries on African culture created a problem for African converts because missionary teachings implied that one could not be African and Christian at the same time. The problem posed by conversion to Christianity is one of the perplexing, vexing and contentious issues in African Christianity. And the responses to this central question of African Christianity– how to be African and Christian– have given rise to different versions of African Christianity. African Christians in the missionary churches– Presbyterians, Methodists, Roman Catholics, Anglicans and Baptists- quietly succumbed to the view that Christianity was somehow incompatible with African culture. But in their own way they have found modes of accommodation between Christianity and African traditional culture that allow them to maintain their African identity within the context of the missionary ideology that sees African culture as incompatible with Christianity.

Figure 8 – Dancing worshippers of the Aladura Church, Nigeria.

Source: *J. Collins/BAPMAF collection)*

Starting at the turn of the twentieth century, there arose an African protest movement that revolted against missionary churches and their views about African culture. This revolt was led by African Christians in the missionary churches who felt that the missionaries were not telling them the whole truth about the Christian faith. The protest movement was fuelled by the translation of the Bible into various African languages. Translation enabled African converts to read the Bible for themselves and this allowed them to interpret the Bible from their own perspectives as Africans. They discovered that the Biblical world and culture were similar in many ways to the world of African culture. African Christians saw a lot of continuities between the Bible and African culture and discovered for themselves a place for African culture and religions in the Bible. This discovery led to the emergence of what has been described as the African Indigenous Churches (AICs). These Churches express themselves in different forms depending on their theological or confessional persuasion, but what binds them together is their attempt to interpret the Christian faith from an African perspective that addresses their needs and concerns.

The movement that brought the indigenous African Churches into being has helped the renewal of Christianity in Africa and transformed Christianity in Africa into a religion that has answers to the needs of African Christians, needs and concerns that were hitherto absent from the missionary agenda of salvation. The early protest movement nurtured in the African indigenous churches created a new form of Christianity that is able to deal with the concerns of African Christians. These are concerns and needs shaped by the African world-view and spirituality which, hitherto, was dismissed by missionary Christianity. The spirit of the African indigenous churches has become the driving force behind the rapid growth of African Christianity. The growth of Christianity through the instrumentality of the Africanization of the faith finds expression today in the African charismatic movement and other pentecostal forms of African expressions of Christianity.

Conclusion

In the historical and cultural analysis of the processes, spread and growth of Islam and Christianity in Africa what stands out clearly is the perception at different times that African religion and culture were a hindrance to the true expression of either Islam or Christianity. However as the chapter has demonstrated, African religions and cultures actually provided the spiritual context and conditions within which Christianity and Islam were planted, nurtured and grown as forms of African religious expression. In sum, the Africanization process in both Christianity and Islam has been the secret of the success of both religions in Africa.

Review Questions

1. Give a historical perspective on the origins of Islam in Africa.

2. Account for the spread of Islam in West, East and Central Africa, noting the key actors in the growth and spread of the religion in all three regions.

3. Critically analyse the impact of Islam and Christianity on African societies.

4. How did African traditional cultures accommodate the new religions (Islam and Christianity) that came into its midst? Discuss critically

5. What accounts for the popularity of African Indigenous Churches and what has been their impact on mainline Christian churches? Discuss critically.

References

Clark, P. 1982 *West Africa and I slam*, London: Edward Arnold Publishers.

Falola, T. (Ed). 2002 *Affinity Redefined, Collected Essays of Ali Mazurui* Vol. 1. Trenten, New Jersey: Africa World Press.

Hilderbrandt, J. 1981. *History of the Church in Africa-A Survey*. Achimota, Ghana: African Christian Press P. 83

Pobee, J.S. 1982. " Political Theology in the African Context" *African Theological Journal* 11(2): 168-75.

Trimingham, S. 1964. *Islam in East Africa* Oxford: Clarendon Press.

Williams, J. A. 1964. *Islam.* London: Oxford University Press.

Endnotes

1. Akrong, A. 1998 " The Historic Mission of the Independent African Churches" *Research Review* New Series Vol 14, No 2 p.58-68

2. Quoted in *Affinity Redefined, Collected Essays of Ali Mazurui* Vol. 1. Toyin Falola(Ed.) Trenton, New Jersy: African World Press 2002. p.115

3. Williams, J. A. 1964. *Islam.* London: Oxford University Press.

4. Peter Clark, P. 1982 *West Africa and Islam.* London: Edward Arnold Publishers. p..2

5. Clark, op cit. p. 5

6. Clark, op cit. p 8-9

7.   Clark, op cit. p.10

8.   Clark, op cit. p.28

9.   Ibid.

10. Clark, op cit. p. 59

11   Clark, op cit. p. 40

12   Clark, op cit. p.72

13   Clark, op cit. p.260

14. Clark, op cit. p. 194

15   Clark, op cit. p. 229

16   Clark, op cit. p. 256

17. Trimingham, S. 1964. Islam in East Africa Oxford: Clarendon Press. p.xii

18   Trimingham, op cit. p.10

19. Trimingham, op cit. p.31

20   Trimingham, op cit. p. 53

21   Akrong, op cit. p.58-59

22   Hilderbrandt, J. 1981. History of the Church in Africa- A Survey. Achimota, Ghana: African Christian Press. p83

23   Hilderbrandt, op cit. p. 89-90

24   J.S. Pobee 1982. "Political Theology in the African Context " African Theological Journal 11(2): 168-75.

CHAPTER 9

TRADITIONAL AND MODERN LEADERSHIP IN AFRICA
Joseph R.A. Ayee

Introduction

The need to study traditional and modern leadership is never as critical as in the case of Africa. In the words of Chazan et. al. (1992) "... leadership is ... one of the many guides to the intricacies of political processes on the continent"[1]. In addition, leadership is important in defining the success (or otherwise) of *good governance*[2] - a rare commodity on the African continent. The richness of the continent's ancient heritage, the wealth of its abundant natural resources, and the vibrancy of its more than 800 million people, conjures the vision of a secure and prosperous future. However, Africa has been reduced to a perilous and parlous state, badly lagging behind other regions of the world in human development. Much of this is explained by the exploitation of the land and its peoples by a century or more of colonialism, whose dark legacy lingers still in the form of skewed cross-ethnic national boundaries and the clandestine pursuit of post-colonial foreign interests represented by multinational corporations. Equally, much is explained through failures, or at least the shortcomings, on the part of Africa's leaders to promote long-term rational policies and programmes that transcend not only national boundaries but also regional ones. Mired in socio-economic deprivation, and vulnerable to the vagaries of global epidemics and the predations of globalization, African peoples are crying out for transformational leadership for their common redemption.

Transformational leadership, unlike *laissez-faire* and transactional leadership, is advocated in Africa because it provides the basis for pushing through radical programmes of political, economic and social reform. Transformational leadership is a leadership style which emphasises not only strategic vision and strong ideological convictions of a leader, but also the personal resolution and political will to put them into practice. The essence of transformational leadership is the capacity to adapt means to ends to shape and reshape institutions and structures to achieve broad human purposes and moral aspirations. Transformational leadership contrasts with the other two leadership styles, namely, *laissez-faire* leadership and transactional leadership. Laissez-faire leadership espouses a leader who is reluctant to interfere in matters outside his/her personal responsibility, while transactional leadership emphasizes the implicit social exchange or transaction over time that exists between the leader and followers, including reciprocal influence and interpersonal perception. Even though features of laissez-faire and transactional leadership have been found to have been used by almost all African leaders, these have not been conducive for development because they have tended to reinforce the status quo[3].

In Africa, the persistent development crisis and the recent phenomenon of failing states are due in part to poor leadership; leaders who are not committed to the development of their societies and who lack honesty and a commitment to democracy. Studies on politics in Africa have pointed out that poor leadership has been a major factor that has contributed to the development crisis on the continent since independence[4]. Indeed, it has been asserted that the trouble with Africa is simply and squarely a failure of leadership. For instance, a World Bank study of Sub-Saharan Africa stated that: "Underlying the litany of Africa's development problems is a crisis of governance"[5]. This has led to persistent instability, violence, ethnic conflict, hunger, disease, poverty, lack of transparency and accountability.

Against this background, this chapter sets out to address a number of issues. First, it defines the concept of leadership. Second, it makes a distinction between traditional and modern leadership by looking at their features. Third, the chapter discusses the importance and challenges facing traditional and modern leadership. Fourth, it highlights the remedies to the challenges and the lessons that can be learnt from leadership in general.

Defining leadership

Despite countless books and studies, no one has developed a widely accepted definition of what leadership is, or what makes some leaders effective and others ineffectual (see Box 1 for some of the definitions). In the absence of any consensual view of leadership, leadership in this chapter may be understood as a *pattern of behaviour*, as a *personal quality* and *as a political value and process*. As a pattern of behaviour, leadership is a social process in which influence is exerted by an individual or group over a larger body to organize or direct its efforts towards the achievement of desired goals without the use or threat of violence. We expect leaders to influence non-coercively and to generate cooperative effort toward goals that transcend the leader's narrow self-interest. Leadership in this definition is a property of the relationship between leader and follower[6]. Those people whom we call leaders are different in at least two respects. First, they have more influence than those around them. Second, they try to influence others to behave in ways that are beyond the mere compliance with the rules and routines of the organization or country[7].

As a personal attribute, leadership refers to the character traits which enable the leader to exert influence over others without coercion; leadership is thus effectively equated with charisma, that is, the leadership having supernatural qualities that provide emotional arousal – a sense of mission, vision, excitement and pride. This feeling is typically associated with respect and trust of the leader[8]. As a political value and process, leadership refers to guidance and inspiration, the capacity to mobilize others through moral authority or ideological insight through a democratic and good governance system.

'Good' leadership, as defined by bilateral and multilateral aid agencies is ethical leadership that promotes the following values: democracy, justice, respect for human rights, accountability, responsibility, duty, freedom of speech, development, personal altruism and integrity[9].

There are three main virtues of leadership. They are its ability to: (i) mobilize and inspire people who would otherwise be inert and directionless; (ii) promote unity and encourage members of a group to pull in the same direction; and (iii) strengthen organisations by establishing a hierarchy of responsibilities and roles.[10] Notwithstanding these virtues, leadership has its vices. Some of its alleged dangers are that it may: (i) concentrate power and can thus lead to corruption and tyranny, hence the democratic demand that leadership should be checked by accountability; (ii) engender subservience and deference, thereby discouraging people from taking responsibility for their own lives; (iii) narrow debate and argument because of its emphasis upon ideas flowing down from the top, rather than up from the bottom[11].

Box 1 – Definitions of Leadership

i.   "Leadership is any attempt to influence the behaviour of another individual or group" (Paul Hersey, The Situational Leader)

ii. "Managers do things right. Leaders do the right thing" (Warren Bennis and Burt Nanus, Leaders: Strategies for Taking Charge)

iii. "Leadership is the ability to decide what is to be done and then get others to want to do it (Dwight D. Eisenhower, 34th President of the USA)

iv. "Leadership is the process of moving a group in some direction through mostly non-coercive means. Effective leadership is leadership that produces movement in the long-term interests of the group" (John Kotter, The Leadership Factor)

v.   "Leadership is the process of persuasion or example by which an individual (or leadership team) induces a group to pursue objectives held by the leader or shared by the leader and his or her followers" (John Gardner, On Leadership)

vi. "Leadership over human beings is exercised when persons with certain motives and purposes mobilize, in competition or conflict with others, institutional political, psychological, and other resources so as to arouse, engage and satisfy the motives of followers (James Burns, Leadership)

vii. "Leadership is a particular kind of ethical, social practice that emerges when persons in communities, grounded in hope, are grasped by inauthentic situations and courageously act in concert with followers to make those situations authentic" (Robert Terry, "Leadership – A Preview of a Seventh View")

Source: Lee Graham and Terrence Deal, *"Reframing Organizational Leadership"*, in F.S. Lane (ed.) *Current Issues in Public Administration*, 5th Edn. (New York: St Martin's Press, 1990), p. 215.

Defining traditional leadership

Traditional leadership connotes authority and legitimacy based on history, traditions and customs. In the words of Max Weber (1947), traditional leadership rests on an "established belief in the sanctity of immemorial traditions and the legitimacy of the status of those exercising authority under them"[12]. The legitimacy of the ruler's authority rests in traditional norms. Traditional leadership is regarded as legitimate because it has always existed; it has been sanctified by history because earlier generations had accepted it. The most obvious examples of traditional leadership are found among ethnic communities and groups. Traditional leadership is closely linked to hereditary systems of power and privilege, as reflected, for example, in the survival of dynastic rule in Saudi Arabia, Morocco, Nepal and Kuwait. These are absolute monarchies under which the monarch claims, even if it is seldom exercised, a monopoly of political power. This contrasts with the constitutional monarchies whereby the monarch fulfils an essentially ceremonial function largely devoid of political significance (for example, in the UK, Spain, Canada, the Netherlands, and Denmark).

Given the fact that the kings and the queens of the UK, Canada, Spain, the Netherlands and Denmark as well as their counterparts in the Middle East have their authority and legitimacy based on traditions, history, customs and status, it is clear that traditional leadership is not a uniquely African phenomenon but rather a global one. Some examples of traditional leadership include kings, paramount chiefs, divisional chiefs, sub-chiefs, and queen-mothers.

Defining modern leadership

Modern leadership connotes a set of impersonal rules associated with an office rather than the office holder. Authority and legitimacy are conferred by rules and regulations, which have been drawn up in a rational framework. In modern leadership, unlike traditional leadership, leaders are subject to the laws; hence the society is characterized by norms of impersonality and the lack of arbitrariness. Some examples of modern leadership include political, bureaucratic, religious, military, corporate and judicial leadership.

At this point, it may be instructive to distinguish between traditional and modern leaders such as presidents, prime ministers and chief executive officers. Unlike traditional leadership, modern leadership links authority to a clearly and legally defined set of rules. The power of the President or Prime Minister is determined in the final analysis by formal, constitutional rules, which constrain or limit what an office holder is able to do. The advantage of this form of leadership over traditional leadership is that, as it is attached to an office rather than a person, it is far less likely to be abused or to give rise to injustice.

Features and role of traditional leadership in Africa

During the pre-colonial period, traditional leadership occupied an important feature of political, economic, social and cultural life of the people in countries like Nigeria, Ghana, South Africa, Botswana, Lesotho, Swaziland, Libya, Egypt, Uganda, and Burundi. It had political, spiritual, military and judicial authority which was perceived to be derived from customs, traditions and practices. Among some ethnic groups, the stool constituted the source of the traditional leaders' legitimacy and authority. For instance, for an Akan chief, the stool encapsulated the souls of the all the departed ancestors. Hence, it was and is treated as an object of reverence. Indeed, the perception then and even now in most Africa countries is that traditional leaders derived their power and authority from the gods and ancestors, who were and are still regarded as divine(see Ch. 7).

One of the most important functions of traditional leaders during the pre-colonial period was leading their people to war either against invaders, or expanding their kingdom or against colonialism. Consequently, in the selection of traditional leaders, the qualities of charisma, personality, bravery and astuteness were taken into account by the kingmakers. Notable chiefs who led their people to war include Chaka, (the 19ᵗʰ century Zulu king in South Africa,) Osei Tutu I (17ᵗʰ-18ᵗʰ Century) and Opoku Ware I (18ᵗʰ Century), Kings of Asante, among others.

In addition to being war leaders, traditional leaders were also the custodians of land – a critical resource in African countries. This point has been reinforced by John Bruce:

> In most of Africa land has been plentiful. Where shifting cultivation has been practised or groups have migrated to settle new territory, traditional authorities have often had an important land allocation function. ... Once cultivation stabilizes, the role of land authorities is primarily that of making first allocations of previously unused land. Where population pressure on land is heavy, chiefs or elders sometimes have the right to take land from larger holdings for new households, though this is unusual.[13]

Even though they are the custodians of land, traditional leaders are forbidden to privately own stool lands since the land belongs to the stool or community.

The mode of selection of traditional leaders differs from one ethnic group to another even though the basic principle is that it is hereditary, that is, one must belong to the royal family before one can either be elected or appointed. In most African countries, succession either by election or appointment of male members of the royal patrilineage or matrilineage is the prerogative of kingmakers. The selection process can sometimes take weeks or months because of the consultation process and desire to reach consensus, as far as that is possible, on an acceptable candidate. There is the perception, whether rightly or wrongly, that the selection process has been politicized during the post independence era because successive governments want to use traditional leaders for their partisan interests.

After a traditional leader is selected, he is installed at a ceremony at which he swears an oath of office by which he binds himself to rule in accordance with time-honoured customs of his people. Violations of the oath may attract dismissal or destoolment. This is one of the checks on the powers of the traditional leader. In addition to this, his authority is also limited by indigenous customary rules and regulations and the popular will. In office, his conduct is controlled through a series of consultations and discussions. He cannot disregard the advice of the council of elders without cogent reasons.

There is evidence to suggest that traditional leaders have been involved in rural and urban local governance from the start of colonial rule to the post-colonial state in most African states. During the colonial period, traditional leaders exercised all powers of government in a given domain – judicial, legislative, executive and administrative – in a system of government that was dominated by force. According to Mahmood Mamdani:

> This authority of the chief was like a clenched fist, necessary because the chief stood at the intersection of the market economy and the non-market one. ... The administrative justice and administrative coercion that were the sum and substance of his authority lay behind a regime of extra-economic coercion, a regime that breathed life into a whole range of compulsions: forced labour, forced crops, forced sales, forced contributions, and forced removals. ... Here there is no question of any internal check and balance on the exercise of authority, let

> alone a check that is popular and democratic. The chief is answerable only to a higher administrative authority. ... It is this agent of this fused authority, this clenched fist, who is usually called the chief. To the peasant, the person of the chief is total, and absolute, unchecked and unrestrained[14].

In spite of traditional leadership being described as "full-blown village despot, shorn of rule-based restraint"[15], it is an important factor in African politics that cannot be ignored[16]. In the words of Richard Sklar, "The *kgotla*, the *Alake* of Egbaland, and the *marabouts* of Senegal exert power in their societies regardless of one or another academic interpretation of their roles"[17].

The degree and nature of that involvement of traditional leaders in rural and urban local governance in Africa has varied considerably, but it has continued. Traditional institutions of political leadership (chieftaincy in its various forms) were a formal part of the governmental machinery until just after independence, and were endowed with state and social authority and power. In Anglophone Africa, during the colonial rule, the policy of Indirect Rule made traditional leadership a major official element of the governmental system. In Ghana, for instance, traditional leaders were involved both in local government through the Native Authorities (NAs) and centrally in colonial politics, through the Joint Provincial Council of the Colony, the Asanteman Council and the Northern Territories Territorial Council. The 1883 Native Jurisdiction Ordinance and the 1944 Native Authority Ordinance gave traditional leaders the power to make bye-laws dealing with such local government functions as the building and maintenance of roads, forest conservation and they had the right to fine or imprison those of their subjects who broke the established bye-laws[18]. While the Nkrumah government prevented traditional leaders from participating in elected local government councils in Ghana, all other post-colonial governments have directly incorporated traditional leaders as members of the state-run local government. Even then, the Nkrumah government accepted the continuing existence of traditional councils and the creation of Regional Houses of Chiefs in order to have local governance structures[19].

In Swaziland, traditional leaders have reserved seats in local administration called the *Tinkhundla*, which since 1979 has been used as a mechanism for election for the whole legislature[20]. Similarly, in Lesotho, the 1997 Local Government Act created community councils, rural councils, urban councils and municipal councils and even though the composition of these local authorities is based on election, in each case a minority of positions is reserved for chiefs. For instance, a Municipal Council consists of not less than 11 but not exceeding 15 elected members, and not exceeding three gazetted chiefs (other than principals) who are also elected[21].

While traditional leaders lost virtually all of their governmental, judicial, and land revenue management roles under colonialism[22], they still undertake the following functions, which are relevant to local and urban governance:

i.   embodiment of deep cultural values and institutions such as ancestor and land veneration, taboos and festivals;

ii.   representation of the community and community identification;

iii.   symbolic leadership and patronage of development/youth/hometown associations;

iv.   control and management of lands of the dynasty,

    v.   creation of dynasties of wealth and influence.

Specifically, the most important role that traditional leaders are expected to play in national affairs are:

- Effective participation in national reconciliation process;
- Lead role in fighting for social development of their people;
- Leadership role in the drive to educate their people;
- Serving as mediator or judge in conflict resolution; and
- Linking national leadership to their people.

Most African countries have adopted constitutional provisions recognizing the place and status of traditional leadership through the establishment of National Houses of Chiefs which have jurisdiction in issues relating to traditional leadership, and acts as a consultative body. According to Richard Sklar, denying recognition to traditional leadership will not make it disappear:

> Traditional authorities do not exist as a consequence of their recognition and appointment by governments of sovereign states. On the contrary, they are recognized and appointed to traditional offices, in accordance with customary laws, because those offices are legitimated by the beliefs of the people, who expect them to exist in practice[23].

Notwithstanding its importance, traditional leadership is a highly contested and politicised one because of the mode of selection and the way it carries out its functions. These have often generated deep local conflict in some Anglophone and Francophone African states.

Features and role of modern leadership

The features of modern leadership espouse Max Weber's legal rational authority principles of hierarchical conformation, continuity, legality and impersonality, accountability, achievement, record keeping, specialization, merit recruitment, professionalism, career structure and ethical codes.

In some respects, the subject matter of modern leadership seems to be outdated. The division of society into leaders and followers is rooted in a pre-democratic culture of deference and respect in which leaders "knew best" and the public needed to be led, mobilised and guided. Democratic politics may not have removed the need for leaders, but it has certainly placed powerful constraints on leadership, notably by making leaders publicly accountable and establishing an institutional mechanism through which they can be removed[24]. In other respects, however, what one may call the "politics" of modern leadership has become increasingly significant, helping to contribute to the establishment of a separate discipline of political psychology, whose major components include a study of the psychological make-up and motivations of leaders both in politics and business.

This growing focus on modern leadership may be attributed to a number of reasons. First, to some extent democracy itself has enhanced the importance of personality by forcing leaders be they political, bureaucratic, religious and corporate, in effect to "project themselves" in the hope of gaining support. This tendency has undoubtedly been strengthened by modern means of mass communication (especially television), which tend to emphasise personalities rather than policies, and provide leaders with powerful weapons with which to manipulate their public images. Second, as societies have become more complex and fragmented, people have increasingly looked to the personal vision of individual leaders to give coherence and meaning to the world in which they live. Third, good leadership is essential in all countries, particularly developing ones, if they are to improve the standard of living of people and alleviate or reduce poverty. For organisations, good leadership is essential if they are to produce high quality goods and services. Indeed, the search for better organisations is also a plea for better leadership. Whenever a country is in deep crisis, people look for leadership to find solutions to the crisis. On the other hand, if it is an organisation, which is not working effectively, people look for leadership to make it better[25].

In a nutshell, countries and organisations need leadership. Without a leader, a country or organization is "much like a rudderless ship – adrift in a turbulent environment"[26]. For this reason, the study of leadership, its modal orientations and processes as well as strands and nuances, is an instructive and fruitful endeavour for students of political science, public administration, public policy, organisation and management practitioners. Modern leadership is a hardy perennial that returns season after season to offer hope of reliable and effective ways to either improve standards of living in African countries and thereby alleviate poverty or improve organizations. Yet the hopes have been repeatedly dashed.

Traditional and modern leadership compared

Comparing traditional and modern leadership is not an easy task. This is because of differences in their mode of selection, performance evaluation and, sometimes, attributes. Traditional leadership is regarded as a closed system, characterised by stratification, hereditary succession, legitimacy and personalism. These features are untenable in modern leadership characterised by openness, legal rationality, universalism, equality and change. This notwithstanding, a first step to compare traditional and modern leadership is to look at the prospects of their co-existence. Most African political leaders are faced with a dilemma in trying to cooperate with traditional leadership in spite of agitations for its abolition in some African countries (see Figure 8). This dilemma is captured in the words of Chief Obafemi Awolowo:

> In spite of agitation here and there against this or that *Oba* or Chief, the institution of Obaship and Chieftaincy was still held in high esteem by the people. But the traditional rights and privileges which the Obas and Chiefs wished to preserve were antithetic to democratic concepts and to the yearnings and aspirations of the people. ... The problem which faced me, therefore, was that whilst I must, at the same time, take the earliest possible steps to modify their rights and abrogate such of their privileges as were considered repugnant, to an extent that would both satisfy the commonalty and make the Obas and Chiefs feel secure in the traditional offices[27].

Figure 9 – Zulu Chief and President Ellen Sirleaf Johnson of Liberia

Sources: *http://www.thp.org/files/images/ellen_johnson_sirleaf.jpg Photography by Cachelleink.com Zulu chief- http://media.lonelyplanet.com/ lpimg/11985/11985-32/preview.jpg, photographer-Ariadne Van Zandbergen*

In spite of the dilemma, there is some consensus on the possible co-existence of traditional and modern leadership. For instance, the Kabaka of Buganda, Mutebi II, who was installed in 1993 in Uganda, noted that "African leaders who enjoy national-legal political legitimacy based on being elected in a fair manner, must supplement it with the traditional legitimacy which traditional leaders like Kings possess"[28]. He envisaged traditional leadership as part of "an effective civil society which countervails and enriches the State"[29]. He was, however, quick to add that "If the traditional leader is largely dependent on the State for his survival, he will find it hard to take a neutral position when the State is prompting him to side with it even when he is convinced that the State is wrong"[30]. Similarly, there has been the clarion call in most African states not only to allow traditional leaders to participate in Africa's nascent democracy but also fashion out modern institutions alongside traditional ones. Furthermore, Pierre Englebert has pointed out that there is increasing evidence that states that incorporate pre-existing sources of political authority into their systems, without denying their validity, do better than those that repress them; Botswana, Swaziland and Lesotho are compelling cases in point[31]. He went on to call for the "recognition of the legitimacy and relative autonomy of traditional systems and their integration into the management of contemporary countries. If the post-colonial state is to be legitimated, it cannot afford to destroy, repress, or even ignore these repositories of political legitimacy"[32].

A second way of comparing traditional and modern leadership is to compare the attributes or qualities one expects from both traditional and modern leaders be they political, bureaucratic, corporate or religious. A summary of the literature reveals that the attributes of traditional leadership are almost the same as those of modern leadership, even though the most important qualities are wisdom, patience, integrity, vision and principles (see Box 2).

Box 2 – Leadership Qualities

- Self-knowledge/self-confidence
- Vision, ability to infuse important, transcending values into an enterprise
- Intelligence, wisdom, judgment
- Learning/renewal
- World-mindedness/ a sense of history and breadth
- Coalition-building/ social architecture
- Morale building/motivation
- Stamina, energy, tenacity, courage, enthusiasm
- Character, integrity / intellectual honesty
- Risk-taking/entrepreneurship
- An ability to communicate, persuade / listen
- Understanding the nature of power and authority
- An ability to concentrate on achieving goals and results
- A sense of humour, perspective, flexibility
- Development-oriented, democratic, transparent, accountable
- Leaders are people who know who they are and know where they are going
- Leaders set priorities and mobilize energies
- Leaders have to provide the risk-taking, entrepreneurial imagination for their organizations and communities
- Leaders need to have a sense of humour and a sense of proportion
- Leaders have to be skilled mediators and negotiators, but they also have to be able to stir things up and encourage healthy and desired conflict
- Leaders have brains and breadth

Source: *W.E. Rosenbach and R.L. Taylor (eds.) Contemporary Issues in Leadership (Boulder, CO.: Westview, 1993), pp. 23-26.*

Challenges facing traditional and modern leadership

A number of challenges face both traditional and modern leadership (see Box 3). For traditional leadership, important challenges include bringing development to their traditional areas, succession disputes, and reaching accommodations with central government on their roles in the modern state. For modern leadership, the major challenge is the myriad of problems that it has to deal with simultaneously. These problems include the almost insurmountable challenge of meeting expectations with meagre resources, the need to grapple with continued dependence on an unfavourable international economic order, the need to incorporate a diverse population into a workable whole, and to establish the guidelines for a distinctive African path of not only constructive change but socio-economic development. For instance, in Ghana, the challenge to leadership is captured in Chapter 6 of the 1992 Constitution, "The Directive Principles of State Policy", which enjoins political leadership to establish a just and free society and take steps for the realization of basic human rights, a healthy economy, the right to work, the right to good health care and the right to education.

Other African countries which were governed by either military regimes (like Nigeria and Benin) or one party governments (like Tanzania and Senegal) have also fashioned out constitutions to address issues relating to ethnicity, political liberalization, sustainable growth, public-private sector partnership, minimal state intervention in the economy and creation of jobs to cope with their rapidly growing population.

Box 3 – Challenges facing leadership in the five countries

- Poverty;
- Urban bias in development policies creating an aggrieved countryside full of a ready army of unemployed youths. These disaffected youth have become the cannon fodder for Africa's entrepreneurial warlords;
- Political exclusion as a result of group-based politics, lack of equitable access to resources and discrimination on ethnic, geographic and religious grounds that have contributed to conflict;
- Corruption;
- The invasive impact of the AIDS and HIV pandemic;
- Human rights abuse;
- Personalized politics;
- Lack of articulation of a clear vision for the future;
- Lack of political will to take forward-looking decisions;
- Domestic and internal conflicts;
- Centralization as national leadership is distanced from the grassroots;
- Lack of good governance;
- Lack of a healthy balance between economic growth and human development;

- Illiteracy;

- Weak agricultural growth rates and food crisis;

- The debt crisis;

- Deteriorating social indicators and institutions (especially education, public health and sanitation, housing and potable water);

- Deforestation and environmental degradation;

- Marginalization of gender in the development process;

- Urbanization and unemployment;

- Poor public service delivery;

- Instability.

Source: *Ayee, Leadership in Contemporary Africa: An Exploratory Study (2001), p. 109.*

The record of good leadership in Africa has neither been impressive, encouraging nor enviable. This is because most of political leaders (at national, regional and local levels) and some bureaucratic, traditional, corporate, religious and other civil society leaders have abandoned their preoccupation with societal or public interest and embarked on unethical leadership, which is detrimental to the well-being of their societies. Poor political leadership especially, has contributed to lack of political and bureaucratic commitment, poverty, political instability, war, poor policy formulation and implementation, lack of accountability and transparency, corruption, nepotism, exclusive politics and moral decadence on the African continent.

Some of the factors that have contributed to a bad leadership profile in Africa are listed in Box 4. These factors include partisanship, lack of mentoring of leaders, corruption, clientelism, neo-patrimonialism, promotion of self-interest rather than public interest, and poor enforcement of codes of conduct.

Box 4 – Factors that have contributed to poor leadership in Africa

- Lack of leadership mentoring that has produced a number of half-baked and opportunistic leaders;

- Most of the political leaders lack experience, knowledge and good judgement;

- The selection and recruitment of most leaders (political, bureaucratic, religious, traditional, youth) is not mostly based on merit, ethics and wisdom (rational components) but on non-rational components such as neo-patrimonialism, money and ethnicity;

- Oversight agencies (such as the legislature, political parties, etc) for vetting or approving appointment or recruitment of political, religious, corporate, and traditional leaders have not done their work effectively because of partisanship or politicization;

- Institutions such as local government units, which are to be the training ground for future leaders have become ineffective and therefore do not appeal to potential leaders;

- Leaders looking to public office as a means of pursuing personal or parochial interests rather than societal or general interests;

- The dilemma between leadership and partisanship;

- Poverty which has led to increased societal pressures for monetary and non-monetary rewards from especially holders of public office;

- The premium placed on money, irrespective of its source has eroded moral and ethical fibre;

- The general misconceived perception of unlimited public sector resources;

- Lack of democratic qualities on the part of leaders, who mostly exhibit authoritarian tendencies;

- Lack of transparency and accountability exhibited by the leaders;

- Avarice and greed on the part of leaders;

- Poor data base or lack of it, which does not enable the leaders to formulate and implement rational policies and programmes to alleviate poverty;

- Non-enforcement of codes of conduct enshrined in constitutions;

- Emasculation or cooptation of civil society organizations by political leaders because of lack of resources;

- Winner-takes-all attitude to politics that has promoted politics of exclusion rather than inclusion; and

- Impact of external factors such as policies and programmes of foreign governments and donors. For instance, some foreign countries had backed some African dictators as a way of promoting their (foreign countries) interests.

Source: *Ayee, **Leadership in Contemporary Africa: An Exploratory Study** (2001), pp. 111-112.*

Conclusions: Promoting the development of a politically elastic leadership in Africa

This chapter has shown that even though better and quality leadership is not the cure-all for Africa's lack of development, it would, at the same time, be an important step in the right direction. Leadership must be seen as an institution that champions new causes, preaches revolutionary values, and suggests radical solutions to existing or unforeseen problems. In this regard:

> The difference between a leader and a follower is that the former leads a group, a nation, or a region of the earth, through crisis situations to triumph and prosperity, while the latter simply follows the trends. ... A leader, particularly, a political leader without a vision, is a fraud on society, and a country that is unfortunate to be afflicted with that kind of leadership is doomed to move from one crisis to another[33].

As Buckley[34] noted, the successful political leader is one who "crystallizes" what the people desire, "illuminates" the rightness of that desire, and coordinates its achievement.

African traditional and modern leadership needs to be politically elastic, and more attention needs to be paid to political "software", than to "hardware". In other words, the beliefs governing political action (political software) must be strengthened and enhanced vis-à-vis the rules governing political action (political software). A judicious blend of the two, with more emphasis on political software, should be able to promote a politically elastic leadership in Africa.

To develop a politically elastic traditional and modern leadership in Africa a number of factors should be taken into account. First, there should be the recognition and appreciation by leaders that widespread participation or dissension is compatible with political legitimacy. The outcome is the emergence of functional relationships rather than counter-productive hostility, conflict and fear within states, governments and organisations.

Second, selective controls, incentives and genuine form of decentralization must be vigorously pursued and sustained. Competent and respected local leaders must be offered significant financial and administrative support for various development projects. Thus reliance would be placed on tangible rewards rather than blatant forms of coercion to obtain results. As local leaders gain from the central government a greater share of its resources, they will have freedom to make decisions based on mutual consultation and shared responsibilities. However, because they are now part of the system, they cannot blame the government if things do not work out as planned.

Third, national programmes on leadership-nurturing in Africa must be coordinated and strengthened with capacity-building as the core focus.

Fourth, the methods of selection and recruitment of political leadership at the national and local levels should be re-assessed.

Fifth, perceptions as to what constitute the qualities of the ideal leader and the ideal metric for leadership assessment should be taken into consideration in the design of leadership performance monitoring systems.

Sixth, leadership at all levels must be sensitised on the important challenges facing the public upon which they want the attention of leadership to be focused, such as poverty reduction, exclusive politics, authoritarianism, corruption, gender equity, HIV and AIDS, and conflicts.

Seventh, suppression of the ethics of self-interest by means of firstly, exemplary selfless behaviour on the part of both traditional and modern leaders, and secondly, encouraging an ideology of the collective good. One is of little use without the other. But both together allow the leadership legitimately to employ coercion against those who exhibit an attitude of "enrichissez-vous"[35]. In the view of Lao-Tzu:

> A leader is best when people barely know he exists. Not so good when people obey and acclaim. Worse when they despise him. If you fail to honour people, they fail to honour you. But of a good leader, who talks little, when his work is done, his aim fulfilled, they will say 'We did this ourselves'[36].

There are, however, a host of difficulties in the way of successfully eliciting support behind a quasi-puritanical stance. Chief among them are the unintegrated nature of most African countries, widespread poverty, the absence of laws to protect whistle-blowers and negative activities by foreign interests, which encourage bribery and corruption and distortions in national programmes and policies.

Review Questions

1. Identify and discuss the leadership styles that have emerged on the African continent.

2. What are the ethical dimensions of traditional and modern leadership? How can they promote good governance and development in Africa?

3. Are leaders "born" or "taught"?

4. Why is "transformational" leadership the best form of leadership?

Suggested Reading

Arhin, K. 1985. *Traditional Rule in Ghana: Past and Present*. Accra: Sedco Publishing

Arhin Brempong. 2001. *Transformations in Traditional Rule in Ghana (1951-1996)* Accra: Sedco Publishing

Grint, K. Ed. 2000. *Leadership: Classical, Contemporary and Critical Approaches* Oxford: Oxford University Press..

Ray, D. and P. S. Reddy, (Eds.) 2003. *Grassroots Governance? Chiefs in Africa and the Afro-Caribbean*. Brussels: IASIA.

Rosenbach, W.E. and R.L.Taylor, (Eds.) 1993. *Contemporary Issues in Leadership*, 3rd Edn. Boulder, CO: Westview.

Endnotes

1. Naomi Chazan , R. Mortimer, J. Ravenhill & D. Rothchild *Politics and Society in Contemporary Africa* (Boulder, CO: Lynne Rienner, 1992), p. 168.

2. Governance refers to the exercise of political, economic and administrative authority to manage the affairs of a nation. It embraces the methods that societies use to distribute power and manage public resources and problems. Good governance or sound governance is a normative concept and a subset of governance that refers to norms of governance such as accountability, transparency, the rule of law, vibrant civil society, gender balance and empowerment, participation, a viable private sector. The principal modes of governance are markets, hierarchies and networks. Markets coordinate social life through a price mechanism which is structured by the forces of demand and supply. Hierarchies, which include bureaucracy and thus traditional forms of government organization, operate through 'top-down' systems. Networks are 'flat' organisational forms that are characterised by informal relationships between essentially equal agents or social agencies. Governance can be contrasted with government, which is one of the organisations involved in governance and refers to the formal and institutional processes which operate at the national level to maintain order and facilitate collective action. In short, government is taken to include any mechanism through which ordered rule is maintained, its central features being the ability to make collective decisions and the capacity to enforce them. The core functions of government are thus to make law (legislation), implementation of law (execution) and interpret law (adjudication). For more elaboration on governance and government see Dele Olowu and Soumana Sako (eds.) *Better Governance and Public Policy* (Bloomfield, CT: Kumarian, 2002; Goran Hyden and Michael Bratton (eds.) *Governance and Politics in Africa* (Boulder, CO.: Lynne Rienner, 1992); UNDP, *Reconceptualizing Governance*, Discussion Paper 2 (New York: UNDP, 1997); Andrew Heywood, *Key Concepts in Politics* (New York: Palgrave, 2000).

3. For extensive discussion on the styles of leadership see J.M. Burns, *Leadership* (New York: Harper, 1978); N.M. Tichy and M.A. Devanna, *Transformational Leadership* (New York: Wiley, 1986; N.M. Tichy and M.A. Devanna, *The Transformational Leader: The Key to Global Competition* (New York and Chichester, 1990).

4. See A. Mazrui, "Leadership in Africa", *New Guinea*, Vol. 5, No. 1 (1970), pp. 33-50; A. Mazrui, "The Monarchical Tendency in African Political Culture", in Marion Doro and Newell E. Stultz (eds.) *Governing in Black Africa* (Englewood Cliffs, NJ.: Prentice Hall, 1971), pp. 18-38; A. Mazrui, Pan-Africanism, Democracy and Leadership in Africa: The Continuing Legacy for the New Millennium, Inaugural Abdulsalami Abubakar Lecture, Chicago, February 23, 2001 (unpublished); V.T. Le Vine, "Leadership Styles and Political Images: Some Preliminary Notes", *Journal of Modern African Studies*, Vol. 15, No. 4, (1975), pp. 631-638; V.T. Le Vine, "Leadership Transition in Black Africa: Elite Generation and Political Succession", *Munger Africana Library Notes* Vol. 30 (1977); P. Woodward, "Ambiguous Amin", *African Affairs*, Vol. 77, No. 307 (1978), pp. 153-164; T. Callaghy, "State-Subject Communication in Zaire: Domination and the Concept of Domain Consensus", *Journal of Modern African Studies*, Vol. 17, No. 3 (1980), pp. 469-492; T.M. Shaw & N. Chazan, "The Limits of Leadership: Africa in Contemporary World Politics", *International Journal*, Vol. 37, No. 4 (1982), pp. 543-554; J. Cartwright, *Political Leadership in Africa* (London: Longman, 1982); R.H. Jackson & C.G. Rosberg, *Personal Rule in Black Africa: Prince, Autocrat, Prophet, Tyrant* (Berkeley: University of California Press, 1982); R.H. Jackson & C.G. Rosberg "Personal Rule: Theory and Practice in Africa", in Lewis, P. (ed.) *Africa: Dilemmas of Development and Change* (Boulder, CO.: Westview Press, 1998), Chapter 1, reprinted from Comparative Politics (July, 1984), pp. 421-442. R.H. Jackson & C.G. Rosberg, "Why Africa's Weak States Persist: The Empirical and the Juridical in Statehood", in Atul Kohli, ed. *The State and Development in the Third World* (Princeton: Princeton University Press, 1986); L. Sylla, "Succession of the Charismatic Leader: The Gordian Knot of African Politics", *Daedalus*, 111, No. 2 (1982), pp. 11-28; C. Clapham, Third World Politics: An Introduction (Madison: University of Wisconsin Press, 1985); L. Adamolekun, "Political Leadership in Sub-Saharan Africa: From Giants to Dwarfs", *International Political Science Review*, Vol. 9, No. 2 (1988), pp. 95-106; S. Decalo, Psychoses of Power: African Personal Dictatorships (Boulder, CO.: Westview Press, 1989); World Bank, *World Development Report* 1986 (New York: Oxford University Press, 1986); World Bank, *Sub-Saharan Africa: From Crisis to Sustainable Growth: A Long-Term Perspective Study* (New York: Oxford University Press, 1989); H. Bienen & N. van de Walle *Of Time and Power: Leadership Duration in the Modern World* (Stanford, CA.: Stanford University Press, 1991); J.A. Wiseman *Political Leaders in Black Africa* (Brookfield, VT: Edward Elgar, 1991); J.A. Wiseman, "Leadership and Personal Danger in African Politics", *Journal of Modern African Studies*, Vol. 31, No. 4 (1993), pp. 357-360; Chazan et. al. *Politics and Society in Contemporary Africa*; A. Adedeji, "'L' and 'M' Factors in the African Development Equation", *African Journal*

of Public Administration and Management Vol. 1, No. 1 (1992), pp. 1-13; Africa Leadership Forum, Africa and the Successor Generation Summary report and papers presented a the 10th Anniversary of the African Leadership Forum, Sheraton Hotel, Cotonou, Benin, 26-28 November 1998 (Abeokuta: Africa Leadership Forum, 1999); P.C. Aka, "Leadership in African Development", *Journal of Third World Studies*, Vol. 14 (Fall) (1997), pp. 213-242; M. Ottaway, "Africa's 'new leaders': African Solution or African Problem?", *Current History*, Vol. 97 (1998), pp. 209-213; A.A. Goldsmith, "Risk, Rule and Reason: Leadership in Africa", *Public Administration and Development*, Vol. 21, No. 2 (2001), pp. 77-87.

5.   See World Bank, *Sub-Saharan Africa: From Crisis to Sustainable Growth*, pp. 6-7.

6.   M. Cohen & J.G. March, *Leadership and Ambiguity* (New York: McGraw-Hill, 1974); J.M. Burns, *Leadership* (New York: Harper, 1978); Keith Grint, *The Arts of Leadership* (Oxford: Oxford University Press, 2000).

7.   J. Paige, *The Scientific Study of Leadership* (New York: The Free Press, 1977; E.P. Hollander, *Leadership Dynamics* (New York: The Free Press, 1978); M. Macoby, *The Leader* (New York: Ballantine, 1981); K. W. Kuhnert, "Leadership Theory in Postmodernist Organizations", in R.T. Golembiewski (ed.) *Handbook of Organizational Behaviour* (New York: Marcel Dekker, 1993), pp. 189-202.

8.   B.M. Bass, Bass and Stogdill's *Handbook of Leadership: Theory, Research and Managerial Applications*, 3rd Edn. (New York/London: New York Press, 1990); B.M. Bass, "Leadership and Performance Beyond Authority", in J.R. Pennock and J.W. Chapman (eds.) *Authority Revisited: Norms XXIX* (New York: New York Press, 1985); W.E. Rosenbach, & R.L. Taylor (eds.) *Contemporary Issues in Leadership* 3 edn. (Boulder, CO.: Westview Press).

9.   See J.R.A. Ayee, *Leadership in Contemporary Africa: An Exploratory Study,* United Nations University Leadership Academy Occasional Papers Academic Series No. 3 (December), 2001, pp. 7-12; UNDP, *Public Sector Management, Governance, and Sustainable Development* (New York: UNDP, 1995); UNDP, *Reconceptualizing Governance*, Discussion Paper 2 (New York: UNDP, 1997).

10.   Bass, Bass and Stogdill's *Handbook of Leadership*; J.M. Burns, Leadership (New York: Harper, 1978); Keith Grint, *Leadership: Classical, Contemporary, and Critical Approaches* (Oxford: Oxford University Press, 1997).

11.   B. M. Bass, Stogdill's *Handbook of Leadership: A Survey of Theory and Research* (New York: Harper, 1981); Bass, "Leadership: Good, Better, Best", Organization Dynamics, Vol. 13: 26-40; Andrew Heywood, *Key Concepts in Politics* (Hampshire/New York: Palgrave, 2000).

12.   Max Weber, *The Theory of Social and Economic Organizations*, edited with an introduction by Talcott Parsons (New York: The Free Press, 1947), p. 152.

13   John W. Bruce, "A Perspective on Indigenous Land Tenure Systems and Land Concentration" in R.E. Downs and S.P. Reyna (eds.) *Land and Contemporary Africa* (Hanover, NH: University of New England Press, 1988), p. 25.

14.   Mahmood Mamdani, *Citizen and Subject: Contemporary Africa and the Legacy of Late Colonialism* (Princeton: Princeton University Press, 1996), pp. 23, 53, 58.

15.   Ibid., p. 43.

16.   Jeffrey Herbst, *States and Power in Africa: Comparative Lessons in Authority and Control* (Princeton, NJ.: Princeton University Press, 2000), p. 178.

17.   Richard Sklar, "The African Frontier in Political Science" in Robert Bates, V.Y. Mudimbe and Jean O'Barr (eds.) *Africa and the Disciplines: The Contributions of Research in Africa to the Social Sciences and Humanities* (Chicago: University of Chicago Press, 1993), p. 94.

18.   Kwame Arhin, *Traditional Rule in Ghana: Past and Present* (Accra: Sedco, 1985); Arhin Brempong, *Transformations in Traditional Rule in Ghana* (1951-1996) (Accra: Sedco, 2001). 19 Ibid.

20.   For more on the Tinkhundla local government system, see J.R.A. Ayee, "A Note on the Machinery of Government During the Sobhuza II Era in Swaziland", *Research Review* (NS), Vol. 5, No. 1, (1989), pp. 54-68. 21.Tim Quinlan and Malcolm Wallis, "Local Governance in Lesotho: The Central Role of Chiefs" in Donald

Ray and P.S. Reddy (eds) *Grassroots Governance? Chiefs in Africa and the Afro-Caribbean* (Brussels: IASIA, 2003), Chapter 6: 145-172.

22. Richard Sklar has shown that in most African countries traditional leaders have been restricted to advisory and ceremonial, rather than decisional, roles in the organs of the national government. There is also evidence of political interference in the affairs of traditional leaders. For instance, in 1996, the Nigerian military government deposed the Sultan of Sokoto, the spiritual head of the Hausa-Fulani linguistic group and Muslim community in favour of an evidently more popular, and less threatening, rival. For more on this see Richard Sklar, "African Polities: The Next Generation", in Richard Joseph (ed.) *State, Conflict and Democracy in Africa* (Boulder, CO.: Lynne Rienner, 1999), pp. 165-177.

23. Ibid. p. 169.

24. J.R.A. Ayee, *Leadership in Contemporary Africa: An Exploratory Study,* Occasional Papers, Academic Series, No. 3 (United Nations University Leadership Academy: Amman, Jordan, December 2001), pp. 7-19.

25. J.R.A. Ayee, "Leading Large States" in Christopher Clapham, Jeffrey Herbst and Greg Mills (eds.) *Africa's Big Dysfunctional States* (Cape Town: SAIIA, 2004), forthcoming.

26. Rabindra Kanungo and Manuel Mendonca, *Ethical Dimensions of Leadership* (London and New York: Sage, 1996), p. 2.

27. Obafemi Awolowo, Awo: *The Autobiography of Chief Obafemi Awolowo* (London: Cambridge University Press, 1960), p. 261.

28. Speech delivered by the Kabaka of Buganda, King Mutebi II at Princeton University, New Jersey, reprinted in West Africa, April 15, 1996, p. 577.

29. Ibid.

30. Pierre Englebert, *State Legitimacy and Development in Africa* (Boulder, CO.: Lynne Rienner, 2000), p. 190.

32. Ibid. p. 191.

33. Adebayo Adedeji, "'L' and 'M' Factors in the African Development Equation", *African Journal of Public Administration and Management,* Vol. 1, No. 1, 1992, p. 8.

34. .See W.F. Buckley, "Let's Define that 'Leadership' that Kennedy say we Need", *Press Bulletin,* Binghamton, NY, 4a (September 22, 1979).

35. See H.H. Werlin, "The Theory of Political Elasticity", *Administration and Society*, Vol. 20, No. 1 (May), pp. 47-70. We also borrowed the concepts of "political hardware" and "political software" from this piece.

36. Lao-Tzu quoted in W. Bynner, *The Way of Life According to Lao Tzu* (New York: Capricorn, 1962), pp. 34-35.

SECTION 3: ECONOMY, LIVELIHOODS & SECURITY

CHAPTER 10

DEVELOPMENT THEORY AND AFRICAN SOCIETY:
AN INTRODUCTION

Kojo S. Amanor

An Introduction

Development refers to two different but related phenomena. Firstly, it is a process of immanent historical and social change that characterises all societies as they grow and transform themselves. Different types of development and rates of change characterise different societies in different epochs, but they nevertheless change and develop a history and a historical memory of the past conditions in society. Epochs of change and transition also create attendant social problems that need to be interpreted, analysed and solved by interventions. The process of capitalist industrial development in nineteenth century Europe, for example, resulted in social problems of unemployment, surplus population, poverty and welfare that needed to be solved by planned interventions by the state. These problems constituted the realm that the concept of development arose to solve. With the expansion of world trade, colonialism and imperialism, these problems were exported to other continents resulting in the need to initiate a process of social and economic planning to contain the social dislocations brought about by change. Hence in addition to the process of change in society, development refers to a set of doctrines and theories about the appropriate types of interventions that need to be implemented to bring about progress and social improvement in society or social development. These are underpinned by theories of society, social change, transformation and progress. These concerns first emerged in Europe in the writings of Saint Simone and Compte, laying the foundations for the emergence of both sociology and socialism as bodies of knowledge concerned with social change and transformation.

Development as theory or doctrine is concerned with how society should be organised and who should do the organising. In its most overt political form, development doctrine consists of discourses through which dominant powers within the world attempt to bring other nations under their ambit, to conform with their vision of the organisation of society and their attempts to construct the world in their own image. In this form, development doctrine extols the virtues of the dominant power and provides a blueprint of the policies the power initiated to achieve its present positions. Poor countries are promised development if they learn from the history of the dominant power and conform to its vision of society and social progress. The aim of this chapter is to show the ideologies that lie behind different models of development. Development theories in Africa are based on certain interpretations of African society that may not necessarily reflect the complexity of the reality. They may result from models of society and economy worked out in other societies and developed into general abstract models that are then applied elsewhere. These models frequently reflect dominant policy and political interests in the global setting rather than the internal socio-economic dynamics inherent in various African societies.

This chapter explores the various ways in which development theories deal with contradictions at different levels of society, and with different social and political interests. This includes the contradictions that emerge at the global level between developed and developing countries and global, regional and domestic markets; at the national level between urban and rural society, the state and the peasantry; and at the community and household level between women and men. Development theory poses itself as neutral, as based on science and technology, as creating technical blueprints for social progress. However, development interventions create both winners and losers in society, and these categories emerge from the ideological constructs that underpin various development theories. The chapter examines the underlying political nature of development theories and interventions, and explores how these operate at different levels of society. This reveals conflicting interests and cleavages within society, and processes of social stratification. Development policies may attempt to further and justify specific political and economic interests. They may also be critical of existing policies and attempt to overcome the entrenchment of narrow political interests in power.

Defining and Measuring Development

In the Post-war period, development has usually been defined in terms of economic growth, as the expansion in productive capacity of a nation state. This expansion of productive capacity is usually measured in terms of Gross National Product (GNP), which constitutes the total domestic and foreign output obtained by residents of one country in one year. This is a measure of income - the total income of the country, including what they get from abroad in remittances. Alternatively, economic growth can be measured in Gross Domestic Product (GDP), which consists of the total output of goods and services produced by an economy in a year. This measures the productive size of an economy. The World Bank and other agencies produce tables of per capita GNP, measuring the GNP as a proportion of the size of the population, and ranking various nations according to per capita GNP.

However, the measurement of GNP may not be very accurate for many African countries, particularly where a large informal sector exists. The informal sector consists of people who are not employed in establishments that are regulated by the state and its laws. The informal sector includes small-scale production and family units that are not effectively regulated within the administrative, legal taxation and social welfare framework of the state. Those in the informal sector depend upon their own initiatives to gain a livelihood and for social safety nets that provide them with the equivalent of social security and subsistence in times of unemployment and crisis. They include small-scale traders, agricultural labourers, casual or contract labourers, artisans (mechanics, carpenters, masons, hairdressers, seamstresses, etc.), small-scale miners, and shantytown dwellers.

In African states the informal sector is large. The agricultural sector largely accounts for between 50-60% of the population,the informal sector for between 30-40% of the population ,and the formal industrial, manufacturing and service sectors for 10% of the population in the contemporary period, for a large number of African states. It is unlikely that the measurement of GNP is accurate when the majority of the population are not regulated by the state, and are not covered by the collection of official state statistics based on the regulatory framework. Informal sector livelihoods are often diverse, and involve multiple activities. They are difficult to quantify, value and measure. Research carried out by the West African Long Term Perspective Study (WALPS) suggests that the GNP in West Africa is hugely underestimated (Snrech, 1995). As an alternative measurement of wealth, WALPS attempted to compute rent payments by urban dwellers in West Africa. They estimated that between 1960 and 1990, 66 million town dwellers came into existence in West Africa. Attempts to compute the rent paid by these town dwelling farmers suggested that the Gross Regional product for West Africa should be 20-30 percent higher than official estimates (Snrech, 1995).

Limitations of growth

Apart from questions about accuracy, measurements of per capita GNP do not tell us much about the state of the economy. They do not indicate how many people are gainfully employed, the provision of social security and social services to meet the needs of the population, and the investment of the state in education and training opportunities. GNP does not tell us anything about the relationship between income, work, and the distribution of incomes between people. In some countries, income is distributed more equitably than in others. In some countries also, there are a few very rich people and many poor people, and in others the rich have less wealth and the poor are better off. Some nations invest more of their wealth in welfare and social infrastructure. These different distributions of wealth and provisions for people have different implications for development. Thus, it has been argued that while the GNP of African and South East Asian countries were often not that different in the 1950s and early 1960s, a much larger part of the GNP of South East Asian economies was invested in the education sector and on training in new skills. The economic benefits of this were then reflected in South East Asian GNP economic growth in the 1980s.

GNP records short term utilisation of resources without looking at implications for the future. For example, rapid deforestation through logging will be reflected as a growth in GNP statistics for a particular year. But far from resulting in development and expanded wealth in the future, this may result in environmental deterioration, which will produce far greater and costly environmental problems than the short-term benefit. This may include loss of topsoil and soil erosion, declining agricultural yields, shortage of timber for the domestic market, etc. Thus it is possible to have short-term economic growth without development, particularly when economic resources are used to support the consumptive lifestyle of a small elite class.

In agriculture, development can be measured in increasing yields achieved by adopting new technology. But this adoption of technology may create social and environmental problems. While modern mechanised agriculture may result in rapid gains of profit, some of the longer-term costs of production may be overlooked, such as the cost of water for irrigation, which may in future result in sinking water tables, shortage of water and salinisation. The costs of pollution through fertilisers seeping into streams and drinking water and toxic uptake in the soil may also be very high.

An increasing awareness of the social and environmental costs of production has led to the development of the concept of sustainable development (see also Ch.15,). While there are numerous definitions of what comprises sustainable development, these usually contain some notion of promoting a development in the present that does not undermine the posterity of natural resources for future generations, and which provides for the needs of the majority of humanity and not for the privileged minority at the expense of the majority. However, political interests frequently temper the interpretation of sustainability in global fora. Many states and entrenched interest groups often attempt to blame other groups for environmental destruction, while presenting their own activities as environmentally friendly.

Human rights, entitlements, and capabilities

Amartya Sen (1999, 1984, 1981) has questioned the notion of development based on economic efficiency without considerations of social welfare and well-being. He argues that concepts of fundamental human rights, human entitlements and capabilities should be of fundamental concerns in defining development. Further, he argues that development policies and market outcomes should be judged in terms of their impact on valuable human ends rather than measured by abstract economic criteria. People's entitlements are characterised by their command over things, and their capabilities are determined by their capacity to make choices to develop a life that is of value to them. According to Sen, most cases of poverty and starvation do not arise because people are deprived of things to which they are entitled. They are the result of people not having entitlements. Cases of starvation do not occur because of overall food shortage, but because people are unable to trade their labour to gain the food they need. Thus, an important dimension of poverty is a lack of freedom of action and choice for the poor. Poverty cannot be defined merely in terms of inadequate income. It also consists of vulnerability and a lack of voice and representation. Development should be rooted in people's aspirations. Sen argues that development should be concerned with creating structures which enable people to develop their own solution to problems and which encourages them to develop the capabilities to achieve this. The provision of social opportunities through public welfare, including schooling, basic health care, rights to land etc., encourages people to enter into the market confidently. When people's ability to participate in economic life is made easier, the macro economy will ride on the success of the individual entering the market.

This approach has influenced the creation of new indices of development that go beyond the economic. In the *Human Development Report,* the United Nations Development Programme (1990) now defines development as a process of enlarging people's choices that leads to a long and healthy life, better education, a decent standard of living, political freedom, guaranteed human rights, and self respect.

Modernisation theory and economic growth

From the 1940s to the 1970s, the dominant discourse in development thinking in Africa was based on modernisation theory. Modernisation theory deals with the problems of the transition from traditional society to modern society and with the problems of underdevelopment. It sees most societies as being trapped in a state of underdevelopment, which condemns society to stagnation and attendant problems of poverty. According to modernisation theory, a few societies have been able to overcome these problems through developing appropriate policies that promote economic growth. Through learning from the planning processes created by developed countries, developing countries can develop appropriate strategies through which they will also become developed. Thus modernisation theory reduces development to a technical problem to be solved by the application of appropriate economic planning, science and technology.

In *The Stages of Economic Growth: A non communist manifesto*, Rostow (1960) argues that societies pass through five stages of development in the transition from traditional society to modernity. In the first stage traditional societies were limited by the lack of development of science and technology, which resulted in agriculturally based societies that were organised on kinship. They were characterised by a fatalistic mentality in which social change or improvement was inconceivable. In the second stage of growth, which characterised Western Europe in the seventeenth and eighteenth century, modern industry and trade began to develop and the expansion of production resulted in the acceptance of science in society and the questioning of traditional value systems. In Third World countries this stage was brought about through colonialism. In the third stage of take-off, economic growth becomes normal and capitalist interests become dominant in society. The rate of capitalist investment rises to between 5-10 percent of national income paving the way for the take-off, into sustained economic growth. In the fourth phase, which he terms the drive to maturity, between ten to twenty percent of national income is invested in new productive capacity. Industry matures, expands and new industries develop. New social institutions come into being and new technologies are generated within the nation state. In the final stage of industrial development, a mass consumer market develops as people become more prosperous and manufacturing industries dominate over heavy industry. Rostow argues that by following the blueprint of the already industrialised countries the developing countries can achieve the take-off into sustained growth. While the stages of growth offer a clear path for developing countries to follow, the path is essentially based on mindlessly copying the policies of the USA rather than on developing countries addressing their own particular circumstances. It generalises the particular model of development in the US for the whole globe. In the conditions of the Cold War, it was essentially concerned with promoting US dominance in the world against the Soviet Union, hence its subtitle - *a non communist manifesto*.

The characteristic feature of most modernisation theory is a concept of dualism based on two sectors: a modern dynamic and a traditional backward sector. The road to development is for the modern sector to overcome and displace the traditional sector.

These underlying constructs can be seen in Arthur Lewis' "Economic Development with Unlimited Supplies of Labour" (1958). Lewis starts from the premise that two distinct economic sectors can be found in developing countries: a backward subsistence economy with unlimited supplies of underemployed labour, and a modern capitalist sector employing wage labour. The subsistence sector is characterised by low labour productivity and low standards of living based on family labour. The populations of these developing countries are large, particularly in relation to the capital and technology resources available to them. A large part of the population carries out economic activities that are highly marginal. Much of the labour force is underemployed, working at a low capacity. Underemployed labour includes farmers who work for short periods of the day, casual labour, petty traders, and domestic servants. The underemployed also include the large number of messengers in firms, who are frequently relatives of the boss, and sit around doing nothing most of the time for paltry wages. Petty trading is another large sector. Markets and street corners are crowded with many small stalls, each selling small quantities of the same goods and making little profit. If the number of stalls were greatly reduced the consumer would be no worse off in making their purchases. They may be better off in that retail margins would fall.

Lewis argues that the vast reserve of underemployed labour working within subsistence sectors provides the modern capitalist sector with a large potential labour force. Moreover, this labour can be transferred from the subsistence sector to the capitalist manufacturing sector without adversely affecting food production or the production of basic needs. Since labour is underemployed within the traditional subsistence sector, the movement of labour into the manufacturing sector can be easily filled by the remaining labour within the subsistence economy without adversely affecting production, since there is much slack labour in this sector. This labour can also be employed for cheap wages, since the conditions of low productivity within the subsistence sector generate low standards of living and expectations. By absorbing cheap labour from the subsistence sector the capitalist sector can reap abundant profits. These high profits encourage reinvestment and expansion of the capitalist sector. This process will result in increasing investment in industrial development and economic growth. It will eventually result in more skilled and productive labour and more knowledge of production, leading to higher productivity and higher standards of living. Lewis argues that this growth can only occur in the modern industrial sector since the capitalist class is the only class that can realise profits that can be reinvested for further expansion of production. If increased productivity occurred in the agricultural sector, landlords would siphon off large amounts of the profits from investments in rents, which they would use on consumptive expenditure rather than in productive investment. Thus, the modern capitalist sector is the main sector promoting economic growth and development and developing countries should invest in developing the urban manufacturing sector above the agricultural sector.

Modernisation theory sees the problems of underdevelopment as lying in the backwardness of the agricultural sector, which is characterised by underemployment and low productivity. The solution is to create a rapid expansion of the manufacturing sector. This will absorb surplus labour at low wages and increase productivity, creating large profits for industries that can sustain industrial expansion. The agricultural sector needs to be displaced by an industrial sector and labour transferred from unproductive subsistence agriculture to industry.

A second variant in modernisation theory can be seen in the *vent for surplus* theory of Myint (1958). In contrast with Lewis' approach, which examines an industrial capitalist sector against the background of subsistence agriculture, this juxtaposes integration into colonial trade and export staple crop production against subsistence food production. Myint argues that before the nineteenth century, the developing countries were characterised by sparse population and poor transport facilities. The lack of transport prevented them from developing a diversified economy. Markets were confined to small localities and most producers produced the same goods, so there was limited opportunity to develop exchange. Surplus labour existed because in a subsistence economy with poor transport facilities and little specialisation in production the people were unable to develop suitable investment opportunities. This lack of economic opportunity resulted in labour being locked up in a semi-idle form. People maximised on leisure rather than increasing material goods at their disposal. There was a surplus of land, which people were unable to use productively.

According to Myint, colonialism resulted in the development of transport and communications and the introduction of new consumer goods and markets for new crops. This acted as a stimulus that encouraged the peasants to expand production for the export trade. With the availability of land and labour, this was easily achieved by bringing new land into cultivation and increasing labour. The export crops were easily developed alongside subsistence crops. Colonial expansion enabled surplus labour (under-utilised or underemployed labour) to be channelled into new land for the production of new wealth. Since the domestic market of developing countries was small this expansion of export-oriented production remained the only viable development option for the colonial administration to follow. Thus, colonialism acted as a *vent for surplus* land and labour, creating modern infrastructure and access to international markets that enabled new wealth to be created in the agriculture sector. However, this process of expansion can only continue as long as there is both surplus land and labour available.

Dependency theory and the problem of history

Modernisation theory denies the historical experiences of African countries and people. Their future development is assimilated to the experiences of the West. This denial of the relevance of history is carried out by characterising developing countries as traditional and static. This prevents their present plight been seen as a product of their history. Instead of learning from their own history, they are expected to learn from the history of the West, as packaged by proponents of modernisation such as Rostow. Modernisation theory is essentially based on model building derived from neoclassical economies. It generalises, abstracts and makes presumptions about the condition of underdevelopment, rather than investigating the actually existing historical patterns of economic activity that characterises underdevelopment.

In reaction to modernisation theory several researchers began to explore the structural dimensions of underdevelopment, examining the historical conditions that gave rise to underdevelopment. Out of this movement emerged dependency theory. The central premise of dependency theory is that underdeveloped countries constitute peripheral economies that are highly dependent upon the world market and the major centres of capitalist accumulation. These peripheral economies have overdeveloped export sectors that are dependent upon trade with the major centres of capital, but have no significant heavy industrial sectors and small manufacturing sectors. They lack effective linkages between their agricultural and industrial sectors, which would promote the development of a home market. The peripheral economy imports most of its manufactured goods.

Dependency theory is highly critical of modernisation theory and dualism. It argues that the roots of underdevelopment must be traced historically rather than derived from abstract models derived from economic theory and presumptions of static social systems. It argues that the dualist division between a traditional and a modern sector is not accurate and that what is taken to be a traditional sector is itself the product of colonialism and the incorporation of developing countries into the world economy. The characteristics of underdevelopment are thus shaped by the global structures of world trading systems rather than local socio-economic conditions and cultural constraints.

In "Underdevelopment and Dependence in Black Africa-Origins and contemporary forms", Amin (1972) traces the historical integration of Africa into the world market. He periodises the integration of Africa into the world market into the pre-mercantilist, the mercantilist and the capitalist eras. Three distinct patterns of integration into the world market have also emerged. In West Africa colonial trading companies predominated which held control over the export of colonial agricultural staple commodities and of the import trade, and marketed the produce of independent peasant producers. In Southern and Eastern Africa, the dominant European economic interests were organised around mining and commercial agriculture and Africans were integrated as providers of labour. In Central Africa, large administrative areas were given out to concession companies to exploit.

In the pre-mercantilist era that preceded the 17th century, Africa was in general no more backward than the rest of the world. Complex social formations had emerged with states, social differentiation or classes, and the disintegration of primitive village economies. Complex trade patterns occurred, particularly in West Africa, resulting in the development of long distance regional trade. In trade, West Africa was an equal partner with other areas of the world. Trade with the rest of the world was peripheral to the African economies, which were largely autonomous. African society did not depend upon trade with other areas to reproduce its economic and social life. Africa was economically independent. African societies developed in parallel with the Mediterranean and Arab world, with which they were linked by trade. West African societies supplied the European, Mediterranean and Arab worlds with gold. The trade encouraged social differentiation, states and empires. The movement of mercantile trade from the Mediterranean to the Atlantic created a crisis in Africa and resulted in the decline of both the Arab world and Africa. In West Africa this resulted in a shift of commercial gravity from the hinterland of the Sahara to the coast.

In the second phase, after 1700, the Americas played a decisive role in the accumulation of money wealth by Europe, laying the foundations for the emergence of capital. The plantation economy of the Americas was integrated into European markets, providing raw materials for the development of European industry. America emerged as the periphery of Europe, but Africa emerged as the periphery of the periphery, providing labour in the form of slaves for the development of the plantation economy in the Americas. The involvement of West Africa in the slave trade favoured the development of powerful states near the coast, which raided and subjugated neighbouring peoples. This resulted in the emergence of wealthy slave-raiding states surrounded by subjugated areas that were depleted of labour and wealth. At the global level this resulted in the development of Africa becoming subservient to the development of America. Africa provided labour for the expansion of America and through that for the expansion of the world economy, but subtracted labour from its own development. Amin (op cit.) argues there was much resistance to the Atlantic trade in the hinterland, which took the form of attempts to maintain former trading roots and patterns of trade, and the spread of Islam in West Africa in the nineteenth century as a religion opposed to the Atlantic slave trade.

In the third phase, which began in the early nineteenth century, a transformation of the world economy occurred. This was characterised by the emergence of industrial production in Western Europe, the decline of the slave trade, and the growth of demand for raw materials for European industry. West Africa became transformed into a producer of export crops for European industry. The period of the slave trade had created links between powerful African states and traders and European factors. These links formed the basis for developing export trade. Colonial authority provided support to existing political groups who were able to organise both the appropriation and/or privatisation of land for export crop production and labour. Labour was often recruited for the export crop sector from areas that were originally depleted of their wealth through slave raiding and political subjugation. Colonial policy sought to maintain these areas in a state of backwardness, to ensure that the youth and men of working age were forced to migrate. Taxation was often used to force people to migrate. To meet their tax obligations they had to seek employment in the export crop sector. The basic arrangements that lay behind the development of the colonial economy in West Africa included the following:

1. The organisation of a dominant trade monopoly with colonial import-export houses, in which Lebanese traders formed main intermediaries and African traders were forced to accept subordinate positions;

2. The taxation of the peasants in money which forced them to produce what the monopolists offered to buy;

3. Political support to the social strata and classes that were able to appropriate tribal lands and to organise internal migration from regions which were deliberately left in their poverty so as to be used as labour reserves in the plantation zone;

4. Political alliance with social groups which were interested in commercialising the tribute they levied on the peasantry, such as Muslim brotherhoods; and

5. Administrative coercion, such as forced labour (Amin, 1972).

Through these political interventions the colonial powers were able to reorganise the economies of West Africa, break down previous regional patterns of trade, and establish new patterns of import-export trade that favoured the European trading companies and paid minimal prices to African producers. Amin (1972: 520-521) comments of this area:

> Under these circumstances, the traditional society was distorted to
> the point of being unrecognisable; it lost its autonomy and its main
> function was to produce for the world market under conditions which,

because they impoverished it, deprived the members of any prospects of radical modernisation. This 'traditional' society was not, therefore, in transition to 'modernity'; as a dependent society it was complete, peripheral, and hence at a dead end. It consequently retained certain 'traditional' appearances which constituted its only means of survival. The Africa of the colonial trade economy included all the subordination /domination relationships between this pseudo-traditional society, integrated into the world system, and the central capitalist economy that shaped and dominated it.

In contrast with West Africa, in Southern and Eastern Africa the dominant colonial interests were concerned with mining (gold and diamonds in South Africa and copper in Northern Rhodesia), rather than import-export commodity trade. The major needs of capital was for a large proletariat for the mines and to provide labour for settler farmers in Southern Rhodesia, Kenya and Tanganyika. Proletarianisation was achieved by dispossessing African rural communities of their land - sometimes by violence - and driving them back into poor regions with no means of modernising and intensifying their agriculture. This transformed these societies into labour reserves, and forced their members to migrate to the major centres of European agriculture and mining to make a living and to send remittances to relatives back home. Amin (1972: 519) comments:

> Henceforth we can no longer speak of a traditional society in this part of the continent, since the labour reserves had the function of supplying a migrant proletariat, a function which has nothing to do with 'traditional'. The African social system of this region, distorted and impoverished, lost even the semblance of autonomy: the unhappy Africa of apartheid and the Bantustans was born, and was to supply the greatest return to central capital.

The third area identified by Amin consists of Central Africa. In Central Africa trade had not developed to the degree of West Africa and it was impossible to implement the colonial trade system. Low population densities and a lack of hierarchically organised societies in which wealthy elites had considerable influence over large geographical areas hindered the development of colonial trade within this area. Discouraged, the colonial authority gave the country over to concessionaires who were responsible for the administration of large areas and extraction of surplus wealth. In contrast with West Africa, where peasant production was encouraged and large plantations discouraged, in the Congo concessions were given out to large companies such as Lever Brothers to develop plantations. Attempts to establish a colonial economy base on concessions were associated with some of the worst abuses of human rights.

In contrast with Myint or Lewis, Amin argues that there are no traditional societies in Africa, only dependent peripheral ones. In contrast with the vent for surplus theory, he argues that colonialism did not remove constraints within the traditional static sector but rather undermined its autonomy. Colonialism did not create new opportunities for semi-idle labour, but used political interventions and violence to create labour reserves, to dislocate existing populations, and force labour to migrate to the main export producing areas and colonial enclaves. This displacement of labour impoverished the areas of labour reserves, while the main export producing zones produced cheap commodities for European industry. The political interventions sacrificed the potential of the domestic economic sector to the narrow metropolitan needs of European industry. Colonialism did not create opportunity for idle or underemployed labour in the traditional sector, or lead to an improved awareness of the "laws of the market", but led to the transformation of some areas into labour reserves for the main export crop areas to produce cheap commodities for European industry. Thus, the traditional underemployed sector as defined by Lewis is a product of colonial intervention. Far from creating opportunity for the traditional sector, the potentials of the domestic economy were sacrificed to produce export crops for European needs.

The main calls from dependency theorists have been for a delinking from the world market, and for the building of autonomous regional blocs. However, they do not resolve how this delinking is to be carried out and by what agency. As is clearly evident from Amin's article, dependency in Africa arose out of an alliance between dominant colonial metropolitan economic interests and dominant African political powers and elites. The contradictions are not only between developed and developing countries and the system of world trade, but also within the nation state between different class interests.

Urban bias

Other analysts have tried to identify the roots of underdevelopment with inappropriate national policy frameworks that favour various elite coalitions at the expense of the vast majority of people who are alienated and marginalised by the national development planning process. Michael Lipton (1977) argues that there is a large disparity in the standards of living of the rural and urban sectors in developing countries that is far wider than in the present developed countries during their period of development. In developing countries, seventy percent of the population work in agriculture. They produce between forty to forty-five percent of GNP. But the rural sector barely receives twenty percent of investments. Thus, the wealth of the rural sector is being extracted to finance urban development. Government policies (pre-structural adjustment) have resulted in cheap farm produce and expensive commodities that rural people buy. Subsidies on farm inputs such as fertiliser have gone to rich farmers. An insufficient supply of subsidised inputs to meet the needs of the majority of farming people has resulted in many farmers buying inputs at greatly inflated prices on the open market.

Lipton contends that in developing countries urban elites are strong and able to exert great influence over policy. He defines the urban elites as consisting of businessmen, politicians, bureaucrats, trade-union leaders, workers, and professionals who control the distribution of resources. They dominate the state organs (government, law, civil service, trade unions, police, military etc.). Their power is not only based on economic wealth, but the power to organise, centralise and control the resources within the state. In contrast, rural people are poorly organised, dispersed and inarticulate. They are unable to unite nationally to fight against urban power and to demand that their interests are met. This results in the great disparity in living standards between urban and rural areas. As a result, urban power in developing countries is out of proportion to the urban share of the population or production.

According to Lipton inequality results in inefficiency. Investment in urban growth is costly and does not promote much employment. Urban-bias means that rural based high-yielding labour-intensive options are not explored and that the resources of the state are expended on the development of a few expensive elite and urban-based projects rather than on developing resources for rural development.

Lipton argues that inequalities within rural areas also owe a lot to urban-biased development. The urban areas want to receive surpluses from rural areas for minimal investment. They provide those people in the rural areas who can most provide surpluses with assistance and neglect the majority of small-scale farmers. They form an alliance with large farmers. The aim of this alliance is to extract surplus from agriculture in the form of cheap food, savings, and foreign exchange from export crops in return for favoured farmers having access to subsidies, inputs and services. Often these inputs are only appropriate for the large farmers and are not suitable for small farmers. These policies have harmed small-scale farmers who have been placed in an unfavourable position in comparison with the large farmers, whose activities are supported and subsidised by the state.

Lipton argues that this results in inefficient policies. The small farmers occupy more significant areas of land. Small farmers are also able to produce greater outputs per acre than large farmers when they have access to a supportive policy environment. The rural rich are less efficient producers but get more aid from the state and the small farmers with the potential to bring about greater change get less. Over time this policy of neglecting small farmers and subsidising large-scale agriculture has resulted in declining exports, rising food imports and increasing national debt. It has resulted in the underuse of scarce labour and overuse of scarce and costly capital-intensive solutions. Had these resources been invested in small-scale agriculture they would have been used more efficiently. With rising population growth and high costs of creating urban jobs this strategy has proven unsustainable.

According to Lipton, in recent years there have been changes in agricultural development policies in Latin America and Asia, but in Africa urban bias is still being consolidated. As a result of this urban bias overall agricultural productivity in Africa is low.

Lipton argues that in Africa inappropriate agricultural policies have led to myths about the backwardness and conservatism of peasants, when in fact there is much evidence that they are innovative and rational. These myths include the following:

1. Large farmers are more efficient producers when in fact yields and returns to capital are higher on small farms for most crops and technologies;

2. It is scientific to apply Western capital-intensive methods to landscarce, maintenance-skill-starved, and labour-surplus rural environments;

3. Technologies developed on experimental stations near urban cities can yield useful results without carrying on experimentation on farmers' fields.

Economic development normally involves industrialisation. However, the road taken by Europe and Japan involved developing agriculture before the rural surplus was transferred from the rural sector to the rest of the economy. Most developing countries have attempted to modernise their economy by giving priority to industrialisation. Some countries have followed the path of developing large state-run farms, which would then deliver surpluses to the cities. Other developing countries have attempted to manipulate market forces in order to influence the prices of exports and imports, against the interests of farmers.

Lipton argues that urban bias exists because the rural areas are poorly organised and unable to articulate their demands in a way that will force urban elites to take note. The solution to urban bias is for rural peoples to organise and demand a more equitable allocation of resources from urban areas.

The theory of urban bias has been criticised for equating rural with poor and urban with rich (Corbridge, 1992). There are many poor people in urban areas that are not rural. While it acknowledges that there are rich people within rural areas these are disingenuously transformed into a part of the urban coalition. In reality there are different strata in rural areas with different interests. While small farmers and large landlords may be interested in high prices for food, rural labourers who need to purchase food on the market are not interested in high food prices. Large landowners are also interested in protecting their favoured status in relation to supply of subsidised inputs. Thus, there is no clear association between urban and rural class interests and urban bias.

Some development analysts, working in the tradition of Lipton, argue that the present model of urban growth in Africa prevents a more equitable distribution of resources to rural areas and impedes their development. This encourages the state to be sensitive to the power and pressure of urban dwellers and to focus on meeting urban demands rather than to develop the rural areas. Other analysts argue that urban growth will encourage the development of production and encourage new dynamic processes that will create new demands for rural produce and encourage rural development. This will provide more stable markets than the production of staple agricultural produce for export markets (Snrech, 1995).

Agricultural Markets and the State

Robert Bates (1981) has attempted to refine the urban bias theory by placing agricultural development policies within a political framework concerned with the role of state intervention in building political patronage, and the political interests of those who make policy. He defines agricultural development policy as being concerned with making suitable incentives available for farmers to guide and reward them for improving their farming. From this premise, he argues that problems in agriculture must therefore be related to improper policy incentives that distort the operation of the market. One of these distortions is government policy.

Bates argues that government policies are influenced by political factors. Therefore, it becomes important to examine the political basis for agricultural policies and the ways in which policies are developed to appease and win over powerful political interests and to enable political regimes to remain in power. Bates examines the process through which governments intervene in agricultural markets. Governments intervene in agricultural markets to gain surpluses, which they redistribute to build up their support base. He argues that there are three important agricultural markets:

1. the market in agricultural commodities, including food crops and export crops.

2. the market in factors of production inputs such as fertiliser

3. the market in manufactured goods consumed by rural people.

In the agricultural commodities markets, governments are interested in keeping the farm gate price of farm produce low. This enables them to realise profit through the control of trade (buying cheap and selling dear) to raise funds for state business and industrial ventures, and to finance the large bureaucracy. It also enables them to provide cheap food for urban workers to prevent urban unrest and cheap inputs for local industries. This creates an urban alliance. This can be done through marketing boards that pay farmers minimal prices for export crops or through enforcing control prices. By purchasing export crops from farmers at cheap prices through monopoly marketing boards and selling them at the world market prices, governments can realise a large "economic rent" or surplus, which it uses to build up its political coalitions.

In the market for inputs, governments subsidise inputs to increase the profitability of mechanised farming and encourage large scale production. However, the government cannot afford to subsidise sufficient quantities of inputs to meet the needs of the majority of the farming population. As a result, the beneficiaries of subsidised input programmes are a narrow group of elite farmers with close ties with government. This encourages patronage of the state's input delivery programmes and wins influential supporters and allies in rural areas. The majority of small farmers can only gain access to inputs in the private sector at greatly inflated prices.

Governments intervene in the market for consumer goods to build up local manufacturers. They introduce high tariffs against imported commodities to prevent them competing against locally produced goods. While this promotes the interests of local industrialists, who are often important allies of government, it makes local consumers pay for the costs of industrialisation, while not assuring high quality or competitive commodities.

Thus, the majority of farmers sell their crops at low prices, are unable to gain access to inputs or purchase them in the informal sector at greatly inflated prices, and pay high prices for the commodities they consume. These policies are detrimental to agriculture and do nothing to encourage farmers to produce more. They encourage farmers to retreat from the market. During the 1970s many African farmers retreated from export crop production controlled by state marketing production and went into the production of food crops over which the state could exert little control. Others engaged in cross-border smuggling of export crops. As a result, many African states began to suffer a decline in revenues from export crop production, which intensified the economic crisis of the 1970s.

Bates argues that African governments do not encourage efficient price mechanisms since they would gain little political advantage from this. When markets work efficiently they become invisible. However, when they are inefficient this encourages political patronage. Political interests dictate that the economy should work to promote a system of patronage. By extracting surplus from rural areas, governments can continue to maintain and extend the systems of patronage that they have established to consolidate their power. This includes extracting rural surplus to support the bureaucracy, to maintain a weak state industrial sector, and to appease urban workers who might riot if prices of food were increased

While governments could raise food prices and increase investment in the agricultural sector to encourage food production, they do not do this because rural producers are poorly organised and do not voice their demands. In contrast, urban workers frequently protest against increasing rises in prices and they bring down governments. By returning a portion of what they extract from rural areas, and giving generously to a few allies, governments seek to divide rural political interests. Rural people compete as individuals to receive favours rather than uniting and organising to assert the interests of the mass of rural farmers. Governments can also use economic inefficiency to cultivate patronage. Introducing tough legislation and economic controls that make it impossible for people to go about their economic activities, and then making exceptions to individuals that support the regime is a way of achieving this objective. Rural people seek for personal favours to overcome their problems rather than uniting to represent their group or class interests. The weak level of organisation among rural people results in a fear of being victimised if they come together to criticise government policies or to articulate and voice group interests. Instead of advocating for policy changes, rural people attempt to evade policy regulation and to gain favour by becoming members of patron-client networks.

Bates argues that African governments prefer development projects to efficient market policies. Through projects, resources can be given to loyal supporters while dissenters can be removed from office and from access to resources and rewards. This often results in inefficiency as poorly trained supporters are rewarded with positions in which they have little capacity. Many people see small farmers as the problem in agriculture. In contrast with this, Bates argues that it is government interventions that have been so harmful to the majority of farmers. Entrenched political interests create serious obstacles to change and prevent small farmers from developing their production.

The impact of neoliberal policies on African agriculture

Writing during the early 1980s, Bates was influential in laying the foundations for neoliberal, structural adjustment policies in Africa. Bates advocated for a removal of government control over the economy, the removal of government interventions in markets, for liberalised markets and a greater role for the private sector. These became major concerns in the early stages of structural adjustment programmes. Structural adjustment programmes sought to introduce liberalised markets through less government control over currency rates, removal of import tariffs, divestment of government enterprises and monopoly export crop marketing boards, and through the removal of subsidies.

However, these policies have not resulted in a flourishing of agriculture. With the opening of agricultural markets, local agricultural production often has to compete against the flooding of the market with cheap food produced by global agribusiness, emanating from states in which indirect subsidies and other credit lines for agriculture still exist. For instance, the US retains farm subsidies by decoupling farm payments from commodity prices and through disguising subsidies as infrastructural support. The level of subsidisation in US agriculture is high. McMichael (2000) estimates that the average subsidy to US farmers is over one hundred times the income of a corn farmer in Indonesia. By externalising these subsidies US agriculture is able to dump its surplus production abroad with low prices. By privileging market price as the criterion of agricultural competitiveness, US agriculture can represent African agriculture as inefficient. McMichael (2000) argues that the rhetoric about free markets and competitiveness serves to justify the use of institutional means to extend markets for agribusiness at the expense of small farmers throughout the world. These arrangements have been institutionalised in the World Trade Organisation (WTO). The WTO seeks to regulate the global institutional framework for agricultural trade in the name of free market principles and efficiency. This creates considerable problems for African farmers who have to compete against transnational agribusiness supported by powerful governments and indirect subsidies, without any support from their own governments. While African states have raised producer prices for export commodities under structural adjustment policies, commodity prices are highly volatile and the global food industry is able to build up large stockpiles of primary commodities from around the world, pushing down international prices. Thus, African farmers continue to produce in an unfavourable international agricultural policy environment, in which the concept of free markets and economic efficiency serves to hide the global inequalities prevalent in capitalist agriculture.

The role of civil society and popular participation

During the 1980s neoliberal economic theorists assumed that retrenching of the state would enable the emergence of a genuine capitalist class to develop and replace patronage politics with a more disciplined market-oriented approach. However, this has not been achieved and deflationary trends have often undermined economic growth prospects and the emergence of a prosperous national capitalist sector. In this situation, those that have benefited have been precisely the elites who are tied into influential political patronage circles, and who have been able to take advantage of their national and international political connections to gain preferential access to control economic resources and markets. The privatisation and deregulation of the economy has not led to less corruption, but has enabled many firms to engage in more corrupt activities and illegal activities, since deregulation makes it easier to evade regulation and detection.

This is evident in timber production in tropical Africa, in countries such as Ghana and Cameroon. With the adoption of structural adjustment in Ghana, the timber sector became a major recipient of credits to rebuild the capacity of the timber industry and to promote export-led growth. Many of these timber companies engaged in underhand operations, exceeding their felling quotas, felling undersized trees, under-declaring felled timber, avoiding payments of royalties and export duties, and using timber as a front for reinvesting loans into other ventures (Friends of the Earth, 1992). By the late 1980s it became evident that Ghana's timber resources were being seriously depleted by an unregulated industry, and by the 1990s a series of reforms had been introduced to regulate the industry, protect forests, and build the capacity of the state forestry sector to manage the industry, which was financed by donors.

Lack of accountability in the land sector also makes it problematic for investors to acquire land for their economic ventures. Markets frequently function differently from the precepts of economic theory, resulting in unanticipated outcomes. By the late 1980s the model of free markets was increasingly questioned and a number of commentators began to argue that the market mechanism could only be successful if it was embedded in appropriate social structures and regulated by social institutions. To function properly markets require a regulatory framework that ensures the enforcement of contractual obligations. This requires building the capacity of the state to regulate and monitor economic activities and to create a legal and policy framework for stable property rights. This also requires the development of civil society organisations that can engage in advocacy, lobby government institutions and voice displeasure with policies that favour elites and encourage corruption.

Civil society consists of voluntary organisations that represent the interests of their members to government. This may include community organisations, associations of small-scale producers, trade unions, religious bodies, Non Governmental Organisations, (NGOs), etc.

Top-down approaches and community participation

Modernisation theory has been essentially *top-down*. It seeks to impose decisions and solutions devised by policy-makers, experts and bureaucrats on the people without involving them in decision-making. The viewpoints of the people are dismissed as irrelevant since they are seen as "ignorant", "backward", "conservative" and "resistant to change". This results in a lack of feedback from the intended beneficiaries to the agencies who design and implement development projects. Few channels exist through which the recipients of development projects can make creative inputs into policy and development planning.

Until the 1980s, central governments usually set up their own semi-autonomous state-sponsored development organisations, which were dependent upon the state for support and patronage. These organisations managed development projects with donor and government sponsorship. These projects were used to disburse scarce goods and services to supporters. As a consequence, the development process tended to be subverted by political patronage and economic development gave way to "rent-seeking" activities and corruption. This results in the poor performance of projects since they did not have mechanisms built into them that enabled monitoring and evaluation of performance according to the changing needs of rural communities. In the top-down approach the people are not seen as playing a role in deciding their future, they are merely recipients of decisions taken elsewhere and of the disbursement of goods.

Songsore and Denkabe (1995) show how the top-down structures developed in the Cotton Development Board in the Upper West Region of Ghana led to inefficient administration, in which decisions could not be made in the absence of the executive director, who frequently travelled to Accra. There was a lack of dialogue and meetings between staff and no flow of information from farmers. As a result of this vacuum, project resources could easily be diverted, dubious contracts awarded and charges grossly inflated. Unsurprisingly, the project was unable to meet its targets. Because of a lack of involvement of the beneficiaries -the cotton farmers in the programme- corruption, waste and inefficiency continued to exist unchecked. The involvement of recipients or end-users in the decision-making serves to make projects more transparent, accountable and efficient.

However, communities are made up of diverse groups and elite groups may seek to establish or gain control of community groups to represent their own narrow interests and to capture resources. Governments may also seek to recognise groups that build up its support base as the representatives of the community, reinforcing systems of political patronage. The concept of civil society participation in policy only works when there are strong traditions of autonomous popular organisation and processes of local democracy where people can choose their own representatives and vote out those who do not represent their interests. Without these conditions being met, civil society participation merely reinforces the existing status quo and serves to build coalitions that entrench dominant power relations and economic interests in specific localities.

The question of gender

Modernisation theory tended to focus on market production in rural societies without examining the implication of work within the domestic sector. The household was seen as the basic unit of production, and the male household head represented the interests of the household. The perspectives of women were not taken into account and women's interests were often marginalised and undermined by development initiatives (Pearson, 1995).

In most agrarian peasant societies women tend to have many responsibilities in the domestic sector (see also Ch.4). In looking at work it is useful to divide it into productive and reproductive (domestic), and monetised and non-monetised. Domestic work (such as processing and preparing food for household consumption or child care) is usually non-monetised and does not bring direct financial remuneration, but it is crucial to the survival and livelihood of the household. What constitutes domestic and productive is also socially determined, since many domestic tasks are important to production (Crehan, 1986; Pearson, 1995). For instance where women are responsible for storing seeds and selecting them for the next year's planting, this combines both domestic and productive functions. Many types of farm work carried out by women are considered to be unimportant or peripheral by some men simply because women carry them out (Crehan, 1986).

Figure 10 – Community Focus Group Discussion

Since development theory has largely been concerned with market relations and interventions that lead to growth of markets rather than with household well-being, the domestic sector has been overlooked (Crehan, 1986; Pearson, 1995). Women and men usually play distinct roles in production and household reproduction. These roles are socially defined, although they are often represented as biologically determined. These roles vary from society to society. For instance, in some African societies women make farms in their own right while in others their main role is weeding. In yet other societies women do not go to the farm. While women are associated with domestic work, in many societies men can be hired as domestic servants or work as cooks and chefs. Secretarial work is now associated with women in many African countries, but in the early colonial period the secretaries were men.

Colonial rule often created institutions that reinforced the domination of men and eroded women's power and autonomy (see Ch.4). In areas that were dominant labour reserves, men were encouraged or forced to migrate to mines or cash cropping areas to provide labour. These societies became dependent upon the labour of women in food production to subsidise the livelihood of the household, while men worked in the cash economy (Pearson, 1995). Few opportunities were created for women to work as wage labourers. Where export crop production existed, men became the main export crop producers and women frequently experienced difficulty in getting access to land for export crop production. Women thus became concerned largely with domestic food production on plots released to them by their husbands or their male kin. Within the urban areas few opportunities were created for women to gain employment and women were largely confined to the domestic non-monetised sector.

Modernisation approaches often assume that the male is the head of the household and owner of the farm, which he works with family labour. This assumption undermines the independence of women and their economic interests and marginalises them from development policies. This often has a negative impact on development. Botchway (1993) examines the impact of the Weija irrigation project in Ghana on gender relations of production. The Weija irrigation project failed to examine the existing division of labour within the family and the different incentives that influenced the strategies of men and women. In the project area, women are traditionally the main organisers of harvesting and they are responsible for marketing of food crops. The project was based on contract farming models. In this model, the farmers allocated land on the irrigation plot had to follow farming prescriptions laid down by the project on the specific crops to be cultivated and the farming practices to be used. They had to surrender their crops to the marketing wing of the irrigation authority, which had a monopoly on marketing. Land was allocated to men and it was assumed that pooled family labour would form the basis for farm operations.

Botchway (1993) argues that the family in the Weija area is characterised by an intricate division of labour based on gender. Women are mainly responsible for the harvesting and marketing of crops. Male farmers generally concern themselves with the supply of "bulk money" for the family. They are responsible for major capital expenditures used in meeting extraordinary expenses such as hiring tractor services and paying for hospital and school fees. Women are responsible for the supply of "current money", for incidental expenses that arise regularly in the household, including the purchase of provisions and food. To meet these expenses, women engage in activities that yield dividends in the short term and on a more or less continuous basis. They sell produce like cassava, chilli and maize from the bush plots for cash. But there is always a limit to what they can sell, because of the subsistence requirements of the family. During the dry season activities on bush plots drop to a minimum. The women are therefore compelled to diversify their income-generating source and mainly engage in small-scale trading. On the irrigated plots of the project farm, work proceeds uninterrupted during the dry season, but farmers' wives do not consider this as a viable income-generating activity, since the irrigation project had captured their main economic activity, the marketing of the crops, and paid the men directly for the crops. One woman commented: "I will never step on any of my husband's fields on the project because those plots hold nothing good for me and my children" (Botchway, 1993: 31). The alienation of women from irrigated farming resulted in a lack of availability of pooled family labour for the project's intensive planting programme. The women work solely on their private bush plots and refuse to assist the men in working on the project plots. If the project had paid attention to these local farming strategies and perceptions, it would have taken the need of women for "current money" and trading capital into consideration, to come to a socially acceptable arrangement, where farming units would have been allocated a predetermined part of the harvest for their household use. This would have encouraged women to join men on their household plots, since they would have been guaranteed a portion of the harvest for trading.

Similar developments are described for Gambian irrigation projects by Carney (1988). Lands converted into irrigation plots, which were formerly worked by women, were allocated to men to work with their families on the assumption that men were the real farmers. All inputs were allocated to men. However, historically men had grown groundnuts as a cash crop, and women cultivated rice. As a result of the undermining of their autonomous farming livelihoods, women were reluctant to participate as part of a family team in irrigated rice cultivation and men had to pay women for work done in the irrigated plots. The alienation of women had a negative impact on the project.

Van Onselen (1996) offers a humorous account of how gender interests disrupted the farming aspirations of a South African sharecropper, Kas Maine. Kas had a large polygamous household which he engaged in his farming schemes. At one point Kas decided to grow sunflower, a profitable cash crop. As usual Kas' wives provided the main labour force. Sunflower is a demanding crop and harvesting the heads and removing the ripe seeds is a particularly unpleasant task. After the experience of the first year, Kas' wives realised that not only was it hard work, but since it was a cash crop for their husband, it gave them nothing in the way of food to meet their obligations of feeding the household or money. Kas, however, was delighted with the profit the sunflower brought him and was determined to increase the acreage the following year. Unfortunately for him, just when the sunflower was almost ready for harvest he had to make a journey to the local town and was away for a few days. Taking advantage of his absence, the women went into the sunflower field and trampled all the plants, destroying them and scattering the seed. On his return Kas met stories of how a terrible attack by birds had destroyed the sunflower!

Without taking into consideration the gender division of labour, projects may introduce bottlenecks into farm production, which increase the burden of women without any recompense. In farming systems where men are responsible for land clearance and women for weeding, the introduction of new mechanical or bullock ploughing technology can enable men to expand the areas they clear. Without an associated development of weeding technology, this will result in increasing expenditure of labour by women on weeding without any corresponding increase in remuneration, particularly if weeding is seen as a domestic obligation.

Without sensitivity to the gender division of labour within households and the interests of women, development interventions can erode the autonomy of women, undermine their role in production, and create intolerable burdens of labour without any corresponding improvement in welfare and access to economic resources. Thus, it is important to understand the gender division of labour within households, the economic interests and roles of women, and the impact of technical interventions on their labour and economic interests.

Conclusion

This chapter has examined the impact of development policies on different levels of societies. It shows that there are tensions in development thought between technical prescriptions, social outcomes and political interests. Development is frequently presented as a technical problem to be solved by technical interventions and economic planning. However, this technicist approach serves to detract from the complex historical, social and political dimensions that surround underdevelopment and development.

Summary

1. Development theory is concerned with the processes of change within society and interventions that purport to solve emerging problems or critique existing policies.

2. Development theories comprise both technicist approaches based on technical solutions for development problems, and social and political analysis that reveals the political and social dimensions that underpin the problem of development and development policies.

3 Technicist approaches interpret development in terms of economic growth and increased production. Social development approaches measure development in terms of improved human well-being, greater equity and redistribution of wealth, social provisions for developing human capabilities, and social participation in policy.

4. Development theories deal with different levels of society. They examine global relations in the context of relationships between different states and power blocs and in the context of the emergence of transnational corporations and global markets. They examine national relations between the urban and rural sectors and between the state, elites, workers and the peasantry. The examine communities and households in the context of the relationship between poor and rich households and between men, women and youth within households.

Review Questions

1. Compare and contrast the ways in which dependency theory and modernisation theory examine history, tradition and modernity in African society.

2. Compare and contrast Robert Bates' theory of political distortions of agricultural markets with Michael Lipton's theory of urban bias.

3. How can popular participation result in a more transparent development process?

4. What are some of the limitations of using indices of economic growth to measure development?

5. What are some of the pitfalls which emerge from making development interventions without considering the gender division of labour?

References

Amin, S. 1972 "Underdevelopment and Dependence in Black Africa: Origins and contemporary forms" *Journal of Modern African Studies,* vol.10 (4):503-24.

Bates, R. 1981 *Markets and the State in Tropical Africa: The political basis of agricultural policies*, Berkeley CA: University of California.

Botchway, J. 1993 "Implications of farming and household strategies for the organization of a development project" in W. de Boef, K. S. Amanor and K. Wellard (eds.) *Cultivating Knowledge: Genetic diversity, farmer experimentation and crop research*, London: Intermediate Technology, pp. 27-34.

Carney, J. 1988 "Struggles over Crop Rights and Labour with Contract Farming Households in a Gambian Irrigated Project" *Journal of Peasant Studies* 15: 224-349.

Corbridge, S. T 1992"Urban bias, rural bias, and industrialization: an appraisal of the work of Michael Lipton and Terry Byres", in J. Harris, (ed.), *Rural Development: Theories of Peasant Economy and Agrarian Change*. London: Hutchinson University Library. pp.94-118.

Crehan, K. 1992 "Rural households: Making a living" in H. Bernstein, B. Crow and H. Johnson (eds.) *Rural Livelihoods: Crisis and Response*, Oxford: Oxford University Press, Oxford, 1992, pp.87-112.

Friends of the Earth 1992 *Plunder in Ghana's Rainforest for Illegal Profit: An exposé of corruption, fraud and other malpractices in the international timber trade*, London: Friends of the Earth.

Lewis, A. 1958 "Economic Development with Unlimited Supplies of Labour" in A. A. Agarwala and S. P. Singh (eds.), *The Economics of Underdevelopment*, Delhi: Oxford University Press, pp. 400-449.

Lipton, M. 1977 *Why Poor People Stay Poor: Urban Bias in World Development*, London: Temple Smith.

McMichael, Philip 2000 "Global Food Politics" in F. Magdoff, J. Bellamy Foster and F. H. Buttel (eds.) *Hungry for Profits: The agribusiness threat to farmers, food and the environment*, New York: Monthly Review Press.

Myint, H. 1958 "The 'Classical Theory' of International Trade and the Underdeveloped Countries", *The Economic Journal,* (June) pp.317-337.

Pearson, R. 1995 "Gender Matters in Development" in Ron Ayers (ed.) *Development Studies: An introduction* through select readings, pp, London: Greenwich University Press.

Rostow, W. W. 1960 *The Stages of Economic Growth: A non communist manifesto*, Cambridge: Cambridge University Press.

Sen, A. K. 1981 *Poverty and famines: An essay on entitlements and deprivation*, Oxford: Clarendon.

Sen, A. K. 1984 *Resources, Values and Development*, Oxford: Blackwell.

Sen, A. K. 1999 *Development as Freedom,* Oxford: Oxford University Press.

Snrech, S. 1995 *Preparing for the Future: A vision of West Africa in the year 2020*. Summary Report, Paris: Club du Sahel, OECD.

Songsore, J. and A. Denkabe 1995 *Challenging Rural Poverty in Northern Ghana: The case of the Upper-West Region*, Trondheim: Centre for Environment and Development, University of Trondheim.

United Nations Development Programme 1990 *Human Development Report* 1990, New York: Oxford University Press.

Van Onselen, C. 1997 *The Seed is Mine: The Life of Kas Maine, a South African Sharecropper* 1895-1985. Cape Town: David Philip. 1996; New York: Hill and Wang; Oxford: James Curry.

CHAPTER 11

AGRICULTURAL DEVELOPMENT IN AFRICA
Daniel Obeng-Ofori

Introduction

Africa is largely agricultural, with the majority of the population deriving their income from farming. Agricultural development is therefore intricately linked to overall economic development in African countries. Since 1960, global food production has increased by 145 percent. But in Africa over the same period production has decreased by 10 percent. And although 70 percent of Africans are engaged in agriculture, 250 million are malnourished, with one third of sub-Saharan Africans chronically hungry (Juma, 2011). According to Juma, the development of agriculture, a sector that has been tragically neglected despite its central role in the life of so many Africans, will also anchor the development of the entire continent. Africa's neglect of food production has caught farmers and other rural Africans in a trap of subsistence. Unable to find markets for the food they grow, they produce mainly for family consumption, limiting not only the quantity, but also the variety and nutritional content of their food. Nonetheless, the continent has an abundance of arable land, and less than 4 percent of its surface and groundwater is harnessed (Juma, 2011).

This chapter examines the meaning and scope of agriculture; the historical development of agriculture in Africa; the importance of agriculture to African economies; contemporary agricultural development, the challenges and critical strategic thrusts for accelerated agricultural development in Africa. As Staatz and Dembélé (2007) emphasize, weak economic performance in Africa is closely linked to slow productivity growth in the agricultural sector which is the key determinant of overall economic growth and poverty reduction in most SSA countries. However, as they also point out, sub-Saharan Africa is incredibly diverse, so sub-continent-wide averages about agricultural performance are often misleading, obscuring localized successes and potentialities.

The Meaning and Scope of Agriculture

The term "Agriculture" is derived from two Latin words *"ager"* and *"cultura"* which together means tilling the land or working the soil in order to produce something. Agriculture can, therefore be defined simply as the production of crops and animals for the use of humankind. However, considering the diverse activities involved in agriculture apart from producing food crops, its definition could be more broadly stated as the science or technology and practice of growing crops and raising animals for food and other purposes (Addo-Quaye *et al.*, 1993).

Agriculture is the oldest occupation of humankind and it started when people found that the food around their immediate dwelling places was being exhausted and that they had to travel long distances to obtain food. Humankind eventually settled down to farming because of the realization that their continued existence on earth depended heavily on their ability to provide adequate food for healthy growth and development to improve their living conditions. Land was put under cultivation to produce various food crops. Livestock was kept to rear farm animals such as cattle, sheep, goats and poultry. Fishing was also carried out in the seas, rivers, streams and other water bodies to harvest different types of fish for human consumption.

As the society became complex and more sophisticated with time, more knowledge was developed about the various aspects of farming. Out of problems which arose over the years, intensive investigations were carried out by specialists in the field of agriculture on improved methods of cultivation and livestock husbandry, breeding of improved varieties of crops and breeds of animals, protection of crops and livestock from diseases, pests and parasites, soil improvement, mechanisation and the economics of the process of raising and marketing crops, animals and their products. However, production of crops and livestock is not limited to food only. Industrial crops are cultivated for the manufacture of various items including beverages, medicines, clothing, detergents and other necessities of life. Similarly, by-products from livestock are processed into a variety of products such as textiles, clothing, footwear, and many other items. Thus, agriculture supplies the raw materials for the manufacture of other needs of humankind.

Due to its primordial importance, agriculture also has cultural significance in communities all over the world (See also Chapter 17, this volume). Some communities in Africa celebrate festivals to commemorate or welcome the new agricultural year. Agricultural festivals are related to crop farming, fishing and hunting, and are usually celebrated to mark the beginning or the end of the harvest season. They are also held to thank the ancestors and the gods for a good harvest and the provision of food for the current year. Examples of agricultural festivals celebrated in Ghana are as follows: the **Homowo** or Hooting at Hunger festival of the people of Ga Dangme, variations of Yam festivals of the people of Akyem, Akwapem and Ewe of Peki; the **Kundum** of the people of Nzema and Ahanta, the **Bakatue** festival of the people of Edina (Elmina), the **Ngmayem** festival of Krobo, and the **Bugum** festival of the people of Mamprusi to commemorate end of harvest. The **Aboakyir** festival of the Effutu (Winneba) is a hunting festival. Certain customary rites are performed during such festivals. For example, the **Homowo** season starts in May with customary rites of sowing of the corn or millet **(nmaadumo)** by the seven principal traditional priests known collectively as **Agbaabii**. The actual Homowo day of feasting starts in August and embraces the entire traditional state. Thus, festivals have religious, cultural, social and political significance.

History of Agricultural Development

Agriculture is a major source of the three basic needs of humans: food, shelter and clothing. It has evolved through nomadic agriculture of gathering fruits in the wild and hunting, to large-scale mechanised farming using advanced technologies developed through research.

Nomadic farming

Early people on earth gathered wild fruits, nuts, roots and mushrooms and leaves of various plants. They also trapped fish and wild animals for food. For shelter, the early settlers used caves, hollows and the protection provided by large trees. Leaves and skins were used for clothing. Stones, pointed sticks and sharpened bones were used for killing, carving and skinning wild animals. Obviously these rudimentary tools were ineffective for carrying out the various agricultural activities. These periods represent the stone-age, hunter and gatherer periods of human civilisation. These were periods of insecurity with no secure home or food supply. Certainly human beings could not continue this sort of unsettled life forever. As civilisation developed, agricultural activities also began to change gradually with improvement in their efficiency and effectiveness.

Settled farming

With time, fire for heating and cooking was discovered. The use of bows, arrows, slings and harpoons as weapons for hunting animals and protecting humans became common. It was also realised that settling at one place to cultivate the land for food production was the only way of ensuring food sustainability to support livelihoods. To achieve this goal, rudimentary agricultural tools for cultivation were made from split bones, pointed sticks and carved stones. This heralded the beginning of the settlement period, compared with the previous hunter and gatherer period.

Settled farming first occurred in areas with abundant supply of water throughout the year especially on the banks of the world's large rivers in the Middle East along the valleys of the Tigris, Euphrates and Nile. At this time, the dog and herded cattle were domesticated. The common tools used included **(a) digging sticks** (pointed sticks for breaking soil and for planting seeds); **(b) hoes** in the form of forked pieces of wood sharpened at one end or flint-bladed tools used in the same way as the West African hoe is today; **(c) sickles** (bones or wood curved inward with flint for harvesting cereals and **(d) milling stones** with grinding surface.

The Sumerians were the first people to understand the relationship between seed, soil and water and their importance in food production. This occurred over 6,000 years ago. Among other crops, they grew barley, lentils, wheat and peas, and reared pigs, goats and sheep. The Egyptians were the first Africans to engage in settled farming about 5,000 years ago in the delta and banks of the river Nile. They grew barley, wheat, dates and beans. Simple irrigation system in the form of the **'shaduf'** was first used to supplement natural rainfall.

Early farmers used indigenous knowledge to select for superior quality crops and animals to produce. Early travellers also carried crops from one continent to another. With advances in science and technology, several crops have been greatly improved in yield, quality and resistance against pests and diseases from their wild ancestors.

Tools for farming operations have become more complex and sophisticated over time with metal replacing wooden parts, making them stronger, durable and more efficient. Small-scale farmers use simple tools for clearing of the land, felling of trees, digging the soil and weeding. Examples of simple tools are cutlasses, hoes, axes, pickaxes, mattocks, spades, shovels and trowels. Others are forks, rakes, garden lines, measuring tapes, watering cans, harvesting knives, secateurs and shears.

Mechanised farming

Agriculture has developed from primitive hunting and gathering to the large-scale commercial farms found in different parts of Africa today. These developments have been accompanied by gradual change in the farm tools used to perform various farming activities. Only a few farmers in Africa use modern complex and efficient farm machinery on their commercial farms (See also Chapter 1, this volume). The use of farm machinery has reduced the drudgery inherent in direct use of human energy in undertaking certain farm operations.

The term 'farm machinery' is used to describe the animal, fuel or electric powered implements that are used to make farm operations easier, faster and more efficient. The use of farm machinery to perform farm operations is called **farm mechanisation.** Presently, agricultural mechanisation has advanced to the extent that the design, use, protection and maintenance of farm machinery have become an important area of specialisation in agriculture. All farm machinery can be grouped into two namely, (a) animal drawn equipment (animal traction) and (b) fuel or electric powered equipment.

Animal drawn equipment consists of implements that are powered using the energy of animals. The animals commonly used are donkeys, bullocks, horses, camels, elephants and dogs. Bullocks and donkeys are mainly used in Ghana for animal traction. The practice where animal power is used in powering farm machinery is called **animal traction.** The animals are used to work such implements in the same way as the mould board plough, chain harrow or seed drill works.

Fuel or electric powered equipment is propelled by machines that are powered by petrol or diesel. Some of the major power-driven equipment found on the farm is tractors, motor sprayers, harvesters and chain saws. Common examples of implements drawn by tractors include ploughs, harrows, cultivators, ridgers, seed planters and trailers.

Figure 11: Different agricultural tools and equipment

Importance of agriculture to African economies

The economies of most African countries depend on agriculture. Agriculture employs 64% of the population of SSA and generates 34% of GDP of these countries, with the majority of the poor living in rural areas (FAO, 2006, World Bank, 2006a; UNECA 2004). According to the World Development Report (World Bank 2008), in agriculture-based countries, most of them in Sub-Saharan Africa, agriculture accounted for about a third of overall growth over 1993–2005. During the 1960s, agriculture in Africa grew at about 3% annually, exceeding the population growth rate. However, in the following decade it declined substantially to about 1% (Townsend, 1999). It accelerated to 2.3% per year in the 1980s and to 3.3% in the 1990s. Between 2000 and 2005, it grew at 3.8% per year, and has largely exceeded growth in nonagricultural sectors. From the African Development Indicators of 2003, the average annual economic growth of Africa was 2.7% with the lowest of -5.1% and the highest of 20% being recorded for the Democratic Republic of Congo and Equatorial Guinea, respectively. The contribution of agriculture to these GDP figures ranges from about 3% in Botswana to 43% for the Democratic Republic of Congo (World Bank, 2009).

In Ghana, for example, agricultural performance outside traditional export crops has been poor (ISSER, 2010). The latest report of the Ghana Living Standards Survey (GSS, 2008) noted that the majority of the working population (55.8%) is employed in agricultural activities. The agricultural sector, however, remains unattractive to young people (ISSER, 2010: 199). In Kenya, agriculture is the backbone of the economy, contributing approximately 25% of GDP, and employing 75% of the national labour force. Over 80% of the Kenyan population lives in rural areas and make a living, directly or indirectly, from agriculture (Future Agricultures, 2006). The sector is important for poverty reduction since the most vulnerable groups, such as pastoralists, the landless, and subsistence farmers, depend on agriculture as their main source of livelihoods. Indeed, agriculture is considered the bedrock for the economic development of Africa. Africa can therefore not achieve its planned economic growth and poverty reduction without significant improvements in the agricultural sector.

The need for adequate food production in the world and the proper balance between agriculture and industry is of such concern to the United Nations that the Food and Agriculture Organization (FAO) has been set up specifically to promote agricultural production. The FAO undertakes to channel food supplies to countries which experience famine or are hit by disasters such as floods, bush fires, drought, earthquakes, conflict and wars. It continually evaluates the world's food needs and recommends measures to be taken to forestall shortages in order to ensure that economic development in the affected countries are not hampered.

Thus, agriculture plays an important role in the economies of African countries in terms of food production, provision of jobs and employment, shelter, source of income, raw materials for agro-based industries and others. These are briefly discussed below.

Food production

It is estimated that more than 239 million people in Sub-Saharan Africa suffer from hunger. But African governments, international donors, nonprofit organisations, and other partners are helping Africa's farmers grow more food and increase their incomes. Together, they are proving that progress in agricultural development is not only possible, but can happen. Important food and cash crops grown in Africa include the following:

- *Cereals* : rich in carbohydrates (e.g. maize, rice, wheat, sorghum, millet)
- *Legumes*: rich in proteins (e.g. groundnut, Bambara beans, cowpea, soybean, French beans, lima beans).
- *Roots and tubers*: good sources of carbohydrates (e.g. yam, cassava, potato, sweet potato).
- *Vegetables*: usually served with other foods, are rich in vitamins and minerals (e.g. tomato, pepper, okra, eggplant, cabbage, cauliflower, cucumber, lettuce, onion, spinach).
- *Beverage crops*: for the production of alcoholic and non-alcoholic drinks (e.g. cocoa, coffee, tea, kola, sugar cane, sorghum, maize, millet)
- *Spices*: for flavouring (e.g. ginger, nutmeg, cloves, black pepper, cinnamon, 'dawadawa', bacillicum, onions and shallots, garlic, cumin, saffron, turmeric, cardamom, coriander, cassia).
- *Fruits*: rich in vitamins and minerals (e.g. pineapple, citrus, mango, banana, pawpaw, cashew, water melon).
- *Oils:* (e.g. oil palm, cotton, coconut, shea butter, cashew, soybean, groundnut, sunflower, castor plant, eucalyptus).
- *Animal Protein*: important source of protein, vitamins and minerals (e.g. Milk, dairy products, eggs, meat, fish).

Livestock

Livestock plays a major role in the livelihoods of small-scale farmers, processors and traders in Africa. Livestock production including poultry, sheep, goats, pigs and cattle make a significant contribution to household food security by providing income, quality food, energy and assets in over 80% of rural households in Africa (Table 10). Kenya has one of the most developed dairy industries in Sub-Saharan Africa, with an annual milk production of some 2 billion litres.

Table 10 – Total meat production, import and export projections for 2010

	Production (Million tones)	Import (1000 MT)	Export (1000 MT)
WORLD	**282.6**	**21 331.7**	**21 386.4**
DEVELOPING	**166.1**	**9 796.1**	**7 064.5**
AFRICA	10.5	826.3	122.2
NORTH AFRICA	3.5	264.3	16.8
Egypt	1.7	214.3	3.1
Morocco	0.6	9.6	2.4
SUB-SAHARAN AFRICA	7.0	561.9	105.4
Cote D'Ivoire	0.1	5.3	2.0
Nigeria	1.1	15.1	.4
Ethiopia	0.7	10.4	.6

Source: *http://www.fao.org/docrep/006/y5143e/y5143e0v.htm,*

Employment

In most African countries agriculture provides employment to a large proportion of the population, particularly in the rural areas. For example, about 70% of the rural population in most African countries depends directly or indirectly on agriculture for their livelihoods by producing crops and/or animals and their by-products. There are food crop farmers, seed growers, horticulturists who produce fruits, vegetables and ornamental plants and landscaping, industrial crop farmers, poultry farmers, livestock farmers, farm workers, fish farmers and foresters.

Agribusiness is an important area which deals with the supply of goods and services to facilitate agricultural activities and increase productivity. These include farm management and marketing of agricultural produce and inputs (e.g. fertilizers, agro-chemicals, equipment, tools, implements, farm machinery, seeds and planting materials etc). Marketing of agricultural products and inputs is a very big business which employs a lot of specialists and other workers.

Agro-processing and manufacturing are big businesses employing workers to carry out the various activities in the production chain. Several processing factories have been established to add value to agricultural produce. Primary products such as cocoa, cotton, tea, coffee, tobacco, sisal, hemp etc. are processed into various products. To promote agricultural production, agro-chemical industries are required to provide fertilizers and pesticides for the maintenance of soil fertility, prevention and control of diseases, pests and weeds. Veterinary drugs, chemicals and animal feed additives are also produced in chemical industries. Mechanical industries have been established to produce farm equipment, implements, various types of machinery, animal-drawn implements, hand tools and equipment needed for the cultivation and processing of agricultural products. Also, mechanical workshops have been established for the maintenance of the machines and equipment involved. All these ventures employ workers for their operations.

Increased agricultural production has led to the establishment of many allied industries which constitute avenues of employment. For example, some of the crops and livestock producers market their products for breeding purposes, thereby creating an industry within the agricultural industry. Manufacture of cocoa bags has become an important activity within the cocoa industry, for example.

Agriculture also provides many jobs and employment opportunities for research scientists (e.g. agricultural economists, horticulturists etc); bankers, teachers, agricultural administrators and agricultural resource managers (e.g. foresters and wildlife conservationists). Indeed, in the Constitution of Mozambique, Article 103 states that agriculture is the basis for development (Mucavele, 2007). About 90 % of rural households are engaged in agriculture, and this equates to 80% of the total population (approximately 21 million) dependent on agriculture. Agriculture is the major development sector in Zambia as well. About 97.4 % of rural households are engaged in agriculture, and this equates to 45% of the total population – approximately 4.6 million, dependent on agriculture. Out of the estimated 600,000 farmers, 76 percent are small-scale subsistence farmers (Ibid).

Source of Income

The various occupations in agriculture are major sources of income for individuals and governments from both domestic and international trade which provide revenue to support peoples' livelihoods and national development. Individuals engaged in the production, storage, processing and marketing of agricultural goods and services derive incomes to satisfy their needs. The foreign exchange derived from the export of agricultural products enables governments to import essential capital goods and equipment and to finance national development.

Production of export crops like cocoa, coffee, tea, cotton and rubber among others, contributes to foreign exchange earnings of most African countries (Tables 11 & 12).

Table 11– Raw material production for Africa and the World (Thousand tonnes)

CROP	1993-95		1998-2000		2010 (projection)	
	AFRICA	WORLD	AFRICA	WORLD	AFRICA	WORLD
Coffee	873	5425	961	6 688	1 114	7 033
Cocoa	1573	2564	1 999	2 905	2 500	3 700
Black tea	335	1970	294	2 145	379	2 443
Rubber	303	5785	376	6 797	476	7 870
Raw cotton	1190	16859	*1 275	*19 901	1 740	23 095
Jute	8	2959	8	2 066	6	1 155

*Figures for Cotton are for 1999-2001.

Source: http://www.fao.org/docrep/006/y5143e/y5143e0v.htm, 21.10.2010

Table 12 – Level of Export of Raw Materials from Africa and the World (Thousand Tonnes)

CROP	1993 – 95		1998-2000		2010 (projected)	
	AFRICA	AFRICA	AFRICA	WORLD	AFRICA	WORLD
Coffee	776	776	927	4 455	996	5 510
Cocoa	1492	1492	1 731	2 220	2 335	2 994
Black tea	295	295	*294	*1 008	379	1 139
Rubber	303	303	338	4 773	375	5 488
Raw cotton	-	-	**993	**6 049	1 522	6 530
Jute	-	-	-	948	-	919

*Figures for Black tea are for 2000 only. ** Figures for Raw Cotton 1999-2001.

Source: *http://www.fao.org/docrep/006/y5143e/y5143e0v.htm*

Since the early 1990s, agricultural exports from Sub-Saharan Africa have increased by about 30%. For example, tea accounts for 20% of total export earnings in Kenya. The horticultural sector is the fastest growing industry within the agricultural sector, recording an average growth of 15% to 20% per annum (Kenya Horticulture Council, 2011). The industry contributes to the Kenyan economy through generation of income, creation of employment opportunities for rural people and foreign exchange earnings, in addition to providing raw materials to the agro processing industry. The sector employs approximately 4.5 million people countrywide directly in production, processing, and marketing, while another 3.5 million people benefit indirectly through trade and other activities (Ibid).

Contribution to Gross Domestic Product

Agriculture contributes significantly to the Gross Domestic Product (GDP) of most African countries. Even in mineral rich countries such as South Africa, whose economy has traditionally been rooted in the primary sectors, agriculture still contributes to GDP (see also Ch.1). Primary agriculture contributes about 3% to South Africa's gross domestic product (GDP) and about 7% to formal employment. However, there are strong linkages into the economy, so that the agro-industrial sector comprises about 12% of GDP. Between 2004 and 2009, agricultural exports contributed on average about 6.5% of total South African exports. Exports increased from 5% in 1988 to 46% in 2009 of agricultural production (South Africa Department of Agriculture, 2011). In Malawi, agriculture plays an overwhelmingly important role in the economy. In 2010, the Malawi Confederation of Chambers of Commerce (MCCCI) reported that agriculture was the mainstay of Malawi's economy and contributed about 33.6 % to economic growth (Mucavele, 2007).

A large percentage of Africa's poor, among who are many women, live in rural areas where they depend largely on agriculture for their source of food and income. Lack of formal education and technical skills coupled with inequitable access to land and other important resources for successful agricultural activity leave women highly vulnerable to chronic poverty. In such circumstances, agriculture presents an avenue for self-employment in the area of production and marketing of agricultural products.

Agriculture and Poverty Reduction

Agriculture is likely to remain the principal sector for development and growth in Africa for the foreseeable future. The potential increase in rural incomes that could be derived from agriculture and related activities make it a pivotal sector for poverty reduction. African governments, in their efforts to reduce poverty and enhance food security, have recognised the need not only to increase productivity through improved land and water management, appropriate technologies, and strengthened support services, but also to improve markets, transport, processing and infrastructure in order to enhance the livelihoods of the rural poor.

The agricultural sector in most African countries is dominated by small-scale farmers with less than 2 hectares of land, representing nearly 90% of farm holdings and accounting for over 80% of food crop production. There are basically three categories of farmers in African agriculture: small-scale (less than 4 ha), medium-scale (4-8 ha), and large-scale (>8 ha) farmers. The majority of the small-scale or subsistent farmers are women who constitute nearly 60% of the rural poor.

Agricultural development essentially involves sustainable management of resources for improved agricultural productivity mainly achieved through the application of technology. This involves the development of new and improved crop varieties and animal breeds, mechanisation of farming activities, integrated soil and water management strategies, judicious use of agrochemicals, integrated management of pests and diseases, agro-processing for value addition, and adaptations in socio-cultural practices. This also includes addressing the poor living conditions of most farmers to ensure that agriculture contributes to the well-being of the farmer and his/her family and to the development of the rural areas.

4.1 Characteristics of Agricultural Development

Agricultural development is characterised by the following: agricultural expansion, increased food production, rapid agricultural growth, product value per farm worker, decline in agricultural labour force and decrease in malnutrition. Below are some details of these characteristics.

Agricultural Expansion: This represents significant changes in the nature and or quantity of farm inputs namely, land, labour and capital committed to agriculture. The productivity of the land should be increased by better methods of cultivation and land/soil management. Efficient and productive skilled and unskilled labour which is adequately remunerated is necessary for sustained agricultural development. Capital must be available in appropriate and suitable forms to invest and provide the resources needed for productive activities. Funds should be available to provide buildings, machinery and equipment, labour, land resources and other inputs such as stock feed, seeds, organic and inorganic manure, and animal-drawn implements to initiate and sustain agricultural expansion. Farmers should have access to loans at reasonable rates of interest.

Increased Food Production: An important characteristic of agricultural development is increase in the overall production capacity of the land in terms of higher crop yields, better improved animal products or a combination of both.

Agricultural Growth: This represents growth in physical quantities and market value of agricultural products as well as the growth in the contribution of agriculture to the national economy. In most cases, agricultural growth is accompanied by industrial growth as a result of the interdependence of the two. In many countries, the absolute growth in their agricultural productive capacities has resulted in giant strides being made in industrial development. The market value of agricultural products or commodities is such that it provides enough incentives to farmers for sustained production at a high level. In this way, all those who are dependent on agriculture for their living can maintain a reasonable standard of living.

Product Value per Farm Worker: The product value obtained by the farming business should be capable of ensuring an increase in the income of farm labour, adequate compensation of the farm operator or owner and greater satisfaction and compensation for the extension worker. The only way that adequate compensation can be made available is to ensure that the product value per worker is high enough to justify the high levels of inputs required to sustain increased production in a cost effective way.

Decline in Agricultural Labour Force: The overall rise in total production in agriculture is not dependent upon an increase in the labour force for production, but rather the increase in the productivity per labour. This can be achieved through the use of more efficient methods resulting from training, adequate compensation and improved working conditions of workers. In this way, the number of farm labour will progressively decrease, while total farm output increases. This is one of the aims of agricultural development so that labour previously engaged in agricultural production can be released to other productive sectors of the economy.

Decrease in Malnutrition: Malnutrition refers to inadequate nutrition or undernourishment. Malnutrition is the result of limited production of agricultural commodities or poor combination of available food items in the diet of the people. Sometimes the choice of a wide variety of food items from which an adequate and balanced diet could be obtained does not exist. Agricultural development should ensure availability of a wide range of food items to promote proper nutrition in terms of quality and quantity.

Food security

Food security is a complex concept. It implies 'physical and economic access to balanced diets and safe drinking water to all people at all times.' This means that ample food is grown, processed and transported, and that everyone has either money to buy food or grow it. A nation is **food secure** when all her citizens have access at all times to enough food for their active, healthy life. The root cause of **food insecurity** in developing countries today is believed to be the inability of people to gain access to food due to poverty. Consequently, the problems of food access and poverty were focal points at the second world summit on food security, the World Food Summit of 1996, at which 186 countries made a commitment to reduce the number of chronically undernourished people by half, by 2015. A *Plan of Action* was adopted to 'implement policies aimed at eradicating poverty and inequality and improving physical and economic access by all, at all times, to sufficient, nutritionally adequate and safe food and its effective utilization' (FAO, 1996).

According to the World Food Programme's *Global Update* which provides food security information in terms of trends in food access and utilisation, the main food access indicators reported in December 2010 are food consumption, coping strategies and terms of trade. These indicators reflect food security status and so enable early identification of potential increases in food insecurity. Three categories are used to classify food security trends as: *Improved*, *No Change* and *Deteriorated*. A summary of the food security situation is presented below:

Improved: Burundi, Ethiopia, Lesotho, Liberia, Malawi, Namibia, Niger, Sudan (Darfur), Southern Sudan, and Zambia.

No Change: Chad, Côte d'Ivoire, Democratic Republic of the Congo, Ghana (Northern Region), Guinea Conakry, Kenya, Madagascar, Mauritania, Mozambique, Swaziland, and Zimbabwe.

Deteriorated: Benin, Cameroon, Djibouti, and Somalia (see Global Update, - December 2010).

Globally, more than 34 countries face acute food insecurity and require exceptional and emergency food assistance. Out of this number, more than half are in Africa. Achieving food security is eluding most governments in the developing countries. This is attributed to global increases in population that has outpaced the rate of growth in food production.

Currently many countries in Africa are experiencing profound economic and social crisis and this is seriously affecting its agricultural development. Political and social unrest particularly in Somalia, Libya, Egypt and Côte d'Ivoire is having a serious and protracted economic and humanitarian impact. The protracted violence in Côte d'Ivoire displaced over one million people internally and over 120,000 to neighbouring Liberia (WFP, 2011). Food prices have increased sharply in some countries, compared to the 2010 levels, consequently affecting the purchasing power of households. For instance, pastoralists in northern Kenya have seen a sharp decline in their terms of trade. Households in Kenya are resorting to high risk coping strategies. About six million poor communities in pastoral and high density urban livelihoods have seen their food intake decline below the minimum kilocaloric requirement, primarily due to successive seasons of below average rainfall and decline in purchasing power (WFP, 2011).

Drought has caused widespread crop failure and displacement of livestock on the continent with the case being worsened by the internal conflicts that result in flows of refugees from one country to another. Conflicts on the continent, with its attendant insecurity, have led to the wastage of large hectares of farmlands, further worsening the food situation in Africa.

In recent times, the HIV and AIDS pandemic has caused extensive loss of lives, including trained personnel, so vital for the success of agricultural development on the continent (see also Ch. 2).

Causes of food insecurity

The list of causes of food insecurity is long, complex and multifaceted in scope. They include the following:

- Political instability, wars, conflicts and civil strife.
- Bad weather and natural disasters (bush fires, flooding, drought, pest and disease outbreaks, and plagues).
- Poverty and the alarming rate of human population growth.
- Macro-economic imbalances and trade dislocations.
- Gender inequality and inadequate education (high illiteracy rate of farmers).
- Environmental degradation and poor natural resource management.
- Poor health, especially the HIV and AIDS pandemic.

All the above factors, however, can be related in some fashion to two basic causes: insufficient national food availability and insufficient access to food by households and individuals. The countries that exhibit the highest severity of food insecurity are those with high poverty and food (dietary energy) deficits, consistent with the view that poverty is the most widespread cause of food insecurity.

4.3 The role of women in food security:

In the world's least developed countries, a significant portion of rural households are headed by women. Women are the principal producers of food in subsistence agriculture in developing countries. They account for 70-80% of household food production in Sub-Saharan Africa, 65% in Asia and 45% in Latin America and the Caribbean. In many developing countries women make up close to 80% of the agricultural workforce. Women are also the main producers of the world's staple crops (e.g. rice, wheat, maize) which comprise more than 90% of the diet of the rural poor. Despite their prominent role in agriculture, women do not get an appropriate share of agricultural extension advice and other services. Women own less than 2% land; have access to 10% credit, have limited access to agricultural inputs and only 15% of extension services. Providing women with basic education would help raise agricultural productivity and incomes,because better-educated farmers are more likely to adopt new technologies. In addition to farm work, women are solely responsible for housework including food preparation, caring for children and the elderly in the family and in most cases, engaging in off-farm income earning activities.

However, women's key role as food producers and providers and their critical contribution to household food security, is only recently being recognized. Even where it is highly acknowledged by governments, this is rarely tackled at policy-making levels. To ensure that people everywhere have access to food and natural resources, women's work needs to be recognized and considered in discussions about agriculture (e.g. crop production, animal production, fisheries, forestry and rural development). It will be possible to build a world without hunger only when gender issues are brought to the fore and women are given a voice alongside men.

Some key facts
- More than half of the world's agricultural workers are women.
- Only 15% of the world's agricultural advisers working in the rural areas are women.
- Female farmers receive only 5% of all agricultural extension services worldwide.
- In developing countries, women tend to work far longer hours than men. In Africa and Asia, studies have shown that women work as much as 13 hours more per week.
- In many regions, women spend up to five hours a day collecting fuel wood and water, and up to four hours a day preparing food.
- In Southeast Asia, women provide up to 90% of the manual labour for rice cultivation.
- Women use almost everything they earn from selling agricultural products and handicrafts to meet household needs. Men use at least 25% of their earnings for other purposes.
- In some parts of Africa, women spend as much as eight hours a day collecting water. The average distance walked by women in Africa in search of water is six kilometres a day.
- In the world's least developed countries, a significant portion of rural households are headed by women.

Goal and Objectives of Agricultural Development

The overall goal of any agricultural development strategy for Africa should be to promote sustainable agriculture and thriving agri-business through research and technology development, effective extension and other support services to all stakeholders engaged in agriculture for improved human livelihood. For Africa to become a leading agro-industrial continent, agriculture must be modernised and based on sustainable rural development. To accomplish this goal, the following objectives need to be addressed:

Attainment of food security: Food security may be defined as access by all people at all times to enough food for an active and healthy life. Food security is achieved when all people, at all times, have physical and economic access to sufficient, safe and nutritious food to meet their dietary needs and food preferences for an active and healthy life. The Ministry of Food and Agriculture (MOFA, 2002) in Ghana defines food security as "Good quality nutritious food, hygienically packaged, attractively presented, available in sufficient quantities all year round and located at the right places at affordable prices". The key elements that cut across the definition of food security are quality and nutrition, sufficiency and physical and financial accessibility.

Production of raw materials for industry: Facilitation of the production of high quality agricultural raw materials in adequate quantities to feed agro-based industries for accelerated economic development.

Production of agricultural commodities for export: Effective collaboration among all stakeholders to promote the production of agricultural commodities for export within Africa and globally.

Development of effective and efficient input supply and distribution system: Establish agency to monitor, regulate and disseminate essential information required by all actors in agribusiness, especially the input trade, to forestall possible supply shortfalls and eliminate dangerous, sub-standard or banned products.

Development of effective and efficient output marketing system: Good marketing outlet is paramount to any sustainable agricultural development. Provision of information on market demands and supply chain to all actors should be strengthened.

Formulation and coordination of agricultural policies and programmes: A sound agricultural policy is critical for any meaningful agricultural development. It is essential that these policies and programmes are well coordinated and their impact evaluated and monitored continuously.

Promotion of research and technology development: Demand-driven research should be supported in order to develop appropriate technologies to address the major challenges in sustainable agricultural development. Agricultural research can lift people out of poverty by boosting agricultural incomes and reducing food prices.

Soil and water conservation: Soil and water are probably the most important factors in agriculture and their conservation is essential for sustainable agricultural development. Soil conservation refers to the protection and management of the soil so that its fertility is not destroyed or lost. Water conservation, on the other hand, means the wise and careful use of water and the ability to store for times when it is in short supply.

Improving the efficiency of farmers: For any meaningful agricultural development, those who are actually involved in the basic work of production must be efficient and knowledgeable in the farming business. Farmers should be empowered through training to take informed decisions in all aspects of the farming enterprise, and to increase their efficiency in the context of the total environment.

Improving the standard of living of farmers and the rural environment: One of the major objectives of agricultural development should be the general improvement in the living conditions of farmers and the areas in which they operate. Farmers must enjoy the fruits of their labour and must be brought into the mainstream of social, political and economic life as citizens of the state.

The NEPAD/CAADP framework sets a target of a sustained agricultural growth rate of 6% per year, which CAADP estimates is required to reach the Millennium Development Goal poverty reduction target of halving poverty by 2015. This is a higher sustained rate of agricultural growth than has ever been achieved on the continent. IFPRI analysis shows that West Africa would require an even higher rate, 6.8% per year, to meet the MDG goal for the region as a whole, although even this rate would not assure that each country in the region would meet the target. Thus, a first challenge for SSA is to secure and accelerate its rate of agricultural growth (Staaz and Dembele 2007).

Major Constraints to Agricultural Development in Africa

Review of Key Interventions

African countries have implemented a number of interventions and programmes to increase agricultural productivity. These programmes have been supported by international development agencies. In the 1960s and 1970s, the World Bank supported agricultural development in the form of rural development projects mainly through large-scale schemes to introduce modern agricultural technologies for crops and livestock based on packages of high-yielding varieties, fertilizers, agro-chemicals, credit, mechanisation and irrigation. The number of such rural development projects increased from 38 in 1965-73 to 171 in 1974-86 with credits of US$218.1 million and US$2,976.6 million, respectively (World Bank, 1988). Regrettably, these projects failed to achieve their objectives due mainly to weak intersectoral coordination, lack of integration and beneficiary involvement, failure to build institutional and financial sustainability among others (World Bank, 1988). Examples of such programmes in Ghana include the Volta Regional Development Project (VORADEP) and the Upper Regional Development Project (URADEP).(See also Ch.10)

Since the latter part of the 1990s, a number of African countries supported by the World Bank and other donor agencies, have adopted a sector-wide approach to agricultural development. In Ghana for instance, the Ministry of Food and Agriculture (MoFA) has been implementing the Agricultural Services Sub-Sector Investment Project (AgSSIP) with support from the World Bank. These sector-wide approaches attempt to tackle agriculture from a holistic viewpoint by including research, extension, agricultural financing, marketing, as well as infrastructure, to facilitate agricultural development as an integral part of the programme.

A critical review of the poor performance of the agricultural sector in most African countries has revealed that a myriad of problems militate against the growth of the sector. Some of the major factors that militate against agricultural development in Africa therefore may be conceived in terms of policy, institutional, infrastructural, financial, social, weather and technological constraints as outlined below:

Policy constraints

- Vaguely defined mission and functions of government ministries responsible for agriculture.
- Difficulty in acquiring agricultural land due mainly to the absence of credible land use policies in most African countries.
- Inadequate investment by governments in the agricultural sector.
- Over-reliance on donor funding with its stringent conditions and cumbersome procedures.
- Presence of several poorly coordinated donor-funded projects and NGO activities spread across different parts of African countries with different implementation policies.
- Ineffective monitoring of on-going projects, poor evaluation of completed projects and non-utilisation of lessons and experiences.

- Unfair domestic and international trade policies.
- Weak enforcement of agricultural laws (e.g. fisheries laws).
- Poor dissemination of information on trade agreements and protocols
- Poorly coordinated agricultural and trade policies.

Institutional constraints
- Weak producer organisations in farming communities.
- Limited monitoring, control and surveillance of fisheries and forestry resources.
- Inadequate agricultural extension staff and poor extension delivery systems.
- High attrition rate of trained staff to other sectors due to poor motivation.
- Weak research-extension-farmer linkages.
- Lack of reliable statistical data for effective decision-making.
- Weak enforcement of laws regulating agricultural production.
- Inefficient marketing and agri-business systems.
- Slow progress in decentralisation.

Infrastructural constraints
- Poor access to production areas.
- Inadequate and poor transportation systems.
- Inadequate and inappropriate storage facilities.
- Poor, unattractive and unhygienic packaging.
- Limited irrigation facilities.
- Inadequate energy supply and distribution.

Financial constraints
- High cost of inputs relative to output prices.
- High interest rates and transaction costs on credits.
- Non-availability of medium and long-term capital for expansion.
- Low investment in agro-processing.
- Lack of innovative and flexible financial packages for agriculture.
- Unfavourable timing of credit disbursement.

Social constraints
- Ageing farmers and low interest of the youth in agriculture.
- High rural-urban migration for non-existent jobs.
- High rates of illiteracy among farmers and fisherfolk.
- HIV and AIDS pandemic in many African countries.

Weather/environmental constraints
- Over-reliance on rainfed agriculture.
- Seasonal destruction of arable and range land by bush-fires and floods.
- Poor soils and harsh climatic conditions.
- Prevalence of natural disasters especially drought, pest and disease outbreaks (e.g. locusts, grasshoppers, armyworms, *quelea* birds, mealybugs, spider mites, striga weed, the larger grain borer).

- Poor management of natural resources.
- Encroachment on farmland by mining and estate developers.

Technological constraints
- Slow pace of appropriate technology development through sustained research.
- Over-reliance on imported machinery, spares and other inputs.
- Poor communication networks in farming communities.

The challenge to the agricultural sector is to develop appropriate policies, strategies and programmes to address the above problems.

Critical Strategic Thrusts for Agricultural Development in Africa

In line with the objectives outlined for the accelerated agricultural growth and development strategy, African governments must seek to achieve the following strategic thrusts in their agricultural development programmes:
- human resource development and institutional capacity building.
- improved financial services delivery to finance agricultural activities.
- development and adoption of appropriate technologies.
- infrastructure development.
- development of irrigation facilities.
- processing and value addition of both durable and perishable products.
- improved access to markets.
- gender equity and mainstreaming to enhance women's participation in agriculture.

Human Resource Development and Institutional Capacity Building
Agricultural growth and development in Africa will depend on well-trained and competent human resources both in the public and private sector. The low level of formal education, especially among the rural population, has contributed to low levels of technology adoption. There is the need, therefore, to develop the requisite capacity at all levels to move the sector forward. Public and private institutions engaged in agriculture must address both the human capacity issues and institutional bottlenecks militating against agricultural development. Both private and public sector service providers should be assisted to access training, information (communication systems), technical assistance, machinery and equipment. Effective training-of-trainers' programmes for frontline extension staff and other service providers should be strengthened. Attachments and exchange programmes should be organised for policy makers and researchers. One problem with capacity building in the agricultural sector is high attrition of well-trained staff. Accordingly, appropriate facilities and attractive conditions of service should be put in place to motivate, retain and enhance the productivity of trained staff.

The district and local assemblies and other service providers should be encouraged to provide social amenities for rural communities to entice people to stay in the rural areas. In the same vein, African governments should encourage private sector operators to invest in rural economic ventures to promote rural economic development which is paramount to sustainable agricultural development.

Agricultural development must be science driven. In this regard, scientists should be encouraged, motivated and challenged to produce innovative technologies, including improved crop varieties and breeds of animals, inputs, tools, and machinery etc, for the agricultural industry. As much as possible, new inventions should be covered by intellectual property rights.

Efficient financial services delivery

Funding is crucial to any meaningful agricultural development. African governments and donors must endeavour to provide adequate funds for financing the procurement and distribution of agricultural inputs, on-farm production, processing and marketing of agricultural produce which are critical to accelerated agricultural growth and development. There are domestic and external sources of agricultural finance. Domestic sources are mainly the commercial banks, development banks, rural banks and credit unions. Low national savings rate in most African countries deprives financial markets of funds for investments in agriculture. External sources of finance are mainly through grants and projects sponsored by bilateral and multilateral agencies.

Many problems account for the non-availability and access to financial services to support agricultural development. These include (a) high interest rates and transaction costs (b) the perceived risky nature of agriculture (c) non-availability of medium and long-term credit (d) poor spatial distribution of banks (e) lack of documented assets for use as collateral (f) small-scale operations of farmers and (g) poor record keeping by farmers.

Sources of finance

Domestic sources of credit are derived largely from financial institutions including the banks, savings and loans, credit unions, non-financial organizations such as NGOs, nucleus farm enterprises, traders, processors and solidarity groups. African governments should develop strategies to improve farmers' access to credit. Loans for the agricultural sector in most African countries are mainly short-term. This restricts the availability of credit to activities with short-term duration. It is, therefore, necessary that other arrangements utilising warehouse receipts and inventory credit schemes are actively pursued.

The supply of funds to the agricultural sector is woefully inadequate considering the emphasis placed on agriculture as the basis for development. Currently, the sector relies heavily on external funding which is not sustainable, while the limited credit available is mostly short term. For African countries to obtain the high level of agricultural production there is the need for massive infusion of long term funds to the sector. It may be useful for African governments to establish an Agricultural Development Fund (ADF) in each country, specifically to provide credit for agricultural ventures with long gestation periods. This will enable the countries to mobilise additional funding to reduce dependence on donors and address the need for long term investment. The potential sources of funding for the ADF are (a) taxes on selected food and agricultural commodity imports, (b) internally generated funds, (c) grants and (d) others such as donations from corporate bodies and philanthropists.

Local banks and bilateral/multilateral donor institutions (e.g. FAO, World Bank) should be encouraged to create portfolios that cater for agricultural production with long gestation periods. The poor spatial distribution of credit institutions in most African countries is also a constraint to accessing credit. Most banks operate only in urban areas. Appropriate public institutions such as the Ministries of Finance and the Central Banks should address this imbalance and make banking services more accessible in the rural areas. Rural financial institutions (e.g. rural banks) should also be strengthened to develop appropriate financial products to make credit accessible to farmers. There is the need to build capacities of rural banks to enhance effective savings mobilisation and credit delivery. Farmers should be trained in credit management to help them improve on loan repayment.

Financing of agricultural activities should not be limited to farmers. It should include input suppliers, processors, market intermediaries, warehouse operators, haulers, researchers and extension officers. African governments must also ensure that the provision of credit is combined with effective marketing advisory services.

Development and Adoption of Appropriate Technology

Against the background of limited land and water resources, it is clear that the objectives of agricultural development can best be achieved by the continued utilisation of science and technology to enhance agricultural production and productivity. Limited access to appropriate technology at all levels in the crops, livestock, and fisheries sub-sectors is one of the major obstacles to agricultural development in Africa.

For crops the main challenges that need to be addressed include:

- Development and dissemination of improved varieties of seeds and planting materials in terms of high yields, drought resistance, disease and pest resistance, early maturity etc.

Improved seeds and planting materials should be made available to farmers at affordable prices. Breeders, foundation seed producers and seed growers should be assisted to expand their operations. Seed certification services must be strengthened to remove all bottlenecks in the seed industry. Recent advances in bio-technology research hold a lot of promise for boosting agricultural production in developing countries in Africa. Adequate resources should be provided to the Universities and Agricultural Research Institutions to undertake bio-technology research to increase food production, reduce costs, fight diseases, pests, weeds in crops and animals as well as reduce the environmental damage caused by excessive use of pesticides.

- Improvement in farm operations and post-harvest handling of crops and animals to increase efficiency of production.

The continued use of hoe and cutlass to carry out farm operations is a constraint to accelerated agricultural production. There is an urgent need for African farmers to adopt mechanised farming on a much wider scale. Farmers should be assisted to have access to agricultural machinery and equipment such as tractors, bullock ploughs, planters, harvesters to reduce drudgery and increase efficiency of small to medium scale production. Private entrepreneurs should be encouraged to establish plant pools for leasing of farm machinery and equipment to farmers. Local manufacturing of appropriate tools and implements should be supported.

- Land, water and soil fertility management are crucial to sustainable agricultural development.

The productivity of most agricultural soils in Africa is declining at an alarming rate due to widespread land degradation caused by soil erosion, deforestation, soil nutrient mining, uncontrolled bush burning and other poor management practices. Farming communities should be trained to adopt such practices as mixed farming, use of agro-forestry systems, and effective use of organic and inorganic fertilizers to restore and maintain the productivity of agricultural lands. Due to high cost of mineral fertilizers, improved soil fertility management strategies involving the combined use of mineral fertilizers and organic manures (e.g. farm yard manure, crop residues, compost, green manures) should be promoted

- Pest and disease control at farm level should be done by promoting the adoption of Integrated Pest Management (IPM) strategies to reduce both pre-and post-harvest crop losses.

African-wide biological control of key pests such as mango and cassava mealy bugs, cassava green spider mites, grasshoppers, the larger grain borer etc., should be intensified. Furthermore, farmers should be educated on the safe and selective use of recommended pesticides for pest and disease management. Quarantine service as the first line of defence against the introduction of exotic pests and invasive weeds should be strengthened in all African countries.

- Harvesting and handling procedures should be improved to reduce loss and maintain quality of farm produce.

Currently, appropriate harvesting equipment is not widely available in most African countries. There is therefore the need to support research to develop appropriate prototypes. In addition, current post-harvest handling practices, especially for fruits and vegetables, should be upgraded to maintain their quality and extended shelf life. Farmers should be equipped with knowledge and skills in the optimum stage of maturity for harvesting various commodities for export, appropriate on-farm post harvest handling methods, and on-farm pre-cooling technology and suitable means of transporting perishable farm produce to marketing centres.

- Processing, packaging and storage to add value, increase shelf life, reduce post-harvest losses and promote price stability should be upgraded. Farmers should be assisted to construct appropriate storage facilities for their produce.
- Development of multiple utilisation of agricultural produce and their by-products to achieve zero wastage should be vigorously pursued to increase returns.

For the development of the livestock sub-sector the main thrusts should include the following:

- Production of improved breeds of animals locally should be intensified.

Currently, improved breeds of chicken and small ruminants in most African countries are mostly imported. Livestock breeding centres should be established and resourced to improve the productivity of large ruminants (beef and dairy cattle), small ruminants (sheep and goats) and pigs. In addition serious measures should be adopted to conserve the genetic diversity of indigenous livestock breeds in Africa.

- Production of high quality animal feed all year round at affordable prices should be vigorously pursued.

Appropriate and affordable animal feed such as by-products and crop residues of rice, maize, sorghum, cassava, groundnuts and other leguminous crops should be promoted for use by farmers. In addition, farmers should be supported to undertake intensive fodder production of forage legumes. District and local assemblies may be encouraged to produce forage seed at the community level for farmers.

- Control of animal diseases is a major problem in livestock production in Africa.

Most African governments have liberalised the procurement and distribution of veterinary drugs as well as the delivery of animal health care services in order to improve the efficiency of service delivery. It may be useful for African governments to support the increasing role of the private sector in the delivery of animal health services as is done in some countries (e.g. Ghana, Kenya, South Africa). Public bodies responsible for disease surveillance, quarantine, quality control of vaccines, public health and disease control, planning for emergencies and reporting to international bodies; import-export inspection according to international standards; general formulation of animal health development policies and creating of the enabling environment for the private sector should be strengthened to perform effectively.

- Improved animal husbandry practices. Animal husbandry practices in many African countries have generally been traditional. It is necessary for institutions responsible for agricultural development to intensify livestock extension activities to cover areas such as improved housing, feeding and general management.

For the fishery sub-sector, strategies should be implemented to increase stock. Marine and inland water bodies are the traditional and most significant sources of fish production in Africa. The bulk of the fish is landed by the artisan fishers and suffers high post-harvest losses. Fish stocks from these sources have dwindled over the years. Serious attention should be focused on the following:

- Stock rebuilding and management.

Catches from traditional sources have steadily decreased because of over-exploitation of the fisheries resources. There is, therefore, the urgent need to facilitate the re-building of fish stocks. Introduction of fisheries management plans based on the best available scientific practices (reducing pressure on stocks, protection of spawning grounds and habitats, minimising the use of illegal fishing gear and methods etc.) will result in sustainable increase in fish catches. The public and private sector including traditional authorities and fishermen could form partnership in the sustainable management of these resources

- Development of good landing sites along the marine coast and lakes to reduce the risks faced by fishermen in landing their catches on open beaches.
- Efficient fish processing technology should be developed and adopted by fishmongers to expand production.

The bulk of fish in many African countries is processed either by smoking or salting. Many of the operators in the fish processing business still use traditional methods with low productivity which, in addition, pose health hazards to fish smokers. The use of improved fish smokers should be promoted. An example of an improved fish smoker used in Ghana is the "Chorkor Smoker".

- Appropriate fish storage and marketing facilities are important to reduce post-harvest losses and ensure stable prices.
- Production of fish from aquaculture is not significant in most African countries. This should be redressed by promoting the production of fingerlings, construction of fish ponds and capacity building in fish husbandry and health.

- Efficient dissemination of information on new technology is necessary to ensure rapid adoption. This could be achieved by strengthening farmer-based organisations, private sector participation in extension and research-extension-farmer linkages.

Infrastructural development

Increase in agricultural growth will require major investments in infrastructure such as irrigation facilities, a good network of trunk and feeder roads, storage and processing facilities, fish hatcheries and markets. Investment in rural infrastructure will create opportunities for the private sector to establish businesses in the rural areas. This will in turn minimise urban migration of the youth. The following infrastructure issues need to be addressed:

- Irrigation and water management
- Agricultural land
- Transportation systems
- Rehabilitation of research laboratories
- Farm machinery, equipment and tools

Irrigation and water management: Agricultural production in most parts of Africa is mainly rain-fed. Rainfall in many African countries is unreliable and poorly distributed. About 86% of water resources in Africa are used in agriculture, but only 4% of arable land is irrigated in sub-Saharan Africa. This adversely affects agricultural production and makes investment in the sector risky. Agricultural production can be improved significantly through the provision of irrigation and moisture improvement facilities such as water harvesting, water recycling and improving valley bottom drainage. Indeed, one important way of reducing pressure on water is to recycle water by re-using waste water. Development of the irrigation sub-sector should involve a two-pronged approach, namely:

- Micro and small-scale irrigation focusing on provision of boreholes, dugout wells, tube wells and other simple water harvesting structures. The target beneficiaries are small-scale farmers.
- Medium to large-scale irrigation involving the rehabilitation and construction of dams, pumping stations, diversion structures, canals and long distance conveyance pressure pipe systems. This requires massive capital for the construction, operation monitoring and maintenance. The target beneficiaries are medium and large-scale commercial farmers. Public and private partnerships should be promoted for maximised economic utilisation.

Agricultural land: A large proportion of the total land area of Africa is suitable for agriculture. However, land for agricultural production is scarce in many African countries as a result of degradation, lack of access and cumbersome land tenure systems. There are different categories of land ownership in Africa. In Ghana, for example, three land ownership systems are provided in the 1992 constitution. These are, (a) Public lands (i.e. state land and land vested in the President in trust for the people of Ghana), (b) Stool/Skin lands (Community lands vested in the traditional/other community leaders on behalf of the community), and (c) Private and family/clan lands (owned by families, individuals and clans in the community).

The laws of Ghana do not allow freehold ownership of land by non-Ghanaians for who can-can have access to residential, commercial, industrial or agricultural land on leasehold basis for up to 50 years, subject to renewal from any of the three categories of ownership mentioned above. African governments should guide and facilitate prospective investors to acquire and register their lands. Poor management of land as a resource is a major constraint to agricultural land use in Africa. This becomes obvious especially in livestock producing areas where animals are reared on a free-range basis. Land management implies using land in such a way that its carrying capacity is maintained or improved, and African governments should promote the adoption of proper land management practices and farming systems.

In view of the difficulty in acquiring agricultural land in most African countries, there is the urgent need for both governments and traditional land owners to establish land banks by taking an inventory of agricultural lands in the respective African countries. The District and Local Assemblies/Councils should also establish land banks specifically for agricultural use. This may be complemented with the preparation of soil suitability maps for different areas and such information should be made available to prospective investors.

Transportation systems: The current transportation systems in sub-Saharan Africa are unsatisfactory. Good roads to farming communities are limited and some of them are un-motorable for some part of the year. Vehicles are all-purpose and not specialized for agricultural use. The existing transport networks (roads, rail lines and waterways) need to be maintained and upgraded in the short to medium term. In the long term the road networks must be extended, while rail and waterways should be developed to cart agricultural produce to marketing centres to minimize post-harvest losses.

Research laboratories: Research is critical for accelerated agricultural development in Africa. It is only through cutting edge research that the much needed appropriate technologies can be developed to drive agricultural growth and development. Existing research laboratories must be rehabilitated and re-equipped with modern state of the art equipment to improve research output. Adequate resources must be invested in the establishment of modern laboratories in the universities and research institutions to develop appropriate technologies.

Gender equity and gender mainstreaming: A meaningful and sustainable development must recognize the significant roles played by women in agriculture. Women's ability to produce food can be enhanced by improving their training, access to resources, technology and information. African governments and development partners must develop deliberate strategies to:

- Ensure women's involvement in decision-making in designing, implementing and monitoring of projects in agriculture and related disciplines.
- Ensure women's right of access to productive resources (land, credit, inputs, etc.) and equal opportunities to use and develop their skills.
- Promote gender mainstreaming in agricultural sector activities (e.g. increase in the number of agriculture extension agents, technocrats etc.).

Improved access to markets

Improved markets will ensure that producers of goods and services pay and receive economic prices for their inputs and outputs. Market information should be provided to help producers make informed decisions regarding domestic, regional and international markets. Attractive packaging and informative labelling are key to market dominance. Standards and guidance should be provided to the private sector to improve on packaging and labelling.

Product development and processing

To expand market opportunities there is the need to identify and develop new products. Different processing technologies should be vigorously explored to reduce post-harvest losses and also develop new products for consumers. African governments should support the private sector to establish pilot processing plants for selected commodities.

Agricultural education in Africa has not received sufficient attention. In many cases, the involvement of the private sector and donor agencies is very low. There is the need to expand education at different levels, as well as designing mechanisms by which knowledgeable and productive farmers could be encouraged, promoted and recognized. The relevance of agricultural education and research is another dimension that should be improved.

Conclusion

In spite of the importance of agriculture to the economies of African countries, it faces many challenges. It continues to be the mainstay of mainly small farmers who produce under rain-fed conditions with little external inputs, making farming an unpredictable and risky business. Small farmers in Africa also face problems with accessing credit, reliable markets for their produce both locally and for export, and low productivity. On the international market, they face competition from large scale mechanised farmers from the United States of America and European Union countries whose production costs are heavily subsidised (see also chapter 10).

Whilst agricultural outputs have been growing in most parts of Africa, especially sub-Saharan Africa, productivity is still very low. Yields have been falling for many crops and livestock products in most African countries. For instance yields of the most important food grains, tubers, and legumes in most African countries are not significantly higher in 2003 than they were in the previous twenty years (Ehui and Pender 2003). Low productivity has, therefore, contributed in eroding the competitiveness of African agriculture in the world market with its share of agricultural trade dropping from 8% in 1965 to 3% in 1996 (Ehui and Pender 2003). The reasons for low productivity of Africa's agriculture have been enumerated by many authors and they include market failures, over regulation of markets, macroeconomic instability, government and institutional failures, insecure land tenure systems, lack of credit, soil and land degradation etc.

It is important to recognise that few countries have experienced rapid economic growth without agricultural growth either preceding or accompanying it (Pinstrup-Andersen and Pandya-Lorch, 2001). It is, therefore, important that African countries adopt strategies that could overcome the challenges faced by farmers and increase their productivity. In addition to access to inputs and other factors of production, productivity increases would depend on access to appropriate knowledge and technology which could be achieved through a combination of technical and socio-economic interventions. The technical interventions could border mainly on research, technology development and effective extension.

In the area of research, it should embody all relevant approaches, such as agro-ecological, conventional and biotechnology research methods. Farmers must be actively involved in the identification, conceptualisation, design and implementation of research projects to ensure that the technologies that are developed meet their needs to facilitate adoption.

Agricultural extension interventions would have to be made in line with reform initiatives including partnerships involving farmers and farmers' organisations, and other private sector extension providers; cost recovery options negotiated directly between farmers and extension workers. A radical alternative to traditional extension systems is needed. This alternative should include farmer research, farmer-to-farmer transfer of knowledge, farmer field schools and other farmer-led activities.

In addition to the technical issues, markets, rural infrastructure and institutional reforms in the organisation of the agricultural sector need to be addressed to facilitate the desired growth in productivity. With 19 out of the 25 poorest countries of the world being in Africa, coupled with the low productivity of agriculture, Africa will continue to be the locus of poverty unless adequate measures are taken to reverse the trend. It is, however, important to realise that one strategy would not work for all of Africa, and blanket recommendations for the whole region are therefore most likely to fail.

For agriculture to develop on the continent, governments all over Africa have a major role to play. They must formulate policies that will stimulate people's interest in the field. Policies that tend to reward farmers such as good and stable prices, available markets, and incentives such as subsidies and access to flexible credit, can help to promote agricultural development at local level. Since modern agriculture is capital intensive, heavy government investment in agriculture in the areas of infrastructural development, research, training and others can help to boost the sector's development.

Review Questions

1. Give a historical perspective of agricultural development in Africa.

2. Critically analyse the food insecurity problem in Africa and suggest measures that can be taken collectively to achieve food security in a named African country.

3. Discuss the role of governments in agricultural development in Africa.

4. Give a critical analysis of how women's empowerment and gender equity and mainstreaming could impact positively on food production in Africa.

5. Give a comparative discourse of some donor- funded agricultural development programmes implemented in a named African country and discuss why they failed to achieve the intended objectives of boosting the country's agriculture.

6. The rapid transformation and expansion of the economies of most African countries can to a large extent be achieved through sustainable agricultural development. Justify this statement.

7. Discuss the probable impact of research and human resource management on sustainable agricultural development in a named African country.

REFERENCES

Addo-Quaye, A.A., A. Ibrahim, J. E. Kitson, S. M. Rockson-Akron, C.B. K. Tachie-Menson and J. P. Tetteh, 1993. *General Agriculture for Senior Secondary Schools*. Bombay: H. Gangaram & Sons.

Akinsanmi, O. 1996. *Junior Secondary School Agriculture*. Lagos: Longman

ECA 2004, *Africa Review Report on Agriculture and Rural Development*. Addis Ababa: UNECA. www.un.org/esa/sustdev/csd/csd16/rim/eca_bg2.pdf,

Ehui, S. and Pender, J. 2003. Resource degradation, low agricultural productivity and poverty in Sub-Saharan Africa: Pathways out of the spiral. Paper presented at the 25th International Conference of Agricultural Economists (IAAE) in Durban, South Africa 16th -22nd August 2003.

Dani, A.H. and Mohen, J.P. 1996. *History of Humanity: From the third Millennium to the seventh century B.B.* UNESCO, New York.

IDRC. 1981. *A Decade of Learning - The International Development Centre: Agriculture, Food and Nutrition Sciences Division-. The First Ten Years*. Ottawa: IDRC.

FAO. 1996. *Rome Declaration on World Food Security and World Food Summit Plan of Action*. Rome: FAO.

FAO. 1998. *The FAOSTAT Database*. Rome: FAO.

FAO. 2001. *Food, Agriculture and Rural Development: Current and emerging issues for economic analysis and policy research*. Rome: FAO.

Future Agricultures, 2006. "Agricultural Policy in Kenya", *Policy Brief* 006 , January. www.future-agricultures.org

Gardiner, R.K.A. 1986. *African Agricultural Development: Reflections on the major lines of advance and the barriers to production*. FAO.

ISSER, 2010. *The State of the Ghanaian Economy in 2009*. Legon: ISSER.

Juma, C. 2011. *The New Harvest: Agricultural Innovation in Africa*. Oxford: Oxford University Press.

Kenya Horticulture Council, (2011). ' An Overview of Kenya Horticulture Industry.' http://www.fpeak.org/khc.html

MOFA 2002. 'Food and Agriculture Sector Development Policy' (FASDEP). Accra, Ghana: Ministry of Food and Agriculture.

Mucavele, F. G. 2007. *The True Contribution of Agriculture to Economic Growth and Poverty Reduction: Malawi, Mozambique and Zambia Synthesis Report, Food Agriculture and Natural Resources*. Maputo: Policy Analysis Network (FANRPAN).

Pinstrup-Andersen, P. and R. Pandya-Lorch (eds.) 2001. *The Unfinished Agenda: Perspectives on Overcoming Hunger, Poverty, and Environmental Degradation*. International Food Policy Research Institute. Washington D. C.

Republic of South Africa. 2011. *South African Agricultural Production Strategy 2011-2016*. Pretoria: South Africa Department of Agriculture, Forestry and Fisheries. http://www.daff.gov.za/doaDev/doc/IGDP/AGRIC_PRODUCTION_STRATEGY_FRAMWK.pdf

Staatz, J. M. and N. N. Dembélé, 2007. "Agriculture for Development in Sub-Saharan Africa". Background paper for the *World Development Report 2008*. Draft.

Townsend, R. F. 1999. *Agricultural Incentives in Sub-Saharan Africa: Policy Changes.* World Bank Technical Paper No. 444. Washington D.C.: The World Bank.

World Bank 1997. *Rural Development: From Vision to Action.* A Sector Strategy Paper. Washington D.C.: The World Bank.

World Bank 1988. *Rural Development: World Bank Experience,* 1965-1986. Operations Evaluation Department. Washington D. C. : The World Bank.

World Bank, 2008. *World Development Report,* 2008 . Washington, D C. The World Bank.

World Bank 2009. *African Development Indicators 2009.* Washington, D.C. http://data.worldbank.org/indicator/NV.AGR.TOTL.ZS?display=default

World Food Programme 2011.'Food Security Monitoring', *Global Update* July–December 2010, Issue No. 4. pp.1-16. (31 Jan.),

CHAPTER 12

HUMAN SECURITY IN AFRICA
Richard Asante and Kojo Opoku Aidoo

At the dawn of the 21st century, Africa continues to be adversely affected by growing political, economic, social, health, personal, and cultural insecurities. As noted by the AU/NEPAD in 2001, about 340 million people, or nearly half of the population then, lived on less than US$ 1 per day; the mortality rate of children under 5 years of age was 140 per 1000, and life expectancy at birth was only 54 years; only 58 percent of the population had access to safe water, and the rate of illiteracy for people was over 15- 41 percent (AU/NEPAD, 2001: 1).

However, the 2007 United Nations Millennium Development Goals (MDGs) Report provides a degree of optimism about the future of Africa especially in the area of economic growth, poverty and the control of measles. The Report indicates that the proportion of people living in extreme poverty in sub-Saharan Africa had fallen from 46.8 per cent in 1990 to 41.1 per cent in 2004. In addition, the number of people living on less than $1 a day was also beginning to level off, despite rapid population growth. The Report further showed that per capita income of seven sub-Saharan countries grew by more than 3.5% a year between 2000 and 2005, while another 23 had growth rates of more than 2% a year over this period.

In spite of these gains, the poverty gap ratio in sub-Saharan Africa (SSA) remains the highest in the world, indicating that the poor in SSA are the most economically disadvantaged in the world. However, Africa made the most gains in reducing deaths from measles by nearly 75 % over the same period, from an estimated 506,000 to 126,000. Thus, though, coverage dipped to 49% in 1999, it increased to 64% by the end of 2005 (see Figure 12). This has been attributed to advocacy and support provided by the International Measles Initiative and the commitment of African governments (UN MDGs, 2007: 7-14).

Declining economic fortunes and stalled political reforms have fostered mass poverty, and inequality, social, economic and political tensions have intensified at the same time as there is continuing abuse of political and civil rights. Although several attempts have been made by both Africans and the international community to tackle Africa's development crisis and insecurity, much remains to be done, especially in achieving and maintaining human security. In this chapter, we explore human security in Africa and its dimensions, as well as the scope, nature, causes and ramifications of human insecurity in Africa, together with the responses that have been formulated.

Understanding the Scope, Nature, and Dimension of Human Security

Since the UNDP Human Development Report of 1994 presented an analysis of the concept of human security, it has attracted scholarly attention and debate within the development community and especially in Africa.

Figure 12 – A child being inoculated

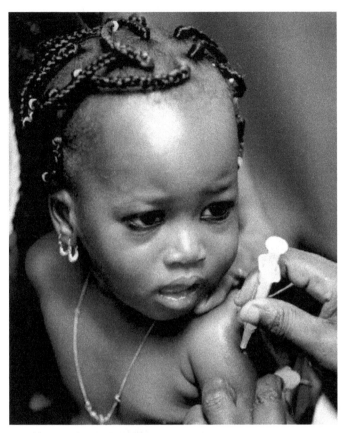

The UNDP defines human security as freedom from chronic threats to security, such as hunger, disease, and oppression, as well as protection from sudden and painful changes in everyday life, at the workplace, at home or in the neighbourhood. The report also identified seven important realms of security namely: economic, food, health, environmental, personal, community and political security. In other words, human security connotes a state of being free from fear and want.[1] For Keizo Obuchi, the former Prime Minister of Japan, the idea of human security involves ceasing all the menaces that threaten the survival, daily life, and dignity of human beings and to strengthening the efforts to confront these threats[2]. In addition, Sen (2000: 2) contends that the prospects of survival have been made more difficult in many parts of the world as a result of public health related issues such as HIV and AIDS, new types of malaria, drug-resistant TB, and violent conflicts and civil wars.

Traditionally, the notion of security was construed by states in the context of state power, national security, or international security, leading to its perception as a top-down concept. Human security on the other hand, is people-centered, and inextricably linked with human rights and human development. The individual human being is the principal object of concern regardless of race, religion, creed, colour, gender, ideology or nationality. Since the pre-colonial era, states and societies in Africa have been concerned with their security and employed different means to ensure a secure territory on the assumption that territory assures the personal security of citizens. Generally, indigenous African societies may be classified into two groups. The first group consisted of societies with centralised authority, administrative machinery, and judicial institutions. The second are societies without a centralised administrative system[3] (also known as acephalous societies). In the former societies, rulers were expected at all times to defend their people and territory from aggressors. However, the rulers were expected to rule justly, to be considerate and conscious of the practices and interests of the people at all times. Though the symbolic power of kings was exceedingly great, there were checks and balances to forestall the abuse of power and tyranny (Adejumobi, 2000: 149-156). Examples of such societies were the Zulu, the Ngwato, the Bemba, the Bayankole and the Kede. In these societies, human security rested on a benign use of state power (see also Ch. 9).

States without centralized authority structures were equally concerned about the security of their territories and their people. For instance, such societies, including the Igbo of West Africa, were organized on the basis of descent and had a well-defined council responsible for maintaining law and order, enforcing rituals, moral values and social order. Here also power was diffused and shared by numerous institutions to forestall tyranny. Other examples of such groups include the Logoli, the Tallensi, and the Nuer. Thus in both the centralised and segmented or acephalous societies, there were mechanisms of social control and legal systems, and rulers strived to maintain a delicate balance between power and authority, on the one hand, and obligation and responsibility, such as protecting their territories and citizens.

Beyond the state, kinship systems and other forms of social networks played an important role in providing the basic security needs of individuals in the pre-colonial, colonial and post-colonial eras. In particular, kinship and lineage networks served as a prime protector for many Africans who were victimised as a result of slavery and colonialism, as well as people who suffered from harassment and intimidation in the post-colonial state (Ekeh, 2004:30-35). However, in the post-colonial period though kinship and lineage networks continue to perform important roles including providing critical social safety nets for members, it has been undermined by economic and political conditions.

From Economic Boom to Crisis

The era of African independence in the 1960s coincided with the period of the boom in commodity prices. Several forest and agricultural products such as groundnuts from Gambia, Senegal, and Nigeria; cocoa from Ghana, Nigeria, and Cameroon; and sisal and coffee from Kenya and Tanzania, yielded enough revenues to produce what some scholars have referred to as the 'golden' period in African development (Deng, 1998). However, after 1965, the fluctuations in the world market led to reduced revenues for African countries and, hence to distortions in their economies. For instance, cocoa exports from Ghana suffered a sharp decline, down to almost 50 percent of its original volume from 1958 to 1965, following the drop in world demand for cocoa. Gambia and Senegal also suffered similar declines in export sales and revenues from groundnuts in the same period. The extractive industries also suffered major setbacks. The fluctuations in the prices of bauxite, copper, and aluminum made unsteady the financial base of the producer countries. The drop in prices of these mineral products in 1975 and 1980 affected the revenue base of Zaire [now the Democratic Republic of Congo, DRC] (copper), Zambia (copper), Sierra Leone (iron ore), and Ghana (bauxite). Worse still, the situation was exacerbated by the oil crisis of 1973 and 1978, following the sharp increases in oil prices by OPEC.[4] Although a few oil-producing countries in Africa such as Gabon, Nigeria and Zaire benefited from the price increases, they also experienced severe economic shocks, especially following the shortfalls in revenues as a result of the fall in oil prices from $36 per barrel in the same period to about $18 per barrel at the beginning of 1983 (Iheduru, 1999: 37).

The strategies adopted by many countries in the context of an unfavourable international economic environment of growing protectionism and decline in international economic cooperation did not achieve the desired results. Consequently, the 1980s became "a lost decade" for African development. By the end of the decade, most African countries in the region were in a worse economic situation than at the time of independence. In that decade alone, per capita GNP declined nearly 10 percent, and capital investment fell by more than 50 percent in real terms. The average annual growth rates of most African countries were negative, and were exceeded by the high population growth of about 2.9 percent. At the same time, the region's foreign debt mounted to about 200.5 billion US dollars, representing 120 percent of GDP and 234 percent of export income, excluding South Africa (UNDP, 1997). The debt burden continues to pose a major impediment to Africa's economic and political renewal, while deteriorating economic conditions have serious implications for human security in Africa.

Perspective on the African Economic Crisis and Human Insecurity

Significantly, there are two major contending perspectives on the origins of the African crisis. On the one hand, the problems of Africa have been attributed to both poor economic policies and political governance on the part of African regimes, and on the other hand, to an unfair international system (Kotze and Steyn, 2003: 73-74; Akokpari, 2007: 22-45). (See also Chapter 13, this volume). The externalist explanatory category suggests that constraints in the international global environment, which are beyond the control of African governments, are the main reasons for Africa's poor economic, political and social performance, thereby undermining human security (Kotze and Steyn, 2003: 73-74; Chabal, 2001; Thomson, 2004). Many African leaders as well as intellectuals hold this perspective. For example, African leaders under the auspices of the OAU (now African Union) argue that the African crisis and economic collapse came about as a result of overwhelming external shocks: soaring interest rates, declining commodity prices, growing protectionism, and growing debt service commitments. Chabal (2001) also asserts that Africa suffers from severe underdevelopment due to an absence of economic growth resulting from the effects of the colonial legacy and Africa's current vulnerability in the world economic system[5].

On the other hand, the internalist explanatory category argues that Africa is not merely the victim of globalisation policies. The social, economic and political problems facing the continent can be attributed to poor economic and political management (see Kotze and Steyn, 2003: 73-74; Thomson, 2004). For example, the Bretton Woods Institutions (BWIs) have blamed the African crisis on inappropriate policies adopted by post-colonial African leaders such as overvalued national currencies; neglect of peasant agriculture; a heavily protected manufacturing sector; and extensive state intervention in the economy. The IMF/World Bank position largely ignores the exogenous causes for Africa's economic plight including the Fund and the Bank's own contributions to past development mistakes, externally funded misguided development projects, declining commodity prices, and world recession.

It has been argued that a neo-patrimonial political system based on vertical links of patronage between political elites and their client constituencies emerged in postcolonial Africa. Political power became highly personalised as a result and political accountability was based on the extent to which patrons were able to meet the expectations and needs of their clients (Kotze and Steyn, 2003: 73-74; Sandbrook and Oelbaum, 1997; Chabal and Daloz, 1999). These factors gravely undermined Africa's quest for human security. In short, the crisis of human insecurity in Africa has domestic, regional and international dimensions.

Many African countries attempted to respond to the economic crisis of the 1980s by embarking on economic reforms along neo-liberal lines, with mixed outcomes (see also Cha.10 and 13). While some countries have made some progress in their macro-economic management, others have failed to sustain economic growth and poverty reduction. Over more than two decades of implementing Structural Adjustment Programmes (SAPS) in Africa, the majority of Africans continue to lack access to potable water, health care and education. For instance, the withdrawal of subsidies on various basic social services and introduction of user fees have impacted negatively on the poor. SAPs further subjected fragile African economies to the volatile international market. In addition, many African countries continue to spend their meager export earnings and other resources on debt servicing instead of on the provision of basic services such as housing, potable water and health care. The unsustainable debt burden that has bedeviled many African countries led many of them to join the HIPC Initiative. Of the 42 countries classified as HIPC in 2003, 34 were in sub-Saharan Africa (UNCTAD, 2004: 17).

Health, Human Security and the HIV and AIDS Pandemic

The security of Africans in the area of health appears to be in jeopardy (See also Chapters 2 & 14 of this volume). In many African countries, expenditures on health have either stagnated or declined in per capita terms. Endemic diseases such as malaria, sleeping sickness, tuberculosis, meningitis and cholera have been on the increase in recent years. The situation has been further aggravated by the HIV and AIDS pandemic.

Globally, it is estimated that about 33.4 million people were living with HIV in 2008, of which two thirds (22.4 million) lived in sub-Saharan Africa, making the region the most heavily affected by HIV worldwide (UNAIDS, 2009: 31-33). As of 2008, more than 14 million children in sub-Saharan Africa had lost one or both parents to AIDS. Women and girls continue to be disproportionally affected by HIV in sub-Saharan Africa, accounting for 60% of all HIV infections. Young women between the ages of 15 and 19 are particularly vulnerable to HIV. In Kenya, young women are three times more likely to become infected than their male counterparts. In southern Africa, nine countries continue to bear a disproportionate share of the global AIDS burden with an adult HIV prevalence greater than 10%. In 2007, Swaziland recorded HIV prevalence of

26%, the highest in the world. South Africa continues to be home to the world's largest population of people living with HIV—5.7 million in 2007 (UNAIDS, 2009).

But there appears to be a glimmer of hope as the epidemic appears to have stabilized in many SSA countries. The rate of new HIV infections in the region has slowly declined. Adult (15–49 years) HIV prevalence declined from 5.8% in 2001 to 5.2% in 2008. By the end of 2008, 44% of adults and children in the region in need of antiretroviral therapy had access to treatment, compared to only 2% in 2003. In Kenya, AIDS-related deaths have fallen by 29% since 2002 (UNAIDS, 2009: 31-33). Drops in HIV incidence were reported among women in Zambia between 2002 and 2007. In Tanzania, national HIV incidence fell between 2004 and 2008. Zimbabwe has also experienced a steady fall in HIV prevalence since the late 1990s. In Burundi, HIV prevalence fell among young people aged 15 to 24 in urban areas between 2002 and 2008 (4% to 3.8%) and in semi-urban areas (6.6% to 4%) during the same period, but it increased in rural areas from 2.2% to 2.9%. In West and Central Africa, the prevalence rate is much lower than in southern Africa (UNAIDS, 2009: 31-33).

The HIV and AIDS epidemic has had negative impacts on food security and other development indicators. The food crises in Lesotho, Swaziland and Zimbabwe have been linked to the death toll particularly among the young and the productive labour force as a result of the epidemic (UNAIDS, 2002: 1). HIV and AIDS has resulted in declining life expectancy,[6] depletion in the stock of scarce productive human resources such as teachers and health personnel, and a major burden on the existing fragile national health sectors. The pandemic also threatens to wipe out the limited gains Africans have made in their socio-economic development over the past decade.

Poverty has been cited as a major reason for the spread of the disease. The intersections among economic hardship, health crises, and internal debt are increasingly affecting individuals, families and communities at the local level. In addition, certain cultural norms, denial, and the culture of silence surrounding the disease, as well as weak or inappropriate government policies regarding the HIV epidemic have aided its rapid spread.

Food Security

Food security is an important component of human security and hence of human development. Africa is highly food-insecure. The continent's current food crisis is a long standing issue (Eicher, 1982: 151) which has been building up over the past decades, and has seriously compromised human security. Africa has experienced both chronic and transitory food insecurity, including recurrent famines. Food security embraces two distinctive issues: the availability of food on the one hand, and the ability to acquire it, on the other hand (Also see Chapters 11 and 15 of this volume). Since the late 1960s, Africa's per capita food production has been declining while total agricultural production also declined in the 1990s. The food crisis is more acute in Eastern and Southern Africa because of climate and soil conditions (see Chapter 1, this volume). In some countries, the crisis has been further aggravated by war, refugee movements and the underlying economic and environmental fragility of the countries and communities affected.

More worrisome is the fact that even in situations where per capita food production is relatively stable, the poor may not have the income or resources to buy it as a result of low income, price hikes, or unavailability of credit. The situation is further exacerbated by famine that has become a recurrent feature in parts of the continent. The most extreme manifestation of this insecurity has been death by starvation and decline in average caloric intake or dietary energy supply. Food insecurity has contributed to growing dependency on food aid and imports. The causes of the continent's food crisis are many and interlocking. They include high population growth rates, environmental degradation, excessive dependence on rain-fed agriculture, civil conflicts and political instability among others (see also Chapter 15, this volume).

Environmental Security

At the beginning of the new millennium, Africa is faced with serious problems of environmental security (see Chapter 15, this volume). Increasingly there is a growing awareness of the problem by African governments, civil society and the donor community, while modest efforts have been made by individual countries, sub-regional and regional initiatives. Examples of sub-regional initiatives include the Permanent State Committee for Drought Control in the Sahel (CILSS) and the Intergovernmental Authority for Drought and Development (IGADD) in Eastern Africa. Regional Initiatives include the African Common Position on Environment and Development which was prepared in 1991 in connection with the United Nations Conference on the Environment and Development (UNCED), as well as the NEPAD Initiative.

Major environmental problems include soil erosion, environmental degradation, deforestation and desertification. These problems are largely generated by poverty, rapid population growth and urbanisation. For example the degradation of the soil is exacerbated by massive deforestation, caused by the over-exploitation of forests and woodlands for agriculture and timber exploitation. The original forest cover in most countries is reported to have already disappeared. The loss of tropical forests is more pronounced in West Africa, which accounts for more than half of the deforestation that is occurring on the continent (see also Chapters 1 and 15 of this volume).

Other countries where deforestation has assumed serious proportions are Guinea, Cameroon, Zaire, Kenya, Ethiopia, and Madagascar (which is reported to have lost 90 percent of its original forest cover and together with it, half the original endemic species). The rate of desertification also appears to be accelerating in areas such as the Sahara, the Kalahari and Namib deserts, and is more acute in North, West and Southwest Africa, rapidly extending eastwards to Uganda, Kenya and Somalia. The rapid rate of desertification has led to severe drought, especially in the Sahel and the Horn of Africa, and more recently in Eastern and Southern Africa.

Political Liberalisation-Human Security Nexus

Worsening economic conditions engendered 'revolutionary pressures' and crises of legitimacy in most of Africa (Ake, 1981). Ruling groups and classes in Africa responded to the crisis of legitimacy by becoming coercive and authoritarian. Coercive authoritarianism has been dysfunctional in the sense that it effectively circumscribed political space and made Africa politically insecure. By the 1990s, the dysfunctionalities of coercive authoritarianism had been recognized by both Africans and the international community, and the last two decades of the 20th century saw a historic shift in the global spread of democracies. Some 81 countries in the world, including 29 in

SSA, took giant steps towards democratisation, but with mixed experiences and outcomes[7]. Rising opposition and external pressures through the 1980s tossed out many long-standing dictators, including Mali's Moussa Traore in 1991, and Malawi's Kamuzu Banda in 1994.

However, in other countries, the transition has been less dramatic. Many have pursued democratisation in the face of massive poverty and pervasive social and economic tensions. On the one hand, some countries have made some progress. South Africa has become a multi-party democratic nation; Ghana, Benin, Mali, Senegal and Nigeria have made progress toward democratic consolidation and stability; relative peace has dawned in Ethiopia after several years of a cruel and debilitating civil war; war-torn Uganda and Mozambique have been relatively peaceful in recent times.

At the same time, many of the countries that embraced democracy have suffered reversal, while many others have only allowed limited political participation in the wake of competition and continuing abuse of political and civil rights, corruption and cross border crime. Increasingly, there is the disturbing trend towards "illiberal" democracies as evident in Zimbabwe, Rwanda, Uganda and Ethiopia. Some African leaders have undermined democracy and personal security by systematically using the security forces to pursue their parochial ends. It is estimated that between 1989 and 2002, national armies intervened in the political affairs of 13 SSA countries, representing a quarter of the countries on the continent (UNDP, 2002: 85).

Even where democratic institutions have been established, they are weak and citizens often feel powerless to influence national policies. Some countries, including the Democratic Republic of Congo (DRC), have lapsed into authoritarianism and have been plagued by conflict. In other countries such as Togo, Burkina Faso, Cameroon or Uganda, one-party regimes have allowed elections, but ended up permitting only limited openings for political competition. Political instability and violence have also marred democratic transitions in Nigeria, La Cote d'Ivoire and Zimbabwe, to mention but a few. In short, several years of both economic and political liberalisation have not produced much dividend in the lives of ordinary people in Africa and poverty continues to increase.

Conflict, Human Security and Development

Since the end of international bi-polarity and the Cold War, SSA has experienced several civil wars and major armed intra-state conflict. The proliferation of conflict, particularly internal conflict, highlights the fragility of African states. Conflict in Africa has resulted in large numbers of refugees and displaced persons. Uganda, Burundi, Rwanda, Chad, Somalia, the Democratic Republic of Congo and Sudan, are some of the countries that have been brutalised by war for several years. The shocking acts of genocide in Rwanda, which resulted in the deaths of over 500,000 people, the flight of 2 million refugees to neighbouring countries and the internal displacement of an equal number of people, illustrate the depth of the tragedy of armed conflicts in Africa.

These conflicts are reflections of economic, social and political demands that have suffered neglect for far too long. In many of these countries, access to power and resources is highly uneven and the opportunities for seeking redress through a peaceful political process are either minimal or not possible. These grievances are often complicated by ethnic and/or religious tensions. In such circumstances, a resort to arms appears as the only solution. This is further aggravated by several humanitarian crises, which have been occasioned by famine, especially in some parts of southern and central Africa.

Africa has also witnessed a surge in armed rebels. The phenomenon of armed rebels is further aggravated by the proliferation of small and light weapons[8]. The uncontrolled accumulation of small arms in the hands of non-state actors is a major cause of human insecurity in Africa. The proliferation of small arms has also increased the lethality of the wars in many African countries, especially in the Mano River Basin states comprising Liberia, Sierra Leone, and Guinea. It has also fueled armed conflict in Nigeria, the citizen crisis in Cote d'Ivoire, and the separatist rebellions in the Casamance region of Senegal and Guinea Bissau. The proliferation of small arms not only aggravates and prolongs conflicts, but also undermines economic activity and intensifies human insecurity. Increasingly the levels of violence especially against non-combatants has increased in volume and intensity as evidenced in the conflicts in Sierra Leone, Liberia, Somalia, Rwanda, Burundi and the Democratic Republic of Congo, while women's bodies have become a site of war, as evidenced in the systematic rapes of women and girls.

Displacement, Refugee Flows and Child Soldiers

Civil wars and other internal conflicts have also caused massive refugee flows and displaced populations, and underscore the intensity of armed conflicts in Africa. Africa is reported to have the highest levels of internal displacement in the world and some of the largest refugee flows (Figure 13). In 2000, almost eleven million people in Africa were internally displaced (DFID, 2001: 10). In Darfur, it was reported that at least 200,000 civilians had died since the conflict started in 2003, and about 2 million remained in camps for refugees and internally displaced persons (West, 2006: 1). The problem of refugees and displaced persons is but one dramatic example of the terrible social consequences of war.

Figure 13 – Internally displaced persons on the road from Goma, DRC

Source: *Roberto Schmidt/AFP/Getty Images*

In the midst of armed conflict, it is often women and children who bear the brunt of the burden, as they constitute a disproportionately high proportion of refugees and displaced persons. Children have become one of the main targets of violence and in turn, are used to perpetrate it. Children are deliberately indoctrinated into a culture of violence and used as specific instruments of war. Militia groups and irregular forces such as the Lord's Resistance Army in Uganda, the Revolutionary United Front (RUF) in Sierra Leone, UNITA in Angola, and RENAMO in Mozambique, forcibly recruited children and initiated them through acts of violence against their own families and communities.

It is reported that of the estimated 350,000 child soldiers worldwide, 200,000 were in Africa (DFID, 2001: 11). A Report published by Coalition to Stop the Use of Child Soldiers in 2004 estimated that since 1991, 200,000 children have carried arms or been recruited as militias in the DRC. According to the 2004 Child Soldiers Global Report, there were an estimated 17,000 children in government forces, allied militias and opposition armed groups in the Sudan in March 2004. Between 2,500 and 5,000 children served in the armed opposition group, the Sudan's People's Liberation Army (SPLA), in the south. Despite a widely publicized child demobilisation programme, in which it claimed to have demobilized over 16,000 children between 2001 and 2004, the SPLA continued to recruit and re-recruit child soldiers[9]. In Uganda, the rebel Lord's Resistance Army (LRA) had abducted more than 30,000 boys and girls as soldiers in the past two decades from the 1980s.

Destruction of Social and Infrastructural Facilities

The protracted armed conflicts in Africa have resulted in the destruction of the already underdeveloped infrastructure. Whole villages and towns have been bombed and stripped of any valuable assets. School buildings, airports, electricity and water supply, hospitals and markets have been razed to the ground. In the process, children of school age have had their education disrupted. For instance, during Mozambique's 16-year civil war, more than 40 percent of schools were destroyed or forced to close, and more than 40 percent of health centres were destroyed. Industries were so damaged that postwar production was only 20-40 percent of prewar capacity, with economic losses estimated at $15 billion or several times Mozambique's prewar GDP. Worse still, the government was compelled to re-direct the state's scarce resources meant for socio-economic development to the prosecution of war as military expenditures kept escalating.

While individual African states court foreign investment to jump-start development, the continent as a whole has been seen as a risk by potential external investors on account of armed conflicts. And in an environment of armed conflict, the primary concern is with survival, not human development and security. In such situations, people's participation in development also becomes meaningless where civil society has broken down totally as in the case of Somalia.

Gender and Human Security

Conflicts in Africa have induced suffering especially on women and girls. In Rwanda, Liberia, the DRC, Sudan, Sierra Leone and Uganda, government forces backed by pro-government militias and rebel groups deliberately used mass rape as an instrument of violence against defenceless women and girls. The situation has been most alarming in North and South Kivu provinces in the Eastern part of the DRC. Though the exact number of rape victims in the DRC is not known, the UN and Aid agencies have recorded several cases of mass rape especially in the eastern part of the DRC. For example, it is estimated that in July and August, 2010 alone, more than 500 cases of mass rape were reported in Eastern part of the DRC.

In February 2008, *Médecins sans Frontières* reported that 75% of all the rape cases it dealt with worldwide were in eastern Congo (McGreal, 2007).[10] According to the UN Special Rapporteur on Rwanda, Rene Degni-Segui, an estimated 500,000 women were raped in Rwanda during the 1994 genocide (Albutt, 2008). Similarly, the UN Special Rapporteur on the Elimination of Violence against Women, Radhika Coomaraswamy, estimated that 72 percent of Sierra Leonean women and girls experienced human rights abuses during the war and over 50 percent were victims of sexual violence (Nowrojee, 2005; Scanlon, 2008: 43). In the Ivorian conflict, it was reported that many women were victims of sexual violence (Human Rights Watch 2007). In Darfur, Human Rights Watch (2008) reported that since the war started, thousands of women had been raped, murdered and uprooted from their communities. In Somalia, UNHCR (2006: 67) reported 256 incidents of rape and sexual violence in 2004 in the Dadaab refugee camp. In Sierra Leone, *Physicians for Human Rights* (2002: 3-4) reported that between 215,000 and 250,000 women were victims of war-related rape. In Sierra Leone, the DRC, Rwanda and Uganda, mass rape cases exposed women to various sexually transmitted diseases including HIV and AIDS. In recent times, some organisations have emerged to assist rape victims. In the DRC, *Heal Africa*, *Médecins sans Frontières*, and International Medical Corps have provided a variety of support services to rape victims. In Somalia, *We Are Women Activists* (WAWA), is also supporting rape victims in that country. Yet these organisations are also faced with security threats.

In Africa, women have played important roles in both formal and informal peace initiatives, despite being the greatest victims of violent conflicts. In 2000, the UN Security Council adopted Resolution 1325 on "Women, Peace, and Security". The Resolution encourages "All those involved in the planning for disarmament, demobilisation and reintegration to consider the different needs of female and male ex-combatants and to take into account the needs of their dependants" (United Nations Security Council 2000, para, 13). Increasingly, women's groups have demanded to be included in processes of resolving conflicts at all levels of society. In recent years, women have become important actors in disarmament, demobilisation and reintegration (DDR) programmes in the DRC, Burundi, and Uganda (Lahai, 2010: 8).

For example, in 2003 Liberian women organized themselves under the auspices of the Women in Peace-building Network (WIPNET) to demand an unconditional ceasefire, a negotiated settlement and active involvement of the international community in the Liberian crisis. During the 2003, peace negotiation process in Ghana, some women held a parallel meeting resulting in 'The Golden Tulip Declaration'. Frustrated by the lack of progress during the peace talks, some women used their bodies as human shields and demanded that an agreement be reached (Scanlon and Muddell, 2008: 25–26). In Sierra Leone, women's groups were instrumental in influencing the outcome of peace talks in that country. In Mali, women were directly involved in building a national coalition to campaign against illicit arms. However, in Darfur, Southern Sudan, and the Ogaden Region of Ethiopia, women have not been visible in the peace processes.

Responses to Human Insecurity in Africa- The African Union and NEPAD

In response to the generally dismal economic situation of the continent, African leaders and the Organisation of African Unity (OAU), now the African Union (AU) have made a series of attempts since the 1970s to craft their own development paradigms. Five landmark strategies, which provide the continent's preferred development agenda[11] emerged in the 1980s and early in the 1990s. They include: The Lagos Plan of Action for the Economic Development of Africa (1980-2000) and the Final Act of Lagos (1980); Africa's Priority Programme for Economic Recovery (APPER, 1986-90); the African Alternative Framework to Structural Adjustment for Socio-Economic Recovery and Transformation (AAF-SAP) 1989; The African Charter for Popular Participation for Development (1990); and the United Nations New Agenda for the Development of Africa in the 1990s (UN-NADAF, 1991). Broadly, these programmes stressed the need for African countries to diversify their economies, promote food-self-sufficiency, popular participation and regional integration as key to promoting development and human security.

More specifically, the failure of SAPs to promote sustained development as well as growing human insecurity led to an outcry for an alternative to SAPs. The African Alternative Framework to Structural Adjustment for Socio-Economic Recovery and Transformation (AAF-SAP), presented by the United Nations Economic Commission for Africa (ECA), was intended as an alternative to the orthodox prescription presented by the World Bank and the International Monitory Fund (IMF). The African Alternative maintains that adjustment must be for the benefit of the majority of the people, and as such, adjustment programmes must be derived with, rather than without the people (ECA, 1994: 169-178).

The AAF-SAP recommended four main goals for achieving development and human security. First, strengthening and diversifying Africa's production capacity. It was argued that Africa could improve human security by strengthening the links between agriculture and industry, and emphasized food self-sufficiency. It proposed that national governments should allocate a minimum of 20-25 percent of total public expenditure to agriculture and particularly to food production. It also recommended land reforms, noting that, since about 85 percent of African women of working age are involved in agricultural production, special emphasis should be placed on granting legal recognition to the rights of women to land. It also called for investment in human resources development as key to social transformation (Ibid.).

Second, AAF-SAP called for improving the level of people's incomes and the pattern of its distribution by promoting policies that would increase the dynamism of the economy and increase incomes. To achieve this goal, debt relief was crucial to freeing financial resources for productive investment. Further to this, it proposed investment in the rural areas where majority of the population live (Ibid).

Third, it recommended adjusting the pattern of public expenditure to satisfy people's essential needs. AAF-SAP rejected the adoption of policies that reduced government expenditure on key essential services. It criticized cuts in wages, elimination of subsidies on consumer goods and services, and retrenchment, and called for expenditure switching from the military to social services and development projects. It also recommended improved transportation and communication links to facilitate intra-African trade and as a way to ease dependence on overseas markets.

Fourth, it called for the provision of institutional support for adjustment with transformation by encouraging the active participation of the entire population and grassroots organization, the full dedication and commitment of African governments, as well as support from the international community, including the Bretton Woods Institutions. Most crucially, it recommended that decision-making be democratized at all levels to enhance accountability (ECA, 1994: 169-178).

Unfortunately, all of these programmes were opposed, undermined and jettisoned by the Bretton Woods Institutions. According to Adedeji (2002: 32) Africans were impeded from exercising their basic and fundamental right to make decisions about their future. Hope (2002) also argues that the Lagos Plan of Action was fraught with lack of political commitment from African leadership, a lack of coordination with other political and economic reforms, a lack of African ownership and control, and lack of resources. The New Partnership for Africa's Development (NEPAD) was adopted in 2001 as Africa's collective strategy for the reversal of this abnormal situation. NEPAD has received support from international donors, including the G8, especially regarding its commitment to good governance, sound macro-economic policies and the creation of a peer review system. It seeks to promote accelerated growth and sustainable development on the continent, to eradicate widespread and severe poverty, and to halt Africa's marginalisation in the global environment

To a large extent, the goals and benefits of NEPAD reflect the broader issues of human security. On the political front, the NEPAD policy attempts to eradicate violent conflict and create enduring stability by ensuring low levels of internal social conflict through the entrenchment of a political system reflecting democratic values, respect for human rights and the application of a consistent framework. Furthermore, NEPAD also affirms a commitment on the part of African leaders to core human security issues including peace, democracy, human rights, and sound economic management as the instruments necessary for sustained development. The inclusion of such considerations as prevention, conflict management, and combating the proliferation of small arms represent the importance NEPAD attaches to human security on the continent.

On the economic front, NEPAD aims to achieve 7 percent growth per annum by 2015; to reduce by half the number of Africans living in absolute poverty by 2015; enrolment of all children of school-going age by 2015. It also aims to eliminate gender disparities in basic education by 2015. NEPAD also seeks to revitalise education and health services, promote diversification and development of infrastructure, and promote the role of women by seeking to reinforce their capacity (AU/NEPAD, 2001: 15).

It is with these principles in mind that the African Peer Review Mechanism (APRM) was established within the NEPAD policy framework to ensure that the policies and practices of participating countries conform to the agreed political, economic and corporate governance code and standards contained in the declaration on democracy, political, economic and corporate governance that was approved by the AU Summit in July 2002.

However, NEPAD has come under severe criticism. NEPAD is seen as not different from earlier initiatives for African development because it pins its hopes for resource and asset mobilisation largely on external sources. For instance, the US $ 64 billion needed to fill the resource gap is expected to come from overseas development assistance (ODA). A serious weakness levelled against the NEPAD initiative is that, like many other African initiatives, the NEPAD document and its contents largely remain known only to African governments, their bureaucrats and the leaders of the G8, but not to the African people. Another major deficiency is that although the HIV and AIDS pandemic is a serious human security issue and regarded as a major problem facing the African continent, HIV and AIDS received little attention within the NEPAD document.

Concerns have also been expressed about the dominant neo-liberal economic framework that underpins the NEPAD initiative. African experiences have shown that increased African integration into the world economy as evident under SAPs led to increased levels of poverty, unemployment, and inequality. It is often argued that like SAPs, the NEPAD initiative is likely to undermine human security, especially in the light of growing gaps between the rich and poor countries perpetuated by the iniquitous global economic relations.

Furthermore, the APRM has also come under severe criticism from various camps. The lack of interest expressed by many African Heads of states in the design and implementation of the APRM has raised doubt about the validity of the mechanism, as only one-third of invited African presidents attended the meeting in Abuja, Nigeria in March 2003, and only 22 countries out of 53 African states had signed the accession document by January 2006. Some critics have argued that the mechanism is fundamentally flawed due to the fact that African leaders themselves will decide on who has complied with its principles, coupled with the fact many of the leaders assumed office through military coups, and many lack credibility and persuasive influence.

The inception of NEPAD was followed by the replacement of the Organisation of African Unity by the Consultative Act of the African Union in July 2002. The AU aims to "promote peace, security and stability on the continent" and reserves the right to intervene in member states pursuant to a decision of the Assembly in respect of grave circumstances such as war crimes, genocide and crimes against humanity, as well as the condemnation and rejection of unconstitutional changes of government."

In 2004, the AU inaugurated the Peace and Security Council (PSC). The PSC is responsible for maintaining peace and security. More specifically, it is responsible for raising and deployment of AU peacekeeping forces, as well as mediation and reconciliation. However, the PSC is currently faced with critical challenges in Darfur, Sudan, Somalia, DRC, and Uganda among others. For example, The African Union forces in Darfur had limited mandate and capacity to protect Darfur and civilians.

In addition, the Heads and Government of ECOWAS adopted a moratorium on the importation, exportation and manufacture of light weapons in October 1998, in Abuja, Nigeria. This underscored the desire of West African leaders to tackle the problem of proliferation of small arms, a major factor fanning human insecurity in the sub-region. ECOWAS leaders followed up on the moratorium by adopting a comprehensive mechanism for conflict prevention, management, resolution, and security in 1999. This protocol effectively replaced the 1978 Non-Aggression Protocol on Mutual Assistance on Defence, and Article 58 of the revised treaty of 1993. Both ECOWAS and the AU have adopted anti-coup protocols including the condemnation and rejection of unconstitutional changes in government, the right of the Union to intervene in a member state in respect of grave circumstance, such as war crimes, genocide and crimes against humanity, respect for the sanctity of human life, rejection of impunity, and political assassination, acts of terrorism and subversive activities, among others.

Conclusion

The concept of human security has gained currency and underscores the security that people should have in their daily lives, not only from the threat of war, but also from the threat of disease, hunger, unemployment, crime, social conflict, political repression and environmental hazards. Thus human security is inextricably linked with human development and needs to be tackled on two fronts: at the macro level through the provision of state security, and at the micro level through removing the obstacles to what Sen (2000) has called 'unfreedom,' to allow for the social and economic empowerment of African people, especially in conditions where pre-existing forms of security provided through kinship and lineage networks have been severely weakened by economic and political crises. This remains a daunting task and a serious challenge for Africa in the 21st century.

Review Questions

1. What is human security? What are the factors that affect it in Africa?

2. Explain the relationship between economic underdevelopment and human insecurity in Africa.

3. From your own personal observations, what are the kinship, lineage and other net -works operational in your immediate environment and how do these provide security to their membership?

4. Suggest ways to improve human security in Africa.

Endnotes

1. The concept of human security has gained currency following increasing recognition that collective efforts are needed to reduce human suffering and insecurity especially where it is most acute and prevalent.

2. Cited in Amartya Sen (2000) "Why Human Security?" A paper presented at the "International Symposium on Human Security" in Tokyo, 28 July, 2000.

3. Saheed Adejumobi (2000) classified indigenous African societies into centralized political systems and segmentary political systems. While the former societies were culturally heterogeneous communities of units, members were bound together by common interests and loyalty to a political superior, usually a paramount chief or king-in- council. The latter societies on the other hand, had no strong centralized authority enjoying a concentration of political, judicial, or military power that was capable of enforcing control by decree over the activities of its members. However, leaders of both societies were concerned with the security of their members at all times.

4. Iheduru (1999) notes that the structure of the African political economy negatively affects its revenue base. The excessive reliance of most African countries on a single or few export products combined with fluctuations in commodity prices affects the total receipt from exports and largely accounts for the distortions in their economies.

5. In an attempt to reverse the effects of dependency engendered by colonialism and to disengage from the global capitalist economy, African governments allocated a strong and increasingly interventionist role for the state in industrialisation. This was done through policies of export promotion, import substitution and state–owned enterprises. These strategies had serious shortcomings and further exacerbated economic problems.

6. The UNDP Human Development Report of 2002 shows that in Botswana, the most affected HIV country, a child born today can expect to live only 36 years and in Burkina Faso, the 20th most affected country, life expectancy has fallen by eight (8) years.

7. The UNDP report of 2002 suggests that several countries that took giant steps towards democracy in the 1990s have returned to more authoritarian rule or stalled between democracy and authoritarianism, with limited political freedoms or dysfunctional politics.

8. The political leadership of the Economic Community of West African States (ECOWAS) have identified the proliferation of small arms as a major threat to national and sub-regional security and have signed the Moratorium on the Importation, Exportation, and Manufacture of Light Weapons in West Africa, to regulate the spread and use of small arms.

9. *Child Soldiers Global Report 2004.* Africa Regional overview.www.child-soldiers.org/document/get?id=743 *(Accessed on 28/10/10)*

10. Chris McGreal (2007). Sexual violence in the Democratic Republic of the Congo is being used as an instrument of war in the ensuing conflict. November 12. (http://www.awid.org/eng/Issues-and-Analysis/Library/ Hundreds-of-thousands-of-women-raped-for-being-on-the-wrong-side) *(Accessed on 28/10/10)*

11. Strategies for African development proposed by Adedeji and the ECA emphasized on national and collective self-reliance and self sustaining development

References

Adedeji, A. 2002. "From Lagos to NEPAD" *New Agenda*, Fourth Quarter. pp.32.

Adejumobi, S. 2000.'Politics and Government' in Toyin Falola (ed.) *Africa* Volume 2- *African Cultures and Societies Before 1885.* North Carolina: Carolina Academic Press.

.African Union 2001. *The New Partnership for Africa's Development (NEPAD).* Addis Ababa: The African Union.

Aheduru, O. M. 1999. *The Politics of Economic Restructuring and Democracy in Africa.* Westport/London: Greenwood Press.

Ake, C. 1981. *A Political Economy of Africa.* Longman, Nigeria Limited.

Akokpari, J. 2007.*The Political Economy of Human Insecurity in Sub-Saharan Africa* .Institute of Developing Economies. Japan External Trade Organization, No.431 (October) pp.1-65.

Albutt, K. 2008. "Rape as an Instrument of War: An Examination of Sexual Violence in Rwanda and the Democratic Republic of The Congo." Unpublished Senior Thesis, Program on Justice and Peace Studies, Georgetown University, USA. http://www1.georgetown.edu/departments/justice_peace/research/theses/theses2008/ albutt_katherine_a.pdf

Chabal, P. and J-P. Daloz 1999. *Africa Works- Disorder as Political Instrument.* London and Bloomington, IN: The International African Institute / James Currey / Indiana University.

Chabal, P. 2001. Africa in the Age of Globalisation, *African Security Review* 10 (2): 383-404.

Chazan, N, R. Mortimer, J. Ravenhill and D. Rothschild. 1992. *Politics and Society in Contemporary Africa.* Boulder, Colorado: Lynne Rienner Publishers.

Child Soldiers Global Report 2004. *Africa Regional Overview.* www.child-soldiers.org/document/get?id=743

Deng, L. 1998 *Rethinking African Development Towards a Framework for Social Integration and Ecological Harmony*. Trenton: New Jersey: African World Press.

DFID, 2001. *Causes of Conflict in Africa*. Consultation Document. London: DFID http://www.gsdrc.org/go/display&type=Document&id=52

Eicher, C.K. 1982. "Facing up to Africa's Crisis", *Foreign Affairs*, p.151 61: 1 (151).

Ekeh, P. 2004. "Individuals' Basic Security Needs and the Limits of Democracy in Africa", in B. Berman, D. Eyoh and W. Kymlicka (editors) *Ethnicity and Democracy in Africa*. Oxford, Ohio: James Currey/Ohio University Press.

Human Rights Watch. 2007. *My heart is cut: Sexual violence by rebels and pro-government forces in Cote d'Ivoire*. http://www.hrw.org/en/reports/2007/08/01/my-heart-cut-0?print (accessed December 10, 2009).

Human Rights Watch. 2008. *Five Years On: No Justice for Sexual Violence in Darfur*.http://www.hrw.org/en/reports/2008/04/06/five-years?print (accessed March 2, 2010).

Kotze, H. and C. Steyn 2003. *African Elite Perspectives: AU and NEPAD. A comparative study across seven African countries*. Occasional Papers. December. Johannesburg: Konrad-Adenauer-Stiftung., Johannesburg.

Lahai, J. I. 2010. "Gendered Battlefields: A Contextual and Comparative Analysis of Women's Participation in Armed conflicts in Africa". *Peace & Conflict Review* Volume 4, Issue 2, (Spring), pp. 1-24.

Nowrojee, B. 2005 "Making the Invisible War Crime Visible: Post Conflict Justice for Sierra Leone's Rape Victims", *Harvard Human Rights Journal*, 18, pp.85-105.

Obuchi, K. 1999. "Opening Remarks," in *The Asian Crisis and Human Security* Tokyo: Japan Center for International Exchange. pp.18-9.

Sandbrook, R. and J. Oelbaum, "Reforming Dysfunctional Institutions Through Democratisation? Reflections on Change in Ghana", *The Journal of Modern African Studies*, Vol. 35, No. 4, 1997, pp.6-44;

Scanlon, H. 2008. Militarization, Gender and Transitional Justice in Africa. *Feminist Africa* 10: 31- 48. http://www.feministafrica.org/uploads/File/Issue%2010/feature%20article%202.pdf *(Accessed on 28/10/10)*.

Scanlon, H. and K. Muddell. 2008 "Gender and Transitional Justice in Africa: Progress and Prospects". Report of the Gender and Transitional Justice in Africa Conference, held on 4–5 September 2008 at the Vineyard Hotel, Cape Town, South Africa. http://www.peacewomen.org/assets/file/Resources/Academic/transjust_gendertransitionaljustice_scanlonandmuddell_2009.pdf ((Accessed on 16/10/10).

Sen, A. 2000 "Why Human Security?" A paper presented at the "International Symposium on Human Security" in Tokyo, 28 July, 2000.(http://www.humansecurity-chs.org/activities/outreach/Sen2000.pdf) *(Accessed on 16/10/10)*.

Thomson, Alex 2004. *An Introduction to African Politics*. 2nd Edition. London and New York: Routledge.

United Nations. 2007. *The Millennium Development Goals Report 2007*. www.un.org/millenniumgoals/pdf/mdg2007.pdf. Accessed on 25/10/10.

United Nations Security Council. 2000. *Resolution 1325*. New York: United Nations.

UNECA 1994. 'African Alternative Framework to Structural Adjustment' in K. Danaher (ed.) *50 Years Is Enough. The Case Against the World Bank and the International Monetary Fund.*. Boston, Ma : South End Press.

United Nations High Commissioner for Refugees, UNHCR. 2006. *The state of the world's refugees: Human displacement in the new millennium*. Oxford and New York: OUP.

UNAIDS. 2009 *AIDS Epidemic Update*. November. Geneva: UNAIDS.

UNAIDS. 2002 AIDS Epidemic Update. December. Geneva: UNAIDS.

UNCTAD 2004. *Economic Development in Africa. Debt Sustainability: Oasis and Mirage?* New York and Geneva: United Nations.

United Nations Development Programme (UNDP), 2002. *Human Development Report 2002. Deepening Democracy in a Fragmented World.* New York: Oxford University Press.

United Nations Development Programme (UNDP), 1994 *Human Development Report.* New York: Oxford University Press.

United Nations Development Programme (UNDP) 1997. *Governance for sustainable Human Development.* New York: UNDP.

West, D. L. 2006. *The Sudan: Saving Lives, Sustaining Peace.* BCSIA: Harvard University.

CHAPTER 13

POLITICAL ECONOMY OF DEVELOPMENT AND POLICY OUTCOMES IN POSTCOLONIAL AFRICA

Lord C. Mawuko-Yevugah

Introduction

Since the attainment of political independence in the late 1950s and early 1960s, African countries have been preoccupied with the issue of economic development. This preoccupation has resulted in fierce debates among various stakeholders on the most suitable approaches and strategies for accelerated and sustained economic growth and development in the postcolonies. While the first few years of the post-independence era witnessed some modest results in terms of economic growth and infrastructural development, by the end of the first decade after independence, the continent had descended into what has been called the 'African crisis' or the 'African tragedy' (Leys 1994; Arrighi 2002). This broadly refers to political instability and economic decay. Thus, by the mid to late 1980s, barely two decades after decolonisation on much of the African continent, a new development orthodoxy- which came to be known as structural adjustment-policies became the main instrument for development policy making and in addressing the 'crisis'. What were the developmental strategies pursued in the post-colonial era? What have been the outcomes of these strategies? What were the implications of the 'crisis' which engulfed the continent in the post-colonial era for the continent's development agenda? This chapter first provides a brief overview of what became known as the "African crisis" arguing that this crisis, which came to be conceptualised as the "failure of development" (Ahluwalia 2001), has its internal and external origins. The chapter will also analyse the competing approaches proposed by different actors and examine the rise, evolution and application of what has become known as a neoliberal development agenda in Africa. It is argued in this chapter that since the early 1980s, this agenda has come to represent a reproduction of policy mechanisms designed to police and regulate the postcolonial state. In order to understand how this crisis evolved it is important to understand the competing ideological orientations which have influenced Africa's postcolonial development process. The chapter will provide a general overview of how 'development' became the rallying point for both the first generation of African leaders in the postcolonial era as well as external bodies that also invoked development as a strategy to maintain their influence in the postcolonies. I will then historicise discussion about the 'African crisis' and the competing policy prescriptions to solve this problem by African leaders on one hand, and the international financial institutions (IFIs) on the other. The chapter will then offer a genealogy of the neoliberal agenda in Africa to the publication of the Berg Report in 1981. The main thrust of the chapter is to show, how as a result of a combination of internal and external factors, the two Bretton Woods Institutions (BWIs)- the World Bank and the International Monetary Fund have been able to establish their hegemony in postcolonial Africa. The chapter also explores the emergence of a new development paradigm in the form of a global consensus towards poverty reduction and partnerships between African countries, international financial institutions and Western donor countries. It traces the emergence of this new consensus to the disastrous implementation of structural adjustment programmes (SAPs). It then explores the transition from SAPs to the new development framework, by mapping out what is new in the development framework, and what persists. The chapter provides a discussion on the shift from the Washington Consensus to the Post-Washington Consensus in the form of the World Bank's Comprehensive Development Framework and incorporation of social development into future bilateral and multilateral lending arrangements. More importantly, the chapter examines Africa's integration into the emerging global development consensus in the form of the introduction of the new partnership for African development (NEPAD). The chapter discusses the growing involvement of China and other emerging powers within the African continent and explore what this means for Africa's long-term development prospects. Finally, the chapter explores possible areas for development policy focus in the coming years in the light of the earlier discussions.

Africa and the challenge of postcolonial development

By the early 1960s, the majority of African countries had attained political independence and the status of sovereignty, thus ushering in a new era of not only state formation, but more significantly, the need to obtain sustained economic growth which would result in the well-being of the people. After all, at the height of the struggle for independence, nationalist leaders such as Ghana's Kwame Nkrumah had promised the masses to 'seek ye first the political kingdom and everything else would be added unto you thereafter'. Thus, there was a huge expectation on the postcolonial leaders to make good on their promise for economic transformation and prosperity for all. As a result, the first decade after postcolonial independence saw the implementation of mainly state-led development strategies aimed at rapid industrialisation and socio-economic transformation. The outcome of these measures was what could be described as healthy or decent growth rates and increased investment. For instance, 21 out of the 29 countries for which there is data available recorded an average growth rate of over 5 per cent a year during the 1960s. In terms of external trade, of the 24 countries for which there is data, agricultural output grew by over 3 per cent while 11 of the 35 countries for which data is available recorded positive external balances. In addition, a quarter of the 34 countries for which there is data available were investing on average over 20% of their GDP, while almost half were investing more than 15% (Mills 2010). Ghana under Kwame Nkrumah epitomised the state-led development agenda of the postcolonial era resulting in increasing investments in infrastructural development and towards the transformation of the colonial economy. As suggested by Dzorgbo (2001), the poor legacy of colonialism at holistic development meant the commitment of huge financial resources by the Nkrumah government into long-term infrastructure and human development. This resulted in the construction of a number of new secondary schools, teacher training colleges and tertiary institutions such as the Kwame Nkrumah University of Science and Technology and the University Cape Coast. The Nkrumah government also implemented an ambitious industrialisation programme, which culminated in the opening up of numerous State-Owned Enterprises (SOEs). The building of the multi-million Akosombo hydro-electric dam, the Tema

Industrial Township and the Motorway, as well as the Industrial Development Corporation (IDC) was aimed at laying the grounds for the country's industrial take-off (Dzorgbo 2001).

In short, implementation of rigorous state-led policies in restructuring the postcolonial economy and investments in socio-economic development resulted in decent growth rates and socio-economic well-being in many African countries during the first decade of independence (1960-1970). However, by the mid 1970s all these gains started to erode, mainly as a result of developments in the global economy, such as rising oil prices, culminating in what has been described as either a 'crisis' or 'tragedy' in postcolonial Africa (Ake 1996; Callaghy 1987; Owusu 2007). The African "crisis" or "tragedy", according to Schraeder (2004) was manifested in "the existence of bloated, corrupt, and inefficient government bureaucracies increasingly incapable of responding to the day-to-day needs of their respective populations". It is thus evident that while external factors played a part in creating the Africa's postcolonial "crisis", domestic factors also contributed to the problem. Owusu (2007) argues that the internal political scene which had become synonymous with military coup d'états, civil strife and ethnic violence and political instability cannot be absolved from contributing to the crisis (see also Ch. 12).

In terms of economic development, the African "crisis" was characterised by a steep decline in the quality of life for an increasing large proportion of the population in several countries and a decline in the rate of growth in all the sectors of national economies. As observed by the World Bank (1986), "the average annual GDP growth rate for low-income Africa declined from 2.7% during 1970- 80 to 0.7% in 1982 and reached a record low of 0.2% in 1983". This was accompanied by a decrease in the average income per capita as well as the average investment per capita in food production; deterioration in the foreign exchange position of the national economy; stagnation of local manufacturing industry with capacity utilisation of industrial plants below economic levels and indices of industrial production reading below negative levels (Barwa 1995). The result was investment levels too low even to maintain or rehabilitate existing production capacity which inhibited the full mobilisation of national human resources in the drive for survival and development (Sawyerr 1988).

Structural adjustment as international responses to the Africa's 'crisis'

In order to deal with the crisis outlined above, African leaders through the Organisation of African Unity (OAU) launched the Lagos Plan of Action (LPA) for the Economic Development of Africa (1980-2000) and the Final Act of Lagos Plan (Maloka 2002). Considered by some of its key proponents such as Adebayo Adedeji of Nigeria as the most comprehensive response by African leaders to the continent's deepening economic crisis, the Lagos Plan of Action minced no words in heaping much blame for the continent's poor economic record on the international exploitative economic system and the inadequacies of the exogenous development strategies being recommended by donors. (See also Chapter 12, this volume). It recognised the over-dependence of African economies and aimed to restructure them on the principles of self-reliance and self-sustaining development (Ake 1996). In order to achieve this, there was the need to reposition the continent in the existing international division of labour, by changing the pattern of production from primary commodities to manufactured goods, and relying more on internal sources of raw materials, spare parts, management, finance, and technology. The pursuit of national self-reliance under the LPA aimed to encourage internally-stimulated production and discourage the reliance on imported inputs. At the same time, there was the need for African collective reliance through pooling of resources, and greater inter-African trade and cooperation to overcome Africa's vulnerability to external forces. However, the LPA and the Final Act of Lagos could not elicit the needed support from Africa's foreign development partners, especially the Bretton Woods establishment. The LPA was criticized by the World Bank for not giving enough room to the private sector and for not conceding to public sector reform to stimulate growth (Nyong'o 2002). The Bank proceeded to undertake its own assessment of Africa's development crisis with the view to devising what it thought were the appropriate strategies for accelerating growth. The publication of the famous Berg Report on *Accelerated Development in Sub-Saharan Africa: An Agenda for Action* (1981) was regarded as the high point of the clash of ideas between Africa and its foreign patrons on their perspectives of the continent's development situation (Browne and Cummings 1983). Like the LPA, the Berg Report as it was subsequently known, also analysed the continent's economies sector by sector, and concluded that two decades after independence Africa had made little progress towards development. But a significant point of departure between the two was that unlike the LPA, the Berg Report blamed Africa's development crisis on bad governance or what came to be known as 'government failures'. It was argued that the state-led development model pursued by many post-independence African countries had not delivered accelerated development. The key argument was that the public sector was bloated and that import-substitution industrialisation as well as foreign exchange control regimes in place were inimical to long-term growth. Consequently, the Report called for the rolling back of the state from involvement in economic activity and the need to give the private sector more room to operate as the engine of development. African countries were asked to open up their economies to more private sector participation and to replace government-led development model with market-led model. This new model had as its key pillars, the rule of the economy by market forces through trade and financial liberalisation, privatisation of public enterprises and removal of subsidies and any form of state intervention. The state was to confine itself to providing the enabling atmosphere for the market to flourish (Ake 1996).

These recommendations later formed the basis of the economic reform packages or the structural adjustment policies handed down to African governments by the World Bank and other donors as conditions for aid disbursement (Nyong'o 2002). African leaders were initially hesitant to embrace these recommendations. But in the face of deepening economic crisis and in order to secure the badly needed donor support, there was little room to manoeuvre (Adedeji 2002). Thus, with few options at their disposal, many African countries during the 1980s turned to the IFIs for financial assistance. In their new-found position of strength, these institutions in turn used policy-based lending to force African governments to carry out far-reaching economic reforms. According to Frances Stewart (1995), in order to reverse the imbalances and restore African countries' economies to good health, the IMF and the World Bank had to impress upon African leaders to undertake one form of adjustment or the other. Consequently, the 1980s has been described as a decade of adjustment for many countries in the region as was the case elsewhere in the developing world (Jespersen 1992; Stewart 1995). By the end of the

1980s, 36 of the 47 countries in sub-Saharan Africa had embarked on structural adjustment programmes (Bello 1994).

The measures central to most structural adjustment policies adopted by countries in sub-Saharan Africa were: reduction/removal of direct state intervention in the productive and distributive sectors of the economy, and restricting the state's responsibility to developing an institutional and policy framework conducive to the mobilisation of private enterprise and initiative. This emphasis on the disengagement of the state from economic activity was based on the conventional economic theory's claim that an optimal allocation of resources can only be obtained in a competitive, free market where prices reflect relative scarcities of the resources (Kim 2005). In other words, to get 'prices right', it was necessary to minimise the role of the intrusive African state, which was blamed for the continent's 'economic crisis'. Thus, it was believed that a lesser role for the state would give freer play to both internal and external market forces and provide the appropriate engine for a resumption of economic growth and development. Consequently, the structural adjustment policies, which came to define the economic policy terrain of many Africa countries, were introduced and broken down in two segments as follows: the first dealt with macroeconomic stabilisation measures spearheaded by the IMF and the second with structural adjustment measures directed by the World Bank. Put together in a broad framework, adjustment measures adopted by countries included the following salient mechanisms: reduction of public expenditure, increase of domestic savings, rationalisation of state owned enterprises and liberalization of the economy, export promotion and promotion of private foreign investment (Hutchful 2002). These measures, it was argued by the supporters of adjustment programs, would provide a macro-economic environment congenial to the small and informal sector entrepreneurs. In its 1989 *Long Term Perspective Study on Africa*, the World Bank projected an annual growth rate in employment in the small and micro enterprises of 6 % over the next 30 years.

In the case of Africa and other regions of the global South, the structural adjustment policies also represented a form of policy conditionality whereby loans from the World Bank, the IMF and regional development banks, as well as aid from bilateral donors and even private finance, became effectively conditional on the agreement by the recipient government to implement often far-reaching economic policy reforms. World Bank and IMF intervention through the conditionality associated with structural adjustment was thus to formally promote economic growth, but through the imposition of a particular model of development and a narrow set of economic instruments. These external interventions significantly constrained the capacity of developing countries to experiment with their own models of development. As Herbold Green (1995) argues, the structural adjustment reforms were based on the assumption that the global economic integration through free trade is the effective route to promote growth and that the benefits of growth will in the long term be beneficial to both the rich and the poor. These measures were aimed at stabilising the domestic economy to make it attractive for private-sector led development and foreign direct investment. As a result, across board, the SAPs emphasised export-led growth, privatisation and liberalisation, and the efficiency of the free market. In terms of specific policies, the SAPs generally required countries to devalue their currencies against the US dollar, dismantle import and export restrictions, balance their budgets and remove price controls and state subsidies. Justifications provided for the introduction of these policies by neoliberal theorists and commentators abound (Bhagwati, 2004; Wolf, 2004; Friedman, 2007; 2008).

Africa and the new global development agenda

The introduction of neoliberal reforms in Africa and elsewhere in the global South in the form of SAPs was aimed at addressing alleged structural weaknesses of their economies and to restore such economies to good health manifested through macro-economic stabilisation, low inflation and high growth rates. And to be sure, the implementation of SAP's austerity measures resulted in a major turnaround in the overall financial and economic performance of many adjusting African countries at least during the early years (Ake 1996). For example, when Ghana launched its economic recovery programme under the auspices of the World Bank and the IMF, the country's economy was experiencing severe difficulties, including high inflation and rising public sector debt. However, a decade after the start of Ghana's reform policies, growth in real GDP recovered, allowing gains in per capita incomes; inflation declined and the general position regarding balance of payments switched from deficits to surpluses, facilitating external payments and a build-up of exchange reserves (Tsikata 2001; Hutchful, 2002). The recovery in output growth, combined with the gradual liberalisation of exchange regime boosted the expansion in the volume of imports to an average of 10 percent a year. The rising external financing requirements have been covered in part by modestly growing inflows of private capital, including direct investment and by increase in the inflows of official external assistance. The inflows of official grants and concessional loans rose from the equivalent of less than 1% of GDP in 1983 to about 10% of GDP by 1990 (Hutchful 2002). In terms of microeconomic stability, the recovery efforts have proved to be successful in terms of short-term growth. In 1986 GDP in real terms increased by 5.3 %. Per capita real income grew by 2.6 %; agriculture output increased by 4.6%, while services expanded by 5.4% (Government of Ghana 1987). The country's infrastructure, which was almost non-existent at the onset of the adjustment programme in 1983, also witnessed an appreciable level of repair and development. In the view of Donald Rothschild (1991), the implementation of the SAPs in Ghana "reversed the decline of recent years". For his part, Gibbon (1992) rated Ghana as being among Africa's most successful countries, pointing to the appreciable macroeconomic outrun as a result of the implementation of SAPs. Notwithstanding the above initial successes in the implementation of SAPs across Africa as was the case in Ghana, by the end of the 1990s and the start of the millennium, Africa had very little to show for years of economic reform and the promised better development outcomes. In particular, structural adjustment did not result in the eradication of poverty and the growth of social well-being on the continent as envisaged at the launch of these programs in the 1980s. To the contrary, many African countries continued to accumulate more debt and were increasingly unable to provide basic social services. The debt crisis which was partly the catalyst for the introduction of the SAPs, had if anything worsened, despite the therapy prescribed by SAPs, and Third World debt rose from $785 billion in 1982 to $1.3 trillion in 1992 (Bello 1994, Chossudovsky 2003). The composition of debt also changed with a larger portion owed to the IFIs than to the private sector.

The failure of the structural adjustment policies and the neoliberal agenda in general in achieving sustained levels of poverty reduction and social development has resulted in widespread criticism and opposition both at the local and at the global level. One of the central criticisms of the SAPs was that they lacked "country ownership" and that they had been prepared without any consultation with representative institutions from the societies in which they were to be implemented (Botchwey et al. 1998; Collier 2000). According to Boafo-Arthur (1999), "the implementation of structural adjustment was without citizen participation or input in the formulation and implementation of the various policies". Thus both governments and civil society were totally excluded from the structural adjustment process. According to Stewart and Wang (2006), lack of country ownership and the widespread perception that the structural adjustment policies were donor-imposed is also blamed for the failure of these policies to deliver on economic development and poverty reduction in developing countries. In apparent response to the mounting criticisms, the international donor community led by the BWIs introduced what Soederberg (2004) calls, "a new development architecture" in the form of donor support for poverty reduction strategies. This, among other things, includes attempts to incorporate a new poverty alleviation discourse into the World Bank's Comprehensive Development Framework (CDF) and to incorporate the ideas of social development into the theory and practice of development, emphasize greater country ownership of policies by incorporating a role for civil society through the participation of NGOs in the design and implementation of poverty reduction policies (Owusu 2006. But see Chapter 10, this volume). This opening up of space in the development discourse also coincides with the movement towards what Stiglitz (1998; 2002) has called, the 'post-Washington consensus". As part of this new consensus, the international donor community led by the IMF and the World Bank in the mid-1990s launched an initiative to provide special debt relief from public creditors to more than 40 'Highly Indebted Poor Countries' (HIPCs).

In 1999, this initiative was further refined and widened in what has been hailed as a new approach to development co-operation and a move towards an 'inclusive neo-liberalism (Graig 2006). As one of the conditions of this 'new' development architecture, aid recipient countries were expected to produce a Poverty Reduction Strategy Paper (PRSP), which would make clear how they would pursue the twin goals of sustainable growth and poverty reduction. The PRSP was to be results-oriented, comprehensive in scope and partnership-oriented, and involve long-term planning. It was to be produced in an open and participatory manner, involving civil society in the process (IMF 2004). This new emphasis on country ownership through country-wide participation and the assumptions about the positive effects of participation were hailed as representing a paradigm shift from the ineffective donor-led, conditionality-driven aid regime of SAPs to a system that puts the recipient country in the driving seat (World Bank and the IMF 1999). Also, as part of the new aid reform agenda, the Enhanced Structural Adjustment Facility (ESAF) which had served as a medium for financing the structural adjustment programmes was replaced by the Poverty Reduction and Growth Facility (PRGF) (Pender 2001). The 'new' rediscovery of poverty is also evident in a seeming convergence between the United Nations system and the BWIs represented by the introduction of the Millennium Development Goals (MDGs) in 2000 with specific targets towards poverty reduction. Apart from this new multilateral approach, individual countries such as the United States have also rolled out new bilateral aid programmes such as the Millennium Challenge Account (MCA). Introduced in 2002, the MCA aimed at increasing the US's Overseas Development Assistance by $ 5billion a year within five years. As of August 2012, a total of 21 African countries including Benin, Cape Verde, Ghana, Kenya, Liberia, Mali, Rwanda, Tanzania and Uganda had benefited from the MCA, having gone through a rigorous selection criteria which included the following: ruling justly; investing in people; and economic freedom (see http://www.mcc.gov/pages/countries). Put together, new multilateral and bilateral aid packages such as HIPC, PRSP, and MCA focusing on strict selection criteria represent a shift towards 'selectivity' in international development cooperation. This new strategy of bilateral and multilateral development cooperation emphasizing 'good govern-ance' is traced to the work of leading World Bank economists Craig Burnside and David Dollar (1998), who argued that aid only works in countries pursuing sound economic policies. The World Bank's 1998 report *Assessing Aid* concluded that a "good policy environment" is an essen-tial precondition for effective development assistance. The report claimed that if a poor country has high trade barriers, a misaligned exchange rate, unstable prices and weak public finances, it is infertile soil for economic growth, regardless of the amount of aid poured into that coun-try. It is contended that aid does work better in countries with honest governments and sound policies. However, given the social challenges posed by the implementation of these policies for countries in Africa and the unwillingness of rich countries to transform the global economy and to embrace poor countries' demand for fair trade, the new international aid and development agenda may not necessarily translate into poverty reduction and social development in Africa and other regions of the global South. Instead, this agenda could become an attempt by the IFIs and powerful countries like the US to create the conditions for capital and as a safeguard against the proliferation of terrorist groups that might pose security threats to Western interests (We-ber 2004). Thus, taken together, the PRSPs and the MCA can be said to represent not only the reinvention of the neoliberal agenda but also, the reproduction of the developing world in a particular way- heavily indebted and poor; undemocratic, or as the 'other' of the West. Both the PRSPs and the MCA embody the donor-imposed, conditionality laden framework of SAPs and are therefore a perpetuation of neo-liberal capitalist agenda masked in the language of pro-poor or what some analysts call, 'structural adjustment in the name of the poor' (Mawdsley 2007; Malaluan and Guttal 2002).

From the foregoing, it could be surmised that the new international development architec-ture in many ways represents a continuity of ways in which 'development' knowledge and its propagation have been undertaken over the years through the hegemonic practices of dominant actors within the global system. The actors, ranging from Western political leaders to institu-tions of global economic governance by virtue of their enormous wealth and domination over institutions of global governance, are responsible for development knowledge construction. The knowledge which they construct is however biased and shaped by their prejudices and from the standpoint of superiority (see also Ch. 10 in this volume).

Rethinking African development in the new millennium

As noted above, since the beginning of 1980s, the World Bank and the International Monetary Fund have through the structural adjustment policies influenced development policy choices in many African countries. But as also noted, by the end of the 1990s, against the background of increasing opposition and criticism, the international financial institutions signalled a move away from policy conditionality towards country ownership and home-grown development strategies with a focus on poverty reduction and social development. This discursive shift towards what is described as a Post-Washington Consensus or a new global development architecture (see Stiglitz 1998, 2002; Soederberg 2004) also coincided with the broader global turn towards the mainstreaming of social development and poverty reduction in international development cooperation in the form of the United Nations Millennium Development Goals (MDGs). In particular, the MDGs call for a new partnership between richer and poorer countries towards the attainment of agreed-upon development targets, and a refocus of the international development agenda from the earlier emphasis on the narrower indicator of economic growth to investments in social policy and poverty eradication (UNDP 2003: 27). Within the African context, this global consensus towards social development was represented in the introduction of a new continental development blue-print in the form of the New Partnership for Economic Development (NEPAD) (see also Ch. 12). Introduced in 2001 as a part of a broader institutional transformation of the Organization of African Unity (OAU) to the African Union (AU), and seen as an overarching policy framework and vision for Africa's economic and political renaissance, the NEPAD instrument includes four primary objectives: poverty eradication, promotion of sustainable growth and development, increasing Africa's integration into the world economy and the empowerment of women through building partnerships at country, regional and global levels (Adesina et al., 2005). What does this mean for Africa's development? What do the changing trends in global development policy and the changing focus of global development cooperation mean for Africa's development? More importantly, what is the state of African economies at the beginning of the second decade into the new millennium? This segment of the chapter seeks to answer these questions and to offer analysis of economic development outcomes and prospects.

Africa's overall economic performance during the first decade of the twenty-first century and since the introduction of new global development policies including the initiation of the NEPAD development blue-print has provided a mixed-bag of results. In particular, the implementation of governance-related reform policies has resulted in growing investor confidence and the growth in the continent's share of global foreign direct investment. For instance after lagging behind all other developing regions since the 1970s, GDP growth rates rose from the middle of the 1990s to exceed population growth. As a result during the decade of the 2000s, investor interest in Africa rose astronomically in different sectors. There has also been the entry on to the African investment terrain of new players mainly from emerging economies such as China, India and Brazil. The implementation of new aid reform and debt relief policies by global financial institutions and donor countries also enabled many African countries to improve upon their sovereign ratings and to once again access private debt markets. Consequently, during the period 2000-06, sub-Saharan African economic growth output rose to 4.7 per cent from a poor 2.5 per cent during the period 1990-2000 (World Bank 2008).

If the 1970s-1980s were described as 'Africa's lost decade', then the first decade of the 21st century could be accurately described as 'Africa's decade of progress.' This turn-around in Africa's economic fortunes was best captured by *The Economist* magazine in its recent analysis of the continent's sustained economic growth rate. It shows that between 2000 and 2010, six of the ten fastest economies worldwide were African (*Economist*, 2011). These positive developments, with the heading, 'Africa Rising' provide a sharp contrast to a 2000 article by the same paper which provided a rather pessimistic and bleak outlook on the continent at the dawn of the new millennium. At the time, Africa was seen as synonymous with deadly ethnic conflicts, natural disasters, famine, corrupt and authoritarian political leadership and aid-dependent economies. After its review and analysis of the litany of the continent's ailments and challenges at the beginning of the new millennium, the *Economist* posed the question, 'Can Africa Change?'(*Economist*, 2000).

A decade later, the verdict on Africa's development outlook and prospects need to be interrogated within the context of key developments both within the continent and the broader global political economy. Within the continent, the introduction of the New Partnership for African Development (NEPAD) with its clear focus on good political, economic and corporate governance, is seen as one of the boldest attempts yet by African leaders to find African solutions to African problems. As noted earlier, Africa's overall economic performance since the introduction of structural adjustment policies in the 1980s could not be said to be very encouraging. It was within this context that NEPAD was conceived by African leaders with the blessing of Western donors as Africa's response to the growing prioritisation of ideas of good economic and political governance as prerequisites for development. There have been various interpretations of the emergence of NEPAD. One such interpretation is the one offered by critical scholars such as Francis Owusu and Ian Taylor (2006). According to these scholars, the NEPAD initiative with its emphasis on 'partnership' between African governments and their Western donors as well as the promotion of the ideals of good governance, trade and security, represents a convergence of ideas between African leaders and the West as far as postcolonial development policy is concerned. Indeed, according to Owusu (2003, 2006), NEPAD represents a shift or the death of the dependency paradigm of early postcolonial African leaders resulting in their embrace of pragmatic neo-liberalism. While there is some merit in this perspective, I would add that the NEPAD agenda with its emphasis on partnership, good governance and trade, needs to be understood within the context of the discursive shift which occurred towards the end of the 1990s and was occasioned by a number of significant events including the Asian financial crisis, the end of the Cold War, the failure of structural adjustment policies and the processes of globalization. In particular, under the NEPAD blue-print is the emphasis on a Peer Review Mechanism (PRM) by which African leaders are expected to voluntarily submit themselves to their peers for performance evaluation (see Chapter 12, this volume). This, it is suggested, fits perfectly into a new cluster of mechanisms being marshalled by donors to integrate developing countries' economies into the global economic system with emphasis on trade liberalisation and economic integration, adopting standardised governance practices, and the rule of law.

A key dimension of Africa's recent political economy is the continent's growing integration into the global economy. A clear example of this development is in the area of information and communication technologies (ICTs). For instance, liberalisation of Africa's telecommunications sector has enabled new connections with individuals, communities, markets and states both locally and globally. This has fostered an increasing integration of Africa with the global economy. From a low figure of just one-tenth of the global average in terms of Africa's telephone connectivity in the early 1990s, by 2011, Africa accounts for half of the total global figure, even though the global figure itself had increased fourfold to 70 connections per 100 people. The number of subscribers on the continent grew almost 20 percent each year between 2006-11 (Mills and Herbst 2011).

From the foregoing, it is clear that Africa's economic outlook at the beginning of the second decade of the 21st century appears positive with signs that the continent may have put behind it some of the bad practices of the past few decades, particularly in the form of self-inflicted internal challenges. These challenges, which have included political instability, ethnic conflicts and weak institutions, have had negative impacts and implications for the continent's economic development and policy outcomes over the years. Political and governance reform policies implemented since the early 1990s and the introduction of a new continental development blueprint in the form of NEPAD with a good governance agenda have ensured that many African countries are able to create the enabling environment for economic growth and prosperity. The emergence of new global economic powers such as China, India and Brazil has also boosted Africa's economic growth prospects. Recent offshore oil discoveries in a growing number of African countries, together with the continent's already rich natural resource base continue to make the region the preferred investment destination for companies from both the traditional or established powers as well as from the emerging powers.

In particular, the emergence of China as a dominant force within the global economy could have some implications for Africa's economic prospects. Already, China has through a series of high level bilateral and multilateral initiatives sought to project itself as an ally or sympathetic to Africa's developmental aspirations. These initiatives have included China's promise to support debt cancellation in favour of African countries. Over the past few years, China has cancelled the bilateral debt of a number of African countries totalling about $1.27 billion. Also, in 2002, $ 1.8 billion or about 44% of total Chinese global development assistance went to Africa, while Chinese bilateral trade with Africa has grown by 430% between 1989 and 1997, reaching $24bn in 2004 (Tull 2010). The creation of the Forum on China-Africa Cooperation in 2000, as well as the inauguration of the Chinese-African Chamber of Commerce in 2005 have also signalled the deepening of ties between China and Africa, resulting in growing Chinese investments in key sectors of African economies, including mining, energy, oil and gas as well as infrastructural development (Taylor 2004).

It is hoped that Africa will build on current success stories in the overall political economic outlook, particularly in the form of political stability, good governance and sustained economic growth. Nevertheless, many of the challenges remain. Importantly, as noted by Mills and Herbst (2011), "Africa remains an exceedingly poor continent, with an annual per capita income level of approximately US$ 600". Mills and Herbst have also indicated that the key challenge for the continent is to improve upon economic growth rates and to ensure that these growth rates translate into job creation and investments in social services. This is particularly important given the fragility of African states, most of which are still emerging from prolonged ethnic conflicts and civil wars. As a continent with huge numbers of unemployed youth, there is an urgent need to expand upon skills training and employment opportunities. In addition, in many African countries, development issues and outcomes continue to be gendered, resulting in the feminisation of poverty (Adu-Kofi 1998; Tsikata 1995). Many African countries continue to support and encourage cultural practices which tend to discriminate against women and undermine their ability to access educational and employment opportunities (see also Chapter 4, this volume). This needs to change through cultural and policy reform initiatives in order to ensure that women, who constitute over 50% of Africa's population, are part of the continent's economic development processes in a more positive way. The failure of past structural adjustment policies to positively impact Africa's long-term development prospects and the ongoing crisis faced by the neoliberal model call for a rethinking of Africa's long term development policy options and choices. The failure of the SAPs to design country-specific solutions and the fact that the new poverty reduction strategy framework continues to be framed and implemented in the same neoliberal one-size-fits all model suggest that African countries need to explore other options if the mistakes and failures of the past few decades are to be avoided. It is in this vein that the criticisms against the NEPAD initiative, especially in regard to its perceived neoliberal focus and over-dependence on donor support, need to be taken seriously. The fact that African countries continue to depend on external sources, particularly in the form of aid, to support what is supposed to be the continent's flagship development agenda, is very worrying indeed. As pointed out by Dambisa Moyo in *Dead Aid* (2009), the aid-anchored development paradigm is flawed and cannot be relied upon as the basis for Africa's development. African countries need to explore internal sources to finance their development budgets and should endeavour to systematically wean themselves off aid dependence. This will undoubtedly call for the transformation of African economies from the current largely mineral resource and primary agriculture-based, to value-addition and manufacturing. With Africa's huge wealth in mineral and other natural resources and continuing global interest in these resources, there is no reason why African countries cannot trade themselves out of poverty, instead of relying on the current donor-driven and aid-induced development paradigm. Deepening good governance and overcoming corruption can also free up resources for investment in social services. Many African countries continue to grapple with the cancer of massive corruption in the public sector, with recent estimates indicating that not less than $148 billion are lost across the continent annually, due to corruption and mismanagement (De Maria 2008). This too calls for devising an effective and robust approach in dealing with the new players on Africa's geopolitical space, most notably emerging powers such as China, India and Brazil. In particular, the tendency to see these new players as allies and to give them unrestricted access to the continent's resource sectors should give way to developing strategies that enable African countries to engage these new players as true development partners and in making sure that the continent gets true value in terms of investments undertaken by these countries. At the moment these new players, particularly China, enjoy a high degree of support in terms of favourable investment deals across the continent from investments in Angola's oil and energy sectors, to Zambia's copper sector, and Ghana's emerging oil and gas sectors. Chinese companies have also been involved in building infrastructural facilities across the continent ranging from road construction to sports stadia. While there is no doubt about the development implications of these investments and Chinese activities on Africa's economies, there have been instances where concerns have been raised either in regard to the maltreatment of African employees working for Chinese companies or the tendency of these companies to bring their own workers from outside the continent, thereby making it impossible for African workers to access employment opportunities at these companies. Some have argued that African governments are giving China and Chinese companies favourable investment terms not only because of huge and unconditional bilateral loans that China offers African governments, but also because of China's unwillingness to interfere in the internal politics of African countries, including commenting on human rights abuses (Taylor 2004; Alden 2007). While such claims may have some merit, especially given the fierce competition between Africa's traditional development partners from Europe and North America on the one hand and the emerging partners such as China on the other hand over access to Africa's resources, the main consideration for African leaders should be what is in the continent's long-term economic and developmental interests. Thus, the issues of development policy ownership and the need to forge true development partnerships are crucial if Africa is to overcome its current dependence on external forces for its development programmes. Finally, while African countries have successfully manoeuvred the delicate process of political reform as the basis for economic growth, many of the continent's new democracies remain a work in progress. If the continent is to build upon recent modest achievements in economic growth and growing investor confidence, then these democracies need to be deepened and attention paid to building credible and robust democratic institutions. As the recent political uprisings in North Africa and the rest of the Arab world (otherwise known as the Arab Spring), have shown, the days of taking citizens' needs and aspirations for granted are over. Political reform and open societies where people can freely express their views and exercise their right to choose their leaders are the surest guarantees for political stability and the peaceful environment required for any meaningful economic development. In other words, while African countries strive to achieve and sustain high levels of economic growth, issues of voice and representation need to be accorded the same attention. The role of continental bodies such as the African Union and regional economic blocs such as ECOWAS and SADC are crucially important in making sure that constitutional rule and democratic governance remain protected and respected across the continent. The human and financial costs of war and conflict are staggering, as they also derail the continent's development agenda, hence the need to continue to strengthen the pillars of good governance and the culture of democracy as the basis for the continent's economic development and prosperity.

Summary and Conclusion

This chapter sought to provide a broad and critical overview of development policy-making and policy outcomes in postcolonial Africa. It took as a point of departure, the continent's postcolonial 'development crisis' in order to tease out key challenges and debates which have shaped and influenced development policy choices and outcomes in the postcolonial era. The chapter then explored the impacts and implications of the introduction of the World Bank and IMF-sponsored structural adjustment policies for the continent's development since the early 1980s. Tracing the evolution, implementation and the outcomes of these policies, the chapter then shifted to the new poverty reduction-focused development architecture which has come to replace the SAPs since the late 1990s. It also commented on the emergence of the New Partnership for African Development (NEPAD) with its goal of good governance and partnership by linking it to the discursive shifts, debates and developments occurring within the broader global political economy at the turn of the last century. The chapter also discussed and analyzed Africa's economic outlook and development prospects at the beginning of the new millennium. In particular, the chapter explored the implications of key changes within the global economy including the processes of globalisation and integration and the emergence of new global powers for Africa's development prospects. Finally, the chapter takes stock of Africa's performance on key indicators such as job creation, gender equality and democratic governance and concluded that while there has been modest success during the past few years, more needs to be done in deepening and expanding the frontiers of voice and representation as well as in the search of African-led development trajectory that relies more on mobilisation of internal resources and less on aid and externally-guided development policies.

Review Questions

1. What were the differences between state-led development strategies implemented during the first decade of Africa's post-independence era (1960-1970) on one hand and structural adjustment policies implemented from the decade of 1980s-1990s on the other?

2. How can we explain the shift from structural adjustment policies to poverty reduction strategies?

3. The statement, "African solutions to African problems" has been used to describe and justify the introduction of the New Partnership for African Development (NEPAD). Do you agree?

4. What are the impacts and implications of the process of globalization as well as the rise of new powers such as China, for Africa's development?

References

Arrighi, G. 2002 "The African Crisis". *New Left Review* 15 (May-June) (Accessed at: http://www.newleftreview.org/?view=2387).

Adedeji, A. 2002 "From the Lagos Plan of Action to the New Partnership[for African Development and from the Final Act of Lagos to the Constitutive Act: Wither Africa?" Keynote address at the African Forum for Envisioning Africa, held in Nairobi, Kenya, 26 – 29 April 2002.

Adesina, J. 2007 "Development and the Challenge of Poverty", In J. Adesina et. al (eds.) *Africa and Development: Challenges in the New Millennium* Dakar, CODESRIA.

Adu-Kofi, L. 1998 "The Impact of the International Monetary Fund and the World Bank Structural Adjustment Programs on Sub-Saharan African Women". *New England Journal of International Law & Policy* 4:73-108.

Ahluwala, P. 2001 *Politics and Post-colonial Theory: African Inflection* New York: Routledge.

Ake, C. 1996 *Democracy and Development in Africa*. The Brookings Institution, Washington D.C.

Alden, C. 2007 *China in Africa*. Cape Town: Zed Books.

Arrighi, G. 2002 "The African Crisis", *New Left Review*. 15 (May-June) (Accessed at: http://www.newleftreview.org/?view=2387).

Bhagwati, J. 2000 *The wind of the hundred days: how Washington mismanaged globalization*. Cambridge, Mass.: MIT Press.

Chapter 13

Bhagwati, J. 2004 *In Defense of Globalization*. New York and Oxford: Oxford University Press.

Boafo-Arthur, K. 1999 "Ghana: Structural Adjustment, Democratization and the Politics of Continuity". *African Studies Review* 42 (2): 41-72

Browne, R. and R. Cummings 1983 *The Lagos Plan of Action Versus the Berg Report*. Richmond, VA, Brunswick Corporation.

Cheru, F. 2006 "Building and Supporting PRSPs in Africa: what has worked well so far? What needs changing?" *Third World Quarterly* 27 (2): 355-376.

Chossudovsky, M. 1998 *The Globalization of Poverty: Impacts of IMF and World Bank Reform*. London/New Jersey, Zed Books,.

De Maria, W. 2008. Cross Cultural Trespass: Assessing African Anti-corruption Capacity" *International Journal of Cross Cultural Management*. Vol 8(3): 317-341

Dzorgbo, D. 2001 *Ghana in Search of Development: The Challenge of Governance, Economic Management and Institution Building*. England, Ashgate Publishing Ltd.

Economist Magazine. 2000 "The Heart of the Matter" (May 2000)

Economist Magazine. 2011 "African Rising" (December 2011)

Frimpong-Ansah, J. 1991 *The Vampire State in Africa: The Political Economy of Decline in Ghana*. London, James Curry

Gibbon, P. 1992 "Structural Adjustment and the Pressure Toward Multipartyism in Sub-Saharan Africa" In P. Gibbon et al., (eds). *Authoritarianism, Democracy and Adjustment: The Politics of Economy Reforms in Africa*. Uppsala, Scandinavian Institute of African Studies.

Gould, J 2005 *The New Conditionality: the politics of poverty reduction strategies*. London/New York, Zed Books.

Government of Ghana 1987 *Budget Statement*. Tema, State Publishing Corporation

Green, R. 1998 "A Cloth Untrue: The Evolution of Structural Adjustment in Sub-Saharan Africa. *Journal of International Affairs* 52 (1): 207-234.

Grosh, B. 1994 'Through the Structural Adjustment Minefield: Politics in an Era of Economic Liberalization' In J. Widner, (ed.) *Economic Change and Political Liberalization in Sub-Saharan Africa*. Baltimore, John Hopkins University Press.

Hutchful, E. 2002 *Ghana's Adjustment Experience: The Paradox of Reform*. Geneva, United Nations Research Institute for Social Development.

Kim, K. 2005 "Development crisis in Sub-Saharan Africa: globalization, adjustment and the roles of international institutions" In John-ren and D. Sapsford (eds.) *Global Development and Poverty Reduction*. Cheltenham, UK , Northampton/MA, Edward Elgar.

Leys, C. 1994 'Confronting the African Tragedy' *New Left Review* I (204): 33–47.

Maloka, E.(ed) 2002 *Africa's Development Thinking Since Independence: A Reader*. Pretoria, Africa Institute of South Africa,

Mills, G.2010 *Why Africa is poor: and what Africans can do about it*. Johannesnburg, Penguin Books

Mills , G. and J. Herbst. 2011 *Africa's Third Liberation*. Johannes-burg, Penguin Books

Moyo, D. 2009 *Dead Aid*. Farrar. Straus and Giroux

Owusu,F. 2006" Discourses on Development:From Dependency to Neoliberalism". In M. Smith (ed) *Beyond the 'African Tragedy':Discourses on Development and the Global Economy*. Burlington/Hampshire: Ashgate.

Owusu, F. 2003 "Pragmatism and the Global Shift from Dependency to Neoliberalism: The World Bank and Development Policy in Africa" *World Development* 31 (10): 1655-1672.

Pender, J. 2001 "From Structural Adjustment to Comprehensive Development Framework: Conditionality Transformed?" *Third World Quarterly* 22 (3): 397-411.

Rothchild, D. 1991 *Ghana: The Political Economy of Recovery*. Boulder, Col., Lynne Rienner.

Schraeder, P. 2004 *African politics and society: a mosaic in transformation*. Belmont, CA, Thomson/Wadsworth

Soederberg, S. 2004 *The Politics of the New International Financial Architecture: Reimposing Neoliberal Domination in the Global South*. London and New York, Zed Books.

Stewart, F. and M. Wang 2006 "Do PRSPs empower poor countries and disempower the World Bank, or is it the other way round?" In G. Ranis et al *Globalization and the Nation State: The impact of the IMF and the World Bank*. London and New York, Routledge.

Stiglitz, J. 1998 "More Instruments and Broader Goals: Moving Toward the Post-Washington Consensus" WIDER Annual Lectures. http://www.wider.unu.edu/publications/annual-lectures/annual-lecture-1998.pdf.

Stiglitz, J. 2002 *Globalization and its Discontents*. New York. W. W. Norton & Co, Taylor, I. 2006 "When 'Good Economics' Does Not Make Good Sense" in M. Smith (ed) *Beyond the 'African Tragedy': Discourses on Development and the Global Economy*. Burlington/Hampshire, ashgate

Taylor, I. 2004 "The 'all-weather friend'? Sino-African in the twenty-first century" In I.Taylor et. al. *Africa in International Politics: External Involvement on the Continent*. New York: Routledge.

Tsikata Y. 2001 "Aid and Reform in Ghana" In Devarajan, Dollar, Holmgren (eds) *Aid & Reform in Africa* .World Bank, Washington D.C.

Tsikata, D. 1995 "Effects of Structural Adjustment on Women and the Poor", *Third World Resurgence* No. 61/62, http://www.twnside.org/souths/twn/women.htm

Tull, D. "China's Engagement in Africa: Scope, Significance, and Consequences" in *Africa in World Politics: The African State System in Flux*. J.W. Haberson and D. Rothschild (eds.), 4th edition, 39–71 (Boulder: Westview, 2009).

World Bank and IMF, 1999 *Building Poverty Reduction Strategies in Developing Countries*. www.poverty.worldbank.org/files/building_english.pdf

Wolf, M. 2004 *Why Globalization Works*. New Haven, Yale University Press.

Suggested Readings

Abrahamsen, R. 2004b "Review Essay: Poverty Reduction or Adjustment by Another Name?" *Review of African Political Economy* 99:184-187.

Moss, T. 2011 *African Development: Making Sense of the Issues and Actors*. Boulder, Co. Lynne Rienner

Kempe R. 2002. "From crisis to renewal: towards the successful implementation of the New Partnership for Africa's Development," *African Affairs* 101 no. 404

Sandbrook, R. 1985. *The Politics of Africa's Economic Stagnation*. Cambridge: Cambridge University Press, 1985.

Shaw, T. Et. al. 2006 "Political Economies of Africa(s) at the Start of the Twenty-first Century". In R. Stubbs and G. Underhill (eds.), *Political Economy and the Changing Global Order*. (Third Edition) Oxford: Oxford University Press.

Thomas, C. 2004. 'The international financial institutions' relations with Africa: Insights from the issue of representation and voice' in *Africa in International Politics: External involvement on the continent*. I. Taylor and P. Williams,(eds.). London & New York: Routledge.

SECTION 4: HEALTH, ENVIRONMENT, SCIENCE & TECHNOLOGY

CHAPTER 14

IN SEARCH OF HEALTH AND WELL-BEING IN AFRICA
Kojo Senah

> The path to God is the path to health
> (A Swahili wise saying)
> The thief does not recover when sick
> (A Togolese Ewe wise saying)

Introduction

For people all over the world, maintaining good health and promoting well-being is an obsession, if not a passion. This is because health has both intrinsic and instrumental value: it is desired for its own sake and perhaps more importantly, it is the wheel around which the development of societies revolves. From another perspective, health is also a metaphor for individual and communal harmony. However, all societies recognise the frailness of the human condition characterized by pain, illness, injury, accidents and misery. These must, therefore, be handled and explained pragmatically and philosophically in accordance with a society's level of technological development, historical experiences and worldview. Thus, beginning with early human efforts to cure headache by rubbing sick people's head against a rock, today humankind has evolved elaborate explanatory models and sophisticated techniques for dealing with threats to health and well–being. In spite of this, people continuously experience ill health and 'disease' as a result of individual or collective action or inaction. Individuals and societies need to explain and handle these phenomena in order to make sense of their social existence.

In a book containing 1,915 proverbs and wise sayings derived from 41 African countries, Korem and Abissath (2004) have captured the two wise sayings (above) that open this chapter. The relevance of these sayings may be found not only in their broad definition of health, but also and perhaps more importantly, in the nexus they establish in the African context between morality and philosophy on one hand and health on the other. This nexus is the core of this chapter.

Cross-cultural anthropological studies have shown that people all over the world have various ways of perceiving, defining, treating and preventing illness. These differences exist because all human beings are embedded in varying natural settings from which they gain information and techniques for coping with the harsh conditions of the environment. (see also Chs. 6 and 7).

In this chapter, I discuss the social reproduction of health and well-being within the context of Africa. In doing this, I do not pretend to cover the entire ethnography of African societies. However, since the health institution exists in every African society, *mutatis mutandis,* it is most likely that parallels of the examples taken from some African societies will be found, at least in spirit, in many other African societies. Another important issue to consider in this regard is that in focusing on 'the African' there is the danger of essentialism and the suggestion of homogeneity, coherence and timelessness. Indeed, many parts of Africa have varying experiences of the pre-colonial, colonial and the post-colonial situations. These experiences have obviously influenced the ways Africans of different countries perceive their cosmology. This notwithstanding, in a discussion such as this, a certain degree of generalization is necessary in order to articulate the core issues.

Concepts of Health and Well-being

Given the differences in human cultures and social situations, it is to be expected that differences will exist in what constitutes 'health" or "well–being." Perhaps, to the ordinary person, health has a specific meaning, invariably the absence of disease or disease or simply what health practitioners are preoccupied with. However, a careful reading of the literature on health reveals a plethora of meanings which people of various societies and civilisations have attached to the concept. Thus, in order to situate the discussion, it is important that we examine some of these varying meanings of health.

Therapeutic systems of whatever hue are invariably underpinned by ideas prevailing in the socio-economic and cultural formations which harbour them. These systems may be identified initially by implicit and explicit criteria of health to which they aspire and which they intend to cultivate in individuals and communities. For example, evaluative criteria of health are useful for the same reason in development and health policy planning. Therefore, it is useful to identify several common sets of health concepts as a basis for the study of therapeutics. The Wellness Movement in Europe and North America, for example, has recently popularised this approach to the analysis and evaluation of therapeutics. However, this concept has its basis in the philosophy of medicine and science as well as in the history of medicine and to some extent, in the anthropology of medicine. A quick survey of the meanings of health reveals the following:

Health as the absence of disease

The history of this perspective is grounded in classical antiquity of Western medicine. However, its primacy emerged in the nineteenth century following important discoveries by Louis Pasteur and Robert Koch. With Pasteur's discovery of microbes through the lens of the microscope in 1852, followed by Koch's discovery of the tubercle and diphtheria bacilli in 1859, diseases gained tunnel-vision in medical practice: they were perceived as the products of unseen micro-organisms inhabiting or 'invading' the body. These gave primacy to the *germ theory* of disease causation and the related techniques for the elimination or reduction of infectious and parasitic disease that decimated early human populations – small pox, malaria, sexually-transmitted diseases (especially, gonorrhoea and syphilis), yaws, typhus, cholera, measles, trypanosomiasis, and leprosy, to mention but a few. In Africa in particular, this focus on the pathology of diseases has been most beneficial. However, in a way, the germ theory has proven problematic in certain therapeutic encounters: it lends credence to the erroneous view that there are 'magic bullets' or quick fix medical technological solutions to diseases. In the African context, the emphasis on pharmaceuticals and curative medicine as the basis of medical practice or health care delivery has been most inappropriate. Consequently, public health has not been given the needed attention while increasingly, the African epidemiological pattern points to the need to tackle the poor environment and the socio-economic conditions of the people in order to contain the spread of diseases.

Health care as the domain of doctors

A variant of this view is that health is what doctors do. Clearly, this view derives its stereotypic basis from the Euro-American experience where most people leave their health problems to the doctor who is regarded as the engineer to patch up mal-functioning body machines. In modern-day Africa, this view is so strong among health policy makers that almost invariably, the greater portion of the national health budget is devoted to the maintenance of hospitals and the training of doctors and other medical and paramedical staff instead of focusing on preventive health or primary health care.

Health as functional normality

A number of philosophers of medical science have proposed this counter perspective in an attempt to overcome some of the disadvantages of the above definitions of health. In statistical terms, 'normality' refers to a measurable average. However, with regard to health, the concept has proven difficult to operationalise in a measurable and manageable way. In addition, it may be argued that what is normal is not always healthful. Thus, taken from the point of view of statistics, the norm may include, say high levels of malaria or schistosomiasis. Although the situation may also be seen by members of the community as normal even if manageable, this should not be a justification for inaction on the part of health authorities. Consequently, according to some scholars, the health norm must be seen in terms of cohorts or groups defined by specific socio-demographic characteristics such as sex, age and perhaps educational and occupational background. In this way, the functional normality of the elderly would include some disabilities such as senile dementia, rheumatoid arthritis and cardiovascular diseases; that of children would include some childhood diseases such as acute respiratory infection, diarrhoea and helminthic infections; that of work-related roles would include certain unique occupational and physiological hazards such as the musculo-skeletal distortion associated with underground miners or psychological stress relating to factory work. Some philosophers have also raised the issue of goals in connection with functional normality. Thus, goal-oriented health programmes such as malaria and HIV and AIDS education seek to achieve an end product – the elimination of or a reduction in the incidence and prevalence of these conditions. Without a degree of goal-orientation, most health policies and programmes would be impossible to carry out.

Health as adaptive strategy

This orientation is based on the ecological perspective, which argues that human beings ultimately – often biologically – adapt to their environment in such a way as to strike a balance between offensive pathogens and the human host. In this way, human beings develop a high threshold for certain kinds of offensive micro-organisms without falling sick. This perspective has seen currency in many of the studies on African health and health care and many studies have benefited from this perspective. A typical example of this is the current understanding of human defences against malaria in West Africa. However, if this perspective is stretched to its logical limits, the same problem arises here: developing a high threshold for malaria as in the case of West Africans is not healthy. Consequently, not all that is adaptive is healthful.

Positive Health and Health Utopia

Some scholars have proposed this view in order to recognize the value–charged goals of health intervention programmes. For instance, the call by the World Health Organisation (WHO) for "Health For All By The Year 2000" was made in this light. Again, the WHO's definition of health as the state of complete physical, mental and social well–being, in a related way, also invokes an utopian image of perfection. These approaches to health are recognized to be value-related, goal-oriented but often problematic; they are at best advocacy stances. As will be discussed shortly, many indigenous African definitions of health would find a perfect fit here, with overriding notions as 'balance,' 'harmony,' or 'morality' propagated by therapeutic acts and attitudes that address the quality of life in the community.

Social Reproduction as Health

This essentially Marxist persuasion refers to the perpetuation of a particular social order in terms of the quality and quantity of health indications. In Marxian terminology, the notion of social reproduction is used exclusively to refer to the reproduction of labour in the interest of the bourgeoisie who control the means of production and the state apparatus. Ill health is thus the result of the way society organizes its production relations. Thus, as Engel argues (see Samson, 1999) the state commits murder if thousands of workers are deprived of the necessities of life or if they are forced into a situation in which it is impossible for them to survive. In a similar view, some Marxists argue that the continued general desire for large families in Africa—a health risk for women, especially— is a measure of the economic peripheralization of Africa in the globalised capitalist economy (see also Ch. 2). Within this context, it is argued that the only rational reaction of African parents is to increase offspring to maximise their opportunities in what remains of a peasant or horticultural economy while at the same time hedging their bets for a stake in the very precarious and exploitative labour market where they are increasingly driven by land loss, disadvantageous market conditions and inflation. In this regard, diseases are state-inflicted, they argue.

In sum, each of these perspectives examines the concept of health and well-being from a particular perspective. This is understandable, given the varied meanings attached to the concepts. In spite of these variations and the shortcomings of each of the perspectives, together they provide a broad framework within which to discuss the core issues of this chapter. In the next segment we shall examine how the concepts of health and well–being play out in the African context.

Anthropology and African Therapeutics

To a large extent, ethnographic works on health and healing practices in Africa are very respectable. Often discussed within the context of religion, witchcraft and magic, African therapeutic modes attracted considerable attention for two main reasons: first, in the early period, European traders, missionaries, explorers and colonial administrators, often cast in the mould of arm-chair anthropologists, provided ethnocentric accounts of various African religious/health practices in order to showcase the perceived high degree of 'primitivism' of Africans and thereby to justify the need for European support to evangelise or 'civilise' Africa (see Ch. 8). In the case of missionaries, their aim was to destroy or 'undo' native societies in order to create a counter-culture, an entirely new social structure based on the European mode. Miller (1994: 131-132) captured this point more forcefully when he observed thus:

> Missionaries sent to Africa typically believed that their special calling was to guide the natives to salvation by teaching them a way of living radically different from what they had previously known. The new life would be centered on the villages, churches and schools attached to the Mission's stations and outstations. Converts were required to accept European names, dress, customs and family forms and to assume positions in their new lives that were subordinate to the missionaries in the Christian community.

Consequently, missionaries dispatched volumes of ethnocentric ethnographic accounts to their respective European mission headquarters. Although some of their accounts may sound ludicrous today, they are nonetheless worth re-stating if only to demonstrate the degree of European ethnocentrism with regard to cultures of Africa and those of other non-Western societies. For instance, in 1851 Stanger, a German missionary, wrote about the Krobo in the Eastern Region of Ghana thus:

> They worship the fetish like all Negroes in this area. The only remarkable thing about them is that on this mountain (Krobo Mountain) there are also a number of cheap harlots who cannot marry. The fetish, they say, has initiated them into this sinful life. The religion of the people is really nothing less than a devil's institution, a cover for all evil and sin and it takes different forms at various places.... (quoted in Steegstra, 2004: 97).

Writing in a similar vein about the life of the people of the Gold Coast (now Ghana) in 1852, another missionary, Johannes Zimmerman, wrote in *Der Evangelische Heidenbote* (The Heathen Messenger) thus:

> Oh, what a sinful life is such a Negro life. And could a healthy moral life be able to unfold itself here? Where, the soul has no living, holy and merciful God to hold on to, she has to perish in the abyss of immorality and wickedness into which the Negro peoples are immersed. The devil of animal lust, in particular, holds them captured, and not just men and women, young men and young women, but children

between the ages of six and eight suffer in these chains... (quoted in Steegstra, 2004: 96).

Kanogo (1993) describes similar negative attitude of early missionaries toward cultural practices of the Kikuyu in Kenya. Over the years, these early negative perceptions of indigenous African religions and social life have persisted, especially within the ranks of Western and missionary educated Africans.

The second reason for the high focus given to African religion is that from a totalistic perspective, religion invariably explains the entire social structure of traditional societies to the extent that religious values embody other social institutions such as the family, socialisation, economy and politics. As Rattray (1929: 2) argued in the case of the Asante, "Religion is the keystone of the whole legal structure." It was no accident, therefore, that in their bid to change the value structures of colonial people, the colonial authorities employed Christianity and Western education simultaneously.

The beginning of the twentieth century, especially the post-Second World War period, saw a resurgence of interest in indigenous religious and healing practices. Coinciding as it did with the birth of modern anthropology and the desire of colonial authorities to understand the usages and nuances of the colonised so as to facilitate colonial rule, latter-day Western anthropologists undertook fieldwork ostensibly to debunk the impressionistic and ethnocentric characterisation of non-Western cultures. In the study of African religions, the new orientation was to demonstrate, among others, that African cosmological notions and health-seeking behaviours had internal logical consistency not entirely different from European thought-processes based on cause-and-effect relationship or simple syllogistic reasoning. In these studies, the healer often described— albeit condescendingly— as the "witch doctor," "medicine man," or "juju man", was depicted as routinely engaged in meaningful ceremonies and rituals to restore patients to states of spiritual, social and psychological harmony. Hitherto, for many people, the mere mention of African medicine was apt to conjure up the fearsome image of the witch doctor... clad in fur and feathers, prancing around a fire, to the inexorable rhythm of the tom-tom. Although these latter-day foreign anthropologists have contributed significant insights into African ethnography, often their transitory experiences and lack of deep insight into the social structure of African societies led to distortions in their observations and interpretations. Thus, for instance, in an attempt to explain the causes of witchcraft and the perceived state of psychological insecurity among Ghanaians in the early 1960s, Field (1960: 38) observed thus: "Witchcraft exists only in fantasy, in the minds of certain mentally sick people, and is bewilderment to others. It is therefore, likely that if depression were to die out, belief in witchcraft would die out also..." Paul Stoller (1989) who became a "sorcerer's apprentice" during his field work in the Songhay region of West Africa but had to flee because of witchcraft attacks, would certainly be amused by this assertion.

The fallacy in Field's observation is clear to any student of the Ghanaian and African social scene. In spite of the great social and technological advances recorded over the years, a good number of Africans, literate as well as illiterate, still believe in this extra-sensory phenomenon. Clearly, post-modernism has its socio-psychological correlates. However, witchcraft beliefs and practices afford a striking insight into the structure of a people's cosmology; it provides them with the tool to contain their morbid fears and wish fulfilments. With this orientation, Geschiere (1997) suggests a new perspective that focuses on the 'modernity of witchcraft.' In this perspective, witchcraft is seen as both a resource for the powerful and a weapon for the weak fighting against inequalities; it is a way of dealing with the harsh realities of modernity.

The Cultural Context of Health and Well-being

An appropriate starting point for understanding the meaning of health and well-being in any society is to appreciate not only the concepts and their related values but also the socio-cultural environment that harbours them. This is because the health institution of any society has broad ranging ties with the cosmology of a people. It is within this theoretical framework that the African concept of health and well-being must be appreciated.

One important characteristic of the African concepts of health and well-being is their relationship to the communitarian character of African moral and political thought. This communitarian spirit is often demonstrated in several aspects of African life, but more especially in the exchange of greetings. As Steegstra (2004: 22) has observed, "Greetings among the Krobo can be very extensive. You always start with asking about someone's home (extended family) and the immediate family, before asking about the person's own well-being. In the greetings the community comes before the individual." In Togo, the southern Ewe often mock at their northern Kabre compatriots for the latter's exceptionally lengthy mode of greeting. In a jocular way, it is said that even in the middle of a busy street, the Kabre exchange their characteristically long greetings and sometimes they are run over by a passing vehicle! Indeed, the veracity or otherwise of this statement is not the crucial issue. The point of emphasis here is that in Africa, personhood is defined in part, by inter-subjectivity, by the connection among the body-self and socio-familial conditions and spiritual concerns.

The communitarian characteristic of African societies has generated much discourse and scholarly works. Indeed, in the period of the Cold War, especially between 1960 and 1970, communitarianism provided the elixir for the newly evolving ideology of African socialism, espoused by Dr. Kwame Nkrumah, Julius Nyerere and Leopold Senghor. Basically, it is argued that the communitarian character of the society provides the African with the sense of community-belongingness. Accordingly, as Dickson (1979: 4) has observed, this is "A characteristic of African life to which attention has been drawn again and again by both Africans and non-African writers on Africa. Indeed to many, this characteristic defines Africanness." Making a similar observation on the social life of his own ethnic group, the Gikuyu, Jomo Kenyatta (1965: 297) observed thus: "According to Gikuyu ways of thinking, nobody is an isolated individual. Or rather, his uniqueness is a secondary fact about him; first and foremost he is several people's relative and several people's contemporary." On the same phenomenon, Mbiti (1970: 141) also writes that in African societies, "Whatever happens to the individual happens to the whole group and whatever happens to the whole group happens to the individual." The individual can only say: "I am because we are; and since we are, therefore I am." From this anti-Cartesian perspective, Ifeanyi argues that this African view emphasizes the ontological centrality of the community: "As far as Africans are concerned, the reality of the communal world takes precedence over the reality of the individual life histories, whatever these may be." Consequently, he concludes that the community defines the individual personhood and not some isolated static quality of rationality, will or memory (see Gyekye, 1997).

The rapid social changes taking place in contemporary Africa have had their significant impact on traditional social structures. Foreign religions, especially Christianity, Western education, monetised economy and migration pose considerable challenges to the stability of the norms and values that support the traditional social structure. Today, a casual look at the African family, especially in the urban setting, reveals a gradual process of nucleation leading to weakening of the proverbial African family bond. Also Christianity and Western education continue to undermine the underlying ideology of African traditional religions. Against this background, it may be stated that the view of the African construction of personhood might have been overstated. However, while this contestation has some merit, its generalization is problematic: Africa is not only largely rural but also the processes of globalisation and consequent marginalisation have led to recrudescence for the need to adhere to or maintain certain core African norms. Consequently, the call by WHO for the integration of indigenous African healing modes into national health care systems must be seen in this light. Another relevant advocacy is the call also to infuse into colonially inherited Western systems of governance, some of the democratic and human rights elements of traditional African political systems. Indeed,

Figure 14 – Mengo Hospital, Uganda

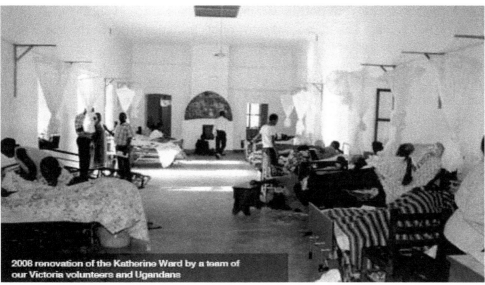

2008 renovation of the Katherine Ward by a team of our Victoria volunteers and Ugandans

Source: *http://www.ststephensanglican.net/?p=336*

it may be argued further that the current explosion of religious revivalism, manifested by the emergence of numerous pentecostal/charismatic churches, is an offshoot of identity contestation in a globalised world. From this point of view, it is still reasonable to say that in the contemporary African context, a person's identity largely derives from a cultural context, the community, which continues to play important roles in his/her life.

Chapter 14

Individual versus Collective Well-being

The communitarian construction of personhood has critical relevance for defining individual and collective health and well-being in Africa (see also Chapters 6 and 7, this volume). In the African sociological context, a community is not simply an aggregation of people linked by enduring primordial ties; they are also linked by a cosmology that binds them in some relationship with the supernatural realm. For this reason, in the African context, the self is very porous to the extent that it is open to influences by other beings, human as well as non-human.

In two of the thorough compendia that survey the nature and the philosophical basis of African religions, Mbiti (1969; 1970) has shown that across cultures, African societies perceive a three-or four-tiered cosmology made up of a pantheon of gods, malevolent and ambivalent spirits and human-spirits, all of which guide the conduct of human beings. At the head of the pantheon is an *Otiosus Deus,* an all-powerful, all-knowing and ubiquitous God who is credited with creation. Knowledge of God is expressed in attributes, names, proverbs, songs, libation, folktales and religious ceremonies. For instance, among the Ga, God is known as Ataa-Naa Nyomo, portraying his bi-sexual attribute (see also Ch. 7). A similar attribute of God (Mawu-Lisa) exists among the Fon of Benin. The Akan refer to him as Onyankopon (the Great Friend), Amosu (the rain maker) or Amoawia (the giver of sunlight). To the Zulu and Banyarwanda, God is known as 'the Wise One' and to the Baganda, he is 'the Great Eye.' That God is no stranger to the African is captured in the Akan saying: 'No one shows a child the Supreme Being.' Also various folktales demonstrate his relationship with human beings. Essentially, however, he is said to live far away and therefore has delegated some of his responsibilities to the lesser gods on earth.

The lesser gods, also known as nature-gods, include animate and inanimate objects – hills, mountains, rivers, the sea, animals, totems, trees, etc. These lesser gods are often divided into two categories – the ancient tutelary deities and the more recent medicine cults. The first category of deities is usually owned communally; they are believed to have been worshipped from time immemorial. In Ghana, some of these de-localised powerful deities and cult houses include Yewe, Togbi Adzima, Hogbato, and Emi, all in the southern Volta Region. Others include Kukula in Navrongo, Kwaku Fri in Wenchi, Apoo in Techiman, Akonedi at Lartey and Antoa in the Ashanti Region (see also Allman and Parker, 2005). As multi-purpose deities, their clients include people with complaints of alleged miscarriage of justice, men and women with fertility problems, clients who desire progress in their businesses and other endeavours of life, people seeking protection against enemies, bullet, snakebite, road accidents and other misfortunes, and people anxious to recover lost property or desiring to be cured of their chronic ailments. The second category of deities are in most cases objects or instruments used in the practice of magic and which have been elevated to the status of a god through the establishment of a priesthood and a followership.

Next to these are human-like spirits represented by the living-dead. These include the spirits of the dead and those of dead ancestors and ancestresses. Also included in this cohort are the malevolents – witches, wizards, sorcerers and animals (such as the owl) that portend evil. Many devout African Christians deny the existence of these and instead reconstruct their religious cosmology featuring Christ, the saints and the angels in opposition to the devil or demonic forces. In their daily lives, however, the fear of these elements is evident. It is in this regard that some anthropologists have argued that acceptance of Christianity does not radically alter the mental structure of the Ghanaian, or for that matter the African; Christianity operates only on the surface of his/her skin.

The Ndembu of Zambia, have a four-tiered cosmology. Thus the Ndembu religion recognizes four main elements: a) belief in a high God; b) belief in ancestors or shades; c) belief in the intrinsic efficacy of certain animals and vegetables; and d) belief in the anti-social destructive power of witches, wizards and sorcerers. All over Africa, belief in these spirits is very strong; it has been so since time immemorial. Writing on the attitude of the people of the Gold Coast (now Ghana) toward these supernatural elements, Casely-Hayford (1903: 102) made some interesting observations over a century ago. Given its relevance and currency I have quoted him in extenso:

> The native of the Gold Coast profoundly believes in the world of spirits. He believes that the spirit in man never dies. So vivid is this faith that he holds open and direct communion with his dead friend, not through a medium but as it were face to face. You should watch him as he takes offerings of food and drink to the graveside. There, he carefully sets a chair for the dear one gone before, then places the meal in order and pours out a libation, addressing the spirit of the departed the while. He earnestly believes that the relative hovers around him by day as well as by night and he has both the physical and the spiritual sense to perceive its presence. He sees in the mammiferous bat winging its flight from room to room at night in the home once dear to the loved one, who is supposed to dominate it, a kindly providence which does not leave him all forlorn in his grief, but sends the spirit of the departed back occasionally to watch and to protect. He even speaks to it in endearing terms at times and would fain belief that it understands and is in full sympathy with him.

Although this observation was made a little over a century ago, its currency is still evident not only in Ghana but also in many other African countries, social change notwithstanding.

Another significant aspect of the African cosmology is the relationship between personhood and the spiritual realm. In many African societies, a person is not simply a mass of flesh, muscles and bones; he/she also possesses spiritual elements often invoked in times of serious ill health or death (Figures 14 and 15). Indeed, in many African societies, one critical importance of post-mortuary rituals is either to facilitate the transition of the spirit of the dead into the realm of the departed and or to invoke the spirit to avenge his/her death if foul play was suspected as the cause of death. The Ashanti believe that a human being is formed from the blood (*mogya*) of the mother and the spirit (*sunsum* or *ntoro*) of the father. Besides inheriting one's mother's blood, every person is believed to receive a *sunsum* and a *kra;* the latter is a life principle, a small indestructible part of the Creator that is given each individual on creation and with it, one's destiny. The *kra* returns to God when a person dies. Among the Ga and Ewe the mode by which these personal spirits exit are the same, though their mode of acquisition differs. The Ga refer to this spirit as *kla;* the Ewe call it *se, dzogbese or kpoli.*

The relevance of the African cosmology is that the African believes that his/her well-being is closely linked with the spiritual realm; the spirits can reward or punish him/her for appropriate or inappropriate conduct. For instance, among the Ga and Ewe, it is believed that one can literally bring harm or ill luck onto himself of herself through acts which may cause shame to one's *kla* or *se.* Indeed, so vital is *se* to the Ewe that this spiritual entity is literally 'bribed' through naming to show love or benevolence or at least to facilitate one's prosperity. Thus, such Ewe names as *Seyiram* (my spirit has blessed me), *Sena or Senam* (my spirit giveth), *Seli* (my spirit liveth) or *Selom* (my spirit loves me), are all cast in the spirit-praising mode.

Punishment from the spiritual realm may be physical or non-physical and may be visited not only on the offender but also, in some cases, on his/her innocent relations several generations later. Among the Ewe of south-eastern Ghana, such ailments as leprosy, lunacy, incurable ulcers, blindness, infertility, oedematous (swelling) conditions and in some cases, HIV and AIDS, are perceived to have supernatural dimensions. As Nukunya (2001: 87) has observed, "The dreadful thing about supernatural sanctions stems from the fact that there is no time limit to the efficacy or manifestation of their results. Sometimes they are so rapid that by the time the complainant returns from the cult house, the result has already come." Presumably, therefore, a goat-thief and his descendants may be inflicted with madness while the chronic adulterer may be punished with an oedematous condition or with a perpetually swollen penis; his descendants would not escape this punishment also. What this implies is that in the African context, 'illness' beside its multiple causation, has high content of morality: a morally bankrupt person may pay the price of his/her immorality with ill health and lack of prosperity. Not unexpectedly, the Togolese Ewe believe that a thief does not recover when sick.

The nexus between morality and health and well-being exists in other African societies. The Ndembu of Zambia conceive of disease or illness (*musong'u*) as a species of misfortune (*malwa, kuhalwa, kuyindana* or *kubulo katooka*). Misfortune is a class term that includes bad luck at hunting, reproductive disorders, physical accidents and loss of property. The Ndembu, like the Azande of the Sudan, consider that mystical forces generated or evoked and directed by conscious agents cause calamities or adversities of all kinds. These agents may be alive or dead, human or extra human. They may operate directly on their victims or indirectly through mystical intermediaries. Ancestral shades cause suffering directly; living sorcerers and witches work evil through medicines or familiars or through a combination of both. Among the Bemba also of Zambia, individual culpability can affect other innocent relatives and in some cases, the entire community. It is reported that one of the foulest acts of all is for a girl to bear a child before she has been initiated or before one of the more abbreviated rites now performed at puberty is carried out. Her child would then be considered a creature of ill-omen – *wa mputula* – who would bring misfortune on any village in which it lives; the child would be a portent of evil. It is considered to be capable of stopping rainfall, to make the granaries empty quickly and to bring dissension. The father and mother of such a child are, therefore, driven out into the bush with their baby to save the community from danger. It is also reported that the penalties which fall on those who come in contact with polluted fire are always envisaged as illnesses, mainly of the chest (*cifuba*). It is important to note also that the punishment falls on the innocent and not the guilty. The adulterous woman who touches her hearthstone causes her husband to fall ill 'of the chest' if he accidentally comes near the fire. The father who is impure through illicit intercourse 'kills' his child with fire (*ukumuipaya umulilo'*) so that the baby starts to waste away and then dies sooner or later. Among the Baganda of Uganda, it is believed that if certain specific offences are committed immediate disease or death would result. These include eating the totem animal of one's clan, violating the avoidance rules between relatives-in-law and breaching sexual regulations, especially adultery. Among the Bariba of Benin, it is reported that a birth always has the potential for being abnormal. The primary indication of a 'bad' delivery is that a child is born with the marks of the supernatural. These include a breech birth, premature birth or a child born with extreme congenital malformations. It is believed that such a child is a witch (*bii yondo*) capable of killing its mother during delivery or of growing up to provoke havoc among its patrilineal relations. Customarily, therefore, such a child is killed shortly after birth. The Bariba 'witch' children have their parallels among the Kassena and Nankana in the Upper East Region of Ghana where such children are also killed. Among the Hehe of southern Tanzania, when one falls ill, this may be attributed to misfortune from several sources, natural and supernatural: worry; impure water, faulty inheritance, witchcraft or to legitimate retribution for the violation of Hehe norms.

The discussion so far points to a situation where from the African perspective, ill health, lack of well-being or prosperity may result from several sources – natural and supernatural. Also these may be occasioned by a personal or another person's misdeed and may affect not only the perpetrator but also innocent relations and in some cases the entire lineage or the community several generations later. Geurts (2002: 138) confirms this observation in her study of the Anlo. She writes: "If a person committed murder or theft, penance did not end with any imagined boundaries around the individual but plagued the lineage for eternity."

The primacy of the supernatural in the causation of ill health or disease is very evident. This has often led to the debate as to whether or not the African or the non-Westerner, for that matter, appreciates the natural aetiology of diseases. This discourse has a long history in anthropological tradition. Of particular importance in this regard is the work of Lévy-Bruhl, whose reflections on the so-called pre-logical and mystical nature of primitive belief systems exercised considerable influence on early – and to some extent late – anthropological explanations of the life of *'la penseé sauvage,'* (the noble savage). Lévy-Bruhl insisted that there were fundamental differences between the pre-logical, animistic and anti-experimental mentality of primitive man and that characteristic of 'scientific thinking'. He contrasted the 'mystical aspect of primitive mentality' with the rational aspect of 'scientific society' (Lukes, 1970: 201). It is somewhat unfortunate that Lévy-Bruhl chose the term 'pre-logical' to describe primitive mentality, for to be fair to him, he clearly did not mean to imply that primitive thought was illogical, but rather that it was not in accord with the 'rationalist' logic of Western thought. Taking issue with Lévy-Bruhl, latter-day anthropologists have argued that the so-called scientific cosmology is as much a function of culture as is the magical perspective of the 'noble savage,' a function of primitive culture.

In spite of this explanation, the debate continues. For instance, while Warren (1979) has argued that among the Bono of Ghana, most diseases have nothing to do with any spiritual forces, Twumasi (1974) and Mendonsa (1997) have argued that among the Asante and Sisala, respectively, their aetiological lexicon hardly gives room for the natural causation of diseases. Also writing on the aetiology of diseases among the Baganda several decades ago, Mair (1934: 254) observed: "When attempting to ascertain the reason for someone's death, it is uncertain if the Baganda even consider 'natural causes' as a possible explanation." Today, this observation appears to be as current as at the time it was written. It is certainly not the orientation of this chapter to examine the pros and cons of these positions. What may be said by way of compromise is that there is no known society however high or low in technological development that can be described as entirely positivistic or outright supernatural in its social organization. Even in a technologically advanced country such as the USA, the number '13' elicits phobic reactions unwarranted by any scientific rationalisation.

Modus Vivendi

The epidemiological profile of Africa shows that the continent carries a heavy disease burden. Africa's diseases are mainly infectious and parasitic; they include measles, tetanus, cholera, typhus, syphilis, gonorrhoea, tuberculosis, trachoma, schistosomiasis, trypanosomiasis, lymphatic filariasis, yaws and HIV and AIDS, to mention but a few (see also Chs. 1 and 2). In recent times, however, degenerative disease such as arthritis, gout, cancers, hypertension, and cardiovascular and neurological diseases have begun to exact their toll, especially among the African elite and urban dwellers. While from the point of view of standard medical practice the causes of these conditions are heavily influenced by the environment, from the perspective of many Africans the causes may have spiritual dimensions also. In the face of these actual or potential threats to health and well-being, how do Africans negotiate their health needs? An adequate response to this question requires some insight into the health-seeking behaviour of Africans against the background of existing health services and facilities.

A number of anthropologists who have studied the African religio-medical space have been impressed by the vast array of health resources available to the sick. Often, for ease of discussion, these resources are categorised into two main domains – allopathic (biomedicine) and 'traditional' medicine – although such medical practices as acupuncture, homeopathy, naturopathy, osteopathy, etc., which represent an interface of the two domains are hardly mentioned. In studying the two medical domains, the major focus has been on the nature and rationale of the interplay between the two. From this perspective, some medical anthropologists and health planners have advocated for the integration of or collaboration between the two domains. However, for some health policy makers in Africa who kick against such moves, the continued existence of and in some cases, the preference for indigenous healing by some people remain an anathema, although these policy makers accept in principle, the tenets of the Primary Health Care concept. Now, we shall take a quick look at the constituents of Africa's health 'supermarket.'

Allopathic Facilities

In Africa, allopathic facilities include hospitals, clinics, maternity homes, medical laboratories, pharmacies and chemical shops. While these bio-medical facilities provide a range of services, they are generally inaccessible to most Africans because their infrastructural requirements (electricity, water, good roads, personnel, etc.) restrict their operations to the urban areas (Figure 14). Besides, their services are relatively expensive even when they are public– or mission-owned. Generally, they are used for the treatment of conditions thought to be severe and to have natural origins. Even in cases suspected to have supernatural origins, allopathic services may be used for the treatment of the physical manifestations of such conditions.

In Africa, the most popular representation of allopathy are pharmaceuticals or cosmopolitan medicines. These are often found even in the most remote rural areas where health facilities and personnel do not exist. In West Africa, an extensive network of legal as well as illegal institutions and persons distributes pharmaceuticals. These include health facilities, pharmacies and registered as well as unregistered chemical shops. Individuals include nurses, market women, businessmen and women, friends and relatives. Medicines distributed in this network include both ethical and non-ethical ones. As Bledsoe and Gouboud (1988) have observed therefore, in Africa pharmaceuticals are as available as coca-cola. The 'coca-colaisation' of these products has led to their indigenised use while reinforcing the 'pill-for-every-ailment' ethos. One significant consequence of this state of affairs (not to mention the financial and health implications) is that Africa has not given public health concerns the desired attention when indeed, much of her health burden is related to a wide range of insalubrious environments.

Interface Facilities

For want of appropriate nomenclature, Asiatic medical traditions such as acupuncture, homeopathy, hydropathy, aromapathy, etc. have been designated as constituting an interface between allopathy and indigenous healing modes. These practices are based on the principle of natural healing and so they make less use of synthetic medicines. In Ghana, these practices emerged in the early 1970s and are commonly resorted to for the management of degenerative disorders such as hypertension, diabetes, stroke, cancers, obesity, cardiovascular and neurological disorders. Although they are very few in number and restrict their activities to the urban areas they are very popular. Due to high demand for their services, a number of 'health shops' have also emerged in the urban areas to provide supportive services; these health shops sell raw or processed herbal preparations from countries such as China, Germany and Australia as well as foods required by those with degenerative disorders. Products here are relatively expensive and as is to be expected. It is mainly the elites who patronise them.

The Indigenous Domain

In the non-Western world, the indigenous health care domain is often the largest. Often referred to as 'traditional,' 'holistic,' 'complementary,' or 'alternative' medicine, it is not a monolithic system but a pot-pourri of therapeutic modes. WHO (1978b) defines traditional medicine as "All knowledge and practices used in diagnosis, prevention and treatment of physical, mental or social imbalance which rely mainly on practical ancestral experience and observation handed down verbally or in writing." The indigenous domain has two sub-sectors—the popular and the indigenous-specialist, designated in the literature as folk. The popular sector refers to the lay, non-professional, non-specialist domain where ill health is first recognized and defined and health care activities are initiated. In Africa, women undertake most health promotion activities.

For this reason, they are more knowledgeable in traditional and modern pharmacopoeia for the management of common ailments such as cold, cough, constipation, measles, malaria and all manner of body rashes. In the rural areas of Ghana, women use concoction and decoction popularly called *odido* or *okumdadao* as prophylaxis against many childhood diseases. In this regard, knowledge of the local flora is very vital for rural women. In the urban areas where the vegetation has been destroyed, several local markets have sections where medicinal plants or herbs are sold. In Accra, the Timber Market is reputed for the sale of such goods.

In the indigenous domain, however, it is the specialist (folk) sector that has received the greater attention, ostensibly because of the anthropological focus on healers. According to WHO (1978b) healers are people recognized by the society in which they live as being competent to deal with health and health-related issues.(See figure 15). Their esoteric knowledge is derived from practical experience, ancestral sources or from magico-religious realm. Healers are found in every African village. They carry out the art of healing the sick and ensure social equilibrium between individuals and communities on one hand and the spiritual realm on the other. Since in every homestead and village people fall sick or meet with accidents and misfortune, healers are considered a very important communal resource .They are the ones who come to the rescue of the individual in matters of health and general welfare. Every homestead is, therefore, within reach of at least one healer. In Ghana, the Ministry of Health estimates that while there are about 4,000 Ghanaians for one doctor, there are 400 Ghanaians for one healer.

Figure 15- Sangoma, South Africa

Source: *http://www.southafricalogue.com/travel-tips/sangomas-tsouth-african-shamen.html*

In Africa, there are several types of healers most of whom perform overlapping functions. For this reason it is often very difficult to classify them. Thus, the healer classifications as found in the literature seem to be purely an academic exercise. This notwithstanding, in an exercise such as this, there is the need for some kind of classification if only to present a holistic picture of the health seeking behaviour of Africans. Thus, using my classificatory arrangement of Ghanaian indigenous healers the following picture emerges:

Herbalists

These are men and women who specialise in the use of plants, minerals and anatomical parts of animals to effect healing. They know the names and nature of herbs, trees, roots, seeds, bones, bird and animal excreta and many other things for making medicines. They diagnose diseases and people's problems and prescribe a cure. They are well-respected in their communities. Their practice may or may not include magico-religious rituals. Herbalists may operate at fixed locations or carry out their activities as itinerant practitioners moving from place to place or from one busy street corner to another. Some even ply their wares in vehicles, especially those that go on long-distance journeys. In Ghana most itinerant herbalists are women; they specialize in the sale of 'women's medicines' also.

Herbalists claim to have medicines for all diseases. For this reason, they deal with a wide range of health problems and their clientele cuts across the socio-economic strata of the society. As a result of the useful role such healers play in their communities, some mission hospitals have involved them in the delivery of specific range of health care services. However, in view of the fact that the activities of healers are not effectively controlled by state regulatory agencies, a number of quacks exist among their ranks.

Islamic Healers (*Malami*)

In most of the works on African healers, this category of healers is either not mentioned or is assumed to be a part of the omnibus class of herbalists or healers. The need to give them a separate class is informed by the fact that their mode of treatment appears to vary considerably from mainstream herbalists. Islamic medicine is certainly not confined to those regions of north Africa that are culturally and historically identified with the Arab World. Indeed, in many Islamized societies of Africa south of the Sahara, from Senegal on the Atlantic Coast to Somalia and Zanzibar on the Indian Ocean, Islamic medicine has been adapted to meet local needs. There is today hardly a village containing a sizeable Muslim community without its own Muslim medical practitioner popularly called *malam*.

According to Gallagher (1985), Islamic medicine uses six main modes of treatment. These are:

Rubutu. For this treatment, appropriate verses from the Holy Qur'an are written on a board. The ink is then washed from the board and the solution is then given to the sick person to drink. Rubutu may be used as a curative medicine, but is more often employed as a tonic to preserve health and bring good fortune.

Laya. These are amulets worn on the body or placed in an appropriate place in the house. They contain pieces of paper with Qur'anic verses believed to ensure protection. These are normally preventive medicine and are particularly employed to protect children from the many childhood diseases.

Tofi. This involves transferring the power of the therapeutic spoken word by rubbing the malam's saliva on the centre of the pain. Tofi is used especially for headache and scorpion sting.

Kamun Kai. This technique is used to treat headaches. In this treatment the patient's head is grasped by the malam while therapeutic passages are recited from the Qur'an.

Addu'a. This refers to the invocations that follow the five-time daily laudatory prayers or specifically to medical invocations in these prayers.

Rokon Allah. This is a supplication commonly employed when the malam does not know the actual treatment for a particular condition.

Beside these, Islamic healers also engage in minor surgery when they make tiny incisions on a swelling and draw blood using the horn of an animal. As part of the therapy management they may also instruct the sick to give alms (*salaka*) to the poor.

Neo-herbalists

These cohort of healers emerged in Ghana especially from the 1970s. Unlike their 'traditional' counterparts, they are fairly young, literate and profess Christianity or Islam. They organize their practice along the lines of Western medical bureaucracy. Thus, their clinics have a consulting room, a dispensary, patients' records office and waiting room sometimes fitted with air conditioners and television sets. Most of the healers now have complimentary cards and mobile phones as part of their symbolic break with past traditional healing. They also use thermometers, sphygmomanometers, weighing scales and in some cases, stethoscopes. In the clinic, they wear white long coats as in the fashion of Western doctors. Their clinics are often located in the urban centres and are easily identified by signboards indicating their location and the range of diseases they can handle. A typical signboard I saw recently carried the following message:

HEALTH FOR ALL HERBAL CLINIC

LOCATION: Oworam near Asamankese in West Akim District, Eastern Region

P. O. Box 35 Asamankese   **Tel.** 027 609236   **Mobile:** 020 8153438

Diseases We Treat

- Stroke
- Typhoid Fever
- Malaria Fever
- Chronic Wounds
- Infertility and Low Sperm Count
- Retention of Urine
- Sexual Weakness and Impotency
- Piles (Kooko)
- Hypertension

Diseases We Control

- Diabetes
- HIV Controller

For all your problems rush and see Dr. X (name withheld). Family planning powder available.

Clearly, as the above example shows, neo-herbalists, just as their 'traditional' counterparts, also focus on the treatment of degenerative diseases. However, treatment is often devoid of magico-religious rituals. Also neo-herbalists who manufacture herbal medicines on a commercial basis advertise their wares on the radio and television. In villages and towns they advertise using vehicles fitted with public address systems. Their services and products are highly patronised in spite of official protestation that most of these products have not been certified as wholesome for human use or consumption.

Traditional Birth Attendants (TBAs)

These indigenous midwives, officially referred to as 'traditional birth attendants,' are usually old women who assist pregnant women with birthing. They also handle health issues relating to women and children. They are found in every village in Ghana. Due to the fact that most children in Ghana are delivered by TBAs, since the early 1980s, the Ministry of Health has upgraded the skills of over 6000 of them as part of the Primary Health Care programme. Basically they are taught to recognize risk factors in pregnancy and to refer appropriately. They are also taught how to handle blood and the umbilical cord. In the rural areas, traditional midwifery is not a profession. For this reason, in most cases, their services are paid for in kind.

Circumcisionists

In Ghana, this group of health workers is commonly referred to as *wanzam*, possibly a derivative from the name *wanzami* given to Hausa barber-surgeons. Although their main job is circumcision of male children, they also practise some herbalism and make body incisions into which protective medicines may be rubbed. In some parts of the rural north and also in southern urban communities where northern migrants live, there are women who practise female circumcision though the practice is illegal. To some extent, such women also attend to a limited range of women's health problems.

Diviners/Soothsayers

In many parts of Africa, diviners or soothsayers abound and operate as mainstream healers. Thus, the Kamba of Kenya distinguish between an ordinary diviner (*Mue wa kwausya*) and one who divines and treats (*Mue wa kwausy na kuiita*).Their main function is to find out hidden secrets or knowledge and pass them on to their clients. They deal with the question of why something had gone wrong or who may have used magic, sorcery or witchcraft against the sick, the barren, the impotent or the person who is not experiencing prosperity or well-being. Across the world ten varieties of divination techniques are identified. Of these, the following are commonly practised in Africa:

Ordeal: drinking a poisonous potion or swearing a communal sacred oath to proclaim one's innocence;

Possession or falling into trance: to enable the diviner to better reveal the future or the culprit of an offence;

Necromancy: by which signs from the spirit of the dead are sought. Among the Ewe and the Ga, the spirit of the dead may be invoked to reveal the actual cause of death. This the dead may do by causing the death of the culprit or inflicting diseases, misery or restlessness on him/her until he/she confesses;

Nature type: by which the behaviour of animals and the elements is used to identify a culprit or to indicate coming events. In many West African communities death by lightening portends evil and a person who dies this way is said to have committed a grievous offence.

Mechanical type: involving the manipulation of innumerable number of objects. Patterns formed by their positions determine an oncoming event. Among the Yoruba and Ewe, Orunmila and Afa, respectively are deities responsible for disclosing events in the extra-sensory domain. According to Nukunya (1969c) Afa divination involves casting onto a mat or board, a chain containing a pair of four half-split palm kernels, nuts or similar objects, some falling face up, others face down. For each of the 256 possible positions, there are a number of verses or pithy sayings interpreted to determine the cause of sickness, bad luck, a run of misfortune, etc. Between the Yoruba Ifa and Ewe Afa divination modes is the Dagbon practice which centers around the manipulation of a stick and a number of small objects such as buttons, blood encrusted horns, beads and nails each representing a particular character or social phenomenon (Oppong, 1973).

Miscellaneous divination: This includes a large category of divinatory modes that do not fit into any of the types above such as multiple deaths, chains of misfortunes and fairy-calling.

Given the overbearing presence of the spiritual realm in the daily life of Africans, diviners are regarded as very influential personalities in the society. In spite of this, diviners are said to be powerless in matters of fate: they may reveal one's ill fate but may not have the power to mitigate its course. Thus, as the Sisala (of Upper West Region of Ghana) commonly say, "Diviners tell lies and people die; they tell lies and people live."

Shrine Devotees

These are men and women called to serve particular deities for the rest of their lives. Often, the deities served are multi-purpose and trans-national: they deal with all manner of issues and can dispense justice even beyond national political boundaries. Their services are open to all irrespective of place of origin. In Ghana, Togo and Benin, shrine devotees are often identified by their mode of dressing; they often wear dreadlocks or are cleanly shaven; they wear a piece of loincloth and walk barefooted. They also present facial and body incisions often done with geometric precision. In some instances, these devotees may engage in healing and divination.

Orthopaedics and Physiotherapists

Although these healers may be classified as herbalists, one of their distinguishing characteristics is that unlike herbalists, they tend to focus essentially on the management of fractures. In Ghana, they are very popular; people with fractures admitted to hospital often opt to be treated by these healers. In Ghana, a few mission hospitals work with some of them.

Faith Healing

Many of the studies on African indigenous healing have often excluded this category of health resource available to the contemporary African. This is indeed understandable: in Africa, the origin of religious sects may be traced to the desire of the colonised African to create a counter ideology and political space. Since the early 1970s, however, much of sub-Saharan Africa has witnessed a religious renaissance with an exponential increase in the number of these sects.

Of particular interest to this chapter, however, is the fact that religious sects as popular religions have become basically materialistic with their 'prosperity gospel.' They also undertake healing often at little or no cost to the sick. Reflecting on the bleak and unpromising economic and political reality of Africa today, it may be argued that popular religions are expressing themselves in terms of the apparent hopelessness reflecting the non-fulfilment of the expectations of the mass of the people. Religious faith is thus regarded as the key to this worldly material favour. As Kabongo (1982) has summed up, "Africa at prayer looks for a miracle; it is a daily appeal for the ultimate solution to illness, poverty and misery. That is Africa of the night, of Saturdays and Sundays. Africa of the week and of the day 'manages', and corrupt and corrupting individuals die between the two worlds, struggling to survive." In many parts of sub-Saharan Africa, these sects now provide prayer camps where the severely sick or emotionally disturbed are admitted for treatment. They also organise crusades where the sick and the disabled are promised instant healing. They provide alternative medical space for those to whom bio-medical interface and indigenous healing services are inaccessible. Indeed, a recent advertisement of the Kingsway International Christian Centre, a popular London-based charismatic church with branches in Ghana, captures this point more forcefully thus: *It is our vision to be a place where the hurting, the depressed, the frustrated and the confused can find life, acceptance, help, hope, forgive-*

ness and encouragement. ***A place for the total healing of the total man and the total nation*** (emphasis added).

Patterns of Prosperity and Health-seeking Behaviour

Against the background of the issues so far discussed, one may immediately appreciate the complexity that describes the African concept of health and well-being. From the complexity, however, it should be obvious that in the search for health and well-being the African must literally go 'shopping,' deciding at each stage which health 'supermarket' is pragmatically relevant for his/her situation. As numerous studies on the combined use of allopathy and indigenous modes of treatment have shown, the vast majority of Africans know very well which options to choose for particular diseases. They make distinctions between diseases suitable for Western health care centres and diseases best handled by the healer or the wonder-working prophet. As Green and Makhubu (1984) have found in Swaziland for most Swazi, health problems fall into three categories: those best treated by traditional healers and those that fall in between, in which either type of treatment or a combination of the two may be effective.

However, several anthropologists have also studied patterns of utilisation of health resources in medically plural societies in an attempt to understand what has come to be known as the 'hierarchy of resort' or the ranking of and subsequent utilization of health facilities. The difficulties that have attended these studies are due mainly to the fact that definition of health problems and utilisation of health facilities are heavily influenced by several intervening variables relating to the sick person's socio-demographic characteristics, the community's perception and definition of his/her condition, the resources available to deal with the health problem and the health facilities readily available to competently handle the problem. In other words, African consumers of health care, like consumers everywhere, pick and choose treatments available to them. In a pluralistic medical system, sometimes the choices are consistent with the tradition or the indigenous belief system, other times they are not. Conceivably, therefore the African may auto-medicate and/or visit the hospital, the healer, and the prophet, with his hernia or elephantiasis, without feeling any sense of contradiction as the Westerner may perceive, because to him all these health facilities are along the same continuum; their explanatory models may differ but together they constitute one cosmology, indeed the best of two worlds.

In an attempt to provide a cross-cultural model for determining the level of utilisation of a health facility, Tanahashi (1978) has proposed what has come to be known as the four 'A's. According to his model the level of utilisation of a health facility may be assessed by the degree of its availability, acceptability, accessibility and affordability. If these criteria are framed as questions, the following questions may be asked: In times of ill health, what health facilities are readily available? Are the services offered acceptable for the condition being experienced? How far is the health facility? How much money is available to meet the cost of health care – actual as well as incidental? It may be argued that while these questions are relevant even in times of minor ailments, in the African context, conditions regarded as very serious demand further questions. For instance, in order to arrive at a home-grown diagnosis which may determine subsequent health pathways, it may be relevant to know the moral character of the person who is sick, his/her age and sex, his/her social standing in the society, the severity and or rarity of the illness, the antecedent events before the onset of the sickness and the degree of involvement of the kin group in the therapy management process, among others. Presumably, therefore when a known thief is seriously ill, the most likely diagnosis is that he is being punished for his misdeeds. In this regard, catharsis may be part of the crisis management. In the Ghanaian context, Jahoda (1970) and Parker (1998) have shown that this thought pattern is common even among students in the University of Ghana or among Ghanaian university students, for that matter. The current wave of pentecostalism sweeping through many Ghanaian secondary and tertiary educational institutions coupled with the diabolization of society and every misfortune, affirm this view. Even among the elite, morbid fear of the demon has led to a new craze of sticking glossy scriptural injunctions on vehicles. Some of these read as follows: *Keep off! Jesus is in control; I am covered by the blood of Christ; No weapon fashioned by the enemy shall prevail against me; The devil sells you pleasures but does not tell you the cost; Christ crosses crisis; Angels on guard, keep off!*

Indeed, the fight against the devil, witches, wizards and sorcerers is captured in daily discourse and 'defensive' or 'preventive' behavioural patterns along the West Coast of Africa. Individuals may acquire small personal gods to protect themselves against misfortunes; children are protected from diseases and evil eyes with magically charged amulets, notched coin or a cross tied onto their waist or wrist or hung on their neck; the Christian may lay her sleeping infant in a cot or on a mat with a Bible under its pillow or mat. In the market, women selling all manner of goods may place a piece of red pepper or charcoal on their wares to drive away evil eyes. They may also bite off one of the four edges of any paper currency used by customers (especially those suspected to have evil eyes) in the payment of goods bought, in order to prevent it from 'flying away' with the rest of the day's sales. Some of the market women also begin the day's activities with a short 'devotion' conducted by themselves or by wandering preachers who visit the markets early in the morning to evangelise. On university campuses and in many workplaces, several prayer groups have emerged. Their prayer sessions are often characterized by what Turner (1981) calls the *ngoma mode,* to wit, attacking the demon, singing, handclapping, stamping of the feet, glossolalia ('speaking with tongues') and catharsis. Indeed, behaviours adopted to enhance health and well-being are many and varied. However, as pointed out earlier, witchcraft beliefs are an important support and resource for the powerful, just as they are a vital weapon for the weak in their fight against social inequalities. In the search for health and well-being , nothing can be left to chance.

Conclusion

The quest for health is one eternal preoccupation of humankind. In this quest, human beings have created social institutions and relevant norms and values that go with them. In the African context, health and well-being are promoted or constrained not only by natural circumstances but also by extra-sensorial factors. In this regard, one may suffer from both physical and moral ill health. The latter may result not only because of one's act of omission or commission but also because of the misdeeds of others. In a system such as this, where human beings are constantly engaged in negotiation for survival with both nature and the spirits, elaborate systems must be developed not only to contain ill health and wrong doers, but also to 'bribe' the entities of the spiritual realm. Thus collective existence is often premised on collective effort to come to terms with the social physical and the extrasensory world. This, however, should not be interpreted to mean that the African lives his/her daily life in the fear of his or her neighbours and the spirits; it is when events defy the 'normal' that the role of human beings and the supernatural comes under the searchlight.

A casual observer of the African medical scene will easily be impressed by the range and complexity of health facilities available in times of ill health. While the existence of these facilities and their mode of use may be problematic to the Western mind, to the African, these facilities represent meaning systems along a continuum of health care. They represent the best of different worlds and are used meaningfully as and when the need arises. Western health care practitioners in Africa must understand that Western institutions and values—indeed any alien system—make sense to non-Westerners only when these are indigenized, that is to say, reinterpreted and reincorporated into existing social structures. If this truism is accepted, doctors will make much more impact than when they insist on reproducing carbon copies of Western medical practices. In the African context, enjoying good health and promoting one's well-being involves coming to terms with nature and the spiritual realm. The reality that emerges from this stance is as logical as the law of thermodynamics, for as the common saying goes, when people see situations as real, they are real in their consequences.

Review Questions

1. Africans may visit the healer, the doctor, the mallam and the pastor with the same disease. How would you explain this medically plural behaviour of the African?

2. How can indigenous healing systems contribute to the health and well-being of the African?

3. In what way can the African concept of illness causation explain the communitarian character of African social control mechanisms?

4. How does the communitarian character of African societies affect the health and well-being of the individual and the society?

5. Discuss the role of morality in the incidence of diseases in the African context.

References

Allman, J. and J. Parker. 2005. *Tongnaab: The History of a West African God*. Bloomington: Indiana University Press

Bledsoe, C. H. & F. M. Goubaud 1988 "The Reinterpretation and Distribution of Western Pharmaceuticals: An Example From the Mende of Sierra Leone", in S. van der Geest and S. R. Whyte (eds.), *The Context of Medicines in Developing Countries*. \Dordrecht: Kluwer Academic Publications, pp253-76.

Casely-Hayford, J. E. 1903. Gold *Coast Native Institutions: With Thoughts Upon A Health Imperial Policy For The Gold Coast and Ashanti*. London: Sweet and Maxwell Ltd.

Dickson, K. 1979. *Aspects of Religion and Life in Africa*. Accra: Ghana Academy of Arts and Sciences.

Field, M. J. 1960. Search *for Security: An Ethno-psychiatric Study of Rural Ghana*. London: Faber and Faber.

Gallagher, N. E. 1985. "What Happened to Islamic Medicine?", in Brian M.du Toit and I. H. Abdallah (eds.), *African Healing Strategies*. New York: Trado-Medic Books. Pp. 47-57.

Geschiere, P. 1999. *The Modernity of Witchcraft*. Charlottesville: University Press of Virginia

Geurts, K. L. 2002. *Culture and the Senses*. Berkeley: University of California Press.

Green, E. C. & L. Makhubu 1984. "Traditional Healers in Swaziland. Towards Improved Cooperation Between the Traditional and Modern Health Sectors". *Social Science & Medicine* 18, 1071-1079

Gyekye, K.1997. *Tradition and Modernity*. New York: Oxford UniversityPress.

Jahoda, G. 1970."Supernatural Beliefs and Changing Cognitive Structures among Ghanaian University Students". *Cross-Cultural Psychology* 2, 115-130.

Kabongo, I. 1982.'Deroutante Afrique ou La Syncope D'un Discours' *Revue des Canadienne des Etudes Africaines,* 18(1):13-22.

Kanogo, T. 1993. "Mission Impact on Women in colonial Kenya", in F. Bowie, D. Kirkwood & S. Ardener (eds), *Women And Missions: Past and Present: Anthropological and Historical Perceptions*. Providence, R. I: Berg,pp. 165-186.

Kenyatta, J. 1965. *Facing Mount Kenya*. London: Heinemann.

Korem, A. K. & M. K. Abissath (2004).*Traditional Wisdom in African Proverbs*. Accra: Publishing Trends Ltd.

Lukes, S.. 1967. "Some Problems About Rationality", in B. R. Wilson (ed) *Rationality*. Oxford: Basil Blackwell, pp 200-211

Mair, L. 1934. *An African People in the Twentieth Century*: London: Routledge & Sons

Mbiti, J. S. 1969. *African Religions and Philosophy*. London: Heinemann.

_____ 1970 *Introduction to African Religion*. London: Heinemann.

Mendonsa, E. 1997. "Characteristics of Sissala Diviners", in A. C. ehman and J. E. Myers (eds.) *Magic, Witchcraft and Religion: An Anthropological Study of the Supernatural*,. Mountain View California: Mayfield Publishing Company. pp 278-288.

Miller, J. 1994. *The Social Control of Religious Zeal: A Study of Organizational Contradictions*. New Brunswick: Rutgers University.

Nukunya, G. K. (1969). "Afa Divination in Anlo: A Preliminary Report". *Research Review* 5 (2): 9-26.

_____ 2001. *Tradition and Change*. Accra: Ghana Universities Press.

Oppong, C. 1973. *Growing up in Dagbon*. Tema: Ghana Publishing Corporation.

Parker, P. P. 1998. "Witchcraft Beliefs among Ghanaian University Students." Unpublished Long Essay, Department of Sociology, University of Ghana.

Rattray, R. S. 1929. *Religion and Art in Ashanti*. Oxford: Clarendon Press.

Samson, C. (ed.) 1999. *Health Studies: A Critical and Cross-Cultural Reader*. Malder: Blackwell Publishers Inc.

Steegstra, M. 2004. *Resilient Rituals*. New Brunswick: Transaction Publishers

Stoller, P. 1989. *In Sorcery's Shadow: A Memoir of Apprenticeship among the Songhay of Niger* . Chicago: University of Chicago Press

Tanahashi, T. 1978. "Health Services Coverage and its Evaluation". *Bulletin of World Health Organization* 54 (2):295-303.

Turner, V. 1981. *The Drums of Affliction*. London: Hutchinson Publishing Group.

Twumasi, P. A. 1974. *Medical Systems in Ghana*. Tema: Ghana Publishing Corporation.

Warren, D. M. 1979. "The Role of Emic Analyses in Medical Anthropology: The Case of the Bono of Ghana", in Z. A. Ademuwagun et al. (eds) *African Therapeutic Systems*. Waltham, Crossroads Press.

World Health Organization (WHO) (1978). The Promotion and Development of Traditional Medicine. Report of a WHO Meeting. *Technical Report Series* 622. Geneva: WHO.

Suggested Reading

Ademuwagun, Z. A., J. A. A. Ayoade, I. A. Harrison and D. M. Warren (editors.) 1979. *African Therapeutic Systems*. Los Angeles: Crossroads Press.

Appiah-Kubi, K. 1981. *Man Curses, God Heals. Religion and Medical Practice among the Akan of Ghana*. New York: Friendship Press.

Ashforth, A. 2000. *Madumo*. Cape Town: David Philips Publishers.

Bowie, F. 2000. *The Anthropology of African Religion*. London: Blackwell Publishers.

Mullings, L. 1984. *Therapy, Ideology and Social Change: Mental Healing in Urban Ghana*. Berkeley: University of California Press.

Endnotes

1. Ghanaian policy makers were always happy to note the advice they received from Nicholas Kaldor during the preparation of the Seven-Year Development Plan 1963/64-69/70.

2. There is, however, a growing view that private capital flows to Africa are much more significant than some official data from international financial institutions would suggest (Bhinda et.al 1999. Bhinda et.al, suggest that FDI flows to Africa more than tripled in the 1990s and that the growth rate was comparable to that in SE Asia and Latin America. They note that "FDI is diversifying its source and recipient countries and sectors, largely due to innovation by non-OECD investors". The under-reporting by countries is attributed to a poor monitoring capacity.

3. But Bhinda et.al 1999 believe that this is due mostly to poor information being sent to investors all the time about Africa.

4. Listening to various call-in programs on the numerous radio stations in Ghana, both urban and rural, about joining the HIPC initiative gives an indication of how little room governments are now given by their populations.

CHAPTER 15

ENVIRONMENT AND DEVELOPMENT IN SUB-SAHARAN AFRICA

Osman A.R. Alhassan

Introduction

Environmental issues such as deforestation, soil and water pollution, indoor air pollution, biodiversity loss, poor sanitation and overcrowding in urban environments have attracted much attention since the early 1970s. In rural environments, traditional agricultural practices coupled with energy requirements have created serious soil and vegetal degradation that frustrate the survival strategies of such communities. In many parts of the developing world, planning and managing the use of natural resources has become one of the highest priorities because environmental resources have become increasingly scarce leading to a general decrease in the life-support capacities of productive ecological systems. The pervasiveness and understanding of these environmental issues as carried by intellectual discourses and the media have awakened and informed the policies and programmes adopted over the last decade by countries in Sub-Saharan Africa (SSA).

Africa is a large continent with many different dynamics. Since the 1960s, many countries have experienced persistent and severe economic and environmental problems as well as political and social turmoil. The lack of sound economic policies often due to the lack of broad participation by relevant stakeholders in the decision making process is often cited as partly responsible for the sub-region's dismal economic performance. Others argue however that the most serious threat to SSA's development agenda has to do with its complex environmental nexus, in particular its rates of population growth and urban expansion which have led to poverty, perpetuating excessive pressure on the natural resource base which further aggravates the environment (see also Ch.2). Yet there are other viewpoints that see deterioration in terms of trade and lack of financial resources for investment as key factors that have made it difficult for many countries to develop patterns of livelihoods that would reduce pressure on the natural resource base.

As the Brundtland Commission observed in its report on environment and development, "the environment *is where we all live* and *development* is what we all do in attempting to improve our lot within that abode" (World Commission on Environment and Development, (WCED) 1987: xi). The two are therefore inseparable and any society that is seen to be living in prosperity can only be contextualised within its interactive environment. The environment does not exist as a sphere separate from human actions, ambitions and needs and any attempt at improving human access to housing, safe water, adequate food and nutrition, and other basic needs, depends on a healthy and productive environment.

Figure 16 – Akagera National Park, Rwanda

This chapter attempts a broader debate on Sub-Saharan Africa in terms of the relationship between the human and natural environment on the one hand, and socio-economic development dynamics on the other. While the natural environment has provided the base for the region's development, the social, economic and political circumstances that have shaped the direction of development have to a large measure determined benefits derived from the natural environment.

In analysing the role of the environment in the overall development efforts of SSA, the discussion not only links overall development with key environmental components such as water, land, waste products and energy resources, but also discusses alternative ways of realising the full benefits of the immense natural and human resources for the common good of its peoples. The redefinition of development priorities through the adoption of more appropriate and feasible technologies is recommended to make national development both attainable and sustainable. It concludes by drawing attention to some current developments that could harmonise the environment-development linkage to propel SSA into sustained socio-economic development.

Salient Characteristics of Sub-Saharan Africa

The chapter on the geography of Africa has provided rich insights about the continent and only a brief survey will be made here (see Chapter 1). Africa is a large and complex continent with fertile tropical forests; a landscape devastated by wars, conflicts, and drought; and a place where rich cultural traditions reach back to the dawn of humanity. It also has enormous mineral wealth and agricultural potential but is ranked lowest among world regions on almost all indicators of socio-economic development including health.

Most of SSA experiences tropical weather with seasonal rainfall and extreme variability in climate, water availability, soils, and vegetation. Most of the moist forest and guinea savanna have enormous agricultural potential in food cultivation and livestock rearing. However, agricultural viability depends on water availability; many countries in the Sahel region concentrate on livestock rearing due to a combination of population pressure, variable and scanty rainfall, and poor soils. Such climatic variation is without doubt critical to the practice of economically productive agriculture, and consistently impacts directly on the activities of a vast proportion of the population. SSA offers an immense natural resource potential that has been crucial in its socio-economic development. However, there are many environmental constraints that reduce the capacity of its people whose vulnerability only increases within existing economic conditions.

The Context of Environment and Development in SSA

The definitions of environment and development demonstrate that the two do not only go hand-in-hand, but are inseparable. Many key development problems such as poverty, inequality, and rapid population growth place unprecedented pressure on the lands, forests, waters, and other natural resources which together form an essential part of the environment. Similarly, the environment does not exist as a sphere separate from human actions, ambitions and needs, and any attempt at improving human access to housing, safe water, adequate food and nutrition depends on a healthy and productive environment.

There are varying definitions of development.[1] However, as expressed by WCED (1987) development implies change that is desirable. What constitutes development depends on the social goals that are being advocated by the society or country in question. Development is a list of attributes such as increase in real per capita income, improvements in health and nutritional status, educational achievements, access to resources, a fairer distribution of income, and increase in basic freedoms. Implied in the statement above is the fact that we can have economic or social development, or both.

National income is an indicator of human well-being. However, human well-being in terms of resources available to people does not depend on economic growth and levels of national income alone. It also depends on how these resources are used, whether for developing weapons, producing basic food requirements, or providing clean water and education. (See also Chapter 10). Economic development depends on the extent to which social goals are met, that is the provision of social amenities plus equity in its distribution. According to Seers, development is appreciated and understood by asking what has been happening to (i) poverty, (ii) unemployment, and (iii) inequality[2]. He proposed that if all three variables have declined from higher levels, then development has certainly occurred. If on the other hand one or two of these variables have worsened, then it would be difficult to call the result development.

Issues of good governance and social justice have also shown how impressive growth rates may not necessarily translate into benefits for the majority of people. For example, although Nigeria exploits oil and earns substantial income, this wealth is not reflected in its national accounts, or in positive impacts on most of its population. On the other hand, Cuba has for many years stood high in equitable distribution of social services and benefits to its people, even though that country with its impressive social infrastructure cannot be compared with many countries in SSA which have more resources, yet are inequitable in their distribution. Equitable distribution of income rather than resource endowments also counts in the standards of living of a country's population.

Chapter 15

As a result, the UNDP's Human Development Report (HDR) presents an extensive set of indicators on important human development outcomes achieved around the world. These indicators include access to clean water, democratic participation in decision making, equal rights for men and women, high life expectancy at birth, and reduced child mortality rates. Human Development (HD) therefore is the process of enlarging people's choices, by expanding their functioning and capabilities. It is nourished not only by expanding incomes, or infrastructure such as schools and hospitals, but also by care and social reproduction, the empowerment of most vulnerable groups and a clean environment. Human development is therefore a process as well as an end.

Since the late 1980s, sustainable development has replaced many economic and social development paradigms and has acquired wide usage, with a stress on the close linkages between the environment and development. Sustainable development received its most popular exposition in the highly influential World Commission on Environment and Development (WCED) Report in 1987. It defined sustainable development as *"development that meets the needs of the present generation without compromising the ability of future generations to meet their own needs"* (WCED, 1987: 43). Sustainable development came to overshadow other development paradigms mainly because of its clarion call for the integration of politics, culture, and economics in key policy decisions intended to improve the lot of humanity. Sustainable development has two key inherent concepts: (i) the concept of needs, especially the felt needs of the poor majority of people, and (ii) limitations imposed by the state of technology and social organisation on the environment's ability to meet both current and future needs[3].

Sustainable development emphasises human needs and aspirations as a major objective of development. The essential needs of the vast majority of people in SSA are food, clothing, shelter, jobs and incomes. These economic and social development goals involving a progressive transformation of economy and society must be defined in terms of sustainability or inter-generational equity where the needs of the present should be met, bearing in mind a shared responsibility that ensures that the same resources are readily available for future generations. This is only possible if economies, society and ecology are given due and careful consideration in their structural integrity and functional relationships (WCED, 1987).

The majority of people in SSA rely on the land for their sustenance and there are indications that this trend will continue as the discussion in Chapter 11 on agricultural development has clearly indicated. But prosperity in crop and animal production in the future, as well as the employment avenues agriculture will create would depend on today's use patterns, as well as on human restorative interventions. We cannot expect to have development on a sustainable basis if we deplete forests[4], pollute soils and water resources, degrade living environments and allow populations to grow and urban areas to expand beyond tolerable limits, reiterating the close relationship between the environment and development (World Bank, 2008).

It is not surprising that the Millennium Development Goals, which is a declaration of the determination to rid the world of poverty, has a key component that aims at ensuring environmental sustainability. This is in recognition that the environment provides the sustenance for humankind and requires the achievement of sustainable development patterns in order that the preservation of the productive capacity of natural ecosystems will be adequate to meet the needs of future generations.

Environment and Development Correlates in SSA

Differences in development have often come about as a result of the capacity of both natural and human environments to facilitate it. Natural resource endowments feature strongly in development debates as resources most often determine the levels of physical development in many countries in SSA.

Agricultural Resources and Development in SSA

Chapter 11 discussed in some detail the practice of agriculture in SSA including major policies, practices and challenges. The present discussion therefore limits itself to the salient associations between agriculture and development in the continent.

In year 2007, agriculture accounted for around 32 % of GDP in SSA and employed about 50% to 70% of the labour force. It also represented a major source of foreign exchange and its development remains crucial to economic prosperity such as providing sustenance, employment, incomes, and hopes of improving living standards in the sub-region.[5] Much of the development expenditure of SSA is driven by agricultural exports. Agriculture has been increasing its share of sector revenues since independence, and by 1990, agricultural exports as a proportion of total exports were as high as 98% in Sudan, 93% in Burundi, 91% in Malawi, 86% in both Uganda and Rwanda, 85% in Mali, 76% in Ethiopia, 68% in Kenya, 66% in Côte d'Ivoire, 63% in Chad, and 62% in Tanzania. Ghana recorded 41% of its total exports from the agricultural sector alone, and seven other countries in SSA had agricultural exports as a percentage of total exports of over 40% (FAO, 1992). This trend continued in the 1990s. The value of the agricultural sector exports (including fisheries) grew by 34 percent during 2002–06, with an average annual growth rate during the period of 8 %, though the growth in export value in agriculture lagged significantly behind the growth in mining and manufacturing. Merchandise exports also declined (from 18 % in 2002 to 9 % in 2006).[6]

Yet another indicator of well-being is resources available to populations in various countries. According to the UNDP (2003: 200)[7], over 35% of the population of SSA lives below US$1 a day. The proportion ranged from 12% in Cote d'Ivoire; 23% in Kenya; 33% in Cameroon; 45% in Ghana; 62% in Niger; 70% in Nigeria; 73% in Mali; and 82% in Ethiopia. Except in resource-rich Nigeria where bad governance, corruption, and a highly skewed income distribution might have accounted partly for the high proportion of people living below US$1 a day, better resourced countries such as Kenya and Côte d'Ivoire all recorded lower proportions of those living in such stark conditions. Worse conditions occurred in countries such as Niger, Mali, and Ethiopia where the climate is quite hostile and natural resource endowments are relatively lower. Here again we see the correlation between environmental endowments, at least in water and soil nutrient quality, and living conditions.

For instance, Ghana's cocoa exports have turned out to be favourable only when market prices are considerably higher, rather than through physical expansion of production. A close look at the revenues accruing from cocoa during the last few years attests to this. Cocoa earned the country $802.2 m in 2003, compared to $474.4 m in 2002, an increase of 69.1%. This was attributed mainly to higher production in 2002/2003 where purchases totalled 496,869 tonnes, the highest level since 1964, and higher world market prices. Despite the very high production,

Chapter 15

the volume of cocoa exports increased by only 11.4% from 2002 to 2003. But the unit price of cocoa beans rose by 56.6% from 2002 to 2003. So while beans exports increased by 11.4% in volume from 2002 to 2003, its export value rose by 72.3% to reach US$ 676.1 m in 2003. Also, the value of cocoa products increased by 54.0% even though the volume of cocoa products decreased by only 17.8% in 2003 (ISSER, 2004). And while there have been significant increases in cocoa production since 2008, it is the steady international market price that accounts for substantial revenues that can be used for socio-economic development (ISSER, 2010: 120-122).

The above discussion about Ghana's success in the cocoa sector is similar to that of most African countries which rely on sales from agricultural products to finance development projects. Not only do the primary products not serve as staple food for the population, but also the unit price of these primary products in international markets at any particular point in time is what matters, rather than high production and export volumes. It is therefore not surprising that a number of agriculturally vibrant economies in SSA rely on food imports. This is because these major primary products (and exports) do not service the food needs of its people, and also because these products on many occasions do not attract good prices in international markets thus constraining the foreign exchange earnings of these countries. In other countries such as Nigeria with a high potential for food production, the near collapse of the agricultural sector following the oil boom has resulted in heavy dependence on food imports since the 1980s. This syndrome of heavy food imports and associated debt burdens in the face of potential agricultural resources makes it difficult to establish a close relationship between agricultural resource endowments and socio-economic development in many countries in SSA.[8]

Again, the World Bank's World Development Report (World Bank 2008) emphasised that Sub-Saharan Africa is a region heavily reliant on agriculture for overall growth, yet public spending on farming is only 4% of total government spending. Yet for the poorest people, it is estimated that GDP growth originating in agriculture is about four times more effective in raising incomes of extremely poor people than GDP growth originating outside the sector. The Bank further stressed that Sub-Saharan Africa has the environment, albeit not always enabling, that can serve as an impetus for growth in agriculture for poverty reduction. The report concludes that agriculture can offer pathways out of poverty if efforts are made to increase productivity in the staple foods sector. The sector must therefore be placed at the centre of the development agenda if the goals of halving extreme poverty and hunger by 2015 are to be realized.

Mineral Resources and Development in SSA

To a large extent, mineral production has been extremely important in the economies of SSA. It has contributed to the export earnings of countries as well as attracting foreign investment capital, creating jobs and improving incomes. The presence of diverse mineral supplies within the region has therefore been a potential source of social and economic development though mineral exploitation has also resulted in the destruction of biological ecosystems and left much of the productive environment in ruins.

Mining provides direct and indirect employment, revenues and economic development. However, mining and the waste generated from active and inactive mining sites from ore beneficiation, and their impacts on human health and the environment is acknowledged to be a serious and continuing problem facing government agencies, industry and the general public.

312

Attempts to control these are becoming one of the top priorities of many governments as well as global financing institutions, and the global demands for environmental consciousness may improve the environment in many mining areas.

The method of production for small-scale diamond mining ranges from very basic methods of digging, washing and sifting to the use of equipment such as water pumps and excavators. The most common method is the highly labour intensive process where large groups of people dig the earth and wash and sift the ore for diamonds. Like gold mining, the environmental impact of small-scale diamond mining is severe. The areas suspected of containing diamonds become exposed and unsuitable for farming. Miners not only remove vegetation and economically valuable trees but their activities also divert water flow and increase surface runoff. In the Upper East Region of Ghana, small-scale mining carried out on hilly areas around Tongo and Bongo has created serious flooding and erosion around slopes.[9]

Figure 17– Goldfields Mine Site, Damang, Ghana

Source: *http://www.geoconnexion.com/newspics/4620_a.jpg*

Mining activities expose communities within the vicinity of mining areas to a wide range of health problems. During heavy rains, dug-out areas hold stagnant pools that become breeding grounds for mosquitoes and increase the incidence of malaria. People who come into contact with water sources contaminated by mine wastes are exposed to disease. Mining activities cause heavy silt to flow into river beds and creeks, which reduces fish populations. Toxic wastes in the water sources contaminate marine life, making them unfit for human consumption. The negative impacts of mining activities on human habitats, especially in areas where mining is more concentrated, result in severe health and social costs for local communities and governments. Concentration of surface mines in the Western Region of Ghana, especially around the Wassa West District, has alienated about 1,040 sq km of land from other land users.[9] As land becomes scarcer, it is likely that women, young people, migrants, and secondary rights beneficiaries would find it more difficult to make a living. The evolving nature of customary land tenure does not assure these vulnerable groups any leverage, and rather tends to perpetuate their landlessness by alienation.

Another case in point is the relationship between mining activities and malaria incidence. Though many countries in SSA have a complex of problems that collectively account for its high levels of infant mortality, a major cause of this mortality is attributed to malaria. In Sierra Leone for instance, the high levels of infant mortality (at 316) and under-five mortality (at 182) is promoted by environmental factors, namely mining activities around human settlements which provide thousands of breeding grounds for the malaria parasite. Even though Sierra Leone has one of the highest renewable internal freshwater resources per capita- 28,957 cubic metres as at 2005, fresh water sources are also polluted adding to the disease burden of the country (World Bank, 2008).

Indeed, according to the World Bank, Angola represents a mixed story of economic success because of the disparity in living conditions between its urban and rural populations. With an urban-rural population ratio of 57% to 43% respectively in 2006, 79% of its urban population had access to improved sanitation facilities while only 16% of its rural population had access to improved sanitation facilities (World Bank, 2010:194). Again Angola's education expenditure, including salaries, in 2008 was a meagre 2.3 % of Gross National Investments (GNI). This compares with an average of 3.3% for SSA, 3.7% for Ethiopia, 4.7% for Ghana, 6.6% for Botswana and 7.3% for Namibia. Angola's figure is however better than that of Nigeria whose education expenditure in 2008 was only 1% of its gross national investment (World Bank, 2010: 194-215). The illustration using Angola and Nigeria underscores the fact that physical resources alone may not constitute development for a country if the gains are not equitably distributed.

The extent to which mining benefits countries in the sub-region depends on its prudent management. Botswana's per capita income has quadrupled between 1975 and 2001 (from US$ 813 to US$ 3,066) because the revenue from diamonds has been invested in health, education, and restoring the environment. The same cannot be said of developments in Angola and Namibia which are both high grade diamond producers, with Angola having oil in addition[10].

Under the current global restructuring programme, mining arrangements are not fair to local communities endowed with these mineral resources. Not only do local communities receive less than a fair share of the net economic benefits from minerals, but they also lose their long-term productive base because of the serious environmental imprints left after mining is completed. The upsurge in mining in SSA has followed the introduction of new mining and processing technologies which have far reaching environmental implications.[11]

Forest Resources and Development in SSA

One essential element of development in SSA is her forest resources. These, like other natural resources, are moderated by the institutions, level of technology, and the demands placed on these resources to meet human needs. These in turn mould the human and physical environment of the region. Coastal West Africa has experienced one of the most drastic forest cover reduction rate even though log and timber revenues have also accelerated the development of countries with forest resources. Ghana for instance relied immensely on exports of forest products during the 1980s when cocoa prices fell drastically. The same can be said of Nigeria, Liberia, Cameroon, and La Côte d'Ivoire.[12] The situation has not changed much except that there are no longer forests to exploit in many countries.

Table 13 below shows forest areas in selected countries in Africa from 1965 to 2000 and some projections for 2010. A noteworthy observation is that forest cover has dwindled significantly over the period under consideration in these countries, except in Gabon and Burkina Faso. Fifty-six percent of the land area of the forest regions in Africa in 1965 had dwindled to around 32% of the land area in 2000.[13] Cote d'Ivoire, Ghana, Malawi, Niger and Ethiopia in that order have lost more significant proportions of their forest stands. Furthermore, data collection deficiencies all over the sub-region suggest that the situation in these countries might actually be worse than portrayed here.

Table 13 – Actual and Projected Forest Areas in Selected African Countries (1965-2010)

No.	Country	Forest Area (in thousand hectares)					
		1965	1980	1987	1990	2000	2010 Projection
1	Ethiopia	27	16	10	4.5	4.2	3.3
2	Congo D.R	80	78	65	62	60	56
3	Malawi	54	54	46	35	27	23
4	Tanzania	51	49	48	45	44	42
5	Burkina Faso	30	26	25	27	26	25
6	Madagascar	31	27	25	22	20	18
7	Ghana	43	38	36	33	28	24
8	Cote d'Ivoire	60	31	20	31	22	17
9	Gabon	78	78	78	85	84	86
10	Niger	31	19	4	1.5	1.0	1.0
Average for Sub-Saharan Africa		56	48	44	35	32	29

Sources: 1. Figures for 1965, 1980 and 1987 derived from p. 279 of The World Bank (1989); *Sub-Saharan Africa: From Crisis to Sustainable Growth*
2. Figures for 1990 and 2000 derived from UNDP (2003: 220)
3. Projections for 2010 derived from World Bank, 2008:165)

The details in Table 13 however represent a partial view on forest loss. A look at forest cover and the rates of depletion of such forests as shown in Table 14 will provide a better understanding of the state of these forests. As can be seen in the Table, the exploitation and removal rates are particularly high for Côte d'Ivoire, Ghana and Tanzania, but the other countries also exhibit high rates of deforestation though not at the same rate as the Cote d'Ivoire where forestland is daily converted into cocoa and coffee plantations. Only Gabon and Niger are projected to halt deforestation through prudent measures by 2010.

Table 14 – Some Environmental Indicators for Selected Countries (1980s and 2007)

No.	Country	Environmental Indicators in % per year				Forest Area (000 sq km)#	Average Annual Defor-estation (in %)#
		Deforestation Rate*		Reforestation Rate+			
		1980s	1990s	1980s	1990s	2007	2000 -07
1	Ethiopia	0.3	0.3	0.01	0	127	1.1
2	Congo D.R	0.2	0.27	0.001	0	1330	0.2
3	Malawi	3.5	4	0.5	0.7	33	1.0
4	Tanzania	0.3	0.35	0.25	0.8	344	1.1
5	Burkina Faso	1.7	1.9	0.02	0.04	67	0.4
6	Madagascar	1.2	1.0	1.1	1.2	128	0.3
7	Ghana	0.8	0.92	0.02	0.01	53	2.0
8	Cote d'Ivoire	5.2	5.9	0.5	0.3	104	-0.1
9	Gabon	0.1	0.1	0.07	0.01	218	0.0
10	Niger	0.3	0.5	0.03	0.01	12	1.0
Average for Sub-Saharan Africa		0.4	0.5	0.05	0.03	-	-

Sources: 1.* Figures for 1980s derived from p. 291-293 of World Resources Institute (1990-91);
2.+ Figures for 1990s derived from World Resources Institute (1996-97).
3 # Figures derived from World Bank (2010) World Development Indicators, p. 166-168.

Again as demonstrated by Table 14, it is only in Madagascar whose reforestation efforts in the 1990s edged out deforestation in the same period. There was also a considerable decline in the rate of deforestation from 2000 to 2007. While all the other countries made interventions in reaforestation, these were too minimal to offset the loss in forests and other wildlife resources, and not much had been done in these countries as at 2007 to be able to halt the increasing rates of forest destruction in SSA.

The reasons for forest depletion are sometimes obvious. Most countries earn substantial revenues from log exports and this helps meet budgetary requirements. Thus, one principal reason for declining forest cover is massive exports of logs and timber. Most of the forests rely on natural regrowth, but traditional agricultural practices as well as the demands for fuel wood as the principal energy source for many countries in SSA make replenishment slow.

In the ensuing section, a discussion of energy and environment is made. As Africa uses a lot of traditional bio-fuels, the impact on forests is immense, especially as a significant amount of this bio-fuels regenerate through natural processes.

Energy, environment and development in SSA

The links between energy, environment, and development in Africa are crucial. This is partly due to the stress energy demands make on the physical environment, and the subsequent implications this has for development. According to the *World Energy Outlook 2004* (OECD/IEA

2004), wood energy constitutes a major source of energy in developing countries, especially in SSA. Four-fifths of the population of Sub-Saharan Africa rely for energy wholly or partly on wood fuel and this accounts for 75% of total energy consumption, although woodfuel share ranges from 61% to 86% (OECD/IEA, 2004).

According to current best estimates, African woodfuel consumption reached 623 million m³ in 1994. This means Africa has the highest *per capita* woodfuel consumption (0.89 m³/year) compared to other continents, an African on the average consumes almost three times as much woodfuel as his/her Asian counterpart (0.30 m³/year).[14] While fuelwood (or firewood) traditionally accounted for a major part of total woodfuel consumption, the demand for charcoal is growing among the urban population and likely to increase substantially in the future with increasing population, given that countries may make insignificant progress in the shift to the use of other energy alternatives such as electricity, LPG, and solar due to slow national growth and inequalities in the distribution of economic gains. This will increase the economic, social, and environmental impact on development in the region.[15]

Table 15 below compares wood fuel consumption as at 1997, against electricity consumption as at year 2000. The lack of reliable woodfuel data for 2000 has necessitated a comparison using different base years. Globally, only about 10% of the world's energy consumption by human societies is from wood. Yet in developing countries, some three quarters (or 77%) of the fuel supply is from biomass. In SSA, this proportion is as high as 96% in Ethiopia; 92% in Congo D.R., Cote d'Ivoire and Tanzania; 89% in Malawi; 88% in Niger; 78% in Ghana; and 33% in Gabon (UNDP, 2003: 302-303). Demand for wood in Sub-Saharan Africa averages about 1.7 metric tonnes of dry wood per capita per year, and given increases in demand from growing populations and from urbanization, shortages are becoming apparent.

Table 15– Energy Use in Selected African Countries

No.	Country	Woodfuel/ charcoal (as % of total energy) (1997)*	Electricity (in kW. Hrs) (2000)+	Population (in millions) without electricity (2009)#
1	Ethiopia	95.9	16	68.7
2	D.R. Congo	91.7	148	58.7
3	Malawi	88.6	-	12.7
4	Tanzania	91.4	37	37.7
5	Burkina Faso	87.1	-	12.6
6	Madagascar	84.0	-	15.9
7	Ghana	78.1	424	9.4
8	Cote d'Ivoire	91.5	-	11.1
9	Gabon	32.9	**697**	0.9
10	Niger	80.6	-	-
Average for Sub-Saharan Africa		72.7	112	23.5

Sources: 1. *Figures for woodfuel derived from World Resources Institute (1996-97)*
2.+*Figures for electricity are extracted from OECD/IEA, 2000.*
3.#*Figures for population without electricity from OECD/IEA, 2009, Tables 1 & 2.*

Consumption of electricity is quite low among the countries under consideration. For the same period per capita consumption figures were as high as 245,422 kW Hrs for Norway; 12,331 for the US; 1,878 for Brazil; and 4,018 for Malta. Gabon and Ghana had moderate consumption of electricity while other countries recorded insignificant use. Ghana's appreciable use was due to her relative electricity endowments while Gabon is a relatively affluent oil-rich country in SSA capable of providing electricity for its people. Indeed, many countries as indicated in the Table do not have records for electricity use which goes to corroborate the details in the last column of Table 15 where a significant proportion of the population lack electricity[16]. This also implies the insignificant use of electricity compared to wood fuel. Indeed, the more recent data on populations without electricity could also suggest the lack of good recording due to the insignificant use within the total energy mix. Above all, electricity is expensive and unless it is subsidized, its use among the majority of poor rural dwellers will be restricted.

The use of electricity and other modern energy forms can be associated with some level of development. It is a clean energy source which is efficient and capable of promoting productive activities, especially agricultural processing and artisanal activities, including the manufacture of rural farm implements. In many parts of SSA, infrastructure is poor and electricity does not permeate vast areas of countries, especially in rural areas where such power is needed to boost processing activities and make agriculture more lucrative. Even in countries with high per capita electric power consumption such as Gabon and Ghana, this is mainly enjoyed mostly by urban dwellers, and a significant proportion of rural dwellers who need energy to process and preserve food either lack access to electricity, or cannot afford to use it due to cost considerations even when the service is available.

Indoor and outdoor air pollution put a major burden on world health. More than half the world's people rely on dung, wood, crop waste, or coal to meet basic energy needs. Cooking and heating with these fuels on open fires or stoves without chimneys lead to indoor air pollution, which is responsible for 1.6 million deaths a year—or one death per every 20 seconds. In many urban areas air pollution exposure is the main environmental threat to health. Long-term exposure to high levels of soot and small particles contributes to a range of health effects, including respiratory diseases, lung cancer, and heart disease (World Bank, 2010: 206).

The high energy prices countries in SSA encounter have stimulated the cultivation of biofuels which promise to help developing countries reduce high oil import bills as well as new opportunities for mitigating climate change. These new initiatives whose economic viability is yet to be seen in the future, are however creating some concern in many countries in SSA. Many consumers in SSA, most of who are very poor, are already paying higher prices for food staples as grain prices rise in both local and world markets directly due to the diversion of grain to biofuels production, or indirectly due to land conversion. This poses tremendous social costs (as a result of rising food prices) and environmental (deforestation) risks. Like any other development alternative, biofuel production offers opportunities as well as challenges and governments of SSA need to devise policies and programmes on biofuels, especially certification systems to mitigate the potentially large environmental footprint of biofuels production (World Bank, 2010: 37-71).

Water as a Constraining Factor in Development in SSA

Africa is the world's most urbanizing continent and there are already more people living in urban settlements in Africa than all of Western Europe and North America (UN Habitat, 2006). Most of this growth is unplanned and driven by both natural growth and migration from rural areas. In spite of the numerous problems rapid urban growth may bring, it also has many advantages. Urban areas are the motors for generating economic wealth of nations, the location for the accumulation of physical assets and infrastructure, the concentration of human capital, and a place for cultural and political exchange of ideas and innovation. Yet an increasing number of urban residents in Africa lack basic services including water and sanitation to facilitate economic growth (Pelling and Wisner, 2009: 19-20).

The lack of potable water remains a serious health hazard in Africa constraining poverty reduction measures and overall economic development. This is especially the case for close to 72% of African urban dwellers who live in slums. Not only is diarrhoea still one of the major causes of infant and child death, but water scarcity worsens the sanitation situation and increases health risks, especially in crowded areas. In addition, malaria is also a water-related hazard linked to improper and inadequate drainage. Between the two of them, diarrhoea and malaria kill 6 million African children each year.[17] Many of these children are in cities, despite the fact that in theory, there is better access to medical attention for these children and their mothers. Indeed, though the child mortality rate declined from 141 per 1,000 in 1990 to 104 in 2008, and substantial decreases occurred in maternal deaths, Sub-Saharan Africa remains off track to meet the income poverty goal[18].

Such diseases are a function not only of the presence of disease vectors such as water quality, but also of the quantity of water a household can command as well as the provision of safe waste removal. The productive capacities of most urban environments in Africa are under-utilized, because the potential health benefits of water supply and sanitation improvements are lacking. A study by Songsore et al. (2010) in the Greater Accra Metropolitan Area (GAMA) in Ghana showed the close relationships among water, human health, and development. An estimated 20-30% of the urban population in the metropolis depend on water vendors for their supply. Those who use water this way tend to buy smaller quantities and therefore may suffer compromised standards of hygiene in food preparation and hygiene. Household water requirements may, and often does, account for 15 to 25% of a typical household's budget, thus leaving less income for other basic necessities such as food and energy, and may add up to existing health burdens.

In a bid to reverse water scarcity and promote agriculture, many governments embarked on irrigation through big-dam projects. The Akosombo, Kariba and Kainji dam projects all made some provision for irrigated agriculture although cheap energy supply for industrial development was the main reason for constructing these dams. In addition, smaller dams were constructed solely to irrigate and increase production of agricultural exports in cereals, fruits and vegetables. Notwithstanding their moderate sizes, these dams were still big projects and did not allow easy local level management of the water resource. The consequence has been the inability of local farmers to effectively use these water resources, as well as manage these dams. In many areas where animal and human populations had grown rather fast, water resources have been subjected to severe pressures, and coupled with poor land use practices, most of the dams silted and dried up over time. Thus the lack of water became a critical factor hindering production as farmers and animal herders have had to rely on rain-fed agriculture with its attendant problems (World Bank, 2008).

It has been observed that the irrigation technologies adopted by SSA were quite sophisticated and did not make room for indigenous control and management. For the natural environment to support agriculture fully, human interventions must be appropriate to the needs of the local environment, as well as being sustainable (FAO, 2006). The Tono and Bontanga irrigation projects in Northern Ghana have sophisticated designs which make them technologically inappropriate because they are capital intensive and it is costly to maintain the infrastructure. This makes it rather difficult to manage at the local level. As the government's maintenance efficiency declined, these irrigation projects became difficult to manage and users had to find extra resources for the maintenance of the few canals.

In the process, irrigated areas became expensive and out of reach of the majority of farmers, especially women. But it was possible for few relatively rich farmers to acquire irrigated fields and control the land. Most of these relatively affluent farmers with irrigated lands were absentee farmers who exploited the labour of local farmers who could not afford to lease or rent irrigated plots. It is perhaps in this light that indigenously designed irrigation is most appropriate as it is cheaper to design and also easier to maintain and make agriculture more sustainable. One such experiment is the Kerio Cluster indigenous irrigation in Kenya.

The diversion of streams and local canal networks along the east wall of the Rift Valley in Kenya, the *Kerio Cluster,* is an example of a small-scale indigenous intervention in agriculture that translates into a local productive base capable of sustaining itself for decades.[19] Described as the most complex and extensive indigenous water management system in Africa south of the Sahara, the Marakwet people have over the past century applied considerable engineering skills to exploit what Potter et al. (1999) term "the challenging ecologies of the Rift Valley" to enable permanent settlement and the cultivation of cereals and vegetables across the valley floor. The Marakwet have constructed dams, furrows, channels and terraces to divert and carry the water from the minor streams of the plateau to the fields of the valley floor. Earth and stone channels with simple brushwood and stone dams are used to modify the variable flow of the natural streams, and to carry water to the majority of fields between the foot of the escarpment and the banks of the Kerio River. This way, many hundreds of households sustain their livelihoods, live normal lives, and contribute to ecological stability.

Africa has substantial natural and human resources that can be used to make local and regional gains in food security. Such gains can be achieved through methods such as applying biotechnology to develop new crop varieties. An example is the development of *New Rice for Africa (NERICA)* varieties by the West African Rice Development Authority (WARDA), with support from other partners. Key to the effort was WARDA's rice gene bank of 16,000 rice varieties which are preserved as seed in cold storage, duplicated at the International Institute for Tropical Agriculture (IITA) in Nigeria, and the International Rice Research Institute (IRRI) in the Philippines (Ramsay and Edge, 2004). With the physical constraints the environment poses, especially with water deficits, what SSA needs is more research which can come out with crop and livestock varieties that can withstand the weather. NERICA is resistant to local stresses such as weed suppression, grain quality and lodging resistance and high yields, among others.

These rice varieties can provide 50 percent more grains than current varieties when cultivated with traditional rain-fed systems and without fertilizer. Irrigation systems can be improved by researching the availability of water for distribution and cost effective utilisation, measured in terms of its quality and quantity. An interdisciplinary approach, including greater utilization of *local knowledges*, can help increase agricultural yield through science-based information, assessment and prediction, together with extension work and good communication with the farming community (see Ch. 1). In addition, science-based climate variability forecasts and assessments can help decision makers take appropriate measures to improve food availability, and subsequently reduce poverty and hunger.

There are about 1.64 million hectares of rain-fed upland rice in West and Central Africa, employing about 70% of the region's rice farmers. Around 80% of the upland cultivation is slash-and-burn agriculture, with other labour-intensive activities namely, land clearing, weeding and harvesting. About 40% of West Africa's 4.1 million hectares of rice is upland or dryland and grown like maize. Experience shows that each slash-and-burn crop produces less than before, and exerts much more pressure on a fragile ecosystem. This is the reason why NERICA is welcome news for all farmers working within the margins of fragile ecosystems where extra effort gives a return not commensurate with inputs invested.

Pests as a Physical Environmental Constraint to Development

Besides the discussion of physical environmental barriers such as water scarcity to development in the sub region, the effect of pests and diseases on agriculture is already well known. The UN FAO and national governments on the continent are concerned about the extent to which pest control remains a daunting problem, often translated into post-harvest losses that further constrain Africa's agriculture and make its food security situation precarious (see Chapter 11).

A serious environmental hazard that translates into poverty and misery in SSA is the effects of locust invasions over the past decades, with the 2004 cropping season as one of the most serious. It affected the whole of the West African— Sahelian region- Mauritania, Senegal, Mali, Niger, Burkina Faso, Nigeria, and then spread into several outlying areas, including Darfur in Sudan. All these countries suffered large-scale loss of pasture land and crops from millions of invading locusts that devoured all vegetal matter in its way. The massive locust invasion in Northern Mali in particular destroyed 70% of rain-fed crops and over 40% of livestock pasture in the regions of Gao and Timbuktu (FAO, 2006).

The livelihood of the majority of the people has since then been under serious threat as pastoralists were forced to move their livestock much earlier in the season to the few areas where pasture remained. This has created greater pressure on these areas and brought together larger amounts of cattle with the threat of the quick spread of diseases. As animal health experts have warned, Contagious Bovine Pleuro-Pneumonia (CBPP) is capable of spreading quickly through herds, with devastating effect. CBBP has already been seen in cattle in Northern Mali and Central Niger. There is no effective treatment for the disease, making the need for vaccination of cattle urgent. Animals have come under serious danger since the invasions and threatened the livelihoods of pastoralists and agro-pastoralists in the whole of Northern Mali.[20]

A number of options have been advocated to resolve the menace of pests. Though some seasons have brought severe devastation to the majority of poor farmers and herders, food losses attributed to post harvest losses are not new in Africa. Improving transport networks is the first solution to curtailing post harvest losses. Promoting the use of bicycles in rural areas should be encouraged and governments should invest in bicycles for poor farmers. The use of donkeys and carts can also help to convey food from rural hinterlands to market areas. In addition, indigenous technologies for preserving food need to be encouraged, and policy makers should not see these as simplistic, primitive and/or inferior. Food deficit countries in SSA should also encourage appropriate technologies in food preservation as this will improve food stocks, enhance food security, and thereby offset some of the natural disasters that strike unannounced.[21]

Population and Urbanisation as a Setback to Development in SSA

The dynamics of demography have been treated in detail in Chapter. 2 and only a brief discussion is offered here on the effects of these demographic dimensions on the environment. Suffice it to say that at any level of development, the human impact on the environment is a function of population size, technology, and per capita consumption. A rapidly growing population means enormous challenges to development as many mouths have to be fed and many people sheltered and clothed. The high population growth rates in most countries in this region thwarts rather than promotes socio-economic development, as a large proportion of the population is less than 25 years, with immense needs for education and training.

Another demographic dimension is the spate of urban growth and the consequences on socio-economic development as discussed in Chapter 2. In many countries in SSA, urbanisation is a major component of growth, often creating major problems for governments and city authorities. While these few cities have a fair share of infrastructure and socio-economic facilities, the population often outstrips infrastructure and services. Ghana is a clear example of such urban development. It is estimated that by the year 2025, 58 % of Ghana's population will reside in urban areas, with 30% located in the four largest metropolises (GSS, 2004). The same can be said of countries such as Nigeria, Senegal, Kenya and Namibia which have majority of its population in rural areas, yet have a few urban centres accommodating more than a proportionate share of urban dwellers.

The last but the not least demographic factor in the region is that of population distribution which is quite uneven, often exacerbating negative impacts on the environment. A survey of SSA shows that crude population densities vary; small sized countries like Rwanda, Burundi, and the island country of Mauritius have high densities. Countries such as Democratic Republic, of Congo, Angola, Namibia and those within the Sahelian region (Mali, Niger, Mauritania and Chad) have low crude densities (see see also Ch. 1).

Many examples exist in Africa where population concentration is not the best for sustainable environmental and economic development. These are often described as core areas and in rural settings they have the tendency of aggravating ecosystems and retarding the productive base of the environment. For instance most of the degradation in Cameroon is associated with the south-western enclave (Ebolowa-Yaounde-Douala-Kumba) where 15% of the country's land area is inhabited by 75% of the population (Aryeetey-Attoh, 2003). Though this rich forest zone has diverse agricultural potential for cocoa, coffee, timber and rubber, coupled with manufacturing in aluminium smelting and oil refining, the area is being degraded and the sustainability of its ecosystem is threatened.

Such pockets of high densities pose serious environmental problems because of pressure exerted on land and water resources by humans and animals. For rural development to succeed there needs to be prudent measures aimed at conserving land resources, as well as encouraging population redistribution in order to free the land from excessive human pressure and make its use sustainable. This is particularly important judging from the evidence that Africa is not only urbanising faster than any other continent, but also the fact that the process of urbanisation in Africa results more from the "push" of environmental and agricultural failure rather than from the "pull" of urban opportunities.[22] Such a situation has weakened municipal governance because it has exacerbated the problem of waste management in cities, as well as killing urban agriculture which hitherto has been a vibrant economic activity. The constraints of urban waste and declining urban agriculture are explored in the following section.

Poor Urban Waste Management and Decline in Urban Agriculture

A serious environmental concern that impedes productivity in urban areas all over SSA is the wastes that are left uncollected, often forming landscapes of their own. The productivity of residents in poor urban neighbourhoods is diminished by exposure to household environments characterised by indoor air pollution, bug-filled outdoors, near-the-door faeces, and far-from-the-door water. Indeed, community and public health specialists have estimated that millions of urban residents are unproductive for some substantial periods within the year due to disease burdens associated with their work and living environments.

Associated with waste is the notion of spatial discordance of areas where bigger settlements such as the big urban areas increasingly rely on smaller ones in the countryside for resources needed to support the bigger settlements. This is particularly true for many of the administrative and capital cities in SSA, and as urban expansion intensifies, not only is competition for residential and industrial land eating up chunks of fertile peri-urban crop and vegetable fields, but rural lands also serve as reservoirs for urban waste. In recent years the dumping of high plastic-content wastes has devastated already impoverished local economies that are based on agriculture and livestock. Traditionally, urban wastes were used to fertilise outlying farm lands because these were predominantly organic wastes. Today, plastic and metal content in urban waste in Africa exceed tolerable limits which make recycling difficult. The indiscriminate diffusion of such waste in the environment is having a dramatic impact not only on public health, but especially on food safety for local populations. The dumping of plastic wastes damages farmland soil and is responsible for increasing livestock mortality rates where grazing lands have been contaminated.

According to city waste managers, waste dumps in African cities have between 10-20% of its constituents being plastic waste and scrap metal. A high proportion of these waste dumps consist of both organic and inorganic waste. Because of this mix-up, it is difficult to sort. This is particularly the case when waste has been left for long. But probably the greatest problem for producers of compost from urban waste is contamination with inorganic waste such as broken glass, toxic materials and biomedical waste.

Managing urban waste is a serious problem for many countries in SSA. The main technological and economic challenges facing local governments are (i) how to provide effective and reliable waste collection service, and (ii) how to dispose of waste in an environmentally acceptable and sustainable manner. Prudent management of urban waste involves costly activities whose short term returns are by and large intangible. In the long term however, an effective waste management system holds the key to viable economic progress which depends on a protected and productive environment.

Tables 16 and 17 illustrate the problem metropolitan and municipal authorities encounter as they attempt to manage waste in the five largest cities in Ghana.

Table 16. Waste Generation and Collection Coverage in Ghana's Five (5) Major Cities

City	Population	Daily Waste Generation (Tonnes)	Daily Collection Coverage (Tonnes)	Daily Percentage Coverage
Accra	3,500,000	1,800	1,200	66%
Kumasi	1,300,000	1,000	700	70%
Tema	500,000	250	200	80%
Tamale	320,000	180	85	47%
Sekondi-Takoradi	300,000	250	200	60%

Source: Mensah, (2004) Waste Management: The Technical and Economic Challenges Facing Local Government. Institute of Economic Affairs, Accra.

Table 17 – Waste Collection Costs and Recovery in Ghana's Five (5) Biggest Cities

City	Monthly Cost for 100% Service Coverage (million ¢)	Monthly Cost of Current Service Coverage (million ¢)	Monthly Cost Recovery (million ¢)	Monthly Cost Deficit (million ¢)	Monthly Cost Deficit (%)
Accra	4.50	2.00	0.750	1.250	63%
Kumasi	2.40	1.50	0.450	1.050	70%
Tema	1.20	0.90	0.300	0.600	67%
Tamale	0.22	0.08	0.008	0.072	90%
Sekondi-Takoradi	0.60	0.40	0.250	0.150	38%

Source: Mensah, (2004) Waste Management: The Technical and Economic Challenges Facing Local Government.

As indicated in Tables 16 and 17, though much of the efforts of city authorities in Ghana have so far focused mainly on collection and disposal at dump sites, the challenge for waste collection remains formidable. Nearly 80% of the cost of solid urban waste management is attributed to collection and transportation to disposal sites.

The waste nuisance has not changed much in Ghana since 2005 as urban growth continues to outpace municipal service delivery. The country currently generates an excess of 11,000 tons of waste per day, with conceivably higher waste accumulation in major cities making them filthy and disease-prone. In November 2011, a fleet of trucks were presented to various assemblies to enable the Metropolitan, Municipal and District Assemblies (MMDAs) deliver higher quality waste management services in their respective areas. This is expected to provide a logistical resource base, which other private waste management operators can fall on to beef up their equipment holdings and enhance their operational capacities. It is clear there is the need for serious investments in waste management to further change the face of the waste management industry. There is also the need to incorporate unorthodox waste pre-collectors (cart-pushers) into mainstream operations by helping them acquire affordable and appropriate waste collection equipment on very flexible terms.

Of particular note are the relatively small amounts of plastic waste being generated, but many countries in Africa have problems in sourcing the necessary funds to solve problems linked to waste collection and safe disposal. These countries are among the world's poorest, where average household incomes are often small. The management of solid urban waste, in particular plastic waste, therefore represents a major problem and not many attempts have been made at large-scale composting as a way of resolving urban waste problems.

There are examples of limited recycling efforts in Africa which are worth emulating if the urban waste menace is to be tackled with all the seriousness it deserves. An Italian organisation called *Lay Volunteers International Association* (LVIA) is promoting a number of plastic recycling and public awareness projects in Africa. Efforts in Senegal and Burkina Faso have been encouraging and are considered *best practices* worthy of emulation. Following recycling successes in Senegal, the World Bank funded a project in Ouagadougou, capital of Burkina Faso, where this best practice has been replicated successfully.[23]

The project aims at constructing Burkina's very first plastic recycling plant. Besides the promotion of international cooperation, serious environmental problems in and around the city will be dealt with by integrating the involvement of public and private institutions (including local associations and businesses) to create a "market-based" system for recycled plastics. Such a system is also expected to help fight poverty in one of the poorest countries in the world. Once completed, the centre will provide income for people who gather and bring in plastic wastes. A cleaner environment will be achieved and in the near future, objects of public utility may be created from the garbage that caused havoc to the environment and constrained development. It is anticipated that the project will be replicated in other African countries.

At the core of the problems of solid waste management is not so much the absence of adequate legislation and policies, but more the absence of an environmentally stimulated and enlightened public, failure to commit adequate resources into managing wastes, and the lack of compliance and enforcement. Government policies on the environment are piecemeal where they exist and are poorly implemented. Public enlightenment programmes on better waste management lack the needed coverage, intensity and continuity to correct apathetic public attitudes towards the environment. Activities of local authorities and other state and non-state environmental agencies and actors have been hampered by poor funding, inadequate logistics and personnel, inappropriate technologies used in managing urban waste, and an inequitable taxation system.

Energy as a Development Constraint in SSA

Energy remains the most paramount driving force for development in SSA; first at the level of low energy supplies which constrain the growth of domestic production and growth, and secondly at the level of the huge import bills that characterise the budgets of many countries in SSA. These problems have often resulted in huge budget deficits and mounting debt burdens. It has therefore been argued that getting reliable and cheap energy sources remain the driving force for the accelerated development of the region.

As at 2004, SSA had the lowest electrification in terms of world electricity production. Africa's power generation represented a mere 3.1%, and only 23% of Africa's population had access to electricity. Further, much of the available supply is unreliable and subject to power rationing and/or unscheduled power cuts (ECA, 2004: 117). This picture is corroborated by the IEA's 2002 Annual Report which estimates that nearly two-thirds of the growth in energy demand will rise in developing countries. Thus while the proportion of the world's population without access to electricity will fall by around 33% by the year 2030 (that is from the current estimated figure of around 2.1 to 1.4 billion people), SSA will experience growing energy crisis in many parts of the region as discussed earlier (see Table 15).[24]

Though natural gas use in SSA has been increasing since the 1990s partly as a result of some governments' policies to promote its use and cut down on depletion of forests and wood stock, the rate of increase has been minimal due to costs associated with its use. So the overriding reason for promoting LPG has been to explore efficient and cheap energy sources to augment the current shortfalls, as well as increase its use in domestic production. However, the serious constraint remains the ability for countries to finance the required energy infrastructure which is a huge challenge, and only governments with serious commitments can embark on projects to improve energy supplies.

While it is not clear how this energy infrastructure would be provided to improve energy supplies in the region, some interventions aimed at harnessing and increasing SSA's energy requirements are ongoing. In 2004, a collaborative initiative between Nigeria, Benin, Togo, and Ghana was set up to construct and implement a West African Gas Pipeline (WAGP) Project. This was aimed at transporting natural gas from Nigeria across a 678 km terrain to consumers in Ghana, Togo, and Benin. The estimated US$ 590 million project is considered a very big venture and has become necessary for obvious reasons enumerated above.

The implementation of the WAGP, begun in 2011 is expected to supply clean energy at lower cost to growing markets and encourage economic integration. As indicated earlier, many countries in West Africa do not have the required energy to drive economic growth, and significant progress is expected to be made with the implementation of the WAGP which will make energy available in many of these countries.

Gender and the Environment

The discussion in this section relates gender to environmental management and its logical extension to development. Two key areas focused on are (i) gender and agriculture, and (ii) gender and traditional energy such as woodfuel. These practices involve women using the physical environment directly, and the outcomes provide some perspectives on the development prospects for both women and their wider communities.

Gender and environmental management

Gender impacts on the environment in different ways because of the multiple roles women and men play in environmental management. Two competing theories have been advanced to aid the analysis of gender and the environment. According to Barrett and Browne (1995), two theoretical perspectives have been particularly relevant in the literature and policy framework concerning gender and the environment.[25] The first view labelled a *women and environment approach* emphasises the important role of women as environmental resource managers, stressing their unique vulnerabilities to decline in resource availability. This perspective is said to have grown out of the debates in the 1980s concerning women's roles in the development process. Advocates of this viewpoint deem it necessary to treat women as a separate entity so that specific environmental programmes can be developed to assist women overcome specific vulnerabilities that confront them (Dankelman and Davidson, 1988).

The second approach proceeds from the philosophy of feminism and has developed a branch known as eco-feminism, which assumes that women have a natural affinity with nature, and that this contrasts with men's urge to control and manipulate the natural world. As has often been emphasised in this chapter, the environment determines development and this viewpoint places women centrally in the management of the environment for sustainable development. However, these viewpoints have been criticised for assuming a simplistic nexus between women and environmental management.[26]

The first view which emphasises the important role of women as environmental resource managers making it necessary to treat them as a separate entity appears to be oversimplified. Environmental management is a collective responsibility, especially as in many parts of Africa where most of it is carried out along family lines with both men and women taking part. The eco-feminist viewpoint can also be criticised for its assumption of women's closer affinity to the environment and on the ground that it essentialises women and does not get beyond a biological explanation. Ironically the eco-feminist explanation imposes heavier burdens on women to manage the environment and exposes women to blame for environmental problems since its management is seen as lying squarely within their domain.

Gender and agriculture

Women play major roles in agricultural processes in Africa and in the processes that translate agricultural production into food and income for many households (see also Chs. 4 and 10). But as has been the evidence across SSA, most of women's agricultural production has been for household consumption, even though changes in land rights and agricultural practices have in some areas increased women's access to commercial agriculture and thus enabled them to earn substantial incomes. But the contexts for women's agricultural production depend crucially on local practices related to access to land, security of tenure, and access to credit, technology, and training. In much of rural Africa, entrenched communal land holding and user rights have limited women's access to land and other rights through marriage, though sometimes women's birthright also determine their access to productive land. While the nature of women's rights and their roles in agricultural production depend on specific cultural practices and particular contexts, both their roles and the bundle of rights they have are determined by men who are mostly the heads of households.

Constraints faced by women in access to land and limited rights in land compared to their men folk impose physical limitations on environmental management, and consequently women's development prospects, considering that agriculture provides food and incomes for the majority of people. Over time, these cultural practices become institutionalised and place enormous restrictions on women's access to other environmental resources. In spite of these constraints, women's contribution to agriculture in SSA remains higher than men. Gender roles affect environmental management because men normally do the land preparation and clear most of the brush through slashing the vegetal growth and setting fire to the brush during land clearance. Women also have defined roles such as assisting in planting, weeding, harvesting, and processing of food crops. In many societies across Africa, marketing of surplus home produce is also the sole preserve of women.

These gendered limitations have impacted negatively on the management of natural resources and achieving levels of development which would have been better without such limitations imposed. In many countries new policies often build on old traditions and practices, and land reforms in Africa have actually not impacted favourably on women's environmental resource management. Examples often cited to buttress this point is the status of women in agriculture in Kenya and Zimbabwe where land reforms have been embarked upon for several years. In these countries, even where husbands and wives jointly owned parcels of land, registered documents were in the name of the husband alone, and divorce automatically excludes the wife from growing crops on the land. Only widows, but not divorced or unmarried adult women, are eligible to be permit holders.[27] An IIED report showed that even though women in Niger have for centuries been very active in agricultural production, acute land shortage arising out of population growth has led to married women being denied access to land, and in extreme cases some have lost their farming skills because there is no land for them to put such skills to use.[28] These are women who hitherto had access to land and increased their social status through surplus accumulation of agricultural produce. Reference was made to the fact that these women who accumulated surpluses from farm production would hold a large feast for the community, and join the ranks of the *tambara*, a respected group of women with the right to speak out.

Women are central to environmental management even though they tend to have secondary status which gives them derived rights to productive land. Because the majority of women have limited land which is in most cases is also relatively marginal in terms of productive capacity, they have tended to be better managers knowing well that they stand to lose if they do not adopt prudent management practices. Thus to a large extent, the view that stresses women's unique vulnerabilities to decline in resource availability, emphasising their important role women as environmental resource managers is well placed. There is therefore the need to develop environmental programmes to assist women overcome these particular vulnerabilities as the majority of women in Africa do not have control over land which is the most important environmental resource necessary for achieving some appreciable level of living conditions, otherwise termed development.

The lack of control of land also means women are deprived of making contributions that could make the environment more productive. For example in paddy rice production in West Africa, especially in Senegal and Gambia, women have adapted several varieties of rice and have for many centuries contributed immensely to feeding their populations and securing incomes for other household and community needs. These production processes have also led to genetic diversity and long-term sustainability of these wetland environments.[29] Yet it is these very women who suffer practical vulnerabilities as mentioned earlier. Carney has shown that changes in agriculture have altered not only the environment, but also the relations between men and women in the Gambia. The acceptance of international development assistance by Gambia resulted in the conversion of most wetlands into irrigated agriculture land. This made rice farming an all year round activity, further leading to conversion of small left-over patches of wetlands. This transformation created tensions within rural households on two fronts. In the first instance, lands that were used by women for the cultivation of traditional crops for household consumption came under pressure and most of such lands were converted into paddies, now owned by men, who had formerly not been as well represented in paddy rice cultivation as their female counterparts. In the second instance, increasing demands on household labour following conversions of wetlands into paddy fields weighed heavily on women who were called upon to provide free family labour on rice fields which were finally sold in the market and pocketed by husbands, fathers, and brothers (see also Ch.10).

Understanding the links between gender and the use of the environment not only reveals the kind of environmental problems that arise from its use, but also the kind of alterations it makes to gender relations at both household and community levels. These are important for understanding the links between gender and environment on the one hand, and the links between environment and development on the other hand. It is also of strategic importance to make these explorations because the increasing spate of negative impacts resulting from the use of the environment are a result of the loss of women's specialised knowledge systems which have enabled specific environmental conditions to be exploited. Thus this view supports elements of the eco-feminist viewpoint that women are better managers of the environment.

Gender and traditional energy resources

As shown above, energy is an important environmental resource and critical factor in development. Since women are central in the production and procurement of household and community energy, they are very crucial in any consideration of environment and development. This is particularly the case in domestic energy acquisition which is the sole responsibility for women in many households. The importance of woodfuel as an important energy source was discussed earlier, and the present discussion concentrates on the constraints women face in domestic production and income generation activities. An understanding of the role of women in energy and income generation activities directly provides the necessary underpinnings for understanding environmental resources and the well-being of households in SSA. In other words, the way and manner women use the environment for energy determine to some extent the living conditions of the households and communities they provide for.

It is a well known fact that populations in SSA have grown rapidly with immense pressures on natural resources and serious implications for resource availability and use. As urban areas extend to occupy rural lands, agriculture and woodfuel prospects reduce since such lands used to supply the needed energy for domestic and commercial use. As bushes get distant from homes, the physical scarcity of fuelwood imposes development constraints on households as women spend more time on obtaining fuelwood to the detriment of other domestic chores such as child care, management of the home environment and income generating activities, and their welfare.

In many environments, not only do women experience physical scarcity of fuelwood due to expanding settlements and agriculture, but socio-cultural scarcity, otherwise known as institutional scarcity. The norms and practices that society imposes on them are more or less institutionalised, and as was observed in the discussion about women's access to land in many traditional societies across SSA, the social relations for a woman might determine her level of security as far as energy resources are concerned. These institutionalised rights are derived, and marriage is one way women can access such rights. Physical scarcities also become institutionalised as men and women begin to compete for resources. New rules can be made to favour men, as was mentioned in wetlands conversion into irrigated rice fields in Gambia.

The environment is a constraint to development in many parts of Africa, especially in the Sahel where women's efforts in providing energy for both household and commercial use places enormous burdens on their time and health, especially in their income generation activities. Fuelwood and other forest products such as wild edible fruits and vegetables including mushrooms, materials for mats and straw, and sticks and grass for compound fences and roofs, have become difficult to acquire, and women spend several hours daily to travel long distances to be able to acquire these essential items.

A research into cooperative integration of ecosystem management in West African savannas found out that men were in the habit of setting fires to bushes to aid the hunting of bush meat. In many communities in SSA, while women use environmentally friendly tools such as machetes and axes for harvesting fuel wood, many men use chain saws for foraging fuelwood, and/or fire to convert fuelwood into charcoal, an energy source that is increasingly becoming popular with most poor urban households in SSA.

Thus far, the nexus among gender, environment and development is clear. Women's representation in the use of environmental resources such as in agriculture and woodfuel acquisition practices is quite significant. How easily women perform these essential activities may be considered as progress, and may not only provide clues regarding the well-being of society, but also provides grounds for assessing the environment. In the same manner, women's rights to these resources will determine the extent to which they exploit these resources.

As is the case in Ghana, many women do not have direct access to land, or equal opportunities to use land, as their male counterparts. This means the human environment, including the institutions that manage land access, is not always conducive for women's work and welfare. Though women have been noted in the discussion to have various skills for harnessing environmental resources,they are often not given the opportunity to exhibit those productive skills. Women's lack of access to agricultural land and fuelwood resources in part explains their economic conditions since many rural women need these resources if they and their families hope to enjoy sustainable livelihoods.

Conclusion- Appropriate technologies for environmental development

Sub Saharan Africa is blessed with enormous amounts of natural resources. Many of the countries in the region have large deposits of minerals such as gold, diamonds, copper, crude oil, forests and wildlife. The region also has wood resources and water systems that provide water for domestic, agricultural and industrial use, and rich fertile lands suitable for cash and staple food crops, as well as fruits and vegetables, and vast stretches of grazing land for livestock rearing.

A number of options are open and include the use of appropriate technologies. While these have been acknowledged by scientists, policy makers, implementers and donor agencies, they have not been pursued to their logical conclusions. Sophisticated western technologies acquired for use have often turned out to be inappropriate because the human expertise within the countries and especially in rural areas where most of these technologies are needed cannot adopt, adapt, and sustain such technologies.

These technologies have also proven to be very expensive to operate and maintain. In many parts of Nigeria, Ghana, Liberia and Niger for instance, farm equipment such as tractors, ploughs, combine harvesters, seed threshers and irrigation pumps are not serviced regularly and become inoperable in short periods of time. Both the technologies to maintain these equipment (especially in the rural environments where they are located), and the recurrent expenditures to make them serviceable have often been difficult to provide.

It is important to revisit the use of appropriate technologies for the sustained exploitation of natural resources for the maximum benefit of the continent. For instance the use of small solar lamps for adult learning in rural areas has proved to be quite cheap and more sustainable than bigger solar lighting experiments that were experimented upon in many parts of SSA in the 1970s.

The use of appropriate technologies remains central in increasing productivity and improving living standards. Many approaches to rural development in SSA have been overly technocratic, subscribing to machines, fertilizers and improved seeds. While this may have resulted because technical decisions were taken without the necessary background consultations and information, it is clear the distributional implications and its overall impact was overlooked or suppressed in some cases. As Green (1986) observed about the inappropriateness of rural development technologies in many developing countries, initial improved maize and rice seed development choices were made by concentrating breeds to be used with high levels of water and fertilizer inputs without reference to the fact that it excluded poor peasants whose lands were in dry, non-irrigable areas, and who could not afford the cost of major inputs.

While modest achievements were made in Ghana in the early 1970s towards self-sufficiency in food when the 'operation feed yourself' campaign was launched, it soon became common knowledge that government, quasi-government institutions, absentee business farmers, and politicians were those who acquired huge chunks of land, farm machinery and equipment, chemical fertilizers and improved seeds, and cash credits that were disbursed by the banks for increasing agricultural productivity. In the end, ordinary farmers had very little to gain from the new incentives that were supposed to radically and positively transform their lifestyles (Brown, 1986).

Suffice it to mention that though no elaborate discussion is made on climate change and disaster risks in Africa, these two issues are gaining prominence as they affect the environment and development prospects for the region. In the last decade or so, climate variability has been a major driver of armed conflicts in Africa with heavy human losses and economic costs. Climatic factors have been cited as a reason for several conflicts in Africa; Darfur, Ethiopia, Niger, and Senegal to mention but a few. In North-western Kenya, drought has brought conflict among pastoralists who compete for grazing ground and water. Future warming is likely to increase the number of the poor and destitute, conflicts and deaths from war, many internally displaced people and refugees, all of which will compound the fragility of African environments and threaten sustainable development.

In the West African sub-region, Ghana, Nigeria, Sierra Leone, Benin, Burkina Faso, Cameroon and Guinea have since 2001 been consistently distressed by disasters which have made the populations of these countries poorer. In 2005, 2007 and 2010 in particular, floods ravaged most of West and Central Africa, leaving in their wake high levels of human suffering. In the Sahelian countries, drought, pest infestation and periodic livestock diseases have set populations wandering in search of land and water to survive on. Indeed, at the global scale, Africa is recognised as having a complex disaster risk profile that includes both slow and sudden onset disasters, which often become protracted. These protracted emergencies also assume complexities that result in large internal disruptions as well as refugee displacements with its accompanying human suffering. In addition to policy formulation and strengthening conventional institutional capacities, Africa needs to develop a disaster risk reduction programme in order to institutionalise training programmes as a critical capacity building effort at national and pan-African level to advance disaster risk reduction efforts on a more sustained basis.

Some of the serious challenges that would confront SSA's development include degraded environments which are the resource-base for the region's development. There are many experiences and lessons learned about population impacts on land resulting in disappearance of forests and watersheds, soil erosion, flooding, and air and water pollution. In parts of rural Mali, Senegal, Ethiopia and Uganda, the impact of population growth in rural areas often push communities into unsustainable practices such as continuous cropping on fragile soils which leads to pronounced vegetation, soil and water degradation. Rural development efforts tend to suffer from population increases as agricultural production and productivity suffers, reduces employment avenues, and in turn sets a spiral of rural-urban migration with its complex dimensions and untold hardships on vulnerable populations.

Review Questions

1. What are the major natural resource endowments of Sub-Saharan Africa? How do these resources enhance or impede the region's development.

2. Why is it often asserted that water scarcity is the most constraining development factor in many countries in SSA?

3. To what extent does the use of woodfuel as a major energy source in SSA constrain the physical environment as a resource base for development?

4. Do you agree that rural development is synonymous with national development in SSA? Use examples from some African countries to illustrate your viewpoint.

5. What indigenous production technologies exist in SSA? With illustrations discuss why these technologies remain the most sustainable way of development in Africa?

References

Aguwamba, J.C. 1998 "Solid Waste Management in Nigeria: Problems and Issues". *Environmental Management*, Vol. 22, No. 6, pp. 849 857.

Aryeetey-Attoh, S. 2003. *Geography of Sub-Saharan Africa*, (2nd Ed). Upper Saddle River: Pearson Education Inc.

Economic Commission for Africa 2004 *Unlocking Africa's Trade Potential*. Economic Report on Africa 2004. Addis Ababa: ECA

FAO (2005) *Irrigation in Africa in figures – AQUASTAT Survey 2005*, pp 5-6

Green, Reginald 1986 "International Development Agency World Views on Rural Development: Who or What is Central?" In Dembo, David; Clarence Dias; Ward Morhouse; and James Paul (eds). *The International Context of Rural Poverty in the Third World: Issues for Research and Action*. International Center for Law in Development/Council on International and Public Affairs, New York. Pp. 145-166.

Mensah, Anthony 2004 Waste Management: The Technical and Economic Challenges Facing Local Government. Lecture Presented at the Joint Policy Forum of the Institute of Economic Affairs (IEA) and the Ghana Academy of Arts and Sciences (GAAS) on Waste Management in Ghana, Accra.

Organisation for Economic Cooperation and Development/International Energy Agency 2004, *World Energy Outlook 2004*, OECD/IEA, Paris

Organisation for Economic Cooperation and Development/International Energy Agency 2000, *World Energy Outlook 2000*, OECD/IEA, Paris

Pelling, M. and Ben Wisner 2009 "African Cities of Hope and Risk". In Pelling and Wisner (eds) *Disaster Risk Reduction: Cases from Urban Africa*. London: Earthscan Publications.

Songsore, J, J.S. Nabila, Yvon Yangyouru, E.K. Bosque-Hamilton, Sebastian Avle, Paulina Amponsah and Osman Alhassan, (2010) *Environmental Health Watch and Disaster Monitoring in the Greater Accra Metropolitan Area (GAMA), 2005*. Accra: Ghana Universities Press.

The World Bank 2008 *World Development Report 2008: Agriculture for Development*. Washington D.C. The International Development Bank.

The World Bank 1993 *Sub-Saharan Africa: From Crisis to Sustainable Growth*. Washington D.C: The World Bank.

UNDP 2003 *Human Development Report: Millennium Development Goals*. New York: UNDP.

United Nations Environment Programme 2010 *Global Environment Outlook: Environment for Development*. New York: UNEP.

UN Habitat 2006 *United Nations Human Settlement Programme State of the World's Cities, 2006/7* London: Earthscan.

Endnotes

1. David Pearce, Edward Barbier and Anil Markandya 1990 *Sustainable development: Economics and Environment in the Third World,* London: Earthscan Publications Limited, present different perspectives on development in the developing world reflecting the context of the problem and discussion.

2.. Seers, D 1967 *The Meaning of Economic Development* articulates reason why these are considered indicators of development to any society arguing that "the focus on national income as a target for achieving poverty reduction avoided the real problems of development" and recommended "redefining how development was measured".

3. The Food and Agriculture Organization of the United Nations (FAO) *Global Forest Resources Assessment 2005* provides detailed information on forest cover in 2005, and adjusted estimates of forest cover in 1990 and 2000.

4. See the World Bank's *World Development Report* 2008 which states among others that agriculture can offer pathways out of poverty if efforts are made to increase productivity in the staple foods sector and generate jobs in the rural non-farm economy.

5. See US International Trade Commission (USITC) on SSA 2008. *Global Trade Atlas (2006): Reporting Countries' Total Global Imports.* Second Annual Report, (USITC) Washington, DC where six SSA agricultural subsectors including cocoa and cocoa products, fresh fish and fish products, fresh and dried fruit each generated total export earnings of more than $1 billion in 2006.

6 See the UNDP's *Human Development Report on the Millennium Development Goals.* This was a global compact among nations to end human poverty.

7. Indeed, the Economic Commission for Africa 2004 publication, *Unlocking Africa's Trade Potential. Economic Report on Africa 2004.* Addis Ababa: ECA, estimates that much of SSA's debt burden is from two main sources; crude oil and food imports. (full reference needed

8. The Environmental Protection Council (EPA) in its 2005 annual report elaborates on the environmental impacts of small scale surface mining in Ghana.

9. See Akabzaa 2004 *"Mining and Land Resources in Ghana"* Cresta Royal Hotel, Accra, July 11: Roundtable Discussion on Environment organized by the Environmental Protection Agency,

10. The Human Development Report 2003 *Human Development Report*: Millennium Development Goals cites Botswana as an example of a country with prudent management of its natural resources, enabling its environment to be more productive.

11. The Third World Network, 2001: ix) for instance noted that surface mining and heap leach processing has left serious ecological damage to the environment which cannot be repaired.

12. Huq (1989) Huq, M.M. 1989 *The Economy of Ghana: Twenty Five Years After Independence.* Hong Kong: Macmillan Press, documents how forest resources have often been used for foreign exchange without due regard to who manages it and how management can be enhanced if the benefits from forest revenues are shred with communities that actually manage these forests.

13. See the UNDP 2003 *Human Development Report: Millennium Development Goals.*New York: UNDP, 14.Amous 2006 documents, using the FAO Forestry Division's Regional Studies (Wood Today for Tomorrow (WETT) data, the significant role of wood energy plays in the energy mix in Africa.

15. One of the readily perceived socio-economic ramifications for development is the fact that in the household, women are generally tasked with fuelwood acquisition for domestic requirements, and would spend more time for fuelwood gathering. This adversely affects the well-being of many.

16. See OECD/IEA (Organisation for Economic Cooperation and Development/International Energy Agency) 2010, *World Energy Outlook 2008*, OECD/IEA, Paris,.

17. See UNICEF (2008) *The State of Africa's Children*, UNICEF, New York, www.unicef.org/childrensurvival/files/SOAC.pdf accessed 30 May 2011 & BBC 2008 "Malaria drugs urged for children, BBC Online, July 11, available at http://news.bbc.co.uk/2/hi/africa/7501477.stm

18. See World Bank 2010 *The World Development Indicators (WDI) 2010*, Washington, D.C.

19. See Adams, W.M., and Anderson, D.M. (1988) "Irrigation before Development: Indigenous and Induced Change in Agricultural Water Management in East Africa". *African Affairs*. Vol. 87, pp. 519-35.

20. The FAO 2005 noted that while food shortage in the Sahel was already a problem, the locust invasion has turned a gradually worsening problem into an acute food shortage.

21. See <http://www.fao.org/NEWS/GLOBAL/LOCUSTS/Locuhome.htm>.

22 According to the United Nations Environment Programme (UNEP, 2011), *Climate Change, Conflict and Migration in the Sahel*, Châtelaine, Geneva: United Nations Environment Programme, shortage of freshwater and its poor quality are the two greatest limits to development in Africa.

23. See Diop's 2003 *Technical Report on Recycling Plastic Waste in Africa* presented to the National Habitat II Committee, Ex Camp Lat Dior, Dakar.

24. For instance, there is a growing energy shortage in many West African countries whose electricity supply has been seriously constrained over the last two decades due partly to climatic change, population increase and increased demands for energy.

25. See Barrett, H. and Angela Brown 1995 "Gender, Environment and Development in Sub-Saharan Africa". In, Tony Binns (ed), *People and Environment in Africa*. New York.: Wiley Publications, pp. 31-38.

26. Boserup E. 1990 "Population, the Status of Women, and Rural Development". In G. Nicole and M.Cain (eds), *Rural Development and Population: Institutions and Policy*, Oxford: University Press, Oxford, pp. 45-60. Boserup for instance noted that these assumptions are contradictory to feminism and ignore the function of social relations in allocating roles, and that women are often subordinate to men and do not necessarily have their own way of doing things.

27. According to Tony Binns 1995 *People and Environment in Africa,* New York: John Wiley and Sons Publishing, an estimated 90% of permits in resettlement schemes in Kenya and Zimbabwe have been allocated to male household heads even where they are absentee farmers.

28. See International Institute for Environment and Development (IIED) 2006 *Annual Report on Natural Resources*. London: IIED,

29. See de Blij, H.J. and Alexander B. Murphy 1999, *Human Geography: Culture, Society and Space. Ne York*: John Wiley and Sons, Inc. pp. 187-224.

CHAPTER 16

SCIENCE AND TECHNOLOGY FOR AFRICA
Marian Ewurama Addy and Ebenezer Laing

There is a land that takes from the past to care for the future.
There is a land that looks to the heavens for answers and finds them from within.
There is a land with gold in its soil and magic in its plants.
This land is Africa.

Introduction

Science, just like art, requires knowledge which can be acquired through experience, study or observation. However, in science one pursues knowledge covering general truths, especially knowledge obtained through what is generally referred to as the scientific method. This method, which deals with principles and procedures for the systematic pursuit of knowledge, usually begins with empirical data or knowledge. It involves recognition and formulation of a problem, and the collection of data through experimentation, observation, making assumptions or hypotheses, theorising, and such other forms of data collection so as to solve the problem, approaching the solution with what is valid and therefore generally acceptable and universally applicable. Central to the scientific method are objective or independent verification and, most importantly, the willingness to modify or completely abandon theories when confronted with new knowledge or adverse findings which go against a former dogma. Generally, the use of the scientific method results in the ability to predict.

The accumulation of empirical data or knowledge, through observation and experimentation, are not lacking in African knowledge systems. However, there is (an apparent) lack of hypothesising, theorising and furthering the knowledge processes which are associated with the scientific method. Data and knowledge accumulation within the African context generally tends to be a form of art. The people with such knowledge, which may be specialised knowledge, tend to keep it to themselves and their offspring, excluding all others, thereby mystifying the knowledge. The group that possesses the knowledge tends to control its dissemination. Members of this group are generally less susceptible to change. In spite of the abundant store of knowledge from the study, observation and accumulation of empirical data in this art form, this system of knowledge cannot be called science, at least in the Western tradition. As stated by Henri Poincare, science is built of facts the way a house is built of bricks; but an accumulation of facts is no more science than a pile of bricks is a house.

There are many indigenous knowledge systems in Africa. Documenting and systematising them would make them better, thus providing what may be considered as a significant meaning of the term "development", that is, moving from the original position to one providing more opportunity for effective use. For the most part, indigenous knowledge, that is, knowledge that the people in a community had before formal education, is neglected. Yet, such knowledge should form the basis for development as defined above, providing the original position from which more opportunity for effective use may be measured. For such development in Africa, there is a need for a new style of learning, one that integrates modern knowledge with indigenous systems of knowledge.

The quotation that is cited at the beginning of the chapter appeared as a background statement on the stage at a formal opening of a regional science office for Africa. The first line of the quotation is reminiscent of the *Sankofa* bird, the bird in the Ghanaian fable which reminds one neither to forget nor ignore one's past, but rather to go back to using or referring to it. In similar fashion, Africa needs to be reminded of its past because sustainable development is assured when the present and future are built on the lessons and wisdom from the past. In some regions of the world, the past is history, not to be remembered, and only the advantages that modern development brings is what is acclaimed, especially in science and technology. Thus old technologies are often regarded as something to be discarded, but that should not be allowed to happen in Africa.

The second line of the quote could be related to the oft-noted spirituality of the African who must use not only what she/he has physically, but also what is within him/her in order to get answers, or in order to get things done. The application of science for development tends to leave out the human dimension in development. Perhaps, we in Africa can enhance the value of the scientific enterprise by highlighting the importance of keeping our common humanity in mind in whatever science we do and apply. Generally, Africans are said to have a love of community and tend to have compassion, which is the basis of morality. Some of these humanist values can be infused or brought to bear on the tremendous advances that have been made in science and technology.

That there is gold in the soil and magic in the plants of Africa is unequivocal. This third line of the quote indicates how rich Africa is. It also indicates the level of science and technology that the continent needs. Gold and magic make a powerful combination. However, here the poem is not alluding to the Midas touch, but rather to how science and technology must be brought to bear on what we have on the continent before we can use them to our advantage. The gold is in the soil and we must work to bring it up and out of the soil as pure gold, as it is of little use as the ore. Africa therefore has many developmental problems that ought to be resolved by recourse to home-grown (whether adopted, adapted or otherwise) scientific and technological solutions. Africa needs science and technology to grow economically. Technology is the engine of economic growth as it creates jobs, builds new industries and improves our standard of living, while science is the fuel for technology's engine.

For Science and Technology (S&T) and ultimately Research and Development (R&D) to play their proper roles as vital instruments in the material development of the resources of Africa, they need to be pursued vigorously and effectively. Both human resource development and the provision of physical facilities for S&T education require adequate financial resources. Unfortunately present provisions are inadequate for the essential roles that S&T must perform in socio-economic development. Ultimately, it is up to the national governments in all African countries to exercise their political will in assigning S&T and R&D high enough priority in their national development policies and plans, and to allocate adequate funds to S&T for its function in socio-economic development. The role of scientists and technologists may be to find convincing arguments and demonstrations to persuade their governments to invest more in science and technology, both on short-term and long-term considerations. It is well known that this does not happen, even when there are scientists in government. However, a number of countries on the continent seem to be on the correct path.

A. What are the Challenges?

Many African countries labour under the combined disadvantages of increasing population without corresponding improvement in the basic necessities of life such as the provision of food, clothing and shelter, and the provision of health and educational facilities (see Chapters 1, 2, 11 and 12, this volume). Many countries still depend, to a great extent, on external assistance for a large part of these essentials. Many still employ technologies that do not use starting materials or energy efficiently, technologies that exert undue pressure on the natural resource base. There are cooking stoves which are wasteful on fuel, a situation which contributes to deforestation and depletion of soil quality (see also Chapter 15, this volume). There are also cultivation systems that may have been useful in the past when populations were smaller, but which now are unable to allow soils to regain their fertility through fallow. Many farmers, artisans and other workers are unable to derive full benefit from modern tools for lack of understanding of the scientific basis of the functioning of these tools or precautions concerning their proper use. There are also examples of people being incapacitated or even dying from the improper application of agricultural chemicals as fertilizers or for control of pests and diseases of crops or farm animals.

Some key economic and developmental problems which Africa faces and which require scientific and technological solutions are:

- Generally poor health services, especially for maternal and child health;
- Persistent and severe shortages of fuel in non-oil producing countries;
- Periodic famines and post harvest food losses;
- Inadequate shelter, qualitatively and quantitatively;
- Poor water quality and general environmental sanitation;
- The scourge of HIV and AIDS.

Some challenges are associated with all of the above and the major one is science education.

1. Science Education

General education is important in preparing citizens to contribute to national development. Science and technology education in particular, enables citizens to exploit their natural resources for their own use and for exchange with other countries for income. General S&T education is important for citizens of the modern world to appreciate scientific reasoning and the products of technology. Science and technology education further enables the modern citizen to enjoy the benefits as well as reduce undesirable effects of modern technology.

These are some of the compelling reasons why funding for S&T education should receive top priority. With relevant science and technology education there is the possibility of generating substantial income from such relatively simple activities as rearing mushrooms or the African giant snail, collecting butterflies, or rearing bees to avert the abject poverty that is found in rural areas. With sound scientific education there is also the possibility of improving production yields of both cash and food crops, reduction of post-harvest losses through refined storage methods and through manufacturing and quality assurance of the manufactured products. But efforts at relevant science education at all levels on the continent are few and far-between.

Relevance is important in the training of scientists in order to have graduates who are able to solve local problems. Depending on what we use as examples, we can produce a scientist who is ready and able to solve the problems that are important to people at the local level, or a scientist who regards science as something exotic and therefore unrelated to the realities of the life that s/he faces locally each day. It would appear as if there is more production of the latter scientist around Africa. An example is the basic school science teacher, who refuses to lead his/her class in an activity because s/he has no glue, whereas s/he may know of a tree on the compound which has gummy latex capable of making things stick together.

Sometimes, science teachers complain about lack of resources. Whereas lack of resources could hinder relevant science education because certain things must be purchased, sometimes the problem is the lack of resourcefulness on the part of the science teacher. Resourceful teachers can "use" their students at all levels of the educational ladder to collect, collate and document indigenous knowledge systems, such as medicinal uses of plants in their environment. Such an exercise would indicate not only application of science, but also involvement of the community and the integration of indigenous knowledge with scientific knowledge.

Whether in the middle of the desert or in the thickest rain forest in Africa, one can find materials in the environment to use for science education. When it comes to the study of medicinal plants, a teacher can design a project which includes assigning students to collect information on such plants and their uses from the community. By discussing the assignment with the students in class, the teacher, together with the students, may identify, classify and give the plants their scientific or systematic names. Such an exercise, planned and executed properly, could give the teacher enough data on medicinal plants of the country for the production of a book on local medicinal plants.

The African Primary Science Programme (APSP) preceded the Science Education Programme for Africa (SEPA), a non-governmental programme dedicated to relevant science education at the pre-tertiary level with a lot of local content, including science teacher education and evaluation. SEPA was an attempt to introduce problem-solving, practical oriented, community-based approach to learning science at an early age. The programme had to fold up for various reasons, including non-payment of annual dues by the African nations who owned the programme. The start of science and technology education is usually late in the scheme of things. When it does begin, the manner in which the topics are presented, as single subjects somehow unfamiliar, unrelated to each other and to the occurrences of everyday life, tends to make a lot of students shy away from such subjects. The use of the environment as a wider laboratory for teaching science is what SEPA and its predecessor, the APSP, sought to achieve. The programmes should not have been allowed to fail.

Apart from lack of relevant science education, there are other weaknesses in the science and technology enterprise in Africa which contribute to the underdevelopment that characterises the continent. They include the following:

2. Dichotomy of Indigenous knowledge and Modern Scientific Knowledge

Whether in national policies or in practice, it is not clear if indigenous knowledge and scientific knowledge are regarded as two cultures which should co-exist. If co-existence is the model, it is not clear whether the two systems should run along parallel lines, with one system being tolerated while the other predominates, or whether the two knowledge systems are to be integrated. This dichotomy must engage our attention because in many African countries it appears as if there are two worlds; one of the citizens who dwell in the big cities and tend to use the modern mode of doing things and are convinced that that is the way to go, whereas the behaviour of citizens in the rural communities, who are in the majority, seem to suggest that no improvements have occurred in their day-to-day activities compared to their peers in the big cities.

For the majority of Africans in the rural areas, science should be used to provide the basic necessities of life. For this majority, the acquisition of the capabilities for doing science must come first before the consideration of the use of science to provide for or improve the basic necessities of life; hence science education for them as well for the others. In addition, we should provide the science education not at the expense of our culture, but in its milieu. As Lydia Makhubu, one time Vice Chancellor of the University of Swaziland, and President of the Third World Organisation for Women in Science stated:

> The greatest challenge, therefore, facing advocates of science-led development in Africa today is devising mechanisms to fuse science and African cultures in such a way that science becomes a driving force for the improvement of the overall quality of life for all people. (Cited in Clayson, 1997)

3. Coordination and Collaboration

There are relatively large numbers of small countries in the same ecological zones around Africa which face similar problems. Therefore, there ought to be more coordination and collaboration among countries in applying scientific and technological solutions to problems. More often there is competition which could be due to lack of knowledge of what each country or region is doing. Sometimes there is lack of coordination or collaboration even among the scientists within one country. Communication services, whether electronic or otherwise, compound the problem, because they tend to be expensive, in comparison with the means of those using the services.

In Africa, government policies, cultural claims, complexities of boundaries set by the colonialists centuries ago, national or ethnic pride which does not encourage some groups to be out-going, lack of innovation, invention and inventiveness and other issues arising from control over Intellectual Property Rights (IPRs), are some of the key factors which negatively influence cooperation and collaboration.

4. Making tools and equipment

Infrastructural support for science and technology is dependent heavily on equipment and tools. Designing and fabricating or manufacturing these tools and equipment locally is one weakness in science and technology in Africa. If Africans are not in the business of designing and making the tools that we need, who is going to make the tools that are appropriate for our needs? Technology is any tool or technique, product or process, physical equipment or method of doing or making, by which human capacity is extended. We cannot improve our technology or extend our capacity if we do not make our own tools, not to mention the cost involved in always buying technology from others.

5. Preventive Maintenance

Because we do not make the tools and pieces of equipment necessary in science and technology, and because we do not have a "hot line" to the manufacturers, maintenance of these items, especially preventive maintenance, is very crucial. Yet, in Africa, there is low awareness or implementation of maintenance, especially preventive maintenance of equipment. The few technicians and technologists charged with the maintenance of tools and equipment are either poorly paid or not recognised with respect to the importance of their jobs.

In an article entitled "Properly functioning scientific equipment in developing countries: Problems and Prospects," Oman et al. (2006) reiterated the fact that the most important factor in the technological development of a country, besides having a critical mass of trained staff, is the availability of properly functioning scientific equipment. They identified the main constraints to the proper procurement and use of scientific equipment in developing countries as i) access to sufficient funding, ii) coordinated and wise selection of equipment type and equipment brand, iii) purchasing and transport, iv) installation, v) demanding climate conditions, vi) unstable power supply, vii) maintenance, viii) servicing, and ix) adequate and visible policies and guidelines. They proposed firm action plans addressing each of the constraints and concluded that new, firm, and long-term initiatives to improve the scientific infrastructure should involve devoted stakeholders and must receive support from national authorities and international aid organisations. Activities which were proposed included: i) management of supplies of spare parts and repair equipment, ii) provision of technical expertise, iii) management of databases for information, iv) arrangements of meetings and training courses, and v) encouragement of the development of policies and guidelines at national and/or institutional levels.

Lack of competent technicians and support staff was identified as another major constraint to scientific research. As a consequence of the low number of technicians in relation to the number of researchers at many universities and institutions, researchers in many developing countries have to rely on foreign expertise for repairs. Experience has shown that in some cases, it is easier to purchase new equipment than to repair the existing pieces, even when the limited funding that many developing countries have to purchase new equipment is considered.

6. Over-dependence on external factors or donors

Africa tends to be over-dependent on donors and other external influences for the direction of scientific and technological development. Institutions that relate to well-endowed international funding agencies may be able to attract funding for special research projects. In some institutions, work would have come completely to a halt, but for the ongoing externally funded research projects. If this dependence could be regarded as a period of embryonic development into adulthood and independence, it would not be such a big problem. Unfortunately, the dependency syndrome appears to be long lasting, with the result that many African scientists are unable to conceptualize or conduct research that may be of social significance to local communities.

Such dependency could have negative consequences because of restrictive conditions that are usually attached to donor funding, such as restrictions on the sources for the procurement of equipment. Such a condition may need to be carefully examined to ensure that recipients are not left in a situation where after sales service and maintenance facilities may only be available in the donor country.

7. Low Support for Science and Technology

It is well known that most developed countries devote a lot more resources of up to 2.5 to 4.0 % of their GNP, to research and development, compared to developing countries, which on the average devote less than 0.5 per cent. The investment of resources is one of the contributing factors towards the ever widening technological gap separating rich from poor countries. Some of the indices which illustrate the magnitude of the investment gap are the number of scientists and engineers in research and development and the number of patent applications. Of all the weaknesses in the S&T enterprise in Africa, funding is the weakest link. Ideally, funding to support S&T and S&T education should be:

- Adequate
  - o To meet the needs of all aspects of the scientific endeavour;
  - o To support required personnel and physical facilities;
  - o For training;
  - o To provide learning resources;
  - o To make communication facilities available.
- Based on sound policies and plans which are reviewed periodically and updated;
- Timely, in that approved funds should be released at the right time to enable the S&T institutions function efficiently. It is possible in some African countries that release of approved funds is late, or, in extreme cases, there is outright cancellation or withdrawal of previously approved funds for S&T or R&D work, especially towards the end of the financial year. Such a move can only hinder the smooth functioning of the institutions;
- Properly applied, for the approved or justifiable purposes and economically and accounted for, on the part of the managers of S&T (directors and management boards) of S&T institutions;
- Paralleled by other essential requirements or supporting conditions in the environment of S&T, for full effectiveness. In this connection, the definition given by the International Council for Science for capacity building in science is worth quoting:: "*Capacity building in science consists of activities that lead to the establishment or strengthening of a corps of qualified scientists with supporting infrastructure - including facilities and working conditions - that enable them to conduct research, education, training and advisory work, particularly in areas of direct social significance.*" (Ravichandran and Daniel, Eds.,1994)
- In the right denominations or categories. For example, where necessary, the foreign exchange component should be adequate for its purposes. In terms of ability to purchase necessary imported items, foreign exchange components may be inadequate, even when the amounts required seem large when expressed in local currency. The ratio of emoluments (salaries) to recurrent non-pay component should be such as to assist and not hinder the operations of the S&T institutions. Sinking funds should be established and regularly maintained to enable institutions replace essential equipment at the right time, rather than allowing all operations to grind to a halt, while searching for fresh funds;

- Supported by stakeholders. Stakeholders in particular fields, especially employers, should plough back some of their earnings to support R&D and related S&T in the subject areas closely related to their interest;

8. Funding

Provision or apportionment of the available funds between the different constituencies of S&T may be unequal or inefficient. Typically, long-term research suffers at the expense of short-term research. Whenever large grants become available, the more influential members of the S&T community will rather purchase the highly expensive and impressive equipment, without sufficient provision for its regular maintenance, with the result that the investment does not yield its full benefits. In the meantime, opportunities to acquire smaller yet essential items may have been lost. Institutions that by reason of sheer chance are in the public eye, may have their research work funded while others may have no such luck. When funds become scarce, S&T work requiring less expensive resources continue at the expense of work requiring more expensive inputs, irrespective of the relevance or importance of the work. Thus attention received by different aspects of the total research effort may be uneven or possibly even inequitable.

The causes of the short-fall in funding of S&T institutions in Africa are many and include:
- Lack of appreciation that S&T require investment;
- Misplaced priorities often resulting from a short term view of development;
- Actual (genuine) poverty;
- Disillusion with the technological society;

Certain indirect effects of the deficiencies in funding may be delineated with regard to remuneration of personnel in S&T, be it teachers, researchers or administrators. Thus:
- Their attitude to work becomes half-hearted;
- They take on second jobs to supplement their pay and they thus lack time to keep up with developments in their areas of science or research, or with new approaches to teaching of the subject or of conducting research;
- They have no desire to market their subject to the next generation through popularisation or demonstrations. As a result, students do not see ahead their potential contribution to S&T

B. Which countries seem to be doing well?

Indications that the continent is poised to take science seriously by way of injecting the much needed funds into it have come from a number of countries including the following:

Nigeria

Nigeria appears to be investing some of its vast oil revenues to boost the country's science and technology. In 2006, the government of Nigeria approved plans for US$ 5 billion in a Science and Technology endowment fund for the establishment of a `politically independent`` agency similar to the US National Science Foundation (NSF), to manage the funds. It is envisaged that the funds will be supplemented by donor agencies and the private sector. Prior to that, a number of initiatives tended to indicate the Nigerian government's commitment to science and technology, probably because of the background and enthusiasm of the country's minister responsible for science and technology during the period. Among these is the Nigerian Natural Medicine Development Agency of the Federal Ministry of Science & Technology, and the Raw Materials Research and Development Council, which provides grants for research work.

In 2003, UNESCO recommended the establishment of regional science policy forums to facilitate interaction between scientists, technologists, engineers, on one hand, and policy makers on the other. The aim of the Forum is to strengthen the role of parliament in policy making in science, technology and innovation. The first Forum in 2004 was held in Cairo (Egypt). In 2006, one such Forum was launched in Abuja as the Nigerian Parliamentarian S&T Forum. Participants in the Forum included the President of the Nigerian Academy of Sciences, President of the Nigerian Society of Engineers, senior officials of science-based ministries, Directors-General of research institutes, representatives of civil society and the media. In between these two Forums were others in Chandigarh (India), Buenos Aires (Argentina), and Tehran (Iran).

Establishing this forum may be regarded as a natural follow up to Nigeria's commitment to the development of her S&T. In 2001, the Nigerian government demonstrated its commitment to starting off a space programme by adopting a policy with the objective of launching its own satellite and space research programme to improve communication links, including that of predicting the weather and having remote sensing technology for detecting signs of fire and flood. The satellite, a low Earth orbit remote-sensing micro-satellite, was launched in 2003. In 2004, the Nigerian government requested UNESCO to establish an international advisory board for the reform of the country's system of science, technology and innovation.

Another area where the country appears to be doing well is in the public understanding and acceptance of science. Nigeria has huge natural gas reserves being exploited by the Nigerian Liquified Natural Gas (NLNG). The company has institutionalised a prize for science, aimed at creating awareness, stimulating competition and rewarding and recognising excellence in science and technology. According to NLNG, by instituting a significant prize for science, NLNG seeks to bring science and scientists to public attention, as well as help the scientists to bring about improvements in the living standards of citizens.

Rwanda

Rwanda's premier science institution, the Kigali Institute of Science and Technology (KIST), set up in 1997, is considered to be one of the biggest successes of Rwanda's post-genocide government. KIST trains a large number of computer technicians, over 3,000 students, offering both degree programmes and "fast track" courses of approximately four months duration. The project is successful because, unlike much of the rest of Africa, Rwanda is small, densely populated, and therefore it has been much easier to connect different regions with fibre optic cables that can bring telephone, Internet and television services literally to the doorsteps of the people. Although the programme benefits government and businesses, having schools online and the unavoidable increase in the number of people with such training, is sure to bring benefits to the entire population.

In March 2006, Rwanda's president created a new Ministry for Science, Technology and Scientific Research, splitting it from an existing Ministry for Education and Science. The new Ministry was placed under his direct supervision in the President's Office, to accelerate the integration of science and technology into all sectors of the economy. The move is also to ensure that plans to turn the country into a regional information and communications technology hub stay on track.

South Africa

The National Research Foundation (NRF), South Africa's national science funding agency, is well resourced and operates a number of research facilities. Access to the national facilities is open to all South African and foreign researchers, subject to the usual international criteria of peer review.

The South African Astronomical Observatory (SAAO), with its headquarters in Cape Town, and a field station at Sutherland, is one of the NRF's facilities. Space science is an area of focus in South Africa, with astronomy and astrophysics as the areas most strongly represented. The development of modern astronomy in South Africa was driven by the need for accurate star positions and time for navigation purposes, and the SAAO has its origins from the Royal Observatory at the Cape of Good Hope, the first permanent observatory established by the British Admiralty, and it is the oldest continuously operational modern observatory in Africa.

The telescopes at Sutherland are all reflectors, with mirrors of 0.5, 0.75, 1.0 and 1.9-m diameter. The Observatory has an active programme of instrumentation development and its work is representative of much of modern astrophysics, with activity in the areas of solar system studies, solar physics, stellar astrophysics, Galactic structure, Magellanic Cloud studies, and extragalactic astronomy. Much of the work is done in collaboration with astronomers from around the world.

A number of South African universities offer degree programmes in different areas of space science. To promote the development of astronomical research in South African universities, the national facilities have introduced programmes whereby students may pursue research degrees under expert supervision at the national facilities while still registered at their own universities. At the University of the Orange Free State in Bloemfontein, the Department of Physics and Astronomy offers a number of undergraduate courses in astronomy as part of the Physics BSc. degree programme.

For the public understanding of science, there are planetariums in a number of cities as part of the South African Museum, offering a variety of public shows as well as popular astronomy courses. These national facilities are committing significant resources to improving science awareness at all levels, and they employ full-time public relations and education officers who liaise with education authorities and the media.

In 2006, the government of South Africa approved the establishment of the South African Space Agency. This body is to coordinate and implement the country's space science and technology programmes. The country's second satellite, an 80 kilogramme micro satellite, is being built as part of a national science programme. The second satellite that was launched into low Earth orbit at the end of 2006 has been named "Sumbandila," which means "Lead the Way." (Figure 18)

Figure 18 – Sumbandila- 'Lead the Way'- First South African Satellite

Source: *http://www.satnews.com/images_upload/620347798/South_Africa_Sumbandila.jpg*

Thus South Africa leads the way in terms of space science, technology, research and innovation on the continent. The first satellite, Sunsat, was built in 1999 by Stellenbosch University staff and postgraduate students. Out of the success of Sunsat a company, SunSpace, emerged, and it is now building a second satellite, managed by the same University. A number of lessons of collaboration between university, research institutions, local and foreign industry may be learnt from this venture: the university trains postgraduate students in, and conducts research into, satellite engineering and software development; the Council for Scientific and Industrial Research's Satellite Applications Centre will be responsible for operating, tracking and monitoring the satellite, and the costs of the project include the cost of the launch by a foreign space agency.

The new satellite will be used to support, monitor and manage disasters such as floods, oil spills and fires. As stated by the staff at the Science and Technology Department, space assets such as satellites are no longer merely a matter of prestige for a country, but essential tools, necessary to understand the earth system in order to improve human health, safety and welfare, to protect the environment, reduce disaster losses and achieve sustainable development.

In South Africa, until recently, there used to be one Department for Arts, Culture, Science and Technology. A combination of all these disciplines under one umbrella would sound like a good idea, since it implies that development using science and technology would not take place outside the realm of arts and culture. A new Science and Technology Ministry was created and it seems as if the separation has given new life to science and technology in the country. Perhaps more emphasis was placed on science and technology after the separation, indicating the importance of isolating and giving science and technology more space to grow and be strong enough for its incorporation into all sectors of the economy, as South Africa appears to be doing. A lesson to be learnt here is that an early attempt to develop S&T within the cultural context, without first giving it solid foundation, including financial backing, would not work. Yet, if we should recognise that science is a knowledge system, much in the same way as indigenous knowledge systems, we can develop paradigms to use the two for sustainable development.

Uganda

In 2006, The World Bank approved a thirty million US dollar (US$30 million) loan to support scientific development in Uganda. The money, which is from the International Millennium Science Initiative, is to help increase the number and quality of scientists produced by Uganda's universities and research centres, to boost the country's scientific and technological productivity in industrial, agricultural and other sectors.

The project, which will fund new undergraduate courses in science and engineering, as well as new research centres, among other support and collaborative projects, is expected to encourage researchers to remain in the country and devote their skills to research and training. Cabinet and parliamentary approval is necessary for such a project to indicate government commitment that is necessary for the success of such a project.

C. What should be done?

Some efforts have been made by African governments to solve the many problems of S&T on the continent. One such effort was the meeting in Senegal in 2005 of African Ministers and senior government officials to discuss what should be done to enhance S&T capacity. During this meeting, a Consolidated Science and Technology Plan of Action was endorsed. The Plan, worth more than US$160 million, set out a number of projects to boost science in Africa. Heads of the African Union member states are to continue with the effort, and the officials of the Science and Technology Commission of the New Partnership for African Development (NEPAD) have identified 21 priority areas in the plan of action, including a survey of Africa's current scientific efforts. It is important that each project, intended to be an African-led initiative, is embraced by all. Political commitment is not only needed, but African leaders also need to demonstrate such commitment by buying into the idea and giving high priority to strategic investments in the projects within the Plan.

In order for the Plan to succeed, there should also be commitment and involvement on the part of African scientists towards the projects. The major contribution that African scientists can make is to build effective systems for innovation as systems developed outside the continent may not be suitable for our situation, and they must design and fabricate what is most appropriate for the continent, using indigenous as well as exogenous knowledge systems.

The international community's acknowledgment that development requires significant input of scientific knowledge, including that expressed in the Millennium Development Goals, would suggest that development partners and other non-governmental organisations are likely to assist and support S&T projects on the continent. In 2005, the Commission for Africa, a

17-member international body set up to review challenges facing Africa, concluded that specific action for strengthening science, engineering and technology capacity "is an imperative for Africa." Innovation ought to be a component of this specific action.

1. Innovation

Innovation is the introduction of something new—a new idea, method or device. The novelty is due to changes made to an old idea or device or an existing way of doing things. It is different from invention, in which the newness is more complete and far reaching. Innovation does not require starting afresh, but rather an old existence.

On the hand, tradition, by definition, can be the transmission of information, beliefs and customs by word of mouth or by example, from one generation to another without written instruction. It can also be an inherited pattern of thought or action (as a religious practice or a social custom) or cultural continuity in social attitudes and institutions (see also Ch. 6).

With respect to the first definition of tradition given above, the phrase to note is "without written instruction." Perhaps it is advantageous that the information, beliefs and customs are handed down without written instruction because the implied absence of (reliable) documentation could be interpreted to mean that these traditions are not carved in stone and therefore may be modified in accordance with prevailing circumstances. But modifications may not necessarily be an innovation. Therefore the school of thought that holds that traditions are so sacrosanct that the saying, "The old order changeth, giving place to new" should not be preached, should be seen as a thing of the past.

The second definition, stressing the inherited nature of tradition, provides yet another avenue for modification which could lead to an innovation. The environment can, and does modify an inherited pattern. There are examples of identical twins, with the same set of genes, who grow up to become different people when they are raised in different environments. Indeed, the modification can be to such an extent that innovation results. This is true of natural phenomena such as the inheritance of genes, and it is certainly true of tradition, which is not even the inheritance of something definite or physical, but rather the inheritance of patterns of thought or action. Modification is possible because a pattern is nothing more than a model proposed for imitation.

The third definition emphasises the continuity aspects within tradition, but places it in a social context. Culture, social attitudes and institutions are dynamic concepts and therefore it is possible to change or modify them and through the modification, introduce something new. It is therefore advocated that we should use innovation within a tradition to provide us with a unique way of developing our resources through science and technology.

Innovation is a component of science and technology, especially when it is considered in the context of discovery. As science progresses, especially when scientists interact with industry and society at large, new ideas are generated, methods and devices are produced to drive new technologies, or new and better ways of doing things. The people in the field tell the scientists what they would like to have or use, and this is what drives the scientists to make the necessary modifications to come up with the type of innovations that society wants or is likely to use. Even without the initial input from society, scientists could add novelty in what they are doing and try and sell the innovation to society if what they find is useful, although it is better to interact with society before putting more efforts into the innovation.

Innovations come out of science and technology all the time and with a few from within our continent, and include:

- Pen or flash drives instead of floppy diskettes or compact discs for computers;
- Mobile telephones instead of fixed line telephones;
- White board instead of black board in the classroom;
- Digital machines instead of analogue ones.

As is well known, diverse human beings want new things; they keep buying new items and that is why innovation is driving the large economies of the world. Thus if African economies are to grow, we will have to innovate. Innovation in science is normal because any inference or prediction, which is a hallmark of any scientific endeavour, illuminates the path to innovation.

The question could be asked whether there are any innovations that we can be proud of as Africans? In Ghana, there is a B.Sc. (Honours) degree programme in Herbal Medicine at the Kwame Nkrumah University of Science and Technology. The goal of the programme is:

> Primarily to train personnel who are knowledgeable in basic sciences,
> medical, pharmaceutical and social sciences, to be competent to practice
> as health professionals, using available facilities to deliver acceptable, safe
> and affordable health care.

The entry requirements are no different from those required of students entering other programmes in science offered by the University. The outline of the syllabus for this 4-year degree programme in the College of Health Sciences, shows a variety of subjects that students can offer: from biochemistry and mathematics/statistics, as examples of the usual science subjects, through typical subjects expected in a medical programme such as human anatomy and physiology, pathology, pharmacology and toxicology, to courses in communication and diagnostic skills, ethics, herbal compounding, phytochemistry, sociology, culture and tradition.

The rationale for establishing such a programme is that although traditional health care is a valuable asset already existing in the community, lack of trained practitioners has tended to create a negative image for the practice and the products used (see also Chapter 14 this volume). The resource base for this health care system is local and cheaper, compared to other health care systems. Scientific training of the practitioners will not only improve the image of the herbal practitioner, but it will also enable collaboration with allopathic or conventional medical practitioners, which will further boost the healthcare delivery system in the country.

Some people may not regard the offer of a science degree programme in Herbal Medicine as a worthwhile innovation. However, this is a programme that recognises an indigenous knowledge system of health delivery and sets out to train scientists to learn more about it, with a view to adding value to it. In such a programme, science enhances an existing knowledge system, but does not subsume it. The programme will become even better when post-graduate research is added, because it is at that level that scientific research can be pursued in earnest, and the triad of research, teaching and extension, can be pursued earnestly.

Innovation is more acceptable if it occurs within tradition because the novelty is bound to be mild or gradual and not drastic, as is expected with invention. If a farmer notices a new variety of maize, it is more likely to be accepted by all, since the variety emerged through a well-known farming practice of (cross) breeding. But if the new variety is through DNA manipulation, a process unfamiliar to a larger section of the population, acceptability could become a problem. We are all familiar with the controversies surrounding acceptability of genetically modified crops, even by people in countries in which these crops have been produced, and their possible negative impact on the environment.

There are a number of reasons which justify modification of tradition. Sticking to traditional systems may not lead to development because of the dynamic nature of things; we have to change with the times but many indigenous systems in Africa tend not to change or do so very slowly. At the same time, national boundaries, real or virtual, have changed because of world-wide trade and regional integration, and a country is not likely to be successful if it clings to its age-old traditions and fails to consider the changes that are taking place.

Indigenous methods do not necessarily give the best outputs or products for development. The methods used by the indigenous system for knowledge acquisition from nature depend on empirical data which could have limitations when the environment changes. There is therefore a need to interface indigenous methods with the modern scientific method which is dynamic.

In many African countries, the modern scientific systems alone are not appropriate for human development partly because the proportion of the populace which can access or understand these systems is low. Another issue to consider is that although modern scientific methods could be good, science does not have all the answers, and its products could be harmful. Above all, there is the view that there is no substitute for the role of indigenous knowledge in human-centred development. And in our attempts to utilise science and technology we have tended to overlook or ignore African indigenous knowledge systems and adopted a more or less foreign system, thus creating problems for ourselves, including the problem of development. This is true not only of science, but also of the systems of governance around Africa. Multiparty democracy, as a modern system of governance, with its notion of law and order, is understood only by a small minority which tends to rule as if the entire country understands the system. Some people are of the view that the dividends to be derived from multi-party democracy are either questionable or are yet to be realised by the many traditional societies that exist around Africa (see also Chapter 6, this volume).

While it is true that many of us want the new items that innovation brings, it is also true that most of us cannot afford them when they come as products. But the vanguard minority can, and does acquire these items, leaving behind the majority, which is often a recipe for disaster and no development. On the other hand, if we set out to have innovations in our traditional processes, technologies and products, we are likely to have better and cheaper products, with more people patronising the new products. The improvements from such innovations would spread and true and sustainable development would be our reward. Such improvements would be reflected in human development, the indicators of which are education, health and livelihoods, for the majority, if not for all of the people.

In order to achieve sustainable human development, it is imperative that the good tenets of the indigenous systems ought to be recognised, isolated and used as a basis. We have already started doing some of this. Here are examples which we believe are worth considering in our human development efforts:

An innovation in science education can be found in the School and Community Science and Technology (SACOST) project based at the University College of Education, Winneba, in Ghana. The philosophy behind this project is that the scientific principles in our indigenous technology systems should be isolated and used as a basis to teach science to our children. The research stage of the project, i.e. documenting the scientific concepts and processes in indigenous manufacturing processes or technologies, has been accomplished. The next stage is for the outcomes to be integrated into the school system, and hopefully, it should not be long before the final outcome of this innovation in the educational system occurs, to assist in the correct approach to the teaching and learning of science for human development.

Another example is the almost in-exhaustive list of scientific principles underlying the local food processing industry. If these were to be utilised, we would have innovative ideas to improve, enhance and boost local food products. In Ghana for example, the teaching and learning that takes place in the Hospitality Industry Departments within the Polytechnics for example, could benefit a great deal from using these innovative ideas to come up with nutritious local food products which could replace the products in the fast food industry, a lot of which are not only imported with hard currencies, but could be less nutritious or even harmful. Such local substitutes could also boost our tourism industry. However, the research must be done first before such an industry could take off and thrive.

Work on herbal medicine used for the management of HIV and AIDS in Burkina Faso has given evidence on how innovation within tradition, involving collaboration between people with indigenous knowledge and those with scientific knowledge, can lead to wealth creation for a community. Herbalists or traditional medical practitioners (TMPs) are the custodians of indigenous knowledge with respect to local treatments for disease. But most of the time, scientists and clinicians either ignore them, or treat them with contempt, and governments also tend to ignore them. The TMPs in Burkina Faso believed that they had an herbal treatment for HIV and AIDS, but they did not keep the knowledge to themselves and they were not ignored, probably because they came together and spoke with one voice. Scientists teamed up with them to collect data showing that the herbal preparation reduced viral load, thus providing an evidence-based approach to solving the health problem. The government contributed by requesting financial help from developing partners through the African Regional Office of the World Health Organisation. Now Burkina Faso has an effective plant-based anti-retroviral therapy that belongs to the people! In this way, wealth will be generated and it will be common wealth.

On the continent and elsewhere, people tend to think or behave as if herbal preparations that are used to manage HIV and AIDS only treat opportunistic infections, or as if a drug good enough to reduce viral load such as the conventional drugs (ARTs), cannot be obtained from herbal preparations and that such therapies must always come from outside the continent, with nothing good seemingly coming out of Africa. It is because of such attitudes that some scientists and clinicians will not even think of looking for effective drugs from among the armamentarium of the TMP. It is the same attitude that prevents policy makers from providing the necessary resources for the scientists, clinicians and the TMPs to do the research. Rather they go begging for the countries which produce the ARTs to reduce the price so that the drug will be affordable, instead of looking inside to produce something local that others can also use and pay for. The Burkina Faso experience is an example of how Africans can inject innovative science and technology into indigenous systems to create national wealth, common wealth or wealth for all to share.

2. Inventions

Unlike innovation, in invention, something completely new is brought into existence and not by addition to an existing one; there is creation of an idea, method or device. Africa needs to develop this culture, especially among the youth. Although it would be better to develop this culture in everyone, invention is through imagination, ingenuity and experimentation, and young people have less of the experiences that tend to make people set in their ways and become less amenable to change. But in general, the youth are more prepared and free to explore, to be adventurous and try things out, and they are also more likely to delve into the unknown because they tend to dream dreams and take risks. For these reasons, we should recruit the youth into S&T programmes and challenge them to invent.

The number of patents held is supposed to be an indicator of S&T activity, and Africa is far behind in patents which come with inventions. Apart from the lack of resources which would contribute to the inventions leading to patent applications, there could be other factors for the situation in Africa. Institutions of higher education are the citadels for the creation of new knowledge which may be exploited for industrial application. Yet, there are many institutions of higher education in Africa which have no offices where scientific research output is examined for its intellectual property and protected before it is published, whereas such an institutional arrangement is commonplace in universities in industrialised countries, and African institutions must have such offices to help with the steps required for patent applications.

Inventors in Africa stand the risk of being marginalised when it comes to protecting their intellectual property solely because of costs. But patents do not come cheap and are granted for products and processes which are novel, have inventive steps and are of industrial application. However, the mere fact that a product or process has been patented does not mean that profit is going to accrue and be shared, as it requires someone to use the invention in an industrial application successfully, yielding profit, out of which the inventor will receive compensation for his or her intellectual property. The fees are high and therefore, filing and renewing the application are both expensive. According to one source, "the amount spent on patenting inventions has gone up from £ 90,000 to £ 400,000 in the last few years." (Sanders, 2003) Meanwhile, the person who filed the patent application must renew the application, which means, he or she must continue to pay fees periodically even when the patent has had no successful industrial application.

If governments or others should help inventors to acquire and keep patents, then the inventors also ought to learn to balance what is due them with the love for the community. Much as there is a need to protect intellectual property rights, protection should not be at the expense of the society at large. A balancing act, including love of community and ethical considerations, is what is needed because of the impact of Intellectual Property Rights (IPR) on development through industrialisation. The cost of industrialisation can be reduced by a not-so-stringent enforcement of IPR, and the following example from the pharmaceutical industry can be used to illustrate the point.

Patents may be acquired for a process or for a product. Prior to the agreement on Trade-Related Aspects of Intellectual Property Rights (TRIPS) promoted by the World Trade Organization (WTO), some countries allowed patents on processes, but not on the final product of that process. With this "relaxation", local industries used different methods to produce generic drugs similar to, but far cheaper than, the original brand names. In Africa, we should learn to explore avenues for protecting intellectual property or indigenous knowledge without blocking development and we can do this through novel institutional arrangements. There is a need to evolve national or regional intellectual property regimes that deal with protection of indigenous knowledge, *sui generis*, that protect all forms of usable knowledge, traditional or otherwise.

It can be argued that Africa has suffered because we have failed to do this. Take for instance, the process of *garification*. In the making of *gari,* a dual process of drying and cooking takes place simultaneously. This process of *garification,* which confers special properties on its products, was not previously known in the food technology industry. Food was dried and cooked in succession, *not together*. The new process is now known internationally, and in the food technology business, engineering designs have emerged to take advantage of this dual processing technique. Scientists from West Africa, spearheaded by Nigerian scientists, pioneered this technique. Obviously, the scientists, working with indigenous food technologists, must have recognised the unique processing technique and written about it. This was an indigenous knowledge system, but they neither protected nor sold the knowledge. *Garification* has been adopted and continues to be utilised in the food industry now, but no scientist, technologist, scientific or technological institutions or groups in the *gari* making countries in West Africa have benefited from this utilisation. In today's techno-science society, this is a great loss to the individuals, to the nations and to the region.

African scientists must therefore learn the process for deriving maximum benefit from their products of endeavour. They should protect their usable knowledge or intellectual property and use the knowledge that they have either created, helped to create or have acquired, and to benefit financially therefrom. The early scientists were philosophers, interested in knowledge of natural phenomena for its own sake. Over time the knowledge was utilised generally for the benefit of humankind, although there were some abuses. For scientists of today, usable knowledge has become the key to success because it creates wealth. However, because of how greedy human beings have become, reaping where they have not sown, this knowledge must be protected. Unfortunately, protecting usable knowledge has its own disadvantages, including restrictions of the benefits of scientific knowledge to society. The right of an individual to property, including intellectual property, is a legal issue. African scientists therefore, ought to liaise with professionals in law in order to deal with this aspect of their work, especially since current patent laws do not pay much attention to the knowledge of indigenous people on which some scientific activities are based.

There are many stages of invention: an idea occurs to someone due to inspiration, curiosity or new knowledge. However, the idea must lead to creating or building something that will lead to the solution of a problem; the idea must be put into practice. If the originator of the idea cannot put it into practice, someone else may be able to. Therefore, disclosure is important as the idea is no good in people's head. Yet, in Africa we tend not to disclose or even to record because we tend to think that we are better protected when we do not disclose. The concept of intellectual property rights is not well understood and in some cases has not served us well, probably because of more communal and less individual ownership of (indigenous) knowledge, and therefore we tend to shy away from it. But more (or additional) knowledge is necessary for a successful invention, and this is obtained as people try to put different ideas together and into practice. Other people's contribution is important to the success of the invention because there is a social component to it and because it must be useful in practical terms, and not merely brilliant in exposition, when nobody can carry it out in a relatively simple manner.

Invention is a solution to a specific problem and hence the need for the practical approach which also builds in the experimentation needed in this hands-on approach. This calls for the existence of research laboratories where young scientists can try their hand at possible solutions to problems, and where ideas will generate into problem solving devices. Industrial research laboratories which are properly and appropriately equipped are also needed to attract and retain African youth in the S&T enterprise for solving problems of industry. These are the reasons why centres of excellence and scientific and technological institutes need to be established. With such research laboratories in place, young scientists will be less likely to receive only theoretical learning, allowing them to explore more and be taught less in S &T.

3. The *Sankofa* idiom

Processes or methods that existed in Africa in the past, which could help us achieve our goals in any aspect of science and technology for our development, ought to be explored. Thus in several educational systems around Africa, a subject known as "Nature Study" used to be taught. Indeed, it was nature study or the study of nature, and students went outside the classroom into the environment and made use of whatever material was there for their study. These were usually plants and animals, and the teacher would be with them, leading the way. There were hardly any text books, and more often than not, students would bring things back into the classroom to draw and label. It is suggested that science in the basic schools should go back to "Nature Study" since after all, science is understanding nature. It does not have to take a particular form as long as the students study and try to understand the things of nature around them. Nature Study can be modified to include take home assignments which will encourage the adults at home, especially the parents, to learn with the children, in a bid to arouse their curiosity.

4. Set Priority Areas

It may be worth our while to identify a number of priority areas on which science and technology teaching, research and extension will be based. We may want to focus on:
- Science education at all levels, incorporating indigenous knowledge systems;
- Specific research agendas with the creation of centres where world-class research of social significance to Africa can take place, preferably with the involvement of the private sector. The focus of the research could be on:
  - Food safety and food security;
  - Fuel or energy;

    o Public health systems in general or maternal and child health specifically;
    o Endemic and pandemic diseases such as HIV and AIDS, malaria and tuberculosis;
- The environment or ecosystem assessment to include issues on biodiversity; and,
- Cultivatingtheinterest of, and engaging policy-makers. Perhaps scientists and techno-logists serving in government should adopt the attitude of ambassadors, providing links between the S&T community and government, and also canvassing for allocation of more resources to S& T.

Whatever priority areas are chosen requires careful and excellent work, and ensuring that the results of the scientific research and technological advancement benefit African people. A good example is the work carried out at the International Centre for Material Science & Technology. This Centre, listed as a Centre of Excellence in The Third World, is located within the Building & Road Research Institute, one of the institutes of the Council for Scientific and Industrial Research (CSIR) in Kumasi, Ghana. Research activities of this Centre include:

- Housing and shelter construction;
- Development and better uses of local building materials;
- Development of laterite soil;
- Building materials for housing;
- Construction techniques and management;
- Lime production for use in paints and soil stabilisers;
- Structural analysis and uses of materials and manufactured components such as timber in construction; and,
- Housing statistics.

To be made a Centre of Excellence for research activities related to improving the basic necessities of life such as housing, is indeed something that Africans should be proud of. However we could ask whether these activities are considered worthwhile in science and technology?

5. Involvement of other stakeholders

It is imperative that all stakeholders consider the role that they should play for innovation within tradition to move the continent forward. Apart from the role of scientists, technologists and technicians, other members of the community, in addition to governments and regional organisations, also have a role to play in ensuring that the S&T enterprise is properly managed for the development of the countries within the continent. Community members can play an advocacy role, but such a role is possible only when they are conversant with the benefit of science to the community. For that to be possible, public understanding of what science can and cannot do, is an essential component of science education programmes.

It appears as though irrespective of what Africa does with respect to its S&T agenda, there would be a need for research cooperation and collaboration, whether at the national, international (regional, continental), or at the global level (see Figure 19). For cooperation and collaboration in science and technology, African countries need to pool resources, including talent, share costs, and increase the private sector's interest and participation in science. First the collaboration ought to be among Africans. It is only after such collaboration that we should look outside where we can find some long standing partnerships that could be exploited. An example is the long history of research collaboration between Africa and Europe as exemplified by bilateral cooperation agreements as well as multilateral ones such as the one found between African/ Caribbean and Pacific (ACP) countries and the European Union (EU).

Figure 19 – Mbita Point Research and Training Centre, Kenya

Source: *http://www.nasa.gov/centers/langley/images/content/118318main_mbita_training.jpg*

In 2001 an ACP-EU workshop on development and national S&T policy was held. An outcome of the workshop was a recommendation stressing the need:

- For dialogue among all the stakeholders involved including the private sector, civil society, the grassroots, research community and the policy makers, and the establishment of a research bridging facility which would provide for activities designed to bridge the gap between policy makers, end-users and researchers.
- To undertake studies that analyse the S&T landscape, promote the participation of stakeholders in such studies to enhance ownership of the results, and promote capacity building to ensure that such studies do take place.
- For an S&T Observatory, a form of a clearing house, in the Africa region, to collect and share information on latest developments in S&T and their applications, an Observatory with an antennae linking up with the private sector, civil society and regional networks.

For the future, Africa needs to look at new opportunities worldwide for strengthening science and take advantage of those of immense benefit to Africa. Here are some of the opportunities:

1. Science, technology and innovation for achieving the United Nations Millennium Development Goals

At the United Nations General Assembly in September 2005, there was a joint statement from international scientific, engineering and medical organisations to the Heads of State and Government who met during the General Assembly. The organisations decided to take a number of actions and committed themselves to working with appropriate partners to help with the implementation of their actions. The statement is of relevance to Africa because it recognised that science, technology and innovation are essential components of effective strategies and programmes for reducing poverty and its many associated problems, and many of the countries on the continent are among the poorest in the world. According to the statement, in order to enable developing countries to pursue the evidence-based policies required to achieve the Millennium Development Goals, they will need sound mechanisms and essential infrastructure for applying scientific and technological knowledge to national problem solving. The need for sustainable national structures and strategies to provide and maintain a source of well-trained knowledgeable people was also part of the statement

Africa ought to dialogue with members of the organisations who came up with the joint statement for the implementation of their actions. The actions of helping to revitalize the universities and support the creation of centres of excellence in science, engineering and medicine, and investing international funds to support scientific, technological and innovative capacity for addressing the Millennium Development Goals are most important. There is a general awareness that governments alone cannot achieve the MDGs and that partnerships are necessary, with much of the action at the local level, while involving all relevant stakeholders.

2. The Inter-Academy Council

The Inter-Academy Council (IAC) is a body formed partly in response to an appeal by the Secretary General of the United Nations to national science academies to mobilise their best scientists and provide expert knowledge and advice to the United Nations and other international organisations. An IAC report entitled "Inventing a Better Future: A Strategy for Building Worldwide Capacities in Science and Technology," the product of an international study panel of renowned scientists convened by the IAC, proposes new initiatives to strengthen national scientific capabilities worldwide and to foster global cooperation (IAC 2006). Africa should implement the relevant recommendations which are that every nation develops an S&T strategy that reflects local priorities, including support for basic science, education and training, which will allow it to achieve local competence in selected areas of national priority.

Although there appears to be nothing new in such a recommendation, the fact that the report stresses the essential nature of local S&T capacity for using and contributing to the world's valuable store of knowledge, and the fact that universities have a critical role to play in building the S&T capacities, means that Africa will do well to take the issues mentioned in this report seriously. It actually makes a statement to the effect that "Stronger S&T capacity in the developing nations is not a luxury but an absolute necessity if these nations are to participate as full partners in the world's fast-forming, knowledge-based economy" (ibid). The report also mentions the opportunities opened up because of the advances in information and communication technology, which developing countries can use to remedy the situation. An example is the proper harnessing of digital technologies for the catch-up game and therefore the need for the countries to provide adequate infrastructure and trained technical personnel in ICT for both learning and research institutions, leading to creation of world-class research institutions. A second IAC report addressed specifically ways to increase food productivity in Africa (IAC 2004).

3. The Nelson Mandela Institute (NMI)

A World Bank initiative, The Nelson Mandela Institution for Advancement of Science and Technology in Sub-Saharan Africa, aims at establishing a number of centres of excellence in African countries, to be known as African Institutes of Science and Technology (AIST). Such an initiative is important because centres of excellence are very few on the continent, compared to centres in the industrialised world. In a document from The Academy of Sciences for the Developing World (formerly Third World Academy of Sciences, TWAS), listing Centres of Excellence in the South participating in a TWAS-UNESCO Associate Membership Scheme, there were only 9 of such centres or approximately 10 percent, from Africa, out of a total of 88 such centres listed! (http://sites.ias.edu/sig/systems/Olang.pdf)

4. AU/NEPAD

The African Union (AU)'s Commission on Human Resource Development has a science and technology component, just as the AU's predecessor, the Organisation of African Unity (OAU) had an S & T component, the Scientific Technological and Research Committee (STRC).

The New Partnership for Africa's Development (NEPAD), also has an S & T commission as indicated above. The environment is one priority area that the NEPAD S & T commission has identified, with programmes in land degradation, drought and desertification, conservation of wetlands, integrated approaches to wetlands management, conservation and sustainable use of marine and coastal regions, application of remote sensing for integrated management of ecosystems and water resources in Africa. In addition, there is a relationship between UNESCO and NEPAD, and there are UN Clusters for Cooperation with AU/NEPAD. With such relationships, it is up to the scientists, researchers and policy makers on the continent to exploit the relationships and make them work to their advantage. There is a need to coordinate all these S&T activities in the various organisations, including the newly established ICSU Regional Office for Africa, which is hosted by the National Research Foundation of South Africa.

5. Funding

In 1987, Chief Olu Ibukun, then of UNESCO, made some suggestions with respect to mobilisation of financial resources for the scientific and technological development of Africa. These suggestions are still pertinent and are reproduced below in slightly modified form on account of the passage of time:

- African countries cannot continue to rely on external financing of S&T development in Africa and hence each national government should show greater determination to provide more funds locally for S&T development.

- Each country should strive to obtain the target of 1% of GNP as contribution to R&D as soon as possible, and this target should be reviewed upwards. (The original document suggested an upward adjustment to 1.25 % by the year 2000).
- All African countries which have not done so, should establish a National Science and Technology Development Fund as recommended by the Lagos Plan of Action and study closely at the national level, various other ways and means of inviting contributions to the Fund.
- The possibility should be explored of creating an industrial training levy by which foreign companies executing contractual development projects involving transfer of technology could be compelled to contribute a percentage of their profits for the training of local personnel.
- African Member States should make every effort to meet their obligatory assessments for the functioning of existing regional centres and networks concerned with the development of scientific education, training and research facilities in Africa, and some Member States should, in addition, consider voluntary contributions or grants as encouragement to such institutions.
- Each country should, as soon as possible, review its national priorities taking into account the significant role that S&T will continue to play in development and devote greater budgetary allocation to S&T and its applications. In this respect, some of the expenditures allocated for defence and military purposes could be diverted into S&T development (Ibukun, 1987).

Ibukun adds that financial resources to be mobilised to enable various bodies contribute to S&T development in Africa can include individual and institutional membership fees of associations, learned or professional bodies, government grants and contracts, endowment funds from the public or industries, institutions' own development enterprises, grants or contracts, as well as funds from private sources including foundations.

In prosecuting the S&T agenda for the benefit of Africa, certain institutions and organisations must necessarily be regarded as major stakeholders on the delivery side. The universities have been mentioned. They should be the prime focus for development and the fertile ground from which centres of excellence should spring up. These centres could remain in the universities or could be located outside them, but there ought to be some relationship between the centres of excellence and the universities. In the focus on universities, organisations such as the Association of African Universities should be taken seriously by African government and its programmes in S&T strengthened, through their contributions to them, including their financial contributions.

But it is not only universities which are the major stakeholders from the educational sector. S&T programmes in all tertiary educational institutions belong to this category. The institutions must play their part in teaching/learning, research and extension, and therefore both teachers and learners are equally important and need to be catered for. However, it is well known that although the number of learners in African tertiary educational institutions continues to increase, this is not matched by the increase in the number of faculty. The situation has led to compromises in the quality of teaching and learning at tertiary institutions. Because the conditions of faculty have not been attractive in the past, it is now necessary to put in place certain special measures to ensure that bright and young scientists and technologists are recruited into the mainstream of teaching, research and extension. Recognition of the work of scientists and technologists and better remuneration are likely to be the best incentives to drive people into the field of S&T.

Apart from the money that ought to be set aside so that the universities could be better resourced, governments, from the supply side of the equation, ought to encourage the other organisations in the S&T enterprise, such as the Academies of Science, and the National Research Institutes or National Research Foundations, with meaningful grants to enable them do their work. For Africa, the S&T agenda must include manufacturing, investing and training people. As businessmen/women and entrepreneurs will not do this at the initial stages, governments must step into the breach. The National Research Foundation in South Africa is well resourced and it is quite clear that it is doing well because of its resources. Similarly, when the Ghana Academy of Arts and Sciences was first established in the late 1950s as the Ghana Academy of Learning, it received the necessary resources to perform its functions because of the personal interest of the then Head of State, Osagyefo Dr. Kwame Nkrumah, who was also the founder. Ghana's Council for Scientific and Industrial Research (CSIR) was part of the Academy then.

Without a doubt, Academies and Research Councils must receive resources from governments to enable them do their work. In this connection, it is worth mentioning that the Nigerian government, did not only give a grant of $5 million dollars to the African Academy of Sciences, but also the President of that Academy was made a science advisor to the Head of State of Nigeria. One would like to think that the donation was a reflection of the Head of State's regard for and/or generosity to the Nigerian Academy of Sciences. The concept of science advisors to politicians, including Heads of State and Ministers of State is not new in other parts of the world, but appears to be relatively rare in Africa.

Another group of scientific organisations that ought to be encouraged by African governments to continue what they do best is the group comprising of scientific networks. The continent is huge and made up of small independent countries. The differences in the geographical areas are also to be appreciable, whereas the problems in each geographical region tend to be fairly similar (see also Chapter 1, this volume). Communication is difficult and expensive, whether physically or electronically, and most boundaries are artificial. Therefore it is prudent to have regional science associations which will deal with regional problems such as desertification or forest resource management, or how to develop natural products for domestic use and for export. If scientists were well paid and the materials needed to research and find possible solutions to the problems that they tend to deal with were available, these voluntary and independent associations and networks, just like other associations, would operate on their own and not look up to government for resources.

Review Questions

1 Discuss the contribution to science or technology, or the application of S&T to development in your country of one of the following:

- A named scientist/technologist of your country (one male, one female);
- A team of scientists and technologists;
- An interdisciplinary team;
- A news item on S&T that caught your attention.

2. Distinguish between an innovation and an invention, giving examples from your country.

3. Debate the following statements:

   - There is no substitute for indigenous technology;
   - The many languages of Africa pose a barrier to development through S&T;
   - Both knowledge and discernment are quintessential in the development of local technologies;
   - 'In art, nothing worth doing can be done without genius. In science, even a very moderate capacity can contribute something to a supreme achievement.' (Bertrand Russell)
   - 'It is the lone worker who makes the first advance in a subject: the details may be worked out by a team, but the prime idea is due to the enterprise, thought and perception of an individual.' (Sir Alexander Fleming)

4. With two colleagues examine the following statements:

   - Problems of the real world invariably require an interdisciplinary team for their solution. Do you agree? Marshall arguments for and against.
   - Communication with the target community in the right register, as regards language and assumed concepts or background knowledge, is essential to all extension efforts. In your experience, was this so when you attempted to enlighten a lay person on a scientific or technological issue?

References

Clayson, Alison. 1997 *Voices, Values and Development: Reinvesting in Africa South of the Sahara*. Paris: UNESCO. p.24

Ibukun, Olu 1987. 'Mobilization of financial resources for scientific and technological development in Africa.' Premier Congrès des Hommes de Science en Afrique. Documents de Référence. Volume II. *Mobilization of the African Community for Rational and Human Management: Financial Strategies*. Brazzaville, 25-30 June. pp. 179-187.

InterAcademy Council 2006. *Inventing a Better Future: A Strategy for Building Worldwide Capacities in Science and Technology*. Amsterdam: IAC (March)

InterAcademy Council 2004. *Realizing the Promise and Potential of African Agriculture*. Amsterdam: IAC (June)

Öman, C. B, K. S. Gamaniel and M. E. Addy. 2006. 'Properly Functioning Scientific Equipment in Developing Countries.' *Anal. Chem.*, 78 (15), pp 5273–5276.

Ravichandran, V. and R.R. Daniel, (Eds.)1994. *The Role of Science in Food Production in Africa*. Proceedings of a seminar, Accra, Ghana, 5-6 April 1994. Madras, India, Committee on Science and Technology in Developing Countries International Biosciences Network (COSTED-IBN)/Vinkaar Publishing Pvt. Ltd.

SECTION 5: ARTISTIC EXPRESSION AND PERFORMANCE IN AFRICA

CHAPTER 17

THE HERITAGE OF LITERARY ARTS IN AFRICA

Esi Sutherland-Addy

Introduction

> "The landscape of creative practice in Africa today is marked by, among other things, the co-existence of multiple forms and media of artistic expression some of which claim indigenous ancestry in Africa itself while others trace their origin to cultures outside of Africa." (Mbaye Cham, 2002:2)[1]

This chapter treats two main forms of artistic expression, namely literature and drama. The view we take here is that there are many ways in which both literature and drama are dependent for their full manifestation on verbal aesthetics and expression and can therefore be usefully discussed together. In our treatment of drama, we shall however acknowledge the fact that it includes expressive, symbolic and representational acts which go much beyond, and indeed sometimes, manifest without verbal expression. For convenience, the expression 'the literary arts,' will be used when referring to both art forms. A working definition of the term 'literary arts' is provided in part one of the chapter which explores oral and written literature as two major categories of literature that can be distinguished in both form and content. However, a generic approach is introduced which admits both oral and written forms in order to more accurately portray the interface between the two. Part two of the chapter essentially identifies and delves into the dramatic heritage, exploring its place in African societies and demonstrating the extent to which other forms of literary arts find their expression through drama. The evolution of theatre as a post colonial phenomenon is discussed in some detail here. In the penultimate part, there is a summary of dominant issues in the study and practice of the literary arts in Africa, before the conclusion.

PART ONE

The field of literary arts is vast, exciting and dynamic and can be approached from uncountable perspectives. To begin with, the literary arts in the African context will be broadly defined, highlighting the growing significance of a literary perspective in scholarly work on Africa today. In order to contribute to an appreciation of the literary arts, we shall discuss a number of critical elements of language and stylistics as well as the relationship between the literary arts and society. In engaging in the latter discussion, close attention will be paid to the literary artist and to gender. A few of the genres of literary arts have been selected in order to discuss form and content more concretely. While we shall provide a brief introduction to writing in Africa, the sections on narrative, proverbial, poetic and dramatic forms will involve both written and oral forms.

Defining the Literary Arts

The literary arts may be defined according to a set of generic characteristics. Indeed, the intricacies of text classification constitute a significant aspect of scholarly work in the field. There is a wide variety of criteria upon which texts can be classified into different genres or types. Below are a number of genres and the main factor on which they have been classified: mode of production (written/oral); and the level to which prosody is significant (song, rather than chant, or poetry rather than prose). The function of the piece may also be the basis for classification as is the case with the categories of work song, praise poem, ritual drama, poetry of abuse, and drama for development. In the case of the epic/narrative/short story/novel/proverb/play, structure is the basis for classification. On the other hand, the context in which a piece of literary art is produced may be the criterion for classification as we find with court or funeral poetry. The social groups who typically perform particular types of literary arts may be associated with these, as for example women's or children's literature. Again the aesthetic techniques deployed in the construction of the piece may be used to classify the piece, as we find in the notions of comedy, tragedy or *Anansegoro* in the classification of contemporary drama. Finally the basic themes about which a piece is composed may also be used to classify it, such as love (love story/love poem) or political ideology (e.g. Negritude poetry).

These classifications are by no means mutually exclusive. Indeed, in the culture of oral literature or verbal art, some genres may be quite ubiquitous. For example people do not normally go about spouting a string of proverbs on their own, yet proverbs usually embellish names of persons, orations, poetry, and narratives. On the other hand, there are particular forms which encompass many of the genres listed above. The epic for example may be described as a mega-genre, for within it may be found praise poetry, narrative, proverbs etc.

Certainly, as Abiola Irele puts it, "oral literature represents our classical tradition- i.e. that body of texts which lies behind us as a complete and enduring literature, though constantly being renewed, and which most profoundly informs the world views of our peoples, and is thus at the same time the foundation and expressive channel of a fundamental African mental universe" (Irele,1990: 12).

In all societies, great store is set by the mastery of language due to its capacity to carry thought, knowledge, values, meaning and emotion. Nowhere is this more clearly enunciated as in the African context where elegant, aesthetic use of language is a vital element of life. Words, in particular the spoken word, continue to be held in high esteem. Words are not to be uttered lightly as they retain an evocative power. Perhaps formulaic genres portray most vividly the link between words and effect. Songs calling for rain for example are found in the liturgical corpus of several ethnic groups such as the Venda of South Africa and the Lango of Uganda. The Lango Rain-Making Litany presented below illustrates the notion of collective or participatory creativity based on the 'call and response' structure. The respondents, in repeating essential aspects of the principal celebrant's plea for rain, are in fact reinforcing the potency of the invocation. The fact that this text is chanted also adds to its effectiveness as an invocative prayer

Rain-making Litany

[Recitative]	[Response]
We overcome this wind	We overcome.
We desire the rain to fall, that it be poured	Be poured.
in showers quickly.	
Ah! Thou rain, I adjure thee fall. If thou	
Rainest, it is well.	It is well.
A drizzling confusion.	Confusion.
5. If it rains and our fold ripens, it is well	It is well.
If the children rejoice, it is well.	It is well.
If it rains, it is well. If our women rejoice,	
it is well.	It is well.
If the young men sing, it is well.	It is well.
	It is well.
15. An overflowing in the granary.	Overflowing.
May our grain fill the granaries.	May it fill.
A torrent in flow.	A torrent.
If the wind veers to the south, it is well.	It is well.
If the rain veers to the south, it is well.	It is well.

(Okpewho,1992:122)

As can be seen from the above extract, this communal outpouring is expected to ensure the survival of a people in crisis.

Taking this idea from a different but equally significant angle is the notion of words as a source for the survival of the ethos of a people. One of the most vivid statements on the power of the spoken word and its chief custodians can be found on page 1 of *Sundiata, An Epic of Old Mali*. The famous Mandinka griot or bard, Mamoudou Kouyate, whose narration of the Sundiata epic is presented by D. T. Niane, stamps his authority on the narrative which he is about to deliver and on the importance of the spoken word as follows:

"I am a griot. It is I, Djeli Mamoudou Kouyate, son of Bintou Kouyate and Djeli Kedian Kouyate, master in the art of eloquence. Since time immemorial, the Kouyates have been in the service of the Keita princes of Mali; we are the vessels of speech, we are the repositories which harbor secrets many centuries old. The art of eloquence has no secrets for us; without us names of kings would vanish into oblivion, we are the memory of mankind; by the spoken word we bring to life the deeds and exploits of kings for younger generations." (Niane, 1965: 1).

Proverbial Language

While proverbs are found throughout the world and are by no means peculiar to Africa, they certainly take pride of place in the culture of speaking and of the creation of literary art in general on the African continent. It is no coincidence that the griot quoted above makes repeated references to the art of eloquence. Proverbial speech epitomizes sophistication in verbal expression. Thus, the ability to make public statements, richly ornamented with proverbs placed appropriately for rhetorical and aesthetic effect, remains a treasured social skill. Much as proverbs are used to illuminate an argument, the existence of the Akan (Ghana) *kasakoa* demonstrates that sometimes intellectual indulgence which requires that only discerning persons deserve to participate in a discussion, is also an important part of the speaking culture. Indeed this can go to the level of obscurantism as is the case with *Adagana* (Ewe-Ghana/Togo) where there is virtually a new language to be learnt in order to be able to participate in the discourse. The Nzema of Ghana and Côte d'Ivoire say that the proverb, *exele*, is a palm kernel; you have to remove the layers to get to the seed.

According to Yankah (1989) two main types of proverbs may be discerned. Attributive proverbs are short, crisp and quotable e.g. 'One who is suspected of being a thief should not pick up a young domestic animal to play with it '(Yoruba). Non attributive ones on the other hand, are longer statements which may take the form of anecdotes. The Akan saying: 'necessity is the source of thought and ingenuity' is derived from the tale in which tortoise was able to find a way to fulfill the non-negotiable obligation to attend the funeral of the mother of his best friend the crow, even though he could not fly. Equally, the material culture is full of symbolic representations of ideas that readily have verbal counterparts. Insignia of the kings of the ancient Dahomey kingdom or those placed on linguist staffs in Ghana are pictographs and carvings respectively, representing some of these ideas. For example, the hand with an egg enclosed in it on the linguist staff of some chiefs in southern Ghana symbolises the enigma of power – hold it too tightly and you will crush it, hold it too loosely and it will fall and be smashed.

Based on sharply perceptive observation of minute details of environmental and social phenomena, proverbs derive their legitimacy from being considered as gems of truth which have gained their acceptability over time and may thus be said to be traditional. These truths may be empirical, such as the well known "all fingers are not equal" which occurs in many cultures, or as in the Ewe" Honey bees form into a hive. It is not easy to pass them and get the honey." Matters are not so simple when it comes to the following proverb from the same culture in the form of a claim: "Cockroach says it has eaten something up and the mouse is being blamed for it." Here the statement is deduced and distilled from reality and has been formed for rhetorical purposes.

Too often, the emphasis when discussing proverbs is on morality. This limits these gems of discourse to a single interpretation and does not allow for ambiguity or for the fact that there may be proverbs about the same phenomenon which may contradict each other. It also does not recognise the sheer love of rhetoric and debate, to say nothing of verbal conflict. With respect to the latter point, the stinging irony of the following Ga (Ghana) proverb is predicated upon the startling but simple metaphor used: "Abui le ke ole kpee le, kpee o dunaa," which translates as "Oh needle, if you know how to sew, sew up your bottom." This should leave the opponent, caught unawares, gasping with indignation as to the audaciousness of the statement.

On the other hand, the speech of an Igbo orator entitled "Breaking Kola nut" (Senanu and Vincent, 1988: 26-30) is a quintessential example of improvised prayer in which there is a balance between received traditional expressions and the speaker's own ingenuity. The speech is ornate and demonstrates how parallelism and redundancy can be raised to the level of an art form. The following is the third section of the invocation:

It is KOLA I bring
It's all I can offer
A little baby
Can only hold its mother
As far as its hands can go!
KOLA is small
And yet is big!
Like the sacrificial food,
It is more important that it goes round
Than that it fills the stomach.

Our fathers' fathers
And their fathers before them-
All our ancestors-
Saw all the fruits of the land
But they chose kola
As the prime substance for hospitality
And for offerings:
What an old man lying down has seen,
Has a young man ever seen better
Though he perches on the highest tree?
                                (emphasis mine)

Proverbs are often structured in such a way that they can be conceptually broken into two, with the second half of the statement responding to the first, either by confirming it or by providing a contrast to it. In other words, there is an inherent conditionality binding the two halves of the proverbial statement together. The latter proverb in the extract clearly demonstrates this, as does the following *Dagaare* (Ghana) witticism: "Since all lizards fall flat on their stomach, who will ever know which lizard feels pains in its stomach?"

Aside from their role in traditional speech acts and events, proverbs constitute a veritable pool of readymade constructions of literary ingenuity for writers of literature as well as speech makers, advertisers, and composers of contemporary lyrics. Their use poses a particular challenge in the creation of new idioms in non-African language texts.

The Significance of a Literary Perspective

The literary text can be said to be a window into the soul of a society or of an individual, and many pieces of literature or bodies of literary heritage provide an indication of core values and ideas. A compendium of proverbs from a particular society for example is usually recognised as providing a spectacular insight into its dominant philosophical tenets and moral values. N. K. Dzobo goes so far as to say:

"Ewe language and culture are at their depth made up of proverbs whose proper understanding leads one to the soul of the Ewe, their philosophy and to the principles that serve partly to integrate the personality of the individual. More than that, an understanding of them reveals some of the fundamental determinants of moral behaviour. Even though the emphasis in this study is on the moral determinants of behaviour, yet the reader will gain some insight into the philosophy and the collective character of the Ewe" (Dzobo, 1973: 12-13).

There are other scholars who value proverbs because they characterise dialectical issues which exercise the intellectuals of a given society. This shifts the emphasis from morality and consensus to an exploration of the rhetorical culture in which persuasive argumentation and sophisticated use of language seems to be one of the delights of life.

As to the reliability of oral traditions as a source of history, African historiography as a field of inquiry includes a number of methodologies evolved to tap the rich information and perspective stored in the literary traditions of African societies. These methodologies recognise the fact that life and its evolution are conceived of in metaphorical terms, metaphor being an essential element of the literary arts. The initial volume of the *UNESCO General History of Africa* series dedicates the first nine chapters to discussing different aspects of relevant methodologies. Speaking of the oral tradition, Joseph Ki-Zerbo, editor of the volume, says:

"In oral narrative, there are no insignificant details, and that is why everything is recounted without any omissions or else the narrator refrains from telling the story altogether, by saying 'If you haven't time to listen to me I'll tell the story some other day.' This is an enormous advantage for the historian since both internal and external criticism can rely on certain details to bear out or invalidate a text. To take the tale of Tianaba, the mythical Fula serpent, for example, the 'legend' traces its adventures and migration through the Sudanic savannah. In about 1921, Belime, the engineer in charge of building the Sansanding dam, was curious enough to follow the trail of the geographical clues given in the legend and discovered to his surprise that he was following the former bed of the river Niger." (Ki-Zerbo, 1990: 72).

Clearly, the semiotics of mythology, legends, tales and other forms of oral literature should become a major preoccupation of African/Africanist scholars who want to unlock the doors to the indigenous knowledge of the continent. Currently, therefore, fields such as history, anthropology, philosophy, gender and development studies recognise that to achieve a deeper understanding of people and societies, it is important to go beyond cold facts and generalisations. There appears to be a greater appreciation of the inherent quality of the literary arts to provide what factual discourse does not, and that is the ability to evoke the significance of events and patterns in human lives and societies. The intense, perceptive and often empathetic view of the writer/composer sets in sharp focus issues which are either perennial and universal, or of immediate, local relevance. A few examples will suffice to illustrate this point.

Stephanie Newell, an anthropologist, has published a revised edition of the late 19th century Gold Coast novel, *Marita or the Folly of Love*. She gives the reader very useful insights into 'the way the politically, economically and socially westernised educated elite of the Gold Coast negotiated these unwelcome changes in their lives in an early period.' (Newell, 2002: iv). Some questions raised in this book are as relevant today as they were then, notably:

'Does working for the colonial state automatically mean the denial of one's own cultural heritage with all its implications? Does modernity equal Europeanisation? Does economic exclusion automatically mean political protest against the regime? Is Christianity mutually exclusive with indigenous cultural practice? ....' (Newell, 2002: ix-x).

Newell recognises that the novel demonstrates the immense complexity of a colonial society in transition. The issues raised certainly have resonance in the 2nd millennium and this brings to the fore the socio-historical importance of the novel.

Again, the recent history of apartheid in South Africa could be seen from a systemic perspective. However it is also vital to recall that the system was perpetuated by, and had an effect upon, real people. South African writing and performance culture is filled with texts which offer the reader/audience a multi-faceted experience of the system through a poignant representation of the lives of individuals. Writers like Alex La Guma (*A Walk in the Night*)[2] give an insight into the community of Coloureds, a racially-based urban community which carries within it the many ambiguities of the notion of *metissage*, achieved by the unacknowledged intimacy among the races of this multi -racial country, in denial at the time. This is a case in which the fact of being of mixed race is given a significance that has been adjudged as warped in the perception of most of the world community. Just how unjust this phenomenon is comes across very clearly through La Guma's empathetic depiction of the socio-psychological pressure brought to bear on members of this community. On the other hand, White South Africans as a ruling race have been shown by writers like Nadine Gordimer to be in the grips of a deep psychosis which makes it possible for them to perpetuate the system of Apartheid or to accept its benefits.[3] Finally, what makes a play such as *Sizwe Banzi is Dead*, composed by Athol Fugard, John Kani and Winston Ntshona, so important is that this play presents the apartheid system from the point of view of the indigenous Africans. It takes one particular aspect of apartheid, the 'pass' system, and demonstrates its devastating impact on the individual and the society. The sardonic humour employed by the creators of the play only goes to emphasise the dehumanising nature of the system, while demonstrating the power of the human spirit to rise above situations of perpetual crisis. Here people are not merely numbers in a system, and neither is history a matter of cold facts.

The Power of the Word

Clearly, the belief in the power of the word does not lie only in the oral tradition of literature, but also in the canon of written literature. Writing in the mid-19th century, Nana Asma'u, daughter of Fulani jihadist, Othman dan Fodio, sought to back up the crusade through a significant body of literary works, particularly aimed at women.

> "Reasons for Seeking God
> We thank God Almighty, the Omnipotent
> He alone in His Majesty.
> He created the Heavens, seven in number,
> And he created the seven earths.
> And also the sun and the moon
> The rain and the stars, for He is All-Powerful.
> Look at the wilderness and hills
> Trees and the green herb, He created them.
> Why count them out? What do you know of his Power?
> ...."

(Nana Asma'u 1861)[5]

20th century African writing is also replete with works by writers seeking to use their words to achieve transformation of the situation of subjugation of Africa. These strivings were not without their contradictions, but the Negritude Movement which had its heyday between the mid -1930s and the early 1960s, sought to transform the negative image of Africa, firmly entrenched by years of conquest and domination and to assert a powerful African essence (see also Chapter 5, this volume).

Below is an extract from "New York," by the main proponent of Negritude, Leopold Sédar Senghor. The poem foregrounds and idealises the African experience, making it the very spirit in which God created the earth. His imagery comes from the African environment and the words 'Black' and 'Negro' are given a lofty interpretation. Finally, he infuses his verse with a rhythm which is meant to reflect the improvisational exhilaration of African music:

> New York! I say to New York, let the black blood flow into your blood
> Cleaning the rust from your steel articulations, like an oil of life
> Giving your bridges the curve of the hills, the liana's suppleness.
> See the ancient times come again, unity is discovered
> The reconciliation of the Lion and the Bull and the Tree
> The idea is linked to the act, the ear to the heart, the sign to the sense.
> See your rivers murmuring with musky caymans, manatees with eyes
> of mirage
> ----------
> And the ears of God who with a burst of saxophone laughter created
> the heavens and the earth in six days
> And on the seventh day, he slept his great negro sleep.[6]

Chinua Achebe in his essay, "The Novelist as Teacher" makes a firm commitment which can be said to echo the sentiments of many an African writer:

> "Here then is an adequate revolution for me to espouse– to help my society regain belief in itself and put away the complexes of the years of denigration and self -abasement. And it is essentially a question of education, in the best sense of the word. Here I think, my aims and the deepest aspirations of my society meet."
>
> (Achebe, 1990: 44)[7]

In making the above assertion, Achebe stands upon a solid heritage of artistic experience. Oral literary artists and performers are often associated with a particular class, caste, or guild. These may be associated with political entities such as the *imbongi* and *maroki* (Praise singers in the Zulu and Hausa courts respectively), or may be a vocational guild for which the practice of oral arts is a critical part of the practice of the vocation such as the Yoruba *onijala* or master hunter. These specialists have mastery over large corpuses of literature, particularly dynastic poetry (such as the panegyric or praise poetry of the courts), which they are honour-bound to preserve, and liturgical poetry (such as the praise poetry of gods). This poetry is often high-sounding, dense, full of historical or philosophical references, and lengthy. Other specialists, such as the Ewe *Heno* of Ghana, have the gift and duty of composing songs which mostly reflect deeply on the import of current happenings and life's circumstances.

Perhaps one of the most well-known castes of oral artistes is the *Griot* of the Sahel region of West Africa, known severally as *Djeli* by the Mandinka, *Gewel* by the Wolof, and *Jeborey* by the Zarma. Indeed, the term *Griot* (feminine,*griotte)*, which has become widely used, is of French origin. The griots were at the service of families of nobility and served in a variety of capacities all related to their mastery of the spoken word in the past. The *griots'* greatest assets lie in a profound knowledge of the history and philosophy of their society and their ability to present and interpret these in elaborate songs, poems and rhetorical speech. In the past, they acted as advisors to kings, and many a noble warrior went to war with his *griot,* who would have been his teacher as a child. It was the duty of the *griot* to exhort and inspire him by recounting the achievements of his illustri-ous ancestors. Indeed at war, the capturing of the *griot* was a sign of total conquest. The *griot* was also spokesperson for the ruler and was a master of diplomacy and protocol. Persons wanting to approach a ruler would also request the *griot* to speak on their behalf, and this made the *griot* a mediator and advocate. Indeed, today the traditional system of rulership in much of the Sahelian region no longer exists, but *griots* continue to play a significant role in the ceremonial life of so-ciety as in naming ceremonies and funerals. *Griottes,* for example, also act as advisors, mediators and spokespersons during traditional courtship and marriage ceremonies. A *griotte* who has to sit behind the door of a newly married couple during the consummation of the marriage will sing to bear witness (with glad relief), to the virtue of a young woman.

"When they send me to seek the hand of a good mother's child
      I never get weary.
.....Happy is she who finds her match in good time,

For endless waiting is full of snares,
Which lead girls astray from the way of virtue"

(Dior Konate, 1998)[8]

The life of the contemporary oral artist has been drastically affected by changes in social organisation. Many members of artistic castes have become recording artistes and performers for wider audiences, mainly for entertainment. Sons and daughters of traditional *griot* families such as world famous Yousou Ndour of Senegal and Oumou Sangare of Mali, have become icons in promoting African causes in the global arena. Others have abandoned their lofty communal affiliations and moved to urban areas to sell their skills to the highest bidder. They act as praise singers for the wealthy and may invent an illustrious ancestry for such persons provided they are prepared to pay for it!

Society and the Literary Arts

The literary arts are also highly participatory and may therefore embrace a wide range of participants who are not necessarily specialists. An individual may be a statutory member of a social group such as a family or clan grouping, an age set, class, or a militia group. These groups usually have characteristic songs, salutations, praise poetry etc. which they share as part of their ceremonial life. For example, the sub groups of the Ga peoples of Ghana have appellations which they declaim to rouse a sense of national pride. The appellation for the La sub group is: "Dade Kotopon: Wuo gbee, La gbee," meaning "Strong Iron: As the cock crows, the clarion of La also resounds." Again, the Asafo (former warrior) groups of the Fante may be seen as mass-based organisations. They have a rich culture of appellations, song and dance in which all their members participate sometimes in praise of the prowess of their ancestors and at other times taunting anyone who might challenge their greatness.

To speak to the Asafo of Atwia Ekumfi in the Central Region, one must call them by their appellation: "They-Who- Fight- On- The- Move!"

The entire assembly of men will then answer in unison:

"They-Who-Fight–On-The-Move respond!"

The following chorus is from the corpus of Asafo songs from the town of Cape Coast. As may be observed, the song that follows hails longingly, the greatness of one leader, Abaka. It is clear that they are calling to him with nostalgia because of the emphatic nature of the first line and the parallel second line in which an honorary title is attributed to him. In the same breath, the second, presumably current leader, Elder Kwesi, clad in the ignoble metaphor of a hyena, is roundly and provocatively condemned:

It's Abaka we are calling
Our Chief, Abaka, we are calling,
Elder Kwesi, the hyena,
If we follow you
This state will collapse [9]

Here songs play a role in expressing the will of the people as regards affairs of the state.

Again the literary arts serve to bond age-mates during the elaborate initiation ceremonies for groups of young persons. During the *Poro* ceremony of the Mende of Sierra Leone, mask construction, elaborate costuming and body art culminate in elaborate dances and ritual drama.

Another of the major social determinants of literary arts is gender. Inherent in indigenous African social systems are clearly demarcated gender roles which intervene in all aspects of life ranging from ritual to work and play. We shall, in the following paragraphs, explore this phenomenon in some detail.

Generally, literary forms associated with political and military power for example are typically associated with men as performers, male activities, and achievements, as themes, and the male dominated power structure as referent. These include panegyric, libation texts, hunters' songs, the narration of state histories, genealogies and mythologies, and surrogate speech forms on drums, horns and xylophones.

The style of these forms is usually bold and majestic, using highly rhetorical and sometimes archaic language. There are also references to historical, legendary or mythological occurrences as well as philosophical and ontological concepts.

The following is an extract from the praise poem to Basotho leader, Makhaola Lerotholi, who is associated with his progenitors:

> Lion of the descendants of Mokhachane, Makhaola,
> Wild Beast of the son of Libe-of-Makhoana,
> Wild Beast of Kholu-child-of-Ntsuku,
> Wild Beast of Thuhloane, you are a Leopard,
> You, Wild Beast of Matee-of-Mokoteli.
> Young man of noble birth of the home of Letsabisa,
> He came out of the stomach of Thahaki, a Crocodile.
> The Lion Cub emerged from the forest,
> He came out of the ruins of the Son of Mokhachane.
> The Crocodile People emerged before other men,
> They emerged from the sea, the sea meanwhile roaring---
>
> (Kunene 1971:51)

In general, popular literary arts based on gender stereotypes depict women in a rather derogatory light. The following proverbs from the Embu and Mbeere cultures of Kenya illustrate this very well: "It is better to make a mistake when buying a garment than when marrying a woman," "A woman can never be sent to demand a debt (because she cannot be trusted)," and "One who is called woman is like one who is called by death." By way of comparison, proverbs about men include: "There is no cock that serves only one hen," "Men are swift" and "A home without a man is not a home."[10] Fictional oral narratives also typically portray women as flighty and unable to keep secrets, jealous, greedy or passive. It is instructive that women and girls are seldom the protagonists of these tales, much less the trickster figure around whom a corpus of tales is built.

Given the above situation, women's literature affords a glimpse at the hidden political, economic, social and spiritual authority of women, as well as their opinions, aspirations, state of being, and artistic prowess. Women in their own spaces employ artistic means to comment upon and document their daily lives, thoughts and feelings. Women as age-mates, co-wives, new wives and mothers, friends and family members, are vital to the development of the region's oral literary heritage. These women create and recreate themes that speak about their work, human relationships and worldviews, and in the process, their orature captures the vagaries and ordinariness of their existence. Their thoughts, words, and deeds are reflected in the lullabies, work songs, insult songs, and songs of motherhood. There is a fascinating interplay between physiology and social structure which generates factors for defining social categories in West African societies.

We could thus at one level, group prepubescent girls and young women in their early twenties who are assigned domestic chores such as the fetching of water and the pounding and grinding of grain. Inasmuch as there is an aesthetic and affective aspect to the enactment of these tasks, these grinding and pounding songs are imbued with the sauciness of youth. They also reflect the concerns of young women who, as newlyweds, have to take their place at the bottom of the pecking order in polygamous homes.

Such work takes place within a matrix of marriage and blood relations involving the observance of hierarchical protocols. The young wife is a minor in many senses of the word and must observe the protocols owed to her husband, her in-laws, and her co-wives. A Zerma woman from Niger might initiate pounding: "Bissi milahi, the Millet Entered the Mortar. Now we must endure other people's Mothers and Fathers."

In the Dagaare society of northwestern Ghana, work such as grinding, pounding, or the churning of shea nuts into butter may be accompanied by *Dannu* or praise songs. They are so called because, although they also serve as an antidote to tedium and an outlet for the feelings of the women who sing them, they consist of the naming and praising of ancestors and by extension, praising the living as well. A woman who lives with her husband in the compound of his patriarchal family creates *Dannu* in praise of the ancestors of her husband's lineage. Women in this culture have very limited contexts in which to demonstrate their knowledge of genealogy, especially since they are not allowed to sing dirges during the massive public ceremonies that are organised as part of Dagaare funerals. Singing *Dannu* or praise songs while grinding, however, demonstrates clearly their knowledge of history.

Marriage songs are often sung by the young women of the community who envelop the bride in a supportive circle of solidarity, teasing, cajoling and encouraging transition into the state of marriage. Young women in rural communities also take time out to play and indulge themselves. The songs form part of a total dramatic performance involving hand-clapping, significant gestures, and body movements. Songs are often initiated by a self-appointed cantor. Unlike many other forms, this is a truly open forum in which each person in the circle has a chance to sing a verse to which all respond. This makes for a high level of personalizsation of the content of the verses rarely seen in other forms. This means that the life experiences of the individual can be overtly and publicly aired:

"If you ask him money for condiments
He knows 500 francs is enough
He gives 100 francs for that
Expecting her to cut her leg and add it
He is just looking for a pretext so she leaves." [11]

The purpose of the performance—for self-gratification and indulgence—is important as sensuousness for its own sake. The following Ewe song illustrates this point:

> Lala, lala itala, ilol
> Whoever feels like doing it
> Let him come and do it freely
> Let him come and do it freely
>
> (Egbleworgbe, 1975: 48)

Through these songs, we catch a glimpse of life as the young women might have loved it to be. The saucy humour and pungent expressions with which these young women express their fantasy world and appropriate the recreational space for their personal gratification are especially significant, since opportunities for such forthright self-expression as well as the exercise of choice for these women are very few.

While men may take the primary role in the funerary rites depending on the society, women very often take a major role particularly in the mortuary rites and the public expressions of grief. Funeral and burial ceremonies, meant to usher the deceased into their next abode, are of great importance in African societies (see Ch. 14). Funerary poetry is a very significant category of poetry in the universe of the oral literary tradition in Africa for many reasons. Firstly, in the cosmology and ritual life of most African societies, death continues to form a fulcrum around which life itself and its greater meaning are reflected upon and values and beliefs reaffirmed. Poetry serves multiple purposes in the context of the funerals. It carries the text of rituals such as those of separation, reaffirmation of relations between clans, or even different peoples with political relations. Secondly, it serves to narrate and interpret the historical trajectory of the peoples or clan to which the deceased belongs. Thirdly, it is the supreme vehicle for expressing the range of emotions and sentiments which death engenders such as sorrow, rage, national pride, pain, betrayal, love etc. The content of funerary poetry is therefore highly charged emotionally and is destined to generate a catharsis among the mourners.

Kwabena Nketia in his seminal text, *Funeral Dirges of the Akan people*, provides a detailed analysis and anthology of dirges as a women's art form. These are performed at different points of the ceremony. These ceremonies are often highly dramatic such as the moment a wake opens. It is the moment for exaggerated gestures of distress such as laying the hands on the head or stomach or stretching out the arms. Sereer women of Senegal, when returning from the burial of a young woman, may dress like and imitate men, make up their faces in charcoal and perform short aggressive dramatic skits.

Poetic Forms

Generally speaking, African literary culture at its most refined and most complex, is often expressed in poetic form. Babalola distinguishes between various forms of Yoruba poetry based on voice tone. He states:

"There are subtle differences between the voice tone of *ijala* and those of other forms of Yoruba song such as *rara* (chants in praise of a noble citizen), *ege* (laments for great men), *ofo* (magical incantations), *ogede* (a kind of *ofo*, supposed to be most efficient), *ewi ogun* (songs for the god of war), and *oriki* (praise names)."

(Babalola 1966:13)

Lofty and sometimes obscure language is used in praise poetry such as the religious poetry in praise of each of the gods in the extensive Yoruba pantheon. *Ijala* poetry to the god of iron, Ogun, is a case in point. From the above, it is clear that poetry is often reflective and meditative, enabling the author to explore in depth a single thought. It is characterized by the combination of beautiful language and disciplined structure in order to evoke emotion. The following Ewe lament demonstrates a carefully structured piling of metaphors which build the emotion of loneliness and abandonment to an intense crescendo:

> My wings are plucked; woe is the day
> Shall I ascend the tree by foot?
> A buttress- that's a mother's son:
> If you haven't it, down falls your house.
> All-purpose cloth, a mother's daughter is.
> If you haven't it,
> You're cold-exposed.
> Relations on the father's side,
> Relations on the mother's side,
> None. In whom shall I confide?
> Oh, brother!

(Adali-Morty 1967: 8)

In Ewe, the effect is achieved not only by the metaphors, but also by the repetition of the particle 'o' which in that language represents pathos. We present the last five lines in the original language to demonstrate the use of the particle 'o', as well as to demonstrate the use of various tropes such as parallelism (compare the 9th and 10th lines which only differ in the first syllable).

8. Avuvo wo wo kpoo
9. Toko mele nunye o;
10. Noko mele nunye o
11. Mee ade nanyanyeawo na o
12. Navie!

(Adali-Morty 1967:7)

Structurally the one-word line that ends the poem is a radical structural shift from the preceding lines and this structural contrast also helps to highlight the sense of distress experienced by the persona in the poem.

Chapter 17

Nowhere is the anguish and passion of African writing more evident than in its poetic itera-
tion. For example, the poets of the Negritude movement sought to defy the dominant perception of the African by putting a positive spin on terms such as 'black' and 'negro,' and thereby
subverting the dominant interpretation; by making Africa a recurring motif and by evolving a
poetic style which was meant to reflect the rhythms of Africa (The Negritude Movement is discussed further below). This nostalgia for Africa remains. Abioseh Nichol of Sierra Leone was to
write, "The Meaning of Africa" in the early 1960s in which he says:

---You are not a country, Africa,
You are a concept,
Fashioned in our minds, each to each,
To hide our separate dreams
---I know now that is what you are, Africa:
Happiness, contentment and fulfilment,
And a small bird singing on a mango tree. [12]

Poets are in search of a language all their own which can accommodate their aspirations, reflections and experiences as Africans. For many writers, the process of creating an idiom of their
own has involved a conscious turning to their African heritage and incorporating into their
writing, literary forms and poetics into which they breath new life thus 'reconnect(ing) themselves to the continuum of literary performance and living traditions' (Chipasula 1995 :xxi).
Noemia de Sousa of Mozambique, Atukwei Okai and Kofi Awoonor of Ghana, each in their own
way, show these continuities in their works. De Sousa is highly reminiscent of negritude poetry:

Joao and Mozambique were intermingled
Joao would not have been without Mozambique
Joao was like a palm tree, a coconut palm
A piece of rock, a Lake Niassa, a mountain,
An Incomati, a forest, a macala tree
A beach, a Maputo, an Indian Ocean
Joao was an integral and deep rooted part of Mozambique
Joao was young like us.

(Extract from "The poem of Joao")[13]

Okai for his part has created extravagant rhythms in his works and has an obvious focus on
the performative aspects of poetry. For example, his poetry often includes invocations as may
be found in traditional libations and appellations:

"The Fontomfrom keeps on
Booming and moaning and booming!
Fontomfrom!....Fontomfrom!....
Fontomfrom!....Fontomfrom!...
I am the Fontomfrom! –
I am Africa!"

(Extracted from "Oath of the Fontomfrom")

376

Kofi Awoonor's work is recalled here to represent those like Kofi Anyidoho and Ocot P'btek (Uganda), who have had the privilege of being born into families of talented oral artists and who have taken the trouble to study this literary heritage. In the case of Awoonor, his poetry is heavily influenced by poetic forms of the Ewe people of Ghana, such as the poetry of lament and of insult.

The following extract is from "Songs of abuse: (i) To Stanislaus the renegade":

This is addressed to you, Stanislaus, wherever you are.
Listen you punk, the last time we met you were selling
Faulty guns in Addis
I heard you panting afterwards in a Cairo whorehouse
Before I knew you had split with my spring overcoat
A cashmere job I danced for in a bar in Kabul.

What is this I hear about you preparing to settle in the
Congo?
To grow hashish in the valley of the Zaire?
I will be waiting for you; for every gun you buy
I shall command a thousand assegais, for every sword
A million Ashanti machetes and Masai spears
I am not afraid of you any more. Those days are past
When you stole my school fees and my catapult
And fled into the cove beyond bird island
I too came of age.

(Okpewho, 1985: 85)

Narrative

We speak of narrative rather than prose because in African oral literature, a narrative may be presented in a spoken, chanted or sung form. Some narrative genres such as the folk tale, may be presented in all three ways. Written forms such as novels, short stories, and epics may also be classified as narratives. According to Naana J. Opoku-Agyemang, 'the folktale is popular literary art in the true sense of the expression; it is a literary art form directly created, controlled and enjoyed by the people across space and time' (1999: 16). The tale may be told by men, women and children, although there are specialists who tell tales at social functions. Audiences are often mixed and have a vital role to play in making the performance complete. Their responses to formulae to opening and closing a story-telling session as well as to songs which form a part of particular stories, or which serve to create the right mood for story- telling are critical. This is apart from off-the-cuff comments which both create humour and keep the storyteller on his/ her toes.

However, the power of the tale to evoke the underlying grid of social relations or value systems makes it a vehicle for addressing strong psychological needs and social tensions. Storyteller and audience share cultural knowledge about the attributes of all characters featured as well as the significance of particular occurences. The existence in many African cultures of the trickster, such as the Tortoise (Yoruba), the Hare (Sahel), and the Spider (Akan, Hausa), provides a colourful character around which to weave stories about the complexities of human behaviour and interrelations among people. This particular quality of the tale draws in the story teller's own personality, state of mind or experiences which may be discerned by a close comparative study of the corpus of texts told by a particular story-teller or group. There is reason to believe that particular storytellers may choose to perform types of tales which reflect their anxieties or needs.

A striking example of this phenomenon is provided by Sabine Steinbrich in her essay, "Images of the Powerful in Lyela Folktales" (Furniss and Gunner 1995) in which she presents two versions of the tale, "Orphan, King and Old Traitress," told by a young woman and an old woman respectively. Each of these women provides the tale with markedly different denouements. In summary, an orphan finds a pair of magic pots in the bush and is persuaded by an old woman to share his secret with her. She however reveals the secret to the king who seizes the pots. The orphan returns to the bush and finds a couple of whips which beat who ever recites a particular formula. Again the old woman finds out about these and learns the formula and is beaten. She again reports the find to the king who again confiscates the whips, pronounces the formula and is whipped. He therefore calls her to punish her. In the young woman's version, the old woman swallows a clay pot and claims she is pregnant to avoid punishment. She is however forced to repeat the formula and is whipped until the pot in her stomach breaks into shards, which she then defecates. She then dies. This version particularly in its final episode emphasises the marginalization of the old woman and her association with evil. She is subjected to mockery and contempt by society. However when this tale is told by Juliette Kanzie, who is in her 60s, she identifies completely with the Old Woman, making her the protagonist who goes to the forest to find the pots and the wily one who at the end defeats the king through her wisdom and ability to manipulate language. In the final episode of her version, the Old Woman is able to place the king in a position where he is the one who utters the full formula and is beaten by the magic whips. As Steinbrich demonstrates, the older storyteller has applied poetic license to make the marginalised character triumph in a personalized retelling of the dominant plot. But whatever the ending of the story, women emerge as persons who cannot be trusted and who may indeed end up polluting the power of the rulers of the state.

> "The matter is really quite simple. Literature, whether handed down by word of mouth or in print, gives us a second handle on reality; enabling us to encounter in the safe manageable dimensions of make-believe the very same threats to integrity that may assail the psyche in real life; and at the same time providing through the self-discovery which it imparts a veritable weapon for coping with these threats whether they are found within problematic and incoherent selves or in the world around us."
>
> (Achebe, 1990)

The above quotation by Chinua Achebe[14] serves as a reminder of what a story is, and makes it possible to speak of folktales in the same breath as one might discuss written literature and therefore acts as an apt segue into the next section where a rapid overview of the heritage of written literature will be presented.

The Written Heritage

Literary texts by Africans date to the period of ancient times. 6000 years of writing in Ancient Egypt includes poetry and fiction. More recent texts are the sacred texts in the Ge'ez language, going back 3000 years. Swahili *Utenzi* poetry made its mark beginning over 300 years ago. This was highly influenced by Arabic poetic conventions. Indeed, Arabic lettering became the preferred form of writing in areas which were swept by Islam. Therefore, we have for example, the famous literary works of Hausa and Fula poets. The family of Othman Dan Fodio, the 19th century Fulani jihadist and founder of the Sokoto Caliphate, included a significant number of scholars, including several women. The most famous of these women was his daughter, Nana Asma'u. She became very famous throughout the Islamic world of West Africa for her religious poetry as well as her odes.

To this lot should be added writing by expatriate Africans, some of whom were born on the African continent, but found themselves in other realms through enslavement, or the agency of adoptive parents seeking to do them good. Some of these are the late 18th century ex-slave and writer, Olaudah Equiano, originally from Iboland in Nigeria, and Phyllis Wheatley, originally from Senegal, who was writing in the mid 19th century.

Writing in European languages began more consistently in the late 19th Century. By putting together of all the episodes of the serialized 19th Century novel, *Marita, or the Folly of Love* in 2002, Stephanie Newell brought to critical attention the first West African novel in the English language, published on January 20th 1886. Its authorship is a source of debate as it was simply signed 'A Novel by a Native.' Throughout the first 50 years of the 20th century, writing in African and European languages began in earnest. Frequently cited works include *Moeti oa Bochabela*, written in Sesotho in 1909 by Thomas Mofolo, and inspired by Bunyan's *The Pilgrim's Progress*, and poetry by the Nigerian poet, Denis Osadebay. Osadebay's work has been noted for the influence of Christian hymnology of the day.

A distinctive trend which emerged during this period was nationalistic and racially conscious writing. The famous collaboration between Leopold Sédar Senghor, Aime Cesaire and Leon Damas in Paris, marked by the establishment of the journal, *L'Etudiant Noir,* in 1934, exemplifies the meeting of minds of Africans on a global scale, such as the cross-fertilisation with the Harlem Renaissance. In a "melting pot" of a new generation of artists and thinkers, Africans crossed borders of race and nation, to dream of an egalitarian world. From afar, these brothers of African descent had an overview of the continent and were caught between the desire for direct confrontation and the desire for reconciliation.

By the beginning of the twentieth century, the elite of Anglophone Africa was producing theatre, fiction and some poetry. Such novelists and short story writers as J.E. Casely Hayford, Adelaide Casely-Hayford and R.E. Obeng of the Gold-Coast, expressed early political consciousness in works like *Ethiopia Unbound: Studies in Race Emancipation* (1911) by J.E. Casely Hayford, which paved the way for a most prolific and now renowned literary production in the second half of the century.

Defined broadly, politics has been a major preoccupation of African writers, particularly in imaginative writing taking on the political evolution of the continent from a variety of angles. Indeed, writers have brooded over the continent and the way it has been governed. Ferdinand Oyono, in a series of satirical novels, lashes out at the French colonial enterprise, demonstrating with sardonic humour, the ironies of the system. The outpourings of the 1960s and 1970s took a different turn, as writers confronted the bitter realities of independence and its aftermath. The corruption of the state, and the capitulation of the intellectual and technocratic classes, was a major preoccupation of Chinua Achebe (*No Longer At Ease, A Man Of The People*), Ayi Kwei Armah (*The Beautyful Ones Are Not Yet Born*,*Why Are We So Blest*), Wole Soyinka (*The Trials of Brother Jero, Kongi's Harvest*), Ngugi Wa Thiong'O (*Petals of Blood*), Ama Ata Aidoo (*No Sweetness Here*), and Sembene Ousmane (*The Money Order, Xala*). In the above works, political leaders are caricatures, foisting an unsavoury climate of greed and patronage on their people. The intellectuals and technocrats are also depicted as spinelessly capitulating either by joining in, as Obi does in *No Longer At Ease,* or opting out, as Teacher does in *The Beautyful Ones Are Not Yet Born*. Men like Fiifi in "Everything Counts" by Aidoo, simply have no mind of their own, and are unable to tear themselves away from Europe.

Writers are not however, a monolithic group of artists, and even within a recognisable framework, they are motivated by a wide spectrum of concerns, beyond the nationalist concerns of earlier writers. Tsitsi Dangaremba of Zimbabwe, and Buchi Emecheta of Nigeria, have dared to question norms and social strictures under which women have operated. In Emecheta's prolific narrative, marriage is a state of miserable oppression and motherhood a state of anguish. Again, writers such as Amma Darko and Alex Agyei Adjiri of Ghana, and Mariama Ndoye of Senegal, for example, provide a different perspective on the modern African society at the advent of the 21st century. They focus intensely on the growing numbers of the poor and marginalised people of urban Africa, following the years of economic collapse from the 1970s and the negative impact of economic development strategies applied to stimulate growth. Mariama Ndoye's story, "En Route to the 21st Century" depicts the broken promises. Ndoye takes an absurdist view of the situation and constructs her story accordingly. For example, it is constructed without a hero/heroine. The entire assembly of characters constitutes a collective protagonist. From a setting in which a group of ordinary persons are squashed together in a small bus, (car rapide*)*, the story of the miserable, pointlessness of their lives unfolds, as they interact with each other. There is nothing to hope for and no end in sight for them. The story depicts accurately the individual survival strategies adopted by the people and their coping mechanisms in the face of a very unfavourable state of affairs. In similar fashion, a writer such as Tanella Boni of Côte d'Ivoire, reminds us of the debilitating civil wars which have swept through the continent through her collection of poetry, *There are no Suitable Words*.

The growing corpus of written literature for many years has also been dominated by men because far fewer women than men had the opportunity to become either literate, or to speak European languages or both. However, today, there is also a powerful body of works written by women which has served to highlight the different perspectives and objectives of men and-women in the art of writing. It has been observed that many male writers have not consciously concerned themselves with the effect of gender on society. Obi Okwonkwo, the tragic hero of Chinua Achebe's classic novel, *Things Fall Apart*, is often cited as reflecting the model of masculinity in pre-colonial Igbo society. His dedication to hard work, physical activity, acts of bravery, national pride, competitiveness and distant paternalism towards his family, are easily discernible. The female characters in the novel are muted and serve to highlight the hero and his story. They fit in as well they can with their lot as women in the society. When women start writing however, female personalities and their stories are foregrounded. Social constructs such as polygyny, are presented from a woman's perspective, revealing that they cannot be taken for granted. This is the case in the classic, *So Long A Letter*, by Mariama Bâ.

PART TWO

Drama in African Society

One of the most exciting areas of growth in the literature is the heritage of dramatic arts in Africa. Penina Mlama, Tanzanian playwright and theatre scholar, provides a useful summary of the role of theatre in pre-colonial African society as follows:

> 'Theatre was a tool for instruction and transmission of knowledge, values and attitudes in initiation rites, marriage, death, religious rituals or public forums for behavioural appraisal, criticism and control. Dance drama, mime story-telling, and heroic recitations were an essential part of one's upbringing.'
>
> (Mlama, 1991: 26).

According to this representation, theatre played a central role in the ceremonial life of African peoples. This assertion is corroborated in the cumulative life work of scholars like Joel Adedeji, Kwabena Bame and Wole Soyinka,[15] who have assembled convincing evidence to demonstrate that ceremonial and ritual drama, as well as forms of popular drama, abound in traditional African society and are moreover, alive and well in contemporary Africa. Drama often either encompasses, or forms a continuum with other modes of performance such as dance and music. Indeed, the very fact that there is a high level of associative symbolism in the arts means that they can be brought together to reinforce each other in a dramatic performance. The concept of performance is well established in the discourse on aesthetics in many African language cultures. For example, scholars such as Nketia, Sutherland, Collins and Sutherland-Addy[16] have discussed the *agoro* principle. The word *agoro* in Akan reflects play in its many connotations, including total performance. Indeed members of a performance group or the audience, moved by the spectacular performance of an individual, may exclaim *agoro*!, signifying the intensity of emotion and aesthetic satisfaction aroused by the performance.

As a multi-focal event built around one general theme, there are moments and sites of high and low intensity performance in festivals, making them a venue for the exposition of highly valued skills and talent. Enactments in mask cultures like the Igbo *Mmonwu*, Yoruba *Gelede* (Nigeria) and the Chechewa *Gule Wamkulu* (Zambia and Malawi) provide examples of highly intense spectacle involving re-enactment and transformation, to provide a visual symbolism of values of a given society. In the context of a discernible structure which often provides the necessary elements of tension, highly intricate costuming and symbolic, complex movement serve to enhance the theatrical quality of the performance.

Rituals are often at the core of festivals, such as the stylised mock fight engaged in between the followers of Obatala and those of Oduduwa, and form part of the of the Obatala festival of the Ede-Yoruba. This is a festival celebrating the official version of the legend of origin of the ruling dynasty, but enacting the struggle for supremacy between two contending powers offers the losing party the opportunity for a sense of catharsis within the drama. In addition to featuring highly specialized and exclusive rituals, festivals provide for mass participation which may feature parody, role reversal, transsexual behaviour etc, sometimes with comical intent.

A wide range of performative acts have struck scholars as dramatic. Kwesi Yankah describes a spectacular solo act of libation pouring by Nana Baah Okuampah VI, chief of Atwia Ekumfi,[17] which he recorded in 1988. She was one of the few women chiefs who was also a gifted orator, storyteller and singer. According to Yankah,

> "This performance was a combination of effective delivery and drama. The chief's loud agitated voice, rumbling low tone, restlessness, gesticulations, dramatic pauses heightened the theatrical effectiveness of the rendition."
>
> (Yankah 1998: 75)

Yankah also records that "the prayer had a highly evocative effect on both the performer and the audience and was greeted with a unanimous *Mo ne kasa* (Well spoken)! " Thus in ceremonial drama, the individual is as capable of creating a captivating drama as a large "cast" ceremonial drama.

African Popular Theatre

Comedy seems to hold pride of place in the repertoire of popular theatre, whether primarily indigenous or Western influenced. In Mali, young Bamana men perform the traditional satirical *Kotetlon* theatre, which enables them to comment on social foibles. K.N. Bame discusses extensively, the *Okumkpa* plays performed in eastern Ibo land. These plays consist of a large masked cast of members of secret societies, and depend for their humour on imitating the speech and behaviour of named individuals (see Bame, 1991: 48-49). These are compared to the *Kote Koma Nyaga* Mande performances from Sierra Leone, which are described as bearing a close resemblance in structure "namely the opening ballet, the prologue, the presentation of players and finally the 'plays proper'" (ibid: 53).

Concert party theatre, a truly Ghanaian 20th century form, has received considerable scholarly attention.[18] The form originated in the 1920s with the one-man acts of Teacher Yalley in Sekondi (South Western Ghana), who eventually formed the *Two Bobs and the Carolina Girl* in 1930, with their witty dialogue and carefully synchronised dance routines. Based on minstrelsy, the cinema and popular dance music mostly from the United States, they provided entertainment for the small minority of Europeanized gentility. The development of guitar band music which incorporated indigenous rhythms, motifs and the storytelling tradition, combined with other influences like the church-based cantata, to contribute to the blossoming of the concert party. Popular plays usually preceded by music, an opening comedy act, and a melodramatic play, whose most distinctive feature is improvised dialogue, are woven through, with carefully selected pieces of popular and traditional songs (see also Chapter 21, this volume). For the first 30 years of the existence of the concert party, the all-male cast featured female impersonators. Plays, often enactments of life stories with a moralistic twist, also re-interpreted traditional tales and legends.

The dialogue between traditional mythic traditions and modern popular theatre in the Yoruba area of Nigeria has also been closely documented. Unlike the concert party, the Yoruba travelling theatre went beyond comedy and included the 'folk opera,' popularized by Kola Ogunmola and Duro Ladipo, which carried in them the intrigue and flamboyance of the world of the Gods. The tragedy of the once-human god of thunder, Shango, who commits suicide out of hubris, is the subject matter of Ladipo's world-renowned, *Oba Koso*.

Written Drama

The artistic antecedents of literary drama in sub-Saharan Africa were the cannon and aesthetic of the Western theatre tradition, contextualized in the British, French or Portuguese experience. Thus for example, the merciless parody of pretentious westernised Fantes in Kobina Sekyi's 1911 play, *The Blinkards,* is nonetheless set in the popular verse form in which light poetry was written in England at the time. The influence of the West on the form of the play was manifest. Playwrights writing in the early 1960s, had also been through the received model of Western education and experimented with forms such as the Greek tragedies, both in form and content. Ola Rotimi's *The Gods are not to Blame* reworks Sophocles' *Oedipus Rex*.

Kofi E. Agovi ends his trenchant analysis of the formation of a theatrical tradition in colonial Ghana, "The Origin of Literary Theatre in Colonial Ghana, 1920-1957" with a thought provoking statement by the critic, Ime Ikiddeh as follows:

> "...By literary tradition, we take the benefit of Shakespeare for granted, yet in several ways, Shakespeare has come to constitute a real danger both to students and writers in this part of the world... The danger of Shakespeare in Africa is part of a larger disease that has affected our cultural universe since our contact with the West. Its roots lie in colonial education and propaganda, and its manifestation is the distortion of our native sensibilities and values including our very image of ourselves. Given the historical circumstances, this distortion was inevitable but it was not inevitable that the damage sustained in our confrontation with Europe would be so deep and so overwhelming that we would neither recover from it nor be conscious enough of the need for recovery."
>
> (Ikkideh in Agovi,1990: 34) [19]

This may be a rather harsh verdict for it is certain that over time, writers of literary theatre in Africa have taken the vanguard among the most daring literary artists on the continent, experimenting with form and its relationship to meaning. There are certainly those whose concern is with the message such as the agonies of social change and the transition between tradition and modernity. The structure of Zulu Sofola's *Wedlock of the Gods*, is unmistakably inspired by Greek classical tragedy. However, the individuals who die in the prime of their lives were locked into the dictates of a tradition that made a widow the automatic wife of her husband's brother. By exercising her choice to relate to the person she loves, she pays the ultimate price as does he. On the other hand, Ferdinand Oyono Mbia in his comedy, *Three Suitors, One Husband,* playfully enables two lovers to neatly evade the grips of oppressive traditions and follow their hearts. Here again theme prevails over innovation in style.

Wole Soyinka, Africa's best known playwright, approaches his subject matter from two angles. One is to parody corruption, misrule and the erosion of morality in comedies such as *The Trials of Brother Jero*, and satires such as *Kongi's Harvest*. On the other hand, Soyinka's extensive cultural literacy permits him to make liberal reference to thought systems and aesthetic antecedents from different parts of the world. His preference is to draw on Yoruba mythological patterns to elaborate a vision of the essence of man and **his** (author emphasis) attempt to achieve balance and order. In his play, *Death and the King's Horseman,* the inexorable march of destiny is pitched against individual free choice.

The concern of some prominent playwrights is the resolution of social imbalance and inequity through the coming together of social forces which empower the most vulnerable. Writers like Femi Osofisan and Ngugi Wa Thiong'O, are among the most prominent in this regard. Yoruba mythology offers Osofisan the opportunity to demonstrate how extraordinary members of the ruling classes can involve the ordinary people in acts of heroism which empower them. This is the way in which he re-interprets the myth of *Moremi*, the princess who sacrificed herself in order to discover the secret of the Igbos who had been terrorizing her people. By transposing this myth on a contemporary situation in the play *Morotondun,* the inversion of the principle of sacrifice and its demystification from an individual act to a collective one, becomes obvious. In the case of Ngugi Wa Thiong'O, the trial of the legendary Mau-Mau leader, Dedan Kimathi, becomes a vehicle for presenting a version of the Kenyan struggle for independence which does not focus on the hero only, but foregrounds the role of the most neglected members of society such as women and the youth. (See *"The Trial of Dedan Kimathi"*).

Writers like J.P. Clark-Bekederemo in *"The Ozidi Saga"* take form to the next stage and demonstrate their fascination with the discovery of the roots of African theatre in the traditional setting. In their hands, the epic drama, the festival and the story telling drama, are transposed onto the Western-inspired stage. *The Ozidi Saga* stays close to the schema of the traditional Ijaw epic. Efua Sutherland, in search of an authentic contemporary African theatre, developed *Anansegoro*, based principally on the *Anansesem* story telling traditions of the Akan. *Anansegoro* includes features like the story teller/narrator and the participating audience. Many playwrights such as Mohamed Ben-Abdallah, Martin Owusu and Yaw Asare, have subsequently followed her footsteps.

For Mohamed Ben-Abdallah (Ghana) and Were Were Liking (Cameroon), the festival has served several purposes. In their plays, *The Land of A Million Magicians* and Sigue Mura, *Given that a Woman* respectively, the festival becomes a metaphor for representing the multiple layers of the authors' message. Abdallah clearly makes a case for the synergy between different peoples and creeds if the problems of underdevelopment are to be addressed. The festival, which is a central trope of the play, *Land of a Million Magicians,* features the dances of peoples from different parts of Africa. In the case of Liking's play using puppetry, mime and ritual, she confronts the issue of sterility and abortion in a rural setting.

Performance and Development

The notion of development has cropped up often in this book. There is a growing perception that the process, as generally conceived, focuses on the economy, leaving out the cultural dimension, and that this has contributed to the failure of many development initiatives (Mlama 1991 and Sutherland-Addy, 2004). This phenomenon has not been perceived in Africa alone, but also in poor and dependent countries around the world. The same is true of the idea that theatre has a social role, one of which is that of empowering otherwise powerless people to articulate their conditions and act to change them. Popular theatre became a key vehicle against feudalism and colonial exploitation on the Indian subcontinent in the 1940s, and was used in countries like Nicaragua and Mexico against repressive regimes in 1970s South America.

A similar type of popular theatre developed on the African continent. According to Mlama, 'It attempts to create a way of life where people at the grassroot level are aware of the forces of work in determining their living conditions. It aims to make the people not only aware of but also active participants in the development process by expressing their viewpoints and acting to better their conditions.'(Mlama, 1991: 67). *Theatre for Development* has specific characteristics of community mobilisation for analysis of problems, selection of issues for dramatization, creation of interactive drama, performance and post performance discussion. The idea is that this process will in turn generate transformative action in the community. Since the Laedza Batanani Theatre programme was initiated in Botswana in 1974, *Theatre for Development* has gone a long way and developed several different sub genres including 'Theatre for Conscientization,' championed by people like Zaks Mda in Lesotho.

Theatre for Development has entered the academy and has inspired courses in departments of theatre arts such as at the University of Ghana. There are fears however that as theatre gains mainstream recognition as an effective tool of communication, theatre for development could become co-opted for marketing ideas of governments,development agencies, non-governmental organisations and even commercial interests. In brief, the ideas of anybody, but the communities concerned, thus defeating the initial principles on which it was founded.

Summary of Dominant Concerns

We have tried to demonstrate during the course of our exposition that the literary arts constitute a privileged configuration of communication strategies which enable individuals and communities to express their creativity while exploring all aspects of human existence. The literary traditions of Africa are mostly expressed in oral form and encapsulate indigenous knowledge, philosophical thought and belief systems.

The issue of identity is a major theme that is carried by the literary heritage. Underlying much oral literature is the affirmation of a collective ethos (e.g. clan and national appellations). Both oral and written literature also manifestly reflect the struggle for the reestablishment of the equilibrium of Africans and their communities, in the face of the overwhelming and sustained encounter with Europe. Once Africa entered into a relationship with Europe, one of the elements that it has had to battle for is its power to represent itself to the world and reclaim the right to name and define itself. For many literary artists, re-establishing this identity has been their main preoccupation. We have seen this in the negritude movement, as well as militant movements such as the Black Power Movements of the 1960s and early 1970s in the United States and South Africa.

One of the most interesting manifestations of interest in identity is writing which opens up the questions of ancient African civilizations and the transatlantic slave trade. Many Ghanaian writers, for instance, have taken up this issue. Some of these are Ayi Kwei Armah in *Osiris Rising*, Kofi Awoonor in *Comes a Voyager at Last*, Kwadwo Opoku- Agyemang in *Cape Coast Castle,* and Ama Ata Aidoo in the *Dilemma of a Ghost* and *Anowa*. This writing has a resonance with the works of Afro-Caribbean writers like Kamau Brathwaite in the *Arrivants*, Paule Marshale in *Praise Song for the Widow*, and African Americans like Toni Morrison in *Song of Solomon*.

The question of identity is not only treated thematically but also affects the very art of constructing texts. For example the issue of language comes into play. The Kenyan playwright, Ngugi Wa Thiong'O, is perhaps the most vocal advocate for the use of African languages in the writing of African literature. His novel, *Caitaani Mutharaba-ini,* for example, is written in Kikuyu. He and his colleague, Ngugi wa Miiri, worked in community theatre with the Kamiriithu community and together, they produced the powerful play, *Ngaahika Ndeenda [I Will Marry When I Want]*, which shook the political authorities and necessitated the departure into exile of the two writers.

Yet other writers engage in asserting the validity of forms of literature and drama inherited from the indigenous community. Mazisi Kunene of South Africa sought to develop an epic mythopoetics based on the heroic poetry of southern Africa. His monumental epic, *Anthem of the Decades*, examines existential issues through the life of the pantheon of Zulu gods. Likewise, we have discussed the efforts made by African dramatists to explore and adapt a whole range of the literary arts for the stage.

Conclusion

Kweku Ananse, the Akan trickster, attempted to climb up the tallest tree in the forest with all the knowledge in the world captured in a large gourd placed on his chest. However, he was finding it terribly difficult to scale up the tree and could not figure out what to do. It took his small son *Ntikuma*, to draw his attention to the fact that he would make better progress if he placed the gourd on his back. Insanely incensed that this shred of wisdom had escaped him, he impetuously smashed the gourd to the ground, thus scattering wisdom throughout the world. Perhaps if he had applied some of the wisdom entrusted to him and been willing to listen to other views, he may have heard a still small voice whisper one of our favourite proverbs from the Ewe culture of Ghana which states that 'knowledge is like a baobab tree: no single pair of arms can encircle it".

What we have tried to do in this chapter is to open a crack into the world of African literary arts and to discuss broad issues of its form, content and role. The literary arts can also be seen as a product of the imagination; a vehicle for creative expression which has the power of freeing the mind of the fetters of fact, enabling the creation of the world as it might be. It is an affective form of expression which may seek to do some of the following things: reach and stir emotions, intensify the senses of joy, outrage and pathos; engage the mind in re-assessing past situations or present circumstances, or indeed in conjuring up a world that has yet to come into being; and assist individuals and society in seeking a deeper understanding of questions of existence and the reason for being. Last but not least, it is a form of expression which allows individuals and society simply to indulge in the pleasure of aesthetic creativity through words. There is much yet to search for in the literary culture of Africa and more to contribute towards perpetuating it simply by delving into and enjoying its delights.

Review Questions

1. In what ways is Africa itself a focus for literary creativity on the continent?
2. 'There is no such thing as women's literature.' Discuss.
3. Identify continuities between oral and written African Literature.
4. "The literary artiste is both revered and reviled." Do you agree or disagree with this comment?
5. Compare and contrast the attitudes of Buchi Emecheta and Camara Laye to motherhood in their works.
6. African literary artistes are distressed about misrule on the continent. What are some of the literary and dramatic techniques that they have deployed to manifest their discontent.

Suggested Readings

Adali-Mortty, G. 1967. *"Ewe Poetry"* in U. Beier, (Ed). *Introduction to African Literature: An Anthology of Critical Writing from Black Orpheus.* Evanston Il,: Northwestern University

Anyidoho, K, and J. Gibbs. 2000. *FonTomFrom: Contemporary Ghanaian Literature, Theater and Film.* Amsterdam–Atlanta:.

Angmor, C. 1996. *Contemporary Literature in Ghana 1911-1978: A Critical Evaluation.* Accra: Woeli Publishing Services.

Bame, K. N. 1991. *Profiles In African Traditional Popular Culture; Consensus and Conflict;* Dance, Drama, Festivals and Funerals. New York: Clear Type Press Inc.

Dzobo, N.K. 1973. *African Proverbs: Guide to Conduct,Vol. I, Part I:The Moral Valueof Ewe Proverbs.* Cape Coast:The University Press.

Gyekye, K. 2003. *African Cultural Values: An Introduction.* Accra: Sankofa Publishing Company.

Newell, S. 2002. *Marita: or the Folly of Love.* Leiden,Boston, Koln: Brill.

Okpewho, I. 1992. *African Oral Literature.* Bloomington and Indianapolis: Indiana University Press.

Sutherland-Addy, E. 1999. Perspectives on Mythology. Accra: Goethe-Institut.

_____ (Ed.) and Aminata Diaw, 2005 *Women Writing Africa: West Africa and the Sahel Region*. City University of New York: The Feminist Press.

Wilentz, G. 1992. *Binding Cultures: Black Women Writers in Africa and the Diaspora*. Bloomington and Indianapolis: Indiana University Press.

Endnotes

1. 'Oral Traditions, Literature and Cinema in Africa: Dynamics of Exchange' (Unpublished paper p.2) prepared for the Faculty Resource Network at New York University June10 to 14 2002 edition on the theme 'Teaching Africa: Interdisciplinary Approaches.'

2. *A Walk in the Night and Other Stories* , 1962 Ibadan: Mbari Publishers

3. Nadine Gordimer is a prolific writer of short stories and novels. Her works include *The Late Bourgeois World* 1966 London: Gollancz, and *July's People* 1984 London: Jonathan Cape

4. Published by Viking 1976.

5. This poem was originally written in the Hausa Language (Northern Nigeria). This version of it was published in a volume entitled *The Collected Works of Nana Asma'u*. Boyd and Mack (Eds) Michigan State University Press.(1997)

6. Originally in French, from *Ethiopiques* pp.56-57

7. Published in his collection *Hopes and Impediments* (1990), Anchor Books edition.

8. The full song is part of the corpus of songs sung at the exclusively female Laaban ceremony held in Wolof culture the day after the consummation of marriage. The song is featured in the second volume of the *Women Writing Africa* series, published by the Feminist Press of the City University of New York.

9. This text is extracted from Leonard Acquah, (2002). "A Repertoire of Tropes: A Study of Fante-Akan Asafo Song Texts from the Cape Coast Area of the Central Region of Ghana." Unpublished MPhil. Thesis submitted to the University of Cape Coast. Pp.125.

10. See pp. 188-192 of *Oral Literature of the Embu and Mbeere* by Ciarunji Chesaiana, Nairobi,East African Educational Publishers 1997.

11. *Recreating Words, Reshaping Worlds: The Verbal Art of Women from Niger, Mali and Senegal* by Aissata Sidikou.,Trenton NJ:. Africa World Press Pp.247

12. From *A Selection of African Poetry*, with introduction and notes by K.E. Senanu and T. Vincent.

13. Ibid pp.93-94

14. From his essay "What Has Literature Got to Do with It?" published in his collection, *Hopes and Impediments* 1990 Anchor Books edition.

15. The discussion around drama in African society has been a lively one. Examples of relevant works by scholars quoted above are: Joel Adedeji – 'Alarinjo Traditional Yoruba Travelling Theatre in *Theatre in Africa* (Ed) Oyin Ogunba and Abiola Irele, Ibadan: Ibadan University Press 1978;Kwabena Bame *Profiles in African Traditional Popular Culture*.New York: Clear Type Press 1991 and Wole Soyinka *Myth, Literature and the African World*, Cambridge: Cambridge University Press 1976.

16. See Nketia's "The Intensity Factor in African Music" Published in *The Journal of Folklore Research* vol 25 Nos 1-2 1988; Efua Sutherland, based on an intensive study of traditional storytelling performance in Ghana and experimentation with permutations of the form has offered the term *Anansegoro* to describe the form of total theatre inspired by the traditional story telling event (See foreword to *The Marriage of Anansewa/ Edufa* Longmans 1990 . Also see Sutherland-Addy "Women and Verbal Art in the Oguaa-Edina Traditional Area". In the *Research Review* Vol. 14. No.1. Institute of African Studies. Legon. 1998.

17. Atwia Ekumfi is located in the Central region of Ghana. Between the mid 1960s and the late 1990s, this village was ruled by Nana Baah Okuampah the VI.

18. Efua Sutherland's research in concert party drama led to the writing of monographs such as *Bob Johnson* 1970, and was integrated into her plays and university-based outreach and training programmes. *West Africa Popular Theatre* by Karin Barber, John Collins, Alain Ricard, Bloomington, Indiana University Press 1997. Also see John Collins, Chapter 21, in this volume.

19. This quotation was taken from an unpublished conference paper by the Nigerian scholar and critic, Ime Ikiddeh entitled "The Tragic Influence of Shakespeare and the Greeks" quoted in Kofi Agovi's 'The Origin of Literary Theatre in Colonial Ghana 1920-1957." Published in the *Research Review* NS Vol.6 No. 1 1990

CHAPTER 18

AN EXPLORATION OF AFRICAN ART
Kwame Amoah Labi

Introduction

This chapter is a brief exploration of traditional and contemporary African art and the contexts in which they are made and used. It also takes into consideration the factors accounting for their stylistic development. Traditionally, many African societies depended on visual and pictorial forms as means to document events and to communicate. These became important icons, embodiments of aesthetic expression, representations of cultural values and records of history. Based on the earliest African art forms available to us, we are able to decipher the environment, cultural practices, beliefs, historical events and the general conditions existing during the period of creation of the art work, and also establish social, political and other relations among those who created and used them. These art forms include a wide range of two and three dimensional works made in materials such as wood, metal, clay, ivory, skin, leather, plant fibre, stone and composite materials. They were used in the everyday life activities of the ordinary person as well as in the most sacred rituals and ceremonies in the lives of priests and kings.

Some African art used by royals and office holders were characterised by naturalistic renditions such as the Benin and Ife bronzes. These were made to represent Kings, Queens and other leaders. Some of these are believed to have been involved in burial ceremonies. A large corpus of abstract and pronounced stylised works with little detail also exist. These abstractions represent African aesthetics and views, and the unknown world of the supernatural. Both simplifications and exaggerations of forms were conventions employed widely in Africa. These art works have predominantly been produced by men but the Luba, Asante and Yoruba women also produced art. Training was by apprenticeship, and practice was often on part-time basis (Bascom 1973:5-8).

Archaeological evidence, oral traditions, written accounts, current art historical research and publications testify that changes have occurred in the art of the continent and are still continuing. Therefore African art is dynamic. Today, African art includes both traditional and contemporary forms meeting different needs within specific communities. Susan Vogel's classification of the different types of art in Africa in her exhibition catalogue *Africa Explores: 20th Century African Art*, (Vogel 1991), gives a clear picture of the range of art currently being made on the continent. Her classification of art in Africa into traditional art, new functional art, urban and international art is partially representational of the trend of stylistic changes. Vogel has stayed away from suggestions by some writers such as Picton (1989) that traditional art corresponds to the "pre-colonial" period which in itself has been the basis for rejecting such a classification. Some African art historians including Okediji (1992), have criticised such Eurocentric Africanist classification and grouping of African art by dividing it between pre-colonial art, referring to traditional works, and modern art, encompassing those made during and after the period of colonisation. Other classifications have also been done in relation to European perceptions and prejudices. These classifications are beginning to be challenged as some Africans are no more willing to be "boxed up" into such periods. There still exist craftsmen who produce in traditional themes and styles and a large clientele who demand it.

Other writers such as Perani and Smith (1998:3-4) have expanded on this module and argue further that unfortunately the larger variety of African art is dominated by traditional art, as if African art is static. Though this is not the case, many of the traditional forms on the market today are copies of old traditional art with some modifications, thus making its classification as Vogels does, to require some review. New methods of examining African art from traditional to contemporary ones, including works of people of African descent in the Diaspora, are making new revelations on the dynamism of African art in maintaining old ideas yet incorporating new ones, materials and forms. Contemporary art works reveal a reliance on traditional art forms for inspiration and even when African slaves were transported thousands of miles across the Atlantic Ocean, they still found a place for traditional art.

Several factors have accounted for these dynamics and changes as well as continuities in African art. The natural environment, internal socio-economic and political changes and needs, have all played a role. For example, in many centralised political systems, art often served the purpose of enhancing and maintaining the status of the rulers, hence it was the settled groups of people who have displayed the most remarkable and largest range of art as compared to the nomadic, hunter, food gathering, desert and sub-desert societies and pastoralists.

I argue in this chapter that African art is made to meet the social, political, economic and religious needs of her people. Hence, it responds to changing situations. Therefore the theory of causality i.e. cause and effect, have played significant roles in the development of art on the continent. This means that the natural environment and climatic conditions and the ability of local communities to adapt their culture to overcome difficulties and make life organised and comfortable are important factors. Trade, religion and political contacts with Islam and Christianity have all been significant contributors to changes in African art. The current economic and socio-political conditions on the continent as well as education and the impact of western technological advancement in the production of new trade goods and materials cannot be discounted as contributory factors in the history of art in Africa. On the other hand, art has also been part of Africa's history and provides us with significant histo-cultural, scientific and social information. The content, meaning, aesthetics and values embodied in African works of art are therefore important to this chapter. I have therefore, rigorously, selected significant examples which, in my opinion, represent this history and organised them into four themes. They are (i)traditional African art; (ii) the changes and sources of these influences and their subsequent impact on the artists themselves and gender relations; (iii)contemporary art; and finally (iv) the art of people of African descent in the Diaspora.

Art of the African Continent

The African continent is rich in art with some dating back several millennia, as rock paintings found in the desert regions point to. Works in the Tassili region in the Sahara Desert date as early as the seventh millennium. Rock paintings are two dimensional mono or polychrome works executed on rocks depicting wild life and daily activities such as hunting scenes and rituals. Some of these paintings depict extinct animals in the desert such as elephants, rhinoceroses, hippopotamuses and buffaloes, indicating that the Sahara was once populated with these animals with vegetation and environment to sustain them, before desertification set in in the northern parts of the continent. The more recent paintings are of animals still found in the Sahara such as camels and horses representing the environmental and climate changes, and the new animals that survived when the desert set in. Thus the artists responded to environmental changes by incorporating these new animals used in transportation and trade. The weapons in these paintings range from axes, throwing-sticks, bows, javelins and swords to firearms (Willet 1997:45-48). The earliest themes depict hunting. The men in the engravings were portrayed armed with clubs, throwing sticks, axes, arrows and bows, but never with spears. In the latter periods, rams, cattle and other wild animals continued to be drawn (Willet 1997:48-49).

In subsequent themes that followed, the elephant is occasionally represented but other domestic animals are common. The earliest chariots are well drawn with a single shaft and a horse on either side. A few bows are seen with the introduction of new weapons such as spears and round shields (Willet 1997:49). Other sub-themes during the period are horse-riding. The latest group of works represent the principal domestic animal in the desert – the camel. Other animals depicted are antelopes, onyx, gazelles, moufflons, ostriches, humped cattle and goats, which can still be seen in the desert areas (Willet 1997:49).

Similar engravings and paintings are also found in Southern Africa, mainly in Namibia, Tanzania, Zambia and Zimbabwe. Both early engravings and paintings are found in the Apollo 11 cave in the Huns Mountains in south-western Namibia. Some of the rock slabs have been dated 25,500 – 27,500 years. This art of Southern Africa is of considerable antiquity and their radiocarbon dating range from 5590 _+ 600 BC to about 5510 _+ BC.

The early paintings found in this area are characterised by their meticulous rendition in naturalistic style dominated with the use of traditional domestic items. There is no recognisable modern or western subject-matter or accoutrements among them. The artists seemed to have lost patience with the latter works appearing to be less carefully done. In the earlier scenes the engravings and drawings depict people co-existing peacefully with one another. Latter paintings begin to portray ceremonial and battle scenes, and people of other races. The subject matter also begins to vary with the paintings reflecting confrontations, struggle and conflict (Willet 1997:64-65). These rock paintings show environmental and social change among the people occupying the areas of the Sahara and Kalahari Deserts. They tell us a great deal about the original and early animal population, changing social patterns and conflicts which occurred particularly in Southern Africa, with the coming of Europeans.

Works of clay on the African continent are one of the most enduring materials used in the production of art. They are able to survive the high fluctuating climate, insect and micro-organism attacks. Therefore, these have remained in fairly good condition for centuries even after they have been abandoned. Surface finds, archaeological excavations and subsequent studies of these works have extracted remarkable and invaluable information of the past and contributed to our current historical knowledge. Because such art works are rare and provide such useful insight into the past, they are priceless, thus raising their value as evidence of our past and important objects of study in academia, and have acquired high prices on the art market abroad because of their rarity. Recent illegal excavations of terracotta figures in Jenne, Mali, and investigations surrounding *Koma* terracotta in Ghana, show how valuable these are to researchers, governments and the international art market. The International Council of Museums (ICOM) frowns on the illicit trafficking of art objects and encourages dialogue and the involvement of Interpol in cracking down illegal trade in art.

The *Nok* terracotta found in the west of the Jos plateau in northern Nigeria in the mid 1900s, attest to the contribution of such surface and archaeological finds to our knowledge of the past. These are large scale human and animal figures fashioned in both realistic and abstracted forms indicating the level of sophistication of art during the period, thus debunking the idea that African lacked the skills or ability to produce realistic works. Terracotta from different levels of the finds have been dated to between 500 BC and AD 200, indicating how this civilisation and the art forms associated with kingship, religion and their general culture were expressed in sculpture. These works also tell us about the technology used in moulding and firing clay works. The eyes in both human and animal heads have been pierced through to the interior and, often, the nostrils, mouth and ears are treated the same way. The sizes vary in height from about four inches to four feet. All except the smallest pieces are modelled into hollow shapes, thus reducing the mass of the object and making it easy to manipulate by the artist (Gillon 1984:82). All these are indicative of style, cultural values, aesthetics and skill.

The pieces that have come to light are mainly human heads and figures. There is some conformity but, at the same time also, some variations are seen in earlier sub-styles. The proportions of the human body are fairly constant. Whereas in nature the proportion of the head to the whole body is in a ratio of about one to seven, in the Nok terracotta, it is between one to three or four. The pupils of the eyes are almost always perforated, set in triangles or segments of circles, with eyebrows stylised and ranging from half a circle to a straight line. The nose is often broad with wide nostrils. The mouths are thick-lipped, sometimes open, but rarely showing teeth. The ears are treated in a perfunctory fashion as simple and insignificant, and are frequently placed in unnatural anatomical positions (Gillon 1984:77). These tell us of the abstractions and ability to represent important characteristics of their people. It also dispels the notions about the quality and technical competencies of the African artist.

Some of the clay figures are shown in decorative dresses, with pubic coverings, hats and caps. No shoes or sandals are indicated in the terracotta finds. Others show beards and moustaches. Careful decorations and details of dresses and accoutrements on the bodies of the figures are remarkably uniform. Limbs adorned with bracelets, beads of various types, necklets and necklaces are common, but with no rings on their toes, fingers or ears (Gillon 1984:77). These tell us of the fashion and types of adornment of the period and what kind of accessories they would add to their clothing. It was also the style for men to be distinguished by giving them beads. Furthermore, it reveals the existence of other artists such as bead and metal makers at the time, all producing and selling their works. Certainly there was a vibrant market for the artists who produced these. The bust of a deceased person was made as funerary terracotta in Ghana to serve as a memorial of the dead person (Figure 20).

Figure 20 – Clay terracotta Figure of woman and child from Aduamoa, Kwahu, Eastern Region, Ghana used in funeral rites

Source: *IAS Archives, Legon. Photo Credit- Mr. Andoh*

Pottery is used as cooking utensils, water storage containers and bowls for eating. Other clay works include sculptures of human figures used in different social and religious ceremonies. For example, among the Fez in Morocco, a ceramic drum is used for the *ashura* festival and in marriage ceremonies. Pots are also used as medicine containers in several parts of the continent. Among the Lovedu in South Africa, it is believed that the ancestors prefer to be served in pottery (Barley 1994:76). Pots also provide abodes for spiritual beings such as ancestors and deities.

In addition to clay, other inorganic materials from the earth such as metals (iron, copper and gold) were extracted and worked into different art forms. Since the second millennium BC stretching to about 500 AD, different people, whether in farming or hunting communities, have learnt to produce arrows and farming tools to till the land (see also Ch. 11). The quality of smelting and smithing were so high in certain places that early Europeans preferred them to those made in Europe. Frobenius wrote about the metal works of the Songye that "they were so perfectly fashioned that no industrial art from abroad could improve upon them." The Marave blacksmiths of the Zambezi were also renowned for their works and were recognised by the Portuguese for this (Herbert 1984:10-11). Bosman also notes the beautiful gold and silver hatbands of the Fante of the Gold Coast (Bosman 1967:128-129). Mande blacksmiths produce a variety of art works including decorated door locks, stools, lamp holders, iron staffs, farming implements and masks. Other works forged in iron are human figures, portraits, single and multiple iron lamps and iron equestrian figures.

Ironworks were very important in the *Dahomey Kingdom*, Benin. For example, King Gele (1858-89) commissioned an ironwork associated with his *Fa* divination. This was a life size sculpture of a warrior. This piece was originally part of the palace military shrine where it was surrounded by large life-size iron swords and machetes fixed straight into the ground. This symbolised power and was believed to aid in military victory (Blier 1998:116). Musical instruments such as the iron double gongs play important roles in many societies such as the Mangbetu double bell from Rungu in the Democratic Republic of Congo. Similar double gongs are associated with royal authority in many African ethnic groups (Blier 1998:27).

There are a few places, such as the Zambian Copper belt, where copper can be found. Others are in Akjoujt in Mauritania, Hufrat en-Nahas in the Sudan, the Bembe mines in northern Angola, and northern and eastern Transvaal in South Africa (Herbert 1984:15-26). Various combinations of copper give different physical properties which make working in them more malleable. Alloys of copper and tin (bronze) or copper and zinc (brass) are much easier to cast than copper alone and very good examples of copper and other alloyed works are found in Nigeria. The Ife heads of Igbo-Uwuku, Nigeria, represent some of the typical copper and other alloyed works which seem to have come to an end after the cessation of a long artistic tradition that existed between the ninth and twelfth centuries. In Benin, Nigeria, some of the bronze works include "an altar of a hand" made for the *Oba* (king), probably in the second half of the eighteenth century. Another bronze plaque shows a Portuguese carrying a staff of office and surrounded by representations of manilla currency. Some of the Ife works excavated in the mid 1900s were bronze heads (Figure 21). These include the seated bronze figure at Tada, a half figure showing an *Oni* (ruler) of Ife in beaded regalia, heads wearing beaded crowns with plume, miniature figures and the head of a Queen mother. Some bronze plaques represent two leopard heads, an important symbol of the unrestricted power of the King of Benin. Works in bronze such as leopard heads, cocks and aquamanile in the form of a ram were also made (Fagg:1963).

Figure 21 – Torso of Oni, Nigeria

Source/Credit: *Plaster reproduction, Courtesy Ghana National Museum, Photograph Selina Laryea*

The Yoruba bronze works are of great interest since they represent one of the greatest art traditions on the continent. These were discovered around Ife and dated between the twelfth to sixteenth century. Included in the works from Benin are the brass head of an *Oni*, with facial striations, wearing a crown. Also included is a brass work of a royal couple wearing their crowns, ankle-length robes, many beads and other adornments. The man's wrap is tucked in between his legs. The *Oni's* leg is twisted round the right leg of his Queen with interlocked arms. These bronzes from Benin and Yoruba are undoubtedly masterpieces and could represent the work of a generation (Gillon 1984:193-195). Several other outstanding metal works cast in proverbial and geometric forms, include: Asante brass and gold trinkets, metal containers, gold weighing scales, necklaces, armbands and goldweights used in measuring gold dust.

In other parts of the continent wood, stone and ivory sculpture is done. However, the largest amount of sculpture made are in highly perishable organic materials such as wood. But the pervasive nature of wood sculpture in several facets of African cultural life makes it one of the most common art works found on the continent. A few other sculptures are found in stone in Zimbabwe and the Democratic Republic of Congo, and ivory in Nigeria and Sierra Leone. Wood sculpture is not found in every part of the continent, but mainly in the rain forest belts and adjacent zones suitable for agriculture. The religious nature of the African society has led to many sculptural forms being made to reflect its relationship with the supernatural. African masks which inspired European artists, such as Pablo Picasso and Paul Gaugin, were to a large extent connected to boys' and girls' initiation and representations of the gods and ancestors. Masks are closely related to the secret societies which were means of maintaining social order. The most famous and prevalent masks are from the *Poro* secret societies of parts of Liberia, Sierra Leone and La Côte d'Ivoire. In other more urbanised societies such as the Bakuba of Democratic Republic of Congo or the Yoruba in Nigeria, secret societies play the role of policing. Most of these societies are limited to men, but similar female ones such as the *Bundu* and *Sande* exist in La Côte d'Ivoire and Liberia. Masks in general (Figure 22), and the Komo mask in particular, play crucial roles in the Bamana, Mali, initiation rites in which young boys are circumcised and go through various forms of training and corporate discipline.

Masks are not the only objects made. There are various insignia carved in wood. Different kinds of sculptures are made to enhance the prestige of rulers. The sculptures produced are stools, chairs, swords, staffs, sceptres, state umbrellas, royal drums, crowns, sandals, headgear and other architectural designs and decorations such as bas-relief, carved doors and plaques. A vast range of sculpture were made for daily domestic use and commercial activities such as cups, food bowls, mortars, stools, human figures and animals, cosmetic containers, combs, neck rests and game boards (Bascom 1973:10-11).

Figure 22 – N'Kang Mask, Cameroon

Source/Credit: *Courtesy Ghana National Museum, Photograph Selina Laryea*

Parts of wood and animals were processed differently for clothing. The fibres used in the manufacture of cloth in Africa are bark, bast, cotton, raffia, silk, and wool. The most obvious use of these products are for clothing. One or more lengths may be wrapped around the body, tailored into gowns, tunics, trousers and so on. The use of clothing for protection and keeping the genitalia from public viewing are not the only reasons for wearing them. In all these situations, colour and design are of significance. Particular colours, embellishments or shapes have value and meaning. Some colours and decorations may have political or ritual connotations. For example, the ethnic affiliation of a Moroccan Berber woman can be read in the patterns of stripes in her dress. Again, in Benin, chiefs wear red cloth as part of their ceremonial court dress and by association with anger, blood, war and fire, this is regarded as threatening (Picton and Mack 1979:9). Similarly in Asante, the *Asantehene* (Asante king) wears black cloth on the days of court sittings to depict the seriousness of the occasion. Akan *kente* and *adinkra* designs have symbolic meanings and are made to be used within certain social contexts. Textiles are used to distinguish social classes by their design and quality of fibre.

There are several other uses of textiles including clothes for the dead, during burial and other ceremonies. Other spiritual manifestations such as masquerades, priests and priestesses are all clothed in particular attire. Textiles may be used to cover a house to mark an event of some significance (Picton and Mack 1979:10). During annual festivals, some Fante *asafo* companies (socio-political military organisation) of Ghana decorate their *posuban* (military shrines) with long cloth banners (Labi 2002).

Textiles are also of economic value. They have been a marketable commodity used extensively in trade within and outside the continent of Africa. In the seventeenth century, cloths woven in Benin were purchased by Europeans for trade in the Gold Coast. Later on, Yoruba cloths were purchased for trade in Brazil. Some cloths have also been specifically woven for use as currency in the Democratic Republic of Congo and Sierra Leone. In discussing textiles, their economic, social, aesthetic, ritual and other roles emerge through their design and use.

Chiefs, kings and queens have been important patrons of art. Therefore the royal arts accompanying political authority place emphasis on themes of power and the display of rare, prestigious and expensive materials which all underscore political positions. Other royal signifiers include dangerous animals such as lions, leopards and elephants; beautiful weaponry; expensive and elaborate palaces and a corpus of sculpture, jewellery and costumes, which are costly and scarce, and in some cases spiritually imbued objects (Blier 1998: 11). What makes art important is the fact that political status is clearly defined and differentiated by physical features or external means. Akan chieftaincy regalia, namely stools, spokesperson staffs, umbrellas, swords, sandals and headbands are all art works which distinguish chiefs from the ordinary person. (Figure 23) . In the Kuba kingdom, Democratic Republic of Congo, the king is noted for elaborate art which he commissions during his life time. These naturalistic figures depict the position of the ruler as ideal rather than representing an individual king (Figure 24). The cross-legged position of the king with a game board in front of him for example, shows his calmness and firm control of affairs (Hackett 1999:88).

Figure 23 – Nana Wiafe Akenten,Ofinsohene,seated with regalia at 1994 the Adaekese Festival in Kumasi

Figure 24 –Three Kuba Kings

Source/Credit: *Source/Credit: Courtesy Ghana National Museum, Photograph Selina Laryea*

Many African courts and palaces display special seats, drinking vessels, furniture, crowns and musical instruments which all convey the idea of status. All these seek to present certain idealised views of political leaders. For example, in Dahomey the most important royal regalia is the kings' sandals; among the Akan it is the stool; for the Kuba a woven "basket of wisdom;" and in the Yoruba kingdoms of southern Nigeria, crowns are the privileged genre (Blier 1998:14-16).

Architecture is also used as a signifier of political status. The Buganda palace in Uganda epitomises African court architecture. The plan of the capital of Benin City in Nigeria was described as "spacious and well laid out with thirty 120 foot wide avenues. The prominent cardinal positions in the direction of the gods no doubt reinforced the king's identity with the temporal cosmological powers" (Blier 1998:51). In addition to Dapper's description of Benin City based on descriptions and illustrations of those who had been there were the striking brass bass relief plaques which decorated the key compounds of the palace (Blier 1998:60). Just as the royal palaces of the king of Kongo, Democratic Republic of Congo, were rectilinear, like most domestic structures whose walls and roofs were traditionally made of woven plant fibre covering the substructure poles, this form of architectural construction shared the key attributes of both their weaving and basketry techniques. Although the kings' houses were made of similar materials, the houses of the nobles were distinguished by their height and a more solid construction. They were interwoven with designs often marked by gable ends and supported by carved poles with elaborate wall paintings (Blier 1998:204). Benin's king, Ewuare, revolutionised art and architecture and is credited with a series of new buildings, including the queen mother's residence. The Benin palace had much imagery, including birds and snakes (Blier 198: 52). The ancestor statues, carved door frames and veranda posts of the Bafusam in Cameroon, surface decoration of Asante mud houses, and the great Zimbabwe stone architecture are remarkable artistic and technological achievements on the continent.

Artists are seen as people with special skills and spiritual powers. In Benin, artists are believed to work closely with divinities; hence they must remain in a perpetual state of purity. In order to achieve this they have taboos they must either abstain from permanently or periodically, including sexual abstinence and bathing or changing clothes after sexual contact (Hackett 1996:40). Among the Akan, the carver must avoid a woman in her menstrual period. Akan artists propitiate trees they fell for carving because they believe they are potential places for the habitation of powerful spirits. The Dogon bury a cowrie shell at the foot of every tree that is felled as propitiation and other sacrifices from the family altar, including the slaughtering of a chicken (Hackett 1999:41).

The ritual contexts in which many significant African art objects are produced, particularly masks and masquerading, give them the capacity to provide abodes for ancestors, spiritual forces, dispel evil as well as heal (Figure 25). In addition to many of their artistic and aesthetic functions is their ability to make the invisible visible. Many traditional African chiefs, kings and leaders believed to represent the ancestors, have art, regalia and ritual symbols to align, regulate and commemorate this relationship.

Figure 25 – Gabuangu performs Gatambi a Imbuanda, a female mask Nyoka-Munene, DRC, 1989

Source/Credit: *Photo Z. S. Strother*

It is no wonder that drums, stools, spokesperson's staffs, figures and other works can be transformed from artistic works into shrines. Among the Baule of central Côte d'Ivoire, carvers produce sculpture to represent nature spirits and spirit mates who are believed to be spiritual entities that influence and control their affairs to illustrate the link between aesthetics and belief about the spirit world. Through dreams, the spirits reveal to the client, the diviner or carver, their preferences for the choice of wood, form, posture and decoration (Hackett 1999:57). The attractiveness of the figure is believed both to tame the spirits' harmful impulses and to provide a locus where it can be contacted and appeased. Usually those who possess these figures feed and even treat them like life partners by lying beside them (see also Chs. 7 and 14).

In addition to creating works which can become abodes for spirits, carvers sculpt deities which are found in several shrines and houses. Shango is the deified fourth king of the Oyo people in Western Nigeria and offers an example of the range of imagery that may be associated with a particular divinity. The variety of iconography that surrounds the worship of Shango is probably the greatest legacy of Yoruba art. Others are Senufo, La Côte d'Ivoire, and Legba shrine figures of the Fon and Gou, Benin, the god of war and iron; Ifa divination cups (in Benin and Nigeria), and charms from Kongo, Bembe and Suku, Democratic Republic of Congo. Among the Akan, it is not a figure which represents the spirits of the ancestors, but rather a stool of the previous leader which, if he lived and ruled according to the ethos of his or her people, is blackened in a special ceremony with soot, gunpowder, eggs and alcohol, to preserve the memory of that ancestor.[1] Among the Edo people in Nigeria, the Oba's persona and art objects are the primary vehicles of Edo cosmology and political meaning (Hackett 1999:81-82).

The power objects from Kongo, known as *nkisi* (singular) are one of the best examples of art and medicine. Within them may be housed healing objects prepared for a particular occasion. They have the power to afflict and heal. The properties of *minkisi* (pl.) include inflicting disease as well as healing (Hackett 1999:136-7). In Ghana many shrines provide health care services (see Chapter 14, this volume). In these shrines are various art objects carved in the form of the disease or care they are expected to provide. For instance a fertility shrine may have women carrying dolls. The legend of the *Akuaba* doll given to an infertile woman by a priest is a familiar story told in Ghana, buttressing the relationship between art, religion and health delivery. Many priests in shrines are healers. The diagnosis and treatment are said to be given or inspired by the gods they serve.

In the last few centuries, the impact of Islam and Christianity on traditional art cannot be ignored, especially in urban towns. Many shrines and independent churches manifest works of Christian themes such as the struggle against "paganism", sometimes depicted in the form of the seductive water spirit such as "Mami Water", who is believed to provide healthcare. The Islamic talismans with Koranic verses are all signs of external influence actually believed in and sometimes solicited for healing purposes. The abhorrence of Islam on the reproduction of any semblance of humankind has modified traditional representation of human forms.

Musical instruments are made by different types of artists including carvers and smiths working in materials such as leather, wood, metal and ivory, and are played by musicians whose tunes are danced to (see also Chapters 19 and 20, this volume). Among the Mande of Mali, and the surrounding people in North and Central Africa, idiophones are of varied types. Xylophones appear to be common. These are available in different shapes, sizes and tunes. The lamellophone or "thumb piano" is also common among the Shona in Zimbabwe; the Kuba, Zande and Luba of the Democratic Republic of Congo, and the Mamprusi in Ghana. They are made out of any of the following materials: wood, metal, shell, gourd, fibre, plywood, seedpods, bamboo and nails. Other types of idiophones are rattles and an assortment of bells found among the Kongo of the Democratic Republic of Congo, wooden bells from the Ibibio people in Nigeria, and brass bells from Igbo in Nigeria and Dan in La Côte d'Ivoire and Liberia. Among the collection of chordophones on the continent are harps from the Kinandas in Tanzania, harp drum from the Mangbetu in the Democratic Republic of Congo, harp lute among the Grebo in Liberia, Tsogo and Ndjabi in Gabon, and lyre and trough zither from Marundi in Burundi. These chordophones are made in composite materials such as wood, string, leather, hide, pigment, fibre, metal, bead, textile and horn. Other musical instruments are aerophones which include whistles, horns, flutes, trumpets, and membranophones, namely drums, for example, tension or squeeze drums (DjeDje 1999:241-337). All these musical instruments are decorated or embellished in one way or the other.

In Ghana the chief maintains a large group of musical instruments in his court. These include drums, ivory horns, bells and clappers. Chiefs have in their court, musicians who play various instruments for different occasions. Some musical instruments such as the talking drum (*atumpane*) and *fontomfrom* are reserved only for the chiefs' drummers and musicians to play. Some drums are taken to war and on these drums may be several types of decorations and adornment, including skulls of enemies, while others may represent war gods and deities.

Some drums are used for communication, rituals, ceremonies and entertainment. They are played to herald the arrival or movement of the chief, or for him to dance. These instruments may also be played for the public's participation in a dance. Strother emphasises the important relationship between masks and music by quoting a sculptor, Gitshiola Léon, who says the invention of masks always begins with a dance, saying "You can't just invent a [face] mask...you need a dance!" (1998:27). The sculptor is often the last person to be consulted after the performers have finalised the dance, song, rhythm and costume. *Asafo* drummers perform for the flag

-dancer who holds the *asafo* flag– an art work made by a tailor –with which he executes a graceful, athletic and acrobatic dance.

Traditional as they are, African masks still find opportunity to address contemporary issues. Pende masks range from very old traditional masks such as *Giwoyo/Kiwoyo* which is still produced in several places in the Congo. Between the 1910s and 1930s a series of newer masks called *mbuya jia mafuzo* which included life size puppets, maquettes of fierce animals, whirling barrels and wriggling snake dancers emerged in the Democratic Republic of Congo (Strother 1998:175-181, 234). Today, the art of Africa reflects the socio-economic, political, cultural and educational changes taking place, thus impacting tremendously on its practise.

Art and the Dynamics of Change

Traditional sculptural forms as well as contemporary art works are being made to suit different markets and clientele. When the European merchants arrived in different parts of Africa to trade, they came across an already existing ivory, wood and stone sculptural tradition. Portuguese interests in African art became a source of patronage and ivory works were commissioned from African craftsmen for these foreign patrons. These works were made mainly in the Benin and Sherbro area of Sierra Leone. The ivory vessel in the British Museum collection, according to McLeod (1980) was probably made in the sixteenth century in Benin for Portuguese patrons. It portrays two Portuguese officials with an attendant at the side of each of them. The proportions of these figures are more African than European, and above the figures are a ship and an anchor symbolising European technology and sailors. These works included intricately carved spoons, forks, hunting horns and condiment bowls called saltcellars, which were taken to Portugal and Europe. The type of objects and some of the imagery reflect European tastes and preferences. Some of these were European hunting scenes and Portuguese heraldic royal arms found on hunting horns. However the style of carving, especially the treatment of human figures and animals, was based on African aesthetics and style (Perani and Smith 1998:81).

Other interesting innovations and adaptation of Europeans influence into African art are the Yoruba solid wooden palace doors. At the entrances to these palaces are elaborately carved doors. Each door panel shows scenes in square columns relating to rulership, contemporary life and the history of the dynasty. For example, above a square area containing a representation of a king is a cyclist and a man, wearing a colonial helmet, holding a book and facing the cyclist while smoking a pipe. According to Blier (1998:86), whereas the man seated may probably represent a government official with the book or code of laws, the rider suggests a traveller. The Yoruba god Eshu, also known as the trickster, and often depicted with a smoking pipe, is also represented. Included in the reliefs indicating representations of modernity are the messenger and a school child who stand on the far right and left respectively. These two figures in relief on this door panel, suggest sources of traditional and modern authority, and war represented in the lower reliefs, and written law in the reliefs above, through Eshu and the cyclist (Blier 1998:86). In another door, the scene reflects local life, and demonstrates the diversity and changing scenes of life over the years, with a Muslim warrior on horseback juxtaposed with a man riding a bicycle (McLeod 1980:72).

Architecture is a strong cultural marker and a shift in it shows contact with other cultures, designs and technologies. During the first two or three centuries AD, the kings of Axum in Ethiopia, influenced by the Christian faith, built a series of spectacular palaces which have now fallen into ruin. However, archaeological evidence, surviving foundations and ground plans and judging from construction techniques of stone churches built several centuries later in the same area, reveal important information on the windows and doors set in recessed panels in layered stone and mortar walls, with wooden beams supporting the upper floors (Visona et al. 2001: 66). Since this period Christians have used architecture as a means of expressing their faith in the churches constructed between the eighth and twelfth centuries. Stone carvers created at least eleven churches at Lalibela, Ethiopia, a site King Lalibela chose to create a new Jerusalem on Ethiopian soil, named after himself. Here churches were carved from solid rocks. Beginning from the ground level the carvers chipped away the rock from the roof down to the foundations. Many of these rock churches were square or rectangular in plan. An example is the Beta Giorghis church dedicated to St. George, which was in the shape of a cross. Other Ethiopian kings known as Solomonic Kings constructed a series of palaces and churches. Some of them especially Debre Berhan Selassie (Mount of Light of the Trinity), stands out among them and its interior displays features of veiled entrances or "holy of holies", the crucifixion and the Holy Trinity. These paintings and rock-cut churches still provide perfect settings for worship by the Ethiopian Christian churches (Visona et al. 2001:68-73).

One of the famous kings of Mali, Mansa Musa, is known for his pilgrimage to Mecca in 1324. The Islamic architecture that Mansa Musa observed during his travels had an important impact on the development of mud architecture in the then Western and Central Sudan. Among the features of the new mosques are the wall (*quibla*) which is aligned to the sacred city of Mecca. Many Sudanese mosques also have a niche (*mihrab*) in the *quibla* wall, symbolising their relation with Mecca. Two important Timbuktu mosques are the Djingereber and Sankore ones – all reflecting influences from Arab culture.

The Hausa are known for their distinctive mud architecture. The design and organisation of the house is governed by the Islamic practice of wife seclusion and, to this end, the entire house is surrounded by a wall. Circulation from the entrance into the rest of the house is subdivided into quarters for the members of different nuclear families. The façade of the entrance is often decorated with bold embossed, geometric patterns which express the wealth and prestige of the family head. The geometric patterning on these façades may be based on pre-Islamic designs that became modified and were given new expression under nineteenth century Islamic influences.

The use of reinforced mud arches to create vaulted-dome ceilings by Hausa builders began in the nineteenth century and reflect Islamic architectural influences from North Africa and the Near East. Many of these house façades such as the famous "Bicycle house" in Zaria have incorporated symbols influenced by the West. The walls and roof of the entrance huts are built entirely of mud bricks.

By the early twentieth century, a group of wealthy traders and merchants emerged as important art patrons, and royal control over building practices began to break down when the Hausa master builders began working for a new group of wealthy private clients. Traders and merchants began to commission elaborate, embossed façades and domed ceilings for their private houses as a sign of prestige.

European architecture, namely forts and castles, were a source of training and influence on the southern coastal areas and nearby inland communities in Ghana. It is evident that the builders brought from Accra and Togo to construct the Cape Coast Castle used new technologies and masonry skills in construction. This certainly had an impact on Fante architecture. By the mid-twentieth century, many domestic dwellings of wealthy merchants and politicians consisted of houses of one or two storeys, influenced by the new designs and technology.

The impact of Western architecture and skills can also be seen in the construction of Fante *asafo posuban*, military monumental shrines, which were previously simple mounds, totem posts or shrines, and flags. The imposing sizes of the forts and castles with canons were symbols of the power and authority of the Europeans, which influenced construction of the new shrines. European military equipment and transportation, especially ships and aeroplanes, influenced the construction of some new *posuban* (Figure 26).

Figure 26 – *Wombiri Posuban*, **Elmina.**

Credit: *K.A. Labi Photo, 2002*

Clothing has also been imported from the Arab north and Europe into southern and western coasts of Africa. Hausa gowns based on Arab and Moorish dress traditions are the earliest tailored garments found in West Africa. The robe of honour has been an important official garment in the Islamic world since the eighth century, and Arab geographers have reported the official use of robes and turbans in West Africa since the eleventh century. Among the Hausa people the embroidered gown, *riga*, is one of the most important visual signifiers of a man's association with Islam. The gowns are made from cotton or silk cloth, woven on a narrow-band treadle loom by male weavers. After the cloth strips have been tailored into a gown, the front and back are decorated by a male embroiderer with a variety of geometric patterns including spiral, interlace, and triangular motifs. The triangular motifs may signify good fortune and victory in war. Members of the Fulani political elite also wear white turban or one that has been dyed with blue indigo for public appearances. The white turban signifies that the wearer has made a pilgrimage to Mecca.

On the southern coasts where the influence was from Europe, cotton, silk, velvet and woollen textiles and clothes such as shirts, skirts, blouses, trousers, ties and jackets were worn and eventually replaced the traditional bark and woven cloth sewn for a lower wrapper and the upper *kaba* (locally designed blouse). These were early indicators of contact with Europeans. Today the design of traditional clothes draws inspiration from both the Islamic parts of northern of Ghana and neighbouring countries, especially La Côte d'Ivoire. These are worn during private traditional gatherings such as festivals, funerals, naming and marriage ceremonies, and as formal dress for state or public functions.

As a result of interactions between Africans and Europeans, royal art works have changed. Though some royal guilds might maintain a certain stylistic uniformity, local symbols have come to mean different things. For example, prior to the conversion of local Kongo kings and dignitaries to Christianity by the Portuguese in the early fifteenth century, the cross which had hitherto been a prominent indigenous symbol took on a new meaning thereafter. The Christian icon, the crucifix, was used in both political and ritual purposes. Now both indigenous and Christian crosses are used in traditional Kongo rites and rituals, and Kongo rulers employed the cross as another potentially direct access in contacting the gods (Blier 1998:207).

Creation of art in Africa has traditionally been marked by division of labour and is sometimes based on gender. Traditionally, pottery and basketry have been made by women in several parts of Africa. There are very few cultures where both men and women weave. The exception to this in recent years is in Nigeria. Textile production is divided into female and male tasks, with the women spinning the cotton while the men weave. In Nigeria, the indigo dying industry, like pottery, was previously controlled by women. When men took over in the nineteenth century in parts of the country, they introduced technical innovations that distinguished their production process from that of women. In the past Hausa women dyed cloth in large ceramic pots, but male dyers replaced the pots with cement lined pits.

Although ceramics in Africa are largely produced by women, men are occasionally involved. In Northern Nigeria, Hausa women controlled the production before the mid-nineteenth century, but since then men have taken over. They took over the production of utilitarian vessels, including small cooking pots and large pots for carrying and storing water, and while women continue to be involved in pottery, now their role is secondary.

Hausa men also took over the pottery industry and introduced new techniques which continued to the twentieth century. While Hausa pottery continues to be a male dominated industry, in recent years an increasing number of women have begun to make pots. In Islamic cultures, women who are confined to compound houses are now viewed as a ready made labour force. This is because due to urbanisation young males have been attracted to more lucrative jobs in bigger towns and cities, and as a result more women have been trained to make pots. In most parts of Africa, pottery manufacture, including the digging and preparation of clay, and the forming of pots and firing is still the responsibility of women.

Such occupational gender and role reversals are also found in other twentieth-century Hausa art industry. For example, since the mid-twentieth century, Hausa women have worked to produce crafts in an aluminium smithing centre, which had always been a male specialisation. While the men continued to shape the aluminium ladle spoons through the hammering process, women decorated them with engraved patterns. Tuareg male blacksmiths and silversmiths specialise in producing tools, weapons, and silver jewellery, while their wives make portable containers of leather such as water bags, personal wallets, decorated colourfully with embroidered appliquéd patterns and protective amulets. In northern Nigeria and Mali, Hausa and Mande men respectively are the leather specialists. While any Tuareg woman married to a blacksmith can manufacture leather products, the tanning of leather can only be done by postmenopausal women (Perani and Smith 1998:39-40).

Contemporary African Art

New trade goods, political struggles and awareness and daily contact with Islamic, European and urban sub-cultures from the late nineteenth century took roots in African towns and cities, and soon cultural influences and current issues became a source of inspiration and challenge to be transformed into visual forms. These new genres became different from traditional art work. In the urban centres a mixture of artists including sign writers, street artists, large mobile paintings of musical and drama (concert) advertisements, hairstyles, portraits of prominent world leaders, celebrities and various visual expressions of the contemporary socio-politico economic situation began to appear. From the guilds of traditional craftsmen to the studios of modern college-trained artists, art works are sold on the streets, in art markets, at exhibitions (local and international) and in art galleries. The artists range from those who produce for traditional cultural activities and local clientele, to those producing commercial art for tourists and the export market, and western trained artists producing single works for diplomats and wealthy local clients, that are often not reproduced.

The flour-sack painters in the Democratic Republic of Congo are a good example of artists' commentary on political life. In Kisangani, a major city in north-east Congo, and other Congolese urban centres, historical themes, such as the assassination of Prime Minister Patrice Lumumba in 1961, and others expressive of the general economic and political situation, often dominate the scenes of the works of artists. Popular paintings also reflect fashion, sports, politics and entertainment. One of the most popular of these artists in the Democratic Republic of Congo is Cheri Samba (born 1956), who has emerged as a highly successful painter. Many of his themes deal with problems of urban life, from prostitution to crowded streets and the desire to acquire European goods. Some of these themes represent the inadequacies of power under colonial rule and subsequent post-colonial regimes. Unlike Samba, Moke's work, such as the Motorcade with Mitterand and Mobutu, with its threatening symbols of power and sinister authoritarian power, are representations of the political violence that plagued the continent in the twentieth century. Similar themes can be found in Kenya and Zambia by both self -taught and college trained artists (Kasfir 1999:18-22).

In Ghana there are art studios which specialise in a genre including political leaders, renowned sports figures and sign writing. Some of the paintings represent the hopes and aspirations of the local population and their desire for such modern furnishing and interiors of houses, balconies, and their wish to visit important landmarks in Europe, holy religious sites and airports. These scenes are used as backdrops in photographic studios.

Commercial lorry drivers have sought the assistance of sign writers and painters to express cherished ideas on their vehicles through a wide range of proverbs, stickers of national colours, coat of arms, quotations and wise sayings reflecting hope, belief, inspiration or frustration. Other representations employ images of power as well as those which represent violence such as lions, leopards and elephants (Kasfir 1999:18-35).

The ubiquitous passenger vehicles known as the *Matatu* in Nairobi and Mombasa in Kenya, and the *tro-tro* minibuses and articulated vehicles in Ghana are one of the fastest growing urban art culture in Africa, south of the Sahara. In Nigeria many of the writings on vehicles are based on Christian or Islamic faith. For example, "Allah yakiyaye" (Allah protect us), "Jesus my Protector," "The Lord is My Shepherd" and "Psalm 100." Other slogans refer to actors such as Rambo or the challenges facing the owner of the vehicle. Some offer popular philosophical sayings such as "God's Case No Appeal" (Nigeria), "No Condition is Permanent" (Ghana and Nigeria), "Fear Woman" (Ghana) and "Hakuna Matata" (No Problem, Kenya). More recently the vehicle genre has included contemporary issues such as HIV and AIDS with writings on its dangers and prevention, such as "One Man One Wife" and "Zero Grazing," which literally means "keep all cows at home" or men should stay at home with their wives (Kasfir 1999:37).

There are artists trained in Western art schools and institutions whose works are targeted towards the international community through local and international exhibitions. Today, there are several of such art schools. Artists such as Ibrahim el Salahi (born 1930), have become important international figures. He was one of the first Sudanese artists to exhibit outside his country. Salahi trained in Khartoum, Addis Ababa and London and, like many painters in Sudan, he was influenced by Sudanese artists who had no formal training. In his painting, 'Funeral and Crescent,' Salahi remembers the death of his father and the affirmation of his Muslim faith during the funeral. The work has heavy elongated bodies emanating from figures with mask-like appearances lifting upwards towards the lunar symbol of Islam. The colours are soft and represent the earth colours and hues dominating the landscape in Sudan. The painting also represent Salahi's desire to create calligraphic strokes and merge them with the Islamic heritage. Salahi's goal was a combination of Arabic calligraphy and "pan-African" styles and themes in his works during the 1960s and 1970s. Several Sudanese artists left the Sudan to Europe and America, due to political pressures and threats of detention. Some of these are Mohammed Omer Khaalil (born 1936) and the sculptor, Amir Nour (born 1939).

Ethiopian artists also responded to local and international influences as seen in the works of some of the early students of the first art school in Addis Ababa founded by Ale Felege in 1957. Gebre Kristos Desta (1932-1981) was one of the pioneer teachers who had studied abroad and returned to teach. Desta's art included abstracted yet recognisable figures such as the crucifix. Even though he was criticised locally for using European modernism to convey his ideas, he managed to adapt these European styles and themes to the Ethiopian context. After the military coup in Ethiopia in 1974, Desta was forced to leave the country and died as a refugee in Oklahoma, USA. Many other Ethiopian artists, such as Skunder Boghassian, who died in the US in 2003, have faced similar situations.

Contrary to the persecution of artists in Sudan and Ethiopia, during the first two decades of independence from France in 1960, art flourished in Senegal under the acclaimed Senegalese President, Léopold Sédar Senghor. One of the most influential Senegalese artists was Papa Ibra Tall (born 1935). He studied painting and tapestry in France and returned to Senegal to teach at the *Senghor Ecole des Beaux-arts* in Dakar. He founded the *Manufactureurs Nationals des Tap-*

estries in the town of Thies. This became an art school as well as a production centre which has over the years trained and employed several artists. These artists produced images of African scenes and art forms using imported fibre and European weaving techniques. There were other artists such as Iba N'Diaye, who also studied in France and returned to Senegal. He painted in layers, a technique which looked like those of seventeenth century European artists. One of his paintings which have two sheep at the sides with a slaughtered one in the centre, was meant to represent the political violence which plagued the African continent and the ability of Africans to look on unconcerned or to do nothing about it. In the 1980s, many of these artists attracted international interest including Fodé Camara (born 1958), whose work illuminated issues of the slave trade (Visona et al. 2001:126-127).

The Congolese painter, Romain-Desfosses, was in search of fresh and new sources of inspiration and his works and those of his followers gained recognition in Europe. Ghanaian artists such as Saka Acquaye, Ablade Glover, Ato Delaqius, Oku Ampofo and the Akuapem Six, need mention as prominent artists who have made immense contribution to modern and contemporary art in Ghana and Africa, drawing inspiration from local themes and icons while working with western tools and mediums (Figure 27).

Figure 27 – Painting- The Call, London. September 2007- Wisdom Kudowor

Source/Credit: *Photography- Courtesy of Artist*

Today, artists in Africa including traditional carvers, smiths and craftsmen, produce a wide variety of works, following traditional guidelines and practices. Some of these are sold to local clientele and as tourist art in craft shops and at airports. The works of contemporary urban artists and those produced by College artists fill the streets of the cities and art galleries, with some displayed at local and international exhibitions.

New Interpretations and Innovations of African Art in the Diaspora

From the early sixteenth to mid-nineteenth century, approximately 14 million Africans were transported across the Atlantic Ocean in the slave trade (see also Ch.5). Though these Africans left behind the material evidence of their culture, it was ingrained in them. In cases where groups of people from similar language backgrounds and neighbouring towns were gathered together on plantations, the cultures from these different places in Africa were exhibited in the lives of slaves and melted together with others. The Haitian religious practice known as *Vodoo*, for example, is a combination of Yoruba, Kongo and Dahomean beliefs and practices with an infusion of Roman Catholicism. More importantly is its remarkable tradition of sacred art developed for this religion (Thompson 1983:163).

The new cultural elements and forces began to affect the artistic expression of Africans in these new places. Some of the old forms were produced but with new interpretations, materials, techniques and meanings. African architectural influences for instance can clearly be seen in the Americas. A typical example is the kind of broad open porches found in American houses. In many of the places where the slaves had been taken from, the hot weather had made outdoors the focus of social life, and as such outside porches reinforced communal life. The slave quarters and the big house of Mulberry Plantation in South Carolina are rare examples of this. Another example of buildings showing roots in Africa is the Haitian *caille*, with its wattle-and-daub construction techniques using natural materials. Their long narrow designs were translated into a form known as "shotgun" house. Shotgun houses can also be found all over the United States, especially in black neighbourhoods. Many of the houses designed during the period of slavery adapted new materials and hybrids from their new social environment, but also exhibited aspects of African belief and philosophy (Visona et al. 2001:501-3).

Artists of African descent have produced many works representing the new culture in the Diaspora. Edmonia Lewis (1843-1909) was the first woman artist of African descent to gain prominence in the United States. She dealt with racial themes and subjects in her work more directly than most nineteenth century artists of African descent. Her sculpture titled 'Hagar' illustrates how she pursues her African themes. This is in reference to the Old Testament Egyptian servant of Sara, Abraham's wife, who was sent away because she showed disrespect towards her master's wife, after she (Hagar) had a son, Ishmael, with Abraham. She links this to the plight of many black women after the collapse of Reconstruction in Southern parts of America, who were still vulnerable to sexual exploitation (Visona et al. 2001: 506). The sculpture also called "Ethiopian Awakening" made by Meta Warrick Fuller (1877-1968), is an allegorical work depicting an African woman emerging from a deep metaphorical, mummified sleep, into a lively animation.

The Brazilian artist, Eneida Assuncao Sanches (born c. 1963), treats African spiritual and cultural revival from a spiritual dimension. He creates works that look like ritual objects. His greatest interest was in earth materials such as metal and stone. His work *orixa Oxossi* is a tribute to a hunting deity associated with the forest. In other ritual contexts such as the Lucumi/Santeria religion, it is possible to hear African religious songs and drum rhythms still being performed. Many Nigerian, Yoruba and Benin deities can be found in renovated forms in the new ritual settings. For example, the Yoruba *egungun* spirit masquerade continues to be depicted as *egun*. Similar colour symbolism of Yoruba attributes of these deities are used in the *Santeria altars* which are elaborate and adorned with drapes, images and offerings of food and drink to the Yoruba gods namely; Shango, Eshu, Obatala, and Yemoja. More interestingly in Cuba and Brazil is the case where people of Yoruba origins in studying Roman Catholic saints, learnt their attributes and worked out a series of parallelisms linking Christian saints to the forces of ancient deities. Thus, the Virgin Mary was equated with the sweet and gentle aspect of the multifaceted goddess of the river *Oshun*. *Eshu-Elegbara* became one of the most important images in Cuba and it became the custom to make small images of *Eshu* to keep. Some sculpture in Cuba were made in clay, and others in stone, given eyes and mouths either by incision or with paint (Thompson 1983: 23). Concrete renditions of Elegba were introduced in the mid-twentieth century and used mainly in the tradition of guarding homes, similar to its use in Dahomey, concealed behind entrance doors. This has been transferred by black Hispanics from the Carribbean to New York and Miami (Thompson 1983:25). The improvisations of the Bakongo complex system of *minkisi* "sacred medicines" and its system of belief is manifested in four major forms of expression, namely cosmograms which mark the ground for the purposes of initiation and mediation of spiritual power between the different worlds; the sacred Kongo medicines; the use of grave dust; and the supernatural uses of trees, staffs, branches and roots (Thompson 1983:108). Thus traditional African art has been transported from the continent and blended into Caribbean culture.

African art is no longer only owned and produced by Africans on the continent, but are in places such as Europe, Latin America and the United States of America. In these places they have been purchased and kept in private homes, museums and art galleries where they are displayed. New variations and interpretations are produced by people of African descent, and as a result of contacts and cultural influence, these new forms expressed in the Diaspora are a mixture of cultures, religions, beliefs and the use of modern industrial goods, tools, materials and techniques. These art works are now considered important works representing the cultural dynamics between people of African descent, Western culture and Christian beliefs.

Conclusion

From this exploration, it can be concluded that African art today is more varied and dynamic than what pertained several years ago when it was primarily functional and involved largely in political, propitiation and religious contexts. The works were made by people who were born, lived and died in the same traditional and cultural settings. They produced works purely within these cultures. The political, economic, religious and social changes and availability of new materials and technology, and pressure to change and address new themes and issues, have been the propellants for change. These have been from two broad sources: internal changes and pressures to create new art forms, and the external influence of Islam, Christianity and Western education.

The willingness and ability of artists to adapt new themes and technology into their art, while in many instances drawing inspiration from tradition, is an affirmation of the resilience of African culture. Works produced by Africans in the Diaspora, and new syncretic religions such as the *Santeria* and its elaborate art and colour symbolism based on Kuba and Yoruba traditions all support the argument of the deep seatedness of African belief in the supernatural, expressed visually through art. African art is therefore no longer solely the traditional art that has often characterised the genre of the subject, but includes modern forms as well. The African artist lives in a contemporary world and art works also reflect that. The persistence of African traditional forms in both traditional and contemporary art works, in spite of strong condemnation of African art and pressures to abandon it during the period of colonisation, is remarkable, to say the least, but continues to flourish as part of Africa's socio-economic, historical and political development.

Review Questions

1. Discuss briefly whether you agree or not with the assertion that African Art has no history?

2. From your reading, justify your opinion on the future of African Art.

3. Discuss the statement that African art is not static but dynamic.

4. Is there any evidence of influence of African art on the art of the people of African origin in the Diaspora? Cite specific examples to support your argument.

5. Are African artists stuck in traditions or not? Cite both historical and contemporary examples to support your argument.

References

Blier, S. P., 1998 *The Royal Arts of Africa: The Majesty of Form*. New York: Harry N. Abrams.

Brown, D. H. 1993 "Thrones of the Orichas", *African Arts*. Vol. XXVI. No. 4: 44-59.

Gillon, W. 1984 *A Short History of African Art*. London: Penguin Books.

Hackett, R. I. J., 1994. *Art and Religion in Africa*. London: Cassell.

Herbert, E. W. 1984. *Red Gold of Africa: Copper in Precolonial History and Culture*. Wisconsin and London: The University of Wisconsin Press.

Kasfir, S. L., 1999. *Contemporary African Art*. London: Thames and Hudson Labi, K. A. 2002

Labi K. A. 2002. "Fante Asafo flags of Abandze and Kormantse: a discourse between rivals." African Arts. Vol. XXXV, No. 4, pp. 28-37. (Winter)

Okediji, M. 1992 "Algebra of Picton's Complex," in *Principles of Traditional African Culture*. (ed. Okediji)Ibadan: Bard Books 108-26.

Perani, J. and Smith, F. T. 1998 *The Visual Arts of Africa: Gender, Power, and Life Cycle Rituals*. New Jersey: Prentice Hall.

Picton, J. and Mack, J. 1979 *African Textiles*. London: British Museum Publications Ltd.

Thompson, R. F. 1995 "The Face of the Gods." *African Arts*. Vol. 28, No. 1. pp. 50-61.

Vogel, S., 1991 Africa Explores: *20th Century African Art*. New York: The Center for African Art.

Visona, M. B., Poynor, R., Cole H. M. and Harris, M. D., 2001 *A History of Art in Africa*. London: Thames and Hudson.

Willet, F. 1997 *African Art*. London: Thames and Hudson.

Endnote

1.   For details of the blackening ceremony, see Kyerematen, A. A. Y. 1964, *Panoply of Ghana: Ornamental Art in Ghanaian Tradition and Culture*, New York: F. A. Praeger, pp. 15-21; Sarpong P. A. 1971, *The Sacred Stools of the Akan*. Tema: Ghana Publishing Corporation, pp. 36-59; and Labi, Kwame A. 1993 "The Theory and Practice of Conservation among the Akan of Ghana." ICOM-CC 10th Triennial Meeting, ICOM, Washington DC, Paris, Vol. 2 pp. 371-376. Gilbert gives specific details on the blackening process in Akropong in Gilbert, "Sources of Power in Akuropong-Akuapem; Ambiguity in Classification" in W. Arens and I. Karp (eds.), *Creativity of Power; Cosmology and Action in African Societies*. Washington and London: Smithsonian Institution Press, pp. 59-90.

CHAPTER 19

DANCE SYMBOLISM IN AFRICA
F. Nii-Yartey

There is hardly any community in Africa in which a ritual or ceremony of some kind does not take place. But as noted by Turner (1996),

> ... Each type of ritual has its own special drum rhythm, its own "theme song", its own combination of medicines, and its own stylized behaviour, expressed in dancing and gestures and its own type of shrine and ritual apparatus ..."

The details of such ceremonies, whether it is a celebration of birth, initiation into the many areas of societal responsibilities, or honouring the dead, most often entail the establishment of new patterns of social relationships and artistic expression among the communities and people involved. For example, in many African communities, traditional stools are considered as sacred symbols of the presence of the ancestors and both the source and the power of politico-ritual office. Among the Lega of the Central Africa the significance of such stools is projected in dance movements and other dance related actions as the primary vehicle of interpretation. Biebuyck (1977) states:

> When the dancer (preceptor) sits on the stool and waves both hands alternately in the air in a gesture of receiving and thankful joy, it is interpreted as, the performer having achieved a high rank of *Yananio*, (and he) will continue to be accorded all privileges due him in accordance with his new position. On the other hand, if the dancer stretches both arms and legs as far as possible from the stool, he will be considered as an excessive and arrogant person.

Another example of the role dance plays on a rather complex and elaborate scale is within the context of traditional festivals. The *Adae* festival of the Asante of Ghana exemplifies this role within the sequence of events that unfolds during the period of the festival. Dance performances of all types, including recreational dances such as *Sanga, Saaboaa, Sikyi,* and others help to create a festive atmosphere during festivities. On the other hand, more solemn dances like the *Akom* and *Apae* religious dances provide opportunities for public worship and collective prayers that serve to assure believers of the divine presence at the festival (Figure 23).

The dance takes on a different dimension when the king as the political and military head, as well as the spiritual leader and the benevolent father of his people, steps down from his dais to re-affirm this role through dance.

Figure 28 – Akom Dance

Source: *Author Photo*

"… He is offered a sword by an attendant. He grabs the hilt, slowly pulls the sword out of its scabbard, and then brings it to the salute with a swift jerk. With an imperious gesture, he receives a gun and tucks the butt under his left arm-pit. He raises the sword in a salute and prayer, [to God the Almighty] then bends down to touch Earth Mother with the sword. He extends his prayer and salutations to the elements with his sword and gun, arms outstretched. He moves his arms in an embracing gesture, finishing with the gun and sword crossed on his chest He runs anticlockwise in crouched position, in three circles. Glancing to his left and to his right, he pauses. He steps slowly and deliberately to single stressed beats from the drums. His pace increases. He swoops this way and turns that way, catching one imaginary enemy after the other and beheading them. He surveys the fields; there is no foe in sight. Hailed by drums, trumpets, and voices he proudly walks to his dais…" (Mawere Opoku, 1987: 199).

Dance symbolism is not homogeneous but rather, each ethnic group and sometimes, each community, may develop its own peculiar movements, gestures, bodily attitudes and characteristics which may be understood only by members of that particular group of people, as each of these peculiarities reflects the common historical, religious and kinship experiences of the particular community. They represent as it were, a vocabulary of common language, activities and relationships, typifying the world view of those members of the community who are committed to the development and sustenance of their common heritage (see also Ch. 7). Ajayi (1998: 30-31) observes that, "… dance as a cultural indicator, is the tangible element able to turn cultural concepts into perceptible forms narrated in rhythmic movements and contextualized in space…" Therefore, it is in the dance that one sees the music, feels the powerful presence of the Yoruba *Shango* thunder and lightning deity, with its characteristic destructive fury of movement. Likewise as Doople

(1992: 29) notes, dance helps to discern each precise and harmonious gesture made by initiates in the *Beo* dances of Côte d'Ivoire, as they are symbolically led to 'communicate' with God.

In many African societies, verbal communication is considered necessary for the establishment of facts and ideas, but the knowledge and use of symbols, gestures and bodily actions goes beyond words and is deemed crucial and pertinent to the attainment of the proper level of communication for the avoidance of misunderstanding and misinterpretations, especially with regard to public utterances and other forms of communication (see also Ch. 15). For example, among many Ghanaian communities, the use of the left hand in gesticulating or emphasising a point while speaking to other people, particularly, the elderly and social superiors, is considered uncivilised, disrespectful and unbecoming, therefore, unacceptable and frowned upon. Similarly, Ajayi (op. cit.) observes that:

> "... Among the Yoruba of Nigeria, as in many parts of Africa the average person is expected to be highly perceptive of and sensitive to body signals as not every piece of information will be fully and explicitly spelled out verbally and a substantial part of every message is made up of body-coded signals ..."

Gesture as an element of symbolism is an action-oriented human phenomenon. It is considered as an important component of dance in many African communities. There are at least three major gestures discernible in African dance forms:

Random Gesture: These are the gestures we make at random to emphasize or illustrate a point when we speak.

Mimicking Gesture: These refer to gestures mimicking specific actions and objects with the aim of creating a visual image of those objects and actions (Figure 29). An example of this is the *Eseni Egbo* dance of Nigeria in which female dancers hold one hand with the palm turn towards the face, while the other hand dabs the face to mimic polishing up the face. Another example is the Somali "Camel" dance in which the successive dancers leap and dart, springing the neck in long successive rhythmic waves resembling a trekking camel.

Figure 29 – Mimicking Movement in the *Adevu* Dance, Ghana

Source: *Author Photo*

Symbolic Gesture: This type of gesture is more abstract in its manifestation. It is perhaps the highest form of gesture in African dance symbolism. It serves as a substitute and back-up action tool for human communication through the art of dance.

In daily activities of communities, the movement aspects of customary behaviour such as hunting, fishing, gathering and pounding of grains, different forms of greetings and other activities, invariably contribute as resources for the various dance forms. These movements in time are codified and become part of the vocabulary of non-verbal communication of the people. Thus, the body response of a woman in the village pounding millet or yam, using a mortar and pestle, may be generating potential movements for a dance. As well, the movements involved in traditional farming with the hoe, the various forms of traditional African greetings for instance, when consciously organised with the proper timing, the right movement dynamics, body levels, and the proper use of space and the application of other elements of dance, are all resources for the dance.

Dance is an indispensable element in many important rituals and ceremonies in Africa. It serves as a vehicle through which the symbolism and other coded messages are manifested. Nketia (1965) observes thus:

> "...Through the dance, individuals and social groups can show their reactions to attitudes of hostility or co-operation held by others towards them. They may show deference to their superiors, gratitude to benefactors, their own estimation of themselves in the presence of rivals, servants, subjects and others, through the choice of appropriate symbolic gestures..."

Below are some basic Akan gestures, which may be found in other areas of Southern Ghana, especially those that have been influenced by the Akan (Figure 30):

1. The chin resting on the palm of the right hand symbolises:- *"Is this really true"? or am I dreaming"?* This is a gesture often used by bereaved families.

2. The fore-finger is placed on the right cheek, touching the space below the eye, says: - *"Look at what has befallen me."*

3. To knock on the chest with a fist expresses:: - *"I am the greatest"*. This gesture is usually performed by people with high social standing

4. The fist of one hand, placed on top of the other, says: *"Superior among superiors."*

5. Locking the right foot from the inside of the left leg denotes that:- *"I have immobilised you"*

6. The right palm on top of the left fist means: - *"I have got you in a corked bottle, or I have immobilised you.*

7. A crossed middle and fore finger says: - *"We are one".*

8. The elbows of two people touching is a sign of brotherhood or friendship

9. Both hands under the breasts, usually performed by women at the funeral of a husband, conveys: *"Who will feed me and the children in your absence"?*

10. Folded arms across the chest denotes: *"I am all alone".*

11. To hook the ring fingers of both hands means: *"We are linked together as in a chain."*

Figure 30 – Gestures in Akan Dance

Source: *Author Photos*

The human body is the principal tool and symbol of dance. According to Turner (op. cit.), in many African communities, the body is conceived:

> "... as a microcosm of the universe...Whatever the mode of representation, the body is regarded as a sort of symbolic template for the communication of ... mystical knowledge about the nature of things and how they came to be what they are..."

The concept of beauty of form and proper body carriage is therefore, essentially derived from the natural contours of the human body. This is largely conceptualised and symbolised in circular images– curves, spiral and conical shapes etc. For example, the accepted body stance in most African dance forms is that the knees must be slightly relaxed, the trunk of the body rounded or concaved, and the feet well planted into the ground, to give a 'circular' image and 'completeness of being.' From this position, the dancer is enabled to leap, turn and creatively explore the possibilities of movement in relation to the particular dance he or she is performing. Allied to body stance, positions and the symbolic use of space, is the employment of symbolic gestures in the dance as a way of communicating specific thoughts and messages to people (Figure 31).

Figure 31 – Body Posture

Source- *Author Photo*

For example, in the *Revival* religious dance of Jamaica, worshippers in the course of their *worship-dance* hold out their arms to the sides as they fast turn to "receive the 'spirit.'" In the *Kumina* dance of the same people, the right and left hands are held in front and back respectively. When the dancer fast-turns from this position, in clock-wise, and then anti-clock-wise directions, with a 'grabbing' gesture of both hands at the end of each turn, s/he is 'catching' the good spirits (Nettleford 1985).

As has been discussed here, the meaning and functionality of many African dance forms are most often hidden in the context of their performance. To understand and appreciate the dance therefore, one must discern the symbolism of the occasion, the gestures, costumes and their colours, the lyrics of the accompanying songs, the drum patterns and of course, the dramatic experience of the occasion. The *Adowa* dance of the Akan of Ghana for example, may be performed under different contexts. It may be performed at a wedding ceremony of a member, while on another occasion the performance may be at a funeral of a non-member. In each case, the gestures and dynamics employed in the dance, the text of the drum language and the accompanying songs and other details, may differ in some respects.

A good dancer is the one who understands the symbolism and the use of space to communicate to his or her audience. The dancer takes a series of calculated steps along the fringes of the performance area as a way of introducing him or herself and, as it were, symbolically unifying the gathering for a successful performance. This is followed by a careful combination of selected steps from the dance vocabulary at various points on the floor, before going into the complexities and details of the dance, thereby giving meaning to the occasion. Definite prescriptions and proscriptions are made concerning the practice and appreciation of dance as a non-verbal and expressive communication apparatus in many African communities. These include particular modes of sitting, body carriage and attitude, how time and space are utilised, the application of movement dynamics, occasion for performance and even, the sequence of events and the interrelationship between sound and movement. These are commonly structured, observed, shared and understood by most members of the community. The physical arrangement of people within their environment in relation to the various activities may be symbolic of the world view of the community.

During a typical traditional dance performance, the spectators, who are usually active, almost always organise themselves in semi-circular, oblong or sometimes circular formations. For instance, among the Dogon of Mali, the ideal layout of some villages was often said to be entirely symbolic. The Dogon base their philosophy, as noted by Denyer (1978:20) :

> "... On the idea of germinating cells vibrating along a spirit path to break out of a "world egg." "The emphasis on circular images does not however, preclude the use of linear forms or medium other than dance in other situations. In the "Kanaga" spectacular mask dance of the same people, the dancers wear masks on top of which are affixed vertical pieces of wood with cross-bars, one at the top and the other at the bottom of each mask symbolizes an archway which reached the earth in the form of a woman and brought the various seeds that enabled man to live on earth...."

These circular concepts represented here metaphorically by seeds, cells and sometimes snail shells and other circular images, illustrate the basic African concept of re-incarnation or "recycling" of the human spirit and personality (Figure 32). Therefore, when Africans gather to dance or celebrate most life events, the circle remains central to many activities, as captured in the following prayer by the Ga people of Southern Ghana:

> *Wo bole **kutu** wokpe*
> *Wo yenu wonu*
> *Wo kodziano adzowo*
> *Wo see tuu*
> *Wo hie fann*

Literally translated, the prayer means:

> *When we gather in a **circle** to dig a well*
> *May we find water!*
> *When we drink this water*
> *May it profoundly refresh us!*
> *May the past remain in darkness!*
> *May the future be clear!*

419

Figure 32 – Circular Buildings, Northern Ghana

Source: *Author Photo*

The use of properties such as swords, handkerchiefs, costumes and make-up, including preference for certain colours for particular occasions, are all symbolic, to facilitate their effective use in the dance. In many African societies, red, black and other dark colours are used in dances connected with funerals, wars and other situations with grave import for society. In the *Agbekor* dances of the Ewe of the southern part of Ghana and Togo for example, dancers usually wear costumes made of shades of red material to indicate the seriousness of war and the experiences of hardships encountered by their ancestors in the many battles they fought in search of a peaceful place to settle.

On a happy occasion, the predominant colours will be white and other lighter colours. Therefore, the manner in which costumes are worn, the significance of their colours and designs, especially in relation to dance, has its own silent language and symbolism. Among many of the ethnic groups in southern Burkina Faso and in northern Ghana, men for example show their attitude towards particular individuals or society as a whole, in the manner in which they sometimes wear their hats. Among the Kusasi people of Northern Ghana, the way in which one wears one's hat is an indication of what the wearer thinks about himself and about other people (Figure 33):

a. If the hat is worn with the top part falling towards the forehead of the wearer, this is meant to denote the person's *"progressiveness."*

b If the hat falls back, it means: *"All evil thoughts by my enemies will fly over my head."*

c. If it is worn on the left side it indicates that: *"I shall get to know all things said and done on my left side."*

d. If worn on the right, the wearer is saying: *"I shall know everything done on my right side."*

e. If however, the hat is worn upright, the wearer is saying: *"I am carrying everything on my head; - I have a lot of responsibility and power"*

Figure 33 – Ways with Hats among the Kusasi, Ghana

Source: *Author Photos*

The choice of appropriate costumes for the dance is similarly very important to the African. Apart from identifying and establishing the identity of individual positions and the significance of particular occasions in the society, perhaps one of the most important messages dance costumes convey is what may be referred to as "Loco-aesthetic symbolism." Loco-aesthetic symbolism is the phenomenon in which the costume worn by the dancer is designed in such a manner that it dictates or suggests the flow and direction of movement as it is activated by the dancer in the course of the performance. Thus in the *Damba/Takai* dance of the Dagomba people of Northern Ghana and some ethnic groups in Nigeria, large smocks are worn by the dancers over loose pantaloons (Figure 34) . This is essential to the significance and meaning of that dance. As the dancer spin-turns, his action twirls the smock into an umbrella shape, circumscribing the direction of the torso swings of this princely and dignified dance form.

Figure 34 – Damba/Takai Dance, Northern Ghana

Source: *Author Photo*

In several African communities, as in the New World, dance continues to give meaning to the events of life and experiences of the people through the metaphoric enactments of its elements in these events, from the *Kpodziemo* or naming ceremonies of the Ga, and the *Bragoro initiation* ceremony for girls of the Akan of Ghana, to the occupational *Makera* dance for blacksmiths performed by the Hausa of northern Nigeria. In the *Matakan* dances of the Cameroon for example, the dancers pay homage to mother Earth and the ancestral spirits by stamping hard on the ground as they carry pruning hooks to symbolise renewed fertility of the soil and future abundant crops. Similarly, in the dances of the Sara of Chad, young men and women show their temperament and physical beauty by stamping. During initiation ceremony for boys of the same people, a 'rite of death' is performed [through dance] to symbolise rebirth of the initiates as complete men. "...The initiation includes tests of endurance and courage and the teaching of a secret language..." (Huet and Savary, 1995).

The Interrelationship of Dance and the Other Arts

In a Ghanaian performance context, it is often said that "when the music stops the dance also stops." This emphasises the interdependency of the arts and artists as a group activity in Africa. This is also true in other areas of artistic expression. For example, there is a strong relationship between art and oral literature, symbolizing the artistic use of proverbs, historical accounts, stories and situations to aid the memory of the dancer and other artists in their creative pursuits (see also Chapter 17, this volume). Costumes are designed in ways that will emphasize direction of the movement of the dance as in the *Takai* dance referred to above.

In certain dance forms, the integration of the arts is much more pronounced than others. For example, in the *Dipo* puberty dance of the Ga-Dangbe people of Southern Ghana in which girls cross the threshold into adulthood, the dancer's body is decorated with a green and yellow substance, called *"Krobo"* Garlands of beads adorn the girl's waist and neck, and these are wrapped in colourful cloth around the waist and neck as part of the costuming for the dance. (Figure 35).

Figure 35 – DIPO DANCE, Ghana

Source:: *Bell Archive, Accra.*

Instrumental music, song and poetry are rendered and interpreted by the initiates in accordance with the requirements of the ceremony at various stages of the ceremony. Also in the *Giriama* dance for young girls in parts of Kenya, the dancers use make-up and wear costumes to help portray the girls as the very incarnate of womanhood. Even though each of the traditional art forms may stand on its own through its own unique characteristics and modes of expression, it is their combined characteristics and aesthetic impact on performers and audiences alike as well as the creative processes that are required for a meaningful and successful traditional dance event.

In the contemporary period, musical pageants are held in the various African countries to deliver messages of peace and reconciliation to the general public, particularly the youth. This is channeled through the lyrics of the songs and catchy rhythms as was done recently in Ghana dubbed, "Peace Concert", to address an ethnic conflict among some communities in the Northern Region. This programme was organised by the Musicians' Union of Ghana. And in South Africa, similar events have been held in a bid to address the HIV and AIDS menace. Other media have been used to dramatise tragedies and national disasters. Thus an artist captured in sculpture the disaster that occurred at the Accra Sports Stadium in May 2001, in which more than 100 people died. Symbolised in an image showing a man carrying a victim of the disaster across his shoulders, this piece of art serves as a reminder to the public, including policy makers, of this sad event and the care that must be taken to prevent such future occurrences.

Theatre and the visual arts have also become dependable tools for economic and business ventures through advertisements on television, billboards and book illustrations. In effect, the arts today are reclaiming their role as tools for development in African communities. They continue to foster creativity and deep thinking, provide a basis for perseverance and discipline in the society, as well as cataloguing influences and events and their effects on the community.

The transcultural impact of African dance on the New World as a result of slavery points to the spiritual and social importance Africans and peoples of African descent attach to dance. This did not escape the destructive policies of the architects of slavery and colonization, including Christianity and Islam. Both religions realized the potential of cultural activities generally as a unifying force for Africans, both on the Continent and in the Diaspora. Furthermore, dance and other cultural activities were characterised as barbaric and uncultured, and colonizers actively sought to discourage the population, especially those who had converted to Christianity, as well as slaves generally, from participating in them, through subtle, and sometimes, forced segregation on linguistic and other cultural grounds. The African however, prevailed and managed to maintain his identity, both on the continent and in the Diaspora. Particularly in the Diaspora, the use of coded messages and other symbolism, such as gestures, drum rhythms or even a piece of wood, helped to provide the needed communication among the slaves.

Significant among the retention of the African spiritual and cultural heritage in the New World are the *Vodun* and *Shango* traditions from Benin and Nigeria respectively (Figure 36). In Haiti and New Orleans, *Vodun* ceremonies like *Shango* are marked by*"...intense physical [dance], emotional and spiritual outpouring which enable the worshippers to establish contact with the ancestors and a higher being..."* (Snipe 1998). [1]

Figure 36 – Shango Devotee

Source: *http://www.blingcheese.com/graphics/15/shango.htm*

The vitality and nature of *Vodun* finds expression in the *Gbehun* version of the dance which is characterised by the dancers whirling around in rapid succession. The secret formula and techniques for achieving possession and other objectives of *Vodun* are symbolized and kept only within the community of the initiated. Similarly, *Ananse* (the spider) stories which originated from West Africa as an educational tool and a form of entertainment, were taken by captured slaves leaving from Kromantsin in what is now the Central Region of Ghana, to Jamaica. These stories contain moral and witty offerings in which the 'cunning' spider is often disgraced for one 'smart' deed or the other. As has been mentioned in Chapter 17 of this volume, storytelling is a highly interactive artistic event which also includes music and dance.

Valorizing the Arts

It is clear at this point that dance and the other art forms constitute the fundamental experience of life to many Africans and peoples of African descent, through their many facets and well-articulated structures, based on verbal and nonverbal systems of interaction. This enabled our forebears to survive over the centuries. These structures were however derailed during the period of slavery and colonisation which deprived Africa and her severed children across the globe the continuity and appreciation of these essential structures. However, as observed by Nketia (1996), emancipation from slavery and the attainment of independence from colonial rule saw the restoration of

> "...The freedom to drum, sing, and dance in the traditional way in contempo-
> rary contexts... a symbolic affirmation of the declaration of independence while
> the re-conceptualization of the arts as national arts enabled them to be used in
> fostering national consciousness..."

The integrative essence of dance and other artistic and cultural forms helped to underline and maintain institutional frameworks at the national level. This was achieved through the establishment of a number of cultural institutions to promote and develop these art forms together with the ideas and ideals, social relationships, and behaviour of the new and free independent states in Africa and in the Diaspora. Ministries of Culture became part of the political and administrative structures of governments in Africa. Additionally, various institutions were set up as implementing agents.

In Ghana, the Institute of African Studies was established within the academic confines of the University of Ghana at Legon, to research into the arts and culture of Africa and the Diaspora in both theory and practice. In pursuance of this mandate, the Ghana Dance Ensemble and the School of Music, Dance and Drama (now the School of Performing Arts) were set up under the Institute, to give expression to the practical and teaching aspects of the Institute's artistic work. At the national level, another body, the Institute of Arts and Culture, was set up in 1961, outside the academic environment, to advise government on policy matters concerning the arts and culture in Ghana and Africa in general.

In many countries in Africa, particularly in the West African sub- region, where the cultural movement for the liberation of Africa was utilised prominently, particularly in the 1960s, the *Ghana Dance Ensemble*, *Les Ballets Africaines* of the Republic of Guinea and the Senegalese National Ballet, among other institutions, were established. They brought traditional dance forms on to the conventional stage with various levels of modification and additions, to express not only the re-emergence and revival of the 'African personality' and traditions in many parts of the world and within Africa itself, but also to symbolise and celebrate the new freedom and experiences of the people.

Figure 37 – Images of Conflict

Source- *Author photo*

Figure 38 – *Gula Matari*

Source: *Author Photo*

As a result, national arts and culture festivals were instituted in most African countries, especially those with a significant African Diaspora community, to showcase the achievements and the diversity and unity of the people, through interactions and the sharing of ideas and common participation in these events. Efforts were also made to organise inter-continental African and Diaspora festivals of arts and culture. Notable among them were the Pan African Cultural Festival held in Dakar, Senegal in 1966; FESTAC, held in a Lagos, Nigeria in 1977; the Algiers Festival of Arts held in Algiers in 1972, and most recently, PANAFEST, which has been occurring in Cape Coast and Accra in Ghana, at various levels of success since 1994. All these festivals in which dance featured prominently, were held to ensure the revival and the promotion of the cultural values of the peoples of Africa. It was also to create the platform for artists and cultural agents from diverse backgrounds within the African family to meet and exchange ideas and other objectives. In Jamaica for instance, the Institute of Jamaica, originally a colonial institution, brought together the Jamaican Schools of Dance, Art and Music, as well as Theatre, under the canopy of a Cultural Training Centre, with the support of the National Dance Theatre

Company of Jamaica. These institutions and certain individuals within the Jamaican society creatively combined the available artistic and cultural resources of the past and the present, to articulate the pride, pain and passion of the Jamaican people from the cultures of the complex configuration of descendants of Arawak Indians, Spanish, English, Ghanaians and others (Nettleford 1985).

Dance – beyond Tradition

The language of traditional African dance has changed and continues to change as new movements, vocabulary and themes emerge as a result of globalisation and easy access to information technology. The increasing exposure to various art forms both from within the continent and outside by African artists through formal education and other educational systems, have helped to create a climate of interesting innovations in African artistic milieu, and dance is not an exception.

Through the works of pioneers like Mawere Opoku from Ghana, Frankis Camara from Guinea, and a host of other dance practitioners, African dance is acquiring a new vocabulary to articulate these new experiences and impulses of our globalized world. In Guinea, Ghana, Mali and Senegal especially, traditional dances were given a new lease of life on the conventional stage where, creating within the traditional forms, dance innovators managed to make traditional African dance accessible to audiences beyond ethnic and regional boundaries. For example, given that traditional performances often last several hours, and may even stretch into days, they were shortened and dancers redirected spatially on stage. New movement dynamics were introduced to compensate for the gap created between performers and the audience on the proscenium stage. This of course negates one of the most important elements in a contextual dance performance, where spectators are also performers. In Ghana, where one of the first formal dance training schools in Africa was established, these new innovations were encouraged.

The Ghanaian choreographer, Mawere Opoku's *Lamentation for freedom fighters*, was one of the first artistic creations to challenge the sensibilities of traditionalists in Africa. This dance production won the acclaim of dance critics at the *1ˢᵗ Black African Arts Festival* in Dakar, Senegal in 1966. Dance theatre has established itself firmly as a performance genre with proponents who have attained international acclaim.[2]

Africans are being confronted almost on a daily basis, with new challenges and value systems brought about by globalisation with its aggressive market economy and the fast growing communication technology. A significant engagement with these influences is a new form of dance expression on the continent known among its practitioners as 'Contemporary African Dance', for lack of a better term. The language and symbols of this dance form is universal in approach, but draws its inspiration from the African experience and cultural values.

Contemporary African Dance negotiates between the older African culture and the impulses of the current generation. In the forefront of this dance phenomenon are *Ori Dance Company of* Benin, *Compagnie Salia n Seydou* of Burkina Faso, *Tche-Tche* of Côte d' Ivoire, *Noyam* of Ghana, *Company Gaara* of Kenya, *Ijodee* of Nigeria, *Moving Into Dance* of South Africa (Figure 38), *Compagnie Motra* of Togo and *Tambuka* of Zimbabwe. Artistes from Mali, Madagascar, Senegal, and Mozambique, among others, are also engaged in contemporary African dance.

Review Questions

1. What are the four integrated areas of artistic expression in African Dance performance?

2. Discuss manifestations of dance symbolism in the African Diaspora.

3. Give one example of the under listed gestures from your own research:

    a) Random gesture

    b) Mimicking gesture

    c) Symbolic gesture

4. 'The human body is the principal tool for dance.' Discuss.

5. What impact did Christianity, Islam and colonization have on African dance? Give a critical appraisal of the situation.

6. In Ghanaian dance practice, it is often said that when 'the music stops, the dance is over.' What is the significance of this statement? Discuss.

Acknowledgments:

Sketches by David Akushe Amoo
Photographs/ Choreography:
*Images of Conflict: F. Nii-*Yartey (© F. Nii-Yartey/Germaine Acogny)
Gula Matari: Moving into Dance (©Vincent Sekwati Montsoi)

References

Ajayi, O. S. 1998. *Yoruba Dance,- The Semiotics of Movement and Body Attitude in Nigeria Culture.* Trenton, New Jersey: Africa World Press Inc.

Biebuyck, D. P. 1977. *Symbolism of the Lega Stool* Working papers in traditional Arts. Philadelphia: Institute for the Study of Human Issues. 1977, pp. 9 – 26

Denyer, S., 1978. *African Traditional Architecture.* London: Heinemann Books.

Doople, T. A. 1992. *The Eternal Law of African Dance.* Reading, Great Britain: Harwood Academic Publishers.

Huet, M. and C. Savary. 1995. *African Dances.* London: Thames and Hudson Ltd.

Nettleford, R. 1985. *DANCE JAMAICA Cultural Definition and Artistic Discovery, the National Dance Theatre Company of Jamaica, 1962–1983.* New York: Grove Press, Inc.

Nketia, J.H.K. 1965. *Ghana, Music, Dance and Drama – a review of the Performing Arts of Ghana.* Accra: Ghana Publishing Corporation.

Nketia, J. H. K.. 1996 "National Development and the Performing Arts of Africa" In Philip G. Altbach and Salah M. Hassan, eds. *The Muse of Modernity: Essays on Culture as Development in Africa.* Trenton, NJ: Africa World Press.

Opoku, A. M. 1987. "Asante Dance Art and the Court" In E. Schildkrout(Ed.), *The Golden Stool: Studies of Asante Center and Periphery* Anthropological Papers of the American Museum of Natural History. Vol. 65: Part 1. New York 199.

Snipe, T. D. "African Dance: Bridges to Humanity", In K. Welsh Asante, Ed. . *African Dance: An Artistic, Historical and Philosophical Enquiry*. Trenton, NJ.: African World Press Inc.

Turner, V. 1996. *The Forest of Symbols, an aspect of Ndembu Ritua*. Ithaca, New York: Cornell University Press

Recommended Reading

Ranger, T. O. (1975) *Dance and Society in Eastern African 1890-1970, the Beni Ngoma*. London: Heinemann

Endnote

1.. Ofotsu Adinku, also a former student of Mawere-Opoku, created the "Orphan","Eternal Idol" and the "Palm Wine Drunkard" for students of the Dance Department at the University of Ghana in Accra. Nii-Yartey, former Artistic Director of the Ghana Dance Ensemble, in addition to individual productions, co-choreographed pieces with artistes of international repute. These include Jean Francois Duroure, Monty Thompson, Germaine Acogny and Nanna Nielson, with whom he developed *Solma, Musu-Saga of the Slaves, Images of Conflict* (Figure 37) and *Children of Faith respectively.*

CHAPTER 20

MUSIC IN AFRICAN COMMUNITIES
Alexander A. Agordoh

Introduction

Music is an integral part of African communal life from the cradle to the grave and covers the widest possible range of expressions, including spoken language and all manner of natural sounds. Music is used for recreational activities, the performance of rites, ceremonies or festivals, as well as collective work such as the building of bridges, clearing paths, a search party, or fire-fighting activities that in industrialised societies might be assigned to specialised agencies. While much of this chapter will capture essential elements of the indigenous musical traditions as manifested in the more rural settings in which most African societies are situated, it does not lose sight of the rapidly developing urban culture and the part played by the musical heritage in this evolution. Attention must be drawn to Chapter 21 of this volume in which an elaborate expose is provided on how Africans have both influenced world music and appropriated external musical influences to create an immensely important popular music culture. Towards the end of this chapter, a brief allusion will be made to this vibrant contemporary phenomenon.

In several communities, the persons who come together in communal activities generally belong to the same ethnic group. The basis for association for music making may also be a community, that is those who share common habits (such as a group of homesteads, a village, a town or a section of a town) and who live some kind of corporate life based on common institutions, local traditions, beliefs and values. Types of music, both local and instrumental, performed by such communities may be connected with life cycle events, domestic and economic activities, traditional political institutions and religious events

Events in the life of an individual such as birth, puberty, marriage and death are generally marked with particular types of music in Africa. There are hundreds of ethnic groups that constitute the continent of Africa and each has her own way of making music. For example, among the Yoruba and the Hausa of Nigeria, traditional recreational music is made to mark the naming ceremony of a newly born baby. The Bemba of Zambia sing appropriate songs to welcome newly born babies and to mark the birth of twins. But there are other societies in Africa which do not consider the naming ceremony as a musical event. For example in Ghana, it is only the Dagomba ethnic group that employs music in their naming ceremony.

Music can also be performed by children as part of their transition to adulthood. For example according to Herskovits (1967), among the Fon of Benin Republic, a child who loses his first tooth has to sing a special song to commemorate the event. Nketia (1975) also reports that among the Akan and Ewe of Ghana, children form a group to sing a special ritual song of insults for regular bed-wetters. Circumcision and puberty are other important life-cycle events in which music is performed in Africa. Male circumcision candidates in Senegal and the Gambia are taught special songs in the evening while they are at the camp waiting for their wounds to heal. In Ghana, the *Dipo* puberty rites of girls among the Krobo, the *Bragoro* of the Akan and the *Gbotowowo* of the Ewes, all incorporate music. In Central and Eastern Africa, especially in the Samba areas of Tanzania, special songs are sung before circumcision, after circumcision, while the wound is healing, and when the wound has healed and the candidate is returning home.

According to Bebey (1975), during the graduation ceremonies of the *Adinkru* of Côte d'Ivoire called *lohu*, music is performed to mark the graduation of the youth from one age group to another. Among the Dagaaba of North-Western Ghana, the first visit of the bridegroom to the house of his bride is marked by chanted dialogue between his party and his brothers-in-law. The Dagomba of Ghana, the Yoruba and Hausa of Nigeria, are examples of societies in Africa that celebrate their marriage with music making (Nketia, 1975; Smith, 1959).

Among many societies, the celebration of funerals with music is regarded as a duty, and no pains are spared to make them memorable events. Among the Akan of Ghana, funeral dirges are sung in pulsating tones to honour the dead, ancestors, or some other person whose loss the mourner is reminded of. In societies like the Akan and Ewe of Ghana and the Urhobo of eastern Nigeria, the performance of funeral dirges is the sole responsibility of women. Memorial occasions are marked by drumming, dancing, singing, serving of drinks, and giving of gifts of money to the bereaved family. Funeral songs are sung to honour the dead, to mourn them and to cherish their names. They are also sung to comfort the bereaved. The Bemba of Central Africa have songs that they sing on returning from burials and songs for "the renewal of the village fire," extinguished immediately after the burial. The performance of these mourning songs is usually distinguished by their characteristic singing style as well as by the text and body movements that accompany the singing.

Domestic and Economic Activities

There are work songs that do not only deal with labour, but accompany rhythmic work by groups, thus making physical coordination easier. Some societies make provision for a variety of domestic songs, or encourage the use of songs as an accompaniment to domestic activities. For example, grinding songs, pounding songs, and songs sung when the floor of a newly built house is being made, have been noted in many parts of Africa (see also Chapter 17, this volume). In economic life, songs function as an aid to co-operative labour. For example among the coastal peoples, canoe paddling and the hauling up of fishing nets is often accompanied with music as a background rhythm.

Smith (1959) and Nzewi (2009) confirm that among the Hausa of Northern Nigeria music is interwoven into the fabric of social life, ranging from corn grinding songs of women, to the trumpets and horns of the royal family. Illustrative of the complexity of Hausa society is the degree of specialisation among professional musicians known as *Maroka*. The court musicians take the top position, followed by those attached to occupational groups like butchers, blacksmiths, hunters and farmers, and occupying the lowest rung are freelance musicians. The Hausa traditionally believe that work songs lessen drudgery and serve to heighten productivity, by rhythmically co-ordinating and maintaining the tempo of the work, like the grinding of grain or the cutting of meat.

Chapter 20

Music and Politics

One of the most important sets of musical types in African societies, especially, in those with centralised political systems, is music relating to political organisations, such as music of the courts and state festivals. In Africa, one cannot talk about the traditional political system without acknowledging the role music plays in it. Music therefore occupies a very important place at the courts of African kings. Musical instruments are also symbols of the high political status of African kings. For example, among some societies in Africa (with the exception of heads of small villages), every important chief or king has special music played for him on state occasions. Much of this is provided by drums, which are kept in the palace as part of the royal regalia. In some societies in West Africa, it is a moral obligation for the king to see to it that these instruments are well protected. Furthermore, many drums and drum ensembles of kings could not be owned or played without the permission of the king, or could not be played any time other than that laid down by custom. If the king's musical instrument is misused, it is believed the dignity of the dances and the language associated with it are lowered and the prestige of the kingship consequently reduced. For example, among the Akan of Ghana, political hierarchy is marked among other things by the possession and use of musical instruments, or by the size, (physical or numerical) of instrumental ensembles. Hence, while a small village chief can own or play one or two short animal horn trumpets, the more prominent chief may have an additional set of five or seven trumpets called *ntahera*. Again, while the former may have only one or two musical types such as the signal drum– *twenesini* and the *bomaa*, the Asantehene, (the head of the Asante nation in Ghana) has about a dozen or more different instrumental ensembles whose physical or numerical size cannot be equalled by any other chief in the Asante. State drums are regarded as state property and they were in the past regarded as valuable war trophies. To capture a chief's drum meant not only the acquisition of a treasured article, but also a humiliation of that chief. To ensure the effective use of drums on state occasions, court drummers are specially appointed and form part of the central organisation of the court.

Some societies in Africa have mythical symbols of office which may include musical instruments. Among the Ankole of Uganda, this symbol is a sacred drum called *bagyendanwa*, and there is a special cult built around it. The Lovedu of Transvaal in the Republic of South African also have sacred drums: they are said to be four in number and the smallest of them is mystically linked with the life of the queen and the welfare of the state. Similarly, the mythical symbols of the Bambara ancestral pantheon are the *tabele* drum and the *ngoni* harp.

The integrative mechanisms of the state may include festivals, which are organised around major agricultural rites, officially recognised divinities, or episodes from the history and traditions of the people. Such festivals are nearly always great occasions for music making, as well as occasions for public re-enactment of the beliefs and values on which state solidarity depends. There is the fishing festival called *Argungun* for example, which is celebrated by the people of Kebbi State in Nigeria. Yam and cassava festivals are also celebrated in Ghana and Nigeria: the Akan and Ewe of Ghana celebrate yam festivals, while the Urhobo of Nigeria and the people of Avenorfedo in the Volta Region of Ghana celebrate the cassava festival. A rice festival is celebrated among the Akpafu people of the Volta Region of Ghana.

In addition to festivals, there are also a number of ceremonies and rites designed to express loyalty to a reigning monarch, or the monarch himself expressing loyalty to the state or to the

432

ancestors. These include the installation of kings or the assumption of other high political office, all of which are performed with music. For example, when a chief dies in Sukuma land in Tanzania, certain stages in the proceedings are marked by music. And for the new chief who succeeds a dead chief, *ntemi,* a different kind of music, is performed at different stages of the ceremony.

Due regard may also be given to the king's movements, which may be heralded by music. His need for relaxation and entertainment may be met with music and dance. In this connection, the institution of praise singing and historical chants is very important in Africa. The role of praise singers is very vital in some societies. For example, among the Yoruba, in kings' palaces, praise singers or *oriki,* follow their masters wherever they go in the society. The *kwadwomfoo* (male praise chanters) perform the same functions at the court of the Asante king in Ghana. The Sahelian *griots,* as they are popularly known in Francophone Africa, originally were a caste of bards attached to noble families. They played multiple roles, including those of historian and the conscience of society (see also Ch. 17). Today, many of them are itinerant praise-singers who perform at public events. According to Bebey (1975: 24, 27-8, cited in Nzewi, 2009), *griots* are feared because as genealogy singers and satiric minstrels, they ferret out many social secrets:

> "They know everything that is going on and ... can recall events that are no longer within living memory. They are treated with 'contempt' because of their interaction traits that include insulting a patron who did not reward them sufficiently for praise. At the same time ... *the virtuoso of the griot commands universal admiration. This virtuosity is the culmination of long years of study and hard work. [Griots] are extraordinary musicians with outstanding talent who play an extremely important role in their respective societies. Their knowledge of the customs of the people and courtly life in all countries where they exercise their art gives them definite advantages; for the whole life of the people, its monarch, and ministers, is preserved intact in the infallible memory of the griots"*

Because of the vital role music plays in the courts of African kings, one can find different types of royal musicians such as drummers, fiddlers, trumpeters and flutists in the many courts of traditional rulers. Some even form part of the central administration.

Religion

One important aspect of African musical heritage is that it has retained its primary link to communal spirituality. The African view of the universe makes the worship of the gods a vital concern (see Chapter 7, this volume). Music plays a very important role in the worship of African gods, and anyone who has visited a scene of public worship will agree that one of the attributes of the gods is that they love music. The gods descend to the devotees through those who participate in the drama of worship. The most common situation in which African gods manifest themselves is the performance situation in which music affects them. They act through these mediums, who are known to object to the singing of particular songs, or to show displeasure when performance is lacking in animation or vigour. In addition to the priests and other officers, musicians may be selected to provide musical leadership. Special music is reserved for the gods, for it is believed that like the other worshippers, they can be affected by music.

As an element of corporate worship, songs are used as a medium through which the language of worship may be expressed. In addition to the use of songs as a vehicle of worship, they are also a means of stimulating the mediums of the gods into action and keeping them in a condition of ecstasy until their mission has been fulfilled. Once possessed, a medium can call up songs of his or her particular liking, in order that he/she might have the strength to act as required (see also Chapter 19, this volume).

Bodily expressions of joy are sustained at festivals for many hours through music, while for the crowd at ceremonies, the sacred is kept separate from the 'profane' world for as long as the instruments and voices are sounding. It must however be admitted that as a musical type, the music for the gods is essentially the music or ritual of drama which fulfils both a religious and social purpose. It carries with it its own religious ideals which are recognised by worshippers. But it also helps in keeping the community of worshippers together and in bringing them in close communion. For example, as soon as the physical signs of ecstasy are noticed in a medium, a crowd of 'Kple'[1] adherents among the Ga of Ghana burst into a chant to welcome the descending spirit.

Instrumental Resources

Africans attach great importance to the instruments that accompany their music. Various types of instruments exist in Africa, and one of the characteristics of African music is their enormous variety of musical instruments. Far from being a land of only drums, as it was depicted in many early sources, it is rather an area in which varied instruments are classified under the following four categories: *Idiophones, Membranophones, Chordophones* and *Aerophones (see also Ch. 18).*

Idiophones

These are instruments made of naturally sonorous materials that do not need any additional tension, unlike drums for instance. They are instruments that produce sound from their own bodies. Idiophones are the most widespread among the four classes. There are two types of idiophones: primary idiophones and secondary idiophones.

Primary idiophones are those that are held and played as part of the musical ensemble. These include bells, rattles, castanets, percussion sticks, sansas, xylophones etc. Secondary idiophones are attached to the instruments, such as buzzers or bells attached to the ankle, knee or wrist of the moving performer.

Figure 39 – Idiophones

Membranophones

These are drums with parchment heads. The sounds come from the membranes stretched over an opening. Materials used include wood, clay, metal or gourd and coconut shell. Their shapes can be hourglass, rectangular, spherical, cylindrical, bottle-shaped or conical.

Drums can be single or double-headed. They may be played alone as is the case of the signal drum, or in ensembles made up of the same drum such as the hour glass drum ensembles found in many Sahelian cultures, or the polyphonic ensembles found all over the continent.

Figure 40- Membranophones

Chordophones

These are stringed instruments. They are either played with the hand or with a bow, and sounds are produced on them by setting the strings into vibration. There are many varieties of chordophones ranging from the one-stringed fiddle (e.g. *gonje* of West Africa) to musical bow instruments with eight or more strings (e.g. the *mvet* of Gabon/Cameroun). These include varieties of lutes, harps, zithers and lyres (e.g. the *kora* of West Africa).

Figure 41 – Chordophones

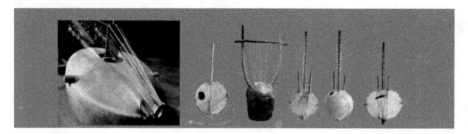

Aerophones

These are wind instruments. They are widespread in Africa, particularly in Central and West Africa. Examples are the horns, trumpets and flutes. Flutes may be carved out of materials such as natural bone or bamboo, or plants with removable pith. Flutes may be notched on plain, end-blown or transverse. They vary in length and size and in the number of finger holes. Trumpets are made out of elephant tusks or animal horns. Others are carved out of wood and they are usually side-blown. These trumpets are often found at royal courts such as those of the emirs of Hausa kingdoms.

Figure 42 – Aerophones

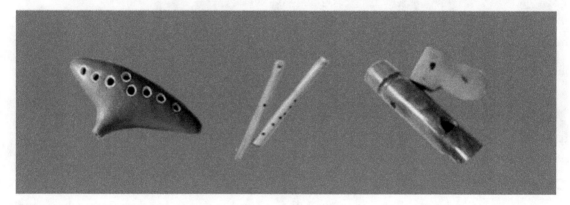

Dance Movement

Although purely contemplative music which is not designed for dance or drama is practised in African societies in restricted contexts, the cultivation of music that is integrated with dance is much more prevalent (see also Chapter 19, this volume). Most Africans are brought up on a dance ethos. Sounds, however beautiful, are meaningless if they do not contribute to an emotionally expressive quality of performance. Indeed in many performances, there is a direct communication between the lead musician, often a master drummer, and the dancer(s). Africans dance for joy, in sorrow or in anger, and for worship.

The importance Africans attach to the dance does not only lie in the scope it provides for the release of emotion stimulated by music. The dance can also be used as a social and artistic medium of communication. It can convey thoughts or matters of personal or social importance through the choice of movements, postures and facial expressions. Through dance, individuals or social groups can show their reactions to the hostility or co-operation and friendship held by others towards them. They can use it to offer respect to their superiors, or to send appreciation and gratitude to well-wishers and benefactors. Dance can also be used to react to the presence of rivals, affirm the status of servants and subjects or to express beliefs through the choice of appropriate dance vocabulary or symbolic movements.

According to Nketia (1965), when a dancer points the right hand or both hands skyward in an Akan dance, s/he is saying, 'I look to God'. When s/he places her or his right forefinger lightly against her/his head, s/he means, 'it is a matter for my head, something that I must solve for myself'. If he places his right forefinger below his right eye, he is saying: 'I have nothing to say but see how things will go'. When he rolls both hands inwards and stretches his right arm simultaneously with the last beats of the music, he means. 'If you bind me with cords, I shall break them into pieces (see also Chapter 19, this volume).

Because dance is an avenue of expression, it may be closely related to the themes and purpose of social occasions, although the guiding principle may be complex. Dancing at funerals, for example, does not necessarily express only sorrow and grief; it may also indicate tribute to the dead or depict group solidarity in the face of crises.

Among the Konkomba of Ghana for example, it is a duty of young men to dance at the burials of elders of their own or related clans, and even of those from contiguous districts if they are sent by their leaders. This is because dancing at a burial can be a symbol of clan membership, as of inter-clan relationships.

The basic movement used in traditional dances in Africa may be either simple or somewhat intricate. In some societies emphasis is on the movement of the whole trunk, while dancers in other societies, like the Ewe of Ghana, Togo, Benin Republic and the Urhobo of Nigeria, emphasise the upper part of the body. There are also dances such as those of the Kalabari of Nigeria and the Northern Ewe of Ghana in which the hips are used in a subtle way. There are others with intricate footwork like the *akom* dance of the Akan and the Ga of Ghana. The Ghanaian dancer/ choreographer and first artistic director of the Ghana Dance Ensemble, Mawere Opoku, revealed through his work the theatrical elements of African dance, demonstrating that dance is to African societies what the conventional theatre is to Western society (Opoku, 1987). As we have seen, these issues have been more fully explored in Chapter 19 on the nature and role of dance in African societies.

Song Texts

Many scholars have discussed the importance of song texts in the lives of Africans. Hugh Tracey (1948) noted that, 'You can say publicly in songs what you cannot say to a man's face, and so this is one of the ways African society .... maintain(s) a spiritually healthy community.' Merriam (1963: 201) also observed that 'song texts, ... can be used as means of action directed toward the solution of problems which plague a community.' While this can take the form of ridicule and shaming or sanctioned legal action, it is also apparent that song texts provide psychological release for the participants. Nketia (1975: 189)) wrote that 'the themes of songs tend to centre around events and matters of common interest and concern to the members of a community or the social group within it'. Thus texts of songs sung in Africa are sometimes a reflection of the concerns of the culture of which they are a part. They contribute to the correction of those aspects of behaviour to which they call attention. They can also serve as direct social control, to effect actual changes in erring members of the society through admonition, ridicule, or in some cases even more direct action.

Performing Groups and their Music

In Africa, we have musical groups that are formed on the basis of age, sex or occupation. We have children's, men's and women's musical groups, although sometimes the group may be a mixed one of both men and women. There are also socio-musical groups of performers that are attached to local institutions and associations. There are also a number of social groups that are usually in the form of associations. Among such groups are warrior organisations. In Ghana, there are *Asafo* companies, which in contemporary times perform civic duties whenever required. Another kind of heroic group is hunters' associations and among the Yoruba of Nigeria, the special music of their association is called *ijala*. Other societies in Ghana also have hunters' music, and examples exist among the Ewe, Adangme, Builsa and the Akan.

Recruitment and Training of Musicians

Since the success of a musical event depends to a large extent on good musical leadership, the recruitment of musicians is something of prime concern to social groups. In Africa, the training of the musician is not done on any institutional basis. Necessary factors include the natural endowment and the person's ability to develop on his or her own. In particular cases where the music is practised by particular families or castes, the child should have been born into such a family/caste. The process is that the child acquires his/her musical knowledge through exposure to musical situations created in the society in which he/she is absorbed, and by active participation in musical situations organised in the society for ceremonies, festivals, worship, and for recreation. As the child is exposed to these musical situations, he/she acquires the musical knowledge through participation and slow absorption until he/she is able to express him or herself fully.

The training of the African child starts right from the cradle by the mother rocking him or her, and singing of lullabies and nonsense syllables to the child. As the child is carried on the back of the mother to ceremonies, songs are sung to him or her. Children are also trained through their games and stories which include interludes of dancing and singing, and the playing of toy drums. Even those who attain distinction usually acquire their musical knowledge through the same process, through slow absorption and active participation. They have to rely on their eyes and ears. Also, important is imitation and correction by others, where this is volunteered. In situations where it is the social duty of the child to take over from his father or her mother or relative in playing an instrument, the child is encouraged to start early. For example, though mourning the dead among the Akan and Ewe of Ghana and the Urhobos and Itsekiris of

Nigeria is the sole responsibility of women, the occasion is also used to help the child to acquire musical knowledge. But there are also specialisations, such as the chanting of divination poetry among the Yoruba, in which the child must go into tutelage with a master diviner in order to attain the required level of proficiency.

Social Control

In African societies, it is not all events that involve the use of music, and Africans do not set aside music for the same set of events. For example, not all societies have work songs or songs for puberty ceremonies. Not all societies celebrate their marriages with music and dancing. Even where similar events incorporate music, the organisation of the events and the emphasis on music may not be the same. Sometimes, the schedule for musical activities is related to the beliefs of a community, the wishes of the gods, or to the reaction evoked from the spirits and forces that are believed to play a vital role in human life (see also Chs. 7 and 14). West Africans in particular are very selective in the organisation of their musical activities and that is why music-making is to some extent socially controlled. Among the Ga of Ghana for example, drumming is banned for three weeks before the annual harvest festival. And among the Urhobos and the Itsekiris of Nigeria, no form of wailing or music making is allowed when a person under the age of forty years dies, no matter his or her social status. In some traditional societies in Ghana, no form of music making or wailing goes on when people die through child labour. These prohibitions are believed to stem the reoccurrence of the event. The implications of all these are that one should not expect to hear music in an African community every hour of the day or every day of week, nor should one expect to hear music on every social occasion or during every kind of collective activity.

Ghana's Musical Traditions

Ghana's musical traditions reflect the variety of musical styles found in West Africa, for although Ghana is a comparatively small country, it is made up of several ethnic groups which have historical, cultural or linguistic affinities with societies beyond its borders. The Northern, Upper East and Upper West Regions, for example, form part of the savannah belt of West Africa, and belong to the Sudanic cultural area. The rest of Ghana consists of the rain-forest belt and the coastal plains. Although about 36 different languages are spoken in Ghana, only 11 of these are recognised officially as written languages. Of these, Akan, in the form of its Twi and Fante dialects, is the most widely spoken. It is also the language whose cultural expressions, including music, have had the greatest impact on other Ghanaian societies.(see also Ch.3).

Distribution of Traditional Music

According to Nketia (1975), the outstanding characteristic of traditional music is the diversity of its forms and manner of performance. Ethnic groups show considerable flexibility in their musical heritage specifically as regards:
1. musical items,
2. instruments,

3. vocal styles, as well as
4. details of form and structure.

The choices that each society makes, however, are not always unique to it and may overlap with those made by others. Thus some societies use similar instruments, but different scales; others cultivate similar types of music, but develop them using different resources, while similar ceremonies and rites may be performed with different selections of music.

Certain patterns of distribution emerge, therefore, when traditional music and musical practice are viewed on regional and national basis. For example, varieties of *jongo* recreational music are performed in the Frafra, Kusasi, Kassena-Nankani and Builsa and Sisala areas in northern Ghana, but not in the South. *Damba* music and dance are performed at Damba Islamic festivals in Dagomba, Gonja and Wa (Waala) areas, but not in the rest of the Upper East and Upper West Regions. On the other hand, a few musical instruments such as the hour-glass drum are common throughout Ghana. These patterns of distribution reflect the continuing social, cultural and linguistic affinities of Ghanaian societies despite separate traditional political identities.

The Dagbon, Mamprusi and Nanumba people for example, speak closely related languages, share cultural usages and are related historically to the Mossi and Gurma of Burkina Faso. A similar situation exists in other societies such as the Lobrifor, Lopiel, Lodagaa and Sisala of northwestern Ghana; the Ga and Adangme of southern Ghana; and the many groups that make up the Akan cluster –the Ashanti, Brong, Akim, Kwahu, Akwapim, Agona, Assin, Wasa, Fante and Akwamu (Also see Chapter 3, this volume). It is thus possible to group together traditional societies in Ghana on the basis of the similarity of their music as well as other features of their culture.

Instruments

The instruments used by Ghanaians include a variety of idiophones or self-sounding instruments. Examples are bells, rattles, xylophones, percussion sticks and hand or thumb pianos, which are primary idiophones. We also have secondary idiophones which are attached to the instruments as buzzers, or to the wrist of the performer or to the body of the dancer. These idiophones are used principally as rhythm instruments and cannot be used to play melodies. A variety of open and closed drums are found throughout Ghana. Of the aerophones, trumpets are the most widespread, and consist of animal horns and cane flutes. Like the flutes, chordophones are less common in the South than in the North. An example of chordophones found in the North includes the *Goje* (Goge) and varieties of lutes called *kolongo, kono,* and *mogola*.

Vocal Styles

Ghanaian vocal styles are varied. Some societies, for example, the Akan and Ga, use an open vocal quality, while the Frafra and the Kusasi use a more tense quality. The use of a high pitch is quite widespread in the North, and is sometimes closely related to the range of melodic instruments such as flutes, xylophones and lutes which accompany the singing. Divergences in vocal style are partly attributable to linguistic factors, for the melodies of traditional music reflect very closely the formation and rhythm of speech.

Melody, Polyphony and Rhythm

The music of different Ghanaian societies do not all conform to the same set of scales: some are heptatonic (7-note scale) varieties, others are hexatonic (6-note) and others pentatonic (five note scale). Polyphonic practices are generally related to scale types and forms of melodic organisation. Most societies which have pentatonic traditions sing in unison, and those which have heptatonic tradition sing in parallel 3rds throughout, as in Akan tradition, or end in unison at final cadences as in the music of the Builsa, Kassena-Nankani and the Kokomba of the North.

In traditional music, the treatment of rhythm is much more uniform than that of pitch. Music may have a linear organisation and may be in free or strict time. In the latter case, the metre is either predominantly duple or based on a combination of duple or triple motifs. An important element in the organisation of rhythm is the ordering of patterns into phases and the control of the length of phrases.

Regional Musical Cultures: **The Mamprusi-Dagomba Cultural Group**

This comprises the Dagomba, Mamprusi Kusasi, Frafra, Namnam and some Gonja communities. This area is a culture of one string fiddle, two-string lutes and hourglass ensembles. There is a tradition of professionalism with strong emphasis on praise chanting. The scale is pentatonic. Islamic influence is particularly marked in the customs and festivals of the Dagomba, Mamprusi and Gonja, but is less so in their music.

The Grusi Group of North-Central Ghana

This includes the Kassena-Nankana, the Builsa and the Konkomba.Musical instruments consist of aerophones and drum ensembles, and three to six flutes and horns. The scale is heptatonic with polyphony based on thirds.

The Lobi, Brifor, Lopiel, Dagaaba, Sisala (and other communities in the Upper West region).

The main instrument is the xylophone played alone, or with the support of a small drum ensemble, and the use of finger bells and ankle bells in dances is prevalent. The scale is largely pentatonic.

The South-Central Akan Group

This comprises Asante, Brong, Akyem, Kwahu, Akwapim, Akwamu, Wasa, Assin, Agona, Fante, Guan and Awutu. The Akan have an elaborately organised court music. Instruments include a large number of drum ensembles, trumpet ensembles and instrumental speech surrogates which are instruments that mime language tones such as talking drums and horns. Akan musical scale is predominantly heptatonic, and polyphony is based on the 3rd as a consonant interval.

The Ga-Adangbe of Southeast Ghana

The Ga, Dangbe and Krobo compose a small group. Their traditions are mixed because of intensive interaction with their neighbours; for example the court traditions and military organization are derived from the Akan. However, there are indigenous musical features which are shared to some extent with the Awutu and Guan, who belong to the Akan group. The main instrument is the drum, and musical types include *Klama* and *kple.*) The scale is pentatonic-polyphony in vocal refrains.

The Ewe of Ghana

Two musical traditions exist among the Ewe of Ghana. Among the southern Anlo-Tongu (in the Keta, Akatsi, Denu, Adidome and Sogakope Districts), the instruments are drums and idiophones like bells, rattles (enmeshed in beads), beaters and handclapping. The musical scale is pentatonic and both men and women sing parallel octaves. Among the Northern Ewe (in Ho, Kpando and Hohoe Districts), musical instruments consist of smaller drums and container rattles, and the musical scale is heptatonic-polyphony in 3rds.

Contemporary Developments

Until the latter part of the 19th century, when British colonisation of the Gold Coast began, many Ghanaian societies were culturally homogenous. Since the 20th century, two distinct cultural expressions have become evident, one embodying the heritage of the past and reflecting the life of traditional societies, and the other resulting from Ghana's contact with Western culture and technology. This duality is reflected in the contrast between the well-established traditions of indigenous music and the evolving inter-cultural musical traditions that serve the new urban institutions such as the ballroom, the café, the night club, the concert hall and the theatre, as well as the educational institutions and the church.

Musicians who practise this new music use both African and non-African resources. While they sometimes use traditional African instruments, they more commonly use Western instruments to play tunes that are basically African in rhythm and melody.

Contemporary Ghanaian music is developing in two particular areas. The first is *highlife,* a form of music which originated in the late 19th[h] century and which is cultivated by dance bands, brass bands and guitar bands. A large number of these developed into touring bands based in the principal cities (see Chapter 21 for a more extensive discussion). The second area is the new Ghanaian art music, which owes its development to the search for an African idiom to replace the Western hymn and anthem, and which is now identified with the church, the concert hall and educational institutions.

The early missionaries succeeded in establishing Western music and musical ideas in Africa through choral music as well as Western instruments like the harmonium, piano and brass band music, as an aspect of the culture of literate Christians. Though these missionaries did not encourage African beliefs and practices and even excommunicated converts who were caught participating in traditional music, these prohibitions underwent considerable change with the spread of Western education and the rise of nationalism from the late nineteenth century.

A new generation of literate indigenous composers and performers subsequently appeared, and so music education is no longer only an aspect of community life, but is also part of the school curriculum. These composers and performers include pioneers like Gaddiel Acquaah, Ephraim Amu and Kwabena Nketia, followed by Nicholas Nayo and Walter Blege, and lately William Anku and William Chapman Nyaho. The recognition and support of contemporary developments in music has not minimised the historical and cultural importance of traditional music. This has continued to occupy a dominant position not only in the musical life of traditional societies, but also through the mass media and educational programmes, at arts festivals and on certain national occasions, as it is regarded as a medium for the expression of national identity. An important creative extension of the traditional mode is neo-traditional music which is inspired by traditional music but is a phenomenon of African modernity and urbanisation. In Ghana, this includes musical types like *Borborbor*, *kpanlogo* and *simpa*. Certain bands like the *Wulomei*, are closely associated with neo-traditional music. (Ch. 21 discusses these features in more detail).

Conclusion

In Africa, as we have observed, music is life, and life is music. The two cannot be separated from each other. In contrast, Euro-American societies have a tendency to divorce music from aspects of everyday life, whereas in Africa stress is placed upon musical activity as an integral and functioning part of the society. As John Collins puts it:

> African music is democratic. Genius and excellence shine from within the whole community, giving inner illumination and providing the opportunity for tuning in to the world of spirit and nature. It is alive within, not dazzling from without like some of the works of Western classical composers and modern rock superstars... African music brings different aspects of life together since it is performed in association with other art forms such as dancing, drama, masked parades and poetry (Collins, 1992: 1-2).

In this chapter, the structure, typology and geographical distribution of indigenous African music forms have been provided. These have also been contextualised through an examination of the musical templates accompanying life cycle ceremonies and traditional institutions. However, it must be understood that as a result of the many years of contact with the West, the two musical traditions – the indigenous traditional forms and the Western forms, exist side by side in Africa. For example, though traditional instruments are employed in worship in the churches, the organ and brass instruments are also used. Thus, although traditional forms are found at the courts of *obas*, emirs and chiefs, governments of Africa use Western instruments in military and police bands to play traditional tunes. National anthems in Africa are also Western-oriented. Western trained art musicians in Africa have combined Western-type harmony with African rhythm in the writing of their music. Clearly, Africans have not done away with Western music since independence, and both the traditional and the Western forms co-exist. A vital aspect of traditional African music is its pervasive and fundamental influence on global popular music, primarily through the retentions among enslaved Africans of rhythms, vocal and instrumental styles, and their descendents have created jazz, rhumba, reggae, soul and hip hop, among other dominant musical trends.

Review Questions

1. Discuss the organisation of music in African societies.

2. 'The African is born with music, grows with it and dies with it'. How can you relate this statement to in the life-cycle in your community? Discuss.

3. One of the most important sets of musical types in African societies is music of the courts and festivals. To what extent is this statement true?

5. Comment on the statement that 'for the African, musical experience is by and large an emotional one, and sounds, however beautiful, are meaningless if they do not offer this experience of bodily movement'.

6. 'You can say publicly in songs what you cannot say to a man's face' (Hugh Tracey, 1954: 237). How does this statement reflect in the role of song-texts in African music?

7. Discuss how the African child acquires his/her musical knowledge.

8. Comment on the statement that 'Far from being a land of only drums, Africa is an area in which varied instruments are found.'

References

Agordoh, A.A. 2002. *Studies in African Music.* Ho: New Age Publication.

Bebey, F. 1975. *African Music, A People's Art.* (Translated by Josephine Bennet).New York: Lawrence Hill

Collins, J. 1992 *West African Pop Roots.* Philadelphia: Temple University Press. |

Herskovits, M.J. 1967. *Dahomey.* Evanston: Northwestern University Press

Merriam, A. P. 1964. *The Anthropology of Music.* Evanston: Northwestern University Press.

Nketia, J.H.K. 1975. *The Music of Africa.* London: Victor Gollancz.

Nketia, J.H.K. 1965 *Ghana, Music, Dance and Drama – a review of the Performing Arts of Ghana.* Accra: Ghana Publishing Corporation

Nketia,J.H.K. 1965 *African Music in Ghana.* Evanston: Northwestern University Press. 1959 "

Nketia, J. H.K. 1959. " African Gods and Music". *Universitas* Vol. IV. No. I:PP 3-7.

Nzewi, M. 2009. 'The Igbo Concept of Mother Musician.'http://rozenbergquarterly.com/?p=1764

Opoku, A. M. 1987. "Asante Dance Art and the Court" In E. Schildkrout(Ed.), *The Golden Stool: Studies of Asante Center and Periphery.* Anthropological Papers of the American Museum of Natural History. Vol. 65: Part 1. New York 199

Smith, M.G. 1957. "The Social Functions and Meaning of Hausa Praise Singing." *Africa.*Vol.27: No1; pp 26-45.

Tracey, Hugh 1948. *Chopi Musicians, their music, poetry and instruments.* London: Oxford University Press

Endnote

1.*Kple* is a religious cult of the Ga of Ghana.

CHAPTER 21

A HISTORICAL REVIEW OF POPULAR ENTERTAINMENT IN SUB-SAHARAN AFRICA

John Collins

Introduction

In many parts of sub-Saharan Africa, art genres have emerged that blend or 'syncretise' local and foreign elements. In spite of their acculturated nature, these new art-styles contain distinctive features that express the identities, symbols and underlying value orientations of their African practitioners and audiences. The ability of these new art-forms to reflect and express the moods and outlooks of Africans undergoing rapid socio-cultural transformations is helped by their often ephemeral and transient nature, and what Karin Barber (1987:12) calls their 'aesthetic of change'. These new popular forms include performance which will be discussed in this paper, popular painting (e.g. Yoruba *Oshogbo* art; see also Chapter 18, this volume) and literature (e.g. Nigerian Onitsha Market literature; see also Chapter 17). Indeed, these new syncretic art-forms go far beyond what in the West is normally called 'art,' for they embrace coffin designs, house decoration and bar murals, portrait photography, hair barbering advertisements and other types of sign-writing, wire bicycles, decorated bread labels, lorry slogans, current jokes and expressions as well as the catch names for printed cloths and hair styles.[1] It should also be noted that the practitioners of popular art tend to be drawn from the intermediate economic layers of African society who neither belong to the peasantry nor the modern elites. They are rather unskilled, migrant workers, artisans, small traders, cash-crop farmers, minor civil servants and so on.

This chapter deals with the transcultural popular performance styles (music, dance and drama) of sub-Saharan Africa that have since the 19th century blended together local elements, with those of Europe, America and Asia as far as India, and have been disseminated through records, radio and the mass media. These influences were initially introduced via ports; thus there is often a pattern of coastal musical and entertainment styles diffusing inland and subsequently becoming more regionalised or indigenised. These Western inputs also contained a Black Diasporic component from the Americas, which acted as a powerful catalyst in the creation of many African popular performance genres. This has been presented as a black musical 'homecoming' (Mensah, 1971), that completed the loop of 'cultural feedback' (Stearns, 1988), producing an 'affinity' (Roberts, 1974), and 'resonance' (Jacobs, 1989), in the African host countries.

Although African popular performance arose within the colonial context, the emergence of distinct regional genres were not only a result of acculturation, but also of musical de-culturation, involving de-colonisation, Africanisation and westernisation. Indeed, in many ways African popular music can be seen as a modern extension of traditional recreational performance that is customarily associated with youthful age-sets and is therefore fast-changing and adaptable (see also Chapter 20). Moreover, the fact that African popular music, dance and drama not only partly draw on tradition but continually interact with a living folk culture has created neo-traditional genres that question the usual folk/pop polarity model of western performing arts.

It should be noted that artistic syncretism occurred in Africa before European contact, through internal trade, war, migration and generational change via youthful age-sets, initiation societies and warrior associations. Because recreational music and dance styles are particularly open to generational modifications, it is from these, rather than the more conservative and slow-changing ritual and court performance, that much of Africa's current transcultural popular performing arts have arisen. Indeed, it could be rightly claimed that contemporary urban African popular performance is a direct continuation of traditional but ever dynamic traditional recreational performing arts[2], albeit with elements from the West incorporated into it. Therefore, although African music has been westernised, at the same time western performance norms have been re-integrated within the context of traditional performance, particularly recreational and other forms linked to the socio-cultural dynamics of generational change.

European Military Bands

The earliest European musical impact on Africa came through regimental bands (fife-and-drum and later brass bands). At first, for obvious military reasons, there was a reluctance to teach Africans European martial marching music. An exception was the formation of the Akrampo Number Six *Asafo* (warrior) Company in 1655 at Cape Coast, Ghana, composed of 'mulatto' soldiers (de Graft Johnson, 1932). However, by the mid-19th century local brass bands had appeared as far apart as the 'native band' of Cape Coast Castle in Ghana (Beecham 1841) and the Cape-coloured one of Cape Town, South Africa (Coplan 1965). These bands played western regimental band music and occasionally, popular dances such as the waltzes and polkas (Figure 43).

Figure 43 – West African Regimental Brass Band around 1900

Source: *J. Collins/BAPMAF collection)*

In West Africa, West Indian troops and their regimental brass bands were stationed by the British in Freetown (1819), Cape Coast (1870) and late 19th century Lagos. In Ghana, these Caribbean soldiers, numbering about six to seven thousand, played Afro-Caribbean music in their spare time, and so helped catalyse the formation of local Fanti *adaha* brass band music that used indigenous and Caribbean rhythms. Incidentally, these West Indian soldiers also introduced elements of Caribbean masquerades that subsequently became popular with Fantis.

These local brass-bands spread through southern Ghana during the cocoa boom of the early 20th century, and a poor-man's *konkoma* or *konkomba* version (using percussion and voices only), appeared in Fanti-land in the 1930s. *Konkoma* spread as far east as Nigeria, and helped establish a neo-traditional variant in the Ghana/Togo area known as *borborbor*. Waterman (1990) mentions that the West Indian troops in Lagos were one of the formative influences on local Nigerian brass band music of the 1920s.

In East Africa brass band music or *beni* was associated with late 19th century coastal Kenyan uniformed parades and later the *askaris* (local soldiers) of German Tanganyika (Ranger 1975). After the First World War, *beni* music moved inland and, paralleling *konkoma*, became indigenised. Western instruments were dropped, the local gourd *kazoo* became important, and the music was played in a typical African cross or poly-rhythmic way, rather than the strict western 2/4 or 4/4 march time (Figure 44). *Beni* also became a focus for youthful conflict with village elders, and an organising factor in the 1935 strike of the African copper miners of eastern Africa. Although initially coastal *beni* was trans-ethnic, its later local offshoots were associated with a specific ethnic group and included the *mbeni* of the Bemba people (Jones 1945), and the *kalela* of Bisa mine-workers (Mitchell, 1956).

Figure 44 – East African Mbeni Group

Source: *J. Collins/BAPMAF collection)*

David Kerr (1995) calls all these West and East African versions, offshoots and parodies of western regimental music 'militaristic mime,' i.e., African theatrical display that involved elements of European military parade-ground music.

Freed Slaves

The music of freed African slaves was another seminal influence on African popular music. The first case is Jamaican *goombay*, a frame-drum music associated with the neo-African myelism healing-cult (Bilby, 1985). *Goombay* was taken to Freetown, Sierra Leone in 1800 by Jamaican maroon rebels freed by the British (Figure 45). From 1900, *goombay* spread to many other West African countries including Mali (*gube*), the Côte d'Ivoire (*le goumbe*), Ghana (*gome*), Senegal, Burkina Faso, Nigeria, Fernando Po and the Cameroons.

Asiko, or *Ashiko*, is an early Pan West African popular music played on frame-drums and musical saw (later guitar and accordion), that was created in the late 19th century by the descendants of Yoruba slaves (*Akus*) liberated in Freetown by the British after their 1807 ban on the slave trade. The British anti-slaving cruisers also operated off the East African coast from the 1840s, and settlements of freed slaves were established in Kenya (like Freetown), by church mission societies. It was from the resulting Christian elite and 'Bombay Africans' (sent to India by the British to be educated), that the local *dansi* of the 1920s emerged, modelled on western ballroom dance-music. More indigenous Luo variants, played on accordions, evolved inland.

Also important were Brazilian slaves who settled in West Africa from the 1840s and particularly in the 1880s. In Lagos they were known as 'Aguda' people who introduced the samba. They made a contribution to the early popular drama of Lagos when they established a `Brazilian Dramatic Society' in the 1880s that put on `Grand Theatre' and performances of humorous pieces and songs for violin and guitar (Echeruo 962:69-70).

Sailors and Stevedores

As the initial European settlements in sub-Saharan Africa were coastal, ports became an important musical interface. In early 20th century West Africa, dockside groups were formed that combined African and imported melodies, rhythms and instruments, including the portable one of seamen— the accordion, harmonica, banjo (originally an African instrument), penny whistle and guitar. The first to do this were the maritime Kru or Kroo people of Liberia, who worked on board European sailing ships from Napoleonic times. In the early twentieth century, they created the distinctive West African two-finger guitar plucking technique and spread their 'mainline,' *dagomba*, and 'fireman'(i.e. steam-ship's stoker) styles up and down the West African coast in their 'kru-towns'. Variants known collectively as 'palm-wine' music or 'native blues,'[3] appeared in Sierra Leone, Ghana, Nigeria and the Cameroons.

In Sierra Leone, palm-wine music was combined with *goombay* to create 'maringa,' first recorded by Ebenezer Calendar in the 1940s (Figure 46). In the Cameroons, this costal guitar music was absorbed into the country's *makossa* music. The coastal 'palm-wine' styles of Ghana (*osibisaaba, annkadammu* and *timo*), moved inland during the 1920s, evolving into regional styles such as *odonson* or 'Ashanti blues,' that absorbed modulations and melodies from the traditional *seprewa* harp-lute.

It was the Ghanaian Fanti guitarist, Kwame Asare (Jacob Sam), and his Kumasi Trio, that in 1928 first recorded 'palm-wine' music, including the famous Ghanaian song 'Yaa Amponsah' (Figure 47). They recorded for the Zonophone Company of London, one of the many foreign record companies that tapped into the lucrative pre-war 'native records' market of West Africa based on a boom in cash-crops such as cocoa. Kwame Asare and the many Ghanaian recording artistes who followed (Mireku, Kwasi Manu, Osei Bonsu, Appiah Adjekum, etc), paved the way for the larger guitar-band of the post-war period.

By the 1920s, Lagos had its own palm-wine and 'native' blues groups (e.g. the Jolly Orchestra). During the early 1930s this was combined with Yoruba praise music and *asiko* by Tunde King and Ayinde Bakare, who were 'rascals' and 'area boys' (Alaja-Browne,1985) of the *saro'*

Figure 45 – Sierra Leone Goombey Group
Source: *J. Collins/BAPMAF collection)*

Figure 46 – Sierra Leone's Ebenezer Calendar in 1984 **(Photo:** *Wolfgang Bender)*

Figure 47 – The Minstrel- influenced Ghanaian Concert Party Entertainers Williams and Marbel in 1923

Photo: *J. Collins/BAPMAF collection)*

Figure 48 – The Kumasi Trio, Ghana, in 1928
(Photo: *J. Collins/BAPMAF collection)*

Figure 49 – East African Taarab Music Group

(Photo: *Graeme Ewens)*

449

(Sierra Leonian) quarter of town. The result was called *juju* music, an onomatopoeic word derived from the sound of the local tambourine, called an *asiko* or *samba* drum. By the mid-1930s *juju* music had become the popular salon praise-music of the Yoruba elite.

Five thousand West African 'coastmen' were recruited by King Leopold for the Congo Free State from the 1880s (Cornet, 1953), as clerks, artisans, sailors, railroad workers and contract workers. It was they who set up the country's first dance orchestra of the Congo River, the Excelsior Orchestra. It was the 'coastmen' and local Congolese mine-workers that helped spread Congo Democratic Republic's earliest recognised local popular music style, *maringa* (Kazadi, 1973). It evolved around 1914 in the coastal Matadi-Kinshasa area, and spread as far as the Shaba mining camps by the 1920s. It was played on frame-drums and *likembe* hand-piano (later accordion and guitar), and was sung in the new evolving trans-ethnic Lingala trade language of Central Africa. It was played in bars for informal dancing, and was frowned upon by local Christians.

It was also the West African 'coastmen' who taught the two-finger guitar technique to local Congolese sailor-musicians, Dondo Daniels and Antoine Wendo. This two-finger technique reached Swahili-speaking eastern Congo (via the navigable Congo River) in the late 1940s and, combined with local traditional *ngoma* musical elements and the imported rumba, was popularised through records by Jean Bosco Mwenda and Losta Abelo. Known as the 'dry' (i.e. non-amplified) guitar style, it gradually replaced the strumming/vamping style of guitar playing of East African musicians such as Kenya's Fundi Kunde who was influenced by the records of American 'singing cowboys' like Jimmy Rodgers. From the 1950s Africanised two-finger picking techniques subsequently were utilised by East African guitarists such as Kenya's John Mwale, and Malawi's Kachamba Brothers. There, like its West and Central African predecessors, it was associated with drinking bars and held in low esteem.

From the 1930s, strummed guitar playing was also a feature of Ndebele/Zulu musicians in southern Africa, and, combined with local mouth-bow influences, was popularised by low-class itinerant artists like Zimbabwean George Sibanda, and South African John Bhengu. In the 1950s, two-finger picking guitar styles were introduced and became incorporated into southern African music styles such as 'jive,' 'twist,' and Zulu working class *maskanda* music. Whether the South African two finger-picking (in Zulu called *utikpa*) style was an independent creation, or stemmed from the 'dry' style from eastern Congo and East Africa (and ultimately West Africa), is a matter of debate.

The Mission-Educated African Elites

Mission schools introduced the sol-fa (i.e. do-ray-mi, etc.) notation and western harmony to Africans. During the 19th century, the educated local elite sang European hymns, cantatas and marches and had their 'dignity ball' of Freetown (Harrev, 1987), Handel Festivals and 'grand theatre' of Lagos (Echeruo, 1962), and 'rainbow balls' of South Africa (Coplan, 1985). However, after the large scale commercial production of the anti-malarial quinine drug[4] and the 1884 Berlin Conference, the 'scramble for Africa' began in earnest. In English-speaking Africa, the 'indirect' system of colonial rule through local chiefs and emirs was instituted. The educated black elites and merchant princes (who formerly acted as middle-men between the coastal British and hinterland areas), were denied institutional power, for with quinine, British traders and district commissioners could live and work in inland areas. As a result, the educated local elites turned towards modern African nationalist movements. Separatist African churches multiplied that played hymns sung in local languages. An early example is southern African *makwaya* (i.e. choir) that combined European hymnody with African-American spirituals and close-harmony singing. Enoch Sontonga's famous 1897 nationalist anthem, 'Nkosi Sikelele Africa,' falls into this category. Similar early African choral composers were Ephraim Amu of Ghana, and Reverend Ransome-Kuti of Nigeria.

In South Africa during the 1920s, *makwaya* went secular and became associated with the re-fined Zulu music of pianist Ruben Caluza. Combined with ragtime and the music of diamond and gold miners (*Sotho focho*/disorder music and Zulu acapella close-harmony 'night-music'), *makwaya* also became transformed into *marabi* associated with working-class *shebeen* bars and prostitu-tion. The African elite loathed *marabi*, but endorsed Caluza's art-music style of *makwaya*, as well as prestigious ragtime bands of the period such as the Versatile Seven and Jazz Revellers, located in Johannesburg's black middle-class Queenstown district, also known as 'little jazz town.' Dur-ing the 1930s, the black elite shifted its attention to big-band swing music, supplied by the Mer-ry Blackbirds, Jazz Maniacs and early Manhattan Brothers that played in Johannesburg's black night-club district of Sophiatown. Similarly, neighbouring Zimbabwe had its own jazz artistes—Dorothy Mazuka, the Milton Brothers and the Black Follies variety show.

As mentioned earlier, the educated coastal Africans of East Africa created *dansi* orchestras that played foxtrots and ballroom music for high-class dancing clubs. In English-speaking West Africa, there was a similar situation as the coastal elites established numerous symphonic-like dance orchestras. The earliest was the 1914 Excelsior Orchestra of Ghana. By the 1920s, these included the Jazz Kings and Cape Coast Sugar Babies of Ghana, the Lagos City Orchestra of Nigeria and the Dapa Jazz Band and Triumph Orchestra of Freetown. In the case of Ghana, it was during the 1920s, when the prestigious dance groups began to orchestrate local melodies, that the term 'highlife' (i.e. high-class), was coined.

Visiting Minstrel Shows, Records and Early Film

White American 'black-face' minstrel groups first visited Africa (Cape Town) in 1859, but made little impact on the local music scene. However, this changed in the 1890s when African-American groups, such as MacAdoo's Virginia Jubilee Singers, began visiting South Africa (Erlmann, 1988), bringing with them 'coon-songs,' ragtime, spirituals and the cakewalk dance. As a result, local African minstrel groups were formed. There were 'coon carnivals' by Cape Town's 'cape-coloureds,' and ragtime bands like the Darktown Negroes were started.

Ebun Clark (1979) refers to minstrel shows in late 19th century Lagos, whilst Nunley (1987) mentions an African Comedy Group in Freetown in 1915. Minstrel and vaudeville sketches be-came popular in Ghana around 1903[5] and in 1918 (Sutherland, 1970). Furthermore, between 1924-6 the African-American (or possibly Americo-Liberian), Glass and Grant team was based in Accra that influenced Williams and Marbel of Accra, and Williams and Nikol from Freetown (Figure 48). This local vaudeville or 'concert party' of the local elites rapidly became indigenised during the 1930s by popular theatre groups such as Bob Johnson and the Axim Trio.

From around 1900, records and silent film became an important source of musical innovation. Early imported records included western classical pieces, popular dances, 'coon-songs,' ragtime, spirituals, singing cowboy songs (e.g. Jimmy Rodgers), and Hindi music (in East Africa). By the late 1920s records by African artistes were being distributed in both East and West Africa, and in 1930 the Venezuelan GV label began distributing Afro-Cuban and Latin-American music. Silent, and later, talking, films introduced comic sketches, dance routines, minstrel acts and 'jazz shorts.'

Islamic Influences

Although not as widespread as the popular music arising out of the African contact with European and American culture, Islam has created popular genres on both sides of the continent. Aristocratic Egyptian music (played on Danbuk clay-pot drum, the *ud* or lute and the *kanum* zither), was taken to the Zanzibar Emirate in the 1870s where, during the 1920s, it became transformed into local *taarab* music. *Taraab* (or *Taraabu*) music was sung in Swahili (the old Afro-Arab trade language of East Africa), employing western violins and accordions with indigenous *ngoma* drums. During the 1930s, *taarab* music spread to the Tanzanian mainland and Kenya, and later absorbed elements from Indian music (Figure 49). It should also be noted that in Tanzania, *taarab* music was, from the early 20th century, associated with a popular form of drama known as *vichekeso*.

Late 19th century *ramadan* festival-music of western Nigeria (female *waka* and male *were* genres), was the basis of *sakara* Yoruba popular music of the First World War period, played on clay-pot *sakara* drum, *molo* lute, and one-stringed *goje* fiddle. It was a praise-music associated with the rise of modern Islamic associations. In the 1940s, combined with *juju* music, *sakara* led to *apala* music, popularised by Haruna Ishola. During the 1970s sung elements of *were*, *sakara* and *apala* (Islamic nasalisation, microtones and melisma) were drawn into *fuji* music that employs *sakara* and hour-glass drums and an eclectic array of western instruments. The term was coined by Ayinde Barrister, and from the 1980s it replaced *juju* as the dominant popular music of Yoruba Christians and Muslims alike.

The Impact of the Second World War

The Second World War not only accelerated the African independence movement, but also deeply affected popular music and entertainment. Foreign troops were stationed in many African countries. American and British servicemen brought with them swing-jazz (as well as rumbas and calypsos), and the associated zoot-suit fashion, jitterbug dance, and nightclub life. Local swing bands were set up such as the Swing Rhythm Brothers, and Bobby Benson's group in Lagos, the Black and White Spots and Tempos (both composed of black and white musicians) of Accra, and the Mayfair dance band of Freetown. In South Africa, the already formed Jazz Maniacs, Merry Blackbirds and Pitch Black Follies of Cape Town played for American and British troops, whilst the American Lieutenant, Ike Brooks, put together the Zonk variety outfit, using local swing artists (Coplan 1979). Swing influenced dance bands were formed, like the Manhattan Brothers and Milton Brothers, as well as the Jazz Crooners and the Evening Black Follies of neighbouring Zimbabwe.

During the 1940s western swing bands fronted important female singers such as Ella Fitzgerald, Sarah Vaughan and Peggy Lee. As a result it was via the swing influened African dance bands that the very first and very tiny generation of African professional female stage singers appeared, such as singer-dancer Cassandra of Bobby Bensons Band, Agnes Ayitey and Julie Okine of the E.T. Mensah's Tempos Band (Figure 50), Dorothy Masuka of Zimbabwean dance-bands and Miriam Makeba of South Africa's Manhattan Brothers.

Figure 50 – The Tempos Highlife Dance Band of Ghana around 1950

Photo: *J. Collins/BAPMAF collection*

In South Africa, the jitterbug dance associated with American swing music became indigenised into the *tsaba-tsaba* dance, popular with young urban Flytaal (African-Afrikaans slang) speaking members of the 'tsotsis' (i.e. zoot-suits) juvenile sub-culture. The Caribbean *beguine* was introduced to Congo Brazzaville by black Martinique soldiers of De Gaulle's Free French army, and in Sierra Leone, calypso bands were formed during the Second World War period by Ali Ganda and Famous Scrubbs.

African troops also fought abroad in the Far East and in North Africa, such as the sixteen thousand *Boma* (i.e. Burma boys) of Nigeria, and the East African Kings' Rifles. Some of the Education Corps members of the East African Rifles learnt vamping guitar and the rumba abroad, and formed Kenya's famous Rumba Boys on their return. Seven Ghanaian concert party actor-musicians of the West African Frontier Force set up a West African Theatre in Burma, and South Africa's Jubulani concert party entertained troops in North Africa where they met Glen Miller, the leader of the most famous American war-time swing band. Local popular music was also used in the war effort. For example Ghanaian *konkoma* highlife (Sackey, 1989), popular concert party theatre, and Nigerian *juju* music (Waterman, 1990), were used for recruiting and wartime propaganda.

The Postwar Emergence of New Popular Music and Entertainment Styles

The impact of wartime troops, the lifting of the wartime ban on record production, the immediate postwar economic boom, the establishment of multi-national recording studios in black Africa,[6] the introduction of electronic amplification, the emergence of mass-independence parties and a new educated generation, all helped shape the numerous popular entertainment genres that mushroomed after the war.

During the late 1940s in Central Africa, local *ngoma* performance, the Afro-Cuban rumba and American jazz (especially its horn section), were fused into what became known as 'Congo jazz' (later *soukous*). It was first sung in Spanish, and later in Lingala. Moreover, an increasingly longer *seben* section was added after the rumba introduction of Congo jazz/*soukous* songs, based on fast traditional dance rhythms and short-form chord changes. Congo-Kinshasa pioneers were Antoine Wendo (1949), Kalle's African Jazz (1953), that included the guitarist, Dr. Nico, and singer, Rochereau Tabu Ley, (who later formed African Fiesta), Franco's O.K Jazz (1956- Figure 51), and Orchestra Les Bantous of Congo-Brazzaville (1959). Congo jazz spread throughout the whole of Africa through records, and Congo Brazzaville's ex-wartime radio transmitter, the most powerful then in black Africa.

In English-speaking West Africa, *maringa*, *juju* music and *highlife* became the dominant transcultural popular music forms. Sierra Leone's Ebenezer Calendar released almost three hundred *maringa* songs during the 1950s and in the 60s, the Afro-Nationals and other electric *maringa* bands entered the scene. Due to rising nationalist sentiments and the introduction of amplification, loud traditional hour-glass drums started to be used in Nigerian *juju* bands, for example by Ayinde Bakare in 1948,[7] and regional variants of *juju* evolved. Most important was that played by I. K. Dairo's Morning Star (Figure 52) and Blue Spots bands of the 1950s and 60s, which enlarged *juju* trios and quartets to full-scale dance-bands that played at working class night-clubs rather than middle-class salons. Immediately after the war, the Yoruba created a comic traveling theatre (partly influenced by local Cantata Bible-plays and partly by the Ghanaian concert party) pioneered by Hubert Ogunde, who staged several plays against the British colonial authorities.

Ghanaian highlife went through two immediate postwar developments. Pioneered by E.T. Mensah's Tempos, the huge pre-war dance orchestras were trimmed down to smaller swing-combo size. The resulting 'dance band highlife' blended in swing-jazz, calypsos and Afro-Cuban percussion, introduced by the Tempos' drummer, Guy Warren aka Kofi Ghanaba. Many bands were influenced by the Tempos: the Black Beats, Rhythm Aces, Ramblers, Broadway and Uhuru of Ghana, the Ticklers of Sierra Leone, and highlife bands in Nigeria run by Bobby Benson, Victor Olaiya, Bill Friday, Rex Lawson and Victor Uwaifo. The jazz influence on Africa was augmented by trips to Africa by Louis Armstrong in 1956 and again in 1961-2.

The small pre-war palm-wine highlife groups of Ghana evolved into larger, post-war 'guitar bands' that borrowed instruments (double-bass, bongos, trap-drums), from the more prestigious highlife dance-bands. In 1952 E. K. Nyame fused guitar band music with the concert party, creating his Akan Trio that had a comic highlife-opera format (Figure 53). This combination was emulated by many others: Kakaiku, Yamoah, Onyina, the Jaguar Jokers, Bob Cole's Trio, the African Brothers, and Happy Stars of Togo. During the early independence struggle from the late 1940s, most of Ghana's guitar bands, concert parties, (and highlife dance bands), backed Nkrumah's CPP nationalist political party, that was aiming at speedy independence from Britain.

In East Africa, local *beni* brass band music died out during the war and was replaced with local variants of the rumba and jazz played, for instance, by the Rhino Boys of Kenya. Their vamping or strumming Jimmy Rodger guitar style subsequently spread to the inland Luo and Luhya. This was followed by the 'dry' two-finger picking guitar style of eastern Congo which, in combination with the techniques and high pitched playing of traditional harps and lyres, created the *sukuti* regional guitar style popular in Kenya and Uganda during the 1950s.

For postwar Francophone West Africa, Afro-Cuban and Latin American dance music was all the rage in the cities. Many elite bands were set up to play this in Spanish or Portuguese. These included La Habanera Jazz of Guinea, the Sor Jazz Band of Senegal, Volta Jazz of Burkina Faso, Alpha Jazz of the Benin Republic, the Melo Togos of Togo, François Lougah's band in Abidjan and Segou Jazz of Mali. Unlike the two Congos, the full indigenisation of the rumba only took place in Francophone West Africa after the 1960s. This will be discussed later.

Immediately after the war, in South Africa a proletarian version of black Sophiatown's middle-class swing music appeared, using homemade guitars and cheap penny whistles. This *kwela* music, together with its sexually suggestive *phatha-phatha* dance, became popular with the *tsotsi* gangs who were becoming increasingly criminalised due to oppressive governmental policies. After the apartheid system was institutionalised in 1948, black urban areas like Sophiatown were destroyed, and its inhabitants relocated to townships. A musical result was the growth during the 1950s of *mbaqanga* or 'township jazz/jive.' This combined elements of jazz, *marabi*, *kwela*, Zulu night-music (e.g. of Ladysmith Black Mambazo), and Sotho *focho* accordion music. Various sub styles of saxophone/guitar/accordion jive arose, the most important being *simanje-manje* ('now-now'), in which a township jive band backed a female close-harmony group and traditional Zulu 'male groaner.' The most famous was Miriam Makeba's (ex-Manhattan Brothers) Skylarks (Figure 54), followed by the Dark City Sisters and Mahotella Queens. The itinerant Zulu/Ndebele style of guitar playing became absorbed into the electric *maskanda* electric guitar bands, popular in working class communities.

The Independence Era

With independence, beginning with Ghana in 1957, many African governments actively supported local popular music in line with their concepts of 'negritude' (Senghor), 'African personality' (Nkrumah), and 'authenticité' (Mobutu). State recording, film and television studios were established. Pan-African festivals were held (the first in Dakar, and the biggest, Nigeria's FESTAC 77), state bands set up, women artistes were encouraged and music unions developed.

In Anglophone West Africa, the Sierra Leone government made Ebenezer Calendar head programmer for state radio, and formed the female police dance-band. Similarly, Nigeria had its all-female armed-forces band, and Ghana's Nkrumah government formed workers' brigade bands and concert parties that included female artistes. Unions for dance musicians and local comic opera groups were established in Ghana (1961 and 1960 respectively) and in Nigeria (1958 and 1971 respectively).

After the 1967-70 Nigerian Civil (Biafran) War, there was an oil boom that created a strong local record manufacturing industry. During the war, highlife (dominated by easterners), waned in western Nigeria, whilst *juju* music waxed and turned again into praise-music, supplied to the oil boom 'nouveau-riche' by *juju* music super-star millionaires such as Ebenezer Obey and Sunny Ade. Highlife survived however in the east and mid-west of Nigeria, played by bands such as the Peacocks, Oriental Brothers, Warriors, Soundmakers, Philosphers' National, Rokafil Jazz, and Victor Uwaifo's Melody Maestros. In neighbouring Cameroon, a local guitar band blend of local palm-wine music with Nigerian highlife and Congo Jazz evolved into the *makossa*.

Tanzania became independent in 1961. In 1967 it declared Swahili the national language. There was a ban on foreign pop, but one hundred-and-twenty 'Swahili jazz' bands were formed, many (for example, Vijana and Juwata Jazz) sponsored by Nyerere's socialist government. These all played a local version of Congo jazz, introduced by musicians and bands (such as Remmy Ongala and Orchestre Makassy), that left Congo-Kinshasa due to its turbulent 1960-5 civil war.

The rise of transcultural popular dance-music evolved later in Francophone West Africa than in English speaking Africa, partly due to the French 'direct' colonial rule in which the colonised either became 'évolués' (i.e. black Frenchmen), or remained as 'indigenes'. This policy, unlike British 'indirect rule' through traditional chiefs and institutions, did not foster cross-cultural exchange. However, with independence (beginning with Guinea in 1958) this situation changed rapidly.

In Sekou Touré's Guinea, and President Keita's Mali, foreign pop music was suppressed and state popular music bands were formed. State radio and record companies were also established to disseminate this music as well as that of the hereditary *griot* (Mandingo *jali*) families such as Koyate, Diabate, Suso, Damba and Kante/Konte. During the 1960s, state bands like Guinea's Bembeya Jazz, and the Les Amazons female police band, and Mali's Super Biton and National Badema (as well as the private Star Band and Baobab Band of Senegal), began the indigenisation of Francophone West African popular music. They combined urban rumbas and Congo jazz with local ingredients from Manding culture, and sang in the Manding dialects of Bambara, Malinke, Dioula and Wolof. An example of an 'Afro-Mandingo' band is Mali's Rail Band formed in 1970, whose singer, Salif Keita, and guitarist, Mory Kanta, were *griots,* and whose Guinean guitarist, Kante Manfila, drew ideas from the twenty-one stringed *kora* harp-lute of the *griots*. Other indigenised Francophone West African popular music genres, such as Senegalese *mbalax* and Malian *wousoulou* will be discussed later.

While most of Africa moved towards independence after the Second War, southern Africa went through a period of increasing oppression. Civil wars occurred in Zimbabwe (1965-80), Angola (1961-74) and Mozambique (1962-75), that held back the emergence of popular music. In Zimbabwe however, anti-Ian Smith[8] *chimurenga* (Shona for 'liberation') guitar-band music (influenced by the local *mbira* hand-piano), was created in the mid-1970s by Thomas Mapfumo and Oliver Mutukudzi. When the Zimbabwean guerrillas returned home from exile in Tanzania, they brought home the fast East African versions of Congo jazz with them. This, combined with *chimurenga*, created the ultra-fast *jit* music of the Bhundu (Bush) Boys and others.

After the 1960 Sharpeville massacre, the political situation went from bad to worse in South Africa. *Mbaqanga* continued to be played in the townships but, with the destruction of Sophiatown and the banning of integrated bands and audiences (the 1959 King Kong musical was the last multi-racial show under apartheid), many of South Africa's jazz musicians went abroad into exile. These included Ibrahim Abdullah (Dollar Brand), Dudu Pukwana, Chris McGregor's Brotherhood of Breath, Letta Mbulu, Hugh Masekela and Miriam Makeba. Ironically, in the United States, Miriam Makeba (encouraged by Harry Belafonte in New York), switched away from jazz-influenced music and became internationally acclaimed for her renditions of South African folk-songs, which (via records and African tours) stimulated many African artistes, especially women.

With the South African apartheid regime's banning of multiracial performances, Gibson Kente (who began his career in `King Kong'), established a popular theatre in Soweto during the mid-sixties. As Coplan (1985:208) observes, at first Kente carefully avoided dramatising the overtly political, and rather concentrated on 'personal morality and social responsibility based on African christianity.' However, with the radicalisation of his audience in the 1970's, Kente's plays began to be more openly political, a trend that was followed by Sam Mhangwane and other younger popular playwright-directors of the period.

It should also be noted that from the 1960s, there emerged a theatrical form influenced by popular drama, traditional ritual drama, and literary university-based theatre (after the Brazilian educator, Paulo Freire), known as 'theatre-for-development' (see also Chapter 17). It began mainly in Anglophone speaking African countries as the theatre schools established in Francophone African countries were more tied to French literary and dramatic traditions.

In the case of West Africa, an early example was the pioneering work done in Ghana by Efua Sutherland, who set up the Ghana Experimental Theatre in 1958, and the Kusum Agoromma concert party in the 1960s, that drew on traditional story telling. Calling this *anansegoro* theatre, she put on plays about family planning and other social issues. In Nigeria during the 1960s, there were the plays of Duro Lapido staged at the Mbari Mbayo Centre in Oshogbo. In Sierra Leone, health educators experimented with theatre-for-development in the late 1970s, and in 1986, the Adult Education Department of Fourah Bay College set up a popular community theatre. As a consequence, Charles Haffner's Freetown Players, the most well-known travelling theatre group in Sierra Leone (established in the 1970s), began to highlight topical issues in their songs and acts, such as the need for immunisation, voter registration, and the dangers of toxic waste dumping (see Malamah-Thomas, 1988).

In other parts of Anglophone Africa, there have been similar policies of using popular drama for national development. An early example was the Makwere Free Travelling Theatre of Uganda, established in the mid 1960s. Barber (1987:33) says that Tanzania's popular theatre was actually instigated by the government and parastatal organisations, after the economic downturn that followed the 1978 war with Uganda. The Lesotho government stimulated popular drama through its National University, which set up a theatre-for-development that employed the Marathali Travelling Theatre to stage plays on the themes of re-forestation and the benefits of cooperative societies. Other eastern and southern African examples of theatre–for-development that began in the 1970s include the Laedza Batanani Theatre of Botswana, the Chikwakwa Theatre of Zambia, and the Kamiriithu Theatre of Kenya.

'Pop' Music of the 1960s and the Experimentation of the 1970s

From the early 1960s, two musical waves swept Africa. One already mentioned was Central African Congo jazz. The other was imported 'pop' music, mainly African-American based rock 'n' roll,[9] twist, soul, funk, followed by soul influenced disco and Jamaican reggae. These were introduced through records and tours in the 1960s by James Brown, Chubby Checker,

Millicent Small, and Ghana's 1971 'Soul to Soul' concert that featured Tina Turner, Wilson Pickett and Santana.

At first, imitative youthful pop bands sprang up, especially in English-speaking Africa: the Avengers, El Pollos and Aliens of Ghana; the Cyclops, Blue Knights and Soul Assembly of Nigeria; the Echoes and Heartbeats of Sierra Leone; the Super Eagles of Gambia; the Chicken Run Band of Zimbabwe; and the Beaters of South Africa. However, during the 1970s, a more experimental 'Afro-pop' fusion phase began, due to a combination of various factors. These included the independence Africanisation ethos and Pan-Africanism. Also important were the black pride, Afro-centric and back-to-roots message found in African-American soul music and 'Afro' fashions, as well as Afro-Caribbean reggae and rastafarianism.

An early pop fusion was the Ewe music of Togo's Bella Bellow. Another was the 'Afro-rock' of Ghana's London-based Osibisa (composed of ex-highlife musicians- Figure 55). Many other Afro-rock bands followed: Hedzolleh and Boombaya of Ghana; BLO, Mono-Mono, the Funkees and Ofege of Nigeria; the Super Combo of Sierra Leone; Harare and Javuka/Savuka of South Africa; and later Angelique Kidjo of the Benin Republic.

Another Afro-pop style was soul-influenced 'Afro-beat,' created in 1969 by Nigeria's militant and controversial, Fela Anikulapo (Ransome) Kuti, (an ex-highlife musician- Figure 56). This style was taken up by the Polyrhythmic Orchestra of neighbouring Benin, the Big Beats and Sawaaba Sounds of Ghana, and Nigerian Afro-beat bands run by Femi and Sehun Anikulapo-Kuti (Fela's sons), Kola Ogunkoya, Dede Mabiaku and Lagbaja. Other Afro-soul fusions were created by Nigeria's Segun Bucknor, the South African Soul Brothers (a blend of *mbaqanga* and soul) and the disco-*maringa* hits of Sierra Leone producer Akie Deen (by Sabanah 75, Bunny Mack and Liberia's Miatta Fahnbulleh). Cameroon's Manu Dibango (ex Kalle's African Jazz), had an international hit in 1972 with his 'Soul Makossa' record and in the early 1980s, German-based Ghanaian musicians created a disco-highlife[10] blend known as 'Burgher' (i.e. Hamburg[11]) highlife.

Soul also influenced the *kiri kiri* 1969 sub-style of Congo jazz (Kazadi, 1973), the same year that the *Zaiko* (i.e. Zaire plus Kongo) Langa Langa band was formed in Kinshasha. This student oriented group was instrumentally modelled on western Beatles-type pop groups, and did away with the horn section of Congo jazz. Influenced by Mobutu's *authenticité* policy, this and other-similar groups (Clan Langa Langa, Zaiko Wa Wa, etc.), used revamped folk-dances (e.g. Cavacha and Zekete Zekete) for the seben section of their songs and did away with the rumba introduction altogether. Ironically ex-Zaiko member, Papa Wemba later became the idol of the young 1980s and 90s 'sapeurs' who wore French designer clothes as a snub to the *authenticité* policy of the increasingly unpopular President Mobutu.

Reggae music became fashionable in Africa in the early seventies. Many Jamaican artistes visited the continent; for instance Jimmy Cliff's Nigerian tour in 1974, and Bob Marley's trip to Zimbabwe during its independence celebration in 1980. At first it was all a matter of local bands doing cover versions in Jamaican patois of the Wailers, etc, but 'Afro-reggae', often sung in local languages, soon began to be composed by the Pied Pipers of Zimbabwe; Ghana's City Boys, K.K. Kabobo, Kwadwo Antwi and Rocky Dawuni; Miatta Fahnbulleh of Liberia; Sonny Okosun, Ras Kimono, Majek Fashek and Evi Edna Ogholi of Nigeria; Alpha Blondy of the Côte d'Ivoire; and South Africa's Lucky Dube.

Yet another form of popular music experimentation that began from the 1960s, was the creation of acoustic popular ensembles, or electric ones that drew heavily on traditional instrumental techniques and folk rhythms. Examples of the former are of two types. First, the music of folk guitarists such as Koo Nimo of Ghana; Francis Bebey of the Cameroons; Pierre Akendengue of Gabon; S.G. Rogie of Sierra Leone; and the blues-*griot* fusion of Mali's Ali Farka Toure. Second, there are the popular music ensembles that have done away with all or most western instruments. These include the *fuji* music of western Nigeria; the 1960s *maringa* influenced acoustic 'milo jazz' of Sierra Leone's Dr. Olu; the Ga cultural groups of Ghana pioneered in 1973 by Wulomei; and the 1990s neo-traditional *sundama* music of Congo Kinshasa.

Figure 51 – Luambo Franco, Leader of O.K. Jazz of the D.R.Congo

Photo: *J.Collins/BAPMAF collection*

Figure 52 – I.K.Dairo and his Blue Spots Juju Band in the 1950s

Photo: *Andy Frankel*

Figure 53 – The Akan Trio Concert Party with its leader E. K. Nyame, and a lady impersonator

Photo: *Cathy Cole collection*

Figure 54 – South Africa's Miriam Makeba

Photo: *J. Collins/BAPMAF collection*

Examples of electro-folk fusion popular from the 1970s are the 'benga beat' of Kenya and Uganda that, like its sukuti predecessor, draws on the local lyre tradition; the mbira influenced chimurenga music of Zimbabwe; the fast polyrhythmic 'bikutsi pop' of the Cameroons that is based on traditional xylophone playing; the previously mentioned Zaiko style of Kinshasa; and the Bete folk rhythm influenced music of the Côte d'Ivoire's Ernesto Dje-Dje (his zigblithi) and Amedee Pierre.

Particularly striking is the string of electro-folk fusions that have been produced in the Manding and Fulani areas of Francophone West Africa since the 1970s. There are the Afro-Mandingo style referred to earlier played by Salif Keita's Ambassadeurs of Mali, Ifang Bondi (ex-Super Eagles) of Gambia, Super Mama Djoubi of Guinea-Bissau, Mory Kante of Guinea and Youssou N'Dour and Toure Kunda of Senegal (mbalax music) (Figure 57). Then there are 'electro-griot' bands that combine the instruments of the griots with western ones, such as those of Guinea's Sona Diabete (ex-Les Amazons), Gambia's Foday Musa Suso (Mandingo Griot Society), Mali's Tata Bambo, Ami Koita and Toumani Diabate and Senegal's Baaba Maal. A non-Mandingo variety of electro-folk is the Malian wassoulou sound based on Fula and Peul hunters music, but ironically popularised largely by women artists like Sali Sidibe, Nahawa Doumbia and Oumou Sangare.

Popular Entertainment since the 1980s

During the 1980s, the popular theatre of Nigeria and Ghana suffered a decline due to the rise of television video. Local video productions expanded enormously and these, to a large extent, drew on the themes of popular theatre. Local video production has also provided a professional occupation for many popular performers.[12] In the 1980s and through the 90s, three new developments emerged in Africa in the realm of dance-music; namely local gospel, local hi-tech computer music and 'World Music.'

Many of the thousands of separatist Christian churches found in Africa, unlike Western ones, allow dance for worship. They have since the late 1970s utilised local popular dance-music bands and commercial records as part of their outreach programmes. Examples of such bands are Nigeria's Charismatic Singers, Imole Ayo's Christian Singers, Sonny Okosun's (ex Melody Maestros) group, and Princess Ifeoma, the Puritans of Zimbabwe and the 'gospel-highlife' bands of Ghana. In Ghana, for instance, about sixty percent of the country's commercial recording output of local music is of danceable gospel music. As popular music has been thought an unsuitable profession for young people to enter, especially women, local gospel music, gospel bands and recordings are paving the way for many African women artists to enter the local music profession.

Disco-music, rap, house-music and ragga using drum-machines, synthesiser and computers have become fashionable with Africa's youth since the 1980s. Many artists have created local versions of this techno-pop: Nigeria's Bolarin Dawadu, South Africa's Sello 'Chico' Twale and Stimela; Guinea's Mory Kante; the Côte d'Ivoire's Magic System; Cameroon's Mone Bile; Congo-Kinshasa's Sousy Kassey; and Ghana's 'burgher highlife' stars, George Darko and Daddy Lumba. The latest techo-pop fashion is vernacular rap such as South African kwaito (Brenda Fassie, Yvonne Chaka Chaka, etc), Ghanaian hip-life, Zimbabwean Zim-rap and the estimated three thousand local rap groups of Senegal.

In the early 1980s danceable African popular music (coined 'World Music' in 1987) became, for the first time, internationally commercially viable. Western super-stars like Peter Gabriel, Stuart Coplan, Bob Geldof, Quincy Jones, David Byrne and Ry Cooder began experimenting in this idiom. An early success was Paul Simon's 1986 South African inspired 'Graceland' album (Figure 58). In a 2000 World Bank Report it was estimated that the total monies generated in sale and royalties of African music on the international (i.e. non internal African) market was about 1.5 billion dollars.[13] There are various causes for this international explosion of African based world music. One is the large number of African musicians who have moved abroad, beginning with the exodus of South African jazz musicians in the 1960s, and followed in the 1970s and 80s by African artistes who settled and/or worked in London, Hamburg, Paris, New York and Toronto. Indeed, Paris became the recording Mecca for Francophone Africa from the mid-1980s, after moving from Abidjan.

Figure 55 – The Ghanaian Afro-Rock Band Osibisa

Photo: *J. Collins/BAPMAF collection*

Figure 57 – The Percussion Section of the band of Senegal's Youssou N'Dour

Photo: *Flemming Harrev*

Figure 56 – Cover of Fela Kuti's 'Zombie' record album released in 1977

Figure 58 – American 'World Music' star Paul Simon and some members of South Africa's Ladysmith Black Mambazo Choral Group

Photo: *J. Collins/BAPMAF collection*

461

A second reason is that with the death of Jamaican reggae star Bob Marley in 1981, international independent recording companies began to look for new black 'pop' styles and superstars, including ones from Africa. For instance in 1982, Chris Blackwell, the manager of Island Records (Marley's label), decided to sign on Nigerian *juju* music star Sunny Ade. Island Record's success was followed by other European and later American independent record companies who released albums of Zimbabwean *jit* bands, Congolese *soukous* artistes (Franco, Mpongo Love, Kanda Bongo Man) and the South African Zulu night-music of Ladysmith Black Mambazo. Currently the focus is on the Afro-beat of the late Fela Anikulapo-Kuti, and the music of Francophone West African artistes such as Youssou N'Dour, Salif Keita, Ali Farka Toure and Oumou Sangare.

The third reason for the global recognition of African popular music at the close of the 20th century is that it is a logical continuation of a process that began during the 19th century, when the popular music of the black diaspora (spirituals, minstrel songs and ragtimes) crossed over to whites. This continued throughout the 20th century, as a succession of international African-American dance-music crazes such as jazz, Afro-Cuban music (*son, rumba, chachacha,* etc), the Brazilian samba, the blues and rhythm 'n' blues, Trinidadian calypsos, Jamaican reggae and raga, soul, hiphop, rap and the zouk and salsa of the Caribbean. These have provided the western world with the nearest thing to a contemporary global 'folk' dance-music. What we are seeing today with World Music is this process completed, the international recognition of black popular dance-music stemming directly from the African continent itself.

Conclusion

During the pre-colonial era, novelty and change in the African performing arts music was largely an internal affair, resulting from the blending of elements from other ethnic groups through proximity, trade, migration, marriage, warfare as well as Islamic Arab contact. Particularly, and continually important, was the youthful re-interpretation and re-cycling of recreational performance styles. Today's African urban popular music can be treated as an extension of the traditional recreational genre, customarily so open to generational modification.

During the 19th and 20th centuries, another novelty that was absorbed by local recreational performers was western popular entertainment introduced through the score-sheets, records and film, and visits by foreign soldiers, sailors and occasionally performing artistes. The people who put African popular performance on stage, on record and onto the dance-floor were largely drawn from the urban masses and cash-crop farmers who emerged as an intermediate class between the national elites and the traditional subsistence peasant farmers. By the early 20th century, these included new rural migrants to the cities, semi-skilled artisans, small traders, seamen, transport workers, farmers, unskilled workers, messengers, school-teachers, school 'drop-outs,' 'area boys,' 'veranda boys,' and minor civil servants. It is from this layer of society that many of the popular artistes of Africa and indeed their audiences have emerged. And because of their lowly status, geographical mobility and being, so to speak, in the middle of things, the popular artiste is in the perfect cosmopolitan position or 'nexus' to produce new African art-forms: by spinning artistic cultural bridges between the old and new, high and the low, rural and urban, local and global.

Popular artistes also provide social commentaries on current events and articulate the ideals and social tensions of the 'street.' Their music, dances and dramas, reflect and articulate and even help create city values and norms, generational identities, class boundaries and changing gender relations. Because of its inter-ethnic nature, popular art also provides African polyglot cities with a common artistic language or 'lingua franca.'

Many African popular artistes were also active in the early nationalist struggle, and as a result many of the first generation of leaders of the newly independent African governments (Nkrumah, Nyerere, Sekou Toure, Keita, etc), put great emphasis on encouraging the local popular arts in the creation of a national and even Pan African identity. More recently, popular artistes have also provided a social and even political critique of the status quo from the point of view of the down-trodden and marginalised. The protest songs of Thomas Mapfumo of Zimbabwe and Fela Kuti of Nigeria against corruption in high places are examples of this.

Just as the American and Caribbean black nationalism of Blyden, Du Bois, Padmore and Garvey had an important influence on African political development, the performing arts of the New World has been a catalyst in the emergence of many African popular music styles discussed in this chapter. The early impact of freed slaves, visiting black missionaries and soldiers from the Americas and later the introduction of ragtime, tap-dancing, minstrel acts, the rumba, swing and calypso music: through records, films and visiting artistes. Since the late 1960s, 'Afro' fashions and Afro-centric ideas have been coming to Africa through the medium of soul, reggae and rap, and have found fertile soil in post-independent African nations. The enormous and resonating impact of the popular performance of the Black Diaspora on that of Africa unites a four hundred year black cultural trans-Atlantic feedback cycle that began with slavery and the retentions and transmutations of African culture in the New World, returned 'home' to Africa from the nineteenth century onwards.

Finally, in the last twenty years, African popular performance, particularly dance music, has become the corner-stone of the booming 'World Music' phenomenon due to a combination of reasons. The continuing internationalisation of Black popular performance that began in the 19th century, the exodus of African performing artistes abroad since the 1960s, and the impact of instant and easy communications resulting from new digital technology. But above all, the global reach and success of African popular performance today stems from the artistes and entertainers themselves, who over the last two centuries have combined and refined traditional and foreign resources to produce contemporary trans-cultural performance styles which are not only aesthetically pleasing and relevant at home, but are increasingly appealing to a cosmopolitan world.

Review Questions

1. Can popular performance text be a good source of information for historians?

2. Discuss the idea that it is the very 'fleeting' and 'transient' nature of popular performance as compared to the 'immortal works' of Western classical art-music, that makes

463

it well so suited to provide social scientists with information on the society they are studying.

3. Discuss the idea that African popular music demonstrates the importance of the masses and 'intermediate' layers of society in the formation of a new African culture, and that this is not just the not the prerogative of elites and intellectuals. Can the popular artiste therefore be a innovative role-model for students?

4. Why is African popular music, dance and drama just as important as art-music in fostering a national and even Pan African identity?

5. African popular entertainment throws light on areas in African urban studies such as social and class tensions, conflict resolution, gender relations and inter-ethnic communication. Think of some other ways popular entertainment is relevant to urban studies.

6. African popular entertainment plays a role in creating, maintaining and re-cycling of youth subcultures in Africa. Is this comparable to the way popular dance-music styles in the West mark out the waxing and waning of their youthful sub-cultures?

7. Do you think the growth of African urban popular performance is a result of African traditional music being westernised, or of western music being Africanised, or both?

References

Barber, K. 1987. "Popular Art in Africa" *African Studies Review*: 10 (3): 1-78, September.

Barber, K, E.J. Collins and A. Ricard 1997. *West African Popular Theatre*. Bloomington: Indiana University Press and James Currey

Bilby, K. M. 1985. *The Caribbean as a Musical Region*. Washington D.C.:The Woodrow Wilson International Centre for Scholars,

Clark, Ebun 1979. *Hubert Ogunde: The Making if Nigerian Theatre*. London: Oxford University Press.

Collins, E.J. 1992. *West African Pop Roots*. Philadelphia: Temple University Press.

Coplan, D. 1985. *In Township Tonight: South Africa's Black City Music and Theatre*. Johannesburg: Ravan Press.

De Graft-Johnson J.C., 1932. The Fanti Asafu, in *The Journal of the Institute of African Languages and Culture*, D. Westerman (ed), Oxford University Press, Volume V, pp. 307-322.

Echeruo, M. J. C. 1962. Concert and Theatre in Late 19th Century Lagos. *Nigeria* magazine, Lagos, no.74, September, pp. 68-74

Erlmann, V. 1988. A Feeling of Prejudice: Orpheus McAdoo and the Virginia Jubilee Singers. S. Africa 1890•-1998. *Journal of Southern African Studies*, vol. 14 (3), April, pp. 332-350.

Graham, M. R. 1988-98. *Stern's Guide to Contemporary African Music*, Vol. I and 2. London: Zwan/Off The Record Press.

Jacobs, J. U. 1989. The Blues: An Afro-American Matrix for Black South African Writing. In *English in Africa*, vol. 16 (2), October, pp. 3-17.

Kazadi, 0. 1973. Trends in 19th and 20th Century Music in Zaire-Congo. In *Musikulturen Asiens, Afrikas und Oceaniens*, (ed) von Robert Gunther, Gustav Bosse Verlag, Regensburg, no. 9, pp. 267-288.

Kerr, D. 1995. *African Popular Theatre*. London: James Currey.

Mensah, A. A. 1971/72. 'Jazz the Round Trip'. In *Jazz Research*, no.3/4, Graz.

Mitchell, J. Clyde. 1956. 'The Kalela Dance: Aspects of Social Relationship amongst Urban Africans in Northern Rhodesia.' Rhodes-Livingstone Paper, No. 27.

Nketia, J.H.K. 1971. 'History and Organisation of Music in West Africa,' Chapter One of *Essays on Music and History in Africa*. (ed) Klaus Wachsmann, Evanston: Northwestern University Press

Nketia, J.H.K. 1973 *Folksongs of Ghana*. Ghana University Press.

Nunley J. W. 1987. *Moving with the Face of the Devil: Art and Politics in Urban West Africa*. Urbana and Chicago: University of Illinois Press.

Ranger, T. O. 1975. *Dance and Society in Eastern Africa 1890-1970*. London: Heinemann.

Roberts J. S. 1974. *Black Music of Two Worlds*. New York: William and Morrow.

Sackey, C. K. 1989. *Konkoma: A Musical Form of Fanti Young Fishermen in the 1940's and 50's in Ghana W. Africa*. Berlin: Dietrich Reimer Verlag.

Stearns M. and J. 1968. *Jazz Dance: The Story of American Vernacular Dance*. London: McMillan.

Sutherland, Efua. 1970. *The Original Bob: The Story of Bob Johnson Ghana's Ace Comedian*. Accra, Ghana: Anowuo Educational Publications.

Waterman, C. 1990. *Juju: A Social History and Ethnography of an African Popular Music*. Chicago: University of Chicago Press.

Zindi, F. 1980. *Roots Rocking in Zimbabwe*. Harare: Mambo Press.

Endnotes

1. See `Travel to Heaven: Fantasy Coffins' by V. Burns (1974) *African Arts* (UCLA) 7 (2)... `Wall Paintings: A Popular Art in Two African Communities' by J. Beinart (1978), *Africa Arts*, 2(1). `Yoruba Photography: How the Yoruba's See Themselves', by S. Sprague, 1978. *African Arts*, 12 (1).. `Wire Bicycles' by M.P. Jackson, 1978. *In Situ* (Zambia) 30. `Nigerian Bread Labels: An Ephemoral Art Form' by J. Middleton (1974) *Nigerian Field*, 29:(2),1974. `No Time To Die' by K. G. Kyei and H. Schiekenbach (1975) Catholic Press, Accra 1975.

2. See Nketia (1971, 1981) for traditional African music dynamics. In his book, *Folksongs of Ghana* (1973) Nketia provides a sequence of changing traditional recreational styles of the Akan of Ghana.

3. The term 'native blues' (or 'Ashanti blues' in southern Ghana) is probably related to the fact that there was a thriving West African recording trade going on in the late 1920s and 1930s and the western companies coined the name 'blues' as the local recording artists were mainly itinerant guitarists, and so resembled the rural blues guitarists of the United States. Also like the American blues, the West African guitar music was slow in tempo.

4. Quinine only became easily available after quinine-tree plantations were established in the far east in the 1860's followed in the 1880's by the by the industrial manufacture of the active chemical

5. Personal communication with C.M. Cole, 1994-1996.

6. Decca in 1947 in Ghana was first.

7. The earlier un-amplified juju bands only used a single samba or asiko frame drum so that the stringed instrument (banjo, guitar) would not be eclipsed. However, with the introduction of the amplified guitar and banjo the 'aural balance' (Chris Waterman, 1990)) could be altered so as to increase additional drums

8. He was the leader of Southern Rhodesia that refused to allow black majority rule and made a unilateral declaration of independence (UDI) from Britain in 1965.

9. A white version of African-American electric rhythm 'n' blues that had evolved in cities like Chicago in the 1940s

10. Disco was a fusion of soul-funk and drum-machine music developed by groups like Kraftwork and Donna Summer in the 1970s

11. Created by Ghanaian musicians who had settled in Hamburg due to the economic collapse of Ghana and its music industry in the late 1970s

12. See for instance on Ghana, Meyer, B. (1998). *Popular Ghanaian Cinema and the African Heritage*. Netherlands Foundation for Tropical Research.

13. See World Bank website : www.worldbank.org/research/trade/africa_music2.htm

CHAPTER 22

A GUIDE TO SELECT REFERENCE SOURCES IN AFRICAN STUDIES

Olive Akpebu Adjah

This chapter attempts to provide a quick guide to a wide range of basic sources of information that will best serve the needs of students and researchers interested in African Studies. It examines materials that provide a general overview of African Studies, reference sources available in the subject area, and other information resources including major libraries and museums, and concludes by providing guidelines for citing references.

Africanist Documentation

This section brings together a number of publications that discuss African Studies in general. They serve as useful sources of information on the state of African Studies, current and future debates, and challenges in Africanist scholarship.

It is essential that one should find out what pieces of information exist at the onset of a research project in order to have an overview of the subject.

i. African Studies in the 21st century

African Studies Centre Research Programme 2002-2006. – Leiden: African Studies Centre, 2002,- pp. 5-10.

The paper argues that African Studies must remain important because Africans constitute one eighth of the world's total population. It goes on to discuss the state of African Studies in the 21st century, and gives an overview of the status of African Studies in the Netherlands.

ii. African Studies outside Africa

Encyclopedia of Africa South of the Sahara/ edited by John Middleton- Vol. 4. – London: Charles Scribner's Sons, 1997. pp. 435-459.

The section provides a listing of major sources for the study of Africa from the Arab world to the present day.

iii. DIKE, K. Onwuka (1964) 'The importance of African Studies'.

The Proceedings of the First International Congress of Africanists, Accra 11th –18th December, 1962/edited by Lalage Bown and Michael Crowder. – Accra: International Congress of Africanists. – Pp.19-28.

The paper argues that Africa, the most colonized continent in the world from the times of the Romans to the present day, has played a part in almost every nation's history. Based on that premise, the writer states the reasons why the study of the African people is important.

iv. HERSKOVITS, Melville J (1964)

'The Development of Africanist Studies in Europe and America'. The Proceedings of the First International Congress of Africanists, Accra 11th – 18th December, 1962/ edited by Lalage Bown and Michael Crowder. – Accra: International Congress of Africanists. – pp. 29-45.

The paper attempts to trace the broad lines along which Africanist Studies have developed.

v. PRAH, Kwesi

'African scholars and Africanist scholarship'. CODESRIA Bulletin. – No. 3 & 4 . – Dakar: CODESRIA, 1998. – p 25-31.

A discussion of the role of western scholarship in the production and reproduction of knowledge about Africa.

For more current discussions on Africanist ideas see the under-listed titles:

i. Alpers A. Edward and Roberts F. Allen 'What is African Studies: some reflections'. *African Issues*. – Vol. 30, No. 2, 2002. – p11-18

ii. *African Universities In The Twenty-First Century/edited by Paul Tiyambe Zeleza and Adebayo Olukoshi*.- Dakar: CODESRIA, 2004. – Vol. 2: Knowledge and Society.
Chapter I is entitled "Perceptions of Africanisation or endogenisation at African universities: issues and recommendations.'

iii. Schmidt, Heike 'The future of Africa's' past: observations on the discipline.' *History in Africa*. – Vol. 34, 2007. Pp. 453-460.

Reference Sources

The listings above help provide an overview on the state of African Studies; however at the start of every research there is also the need to find out sources of information available in the subject area. The best place to begin reading about a topic is from the reference sources. Reference sources, as the name implies, are materials that contain concentrated information, meant to be referred to for specific pieces of information and not to be read from cover to cover. Reference sources provide the necessary introduction to a topic or subject, clarify issues and terms, provide a one-stop-shop for information and help identify other relevant sources of information. They serve as starting points of every research or gateways showing the means by which information can be accessed.

Every library has these special sets of materials in its reference collection housed in a particular area or room. These materials are not allowed out of the library because they are meant for frequent consultation and therefore must be accessible to all. There are basically two types of reference sources; 'self-contained' reference sources i.e. those that contain the needed information e.g. encyclopedia and the 'where to find' reference sources i.e. those which direct to the sources of information e.g. bibliography. Each of these reference materials provides a peculiar kind of information and the use of a particular kind depends on the kind of information being sought. The preface of each reference work describes the scope, arrangement; guidelines for use and currency i.e. date of publication, to help decide if a particular reference work would satisfy a pertinent need. Listed below are some 'where to find' reference sources found in a library's reference collection.

Where to Find Reference Sources: Guides

Guides, as the name implies, are to show the way, serving as finding aids that direct and guide a researcher through the maze of information available. They list all sources of information available in a particular subject or subject areas by pointing to other documents or collection of information. Two Guides that provide general and current scholarly information in African Studies are:

Africa: A Guide to Reference Material. - 2nd revised and expanded edition/ Chippenham: Hans Zell Publishers, 2007. -666p

First published in 1993, this second edition is revised and substantially expanded edition of a classic African studies reference work that evaluates the leading sources of information (other than bibliographies) on Africa South of the Sahara published in English and French, and in a number of other European languages.

This edition contains 3,600 for the most part annotated entries, covering encyclopedias, dictionaries, directories, handbooks, atlases and gazetteers, almanacs, yearbooks, topographic reference sources, directories of organizations, as well as biographical and statistical sources. Each title is described and analysed for content. Following a general section on Africa as a whole (with sub-divisions by special subjects), material is arranged under broad regions of Africa, and then by individual countries.

The book is extensively cross-referenced throughout and contains an author and title index, and a separate subject index with expanded coverage to accommodate the increased subject range of this new edition. It has sections on principal reference sources in the biological and earth sciences, especially on flora and fauna, and on biology, habitat, and geology. Africa: A Guide to Reference Material facilitates rapid access to specific sources for an enquirer seeking to track down information.

Guide to Reference Material facilitates rapid access to specific sources for an enquirer seeking to track down information.

The African Studies Companion: a guide to Information sources; revised and expanded 4th edn./ edited by Hans M Zell – Chippenham: Hans Zell Publishers, 2006. – 864p.

The African Studies Companion, which can be accessed online as well, provides compact, time-saving and annotated guidance to print and electronic information sources, and access to a wide range of sources of information in the field of African Studies. It lists reference tools and online resources, African studies journals, listings and profiles of publishers with African studies lists, of organizations, and much more. It also has a directory of African (as well as African American) Studies teaching and research centres, and those offering African Studies programmes and courses, in all parts of the world. It contains over 300 entries; each entry includes the full postal address, telephone/fax numbers, email address, name of Director or Chair, and links to websites leading to information about faculty and staff, details of courses and programmes, admission requirements, degrees awarded, publications, and contact points. guide offers essential information for over 250 of the continent's leading newspapers and news weeklies, providing full

The guide offers essential information for over 250 of the continent's leading newspapers and news weeklies, providing full editorial and other contact details, email address and website (where available), frequency, political orientation, as well as information about access to searchable online archives. This publication also has an updated and condensed version of a popular guide, designed to help the user get the most out of Google's web search techniques, and at the same time providing a critical evaluation of Google's many web search features, services, and tools. This companion can be accessed online at www.africanstudiescompanion.com.

Bibliographies

Another reference source for information is the bibliography, similar to a map or compass, that helps in the search for information. Bibliographies list books, articles and other relevant sources of information. They could be an entire book or sections in books or journal articles. Bibliographies are consulted to discover materials available on a particular topic or subject area. Some bibliographies are annotated with short descriptions and evaluations, which help in the choice of relevant literature. However, unlike the catalogue of the library which lists all holdings in a particular library, materials listed in a bibliography do not necessarily mean they could all be located in one library. Bibliographies only make the reader aware of materials in existence. It is the first place a student or researcher or lecturer should think of in looking for materials on a given topic or item. An example of an African Studies bibliography is: *Africa Bibliography*. - Edinburgh: Edinburgh University Press. 1985-

Published annually, this bibliography records publications on Africa of interest to students and researchers of African Studies. Subject areas are principally in the social and environmental sciences, development studies, humanities and arts. Arrangement is by region and country, with a preliminary section for the continent as a whole. Each region or country begins with a general section and then the subject fields, in alphabetical order. It lists periodical articles, books, pamphlets and chapters of books listed. It has an author and subject index and is a useful source of information on materials available on particular subject areas in African Studies.

Self-Contained' Reference Sources

The second type of reference sources are the 'self-contained' reference sources, some of which are listed below:

Encyclopedia

The encyclopedia is described as the most useful single source of information (Katz, 1997) serving as a basis of any enquiry work. Encyclopedias are useful sources of background information on any research topic, as they tend to attempt a comprehensive discussion of topics, key concepts and terms. Encyclopedias are produced by a number of scholars and therefore tend to provide balanced, neutral, and widely accepted scholarly information about topics. Because of its universal scope, it is always a good place to start with enquiries for the history of an object, process, custom or practice. There are two types of encyclopedias; the general encyclopedia and the subject encyclopedia. The former, as the name implies, tends to be general in scope and the latter, which concentrates on a particular subject area, provides more in-depth information.

470

Older editions of encyclopedias are also useful because they provide historical information on the state of knowledge of the subject during a particular period (Grogan, 1997).

The encyclopedia has certain special features useful to a researcher. There are useful short bibliographies (list of books, articles etc) found at the end of each article which serve as a guide for further reading. An advantage of the encyclopedia bibliographies, according to Grogan (1997), is the "sheer speed" by which the user is made aware of specific books on a topic. At the beginning of any work it is advisable to consult an encyclopedia, possibly one in the subject area. However to make maximum use of the encyclopedia, one must look at the subject index or table of contents to identify topics discussed and arrangement in the encyclopedia. There is also the need to pay attention to the cross references in the index; the 'see' and the 'see also' references. The 'see' reference directs the user to the preferred term used in the text e.g. woman see female and the 'see also' suggests additional or related information which the user could consult or refer to. However one should not depend solely on information in the encyclopedia, for an in-depth study, but rather as an indication of the history and current scholarly state of the subject to help shape and focus a research work. Some useful encyclopedias in African Studies are:

Africana: the encyclopedia of the African and African American experience/ Kwame Anthony Appiah and Henry Louis Gates (Editors). Basic Civitas Books, 1998. Pp. 2095

A one-volume encyclopedia that attempts to provide a broad range of information to represent the full range of Africa and her Diaspora. About two-fifths of the text dealsexclusively with the African continent: the history of each of the modern nations of Africa; biographies of eminent African men and women, major cities and geographical features; forms of culture- art, literature, music, religion; and some of Africa's diverse plant and animal life.

Encyclopedia of African History/ edited by Kevin Shillington. – Fitzroy Dearborn, 2004. – 1600pp.

The *Encyclopedia of African History* in two volumes, contains about 1,000 entries covering a wide range of topics in African history from the earliest times to the present. It looks at social, economic, linguistics, anthropological and political issues.

*New Encyclopedia of Africa/*John Middleton and Joseph C. Miller (Editors).The *New Encyclopedia of Africa* encompasses the entire continent as well as the many changes that have occurred since 1997, not just in terms of scholarship and historical events, but also in terms of perspective.

Encyclopedia of Africa. Henry Louis Gates, Jr. and Kwame Anthony Appiah (Editors).- -2 Vols. Oxford: Oxford University Press, 2010.

This two-volume encyclopedia covers prominent individuals, events, trends, places, political movements, art forms, business and trade, religions, ethnic groups, organizations, and countries throughout Africa. The A–Z entries are preceded by a chronology and followed by a "Topical Outline of Selected Entries," a two-and-a-half-page bibliography organized by subject, and an index. It also has information about the death of South African singer Miriam Makeba, and the election of a women majority legislature in Rwanda in 2008, the death of former Sudanese president Gaafar Muhammad al-Nimeiry, and trouble with militant groups in Niger in 2009. The "At a Glance" tables in country entries have data drawn from estimates for 2009.

Dictionaries

Another self-contained reference source is the dictionary. Dictionaries are alphabetical listings of words, which set the authoritative standards for spelling, meaning, pronunciation and usage of words of a language or subject. According to Katz (1997), there are eight generally accepted categories of dictionaries. However the most useful category in this case is the Subject Dictionary. Subject dictionaries concentrate on definitions, meanings and sometimes the origin of words, in a given subject area and provides information which tends to be more than just simple definitions but are encyclopedic in nature. Such dictionaries do not only give definitions of terms but provide other descriptive information, brief biographies of persons prominent in the field. Defining a term is often a sensible way to begin an enquiry and subject dictionaries provide synonyms or alternative keywords to use in searching through indexes ,bibliographies and databases. A useful dictionary in African Studies is: *African Historical Dictionaries Series*. – Metuchen, NJ: Scarecrow Press, 1974-2000

In this series of African historical dictionaries, 75 or more titles dealing with individual African countries have been published between 1974 and 2000. They are useful to the Africana scholar and others who may which to place Africa in an understandable context. Each volume contains introductory tables of common abbreviations, acronyms, basic demographic patterns, notes on transactions and spelling issues included where required, maps agricultural regions, ethnic distributions, and important towns. They also contain a chronology of major political and historic events, past and present political leaders, military leaders, religious leaders and other groups of people who made history, and extensive bibliographies.

The African Historical Dictionaries Series provides background information, meaning of unfamiliar terms, information about the history, and politics or economy of each African country.

Directories

A directory is a list of names and addresses of any identifiable group of people. They are systematically arranged, usually in alphabetical or classed order, giving addresses, names of officers and functions. Directories also serve as historical sources of information, providing information about listings of people who were members of particular groups. A useful directory in African Studies is: The International Directory of African Studies Scholars (IDASS)

An online international directory containing records of individuals who have identified themselves as being involved in any aspect of African Studies. It has an index and allows users of the online directory to conduct searches by name or keyword.

Yearbooks

Yearbooks are like diaries of events, in a stated year, either all over the world, or in a particular country. They serve as both current and retrospective sources of information. Some useful ones are: *Africa Contemporary Record*. – New York; London: Africana Publishing Company. 1968-

An annual analysis of political, economic, social and constitutional developments in all countries on the African continent. It provides essays on current issues, country by country review of activities of governments in power, industrial relations and transport, political, social, foreign, economic affairs and any other issues of interest are discussed. In the international affairs section, key documents from international organizations like the Organization of African Unity, ECOWAS, and others are recorded. It has a subject and name index.

Africa South of the Sahara, 2010 –London: Routledge, 2009. – 1588p

The publication has over 500 pages of economic and demographic statistics, wide-ranging directory material and authoritative articles, contributions from over fifty leading experts on African affairs. Articles cover issues affecting the area as a whole, including: Economic Trends in Africa South of the Sahara; Health and Medical Issues in Sub-Saharan Africa; State Failure in Africa; A Century of Development; China's Expansion into Africa; European Colonial Rule in Africa; Peace and Security Architecture and The Threat of Organized Crime to West Africa.

It also contains a political map of contemporary Africa and a chronological list of the dates of independence of African countries. Individual chapters on every country incorporate:

- an introductory survey, containing essays on the physical and social geography, recent history and economy of each country
- an extensive statistical survey of economic indicators, which include area and population, health and welfare, agriculture, forestry, fishing, mining, industry, finance, trade, transport, tourism, media and education
- a full directory containing names, addresses and contact numbers for key areas such as the government, political organizations, diplomatic representation, the judiciary, religion, the media, finance, trade and industry, tourism, defence and education
- a useful bibliography, providing sources for further research.

Users can find detailed information on regional organizations; major commodities; calendars, time reckoning, research institutes concerned with Africa and select bibliographies of books and periodicals.

The Africa Yearbook. Leiden: Brill, 2004-

Published by the African Studies Centre at Leiden University, The Netherlands, it covers major domestic political developments, the foreign policy and socio-economic trends in Sub-Saharan Africa in one calendar year, and contains articles on all Sub-Saharan states and each of the four sub-regions (West, Central, Eastern and Southern Africa) focusing on major cross-border developments and sub-regional organizations.

There is also an article on continental developments, on Africa and the United Nations, and one on European-African relations. The Yearbook is mainly oriented to the requirements of a large range of target groups: students, politicians, diplomats, administrators, journalists, teachers, practitioners in the field of development aid as well as business people.

The Africa Yearbook is the sequel to the German-language ;Afrika Jahrbuch' that used to be published by the Institut für Afrika-Kunde in Hamburg.

Statistical sources

Statistical sources of information, as the name suggests, provide statistical information which answers the questions "How much and how many?" An example of a statistical source of information, published annually, is the:

African Statistical Yearbook, 2011. New York: United Nations, 2010

African Statistical Yearbook presents data on a country basis for 53 Economic Commission for Africa member States.

Biographies

Biographies are written accounts or history of a person that answers the questions who is who?, who has done what?, and serves as a useful source of portraits. They are biographical listings of notable persons usually arranged alphabetically by surname, with biographical identification that ranges from brief outlines to extended narratives. Biographies serve as a useful starting point when writing about people and unlike directories which serve as location tools, biographies provide more information about individuals. It is however useful to check one source against the other for possible omissions. Other sources of biographical information are obituaries in newspapers, bibliographies, periodicals and encyclopedias. In African Studies, one could come across biographical reference work concentrating on people in the history of a particular country or the continent. A useful biographical source is:

Makers of modern history: profiles in history. – London: Africa Books Ltd, 1996. – 733p

Comprising three volumes, *Africa Today, Africa Who's Who,* and *Makers of Modern Africa,* Volumes One to Three respectively, this title consists of 640 life histories of eminent people, who in their various ways occupied a special place in modern African history. Listings are alphabetically arranged, from General Sani Abacha to Sa'adu Zungur, with photographs. Information is provided about the date of birth and death, educational background and their contribution to the development of African history.

Vieta, Kojo T. *The flag bearers of Ghana: profile of one hundred distinguished Ghanaians.* – Accra: Ena Publishers, 1999. - 662p.

This book has biographical information abut Ghanaians who have distinguished themselves. Persons have been classified under broad headings: the Big Six, builders of a new nation (Convention Peoples' Party), the liberators (National Liberation Council), pioneers in Africanisation, challengers of gender stereotypes, the enlighteners, voice of civil society, promoters of the African personality, custodians of our culture and traditions, men of glory and spiritual leaders.

Online reference sources

The internet has become a very powerful tool for accessing reference information. The internet began in America in the 1960s with four computers owned by the Department of Defence, known as Advanced Research Projects Agency Network (ARPANET).The purpose was to swap information between agency sites in the event of a nuclear bomb falling on one of the computers. 1990 saw the first commercial company to provide access to the internet and by 1996, there were nearly 10 million hosts online and the internet covered the globe (Alexander, 2004)

The internet is a network of a number of computers that allows the dissemination, retrieval and communication of information in seconds. They could be connected via telephone lines, cables, microwaves or satellite systems. The internet is not owned by any single entity, but is rather a decentralized network. The World Wide Web (www), which is closely related to the internet, is a collection of documents or websites that one can access, using the internet and web browser software e.g. Microsoft Internet Explorer. People from all occupations use the internet and so are academics, students and researchers. According to Hofsteter (1998) the internet affords researchers an unprecedented opportunity to create an interconnected world of scholarship. He explained further by stating that scholarly papers mounted on the World Wide Web can be accessed with a few mouse clicks. A guide to electronic resources is:

Adjah, Olive A and Adanu, Theodosia S.A. 'A guide to free online resources in African Studies'. Research Review.- NS 20.1 (2004) 49-56.

The paper provides a guide to the huge resources in African Studies that reside on the internet at no cost. Online resources cited in the document include databases, discussion groups, mailing lists or listservs useful to the student and researcher in African Studies. Some online resources are:

JSTOR (all subjects full text)
http://www.jstor.org

JSTOR has more than a thousand academic journals and over one million images, letters and other primary sources. There are about 42 titles on Africa.

PROJECT MUSE (Humanities and Social Science)
http://musc.jhu.edu

A collaboration between libraries and publishers to produce full text journals.

AJOL –African Journals Online
http://ajol.info

A non-profit organization based in South Africa, which provides access to African published research promoting worldwide knowledge of indigenous scholarship.

ALUKA
http://aluka.org

Aluka aims at building a digital library of scholarly resources from and about Africa.

African Studies Internet Resources
http://www.columbia.edu/cu/lweb/indiv/africa/cuvl/index.html

Columbia University's collection of African Studies Internet Resources is an on-going compilation of electronic bibliographic resources and research materials on Africa available on the global Internet, created under the purview of the African Studies Department of Columbia University

Libraries. Electronic resources from Africa are organized by region and country. All materials are arranged to encourage an awareness of authorship, type of information, and subject. The scope of the collection is research-oriented, and it also provides access to other web sites with different or broader missions. Beginning in early 1999, the site became the "official" African Studies web site for the World Wide Web Virtual Library.

Academic Information Africa Studies Gateway
URL:http://www.academicinfo.ref/histafrica.html
The mission of Academic Info is to:

- Improve access to online educational resources by developing an easy to use subject directory covering each academic discipline.
- Increase educational opportunities for students in rural and underrepresented communities by giving them the same online experience as students from communities that are more privileged.

Academic Info tries to add between 250 and 500 new resources each month. A priority is adding digital collections from libraries, museums, and academic organisations and sites offering unique online content. It includes dissertations and preliminary research only if requested by the author.

Gateway to African Studies on H-Net

http://www.h-net.org/gateways/africa/

An international consortium of scholars and teachers, H-Net creates and coordinates Internet networks with the common objective of advancing teaching and research in the arts, humanities, and social sciences. The goals of H-Net lists are to enable scholars to easily communicate current research and teaching interests; to discuss new approaches, methods and tools of analysis; to share information on electronic databases; and to test new ideas and share comments on the literature in their fields.

Discussion /Mailing Lists

Discussion lists or mailing lists are an e-mail discussion forum that allows individuals to subscribe and automatically receive messages posted to the list by other subscribers. Participants may also post their own messages and replies for distribution to the other subscribers to the list.

E-mail discussion lists hold tremendous potential and opportunities to researchers for increasing knowledge and general self-development. They are an excellent and informal method of networking with colleagues, far and near, known and unknown, and are relatively inexpensive. Some information provided through e-mail discussion lists include conference announcements, short courses etc. It is also an avenue where one can contribute to hot issues/debates in one's area of interest as well as have responses to nagging questions.

E-mail discussion lists are available in all subject disciplines. African Studies boasts of numerous discussion lists. Below is a description of a few that may be beneficial to researchers.

The African News & Iinformation Service: Africa-N

The purpose of the African News & Information Service is to:

- To provide news, information, analysis, insight and articles about Africa
- To provide a forum for level-headed discussion on issues concerning Africa in an enlightened manner.

This list does not allow personal attacks on other list users. Neither does it accept articles that are of an inflammatory nature for example, making uncalled for attacks on the religion of others, etc.) The list welcomes discussions, but in an educated and reasoned manner.

To subscribe, send the following one-line command, "SUBSCRIBE AFRICA-N" to "LIST-SERV@UTORONTO.BITNET" or LISTSERV@VM.UTCC.UTORONTO.CA

AFRICAGIS Listserver

AFRICAGIS is an electronic mailing service provided by the Program on Environment Information Systems (EIS) in Sub-Saharan Africa hosted at the Environmentally Sustainable Development Division (AFTES) of the Africa Technical Department of the World Bank, in collaboration with UNDP, OSS/UNITAR and USAID/WRI-NRICG. The Program is specially building a network of institutions, organizations, groups, and people interested in EIS activities in Sub-Saharan Africa.

The objective of this mailing list is to provide a forum for discussion, and specially to promote the use of geographical information systems (GIS) and spatial information on environmental issues as a support tool for decision-making for natural resource management in Sub-Saharan Africa. AFRICAGIS is open to any interested parties. Subscribers can send questions, post information or comments regarding specific GIS topics to the list.

H-Africa Discussion group

H-AFRICA is a moderated electronic discussion group and bulletin board for scholars (including graduate students), librarians, and teachers interested in the African past, including a variety of disciplines and approaches to the history of the entire continent. A part of the H-Net family of LISTSERV discussion lists, H-AFRICA encourages informed discussions of teaching and research on African history at all levels of interest and complexity.

The primary purpose of H-AFRICA is to provide a forum for those interested in the serious study of African history to communicate openly. In this spirit, H-AFRICA welcomes research reports and inquiries, syllabi and course materials, bibliographies, listings of new sources, library and archive information, and non-commercial announcements of books, journals, conferences, fellowships, jobs, and funding opportunities, as well as reports on new software, datasets or CD-ROMs relevant to the African past.

Subscription to H-AFRICA is free and open to professional researchers and teachers in African history or allied fields and to everyone concerned with serious scholarship in the field. To subscribe, send an e-mail message to:

LISTSERV@MSU.EDU with no subject and only this text:

SUB H-AFRICA your first name your last name, your institution. When you include your own information, the message will look something like this: "sub h-Africa Harold Marcus, Michigan State U.").

OTHER SOURCES OF INFORMATION

This section presents other important sources on information.

Periodicals

Periodical literature, in its broadest definition, includes popular magazines, scholarly and technical journals and newspapers. Periodicals as the name suggests, are published at regular intervals- daily, weekly, monthly or quarterly, and each publication is called an issue, and these issues make up volumes. Periodicals or serials are loosely used for the same purposes. "Periodicals" is favoured in the United Kingdom and "serials" in the United States.

There are three main genres of periodicals- the newspaper, magazine and journals. Newspapers are published at rather frequent intervals and contain news, current opinions and affairs, contemporary thoughts on issues and topics, advertisements, news on everyday happenings and other pieces of information that make news. Newspapers are a source a peculiar kind of information which cannot be found anywhere else. Magazines usually have many photographs, come out in a glossy format and contain pieces of information that tend to be on various topics by different authors. Journals on the other hand contain scholarly and research-oriented articles and as Hord (1995) describes them, they come with plain covers, very little or no advertising, and are mostly text with tables and graphs, rather than photographs. Articles tend to be a little longer as compared to those in magazines and usually begin with an abstract, with authors most often having university affiliations or professional titles.

Periodicals are particularly useful in locating current information. This is because they are published at more frequent intervals than books and as a result, the contents are more current and up-to-date. A student writing a paper on a recent and controversial issue like Trokosi, a cult institution in some parts of Ghana for example, would probably encounter no books on the topic, but would discover articles in journals. Periodicals also provide briefer, concise and to the point information, because authors do not have enough space for lengthy discussions.

There is always a deluge of information, scattered amongst a number of periodicals which are difficult to identify and obtain. Most individual libraries display or make available to its users, lists of current periodicals. The most elementary guide to the contents of periodicals is the individual content page which comes with each issue. To help access this important source of information, are Periodical directories. Periodical directories serve as maps to periodicals and make the researcher or student aware of what basic periodicals there are on a subject and where they are indexed. It also provides information about each issue, the year it was first published, and the price. A directory worth looking at is:

Periodical directories

The Serials Directory: an International Reference Book. Birmingham: EBSCO, 1986-

A Guide to periodicals all over the world and in all subject areas, including African Studies. Entries provide title, frequency of publication, publisher's name and address, where periodicals are indexed, and subscription information.

Periodical indexing services and indexes

The catalogue of a library is not helpful when searching for articles in periodicals because periodical articles do not get listed as they do appear in periodical indexes. Indexes are directional aids useful for discovering articles that have been published on a given topic in a particular period, giving enough information as to how it can be traced. They serve as a systematic guide to the location of articles synonymous to a library catalogue. Periodical indexes therefore serve as a key to the content of periodicals. Many periodical publishers produce volume by volume index to contents of issues of their periodicals. However indexing services are also provided by "Periodical Indexing Services" that provide indexes on a regular basis. They usually have the advantage of currency, as most of them are published monthly, quarterly and the cumulative pattern; and most of them assist in speed searching. Indexes could be arranged alphabetically or analytically under appropriate headings or entries reflecting current terminology. Some useful indexes are

Quarterly index of African periodical literature. (Online) -- Nairobi, Kenya: The Library of Congress, 1991-

A searchable quarterly, online index of African periodical literature, indexing over 300 selected periodicals acquired regularly form 29 African countries.

http://www. Icweb2.loc.gov/misc/qusihtml.

The index on Africa

A gateway to information on Africa on the internet with over 2,000 listings, which can be navigated by links arranged by country or subject. This index on Africa was created by the Norwegian Council for Africa, as part of the efforts to raise awareness about Africa and African Affairs. It can be accessed at http://www.afrika.no/index/index.html

Abstracting Services and Abstracts

Indexes help locate articles in various periodicals. However they do not provide information about the content. Abstracts have several advantages over the indexes because they go further than providing the bibliographic citation to the original article to providing information about content. There are basically two sources of abstracts; the author abstracts written by the authors themselves which normally precede the main text of a book or periodical, and the independent abstract compiled by some else, commissioned by the abstracting service, who reads the articles and writes summary of the main content of the document in his own words.

Independent abstracts are usually arranged in a classified order, with each entry accompanied by 50-250 word summary of an indicative or informative abstract. Indicative abstracts only indicate matters dealt with in a document and alert the researchers about the existence of the document. Informative abstracts on the other hand, attempt to convey the message of the original document and incorporate important data, facts, observations and conclusions. Sometimes one can make do with this kind of abstract without referring to the original document. However an ideal abstract should combine the indicative and informative characteristics of an abstract. A useful one in African Studies is:

African Studies Abstract Online
http://asc.leidenuniv.nl/library/abstracts/asa-online/,

Issued four times a year, *African Studies Abstracts Online* provides an overview of articles from periodicals and edited works on Africa in the field of the social sciences and the humanities available in the library of the African Studies Centre in Leiden. Each issue of the journal contains up to 450 titles with abstracts of collective volumes, journal articles and chapters from edited works, arranged geographically. Each issue also contains a geographical index, a subject index, an author index, and a list of journals and edited works abstracted in that issue. Coverage includes all the leading journals in the field of African Studies, as well as a number of journals dealing with Third World countries and development studies in general (Adjah and Adanu, 2004).

Union Lists

When details of potentially useful materials have been identified with the aid of the index and abstract, the next step is to locate copies of the periodicals cited. A student's first step should be the academic or local library. A Union List is a location tool which helps identify where a particular periodical in the closest library could be borrowed or copied. Arrangement is usually in alphabetical order of titles, and notes are added to each title, indicating a shorthand coded form of the name of the libraries which house particular periodicals and the extent of holdings. Union lists could be compiled internationally, nationally, or on local basis. They could be general or restricted to a particular subject area. One such Union List is:

Periodicals in Africa: a bibliography and union list of periodicals published in Africa.- Boston: G.K. Hall, 1977

A comprehensive list of periodicals published in Africa and location of titles held in the United Kingdom. It covers all countries on the continent of Africa except Egypt.

Individual periodicals

Listed next are individual periodicals useful in the study of Africa:

Africa: journal of the International African Institute, 1928-

The journal Africa, published quarterly by the Edinburgh University Press, is the journal of the International African Institute which promotes international research, conferences and publications on African societies, cultures and languages. It attempts to promote the application of research and science to practical affairs in Africa.

African Studies Review, 1957-

African Studies Review is a multi-disciplinary scholarly journal of the African Studies Association, published three times a year (April, September and December). It publishes original research articles and book reviews on all aspects of African Studies.

Research Review, 1965-

The Research Review of the Institute of African Studies, University of Ghana, Legon, is a peer-reviewed scholarly journal issued twice a year. It publishes academic and scholarly articles that emphasize findings of new research in any branch of African Studies. Table of Contents can be accessed at http://www.inasp.info/ajol or http://www.sabinet.co.za. Document delivery service is available to persons under the Programme for the Enhancement of Research Information (PERI).

The Journal of Modern African Studies, 1963-

The Journal of Modern African Studies, published by the Cambridge University Press, provides a quarterly survey of developments in modern African politics and society. Its main emphasis is on current issues in African politics, economies, societies and international relations. This journal is included in the Cambridge Journals Online service and can be accessed at http://www. cambridge.org.

Theses/Dissertations

A dissertation or thesis is an original piece of individual research advancing a new point of view. Dissertations normally contain the results of high quality academic research, often in tertiary education institutions, written into a special form of report, most of which never get published. Dissertations or theses present original contributions to knowledge and relevant pre-existing literature. These works have a detailed list of references to the significant literature of the chosen field of the thesis, serving as a selective subject bibliography as well.

The student hunting a subject for research can find out what topics have already been covered and also have access to bibliographic information available in the subject area. There is however a vast amount of theses literature some of which might only be known to the authors. Some useful guides to dissertations available are the catalogue of a library, theses lists, guides and databases.

Theses on Africa 1976-1988 /edited by H.C Price, C. Herson and David Blake. —London: SCOLMA, 1993. 338pp.

It lists 3,654 items written on all the regions of Africa and on a wide variety of topics, including those not traditionally considered as falling within the scope of African Studies. Each entry lists author, title qualification, university/authority and date. It has an author and subject index to help users who are not sure where a particular item will be listed. This is an essential tool for researchers and students interested in research on Africa.

African Studies Dissertation and Theses on Africa
Guide to sources for dissertations and theses about and from Africa.
www-sul.stanford.edu/depts/ssrg/africa/theses.html

Database of African theses and dissertations (DATAD)

The DATAD database contains citations and abstracts written by authors of theses and dissertations completed in African Universities. Participating universities are from the Cameroon, Egypt, Ethiopia, Ghana, Kenya, Mozambique, Senegal, Tanzania and Zimbabwe. This database can be accessed on http://www.aau.org/datad/.

Libraries

Libraries are storehouses of information, managed by professional librarians with a fundamental role of preserving information for its users. A researcher or student cannot conduct effective research without exploring the wealth of information in the library. All materials listed in this guide can be found in libraries whose basic function is to store and make available the resources they have for use. However a researcher needs to be informed about libraries that are available in the field and there are Guides that serve that purpose. For example there is:

The SCOLMA directory of libraries and special collection on Africa in the United Kingdom and in Europe. 5th Edn, /edited by Tom French. — London: Hans Zell Publishers, 1993. 366p.

Published on behalf of the Standing Committee on Library Materials on Africa (SCOLMA), this directory identifies and describes books, periodicals and audiovisual materials in more than 300 libraries in the United Kingdom and Europe. It contains 392 entries listing the full name and address of each library, name of the chief librarian or person in charge, opening hours, the size of the collection and the type of materials housed in the various libraries.

Individual libraries

Some individual libraries with holdings on the subject area are as follows:

Institute of African Studies Library

University of Ghana
P.O. Box LG 75
Legon
Tel: 233 (0) 302 513390/1
Email: iaslib@ug.edu.gh

The Institute of African Studies Library, set up in 1961, is the research library of the Institute of African Studies. It possesses over 30,000 volumes of collections comprising books and periodicals. The Library boasts of special collections made up of stool histories from Ashanti, the Afram Plains, and the Volta Basins; court records, oral traditions all aspects of African Studies, newspapers dating back to 1932 and research publications produced by Research Fellows in the Institute. The Library is currently housed in the old building of the Institute of African

Studies and is open to the University community and any persons interested in African Studies.
Balme Library
University of Ghana
P.O. Box LG 24
Legon-Accra
http://library.ug.edu.gh

The Balme Library is the main library of the University of Ghana Library System. It coordinates from the main Legon campus, a large number of libraries attached to the various Schools, Institutes, Faculties, Departments and Halls of Residence of the University, most of which are autonomous. The Library is the nerve centre for academic work in the University. All academic related functions such as teaching, research and learning find their support-base in the library, where all types of documents are organised for easy access to members of the University community. It has an Africana Section where materials on Africa are housed. Most of the libraries, together with Balme, have a union catalogue called The University of Ghana Catalog (UGCat), the University's version of the Online Public Access Catalogue (OPAC). The UGCat provides a web interface to the University of Ghana libraries' catalog. The UGCat offers services such as ability to limit search to a specific library, personal search space using my record, course reserves, featured item lists, avenue for suggestions, comments or questions, means to suggest a purchase, and offers multiple means for searching the catalogue.

George Padmore Research Library on African Affairs

P.O. Box GP 2970
Accra
Tel: 233 (0) 302 223526

The George Padmore Research Library on African Affairs was established in 1961 to serve as a monument of the ideals of Pan-Africanism and a memorial to George Padmore. The main aim is to collect materials on Africa, and subject areas covered are anthropology, economics, geography, history and literature. Emphasis is placed on collecting materials on Ghana to build a comprehensive national collection. The library houses over 53,800 books, pamphlets and other monographs. Its special collection comprise the Norma collection, the personal library of the late George Padmore, press cuttings from newspapers all over the world, local language publications, and the collection from the former Drama Studio.

The Nordic African Institute Library

P.O. Box 1703
SE-751-47 Uppsala, Sweden
+46- (0) 18 56 22 00
Fax   +46-(0)18 56 22 90
E-mail: nai@nai.uu.se
Website: http://www.nai.uu.se

The Nordic African Institute Library specializes in the collection of materials that deal with contemporary African issues. The main emphasis in the collection development is on politics, education, economics, the social sciences and African literature. The library houses a total of

50,000 books, reports, pamphlets, 1,000 current journals and a special collection on African government documents.

Schomburg Library

The New York Public Library
515 Malcom X Boulevard
New York NY 10037-1801
212 491 2200

The Schomburg Library, considered as the library with the largest collection in the world on materials on Africa, is a national research library devoted to collecting, preserving and providing access to resources documenting the experiences of the people of Africa. Opened in 1925 as the Negro Division of the New York Public Library at its 135th street branch of the New York Public Library, it houses over 5 million items relating to the history and culture of the people of Africa and the African Diaspora. Collections include manuscripts, rare books, newspapers, pamphlets, oral history, video documentation programmes and photographs. It also has a special collection of masks, weapons and rare items from Ghana.

Archives

Archives contain the organized body of records made or acquired in connection with the transactions of government, governmental agency, institution, organization, establishment, family or individual, preserved for record purposes. Most materials are in the form of manuscripts, hand or type-written, and are unique, fragile, irreplaceable and vulnerable to improper handling. Archival materials are also known as primary sources of information and serve as a rich source of historical information for the researcher in African Studies. A valuable tool to locate archives with Africana collections is: Cook, Chris *The making of modern Africa: a guide to Archives.* New York: Facts on File, 1995. 218pp

This book provides a list of archival materials relating to the history of modern Africa. It has over 1,000 entries on the collections of individuals who have contributed to the making of modern Africa. It covers the period 1878 to early 1990. Arrangement is by personal names, followed by notes on location and holding of each archive.

Individual archives

Some individual archives are:

The Manhyia Archives

Institute of African Studies
University of Ghana
Kumasi
Tel: 233 (0) 3220 33971

The Manhyia Archives situated in Kumasi, is administered by the Institute of African Studies, University of Ghana, to support teaching and learning of Asante's history and culture. It processes and makes available records created or received by the Kumasi Traditional Council; the

Asantehene's Secretariat, the Asantehene and Kumasi clan chiefs' courts, the Asanteman Council and their predecessors. The holdings comprise documents, court record books and dockets, 'native' affairs files, minute books, account books, newspaper clippings, annual reports, maps, plans and Asante stool histories. There are also in stock government gazettes, ordinances, acts, legislative instruments, local government bulletins, commercial and industrial bulletins and other government publications. The Manhyia Archives publishes lists of holdings and is open to all who wish to research into the history of Asante.

Museums

Museums are another form of information resource. They could be a whole building, or portion of a building, established as centers of learning and information, holding resources that tell about the past. Museums preserve material culture in the form of valuable objects that provide historical information. These objects tell a story and place events in context. Some individual museums are listed below:

National Museums

Ghana Museums and Monuments-
Barnes Road
P.O. Box 3344
Accra
Tel: 233 (0) 302 221633

The Ghana National Museum is located in Accra. It was built in 1953 and was opened to the public in 1957. It was established purposely for education, research, acquisition and exhibition, and its collections are made up of ethnographical, archaeological and art objects from various sites and regions of the country and Africa

Individual Museums

Department of Archaeology Museum
University of Ghana
P.O. Box LG 3
Legon
Tel: 233 (0) 302 502278

The Department of Archaeology, at the University of Ghana, was established in 1951 and is currently the backbone of most archeological research in Ghana. The Department runs a Museum which has a collection of over 15,000 items, dating as far back as the 1930s, comprising ceramics, terracotta, stone bones, metal, glass, porcelain and sea shells.

Institute of African Studies Museum
University of Ghana
P.O. Box LG 73
Legon
Tel: 233 (0) 302 513390/1

Object acquisition for the museum of the Institute of African Studies began in 1964 with the main objective of providing information and preserving the ethnographic works of Ghana. The holdings of the museum are about 1,500 objects(Does this include the gold/brassweights?). Included in the collection are works in clay comprising, terracotta heads, figures, smoking pipes and ritual objects; objects made of wood like stools, chairs and musical instruments; metal items like gold weights etc. Others are works made from plant fibre, animal origin, textile collection, photographs of hairstyles, funeral of Sir Nana Agyeman Prempeh, and other assorted photographs and a palanquin (Labi, 1992). In April 2008, the Institute opened an exhibition of more than 1,200 brass works used as weights for the gold trade in the Gold Coast. The brass gold weights were bought from a German collector, Dieter Rottger, by the late Chancellor of the University of Ghana and Gyasehene of Okuapeman, Oyeeman Wereko Ampem II, and subsequently donated to the University in March 2005, to serve educational and tourism purposes. The brass weights, which were used in business transactions, have now evolved from weights into contemporary utilitarian objects. 'Some are designed and cast as coat hangers, drawer handles, candle stick holders and several more.'

Research Registers/Directories

One great risk a researcher takes in conducting a piece of research is that someone somewhere could be working on the same topic precisely in the same field. Research registers are valuable as auxiliary aids to bibliographic control as they indicate possible publications in the subject area. However caution must be exercised in the use of such registers since a large amount of research never get completed. Some helpful guides to research are: *International Directory of African Studies Research/compiled by Philip Baker.* ▬ London: Hans Zell, 1994. 398Pp.

A new revised and expanded edition of the *International Guide to African Studies Research*, providing comprehensive information on some 1,500 academic institutions, research bodies, associations and international organizations involved in African Studies research in all parts of the world. Entries are set in alphabetical order by country and name of institution, with many helpful cross references. A series of carefully planned indexes provides easy access by name of individual scholars, topic or area of research, regional or country, ethnic group and languages, which are the subject of research being conducted by individuals and organizations. It gives substantial insight into worldwide activities in African Studies.

Akpebu, Olive *Publications by staff of the Institute of African Studies, 1961-1991.* *(unpublished)*

A list of publications providing a ready reference, of the results and efforts of staff of the Institute of African Studies, who worked on diverse topics between 1961 and 1991. An attempt has been made to include all books, pamphlets, periodical articles, project reports and unpublished seminar and conference papers. Arrangement is alphabetical by author, and under each author, listings are made chronologically. Information given for each entry includes the author's name, title place and publisher of the publication, and here otherwise stated is the Institute of African Studies, date of publication and pagination.

Research Institutions

Research institutions are organizations dedicated to careful scholarly and scientific study of subjects or issues, and the dissemination of these findings to the benefit of academia and the society as a whole. Some research institutions are:

Institute of African Studies

University of Ghana
P.O. Box LG 73
Legon
233 (0) 302- 513390/1

The Institute of African Studies, located at the University of Ghana, Legon was established in 1961 by the first President of Ghana, Osagyefo Dr. Kwame Nkrumah? The Institute conducts research and teaches in a wide range of fields including History and Politics, Philosophy and Religion, Societies and Cultures, Language, Drama and Literature, Visual Arts, Gender, Culture and Development, and Music and Dance. These researches generate a wealth of literature useful to the study of African Studies. The Institute organizes seminars, lectures, conferences and also publishes the journal Research Review. It also houses a museum and manages archives, including an audio visual archive in situ and the Manhyia Archive at the Asantehene's palace in Kumasi.

The Nordic African Institute

P.O. Box 1703
SE-751 47
Uppsala Sweden
Tel: +46-(018 56 22 00
E-mail: nal@nal.uu.se
    Internet: http://www.nal.uu.se

The Nordic Africa Institute was founded in 1962 as the Nordic centre for research, documentation and information on modern Africa. Its main objectives are to carry out scientific research on Africa; further cooperation and contacts between Nordic and African researchers; serve as a documentation centre for research and studies on Africa; and disseminate information about African research and current African issues. The Institute publishes the following: periodicals: News from Nordiska Afrikainstitutet, monographs, and collective works, current African issues and research reports.

Council for the Development of Social Science Research in Africa

Avenue Cheikh Anta Diop X Canal IV
BP 3304, CP 18524, Dakar, Senegal
Phone: (221) 33 825 98 22 ou (221) 33 825 98 23
Fax: (221) 33 824 12 89
http://www.codesria.org

CODESRIA, the Council for the Development of Social Science Research in Africa, is headquartered in Dakar, Senegal. It was established in 1973 as an independent Pan-African research organisation with a primary focus on the social sciences. It is recognised not only as the pioneer

African social research organization, but also as the apex non-governmental centre of social knowledge production on the continent.

Its objectives are to:

- Promote and facilitate research and knowledge production in Africa using a holistic, multi-disciplinary approach. The Council is committed to combating the fragmentation of knowledge production, and the African community of scholars along various disciplinary and linguistic/geographical lines;
- Promote and defend the principle of independent thought and the academic freedom of researchers in the production and dissemination of knowledge;
- Encourage and support the development of African comparative research with a continental perspective and a sensitivity to the specificity of the development process in Africa;
- Promote the publication and dissemination of research results undertaken by African scholars;
- Strengthen the institutional basis of knowledge production in Africa by proactively engaging and supporting other research institutions and their networks of scholars within its programmes of activities. As part of this goal, the Council also actively encourages cooperation and collaboration among African universities, research organisations and other training institutions;
- Encourage inter-generational and gender-sensitive dialogues in the African academy as a further investment of effort in the promotion of awareness and capacity for the use of different perspectives for knowledge production;
- Promote contacts and dialogue between African researchers and researchers on Africa elsewhere in the world, as well as interaction between the Council and similar international organisations.

Conference Proceedings

Conferences are large meetings, held annually or at regular intervals, at different locations each year by groups of people, where a number of speakers deliver papers or make presentations. Papers usually centre around one major theme, issue, topic or region, and are usually the result of research conducted. The discussions, debate, submissions and decisions of the conference are often printed and circulated to delegates. After the conference, papers presented are collected and published as conference proceedings. So many conferences are held each year and a researcher needs to keep track of those of interest. A useful tool to help identify conferences which had African Studies as a major conference subject is: *Conferences and other events on Africa: past conferences and proceedings. www.columbia.edu/cu/web/indiv/africa/cuvl/confs.html*

This site has a listing of conferences arranged chronologically by the year in which they were organized, from 1995 to date. Each listing has the theme of the conference, place and date and deadline for the receipt of proposals, sponsors and useful links to homepages.

Individual conferences

First International Conference on Africanists (; 11th – 18th December, 1962; Accra)

The proceedings of the First International Congress of Africanists/edited by Lalage Bown and Michael Crowder. – Accra: International Congress of Africanists, 1964. – 368p

A collection of papers of the first Africanists' Congress that discussed issues about the History, Languages, Religion, Social and Economic problems, Literature, Art and Music, Social and Political Institutions, Science and Technology, and Education and Psychology of the African people.

The Centre of African Studies
University of Edinburgh
21 George SQ
Edinburgh EH 8 9LD
Scotland
Tel: + 44 (0) 131 650 3878
Fax: + 44 (0) 131 650 6535
email: African.Studies@ed.ac.uk
Website: www.cas.ed.ac.uk

The Centre of African Studies hosts major international conferences every year. Experts from all over the world gather to discuss topical issues relating to Africa. Papers presented are published as monographs by the Centre. The conference theme for 2011 is 'Global Health Governance and African Health Systems: Issues, Actors, and Outcomes'

Associations

Associations are group of individuals or organizations that have a common goal. Where such organizations are academic, the outcome of meetings, conferences and publications serve as a valuable source of information. One such association is the:

African Studies Association

Rutgers, The State University of New Jersey
54 Joyce Kilmer Avenue
Piscataway, NJ 08854-8045, USA
Tel: 732-445-8173
Fax: 732-445-1366.

Founded in 1957 as a non-profit organization, the African Studies Association brings together people with a scholarly and professional interest in Africa. It is open to all individuals and institutions interested in African affairs. It has four publications: Africa Issues, ASA News, African Studies Review and History in Africa. The African Studies Association of Young Scholars (ASAYS) was recently formed to promote scholarship and professionalism within the community of young Africanist scholars, to provide an opportunity and a forum for the exchange of thoughts and ideas related to Africa, and to provide a bridge between the community of students and the academic and professional realms.

African Language Teachers Association

The University of Wisconsin-Madison
455 N Park St
4231 Humanities Building
Madsion, WI 53706
Tel: 608-265-7905
Fax: 608-265-7904
Email: alta@mailplus.wisc.edu

The African Language Teachers' Association (ALTA) is an organization that works for the advancement of the teaching of African Languages. ALTA aims to develop a culture of African language teaching where its members can share common interests and concerns on the study of African languages, and to link and consolidate efforts of government, teachers, administrators, students and researchers involved in the teaching of African languages. The overarching objective of ALTA is to build a strong organization, which meets the needs of all its members. The Association organises a "Second Language Acquisition Certificate Program for African Language Instructors" to prepare graduate students, teaching assistants who are planning to pursue African language teaching as a profession, and faculty members in the field who need retooling. They also publish African language textbooks, and two journals entitled Journal of African Language and Learning and Journal of African Teachers Association.

Acknowledging sources of information consulted

Citing references

At the end of a research project, in writing up the research report in whatever form- as a terminal paper, article or thesis, it is essential to acknowledge the sources of information or materials used. Referencing or citation is the standard way in which other people's ideas and findings are acknowledged. It is important to cite references to acknowledge the work of others, demonstrate the body of knowledge in which the current work is based and to enable other researchers trace the sources of information (Murdoch University, 2004). Citation should be done at each point that one paraphrases or summarizes another person's work, when a reference is cited in the body of the text, or when someone else's work is quoted directly. Quotations however must be cited in quotation marks and the exact page of the source of quotation indicated. There are various styles of referencing or citation, some of which will be discussed here. However it is advised to check from the lecturer or tutor, or to consult one's university handbook for guidelines or the preferred style.

Recording bibliographic information

There are usually four steps in referencing: record, organize, cite and list (Murdoch University, 2004). In the first step, as one reads along, it is essential to keep note of the sources of information, especially the descriptive elements or bibliographic information which would help trace the document. Every piece of material photocopied, must include the title page as well.

The title page is usually the page at the very beginning of a document that contains all the bibliographic information necessary for compiling the list of materials consulted. For books and in situations where the whole book of an edited work has been consulted the following descriptive elements should be noted:

Author's name (surname first e.g. Adjah, Olive); title of book; place of publication, state or town, not country e.g. Accra not Ghana; publisher not printer; date of publication; edition if not the first, and page number, i.e. the total number of pages of a book, if applicable.

Parts of a Book or Chapters in Books

For parts of a book or chapters in books descriptive elements for such a document are as follows:

Author of the chapter, surname first; title of chapter; title of the book; editor/s; place of publication; publisher; date of publication and page numbers where chapter can be found.

Journal Articles

In listing journal articles, the following should be noted:

Author of the article, surname first; title of article; title of Journal; volume and issue number; date of publication and page numbers where article can be found.

Electronic documents

Some electronic documents are in the form of CD-ROM, web pages, electronic journals (e-journal) or even e-mails. The elements used in the citation of electronic documents depend on the type material consulted. They are as follows:

Author; title of the document; title of the webpage; database name; page or section number; format e.g. Compact Disk- Read Only Memory (CD-ROM); year of publication or date last updated; web address usually called the Universal resource locator (url);e-mail address; date on which materials was accessed. (The date on which the material was accessed is essential since pieces of information on the web often get updated or changed).

Thesis or Dissertation

In listing a thesis the descriptive elements include:

Author; title of thesis; degree for which it was awarded; name of awarding institution and year of submission.

Encyclopedia articles

The name of the author can be found at the end of each article.

author's name, surname first; title of the article; title of the encyclopedia and volume number; place of publication; date of publication and page numbers on which the article could be found.

Organizing bibliographic information

The next step after recoding the descriptive or bibliographic data about the documents is to organize these pieces of information in a way that can be easily accessed at a later date. Information could be stored on a personal computer using Microsoft word or software package e.g. Endnote. Manually, it is recommended that a 5" by 3" card catalogue (the card catalogue found in catalogue cabinets in libraries) be used where the details of materials consulted could be recorded and filed alphabetically. This makes the task of compiling the reference list, at a later date, very easy.

Citing bibliographic information

The third step is to construct the citation within the text of the essay using the appropriate guidelines of the format chosen and every work cited must be in the reference list. The list of all materials consulted can be put together at this point following the citation style in the main body of the essay. This list is normally found at the end of the main essay or at the end of each chapter of the essay. This again depends on the style recommended by the supervisor, lecturer or the university. As a matter of choice some bibliographies may be divided into different groups according to the type of material e.g. books, journal articles, conferences, or according to subject

Citation Styles

There are various styles of citing references; however common to all styles is the need for full bibliographic details for easy location and identification of the materials consulted.

In the Harvard style, sometimes referred to as the author-date style, references are listed alphabetically by author's surname and the date of publication. The Footnote-Endnote citation style, on the other hand uses consecutive numbers within the text which refers the reader to the individual footnotes or endnotes.

Listing bibliographic information

Harvard Citation Style

In preparing the list of materials consulted using the Harvard citation style, listing must be done alphabetically, as already mentioned, using the same name format used in the body of the main text. In the main text of an essay employing the Harvard style of citation, the author's surname and the year of publication are put in brackets at each point of reference, e.g.

> *However research on women's information needs and access to appropriate information, has not received much attention in developing counties* (Marcella, 2001)

Where the name of the author occurs naturally in the text, the surname is taken out of the brackets e.g.:

Lind (1990) argues that illiteracy is the major obstacle to access to information and that women need to be literate as the first step in the process of empowerment.

In preparing the list of references, multiple publications by a particular author, should be listed in order of the year of publication. If an author has more than one document published in the same year, they could be distinguished using the small letters of the alphabet, starting from an 'a' which should be written together with the date of publication. For example:
Adjah, O. *The story of my life* published 1990
and
Adjah, O. *History of the Ewes* also published in 1990,

The listing will be as follows:

Adjah, O (1990a) *The Story of my life*
and
Adjah, O (1990b) *History of the Ewes.*

This should be consistent with the citation in the main text of the essay.
Where an item has no author, it is allowed to list it alphabetically by title or by the first significant word of the title.

With the Harvard citation style, the following rules apply to its use: the surname of the author followed by the initials should be in upper case; the full title of the document must be given, and this must be underlined or put in italics. If the publisher's name has been abbreviated in the original document then it is allowed to record it as it appears on the title page, otherwise the full name of the publisher must be indicated. If there are several places of publication, the one relevant to the county of the edition being consulted should be recorded. Where the reference in the text is a quotation, the page number of the quotation in the original document must be stated e.g. (Adjah, 1990, p2). Repeated citations in the Harvard style does not make a difference e.g. subsequent reference to a citation by (Adjah 1990) would still appear as Adjah 1990 no matter the number of times it is cited. (see http://www2.rgu.ac.uk/library/usered/images/HowtoCR.pdf for further information)

Endnotes/Footnotes Citation Style

In using the Endnotes/Footnotes citation style, listing is done in numeric order in which citations appears in the main text. Endnotes, as the name implies, have the listing of references at the end of a paper or document, and footnotes appear at the foot of each page of the document. Each time a work is cited it gets noted (i.e. goes with a number). In the endnote/footnote style, it is preferred that both the author's surname and other names are written in full at the first instance of citation. In subsequent references to the same material, the author's name is stated followed by either the abbreviation op.cit or ibid. (See list of abbreviations listed below).

e.g.   Adjah, Olive. *The History of the Ewes.* Legon: Institute of African Studies 1990 Amekuedee, John. Cataloguing: Legon: Balme Library 2003
        Adjah, Olive op.cit. p14

It must be stated here that the use of ibid and op.cit is no longer fashionable, instead one could use the author's last name or the short form of a title in subsequent citations of a particular document. e.g. Adjah, p14. It is recommended to have a bibliography, alphabetically arranged, at the end of a report presented, using the footnote/endnote citation style. However, again, this depends on the format approved by one's University or supervisor.

Abbreviations

Below is listed of abbreviations used in referencing:

anon;	Anonymous:	Used in some styles when the author is unknown.
c., ca.	Circa:	Used for approximate dates e.g. ca. 1978.
ed., eds.:	editor, editors.	
et al.:	and others (et alii).	Used when there are more than three authors - use the first author only e.g. Adjah et al. instead of Adjah, Amekuedee, Asare and Bawa
ibid.:	(in the same work, cited just above (ibidem)	Used when the citation comes from the same source as the one immediately before it. The page number can be different. e.g. ibid., p.56.
loc. cit.	(in the place (or work) cited (loco citato).	
n.d.	(no date)	Used when the date is unknown
op. cit.	in the work cited (opere citato)	Used when the citation comes from the same source as one cited previously. The author's name should be attached to indicate the source e.g. Mensah, op. cit., p.99.
p., pp.	Page, pages.	
rev.	Revised.	Used when a book has a revised edition rather than a new number e.g. rev. ed.
trans.	translated by.	Used to acknowledge a particular translator of an item published in another language
v.,vol.,vols.	volume, volumes.	

Source: *culled from Monash University Library Online Tutorials (2003)*

Other Citation styles

Other Citation styles are listed below with subject areas where they are commonly used and web address where more information about the style could be accessed.
American Psychological Association (APA) used in psychology, education and other Social Science subjects.
(http://www.library.cornell.edu/newhelp/res_strategy/citing/apa.html)

Modern Language Association (MLA) used for literature, arts and humanities (http://www.library.cornell.edu/newhelp/res_strategy/citing/mla.html)

American Medical Association (AMA) used in medicine, health and biological sciences.(http://www.liu.edu/cwis/cwp/library/sorkshop/citama.htm)

Turabian designed for use by college students, in all subject areas.
(http://www.lib.usm.edu/~instruct/guides/turabian.html)

Chicago for use with all subjects
(http://www.liu.edu/cwis/corp/library/worksop/citchi.htm

Referencing Terms

Listed below are a few referencing terms:

Bibliography

List of documents consulted, but not necessarily referred to in a specific essay or assignment.

Citation

Another word for a reference. It provides enough and accurate bibliographic information about a document for easy identification and location.

Citation style

Method used to format citations. Commonly used formats are Harvard (sometimes called Author-Date), MLA, APA, Footnote-Endnote styles.

Descriptive elements

The building-blocks of a citation. A few examples of these elements are: author, title, edition, date of publication, internet address, etc.

Endnotes

Where large number of references are cited at the end of each chapter or at the end of the whole work.

Footnotes

Listed at the bottom of the page on which a reference or citation occurs in the text. A number is placed in the text to indicate the cited work and again at the bottom of the page in front of the footnote. Footnotes are used when only a small number of references need to be made.

Reference list or Works cited list

List of all documents referred to in your assignment, essay, theses or project. It is usually included at the end the work. It is arranged alphabetically and formatted according to one of the citation styles (Boyle, 2004).

Conclusion

This chapter does not claim to be a comprehensive guide to all resources available for the study of African Studies. It is an attempt to help researchers and students understand the use of information sources, know when to consult particular reference materials, and to prepare the reference, list using acceptable citation styles. Discussions have therefore centered on the relevance of references sources to the point to which it enhances the study of the African people and their culture.

Reference

Adjah, O. A and Adanu, T.S. A.(2004) A Guide to free online resources in *African Studies*. *Research Review* NS 20. (1) pp. 49-56.

Alexander, L. 2004. The complete beginner's guide to the internet. Mumbai: Jaico Publishing House.

Boyle, M. 2004. How to cite references. Murdoch University Library Publications http://wwwlib.murdoch.edu.au (Accessed 20/12/04).

Dike, K O. 1964. The importance of African Studies, in Lalage Bown and Michael Crowder (eds). The Proceedings of the First International Congress of Africanists. Accra 11th – 18th December, 1962 Accra: nternational Congress of Africanists. – pp. 19-28.

Grogan, D. 1987. Grogan's case studies in reference work (Nos. 2-6). London: Clive Bingley.

Hord, B. 1995. The Research Center Periodical Room. Physical accesss to periodicals. HYPERLINK "http://www.hccs. cc.tx.us/system/library/center/   periodical.html"www.hccs.cc.tx.us/system/library/center/periodical.html. (Accessed 02/12/04).

Katz, W. A 1997. Introduction to reference work: basic information services. Vols. 1-7th Edns. New York: McGraw-Hill Co.

Labi, K. 1992. Institute of African Studies Museum. Legon: Institute of African Studies.

Monash University Library Online Tutorial. 2003. http://www.lib.monash.edu.au (Accessed 20/12/04).

Index

Index

Index

Index

Printed in the USA
CPSIA information can be obtained
at www.ICGtesting.com
LVHW071608091223
766042LV00006B/518